LET'S PANIC
ABOUT BABIES!

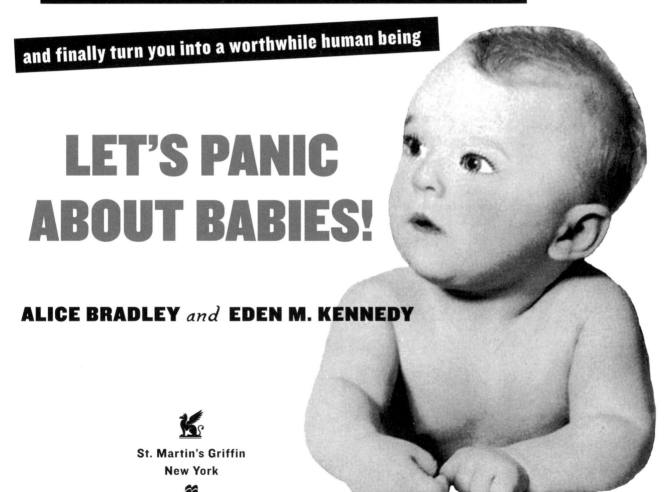

How to endure and possibly triumph over the adorable tyrant

who will ruin your body, destroy your life, liquefy your brain,

and finally turn you into a worthwhile human being

LET'S PANIC ABOUT BABIES!

ALICE BRADLEY *and* **EDEN M. KENNEDY**

St. Martin's Griffin
New York

www.stmartins.com

This book is for entertainment purposes only. Most of the people are fictional.
None of the information contained herein should be mistaken for anything real
or helpful in any way. In the event of actual panic, call a loved one.

Art credits can be found on pages 264-265.

Library of Congress Cataloging-in-Publication Data
Bradley, Alice, 1969–
Let's panic about babies! : how to endure and possibly triumph over the adorable
tyrant who will ruin your body, destroy your life, liquefy your brain, and finally turn
you into a worthwhile human being / Alice Bradley and Eden M. Kennedy.
p. cm.
ISBN 978-0-312-64812-1
1. Pregnancy—Popular works. 2. Motherhood—Popular works. 3. Pregnancy—
Humor. 4. Motherhood—Humor. I. Kennedy, Eden M. II. Title.
RG525.B6493 2011
618.2   2010040325

First Edition: March 2011

10   9   8   7   6   5   4   3   2   1

CONTENTS

Part I

THE
sWELLing

1. IT SEEMS THAT YOU
ARE PREGNANT

Greetings, woman. You are gloriously full with child, living proof of the miracle of creation, or else you wouldn't be reading this. Unless you're just curious. Or you're a man, and you have some sort of fetish. Well, as long as you paid for the book and are not soiling it in a dim corner of your local bookstore, we're okay with that.

But let us return to you, the reader who is actually, validly pregnant, and not at all some moist-palmed pervert. Our first question is: Are you *sure* you're pregnant?

It's a little-known fact that 83 percent of people who believe they're pregnant are not; of those people, 47 percent stuffed an embroidered keepsake pillow under their shirt to see how it would look. The remaining 59 percent are merely confused about how *The Secret* works. And for good reason! A strong desire to manifest the symptoms of pregnancy can result in all sorts of misleading indicators. Vomiting, fatigue, bloating, cessation of one's period: sounds like a normal day at our house! So how is a woman to know?

What You Might Be Instead of Pregnant

Not-pregnant

Hysterical

Recovering from a plate of bad clams

A snake that recently swallowed a full-grown ewe

Pumpkin costume!

Unable to button your pants

Nurturing an eight-pound subcutaneous grapefruit

A man

Only with professional confirmation! But maybe not even then! So-called "blood tests" and "urine-sampling kits" are (probably) no more than a thinly veiled excuse for necromancy. No one knows what doctors actually do with your blood and/or urine or whatever other fluid they demand from you that day. We suspect they shut the door, bury your sample beneath the floorboards, and leap into a mountain of that day's copayment fees.

And yet their "tests" are the only ones that hold up under legal scrutiny, so we must grit our teeth and soldier on.

Here are some ways you may have validly discovered that you were actually pregnant and not imagining things:

- Multiple positive at-home pregnancy tests
- Positive blood test using blood taken from *your very own arm*
- Doctor shakes you and demands that you maintain eye contact while he tells you you're pregnant
- Everyone's congratulating you, and not in a sarcastic way
- You're standing in a bookstore, reading this book *(What are you waiting for? GO TO THE CASH REGISTER.)*
- You bought this book while holding your positive pregnancy test in one hand *(We don't think that's the least bit strange.)*
- Your doctor's lawyer sends you a letter confirming your pregnancy and asking that you not call his office anymore *(Or was it all just a dream?)*
- Swelling of torso increases weekly until baby falls out *(Or have you been hiding someone else's baby in your underpants?)*

BUT HOW DID THIS HAPPEN?

Other Fluids They May Demand from You

1. Sweat

2. Earwax

3. Cry into this vial!

There's no getting around it: you did it with someone. Don't look away from us, or ask what "it" is. You know. *We all know.* You're just making this harder on yourself.

In order for pregnancy to occur, someone's sperm had to get up inside you. This may be a little more technical than we need to get, but specifically, it went up your vagina and traveled into your uterus where an egg was waiting to be fertilized, yearning and yearning for a blissful commingling with its partner-to-be. And lo, life was created.

Here are a few examples of how pregnancy might have occurred. Check off which ones might apply to you!

- ☐ Pleasant bout of lovemaking with your partner
- ☐ Hot quickie in a bathroom stall of an Outback Steakhouse
- ☐ Furtive congress in the backseat of a Honda Accord with your ex-boyfriend
- ☐ Joyless, obligatory coition with your long-time spouse
- ☐ Professional insemination by a trained authority
- ☐ Unsanitary and off-label use of a turkey baster by your lady friend
- ☐ Bizarre sex dream about your old social studies teacher turned out to actually have happened

Did you know? Some people still believe that you can get pregnant without being directly inseminated. Crazy fools! Here are some examples of what will never, ever work:

- Wading in a swimming pool after the high-school boy's swim team finished a race

- Wearing one of those T-shirts that says FETUS across the chest, with an arrow pointing down
- Hanging out with those cheap sluts you call "friends"
- Disturbing a forest gnome's century-long slumber (unless he is actually just a very tiny man and he woke up because you were having sex with him)
- Nuzzling Vince Vaughn's forehead and/or elbow crook (note: this may actually work)

HOW YOU FEEL

Having discovered life stirring inside, you may have any number of reactions. Beatific smiles are common, as are tears of joy, or leaping about the woods singing traditional hymns while hunting for small, delicious animals to sacrifice to your god(s). Or maybe you're just sitting there, reading this book while your ankles swell.

On the other hand, we have to face the possibility that you weren't trying to get pregnant at all. Perhaps you're entering the first flush of menopause and you assumed it was too late to get pregnant. (Surprise!) Or you thought you were too young to start a family, but now that boyfriend of yours seems awfully pumped about this whole baby deal, which is weird because you're barely out of school and is it just because he can't get over how God made his semen so powerful that it broke through the condom?

It's important to know that what you're feeling is entirely normal and correct. But is it? *Not necessarily.*

Here is a guide to the emotions you should be having.

TABLE 1.1 APPROPRIATE EMOTIONS REGARDING PREGNANCY

If you have a . . . → And you are a . . .↓	Partner	No partner by choice	No partner by not-choice	Partner in relationship that is slowly dying	Same-sex partner
Liberal-arts coed	Horror	Horror	Horror	Horror	Bafflement mixed with suspicion
Midlife professional with no desire to raise family	Reluctance intermingled with strange, newfound maternal urges	Unexpected enthusiasm mixed with terror	Ennui	Defiant fury	Confusion
Midlife professional attempting to conceive for thirtieth time	Fear-tinged elation	Fear-soaked elation	Elated hopefulness	Elation touched with resigned sadness	Sexy elation
Nun	Fear, shame	Shame	Crushing guilt and shame	Guilt, regret, shame	Confusion, wonder, urge to perform miracles, overwhelming shame
Thirty-something with considerable financial assets	Satisfaction	Smug satisfaction	Defiant satisfaction	Satisfaction kissed with what-might-have-been	Sexy satisfaction
Person with financial struggles who nonetheless wants to have children	Nervous excitement	Excited nervousness	Excitement with a whopping dose of nerves	Resentment-filled excitement	Sexy excitement
Badger	Apathy	Neutrality	Unconcern	Digging	Scratching

No matter what you're feeling, you're pregnant now, and if you're reading this book you're in it for the long haul. So let's wipe away those tears and other effluents and move on, shall we?

HOW NOT TO SCREW UP

Pregnancy is a strange and bloated time, but more important, it's a time when every single one of your decisions will leave an indelible and unmistakable imprint on your baby *forever*. Every decision you make from now on, even the tiniest choices, will be of the utmost importance. Scared yet? If you're not, you must be drunk. (You need to cut that out, by the way.) The pressure is on now, almost-mother! Fortunately, you've got this book, so at least you're on the right track no matter how many mistakes you've made in the past. And we're sure there were many.

TIPS FOR THE FIRST MONTH

Now that you're pregnant, it's time to straighten up and fly right. Throw out your junk food, pack away those cigarettes, seal up the uranium mine in your basement, and purchase some sensible, crotched underpants.

WHAT TO AVOID

Lead-based paint. If you own a home or enter any structure built before 1978, you're exposing your precious fetus to the deadly lead-filled paint that was slathered on the walls and ceilings in more ignorant times. If you think there's even the slightest chance of lead being anywhere near you, it's your responsibility to get rid of it. Purchase a power sander and get to work! Just release all that lead into the air and let it drift back down and settle into the earth where it belongs. There's no need to interrupt this beautiful, natural process.

Cats. Cats are a known spreader of trichinosis, due to their love of raw pork.

Trichinosis is a fatal disease that will turn you fat and hairless before it kills you. And cats aren't just dangerous for their disease-carrying: they have sharp claws and teeth; they can navigate in the dark using a complex navigation head-system they call "whiskers," thus giving them an advantage during blackouts; and the only flesh they enjoy feasting on more than pig is new-born babies. People who are foolish enough to harbor cats do so at their own peril! Now that you've got a baby on board, however, you're petting for two.

Eye contact with cats. Cats will suck the burgeoning life right out of you, using their infamous feline mind-powers. Avert your eyes, and move along.

Recreational X-rays. There's no doubt that seeing what your insides are up to is good fun, but in the end, your poor fetal intruder is going to resent being saturated with massive doses of radiation. So as much as you think you might have a hairline crack in your pelvis that your Facebook friends just *have* to see, you might want to exert a little something called "self-control."

Endless night-trolling for anonymous sex down by the docks. Let's face it. There's nothing like the illicit thrill of being taken from behind by a mustachioed stranger, but the time for that frivolity has passed. You're not getting any younger, and besides, all that cruising is what got you into this mess in the first place. Really, haven't you noticed that you only get action if you call yourself Steve and wear that Jeff Bridges mask you bought for Halloween? It's time to bid adieu to that brand of dangerous fun. It's gone for the next nine months—along with your waistline!

In fact, while you're at it, also avoid:

Any sex at all. Remember: your baby is watching you! And that's just not right.

Anyone who seems even a little catlike. Cats are known for their ability to shapeshift. Be on your guard!

While avoiding the above, you should *begin:*

A typical upper Midwestern-style birthing hut.

Weighing yourself. It's vital to weigh yourself in the first week of pregnancy, so that you know the specific tonnage you're larding on and how bad you should feel as a result. A baseline weight will help your self-esteem plummet quickly and easily as the months fall away. (For more information on weight loss and pregnancy, see our companion book, *Let's Panic About Lady Shapes!*—with ordering info for our patented line of Sta-Shapl-EE™ salts, teas, foams, and goops.)

Learning to vomit quietly and delicately. There's nothing less attractive than the echoing sounds of regurgitation accompanied by loud moans and pleas for heavenly release. A slight pallor, a few beads of moisture on the brow, a slight rosiness in the lip from recently expelled Hawaiian Punch—these effectively communicate a palatable level of misery, while reassuring the pregnant woman's friends and acquaintances that she will not unleash her lunch on anyone's shoes.

Monitoring your home for traces of radon and carbon monoxide. If you find any of these toxins, immediately move to the country and build a passive-solar bamboo, straw-bale, or used-tire-and-beer-can house from the ground up with your own two blistered hands. If you don't, your radioactive superbaby will be able to light fires by snapping his fingers.

Building your birthing hut. What's more fun than constructing a leaky structure of twigs, laundry lint, and stray bits of roofing material? Not much! Especially when you're getting ready to crawl inside with musty blankets and give birth in

It Really Happened! Lucille's Story

"I still can't figure out how it happened. My husband Bernanke and I have separate beds—actually, they're in different homes—but once in a while I let him borrow my underpants (I'm not sure why, I don't ask) . . . so maybe? Ew. Anyway, when I told him the news, Bernanke tried to celebrate by thrusting his hands down my skirt, but I told him, No thank you, sir! Our baby didn't need to put up with *another* outburst of his filthy nonsense. He said, "How about a kiss, then?" and I threw up into the sink. I immediately recorded this moment into our baby book, so I could add it to my list of Bernanke's cunning efforts to embrace me, while he sobbed into his tie. He's so cute when he's emotional and across the room from me!"

—Lucille Liebestraum, age 46, West Egg, New York

It Really Happened! Delilah's Discovery

"It was about eight in the morning and I'd just put a pan of gluten-free zucchini muffins in the oven. Lacy, 11, Jebediah, 8, and Stump, 6, had just harvested everything out of the garden as part of their home-schooling project on medieval farming methods when I turned around and puked all over Lacy's model of the solar system she'd made out of dried gourds. Boy, was she steamed! I told her that vomit was one of Nature's ways of telling me I was with child, so she went and got the mop and a bucket, and then she said the cutest thing: 'I hope you have another girl because I am sick of cleaning up everybody's shit all by myself while the boys get to work on their Civil War dioramas!' That Lacy! Whenever I assign housework along traditional, gendered patterns she gets as mean as Granny's chihuahua."

—Delilah Lu, age 33, Longmont, Colorado

Sure, satyrs are fun, but you can never get them to commit.

this sacred, holy nest of your own devising. Don't forget to bless your hut when it's done. Make up some crazy dance! Burn a wig! Throw oranges at the neighbor's dog! When you grow up in a society without meaningful birth traditions and are thus compelled to create your own, the sky's the limit!

Taking herbs. We hear that the Chinese developed a working medical system 5,000 years before us, so maybe we can learn a little something from these ancient, wise people. Here's what we found out from the little Asian fellow who runs the corner grocery on Alice's block.

Yo-Yo Ma is indicated in cases of night sweats and plagues of vampires.

Gong Li is effective for heartburn and bosses who look annoyed when you leave early for prenatal yoga.

Chow Yun-fat is excellent for repelling gangsters.

Amy Tan makes you invisible.

Or, if you insist on Western remedies because you're (no judgments) a *racist:*

Earl Grey tea prevents fox-hunting accidents.

American ginger root improves digestion; enables mnemonic retrieval of the names of dead sitcom actors.

Grapeseed extract is a useful source of antioxidants. Also attracts satyrs.

MEANWHILE, INSIDE YOU . . . THE FIRST MONTH

WHAT'S GOING ON UP IN THERE?

No one really knows what's going on within the human body at *any* time, but we can provide you with, at least, an educated guess.

During the first month, most experts agree that the baby is flopping around inside you; most likely near the vagina, because that's where he or she was made. Want to know what he (or she) looks like? Wonder no more.

Here's your baby!   Except this big:

WOULD YOU GUESS...?

Right now, your baby is thinking about . . . nothing at all! He's just a dopey clump of cells.

Despite being a bitty thing and not even knowing how tiny he is because of his astounding lack of brain matter, he's already managed to develop a heart, a digestive system, and a nickname for his placenta (he calls it "Sacky"). All this overachieving has helped instill in him tragic feeling of overconfidence. He's kind of an asshole, is what we're saying. Not to worry: this will be straightened out soon enough.

2. THE FIRST TRIMESTER: ONE-THIRD OF THE PREGNANCY, TWO-THIRDS OF THE ANGST

t's finally sunk in: you are with child. You've been impregnated by the glorious sperm of a man whose penis you may or may not have personally scrutinized. We will try not to judge who or what or *just how* that satisfactory genetic material pierced the maidenhood of your swollen ovum. We hope, for your sake, that he signed a legally binding document before you slipped off the granny panties you'd put on that day in the hope that the mere shame of them would keep you from sleeping with him. But there you were on your second date, cramming them into your purse while he was in the bathroom. Hmm.

Moving on!

HOW ARE YOU FEELING?

DIFFERENT!

LET'S DO MATH!

Doctors calculate that the first day of your pregnancy actually "begins" with the first day of your last period. So whenever you get your period, you're already pregnant in the future, maybe! And when you actually *do* become pregnant, you've actually already been pregnant for two weeks, which means you didn't have to have sex after all! Right? Or maybe the sperm travels back in time? Now we're all confused and dizzy because of numbers.

As the second month begins, you might find yourself feeling . . . full. Bloated. Fecund. Replete. Abundant. Jam-packed with . . . something. Well, that *something* is called a fetus, lady, and while it's only a trifling thing at the moment, there's no denying its presence! It's up inside you, being all *look at me, turning into something,* its cells multiplying and whatnot, your hormones pumping out at alarming rates. No wonder you feel different. You *are* different. *And nothing will ever be the same, ever again.*

Ever.

At any rate, the vague pregnant feeling is often reassuring—so it wasn't a fever-dream after all! It wasn't a hallucination brought on by those mushrooms you bought at that roadside hallucinogenic mushroom stand! You really *are* knocked up. So that's nice.

On the other hand, you feel kind of gross.

BREASTY!

Breasts. Whether they're small or large: if you have them, they're now requesting your attention. They are swollen, tender, and growing increasingly impressive! And it turns out you're not the only one who's noticed. Your partner and/or roommate may slaver at the thought of handling them, but doing so hurts you so much you want to punch your partner/roommate if he/she so much as glances at them. So punch away! Hard! How else is he/she going to get the message/warning?

SLEEPY!

As you enter the second month, it's not uncommon to fall asleep suddenly and/or constantly when walking, speaking, or driving. The feelings of fatigue some women experience during the early months of pregnancy are actually the result

16

of several factors, but the main reason is that your body is diverting blood and assorted nutrients away from your brain and directing them to your needy, selfish embryo. As a result, the "awakeness follicles" in the brain will shut down suddenly and without warning. As Grandma learned during the Great Depression from all the hobos tramping up to the farm in search of a block of government cheese or a grubby brioche: a poor man can quell his hunger by sinking into a deep, dreamless sleep. In the same way, the great Hooverville of neurons that make up your brain is just shutting down for lack of basic nutrition, sanitation, and clean underbritches.

On the other hand, you might just be lazy! Before you get all defensive, here comes Science to *prove* how lazy you are with this illustrative graph:

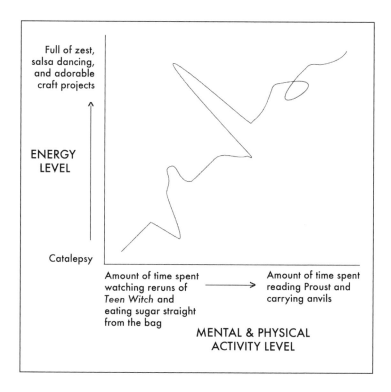

Smells, sights, sounds, and ideas that may induce nausea in the first trimester

Aluminum

Applesauce

Aspic

Baby powder

Banjos

Bath mats

Bertrand Russell

Blintzes

Borscht

Busking

Butter

Buttermilk

Cabbage

Canada

Celine Dion

Chamomile

Cheddar cheese

Things that smell like cheese

The sight of cheese

QUEASY!

If you're like most women, the first weeks of pregnancy have brought on a frequent and awful urge to retch into the nearest file cabinet. No one knows for sure why women experience pregnancy-related nausea, but we suspect it's directly related to something wrong you did in your life, and only you know what that thing is.

If you're not experiencing nausea, well, aren't you the lucky one. Now you hush up about it because no one likes a show-off.

HOW TO HANDLE THE SUDDEN ONSET OF NAUSEA IN PUBLIC

There you are in the produce section looking for an attractive gourd to anchor your horn of plenty, when the ground shifts and suddenly it's too warm, and— Oh, God, why is the smell of blue cheese and bubble gum wafting from that old woman's rain bonnet?

If you can't quickly find an appropriate place to barf, follow the flow chart on the next page to assess your situation and find the best coping strategy for either avoiding or surrendering to your nausea.

SOCIALLY ACCEPTABLE PLACES TO BARF

AT HOME

Acceptable:	*Unacceptable:*
Toilet	Cutlery drawer
Wastebasket	Fish tank
Pillowcase	Dishwasher
Empty paint can	Spouse's pillowcase

Petting Zoo — Baseball Game — Grocery Store — Eiffel Tower

eau de goat — who's smoking a cigar? — aroma of fresh coffee — sense that the floor is moving

NAUSEA IS TRIGGERED

you think you're going to vomit — you don't think you're going to vomit

can you put something in your stomach? — yes → have a sip of water

no → is there a place to sit down? — yes → sit down → **YOU'LL BE FINE**

no → only if you get into this clown car — suddenly you're trapped in an elevator!

can you roll down a window? — are you alone? — yes → take off your clothes

no — yes — yes, but Blinky's giving you the stink eye — no → remove your coat — do you have any mints in your bag? — yes → put one in your mouth

are you showing yet? — no — no → visualize a warm, flat stone in your hands, then place your hands on your stomach and let the warmth of the stone melt into your stomach to create a soothing protective vibration of healing

yes → roll down the window — did that help? — no — yes

not without risking the life of your unborn child — can you open the door and jump out? — yes, you think you can clear the guard rail/ slide down the cable to the mezzanine — **VOMIT**

The word "cheese"

Also the word "chunky"

Chicken piccata

Christian Science Monitor

Christmas trees

Cinnamon

Clouds

The Cold War

The color blue, especially azure, cerulean, and ultramarine

Corn chips

Cougars

Crock-Pots

C. S. Lewis

Cumin

Dacron

Danny Thomas

Deadlines

Death

Delaware

Dust

Eczema

Effluvia

Elephants

Elves

Ennui

Everything

Fabric softener

Falkland Islands

Fanny Brice

Fear

Fire

Furballs

Geckos

Genotypes

RESTAURANT

Acceptable:
Napkin
Bread basket
Mop bucket in kitchen
Your purse

Unacceptable:
Gravy boat
Water glass at next table
Salad bar
Maitre d's cupped hands

AIRPORT

Acceptable:
Potted plant
Black sand ashtray on top of trash can
Cinnabon
Ziploc bag (remove toiletries first)

Unacceptable:
TSA officer's cupped hands
Pilot's hat
Galley coffee pot
Overhead compartment
First Class

SCHOOL

Acceptable:
Bathroom stall
Rear aisle of auditorium
Behind the tennis courts
Guidance counselor's
   cupped hands

Unacceptable:
Test tube
French horn
All over your math quiz
Inside your Jonas Brothers
   Trapper Keeper

AT THE OFFICE

Acceptable:
Receptionist's coffee cup
Empty water cooler bottle
Recycling bins out back
Emergency exit stairwell
Subordinate's cupped hands

Unacceptable:
Conference room table
Overhead projector
Boss's cupped hands
Microwave

AT LARGE

Acceptable:

Fireplace
Spittoon
Porta-Potty
Pothole
Vagrant's lap
Open grave

Unacceptable:

Open manhole
Society matron's lap
Historical landmark
Baptismal font
Hamster habitat
Dolphin's cupped fins

Warning: Do not throw up near your dog. He will delight in the warm snack you have provided him via your mouth. And then you will throw up all over again, and for the rest of your life.

WHAT YOU WON'T HEAR FROM THE OTHER EXPERTS OUT THERE

The first trimester of your pregnancy is when the Uterine Goblins come at night and squat next to your bed arguing about how much pain and discomfort to inflict upon you in the months to come. Have you led an exemplary life, opening doors for old ladies and giving bus seats to one-legged legionnaires? The goblins will reward you with some mild heartburn and an odd patch of freckles on your forehead. If you've spent your life forwarding e-mail chain letters and mispronouncing "paradigm," however, the goblins will know and act accordingly. Brace yourself for the full complement of prolapsed organs, comrade! *The Uterine Goblins decree it.*

Incidentally, if during a routine checkup you mention anything about any kind of goblins—much less ones that control your reproductive organs—your OB/GYN will think you've lost your mind. And then she'll enlist a few members of her office staff to mill around your examination room. Here's a general rule of

Gingivitis

Gravity

Groats

Hair

Hair, the musical

Harry Connick, Jr.

Harry Dean Stanton

Heidegger

Herbivores

Hermit crabs

Hot pads

Hydroponics

Illinois

Inflation derivatives

Integers

Iron

Iron John

Iron Man

Jowls

Kasha

Key lime pie

Keystone Kops

Kitten teeth

Real.

Knishes

Knock-knock jokes

Kohl

Koi

Latex

Logs

Loofah

Magicke

Mah-Jongg

Matching clothing

Matchsticks

Matriarchal cultures

thumb: Is the person you're speaking to displaying a gilt-framed diploma on her wall? Does she open her lab coat and point to her crimson Harvard sweatshirt just as you begin telling her about the goblins? If so, do not tell her about the goblins. We learned this the hard way.

(They're real, though.)

If you mention the goblins to your midwife, on the other hand, she'll give you the protective amulet she saves for those who are gifted with "The Knowing."

QUIZ: WHAT ARE THEY THINKING?

So, you think your pregnancy is far enough along that family, friends, and random strangers will automatically share your joy? Think again! Match the person whom you've just told you're pregnant with the thought racing through their minds while they stare at you in disbelief.

1. Skinny teenage girl in line behind you at Starbucks

2. Your mother

3. Childless girlfriend with fantastic taste in shoes

4. Emotionless male coworker

5. The president of France

6. Adorable five-year-old boy sitting in a grocery cart

a. "What an irresponsible slut."

b. "I am so turned on right now."

c. "I hope it ends up being just like her; then she'll see how hard it is to raise a child!"

d. "Better her than me."

e. "Am I the father?"

f. "I like to touch the cold, bumpy chickens!"

Answers: 1, a; 2, a; 3, a; 4, a; 5, a; 6, a.

QUIZ: WHICH SIDE ARE YOU ON?

Are you going to go for a hospital birth, or will you go *au naturel*? Even though, technically speaking, you have eight more months to figure out how you want to have this baby, you *in fact* have to decide RIGHT AWAY. As soon as you begin to show, your friends, family, and complete strangers will demand to know your philosophical position on epidurals, so that they'll know how to judge you. This quiz will tell you whether you want a medically numbed baby-extraction procedure or an aquatic hippie squawkfest.

1. **YOUR FAVORITE FOOD IS:**
   a. Steak
   b. Kamut Puffs
   c. Jelly Beans
   d. All of the above

2. **YOUR POLITICAL AFFILIATION IS:**
   a. Libertarian pro-choice prescription-drug addict.
   b. Radical Christian gun-control nut.
   c. Apolitical fashionista.
   d. What does this have to do with anything?

3. **HOW DO YOU FEEL ABOUT YOUR ARMPITS?**
   a. I shave them twice daily and use a prescribed antiperspirant/ deodorant. And duct tape.
   b. I don't shave them, but I do rub one of those crystal things in my glorious pit-fur.
   c. I have each hair individually zapped by a laser, and then I'm exfoliated and sluiced with lavender water.
   d. Again, I really don't see the point of this question.

The Mesozoic era

Metallurgy

Michael Madsen

Mittens

Motocross

My Three Sons

The nineteenth century

Nor'easters

Nova Scotia

Old Norse

Paprika

Particle physics

Pi

Pie

Pierce Brosnan

Pierogi

Pince-nez

Platform shoes

Polio

Polygamy

Polygons

Pomeranians

Quinoa

4. WHAT KIND OF FOOTWEAR DO YOU PREFER?

a. Lace-up oxfords

b. Flip-flops

c. Patent leather kitten-heel slingbacks

d. Oh, for God's sake. Moccasins. I go everywhere dressed like Pocahontas.

5. WHAT ARE YOU GOING TO NAME YOUR BABY IF IT'S A GIRL?

a. Something traditional yet modern, like Constance or Olivia.

b. Something traditional yet modern, like Willow or Jade.

c. Something traditional yet modern, like Nefertiti or Supernova.

d. If I tell you, everyone will use it and I'll be really, really mad.

6. WHAT ARE YOU GOING TO NAME YOUR BABY IF IT'S A BOY?

a. I'll name him after his grandfather, Elliot.

b. I'll name him after my favorite band, Sleater-Kinney.

c. I'll name him after my favorite subway stop, Delancey.

d. Seriously, I'm not telling you.

7. HOW DO YOU FEEL ABOUT STRANGERS POKING YOUR CERVIX?

a. It's okay as long as they're wearing surgical scrubs.

b. It's okay as long as they make me a pot of chamomile tea first.

c. It's okay as long as they accept my health insurance.

d. It's okay as long as they promise never to do it again.

8. WHAT'S YOUR FAVORITE COLOR?

a. Orange: it's so cheerful and vibrant.

b. Purple: it's so rich and mystical.

c. Carafe: it's the color of an organic, fair-trade, medium-roast latte.

d. Delicious: it's the color of a margarita.

CALCULATING YOUR SCORE:

Give yourself one point for every A answer you chose, two points for every B, three points for every C, and four points for every D.

0 TO 8 POINTS   SAFETY FIRST! You should go straight to the hospital right now.

9 TO 16 POINTS   LOVE CHILD! You want to give birth in a tide pool, assisted by dolphins.

17 TO 24 POINTS   TRENDSETTER! You're going to do whatever Oprah tells you to do.

25 TO 32 POINTS   WACKO! You're pretending to be pregnant.

Telluride

Testicles and things that look like testicles

The Thames

Toes, especially the fourth one over

Tracing paper

The Ukraine

Ukrainians

Underground bunkers

Vacuum-cleaning

Veal

TEN QUESTIONS TO ASK YOUR PROSPECTIVE OB/GYN OR MIDWIFE

1. Is that diploma real?
2. How do you feel about natural childbirth?
3. Why are you laughing?
4. Can you use these hand puppets to explain the facts of life to me?
5. Why are your hand puppets so hostile?
6. Can I just have the epidural now?
7. Why are you filming my exam?
8. Why do you need my passport?
9. Who is that man with the night-vision goggles?
10. Why am I being blindfolded?

TABLE 2.1 THE EIGHT TYPES OF VAGINAL PROFESSIONALS

	Defining habit	Magazines in waiting room	Shows up to appointments wearing . . .	Preferred pain relief method for laboring women	Pet peeve	Will say to you while you're pushing
HMO Robot	Schedules unnecessary tests without your permission	*HMOs Ahoy!, Popular Mechanics*	White lab coat over another white lab coat	Spinal block, promotional samples	Your birth plan	"I've just laproscopically circumcised the baby in utero."
Woman hater	Puts sanitary paper on all office chairs, not just exam table	*Martha Stewart Living*	Hazmat suit	Morphine, codeine, methadone, valium, oxycontin	Menstruation, bodily fluids, bodies	"Have you no shame?!"
Cranky old nurse-midwife	Doesn't give a shit about anyone's feelings anymore	*Bitch*	Overalls	Suck it up	Thong underwear	"Your baby can sense your ambivalence about motherhood, that's why he doesn't want to come out."
Shaman	Places crystals on your belly during exams	*High Times, Mother Jones*	Patchouli	Tibetan bowls	Episiotomies	"Pain is an awesome way to burn off bad karma."
Ex-con with Internet degree	Shaves women's pubic hair before each exam	*Hustler, Juggs, Good Housekeeping*	White lab coat over free *Maxim* T-shirt that came with his subscription	Roofies	Dull razors, hidden cameras	"Give it to me, baby; that's right, push it out for Daddy."
Kindly old country doctor	Chuckles at all your questions instead of answering them	*Field & Stream, Saturday Evening Post*	Fishing hat	Chloroform, ether	The new nurse who makes him get his own damn coffee	"Get a move on, honey, I've got a date with a bass boat!"
Mousy lady doctor	Moist hands	*Lilith, Poetry*	Sensible shoes	Demerol, humming	Men in the delivery room	"You're so pretty."
Perfect doctor	Acts as your advocate, coach, and best friend through nine trying yet joyous months	None. Instead, the staff reflexologist kneads away your tension while you wait	Incredibly well-tailored lab coat, smart black pumps	Whatever your heart desires	People without Swiss bank accounts	"I accept Diners Club, too."

It Really Happened! Trudie's Story

"My husband and I never planned on me getting pregnant. I really enjoyed my career as a nuclear physicist in charge of radioactive household appliance technology, and I didn't want to have to spend a lot of time and money decontaminating the house and comparison shopping for prenatal vitamins. Ultimately, the little guy snuck up in there anyway, and then we found out that the decontamination shower tent and waste-water-containment bladder *alone* would cost more than his college tuition. Oh, well. With luck, the fetus will enjoy the giant microwave oven-bed I built for us to sleep in at night as much as we do. The warmth and the humming are so soothing after a long day of injecting isotopes into monkey brains, and I've got a little warming drawer—I mean, bassinet— that attaches to my side of the bed. It will go *ding!* when the baby's done . . . sleeping."

—Trudie Oppenheimer, age 39,
Los Alamos, New Mexico

Vinaigrette

Warm fronts

Water: lukewarm, warmish-hot, or cool but not supercold

White

Whodunits

Xenon

Yoruba mythology

Yurts

Zombies

MEANWHILE, INSIDE YOU . . .
THE SECOND MONTH

WHAT'S GOING ON UP IN THERE?

During the second month, your baby is composed of only eighteen cells. Still, he's with-it enough to attach himself to one of your major organs, scraping away vital nutrients using his razorlike proto-incisors and rasping tongue.

Here's your baby! (magnified 2x):

WOULD YOU GUESS...?

This month, the judging portion of your baby's brain is developing, and he's warming it up by judging you. Will he find you to be a sufficient host, an adequate food source, and an acceptable shelter-provider? You can hope. Continue to eat well and stay on his good side.

3. GETTING USED TO THIS "PREGNANCY" NONSENSE

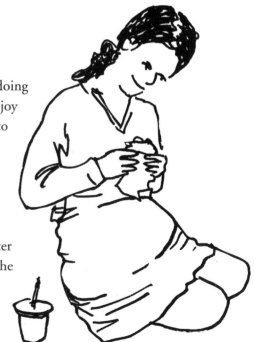

You're nearing the end of the first trimester! Congratulations on doing that. At this point, a normal pregnant woman will find that the joy and excitement she's been hanging on to are slowly giving way to a new reality, one that's puffy and exhausted. Don't despair too much yet! If you let out all your moaning now, you'll have nothing left for later; by the ninth month you'll only be able to speak in an unearthly monotone and no one will want to have lunch with you. No, you'll need to parcel out your despair, month by month, in subtle winces and sobs.

Many women wait until they've cleared the hurdle of the first trimester to announce that they're pregnant. Once you feel comfortable telling the world about your parturient state, you'll soon discover that the world does not actually care. In fact, you might find that the world considers your getting pregnant some kind of character flaw.

Hey, it wasn't the world's idea for you to get a baby in you.

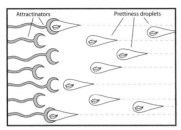

Pre-pregnancy

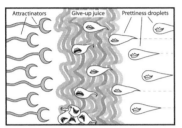

Pregnancy and Postpartum

YOUR BODY IS CHANGING; IT'S WORSE THAN YOU THINK

Why do our bodies fall apart during (and well after) gestation? This is where Science comes in, ladies, so strap on your thinking caps. When you are pregnant, your body begins to create a protein that we call "give-up juice." This basically tells your body: "Hey. You're done. You were attractive enough to score a partner and get yourself pregnant, and that's swell! But now there's no more time for fun and games."

Besides, do you know what would happen if you became increasingly attractive as your pregnancy continued? Your partner would get you re-pregnant! And since your womb has a NO VACANCY sign hanging outside it, Baby #2 would have to wander your insides until he found a safe home somewhere else. Most likely in your liver. And doctors now believe that your liver is probably full of its own children and has no room for yours.

Look how much worse it's going to get!

a. Tender, swollen gums, such that eating anything more challenging than custard causes rivulets of blood to cascade down your teeth. And not in a sexy teenage vampire way.

b. Your extremities swell as your organs migrate and eventually settle in your hands and feet. (Walk and type with care.)

c. You'll never poop again, or you will poop constantly, or both.

d. Your spine will buckle and turn to dust.

e. You'll suddenly find dog food commercials achingly sad.

f. Not to mention reruns of *Full House*. Tearjerking.

g. Also? Sunlight. So poignant.

h. You will be up all night, training your red-eyed glare at your peacefully sleeping partner and wondering if it would be a bad idea to smother him or her with your body pillow, or just your body.

i. Food you'd eaten hours before will spontaneously revisit your mouth.

j. Oh yes, there will be hemorrhoids.

k. You shall pee yourself.

l. You will fall asleep at inopportune moments, like during trapeze practice, or while operating on someone else's brain.

m. You will develop the worst acne you've ever known.

n. You will begin to store food in your cheeks like a squirrel.

o. You will suffer from dry eye, wet eye, excessive blinking, inability to blink, and/or eye-shape and eye-color change. Eye *quantity* should remain stable for the duration of pregnancy.

p. You'll walk like a penguin—a penguin with *hemorrhoids.*

q. Your hair will become shinier and fuller than you've ever known it to be. Note: in some cultures, this is considered a good thing.

r. Your natural body odor will become meatier. Packs of feral dogs will chase you down the street.

s. Your swollen breasts will ache and perspire.

t. Your feet will flatten and enlarge and develop growths, and you will be banned from the pedicure parlor.

u. Your sinuses will become blocked with migratory placenta (keep a roll of paper towels nearby for unexpected sneezing fits).

v. Eating will take on unfathomable importance.

w. As will online Scrabble.

x. Three words: total etiquette amnesia.

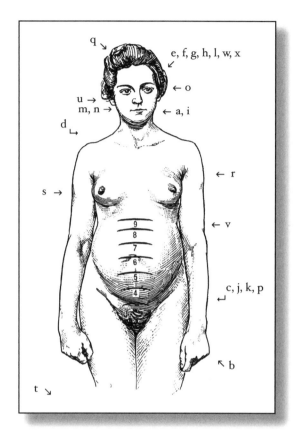

HOW TO DRESS UNTIL YOU CAN BUY PREGNANCY CLOTHES WITHOUT SHAME

Your abdomen is expanding at a rate that will cause your regular pants, upon buttoning, to explode in a cloud of dust, but your pride won't yet allow you to consider the elasticized maternity panels that loom in your future. We understand . . . kind of. We ourselves kept our weight down with the help of steely self-discipline, breathtaking genetics, and Alice's ability to control her colon with her mind. But we hear the gaining-weight thing happens to other people.

Many women in this alarming and swollen time don't know how to clothe their changing body. Some try cinching the gaping waistband of their skinny jeans together with twine; others leave the house wearing nothing but body paint and a broad smile. *Do not do these things.* A beach towel fastened with an oversize safety pin is not a bohemian toga—it merely makes you look like a toddler who's wandered away from the kiddie pool.

Here's a thought: instead of hiding your special condition, why not accentuate it? In many communities pregnancy is considered trendy, so go ahead and flaunt it, Fertile Myrtle!

If you're concerned that the world won't know the difference between morbidly chubby and commendably knocked up, here are a few suggestions to get you started down the path to Unmistakably Pregnant:

1. A serene, I-meant-to-look-like-this expression
2. Empire-waist anything
3. A low-riding tutu is festive!
4. How about an inner tube?
5. Something with a ruffled, pleated, puckered, and/or ruched midsection. They make those, right?
6. A horizontally striped speed-skating suit
7. A T-shirt that reads I AM PREGNANT, NOT FAT
8. A cropped shirt. With a cropped jacket over it. Let your belly breathe!

WELCOME TO THE END OF THE FIRST TRIMESTER

You should only have gained one pound this month, if you've stayed on our plain-yogurt-and-ice-cubes diet, so if you've gained more, you're using this pregnancy as an excuse to turn into a fatty. Which is what all women secretly yearn to be.

If this is your first pregnancy, at three months you may be starting to look a little heavy. All those bastards in the stockroom have organized a betting pool to see if you're lying about being pregnant just to get out of moving those file cabinets all by yourself. If this is baby number two or three, you're probably pooched out quite a bit already, but half the office still thinks you're lying just to cover up three months of binge eating and secret alcoholism. Try to take things in stride. Learn to appreciate their creativity in finding new ways to judge and harass you. Think of it as the hazing process pregnant women go through on their way to joining the sorority of withered old grannyhood.

HOW ARE YOU FEELING?

HUNGRY!

You may experience an increase in appetite, now that your nausea is on the wane. (Please note: if your nausea is not on the wane, you are experiencing karmic retribution. At least, this is what our prenatal yoga teacher told us, and she should know. If you're still vomiting or even just belching, run—do not walk or waddle—to your nearest past-life-regression pavilion.) If you're anything like us, and we know you're trying to be, it used to be that your every-other-day eating routine was governed only by the knowledge that a certain number of calories was necessary to keep your posture rigid and your eyeballs moist. Now, however, you're figuring out that food tastes good. And you want to eat more of it. *All the time.*

This, needless to say, is a terrible mistake that will result in job offers from various traveling carnivals, not to mention your never fitting into those size six pants again. Luckily, we're here with helpful tips on managing both your terrible, boundless appetite and your grotesquely expanding waistline.

THIRD MONTH TIPS: DON'T GET FAT!

Hey, fatso! Yeah, that's right, we're talking to you. Being pregnant doesn't give you license to let yourself go. You're not "eating for two"—you're eating for you plus what is now a tiny demi-baby. In fact, your body will reroute all your nutrition to said baby, so you probably need to eat less than you did prepregnancy, just to keep that thing from growing into some sort of unbirthable (though placid) manatee.

But what's a hungry almost-mom to do? Not snack?! Bite your tongue! (Literally: your tongue can provide you with several important nutrients.) There are all kinds of barely nutritious, calorie-light snack options that will fill the gaping void within you without turning you into a grotesque. Here are some examples!

- 3 apple slices drizzled with one-quarter teaspoon maple syrup
- 2 almond-sized banana-sweetened nut clusters
- 1 celery stick dusted in powdered sugar substitute
- A fistful* of raw bulgur wheat moistened with a sprinkling of pomegranate juice
- 12 mashed raisins nestled in a porcelain espresso cup
- A thumb-sized hill of shredded coconut mixed with all the pencil shavings you can eat!

*Please use child's fist for measurement

It Really Happened! Beanie's Story

"I had the morning sickness something fierce all during my first and second month, but even though it seemed like I puked up everything I tasted or saw or smelled, by the third month I was *faaaat*. Before pregnancy I was a size zero and now all of a sudden I need to buy a pair of size four jeans?! *KILL ME, I'm a whale.* So I called my friend Alex, and I was all, *Girl, I'm going on a Fresca fast even if it makes me barf so hard my eyeballs hemorrhage.* She came right on over with two pints of Overweight Husband™ ice cream and told me that my tiny baby needed me to ingest as many calories as I could, especially if they were made out of heavy cream or chocolate. Miraculously, I found that all this high-fat eating eliminated my nausea! So I decided to not worry about my weight gain and just enjoy my pregnancy. Now I have a beautiful, healthy baby boy! And my ex-husband is so sweet—he still comes over once a week to wash me with a rag on a stick."

—Beanie McCord, age 27, Tallahassee, Florida

DID YOU KNOW? IF YOU HAD BEEN PREGNANT 100 YEARS AGO . . .

TABLE 3.1 A BILLION-YEAR HISTORY OF CHILDBIRTH

Today	100 years ago	500 years ago	1 billion years ago
You have a plethora of pain-relieving options available to you.	How about some nice, calming ether?	Your midwife gave you a worn leather strap to bite down on.	Your cells simply divided in the warm primordial soup.
Give birth in a nice, sterile hospital bed! Or a filthy, rented hot tub. Your choice.	Beds were an option, though some women preferred hay.	Beds stuffed with hay.	Ah, the soup. So primordial, so warm.
Vaginal birth or C-section? Whatever's best for you and your baby.	Typical C-section scar ran from pubic bone to throat (good thing high collars were so chic!).	Only the most rugged women agreed to C-sections (performed by a village barber or smithy).	You just divided right down the middle! It felt a little weird.
Your husband, family, and friends can all be with you and support you through this life-changing experience.	Husbands kept in distant waiting rooms with plenty of tobacco and Glenlivet so as not to be disturbed by all the screaming.	Husbands were out plowing, herding, shearing, harvesting, running off to sea, and/or getting drunk and harassing the mead wench.	Your indifferent soup mates just floated thoughtlessly around you, occasionally bumping into you and burping.

WHAT KIND OF PREGNANT LADY ARE YOU?

There's no question that you are an individual, with a unique mélange of fascinating qualities baked to perfection in the coal-fired brick oven of your soul.

However, once a woman is with child, studies have shown that she will instinctively camouflage her many charming facets to mimic the stereotypical behaviors you'll see below. This is a survival technique that allows her unwitting peers to laugh and feel superior to her (so that they won't want to set her house on fire).

If you have a problem with this brutal reality, we recommend taking it up with Nature herself.

WHICH OF THESE STEREOTYPES BEST DESCRIBE YOU? COME ON, ADMIT IT.

PREGNANT LADY WHO CAN'T HANDLE BEING PREGNANT
- Wears flannel nightgown and slippers to work
- Screams every time the baby kicks
- Stares longingly at grocery store sushi
- Has a birth plan that includes instructions on how to dial 911

PREGNANT LADY WHO LOVES BEING PREGNANT
- Practices beatific smile while knitting tiny baby clothing
- Flips her hair over her shoulder and exults in how shiny and manageable it's become since she got pregnant
- Forces strangers to manhandle her abdomen
- Seriously asks doctor about keeping baby inside an extra month

PREGNANT LADY WHO STUBBORNLY BELIEVES THAT HER LIFE WON'T CHANGE AT ALL AFTER THE BABY COMES
- Wears four-inch heels all the way into her third trimester
- Has her baby shower in a karaoke bar with nine Japanese businessmen
- Makes dinner reservations while pushing
- Plans to take the baby home from the hospital on a Vespa

QUIZ: WHAT KIND OF PARENT WILL YOUR PARTNER BE?

Just as you fit one of a small number of stereotypes, so, too, does your partner. What, did you think we were only going to disparage *you*?

If your partner is a woman, then we commend you for your modern ways and we invite you to switch some pronouns around; we think we've done enough already. If you're the one having the baby, she's probably wearing the pants in the family anyway, if you know what we mean. *(We mean that she plays the guy.)*

1. WHEN YOU TOLD YOUR PARTNER YOU WERE PREGNANT, DID HE:
   a. Weep softly and cling to your abdomen until you had to push him away?
   b. Jog down the street, high-fiving everyone in sight?
   c. Roll his eyes and turn the television up louder?
   d. Jump on his laptop and order a breast pump?
   e. Demand to know what the baby is thinking?

2. THE FIRST TIME YOU SUFFERED A BOUT OF MORNING SICKNESS, DID HE:
   a. Hold your hair back, quietly retching in sympathy?
   b. Shout "Mind over matter, babe!" as you ran to the bathroom?
   c. Ask you to keep it down because he was trying to sleep in?
   d. Google "labor pain remedies"?
   e. Gasp, "What have you done to anger the baby?!"

3. WHEN YOU STARTED TO SHOW, DID HE:
   a. Ask if he could photograph your nude form bathed in early morning light?

b.   Offer to let you hide it under his high school football jersey?

c.   Glare at your abdomen and warn you not to get carried away?

d.   Start making a PowerPoint presentation of your daily belly photos?

e.   Hide under the bedspread with an aluminum foil–covered colander on his head?

4. WHEN IT WAS TIME TO ANNOUNCE THE JOYOUS NEWS TO YOUR FAMILY, DID HE:

a.   Summon your families to a clearing in the woods, where he played a lute and shared the exciting news in rhymed couplets?

b.   Ask you to call everyone, because he's "not so good with feelings"?

c.   Begin the conversation, "Guess what Angelina Jolie here got herself into"?

d.   Send a baby shower e-vite to the admissions office at MIT?

e.   Contact the FBI to inform them that the fetus growing inside you is transmitting messages to the world via the lyrics of Coldplay?

5. WHEN YOU GIVE BIRTH, DO YOU EXPECT YOUR PARTNER TO:

a.   Weep and giggle at the same time?

b.   Cheer you on like you were wrestling a goat?

c.   Smirk every time you suffer a contraction?

d.   Live Tweet the entire process?

e.   Clamber up to the hospital roof, barking like a seal?

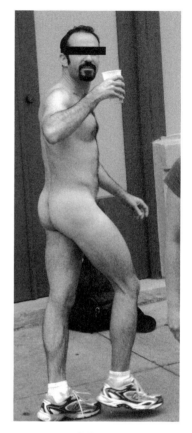

Some men defy classification altogether.

If your answers were mostly As: you've got a SENSITIVE DAD on your hands! Keep plenty of tissues around; you're going to need them.

If your answers were mostly Bs: an EMOTIONALLY STUNTED JOCK is your baby's dad! It could be worse. See next page.

If your answers were mostly Cs: we're sorry, but you're saddled with a TOTAL DICK! Keep hoping and don't let go. Eventually he'll come around and love you. We can feel it.

If your answers were mostly Ds: you've got a BEFUDDLED GEEK to deal with! He may be more connected to his smartphone than to you or the baby, but he'll find a relevant article about it on WebMD before you can say "Han Solo shot first."

If your answers were mostly Es: your guy is CLINICALLY NUTS! Keep knives out of reach and speak in low, hushed tones.

FIRST TRIMESTER KEYWORD SEARCH STRINGS TO MAKE YOU PANIC MORE

The first trimester is a groundbreaking thrill ride from start to finish, it's true. But don't let sensible advice from your doctor or midwife dominate the conversation; why not ask the Internet's opinion on some of the things you've been too embarrassed to bring up during office visits? It will provide a welcome surge of adrenaline to your developing fetus, who is a bit bored him/herself! Try some of these helpful searches:

- Eleven weeks pregnant cross-eyed tuna can dented
- Belly-button oozing ranch dressing
- Stop mother-in-law poking breasts slapping uterus
- Penis bruise "baby head"
- Fetus + odds + extra organs
- PCP during pregnancy bad?
- Nipples leaking Hawaiian Punch
- Dreams baby Brian Dennehy face head

- Okay to take fetus to R-rated movie?
- Pregnant woman smell *and* mayonnaise
- Craving fiberglass
- Parasitic twin names

QUIZ: WEIRD OLD WIVES' TALES: TRUE OR FALSE?

Once the word is out that you are full with child, senior citizens you never knew you were related to will emerge from the woodwork to share their nonsensical old-world "knowledge." Some of these superstitions may have a basis in reality. Do you know which ones?

1. If your unborn baby gets the hiccups, stand on your head to make them stop.
2. Wearing a football helmet daily throughout your pregnancy will turn your baby into a great athlete.
3. Don't let a cat near a newborn baby, as it will lie on the baby's face and suffocate it.
4. If you feel a burning sensation while you urinate, your baby is angry with you.
5. If you look at a toad while you're pregnant, your baby will be born covered in warts.
6. If you have sex while you're pregnant, your baby will be born with a beard.

Answers:
1. FALSE. Nothing amuses the elderly more than watching a pregnant woman try to turn herself upside down.

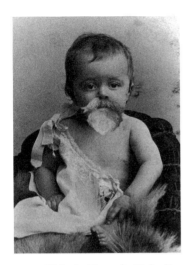

This is Francis Bakoff, 1907–1952, seen here at age six months. Once his parents were outed as having "done it" while their son was in utero, the entire family was sent to live as circus freaks: Francis, of course, as the Bearded Baby (then the Bearded Boy, then the Bearded Man, which was less of an attraction), and his parents, Doris and Jules, as The Married Immigrants Who (It Can Be Proven) Coupled More Than Once!

2. TRUE. What you eat, your baby eats. What you drink, your baby drinks. What you wear, your baby wears. And wearing a football helmet will naturally orient his tiny brain toward that great American sport. That's just logic.

3. VERY TRUE. Your ancient relatives are all too aware of the cat's abilities to suck the fresh life essence from your baby during the night. Before the days of cat monitors, too many babies were lost to the feline lust for new-baby gasses. Take heed!

4. FALSE. If you feel a burning sensation when you urinate, your *ancestors* are angry with you. For marrying a man whose flocks and herds are frail, and whose sepulcher is set with shameful objects of some sort.

5. FALSE. This is utterly ridiculous! Toads are not cats. Don't even get us started on what will happen if you look at a cat.

6. DREADFULLY TRUE. See sidebar for proof.

HOW TO EXPLAIN TO YOUR GRANDCHILDREN THAT YOU'RE PREGNANT

This is for you older ladies.

Because it is vitally important to the ongoing existence of our culture that no one under the age of thirty think about middle-aged people having sex, you pregnant women in the forty to fifty range are going to get a lot of strange looks when your belly starts to show. Children and animals will shrink from your touch. Your doctor will shriek at his first sight of gray pubic hair. Your varicose veins will swell and throb like a second heart! It's kind of like being a superhero who has the power to make people uncomfortable.

Many older women foolishly believe they've already gone through menopause (aka "The Change" or "The Great Desiccation") when in fact they've just failed to notice their period due to early-onset senility. So they dispense with condoms during their bouts of gerontological intercourse, and lo! One day they realize they can no longer dismiss their expanding waistlines as the result of "too much bridge mix at Sandy's euchre parties."

These little surprises are sometimes called "Change of Life Babies," and they're nothing to fear. (Usually.) They're often a blessing, in fact. A ghastly blessing!

BENEFITS TO HAVING A BABY LATE IN LIFE

It can bring you closer to estranged older children who aren't unnerved by the thought of you having sex.

Unemployed older children can now earn money by babysitting.

Baby can be playmates with her own nieces and nephews.

No need to buy a stroller—just climb into your Rascal mobility scooter and put Baby in your lap!

DRAWBACKS TO HAVING A BABY LATE IN LIFE

Breasts may drop beyond arms' reach.

Baby cannot clap hard enough to turn off your lights and TV.

Geritol does not make prenatal vitamins.

Breaking the news to older children can be an icky affair, it's true, but how to explain to *their* children that Gran-gran's got a baby inside her? Here are some suggestions:

1. "The stork's on his way! A stork is a bird that brings babies. Yes, he brought you, too. He didn't? Daddy fished you out of the birthing tub? Oh."

"Take it from me, kids: you can *get pregnant doing it doggy style."*

2. "Grandma's swelling up with love and soon it's going to burst out all over everyone! Why are you crying?"
3. "Look, kid, I'm pregnant. I'm not happy about it, but there it is. Hand me my lighter."
4. "Grandma's got a surprise for you! No, it's not an Xbox 360."

MEANWHILE, INSIDE YOU . . . THE THIRD MONTH

WHAT'S GOING ON UP IN THERE?

Between thirteen and sixteen weeks, that clump of cells will mature into a fuzzy sack of beating organs. With fingernails! Eeeee!

Here's your baby!

This month, your baby's bones begin to "harden," which means "get more hard." Baby is also moving like crazy, but what, did you really think you could feel him kick? He's just a nubbin. Get ahold of yourself.

4. THE SECOND TRIMESTER: TIME FOR INVASIVE TESTING

You're glowing. Don't fight it! All that bonus estrogen coursing through your veins has finally turned you into the woman your mother always hoped you'd be. You no longer have to perform a complicated depilatory/blowtorch routine on your shaggy man-legs anymore. Not only have you lost your mustache and careless swagger, you're one decent manicure short of becoming Julie Andrews. Try to enjoy it. Soon enough you'll be little more than a brood sow flopped and grunting in the dirt, whose existence balances on the whim of a cute, greedy, viciously suckling little piglet.

HOW ARE YOU FEELING?

You're finally out of the first trimester, which means that you are no longer worried. After all, your risk of miscarriage has all but disappeared and it's all smooth sailing from here. Right?

Not so fast, missy. Your miscarriage risk has decreased, sure, but plenty can still go wrong. Have you considered that your baby may be a total jerk? Have you even considered the possibility? HOW ARE YOU GOING TO SAFEGUARD AGAINST THIS?! You're lucky you have us. Now all you have to do is find our guide to molding your baby's personality in utero, which is buried somewhere deep within this book. Good luck! *The clock is ticking!*

Meanwhile, according to the literature your first-trimester fatigue should have eased up, and yet *you are still sleepy*. There's only one explanation: your baby, bored with staring at the same dumb womb day in and day out, has exited your uterus and is now touring your body. You're sleepy because he's lodged in your hypothalamus, which most experts agree is in your brain. As you drift off to napland, try not to worry too much about the baby getting stuck there and continuing to grow until your skull bursts. He's just taking a little field trip, is all. There's a 37 percent chance he can be coaxed back—more, if he likes the smell of Summer's Eve.

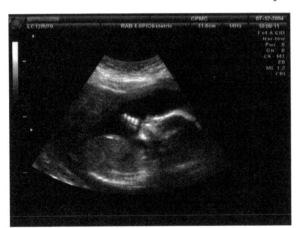

This baby is a dick.

When you're not sleeping, you can be found stuffing your face. If you've been recklessly nutrifying yourself despite everything we've told you, you might find that none of your clothes fit anymore, and instead of looking as streamlined as *we* did, or perhaps slightly more plush, your mom is asking you if you're sure you're not having twins.

If you had listened to us earlier you wouldn't be in this mess. Good news: it's not too late! Even Alice managed to gain an ounce more than she wanted in the first trimester, when the only thing stopping her from retching herself dry was string cheese rolled in confectioners' sugar. In the fourth month she came to her senses and began a daily regimen of berating herself in front of a full-length mirror and only eating fennel. Soon she was able to squeeze herself into her birthing corset without breaking any more ribs.

AMNIOCENTESIS AND RELATED TESTS

Back in the old days, when we were all ignorant savages, a pregnant woman had no idea who or what was growing inside her. Did it have a penis? A vagina? Or an unruly *pegina*? Feet where its hands should be? A sheep's head? Feathers? Birthing was the moment of truth, and the joy everyone in the village felt at the emergence of new life was often subdued by the discovery of the infant's prehensile tail, which foretold that it was destined for the papacy.

It Really Happened! Ann's Story

"After I read Mahatma Beauregard's book, *The Robotic Pregnancy*, I knew I didn't want to have any corporate intervention into my baby's gestation. I grew all my own organic pregnancy food, washed it in rainwater, and ate it raw. I heated my house with the wood from an ancient, self-sacrificing redwood we lovingly pushed over with our bare hands and chopped up with flint axes, and my version of prenatal testing was accomplished when a butterfly landed on my belly one morning and telepathically told me that my fetus was perfect. The completely natural birth of my child, Chuck, was attended by woodland creatures, who held vigil for hours, either in wonderment at the miracle of life or in expectation of the placenta. Chuck was never immunized, was totally home-schooled, and grew to be a strapping man of six-foot-three inches who now, at the age of twenty-three, survives on Dr. Pepper and microwaved taquitos from 7-Eleven. He lives in my finished basement, won't pay rent, and makes his living selling asbestos to the elderly. How do you test for *that*?"

—Ann Pritchard, age 47, Bend, Oregon

TABLE 4.1 AMNIOCENTESIS AND RELATED TESTS

Test Name	What Your Doctor Tells You It's Meant to Detect	What It *Really* Detects	Ways You Can Skew the Results in Your Favor	No, Really, What Can You Do to Make This Turn Out Okay?
Amniocentesis	Down Syndrome or other chromosomal or genetic abnormalities	How much money your child will inherit from miserly relatives	Slip the lab tech a fifty	Slip the lab tech *two* fifties
Blood test for Rh factor	Whether your blood type is incompatible with your baby's	If you and your spouse are going to divorce within a year of the baby's birth	Blow jobs. *Lots of blow jobs.*	Maybe go to dinner and a movie, too. One of those chick flicks.
Carrier screening for inherited genetic disorders	Sickle-cell anemia; cystic fibrosis; Tay-Sachs; and other genetic diseases	How Jewish, French-Canadian, and/or black you are	Learn to enjoy pickled herring/eat poutine/blow out your Afro	Travel back in time and be born to different parents
Chorionic villus sampling (CVS)	Genetic disorders; chromosomal abnormalities; blah blah blah	If/when your baby will knock over a chain of pharmacies	Drink a case of NyQuil	Hide the syringes
Doppler sonography	Measures blood flow to different parts of the baby's body	If the fetus is genetically superior, has supersonic hearing	Watch *Das Boot* a couple of times	Dress in the native garb of the Fatherland
Glucose screening and glucose tolerance test	If you've developed gestational diabetes	If you use Internet pornography to prop up your fragile sense of self-worth	Cancel all your credit cards	Throw your laptop into a hot tub
Group B streptococcus screening	If you carry the Group B Strep virus in your vagina or anus	What a wonderful human being you are	A whole *Silkwood* scrub-down can't get rid of that	Keep telling yourself *it's not your fault*
Nonstress test	Monitors your baby's heart rate at rest and after being nudged with a cold ultrasound wand	How many Olympic medals your baby will win someday	Get a tiny treadmill up in there	Hum the theme to *Chariots of Fire* and ignore the baffled looks from those hospital techs
Nuchal translucency screening	Whether or not there's fluid accumulating in the tissues at the back of your baby's neck	Translucent nuchals!	Get one of those Harry Potter invisibility cloaks	Seriously

Nowadays, we can discover all kinds of things about a fetus while he's still in utero, thus ensuring, among other things, that your child will never be pope. And with early testing, you can enjoy up to six more months to worry and fret over inconclusive or incorrect results. Thanks, Medicine!

PRENATAL TESTS AND THERAPIES WE *CANNOT* RECOMMEND

You want to know every single thing about your kid when he's still inside you and you can't get at him, but how many of these tests are *really* necessary? (Aside from the one that detects psychokinesis—*that* you want to be ready for.) It's dispiriting to learn how many tests your doctor is ordering just to keep his girlfriend in phlebotomy busy. Below are some tests you should absolutely refuse.

Spinal fluid sluice test
Your cerebral-spinal fluid is drained, mixed with Grape Nuts (an excellent source of folic acid), and then reinjected into the base of your skull while you listen to a medley of Raffi-inspired tambourine solos. How intolerable you find this test is said to be directly related to how human your baby will be.
Elaborate, and not recommended.

Nipple density test
"Will your nipples be able to stand up to a teething infant? Let's use this big needle to find out."
No.

Bladder jab electro-saturation testing
Just like it sounds.
Don't do it. Just don't.

Pulmonary vacuum-suctioning therapy
Your lungs are gently sucked out through your mouth, laid on a sterile surgical tray, and covered with a wet washcloth. Said to increase yelling capacity and relieve symptoms of heartburn.
Extremely inconvenient.

Metaphysical horripilation testing
Discovers the range and intensity of your feelings of existential despair when picking through the shards of your hopes and dreams at 4 A.M.
A little journaling could do this without you coughing up your bone marrow.

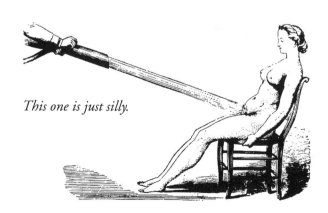

This one is just silly.

POINT/COUNTERPOINT: IS THERE A POINT TO ALL THIS TESTING NONSENSE?

ALICE:

YES, TEST EVERYTHING, CONSTANTLY.

Is there a point to all this testing "nonsense"? Of course there is. Who put "nonsense" in quotes, anyway? Eden, was that you? How dare you. As I was saying: your baby has to learn that she's not going to get out of you before you've figured out exactly what she's made of. After all, a child cannot graduate from high school until he meets the minimum requirements of the state board of high schoolery. (Right? I think I'm right about that.) In the same way, a fetus must not be released from the womb until professionals can establish that she'll be able to handle life amongst the humans and plants.

Besides, comprehensive testing gives you a battery of results you can brag about to your friends—and when they stop calling you back, your local cashiers, neighborhood homeless, and any receptive clergy you come across. (One word: confessionals. They can't run away!) Did the anatomical perfection of your baby's heart move the technician to tears? Does your baby's femur-to-tibia ratio predict a wildly successful future in basketball? Is your child's DNA pattern so uniquely beautiful that your geneticist asked if he could have it tattooed on his chest? You and the rest of the world gets to know all of this thanks to testing. Thanks, testing!

EDEN:

NO, TRUST IN NATURE'S INNATE WISDOM.

All fetuses are perfect just the way they are. Your baby's karma decrees what sort of embodiment he or she will take in this lifetime, so deal with it. I myself was born with X-ray vision and my parents not only supported me unconditionally, they took me to local hospitals so that I could do CT scans on patients during blizzards and blackouts. Children need to see their unique, unpredictable traits as gifts they can use to help others, not just skills they can use to get ahead in an uncertain job market. Although I have to say, after college I was able to support myself quite nicely as a mammogram technician.

QUIZ FOR FETUSES: WHAT KIND OF NURSERY THEME SHOULD YOUR MOMMY AND/OR DADDY CHOOSE?

A. WHAT IS YOUR FAVORITE COLOR?

1. Dark
2. Reddish-dark
3. Dark with patches of not-dark
4. Amniotic orange

B. WHAT IS YOUR FAVORITE ACTIVITY?

1. Dozing
2. Hiccuping
3. Squirming
4. Bluffing

C. WHAT IS YOUR FAVORITE ANIMAL?

1. "Animal"?
2. Foot
3. Whatever's murmuring out there sounds good to me
4. Oh, just let me be!

Baby will feel right at home!

D. FAVORITE SHAPE?

1. Blob
2. Me
3. Ovoid
4. Amorphous

E. WHAT IS YOUR FAVORITE FOOD?

1. Fluid
2. Warm
3. This
4. Tiramisu

F. WHAT KIND OF JOB DO YOU WANT TO HAVE WHEN YOU GROW UP?

1. Submarine captain
2. Chimney sweep
3. Chunnel train conductor
4. Amniotic fluid temperature regulator

Now, add up your score based on the number you chose for each answer, i.e., 1 point for number 1, 2 points for number 2, etc.

0–5: ABANDONED COAL MINE THEME—you like nothing more than a close, dark room where you can escape from the world

6–10: UNUSED SEA CAVE THEME—you want a salty, predator-free environment that will help you chill out

11–15: UNATTENDED WINE CELLAR THEME—those barrels aren't just rustic accoutrements, they're fermenting some top-quality hooch

16–20: DEAD RELATIVE'S WARDROBE THEME—just shut the door, curl up in a musty fur coat, and relax!

MEANWHILE, INSIDE YOU . . .
THE FOURTH MONTH

WHAT'S GOING ON UP IN THERE?

Guess who's peeing inside you? Your baby, that's who. Try not to let this freak you out too badly. If you ingest only distilled water and celery, your baby's pee will be . . . well, slightly less disgusting to fathom.

In addition to whizzing all over your insides, your baby is busily growing a coarse, light-brown fur. He's developing sharp clawlike digits, too—the better to cling to your uterus. You can't shake him loose now!

Here's your baby!

5. WELCOME TO THE SMUG MONTH

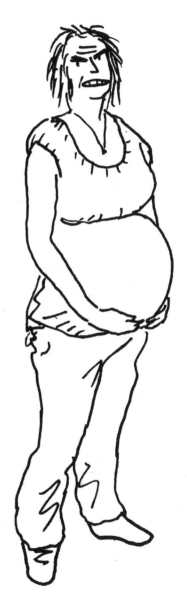

The fifth month of pregnancy is widely known as Rainbow Delight Nougat Dream Fantasia Month, wherein all your troubles magically end and you can't imagine that any new ones will ever crop up, ever. And you think you can take credit for at least some of this. Finally, you've tackled the challenges of pregnancy! Your nausea has abated, no doubt due to wise nutritional choices and/or the strength of your hours of fervent, toilet-adjacent prayer; you no longer fall asleep at every quiet interval, such as when you're drinking cocoa or uncoupling box cars; your sleep is refreshing, your dreams psychedelically dirty; your "baby bump" is adorable and not at all as grotesque as you were afraid it might be; mealtime has taken on an orgasmic significance as you savor each delectable morsel; your complexion is smooth and glowing where once it was oil-slicked and furious; your urine is pure enough to be used to irrigate crops, and yet powerful enough to replace carbon-based fuel. You've saved the environment with your hormones! *Wheee!*

Fifth month: artist's depiction.

Ah, yes. It's all lovely for you, we know. Now wipe that smirk off your face. You can't take credit for any of this. The fifth month is a honeymoon period in which everything will go great, no matter what you do, so enjoy each blissful moment! Things will start to suck again before you know it.

If you are currently in your fifth month and are not having any fun at all, we apologize for the above paragraphs. We recommend taping over them with a sturdy piece of cardboard. A couple of things may be going on with you:

- You're having twins—or more! Thus you have skipped straight over the honeymoon interval and are on the express train to jumbo-size and extra-gassy.
- You have *hyperemesis,* which is Latin for "excuse me, why am I still throwing up?" Hyperemesis is, technically speaking, a medical mystery as well as a cataclysmic bummer. Not only are you still throwing up, you may continue to do so for some time, and God has forsaken you, and also there is no God, you know that now, just as you know that we live in a cold and indifferent universe. The one guaranteed remedy for hyperemesis seems to be delivering your baby. So you have, at most, four more months of constant, relentless nausea. But maybe less! Buck up!
- You are a giant whiner.

BREAKING THE NEWS

Now that you are obviously, clearly pregnant, it is your moral obligation to alert everyone to the moist, swollen state of your sexual organs. Don't make them wonder whether that's a baby bump or if you're just bloated from lunch! Do you know how embarrassing that is for them? Think of humanity! Loved ones and strangers alike fairly ache to give you their approval, unwanted advice, and unnerving, wide-eyed stares directed at your boobs.

Reactions to your News can be awkward, especially from the men around you. This is because only one thing will be on the minds of every friend, family member, and medical professional with whom you share your pregnancy: *You let a man put his penis in your vagina.* Even if you're a lesbian and used donor sperm, once you're big enough to show, every barista who hands you a latte is going to assume you were impregnated during hot heterosexual intercourse that may or may not have brought you to orgasm, and what did your face look like while that happened?

So. You can imagine how turned-on everyone feels around you now.

While it's important to inform the world of your delicate situation, *you must not do it by talking.* Talking about sex and its results is intensely upsetting to almost everyone, and its pernicious effects can ruin lives. Look how badly this could go:

"Welcome to Wendy's! What can I get you today?"
"I'll have a Frosty, and the fetus inside me will have fries, ha ha!"
"Ha ha, congratulations!"
"Thanks!"

Sounds innocent, right? And it was—until the cashier got into a motocross accident later that day because she was imagining a tiny fetus eating fries with its weensy arm-buds and not about the challenges of the off-road circuit in front of her.

Or here's another:

"Hey, Mom, good news! We're having a baby!"
"Oh my God, what did that husband *do* to you?"
"Well . . . you know."
Kerthunk.

How not to break the news.

To overcome all the awkwardness and potential for tragedy, we recommend breaking the news and combating ignorant speculation with the use of *T-shirts*. A pregnancy announcement stretched across your swollen midsection can do double duty: worn to a family gathering it will silently alert your parents, siblings, in-laws, and spouse to your condition; worn in public, it will instruct literate strangers to stand up and give you their seat at the bar. Here are a few telling phrases that we recommend:

- ATTENTION: I AM PREGNANT.

- I AM THIS WAY BECAUSE I ALLOWED
  A MAN TO PUT HIS PENIS IN MY VAGINA.

- THAT'S RIGHT. HIS PENIS, PLUS MY
  VAGINA, EQUALS A BABY, WHICH IS
  CURRENTLY INSIDE ME, DOING ITS THING.

- I ENDURED A BOUT OF SEXUAL
  INTERCOURSE, DISCOVERED THAT
  I WAS WITH CHILD, AND THEN I
  WENT AND MADE MYSELF THIS T-
  SHIRT. ARE YOU STILL READING?

- THE SEX WAS SPIRITED AND
  VIGOROUS; MY EXPRESSION,
  TORMENT INTERMINGLED WITH ECSTASY.

- IT WAS JUST A TURKEY BASTER. DON'T LOOK AT ME LIKE THAT.

SCIENCE CORNER: WHY YOU WILL WANT TO, BUT SHOULD NOT, HAVE SEX WITH ANYTHING THAT MOVES

Midway through your pregnancy, you may begin to find yourself consumed by irresistible and badly timed sexual urges. Several theories abound as to why this is. Some experts have concluded that this is nature's cruel trick, turning you into a ravenous she-beast just as your proportions make you more comical than alluring. Still others (mainly the kinky anthropologists in the crowd) posit that in long-ago, cruder times, a pregnant woman was considered the sexiest female in the community because she had obviously Done It, *and might be up for Doing It again.* Plus, her hindquarters were swollen and pink, and we all know what that means!

Sadly, we live in the present day and not in some ancient pervert tribe, so you cannot and must not cheat on your loved one, no matter how repulsed s/he is by your girth. "Having sex with anything warm and ambulatory" is, as we know, one of the top fifteen relationship killers. (Other top relationship killers include "accidentally" sucking your partner's favorite pet snake into the vacuum cleaner, all-night drunken hootenanny jags, and seething hatred.) And right now you need to hang on to your partner for all you've got, because he or she is the only one who might help you with those 2 A.M. feedings.

So who does that leave available for your sex-making?

- Your husband or partner
- Your husband or partner's life-size replica (preferably constructed with an articulated steel skeleton and flavorless, weapons-grade silicone)

Beyond that, what you do with the small appliances in your home is your business.

Use only as directed.

IMPORTANT NOTE: If you're not in a relationship, disregard the above advice and start cruising your church, drum circle, or local synagogue's singles jamboree. Quick, before you bloat up exponentially. Internet dating is also an option, as you can string along potential dates by e-mail for as long as it takes to lose that baby weight. Do you know how to use Photoshop?

POINT/COUNTERPOINT: SHOULD YOU FIND OUT THE GENDER OR NOT?

ALICE: OF COURSE, AS SOON AS POSSIBLE.

It's essential that you know how to address your baby while he or she is still in utero. While your baby is swimming around in your aquatic baby-growing tank, he's searching for clues to his future identity. He's got nothing better to do. Defining him correctly helps to cement Baby's gender role and keep him from evolving into one of those newfangled boygals, or ladymen, or whatever they're calling themselves nowadays.

I discovered that my baby was a boy at twenty weeks. Oh, how I mourned not having known his sex for almost half his gestation! How often, I wondered, had I referred to him as Girl and/or Boy Baby? How many times had I whispered, "I can't wait to show you your Desert Storm– or bulimia-themed nursery, depending"?! I tried to correct my behavior later on by whispering daily masculine affirmations, but the damage had been done. Just the other day my seven-year-old *boy* complimented me on my *pretty shoes.*

No one else should suffer this fate.

EDEN: NEVER! YOUR BABY'S GENDER MUST REMAIN A BEAUTIFUL MYSTERY UNTIL HE OR SHE DECIDES OTHERWISE.

As we now know, and as countless studies have shown *despite what Alice continues to insist*, gender is a beautiful continuum, a spectrum upon which each individual alights hither and/or yon. The male/female dichotomy is but an illusion! So why would I have my precious baby's sexual identity defined by some *technician* in a *lab coat*? Why, indeed, would I presume to say whether my baby is a boy or girl or glorious pan-gendered evolved being?

This is why I didn't find out what sex my child is. And it's why I still don't know. Quant, my lovely prepubescent offspring, is a mystery wrapped in a gender-puzzle, and he or she can remain that way until him or her decides it's time to identify one way or the other. Or not.

MYSTERIOUS PAINS AND WHAT THEY SIGNIFY

They tell you not to worry about the weird pains, but do they tell you *why* you shouldn't worry? Or what they really are? No. They say nothing. Because they are lying. Fortunately, we are not they. We are us.

- Piercing pain in lower right quadrant: *Your child has gotten hold of a spork.*
- Dull ache down left leg: *You forgot you were pregnant for a minute but now you remembered.*
- Stabbing pain in right eye: *Your partner is looking at naked pictures of Wynona Judd online.*
- Stabbing pain in left eye: *You're stabbing yourself in the left eye.*
- Acidic burning in throat: *Couple of possibilities here: you've been cursed by an old Romany woman; your child is traveling up your esophagus, for the hell of it; you ate something awful, like olive loaf.*

- Taste of olive loaf in your mouth: *There's your answer.*
- Feeling that your pelvis is cracking open. *Why, that's your ligaments loosening!*
- Feeling that you're being torn apart from the inside: *Just some loosening of the ligaments! Nothing to be concerned by!*
- Feeling that STOP TELLING ME IT'S FUCKING LIGAMENTS: *Okay, but. Well.*
- I SAID—: *OKAY! Sheesh. Just take some vitamins or something.*
- Surprisingly painful cramping sensations spreading through your midsection, coming and going in waves, accompanied by the urge to push: *We have no idea what this could mean. Accept the vast unknowableness of your body's strange journey.*

NONPREGNANCY-RELATED TRIVIA YOU CAN DISCUSS WITH YOUR NONPREGNANT FRIENDS!

By as early as your second trimester, your nonpregnant friends ("normals") will have had enough uterine updates from you. If you want to hang on to your friends, now is the time you must think of something(s) other than yourself and *fake interest in the outside world.*

Can you do it? Yes, you can! With this *amazing trivia:*

1. Guess which United States presidents weren't breastfed?
2. Guess how many baby possums are born per litter, on average?
3. Did you know that condoms were originally made out of animal guts?
4. And the first diaphragms were, like, half a lemon!
5. Which creature has the most chromosomes, a fruit fly or a dog?
6. Who is the only player in NBA history to accumulate 20,000+ points in his career, while averaging fewer than 15.0 points per game?

Answers

1. Clinton and Taft? We're just guessing.
2. SEVEN.
3. Gross, right? But it makes sense if you think about it.
4. We're pretty sure the Egyptians did that.
5. Probably a fruit fly. That's why they do so much science on them.
6. Kareem Abdul-Jabbar.

Trivia that you should just keep to yourself:

- Guess how many nipple hairs I have?
- I've discovered seven different positions for having a successful bowel movement!
- My husband is addicted to Rice Krispies.

SURVIVING BED REST: CULTIVATE NEW HOBBIES!

Say, for one reason or another, your doctor has consigned you to bed rest. In the interest of your health and the health of that little lollygagger inside of you, you have to stay put. Weeks and months will pass and there's nothing you can do but wait. You're trapped. Maybe forever. *(NB: Probably not forever.)*

You may be tempted to spend this time languishing on the Internet and whining to strangers, but we're here to tell you: no one wants to hear it, and the ones who *do* want to hear it will turn on you like rabid coyotes the moment you start feeling better.

So what else can you do, if not reach out to the mentally unstable? Plenty! You can still be a productive member of society even flat on your back in a dark, stuffy room surrounded by dirty teacups. Where your body has failed you, your *mind* can now develop obsessive worries you never knew existed!

1. **Try to figure out what you did to deserve this.** Think back. Was it the time you sat under the dinner table and poked at your mom's varicose veins? You definitely did something and the Universe waited until now to punish you.

2. **Plot the demise of your enemies.** Since you have the time, why not spend it imagining deadly pranks that will take teams of science detectives a lifetime to figure out, by which time you'll be dead yourself? For example, invent an undetectable acid that will, over the course of four decades, eat away the elevator cable in your enemy's apartment building until it breaks, but only when she's riding alone inside of it to a height greater than seven stories. That'll show her!

3. **Build a bed-fort.** We don't mean one made out of pillows and sheets. You are not a child. No, you'll be constructing an actual garrison fortified with twelve-pound howitzers, horse-drawn ammunition caissons, a first-aid tent, bunkers, and barracks. Because what if there's a war in your town? And when this war reaches your bed—what then?

4. **Ask your friends and neighbors for assistance.** Whether you construct your fort out of sandbags, logs, or salvaged masonry surrounded by a deep moat with spikes buried beneath the murky waters, you will most likely need to enlist the aid of your more able-bodied compatriots. Start by calling everyone in your book club and then work your way down the list of

cousins, former employers, old boyfriends who still "owe" you, weak-willed neighbors, and people you exchanged business cards with while standing in line at Starbucks.

5. Make a list of those friends and neighbors who refuse to help. Title the list "New Enemies." You can never have too many enemies. Also, here's a little-known fact that only we will tell you: as long as your brain simmers with resentment and revenge-plotting, you can avoid contracting Bed-Rest Madness.

6. Build a deadly catapult. Point it toward your new enemies' homes. A simple counterweight trebuchet is easy and fun to build. Ordering diseased carcasses to fling toward enemy lines might take some time—but then, time is what you have quite a lot of.

7. Chat up telemarketers. After they insist that they cannot ship you any diseased carcasses via the postal service, you can get to talking about more personal matters. Like, "Wouldn't *you* drag slabs of limestone to your friend's bedside? *You* wouldn't think that was too much to ask, would you, Shonda?"

8. Imagine you're on a boat! On the other hand, don't imagine that.

9. Regress into some past lives. We bet it was easy to find help installing the spikes deep within your fetid moat when you were the Macedonian Emperor Constantine VII.

10. Write a best-selling memoir. You can write all about the madcap, whirlwind existence you led before you were trapped in this soft, pillow-strewn prison.

11. Knit all of your baby's clothing for the next thirty years. Well into adulthood, every time your child dresses it will be a reminder of how much you sacrificed so that he might be born. Just let him try and complain that his woolen swim trunks bunch up during free swim at Camp David. LET HIM TRY.

12. Grow a beard. If you're ever going to do it, now's the time.

MEANWHILE, INSIDE YOU . . . THE FIFTH MONTH

WHAT'S GOING ON UP IN THERE?

Baby continues to grow physically, of course, but did you know that he's also growing mentally in ways your dusty adult mind can hardly fathom? Well, fathom this: while you're rummaging through your cupboards for those stale lemon cremes you bought that time you got high with your cousin and giggled at television static for two hours, your baby is busy developing his powers of telekinesis. If, by the end of the month, all your cutlery is hopelessly mangled, you know whom to blame—the unborn wonder inside you!

He can also read your thoughts, so watch it.

Here's your baby!

Aww.

6. OBVIOUSLY PREGNANT = OBVIOUSLY STUPID

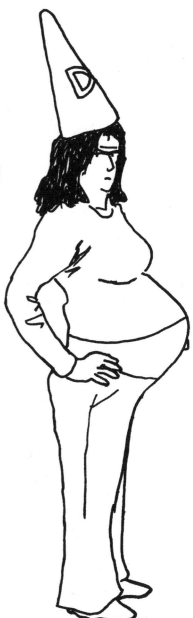

Once your fetus reaches the six-month mark, it officially begins to take more than it gives. And it's given you plenty already: your mother finally thinks you did something right with your life, you can cut any restroom line, you've been getting extra free sheep's milk cheese samples at the local gourmet grocery store, and all those used-baby-furniture salesmen think you're hot stuff. Your fetus knows he's improved your status in the world, and now he wants a little payback: *directly from your brain*.

So, if you're feeling a little forgetful or spacey, here's why: your baby has temporarily developed several prongs that extend from his spine—much like Doctor Octopus in the Spider-Man series, or those grabby things clerks at small, densely stocked grocery stores use to retrieve rolls of toilet paper from high shelves. Baby tests her horrible new appendages by groping around and squeezing nutrients from your vital organs. What's that twinge in your right side? Baby's just curious about your gall bladder! It will probably grow back.

Once your little one figures out how to work her proto-limbs, she'll send them straight up to your precious gray matter. You've had enough time with your brain, and you wasted it playing Frisbee and watching *Murder She Wrote* instead of going to your organic chemistry seminar. Now it's her turn. Who knows— maybe she can do something useful with it.

WHAT BABY'S GETTING FROM YOUR BRAIN

CEREBRUM: Helps you think, speak, and feel

What Baby will discover there: Cake decorating skills; finer emotions (serenity, delight, ruefulness); telepathy

What's left for you: Everything smells like burned toast

BRAIN STEM: Helps regulate the central nervous system

What Baby will discover there: Ability to storm away in a huff; sweater-layering skills; echolocation (if you are a bat)

What's left for you: Hot flashes

HIPPOCAMPUS: Regulates long-term memory and spatial navigation

What Baby will discover there: Your childhood phone number; the ability to walk without running into telephone poles

What's left for you: Deathless grudges

TEMPORAL LOBES: Helps categorize objects

What Baby will discover there: Your extensive knowledge of '80s hair metal bands

What's left for you: Nothing much worth a damn

SO HOW'S THE REST OF YOU?

INCONTINENT!

Have you encountered a dampness in the pants area whenever you chuckle at a Family Circus cartoon? Good news: you're not in early labor! You're only peeing on yourself. This happens because the baby is pressing on your bladder, and because Nature wants to shame you into staying home, where sloppy-pantses like you belong.

Fortunately, Nature can be counteracted with a neat little exercise called the Kegel, in which you rhythmically tighten and release your pubococcygeus muscles. Yep, those . . . no, not your . . . nooo, those are your *arms*. Okay, do you have it now? Good. Now do that 3,000 times a day, in sets of 48, with 45-second breaks in between. Kegel like it's your job, and you may (we stress *may*) stop wetting your pants.

If you're looking for a little variety beyond the basic Kegel, try performing it while doing jumping jacks, yodeling, baking pot pies, or pretending your husband won't leave you after the baby arrives.

HEARTBURNY!

Baby's not only using your poor, battered bladder for a football, he's also pushing his little head up into your stomach in an effort to help you regurgitate that entire lemon meringue pie you mindlessly consumed while reading passive-aggressive threads on Mothering.com. Remember: Jesus may love you the way you are but BABY WANTS A SKINNY MOMMY.

DELUSIONAL!

At six months you may feel like you have *plenty* of time before the birth. Well, don't get too comfy, Miss I-Still-Have-Two-Months-to-Choose-a-Crib: your baby can decide it's time to evacuate right now, if she wants—and she'll do it, too, just to spite you. Baby knows quite a bit about your karma and she's been given clearance to come out early and to try to kill you with it. Payback is a bitch! You should have moved out of that ashram when your mother told you to.

MEET SOME PEOPLE WHO WANT TO TELL YOU WHAT TO DO

Now that there's no hiding your condition from any sighted person, you'll notice that perfectly normal-seeming people want to weigh in on the most intimate details of your life. Why? Some just want to show off their hard-won pregnancy knowledge; others think that their shrewd observation about your physical appearance will shame you into changing yourself into something the world will finally approve of; and still others are carried back to their own traumatic birth and early childhood, and they are drawn to you out of some unconscious urge to be healed.

Rather than coming up with a stinging retort or bursting into blubbery tears, be thankful that you can help strangers with their own weird issues! You are so lucky.

Guy rotating your tires (nodding at your swollen midsection): "Man, you must sure like to eat."
Subtext: "I like to eat as well, but it's okay for me, as I am a dude."
Think: *Do I, in fact, like to eat?*
Say: "Here, you finish my sandwich."

Bookstore clerk who spends way too much time in the pregnancy/child-rearing section: "I hope you don't get one of those third-degree tears in your vagina that never heals and then poop leaks down your leg."

Subtext: "Birth terrifies me so looking at you terrifies me and you're right here and I can't remember what else to talk about. Vagina!"

Think: *Not everyone gets to have strangers worry about their vagina.*

Say: "Would you like a hug?"

Your cousin's colon hydrotherapist: "I hope you did a big cleanse before you got pregnant; so many toxins get lodged in the placenta and cause birth defects."

Subtext: "My mother took an aspirin when she was pregnant with me, and now I'm seven feet tall. *Look how short my pants are.*"

Think: *Oh my God, my colon!*

Say: "I hope it's not too late for me to get a Prenatal Carrot-and-Wheatgrass-Infused Irrigation Cleanse! Do you take Visa?"

The man who walks your mom's dogs when she's out of town: "I hope you haven't stopped going to the gym."

Subtext: "I'm pretty sure you've stopped going to the gym."

Think: *I've stopped going to the gym.*

Say: "I'm going to the gym right now."

Server in overpriced family-chain restaurant: "Whoa—no more jalapeño poppers for you!"

Subtext: "I suspect you would eat the table if it wasn't bolted down, which it is not, because these tables often need to be rearranged if there's a birthday party or whatever."

Think: *That server just stopped me from destroying my self-esteem with all this . . . this food!*

Say: "Ha, ha! Say, how would you like a 50 percent tip?"

Guatemalan high-school teacher now working illegally as your gynecologist's

office cleaner: "You're so beautiful! Oh, you're going to have a happy baby!"

Subtext: "You look like you have a lot of resources at your disposal and you know what you're doing."

Think: *What does this person want from me?!*

Say: "Chupacabra! Run for your life!"

WHAT YOU DEFINITELY SHOULDN'T CONSUME

None of this for you.

You've no doubt already discovered that there are all manner of seemingly benign foods that are in fact *incredibly dangerous* to your helpless, helpless baby. Coffee, for example, will cross the placenta, causing your baby to grow a thick, hairy pelt, and develop a voice like Larry King's. That's common sense.

You're already avoiding all the substances you're supposed to, so you're probably feeling pretty good about yourself. That's where we come in. As it turns out, plenty of so-called medical experts and authorities want to let you relax and think you can recklessly eat more than four or five different foods throughout your pregnancy. Your doctor might even insist that you can occasionally nibble on imported soft cheeses, or relax and have a sip of red wine.

Your doctor is an idiot. You need to know this.

Now, we don't want to take (further) part in any cheap accusations. It's beneath us to imply that anyone's pandering to corporate interests. (By the way, has your doctor jetted off on any Soft Foreign Cheese junkets lately? Why not ask him? Because he'll answer by offering you a cigarette and then he'll go on and on about how it will revive your "t-zone"—that's why.)

We, on the other hand, are not being paid by Big Substance, and we're not afraid to tell the truth. We have an extensive list of everything you should avoid ingesting, inhaling, or standing near—no matter what your doctors claim. Read this and nothing else. Admire how much we educate you!

TABLE 6.1 SUBSTANCES TO AVOID CONSUMING DURING PREGNANCY AND POSSIBLY AFTER

Substance	Contains	Effect on fetus	And this proves it
Lox	Jewishness, Scandinaviatude, that bloated weekend brunchy feeling	Baby will be born covered in capers. Your house will be plagued by reindeer.	Lox comes from salmon, and salmon are terrible mothers.
Soda pop	Bubbles, artificial sweeteners, pretty colors, pep!	In place of brains, Baby's head cavity will be filled with sweet, numbing effervescence.	This might actually be an advantage when the zombies take over.
Brie	Cream of privilege, with a whiff of arrogance	Baby will become smug and pretentious, demanding to discipline the servants and pilot the family yacht wearing nothing but an ascot and a cruel smile.	France
Bologna	Dachshunds	Baby's future home: a van.	You need proof, when you have the specter of *van-living* looming over your child?
Spicy tuna rolls	Spice, tuna, rolls	In boys, spicy tuna rolls cause decreased levels of machismo; in girls, excessive sweatiness.	Seriously, have you ever been to Japan?
Beer	Carbohydrates, underachievement	If it's Pabst Blue Ribbon, you're really in trouble.	Eden's mother never drank but her *father* had a beer once! Thus Eden's cheerleading failures should come as no surprise.
Martinis	Alcohol, money, sadness	What are you trying to prove?	Alice's mom drank martinis throughout her pregnancy, and Alice still cannot tell time.
Clove cigarettes	Emphysema, rebellion	Clove cigarettes are a gateway drug to hacky sack.	Hippies
Ecstasy	Powdered bone marrow, hugs	Baby will use pacifier until he's 30.	*The Cat in the Hat*
Chamomile tea	Flowers, death	Thoughtfulness and sobriety. Hummel figurine-collecting	Guidance counselors

ALTERNATIVES TO ANY AND ALL MEDICATIONS

You don't want to risk Baby's health and well-being just for your *comfort*, do you? You do?

We didn't think so.

With that in mind, here are some pleasantly ineffectual alternatives to medicating yourself!

HEADACHE: Instead of a common and probably deadly OTC pain reliever, try a washcloth soaked in cool water! Alternately, try a washcloth soaked in tepid water! WARNING: *Do not apply washcloth for more than thirty seconds at a time.*

COUGH: No need for cough syrup—just heat up a mug of water. Drink it down and presto: relief!

FATIGUE: Eschew caffeine in favor of a refreshing, energizing hot-water-and-cool-washcloth combo. *That's* the stuff!

SLEEP TROUBLE: A little warm, wet washcloth applied to the forehead should do the trick.

HEARTBURN: Who needs antacids to actually get rid of the problem when you have a healing elixir flowing from your kitchen tap?

PSYCHIATRIC PROBLEMS: Don't take prescription medication for your severe clinical depression or bipolar disorder. Instead, enjoy water. Hot, cold, or warm, whether applied to the face or put *into* the face, nothing helps like water!

BABY-SAFE ALTERNATIVES TO COMMON RECREATIONAL DRUGS

COCAINE: Drink an espresso in a toilet stall in an overhyped nightclub.

HEROIN: Eat an entire chocolate cake with your hands while sitting on a cold kitchen floor.

SPEEDBALL: Drink the espresso and eat the chocolate cake at the same time. Wake up in an unfamiliar hotel room.

ECSTASY: Do a YouTube search for baby pandas. Then have sex with someone.

MARIJUANA: Slip into a tie-dyed caftan, lie down on the floor, and listen to the original Broadway cast recording of *Godspell,* breathing deeply and with an open mouth in time with the music. After fifteen minutes you will be somewhat light-headed. Persuade someone to go buy you a box of Oreos. Tell them you'll pay them back later.

MUSHROOMS: Dump a box of organic raisin-and-hemp clusters (or other cereal that contains at least one ingredient you despise) onto a cookie sheet or large cutting board; pick out all the raisins/ingredients you hate and put them in a bowl. Put the rest of the cereal back in the box and then eat the bowl full of the ingredient you hate, morsel by morsel, meditating on how wretched each bite is. Then go outside and look at a bush for three hours.

GLUE OR OTHER SOLVENTS: Bend over and try to wedge your head between your knees. Stand up quickly! Now fall back against a dirty beanbag chair and groove to the pleasant buzzing and tunnel vision.

LSD: Get your tie-dyed caftan back on, and go out onto the sidewalk and spin in circles until you inadvertently wind up in the middle of the street. All that honking means that people like your outfit! Keep spinning.

BARBITURATES ("DOWNERS"): Tuck a catnip-stuffed calico mouse into your cheek. Curl up beneath your grandma's hand-crocheted afghan and remember how she used to make you soup.

AMPHETAMINES ("UPPERS"): Fill empty medicine capsules with Tang drink mix. Take seventeen capsules every half-hour. Drive until you find an amusement park and then hijack a rollercoaster.

No one made corn chowder like Nana.

KEEPING YOUR JOB

HOW TO HIDE THE FACT THAT YOU'VE GOT BABY ON THE BRAIN

Despite what we told you *(and know for certain)*, science types continue to find no evidence that babies drain the smarts from your brain. They can't deny, however, that a pregnant woman's brains, even if they are still intact *(which they are not)*, are distracted and overwhelmed. You are always mentally calculating the nearest source of on-sale support hosiery to help get you through your work day. It's enough to throw even the most focused prepartum CEO off her game.

You don't want to become unemployed *(or do you?)*, so it's time to start faking it. But how? What's a girl got to do to make it look like she's paying attention to last quarter's sales figures?

PROBLEM #1:   You spent your lunch hour shopping for business maternity underwear instead of using the time to brush up your Japanese for an important client meeting. When you return, the clients are already in the conference room, waiting for you.

SOLUTION: Plunder your stash of rice candy and peanut brittle, and use a glue stick to artfully adhere it all to a sheet of card stock. (Glitter would be a nice touch here, or a small "pig" made from a pink eraser, with pushpin legs and snout.) The clients will be so flattered by your gracious "hospitality tray" that they will buy/sell/agree to whatever your phrase book says.

PROBLEM #2: In a confused and anxious moment, instead of ordering two cases of recycled copier paper for the office, you ordered a table saw and a gross of medical-grade polyethylene bags.

SOLUTION: Pin the order on that hostile IT guy who's blocked your Web access to BabyGap.com.

PROBLEM #3: You illustrated your PowerPoint presentation on "Overcoming the Challenges of the European Derivatives Market" with images from parenting Web sites and dog-grooming magazines.

SOLUTION: Pull the fire alarm.

PROBLEM #4: What was the question?

SOLUTION: Talk about how big your boobs are getting.

PROBLEM #5: Your office manager insists on cleaning out the refrigerator at the end of each month, despite your insistence that the white-chocolate-flavored coffee creamer is still good.

SOLUTION: Using the heel of your hand, smash it into the office manager's nose using an upward motion, thus driving the cartilage into her brain.

PROBLEM #6: You're blanking on your boss's girlfriend's sister's name and she's standing right in front of you.

SOLUTION: Cry.

PROBLEM #7: You can't look out the window, daydream, and knit at the same time.

SOLUTION: Oh, yes you can. Try harder.

MEANWHILE, INSIDE YOU . . . THE SIXTH MONTH

WHAT'S GOING ON UP IN THERE?

Your baby is now around twelve inches long and has eyelashes and eyebrows. No kidding! Baby is also kicking and stretching, and possibly even hiccupping. Some fetuses do that more than others—it depends on how much sangria you've had recently. Baby is also practicing opening her eyes and staring at her dark, aquatic universe. She probably figures it will be like this for the rest of her life. Baby is in for a big surprise.

Here's your baby!

7. THE THIRD TRIMESTER: NOW YOU'RE COMICAL TO EVERYONE BUT YOU

WHO'S EVERYONE LAUGHING AT? IT'S YOU!

You have officially morphed from "noticeably pregnant" to "farcically gravid." This is why people are laughing at you. You are now an absurd waddling creature. Have you really taken a good look at yourself? Because you may be missing out. Go look, right now. Look! Right? Hilarious!

The funniest part is, you think you can't get any bigger, *but you will.* You will grow and grow until you are *not humorous at all to behold.*

HOW ARE YOU FEELING?

FORGETFUL!

You walked out of your house without your shoes again, and why is there a strange breeze flirting with your lady parts? Is it because you also forgot your pants? No? Well, did you remember to pull them up? *There you go.* Your natural pregnant-lady forgetfulness combined with an inability to see the lower half of your body can result in unfortunate wardrobe incidents such as this. Always have your partner look you over before you leave the house. Do not depend on your dog. DOGS DO NOT CARE IF WE ARE DRESSED.

Also, you forgot your underpants.

STAINED!

Your constant need to forage for snacks combined with your increased girth will result, almost inevitably, in telltale hummus-and-bacon stains atop your fetal hump. To counteract this expensive ruination of your husband's old sweatshirts, we suggest tying a tarp around your neck, snacking naked, finding a fork, or having some self-control and waiting the fifteen minutes until dinner's ready. For God's sake.

OUTFITS YOU COULD WEAR TO LOOK FUNNIER

If you're still having trouble developing a sense of humor about all this, why not run with your ballooning proportions and make yourself even *more* amusing to look at? Here are some outfits and accessories to add to your repertoire.

- Undersize tube top
- Clothing that dissolves when you answer the phone. (Invent this, if you have to.)
- Bull's-eye patterns centered over belly, breasts, and buttocks, or ideally a jumpsuit that incorporates all three/five areas
- Wonder Woman costume
- Football helmet
- Naugahyde spats
- Hawaiian-style coconut "bra" you won at that fraternity party ten years ago. (Boy, those were some wild times, huh?)
- Two words: fart machine. In your pants. Okay, that's five words.
- Lederhosen
- Sousaphone

Actually, if you could be followed around by a polka band? That would be ideal.

HOW TO BE MORE TOUCHABLE TO STRANGERS

Get used to the following idea: people want to touch you. Feel you up. Grope your gut. Scrape their callused palms all over your distended midriff. Hurdle the cash register and violate your abdomen with their sweaty, insistent pawing. Drive their truck straight into a ditch, leap out, and plaster their filthy, dirty hands all over your brand-new Scooby Doo maternity shirt. Oh, it will happen. *Again and again.*

You have a nearly full-term baby in there, and accordingly, the world wants to fondle it. Through you! This desire is probably hard-wired into our very beings—we haven't looked it up, but surely *you* have the time to. (Do you really have anything better to do right now?) Anyway, people you don't know can't very well give you an internal exam on the street *(or can they?)*, so the best they can hope for is to palm your belly and be awarded a vague sense of baby-heft through all those layers of skin and muscle and fat. And organs. And blood? Look, we never said we were sure exactly what you were made of. Let's just say "person meat."

So in addition to clothing yourself as hilariously as possible, make sure your outfits are made of fabrics that are naturally touchable and inviting. You'll want soft, sumptuous garments that hug the skin.

- Velour is good, as is velvet. But none of that velvet that can only be petted in one direction. No one enjoys that against-the-grain feel. You'll want a nap that allows for omni-directional stroking. Did Science invent that yet?
- Do you have an old chenille bedspread? Aren't they nice?
- How about some rabbit fur! Or just stuff a warren of rabbits into your undersize tube top.
- Bake a shirt made of cake.
- Not the baking type? It's easy to fashion a garment out of fistfuls of Puffs Plus tissues. This way your belly can be moisturizing and/or antibacterial as well as touchably soft. Your assailants will be sure to thank you.

DO:

- Lean back slightly so that your midsection protrudes and appears more available to the public (this is called "presenting")
- Point at it and waggle your eyebrows at anyone who glances at you on the bus
- Chase people down the street, shouting "TOUCH MY INSIDE BABY!"
- Hold your arms spread slightly apart and cast your gaze skyward,

as if to say, "As I am mother to one, so I am to you all. My body is yours to do with as you will."

- Keep your belly well oiled and exfoliated so that people won't accidentally peel off a sheet of chapped skin (especially those with dessicated elder-claws)
- Make your breasts available for hefting so that perverts don't feel left out

DO NOT:

Wear man-made fibers, hemp, jute, steel wool, wood, banjos, or fire.

ADDITIONALLY, DO NOT:

- Cross arms
- Avert eyes
- Cross eyes
- Avert arms
- Wear biohazard symbols
- Hide an electrified fencing system under shirt
- Imitate a car alarm when someone brushes past you
- Growl or make noises like a copulating bobcat
- Ask people to respect your personal boundaries
- Sue
- Stay inside where people can't get at you

DOCTOR CODE-SPEAK

One of the best-kept secrets in the vagino-medical profession is that lady-parts doctors and nurses have developed a second language full of shorthand code words that they use only with one another in order to quickly and stealthily share less-than-flattering information about you right in front of your face. Just as when a waitress yells, "I need a bun pup with fish eyes!" and the short-order cook knows he needs to make a hot dog with tapioca on the side, when a labor and delivery nurse shouts, "Time to spark a fattie!" it means someone's about to give you an emergency episiotomy using a ballpoint pen.

With zero-hour not all that far away, now's a great time to familiarize yourself with these phrases—so that when you hit labor-and-delivery, you'll know why that nurse is coming at you with a jug of dishwashing liquid and a grapefruit spoon.

WORD OR PHRASE: "Jenny"
MEANING: A particularly stubborn laboring woman, derived from the name for a female donkey

WORD OR PHRASE: "Pull a Tyson"
MEANING: Administer anesthesia in order to knock out an uncooperative Jenny
ALT DEF.: To deliver a baby who resembles a plucked chicken

WORD OR PHRASE: "Johnny Cash"
MEANING: Labia that's been stretched to the point where a laboring woman feels a strong burning sensation; also known as "the ring of fire"

WORD OR PHRASE: "Panko"
MEANING: Pubic hair. The word is taken from the brand name of a bread-crumb-

like product, typically sold in Asian markets, used to give a crunchy coating to fried fish or chicken

Word or Phrase: "Weather balloon"
Meaning: A woman experiencing a hysterical, or false, pregnancy
Alt. def.: A woman who, despite carrying a full-term baby, has gained little or no extra weight during her pregnancy

Word or Phrase: "Dr. Norelco"
Meaning: The nurse or aide designated to shave a woman's Panko

EXAMPLES

"This Jenny won't let me spark a fattie with Johnny Cash. I'm gonna have to pull a Tyson."

"The Panko on the weather balloon in L&D got tangled up in a IV line so we had to page Dr. Norelco."

Midwives, meanwhile, have their own special terms:

Word or Phrase: "Wet hen"
Meaning: A woman laboring in a birthing tub who's just screaming at everyone

Word or Phrase: "HMO"
Meaning: "Hellish Mother in Overdrive." A controlling or otherwise difficult mother who has been banned from the house but nevertheless calls repeatedly in the midst of a home birth, runs her car into the porch, calls in false alarms to the fire department, etc.

Word or Phrase: "Logan's Run"

MEANING: A woman desperate to get pregnant before she hits forty
ALT. DEF.: A high-speed trip to a birthing woman's home, made in an effort to arrive before the baby does

WORD OR PHRASE: "Dog biscuits"
MEANING: The result of a laboring woman in the pushing phase who accidentally poops in the birthing tub

WORD OR PHRASE: "Happy Hour"
MEANING: When a woman's natural endorphins kick in and she's high as a kite

EXAMPLE

"Can you scoop up a couple of dog biscuits for me? The H.M.O. is on a Logan's Run and I need to lock all the doors or this wet hen will never make it to happy hour."

THINGS YOU CAN'T DO FOR MORE THAN A FEW MINUTES

You may have noticed that there are things you can no longer do, like competitive popping and locking, or standing at attention for any length of time without collapsing in a heap.

You may be noticing increased fatigue and soreness. This is because Baby is sucking you dry through a horrible tube growing out of her midsection. Where has your energy gone? Baby has devoured your life essence through your fortifying blood!

BABY NEEDS IT MORE THAN YOU DO. Do not deny Baby.

Baby might give you *back* a little bit of your life force, if, say, you need it for ironing her little clothes. You should talk to Baby about that. However, know that while you're speaking, Baby is quietly siphoning off your hopes and dreams and youth, and if you go on too long they'll all just disappear. *Pfffft.*

DON'T MOVE!

Some experts theorize that there are "hormones" that cause your "ligaments" to loosen in preparation for childbirth. Of course this is all wild conjecture, as "hormones" (as proposed in Einstein's Theory of General Femininity), are elusive subdermal particles that are repulsed by rainwater and sperm. "Ligaments," it is believed, hold your bones together somewhat like rubber bands. As you enter your third trimester, be aware that if you come in contact with rain or experience even a *hint* of optimism, your hormones will direct your ligaments to dissolve, and any sudden movement or spontaneous gesture can cause your limbs to FLY OFF.

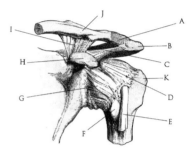

Your shoulder needs all these letters to stay together!

It's now best to remain still and wait until your child has been removed from your person and secured elsewhere (in a playpen or some sort of infant-size club chair) before you budge again. If you want to engage in some low-intensity Aqua-Bobbing™, that *might* be okay—only please consult your physician or the Army Corps of Engineers before attempting it. Otherwise, cover your entire body in bubble wrap, and wait. Remember: your shoulders, elbows, or head could pop right out of their sockets, so make sure that your partner knows how to make a quick splint out of duct tape and old magazines. (It's nice for him to feel useful!)

Other activities you should avoid for now, if you're as fragile as we fear you are:

Camping

Bird-watching

High-jumping

Hula-hooping

Snapping your fingers

Making your own dynamite

Sewing gowns out of velvet drapes and sashaying around town, looking to borrow money from your old boyfriend

If you are, however, more energetic and full of vigor than ever, well, congratulations! It's best to stay active until your ligaments inevitably liquefy—and more important, to lord your excellent physical condition over any pregnant women who might be around you. That means doing jumping jacks in places where weaker pregnant women congregate, such as doughnut shops, bubble-wrap distribution centers, and any place where varicose-vein pressure stockings can be purchased.

POINT/COUNTERPOINT: SHOULD YOU SIMPLY PEE IN YOUR PANTS?

As the pressure on your bladder from Little Miss or Mister Interloper increases, you may find it challenging to get to a bathroom on time. Fortunately, technology now exists that can allow you to simply whiz in your undies without anyone being the wiser. But is this acceptable behavior? Shouldn't you simply ration your intake of Fresca before you head off to the DMV? *(Please note: both Fresca and the DMV will cause birth defects.)*

So what's it going to be: mature, adultlike behavior, or the other thing? Alice and Eden face off:

ALICE:
No.

EDEN:
I don't see why not

EDEN:
Let your womanly stream freely flow!

ALICE:
We have restrooms. We live in a civilized society.

EDEN:
LOL

ALICE:
You don't want to smell like old pee

ALICE:
Or maybe YOU do

EDEN:
Like you've never peed your pants

ALICE:
Not since preschool

ALICE:
Okay, seventh grade

ALICE:
I had bladder control issues

EDEN:
You've got control issues, all right

ALICE:
Which I got past with an iron will and a mental map of every IHOP on Long Island

EDEN:
But what if you're on an airplane

ALICE:
PREGNANT WOMEN SHOULDN'T FLY

EDEN:
And you literally can't get out of your seat without climbing over some OTHER pregnant woman, who's asleep

ALICE:
TWO pregnant women flying? That's absurd

EDEN:
And then the pilot comes on and he's all, The toilets are broken! Everybody has to pee in their pants!

EDEN:
You'd pee in your pants

EDEN:
You'd have to

ALICE:
Well, the pilot is like the captain of a ship, he can marry you and you have to do what he says

EDEN:
Airplane pilots can't marry people

ALICE:
Yes, they can

ALICE:
It says so in the Magna Carta

EDEN:
Wait, what?

ALICE:
It's in the dictionary

EDEN:
What does this have to do with—

Alice has signed off.

FEEL THE BURN! CREATIVE WAYS TO STAVE OFF INDIGESTION

You may have noticed that if you eat or belch or inhale (or exhale) or bend over or lie down (or sit up), your mouth will fill with a deadly acid that immediately corrodes your teeth and burns away your taste buds. Horrifyingly, this stuff has *always been inside you.* Your baby just pushes it up that tube that comes up from your stomach and then floods your mouth with it. Until Baby learns to talk, this is the most straightforward way she has to keep you from standing in front of the fridge and eating a pack of raw hot dogs.

Unfortunately, all the various medications you can take for acid reflux will cause Baby to develop pectoral fins and a translucent, moisture-resistant casing. Your only alternative is to limit your diet to foods that Baby won't notice going by. Here's the complete list of what you should eat for the rest of your pregnancy:

Ice

Plain yogurt

Plain frozen yogurt

Ice mixed with plain yogurt

Crushed ice sprinkled on top of plain frozen yogurt

Sugarless, flavorless Popsicles

Plain yogurt Popsicles

Stomach acid (tricks it!)

Eggplant parm

HOW ARE YOU GOING TO LABOR? HOW?

You should have already figured this one out, but if you have not, we hope you're a good last-minute study! Your baby could just come flying out of you any day now, so you'd better get cracking.

COMMON LABOR METHODS, PROS AND CONS

BRADLEY METHOD
Emphasizes breathing and relaxation, natural birth, and partner support.
PRO: Good excuse to develop personal strength and tap your inner resources
CON: It takes twelve weeks (your entire third trimester) to really absorb all the teaching. Wow, twelve weeks is a long time.

LAMAZE
Emphasizes breathing and relaxation, natural birth, partner support, and bouncing around on giant rubber balls—whee!
PRO: "Giant balls." Heh.
CON: *(Still laughing.)*

WATER BIRTHING
Have your baby in an aquatic environment!
PRO: Baby is born into warm, gentle, familiar surroundings
CON: Not allowed at Sea World (despite their Dolphin Doula® training program) or most public pools

HYPNOBIRTHING
You hypnotize yourself into not knowing you're in labor.
PRO: Just go about your day until a baby falls out
CON: Did you act like a chicken in front of a community-college freshman orientation?

LESSER-KNOWN BIRTHING METHODS

BIRTHING FROM WITHOUT

Please close your eyes and hand this book over to a medical professional immediately so that they can follow our instructions. (Okay, doctor: you'll need a bucket of ether, a liter of chloroform, a rag, a good pair of snake tongs, and a mallet. If you need more guidance, please order our pamphlet, *Here Comes the Stork, with a Little Help From Science!* from your favorite vendor of 1940s medical textbooks.)

PRO: Once the baby's out, you'll be good to go.

CON: Whoever is responsible for your limp, bloodless form will have a lot of dead weight to haul home.

BAD-ASS METHOD

Get a tattoo while you're in labor. Working on the pain-confusion theory, the tattooing will all but eliminate labor pain. Theoretically.

PRO: You're so bad-ass that hepatitis C is frightened of *you*.

CON: The tattoo artist might throw up; the labor pain may simply subsume the tattoo pain and you'll be thrashing around so much the tattoo will end up looking like James Carville, no matter what it was supposed to be; you'll be charged extra if your baby also gets tattooed.

DENIAL METHOD

Baby? What baby?

PRO: Leaves everything to the professionals; absolves you of responsibility.

CON: Hard to ignore the overwhelming sensation that a car is driving over your pelvis.

WAILING/GNASHING OF TEETH METHOD

Why not bring God into the birthing room?

PRO: Gets a lot of attention.

CON: You'll be ineligible for federal funds during the tax year of the birth; pillar of fire may damage labor and delivery room.

DYSON METHOD

PRO: The crevice attachment is revolutionary.

CON: It will take a while for Baby's head to become round again.

YOUR BIRTH PLAN

A birth plan is a document that you, the pregnant woman, should have already prepared either on your own or with a partner, a friend, a midwife, or a local ombudsman. It's a way of organizing your intentions and desires, and getting them rolling together in the same direction so that in the heat of labor, when God forbid a doctor is hovering over you with a melon bailer and threatening to dig out the baby through your navel, you can cry out, "THAT ISN'T IN MY BIRTH PLAN!" and your minions can legally descend and tear at his or her limbs with their filed teeth.

Ideally, you've discussed your birth plan ahead of time with your doctor or midwife so that everyone feels comfortable with your desires. Or—and here's where being a modern person really pays off—you can just go to www.lets-panic. com, print out the following form when the first contraction hits, fill in the blanks when your mucous plug falls out, and fling it at the first orderly you see on your way screaming into labor and delivery.

Dear _____, _____ and various nurses/assistants whose names I will probably be screaming later on;
       primary caregiver   vaginal expert

I am so _____ to have my baby born at _____. I apologize in advance for any _____
      random emotion   national monument   adjective

names I call you during my labor, such as _____ or _____ or _____ _____
            noun   adjective   adverb   color

_____. I did not mean to say that your _____ is _____. I am sure it/he/she/they is/are
  sex organ   family member   adjective

actually quite _____. If I could describe my dream for my baby's birth, it would be _____ and
       euphemism   popsicle flavor

_____. I would like my baby's birth to be like _____. To that end, I have the following requests.
  mythical animals   board game

PRIOR BELIEFS

I actually believe that my birth will be _____ and _____, and that I will not need to _____
                   adjective   adjective   bodily function

or _____ at any point during the experience, so if you want to laugh at me, please: a) Suppress your laughter or
  disgusting bodily function

else my child will think you're mocking him/her and will grow up to become a _____ _____; b) Feel
                                         pejorative   superhero

free to laugh, but only into your _____; c) Laugh right in my _____ because I can _____ it.
                 body part   body part   verb

LABOR

I want to use a _____ during labor because I think _____-ing _____ on a _____
       household appliance   verb   adverb   leafy green plant

will make the pain easier to bear. (See above, re: laughing.) Snacks I want to have during labor include _____ and
                                                           vegetable

_____ because these seem the most palatable coming back up. If I am unwell, I would prefer to _____
  alcoholic beverage   mode of expression

into a _____. Towel-lined, if possible. My favorite essential oils are _____, _____, and
    large container   candy bar   vegetable

_____. My totem animal is the _____. (Do not bring a live one into the room during labor, however;
  bird   movie star

a plush replica or cardboard cut-out will suffice.) During labor, my _____ will _____ my _____
                                           sexual organ   verb   primate

with _____ while singing _____. If you have a problem with this, you can go _____ yourself.
     emotion   patriotic song   verb

DELIVERY

Please note that I am not in control of my _____. I may _____ like a _____. I may
                          emotion   verb   member of the armed forces

start singing songs about _____. Anything is possible. If I _____ things that are _____
               national holiday   verb   adverb

shocking or _____ you right in your _____, I already said I was sorry. By reading this birth plan you
     gesture   type of pasta

agree not to press charges or file any lawsuits against me. No backsies! Once my baby is born, do not scream "I AM NOT

HANDING THIS _____ BABY TO THAT _____ _____" just because of some of the things I
             adjective   profanity   dictator

said, did, or incanted during labor. Grow up, for _____'s sake. They're just words/actions/ancient Romany curses.
                                  name of Greek goddess

I am sure you will be _____ eventually, if you watch your _____.
               adjective   equine quadruped

_____
            signature of pregnant lady

_____
     signature of state-sanctioned vaginal authority

MEANWHILE, INSIDE YOU . . .
THE SEVENTH MONTH

WHAT'S GOING ON UP IN THERE?

This month your baby is heading into the home stretch and finishing up her developmental touches. She will grow up to three feet in length from crown to rump, and will develop the thick layer of subdermal blubber she'll need to insulate her those frigid winter months. Continue to eat all the clams, sea cucumbers, and cephalopods you want, mama!

Here's your baby!

8. THIS PREGNANCY SHIT IS GETTING OLD!

The eighth month is also known as the Really Goddamn Over This Pregnancy month. You feel like you might explode and you cannot *fathom* staying like this for another goddamn *month*. GODDAMMIT. Incidentally, you are now swearing like a dockworker. Even if you were born and raised a plainspoken Mennonite who never so much as used the word "gosh"—because everyone knows which Almighty is being blasphemed by *that* cuss-substitute—you're now a salty-language connoisseur. Every time Baby pummels your ribs at 3 A.M., you let out a stream of expletives that sends your partner scurrying for the village exorcist.

Let it all out! If you don't, you'll only be tamping down those indelicate feelings until you develop a full-body hernia. We'd all prefer that you simply indulged in a case of Potty Mouth for a few weeks. Just don't make this a habit. You want that mouth dialed back to Ellen DeGeneres levels by the time you're ready to kiss Baby on her sweet little fucking fontanel.

(Ooh, you are so *cranky*! It's kind of adorable, how your face gets all red like that.)

Feeling Perfectly Cheerful?

There's only one explanation: *you are clinically out of your tree.*

HOW ELSE ARE YOU FEELING?

BIG AS A WHALE!

So big we can't stop talking about it. At this point you may as well start fastening your pants with packing tape because what are you going to do, buy more pants? That you'll only wear for a month? Your great-grandmother, were she alive, would slap you with a waffle iron if she heard you talk like that. *She* made it through five pregnancies wearing nothing but wooden clogs and a burlap girdle, so what makes *you* so special?

VIRTUOUS!

The eighth month of pregnancy is also known as "cake month," due to all the baby showers that may start popping up on your calendar. It is a delicious, decadent time in your life. Too bad you can't enjoy it. You've been following our Sta-Shapl-EE™ Baby Weight Restriction Program and you're not going to blow it now! If, while being showered, you find yourself wild with hunger and ready to grab an entire plate of canapés and shove it into your mouth, go crazy and nibble on a dried apricot instead. Your baby may be clawing to get out and wrap his lips around a bottle of extra-fatty steak-based formula, but your close friends will applaud your self-control.

THE BABY SHOWER: MAKING YOUR FRIENDS SUFFER AS MUCH AS YOU HAVE

Why a baby shower? For some, it's an opportunity to connect with old friends and let them goggle at your pregnant self (and also at how old your mom looks these days). For others it's a chance to extract payback: now you can force all those people whose showers *you* attended to play humiliating games, give you a gift you'll use for a month, and then wait a year for your thank-you note.

Here are some fun shower themes! Choose one of these, and no one will ever call you unoriginal ever again. Not if you can fucking help it.

TABLE 8.1 FUN SHOWER IDEAS

Party Theme	Because ...?	Food That Should Be Served	Games You Can Make Everyone Play
World War II	The day will most likely live in infamy	Sauerkraut, Kamikazes, Rivets	Pin the Mustache on Stalin, Guess the Armored Tank Division
Gay Paree	Ooh-la-la!	Profiteroles, ladyfingers, absinthe, Gauloises	Competitive scoffing, ménages à trois
Murder Mystery Shower	Someone needs to get to the bottom of Lady Crawfinger's unfortunate demise	I guess we can get some coffee and cake to keep our energy up while we search for the killer amongst us	This is no game, my friends. No game at all.
Mathletes!	Who doesn't love math?	Pie. Obviously.	. . . math.
Beauty Salon	The ladies love to primp and preen	Herbal tea, weak coffee, year-old Luna bar you found at the bottom of your bag	Whose Color Came Out the Brassiest?
New York, New York	It's the last idea and you're tired	Gum, Dexedrine	Who smells?

OBSERVATIONS SOME ASSHOLES WILL SHARE WITH YOU, AND APPROPRIATE RESPONSES

In general, we recommend welcoming the thoughts of the friends, family, and strangers who want to share in your intimate journey. As you enter the eighth month, however, you have exhausted your primary stores of goodwill toward humanity, and your backup tanks are sloshing hollowly with what may be Crystal Light. And even if these others are correct—*even if their points are valid*—it is universally acknowledged that it's your eighth-month privilege to tell anyone who says one word to you about *anything* to fuck off. Letting off a bit of steam is good for you and the baby, so go on ahead and alienate the entire fucking world. They'll get over it. They'd better.

Here are the kinds of remarks you're sure to get:

"No way are you only eight months pregnant. Surely your doctor was wrong."
Suggested response: Stink eye; middle finger

"Only eight months? Are you are having quintuplets?"
Suggested response: Savage braying

"I see you have those swollen ankles everyone talks about. No more strappy sandals for you!"
Suggested response: Wild, animal-like shriek

"Your baby is too big! Are you sure you'll make it to nine months?"
Suggested response: Lunge forward, make clawing motions with hands

"Oh, man, you got to stop eating so much!!" (Note: *Only we can say this to you*)
Suggested response: Hastily improvised shadow puppet play about that person being gored by a rhino

"Shouldn't you get to a hospital NOW?"
Suggested response: a fulmination of biblical proportions

"Keep on keepin' on, beautiful lady!"
Suggested response: Full-on karate-chopping freakout

LAST-MINUTE PREPARATIONS!

Believe it or not, your work isn't confined to just taking care of yourself, Miss Queasypop! You have to start doing some things for this baby that's about to spill out of you. Though it can be hard to look ahead when you're so focused on waddling around in the present, there are several things you can take off of Baby's worry plate so that she can spend her first few days just lying there, pooping herself contentedly in the knowledge that her mother is at least somewhat capable of keeping her own shit straight.

1. *Write a will.* Because you're going to die someday, and how is Baby going to know what to do with all of your old Wham! records?
2. *Lose fifteen pounds.* Don't you want Baby to be proud of you for walking out of the maternity ward wearing your skinny jeans?
3. *Get rid of any cats you still have, because even though you pretended to get rid of them when we told you to back in chapter 1, in reality you just hid them in the garage.* It seems cruel now, but believe us, once that baby comes there will be no more room in your heart for Fluff-Pot and Mrs. Winklestein. It's best to take them to the shelter before they get a whiff of the interloper in their midst and begin filing their teeth in preparation for their first moment alone with him.
4. *Read one of those other pregnancy books.* This is a hilarious joke! *Let's Panic About Babies!* negates the need for all other books. Clear your shelves.

DETERMINE YOUR BABY'S DESTINY BY NAMING IT SO

Your baby's name is the most important gift you will ever give him. (Except for life. Life is the first one, and, okay, next comes love. Then health. Then maybe shelter. *Then* the name. It's up there, is what we're saying.)

Yes, your baby's name is *one* of the most important gifts you'll ever give him or her. Yet some fools believe you should wait until your child is born, as if your baby's appearance and/or nature should determine his name. Huge mistake. This is why so many babies are named "Baby-sized Rottingpumpkin" or "Wrinkly Red-Face O'Screamessy." Do not name your baby what he seems to be when he's born—name him what you want him to become!

The power to manipulate the future is a double-edged sword, however. History shows us that if you name a boy "Billy the Kid," you may have a lovable sociopath on your hands, but you're going to have to have one whopper of a yard sale to cover all those pesky legal fees.

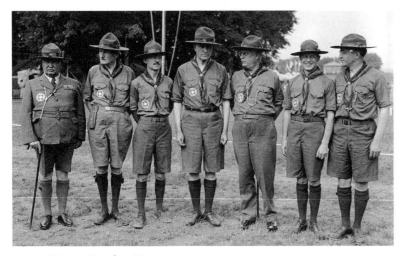

Hagar, Pinchy, Munson, Stretch, Snowflake, Forthright, and President Woodrow Wilson demonstrate the importance of a proper name.

So what's it going to be? Will you create a mild-mannered girl named "Ann" who will hate you because you've doomed her to wander a *dowdy ecru hellscape of boringness*, or a drug-addled recluse who'll get to solve mysteries because he's "Baskerville Holmes"?!

TABLE 8.2 NAMING BABY IN ORDER TO FOSTER DESIRED TRAITS

DESIRED TRAIT	Male	Female
Brakes for small animals	Benji	Chinchilla
Knows which fork to use	Horace	Hortensile
Prone to languish on the fainting couch	Barrymore	Ammonia
Headed for jail	Scar	Lefty
Eats raw eggs for breakfast	Cromagnoid	Ovaria
Can successfully elude police at high speed	LeMans	Spoileretta
One hell of a dancer	Sammy Davis, Jr.	Macarena
Attends cotillions	Bunny	Listerine
Cheerful vegan	Lanyard	Quinoa
Smartypants	Bunsen	Abacus
Little bit of a mama's boy/tomgirl	Fauntleroy	Wayne
Will own a lot of cats	Flens	Cloaca
Will not put you in a home	Kevorkian	Pneumonia
Will practice good personal hygiene	Mitchum	Palmolive
Off-puttingly opinionated	Dobbs	Orman
Diplomatic to a fault	Synergy	Tapioca

CITY TALK: HOW TO GET A SEAT ON THE BUS

City dwellers are tired, angry people who don't give a shit if you're pregnant or not, so it's finders-keepers when it comes to securing a seat on public transportation, a pew at the tabernacle, or a stray velvet pouf at the opera. But what's a mom-to-be with swollen ankles and aching hips to do?

THE TOE CAPPER. Stand right in front of a man who's wearing a suit and fiddling with his cell phone. Drop a bucket of barbecue sauce on his foot. If he leaps up in surprise, say, "Why, thank you!" and take his seat. If he doesn't leap up but merely glares at you, sit on his lap.

THE LEAN AND STARE. Find a person who looks weak and skinny. Like he doesn't get enough food, or love. Now lean in and stare at him. Hard. You know what I'm talking about.

THE DROOP. Find a strong guy who doesn't have a seat, either; put down your bucket of barbecue sauce, then swoon carefully into his arms. He will yell at a bunch of people to get out of the way and give you their seats. (This is a good way to get three seats in a row if you want to lie down.)

THE UNCOMFORTABLY CLOSE BELLY RUB. This is an excellent summer move. Get practically on top of someone with a seat and start fanning your face like you're really hot, which you will be, because the air-conditioning sucks and you're eight months pregnant. Lean forward a little so your belly brushes against your seated target. Whimper. Not working? Lift up your shirt slightly, rub your naked belly, and let out a series of pained bleats. If it's crowded, your target might have to climb over you to get away, so be polite and let her step on your bucket(s) of barbecue sauce as she makes her escape.

COUNTRY CHAT: HOW TO PARK ON THE SIDEWALK

Small-town folk are no more welcoming to your pregnancy than their citified counterparts, but they're often far less confrontational. Use their innate passivity to your advantage.

CHOOSE YOUR SPOT. Handicapped spots are a good choice because they're usually right up front. If none are available, it's sidewalk-parking time.

HONK TO CLEAR YOUR PATH OF PEDESTRIANS. You might have to honk a few times to get the attention of older folks.

GUN YOUR ENGINE. Sometimes old folks are deaf, but they can usually feel vibrations.

SMILE BIG!

PROCEED. You need to get up some speed if you want to make it over the curb.

DON'T FORGET TO LEAVE THE ENGINE RUNNING. This signals that you'll be back soon! Even if you're not really, ha ha! But seriously, you don't want to get a ticket.

WAVE! It's simple courtesy.

If, when you return to your car, there's a police officer (or "lawman") standing next to it, **GO INTO LABOR.**

WAYS TO HANDLE THE CRUSHING FEAR THAT WASHES OVER YOU IN THE DEAD OF NIGHT

There's nothing like staring at your alarm clock as the minutes tick by, clutching a body pillow while your tongue tries to loosen the crushed TUMS-bits still lodged in your back teeth, to start a woman trekking down the sleepless road to Anxietyvania.

Unfortunately, science is still decades away from discovering the actual source of this intense worry and dread that curses women in advanced pregnancy. Most experts believe it's Nature's way of keeping you awake so you can figure out how you're going to provide health care, day care, insurance, food, shelter, happiness, music lessons, a college education, healthy self-esteem, and robust sexuality for the infant writhing within you like a ball of copulating snakes. So what are you doing, "shutting" your "eyes" for a "minute"? Get to work!

Oh, all right. Here a few ways you can relax or get your mind off whatever it is you're obsessing over tonight.

VISUALIZATION

Imagine you're in a garden—or an aquarium. Let's go with aquarium! And there's this thick pane of glass and on the other side is a shark that keeps bumping his or her (it's hard to tell) nose against the glass as if to say, "Hello! I'm really a gentle creature, once you get to know me! Just place your hand against the glass, and then I'll touch the other side of the glass, and it will be like you're communicating with a vicious primordial beast in a calm, controlled manner!" Then while you guys are having your nice little moment, imagine a big jellyfish comes up behind the friendly shark and wraps his or her (also hard to tell) tentacles around the shark and stings the ever-loving shit out of it. The shark is writhing in agony! And the shark is your friend—you must help the shark! You beat both your hands against the glass and yell for the jellyfish to stop, but the jellyfish won't stop, he (she?) keeps stinging and stinging, and now there's a squid joining in, you're not sure WHAT that squid is doing, it's just a big kill-the-friendly-shark clusterfuck, and you're pressed against the glass, sobbing and helpless.

Well! Now you're awake, aren't you? Might as well get up and do some ironing.

MANTRAS

Recite these until you collapse from boredom!

"I am happy and well. As far as I know."

"I am excited to meet my baby, who will probably not eventually abandon me in a nursing home."

"I am safe and sound and one with the universe, at least that part of the universe we know of, not that we know what's in the *entire* universe, and who's to say what's out there, on its way here to destroy us all."

Will probably not get you.

"There is nothing to fear, once you take away serial killers, vampires, and Bigfoot."

DISTRACTION

Give in to your nesting instinct

Start cleaning and organizing your house in such a way that will be easy to maintain even when you're sleep-deprived and indifferent to mold and safe meat handling practices. What do you mean, your house is pretty much clean? "Pretty much"? Have you dismantled your kitchen cabinets so that you can disinfect the wall studs behind them? Have you pulled up your linoleum and sand-blasted the subflooring? Have you set cat traps both indoors and out? We didn't think so.

Begin a list of people you're angry with

Who's wronged you—recently, or not-so-recently? Yes, you can include your third-grade swim coach, who put you in Minnow I when you were so obviously a Minnow II. And who hasn't RSVPed for your baby shower yet? If you're not angry at those people, you should be. Call them now! What do you mean, they're probably asleep? How is that your fucking problem?

When you're done with your tea, take another look at Baby-Safe Alternatives to Common Recreational Drugs in chapter 6.

BIRTH ART: VISUALIZING THE MESSY, EXPENSIVE JOURNEY

Many women like to prepare for the birth of their child using visualization techniques, in the belief that positive imagery will seep down from their brains and into their wombs, helping them get through the experience of birth with more ease and less wailing. It's an age-old midwifey technique that thumbs its nose at scientific doctorly procedures. Even though womens' brains continue to defy sterilization, birth art and visualization may still have some value for women who can't afford prebirth whole-body numbing spray.

DRAW YOUR BIRTH ANIMAL TOTEM

A birth animal totem can protect and inspire you while you're in labor. These are the three best animals. Choose from these three. NO, YOU CANNOT CHOOSE ANOTHER.

THE EMPEROR PENGUIN

Like you, it is flightless. Unlike you, it has to endure the worst conditions anywhere on earth. Your Emperor Penguin totem will help you suck it up and quit your endless, endless whining. Also, the male Emperor Penguin incubates the egg, and that's a nice thing to imagine while you're enduring a thirty-six-hour labor.

THE PLATYPUS

The mysterious platypus defies logic, much as your body does. The platypus is all kinds of crazy. Venomous, duck-billed, otter-footed. Who would mess with the platypus? Not that Australian delivery-room nurse or that doula you hired who won't stop trying to massage your arches, no way. Though the platypus is a mammal, it . . . uh, it also lays eggs. Hmm. No, we're not changing our minds! Platypus!

THE DRAGON

If you're a fantasy-loving lady, you're going to want a dragon on your side while you're in labor. Breathing fire on those who would oppose you; letting you pet its cool, scaly muzzle. Piercing your soul (figuratively) with its opalescent eyes and bestowing upon you the gifts of pain relief, immortality, and a Level 15 Lawful-Good Wizarding rating. Sweet!

DRAW WHAT YOU WANT YOUR BABY'S BIRTH TO BE LIKE

Now, how do you want your birth to be? Let's look at some samples!

That baby really worked up some speed! Notice the blissful smile on the woman's face, as well as the surprised expressions of the doctor, nurses, and Santa.

This is good because it's so specific. Details!

Draw what you imagine your helpers doing while you're birthing. Erase those cell phones, if you don't want them there!

You can also draw a more abstract, *feeling-based* work. What do you imagine labor will feel like?

Now you've got nothing to worry about—and plenty to look forward to!

MEANWHILE, INSIDE YOU . . .
THE EIGHTH MONTH

WHAT'S GOING ON UP IN THERE?

By the eighth month, your baby can open and close her eyes at will. She may have also a full head of hair, sharpened talons, and the ability to create black holes in space with her mind. Well, what do you expect? It's boring in there.

Here's your baby!

9. ONE WAY OR ANOTHER, IT WILL COME OUT OF YOU

You're in the home stretch! All bases are loaded, and you've got the bat, and it's time to kick a home run, or . . . look, we're experts in *parenting*; we never claimed to know anything about sports metaphors.

You're so close to childbirth that you may have *had* your baby already. Look down. Is there a baby on your lap? If so, you are free to move ahead to the next chapter. Unless, of course, you've come here to gloat over the fact that you're not one of those suckers who still have babies *trapped inside them*.

If you have not yet delivered that baby, you are mammoth. Your largeness level has been elevated from COMICAL to TERRIFYING. You look as though you will give birth if you sneeze. People no longer chuckle as they pass by. Now they might gasp, scream, clap their hands to their mouth, weep, vomit, or fly backward out of view, leaving two beads of sweat hanging in midair. All are appropriate reactions; after all, you are defying the laws of nature and God with your ghastly ginormitude. All you can do is nod sadly and offer to get everyone a cool washcloth for their forehead.

Actually, just . . . just go. You've done enough.

HOW ARE YOU FEELING?

OUT OF CONTROL!

Your baby will soon descend so that it can be closer to its eventual place of egress. Baby may have already dropped down into your pelvis, for all we know, and now you feel like you have a small, hairy bowling ball between your legs. This descent is silent and theoretically painless, and will render you able to breathe slightly more easily, as the baby's feet are no longer pitter-pattering against your lungs. Unfortunately, Baby is now massaging your bladder with his elbows, and so your old friend incontinence is back for a visit. Fortunately, you can always claim your water is breaking, and wet yourself without shame! (This works up to three times per bystander, on average.)

RESTLESS!

You may also be suffering from *Restless Leg Syndrome*, also known as the feeling that you're not tall enough, and that your toes are arguing with each other, and that ants are tunneling under your skin. OH DEAR GOD, HERE, JUST TAKE THESE DORITOS TO YOUR QUEEN. This feeling usually strikes in the dead of night, *not because God wants to spend a quiet few hours watching you whirl amongst your bed linens*, but because your body is dress-rehearsing for all those wakeful nights you'll spend pacing and rocking and traveling from room to room with your baby! So thank you, Nature. Thank you for giving mothers-to-be some much-needed spasm practice.

Tell Me More About Restless Leg Syndrome!

Pregnant women have been experiencing the phenomenon of restless legs since the dawn of women being pregnant, but there was no name for the discomfort for many, many years, which meant women were unable to gossip about it in the town square. Known in medieval times as "Demon Legge Sicknesse," Restless Leg Syndrome was thought to be caused by evil spirits settling heavily in the lower limbs, the result of witchcraft gone awry. To remedy the situation, a physician, or "blacksmith," would apply a white-hot poultice made of crushed henbane and the gall of a castrated boar, and then create "release-holes" all over the body of the alleged witch with an awl or dagger. Women rarely survived the procedure. Naturally, this was blamed on the demons.

Sucks for Them. What Else Is Happening to *Me*?

In addition to having the jimmy leg, you are unable to poop. Your body is too busy completing the finishing touches on your baby to worry itself over your voiding concerns. In medieval times, constipation was known as "Demon Faeces Stoppage," usually blamed on evil spirits (again!) setting up shop inside the colon. (The colon was also known as the "Serpentine Demon-Stronghold.") Fortunately, medieval doctors did not favor the release-hole procedure for constipation. Instead, they prescribed mercury colonics, which were embarrassingly effective, astonishingly lethal, and eerily beautiful upon release.

You may be saying to yourself, "Say, this medieval medicine talk is informative, and thanks for that, but how do I treat these problems nowadays?" To which we reply: "What do you have that the medieval pregnant woman did not? That's right: *Google.* Look it up."

If you *insist* that looking it up is *too hard* and *what did you pay good money for if not to get that sort of information, blah blah blaaaaargh*, we then respond: "OH MY GOD, pregnant women today are touchy."

Okay then.

For Restless Leg Syndrome, the best thing to do is help your legs understand that you are not running a marathon. Your legs might be confused, because they have no brains in them. Put on a movie such as *Marathon Man* or *They Shoot*

Horses, Don't They?, then point to the screen, and then at your legs, and then shout at your legs, *"That is not us. Stop doing that."*

As for constipation, we recommend Metamucil and a set of rosary beads. For *praying* with. (What were *you* thinking?)

Did we also mention that you have insomnia? Even when you are able to sleep, you will do so fitfully because of your *crazy dreams*. But what do these dreams mean?

TABLE 9.1 EXACTLY WHAT YOUR DREAMS MEAN

Dream:	What it means:
You're eating your cat.	Your body requires some Vitamin C, which can most likely be obtained from C-rich cat meat. Recommended!
You're flying over Mount Rushmore.	You want filmmaker Wes Anderson to help you escape from the virtual prison of parenthood. *Don't we all.*
You're making sweet love to Brian Dennehy.	You've always had a thing for burly character actors.
You're in your house, but it's not *really* your house. It's pretty different, but still somehow you *know* it's yours. Then your husband walks in, but he's talking in the voice of that beefy gal who anchors the local nightly news. He says the craziest thing, but darned if you can remember it. Then you remember that you're late for your physics final! Which is funny because of course you haven't taken physics since eighth grade. Then you wake up and your pillow is gone. Ha ha, not really.	You are boring and talk about your dreams too much.
You give birth to a hundred tiny Santas, who then turn into gingerbread men and crumble helplessly as you nurse them.	You're resisting the idea of giving birth to a spiritually realized being, so your subconscious turns him into a tasty holiday treat/Eucharist so that you can still ceremoniously ingest your Lord, even as he resists suckling the life-giving nectar that flows from your breasts. Hey, good luck at your next confession!
All of your teeth fall out.	You fell asleep with half a Twix bar hanging out of your mouth.
You're . . . nude.	Are you sure you're dreaming? Because you're at the grocery store. Here, cover yourself with these cloth bags until we can get you to the car.

DON'T READ THIS NEXT PART!

Women in the ninth month of pregnancy often start having intensely sexual dreams that culminate in *orgasm*. This is a mother-to-be's glorious little secret. For God's sake, don't tell anyone, or they'll get all turned on and want to have sex with you. IN FACT, JUST BECAUSE YOU READ THIS, YOU'RE PREGNANT AGAIN. YOU'RE DOUBLE-PREGNANT! You should never have read this.

HELPFUL OBSERVATIONS FROM THE CRAZY PEOPLE ON THE BUS:

- Nap now because you won't get to later! YOU WILL NEVER NAP AGAIN. I should know, I haven't slept since 1976.
- You should already have had that baby! Get to a hospital! Turn this bus around and take this woman to a hospital!
- They have rooms for squeezing at the hospital. They'll just squeeze and squeeze until a baby comes out.
- You're having twins! Twins can read them others' thoughts.
- Look at the balloon lady! She has a balloon inside her! *I'm going to pop her!*
- That lady doesn't have a balloon in her—she's got *snakes.*
- Lady, you did sex.

Things you need to do right now before that baby is born because you'll never get the chance ever again

- Skydiving
- Hang gliding
- Jumping off of something
- Rappelling
- Spelunking
- Murdering
- Making love to Brian Dennehy

Brian Dennehy is an esteemed star of stage and screen. He has been in such movies as *Silverado* and *Cocoon*, and has won a Golden Globe and a Screen Actor's Guild Award. In addition, he was nominated for five Emmys. Five. (How many Emmys have *you* been nominated for?) Mr. Dennehy loves sailing and exudes a natural, earthy musk that women and small mammals are powerless to resist.

PREPARING FOR BIRTH: A FUN WAY TO FOOL YOURSELF INTO THINKING YOU'RE READY FOR THIS

Is your suitcase ready? Oh my God, why isn't your suitcase ready? Hurry up and get your suitcase ready!

Your suitcase really should be ready by now, you know. Not that you should panic, but what if you go into labor and you don't have your suitcase ready? All kinds of things will go horribly awry. You won't have your *stuff*! Which you'll need! So get that suitcase ready!

Suggested contents of suitcase:

- Comfortable gown for birthing in, because that hospital one is so tacky and you're sure you won't gore yours up *too* much
- Phone numbers and e-mail addresses of everyone you've ever met who must immediately be informed of your child's miraculous arrival
- Phone numbers of better doctors and/or hospitals just in case this one turns out to be not as great as you thought
- Unscented massage oils, for when your husband and/or partner and/or doula and/or entire family massage your pressure points and/or perineum
- Snacks that you can throw up easily (Jell-O cups, pudding cups, yogurt cups. Cup-O-Soup!)
- Clean, sturdy bucket in which to throw up (Fact: the hospital will give you one of those little kidney-shaped basins, which is just insulting)
- An iPod dock so that you can catch up on your *Wall Street Week* podcasts

- Pianist to play casual background music that won't interfere with your screaming

If you birth at home, you'll need:

- Tarps
- Econo-sized drum of Purell
- The phone number to one of those crime-scene cleanup crews
- Meals for your midwife and/or shaman
- Inflatable birthing tub filled with 98.6°F water
- 40-gallon flash heater for warm-ups
- Kiddie pool into which midwives can pour cooling water from the birthing tub (husband/partner going through sympathetic labor pains can lie in there, moaning softly, let's just humor him for a minute, okay? And *then* the punching.)
- Weed. (If you're doing this without anesthesia, you might as well be high.)
- You won't need clothes!
- Earplugs for neighbors
- Advance calls to police, fire, and sanitation departments to let them know that any screaming they hear is merely Mother Nature's way of keeping all the streets clear in front of your house just in case you need to hustle, you know . . . anywhere

GUESS WHAT?

If your baby could text you, here's what she'd say!

C U SUN
(See you soon!)

LOLZ
(I am filled with joy in anticipation of our meeting!)

U R AWSM
(I find you admirable!)

U R FXN MI NRSRY RT?
(You're decorating my nursery, aren't you? Nothing tacky, I hope?)

HAY WHAZZUP I RLY W8NT H3LLz YA
(unclear)

Don't forget to try out your birthing tub!

Richard Wagner made some sweet baby-havin' music.

Things you should also have ready at home for immediately after the baby is born:

- Six months' worth of frozen dinners
- Detailed list of which friends brought you frozen dinners and which did not, for later reevaluation of friendships
- Some sort of electrical heating appliance for thawing frozen dinners
- Entire house has been cat-proofed (as well as unkibbled and de-dandered) by a professional cat-proofing service
- Large needlepoint samplers on wall that read BABY IS NOT YOUR ENEMY, YOU LOVE BABY, and SHIT HAPPENS

IS IT FALSE LABOR?

At some point during this last month, you may very well experience what you think is real labor, only to find out that your body is putting you through yet another infernal dress rehearsal by inflicting a bunch of kind-of-painless yet somewhat-unnerving Braxton Hicks contractions on you. Your doctor or midwife will be amused as she explains this to your sweaty face, and you will want to punch her right in the mouth. DO NOT. You're going to need her when it's time for the baby-having. Really, would *you* want to work with a patient who socks you *just because she doesn't like your stupid face*?

SIGNS THAT IT'S FALSE LABOR

- Pain not coming in regular waves
- You can still speak and move
- Doctor on phone says it sounds like false labor

- Nurse is recommending that you leave the hospital until you're really in labor
- Orderlies are chuckling as they haul you out of the supply room, where you were attempting to put on a gown and wheel yourself out on a gurney
- The nurse in triage is wondering aloud how you got in
- Anesthesiologist is refusing to give you an epidural
- Hospital cafeteria lady won't sell you an open-faced sandwich
- Security is escorting you out the door
- Pain slowly fading
- Now you feel silly
- It's over and there's no baby anywhere you can see

POINT/COUNTERPOINT: MEDICATED VS. NATURAL CHILDBIRTH

ALICE:

I would never judge any woman who opted for natural childbirth, who decides she'd rather labor for hours, days—even weeks—without an ounce of relief than take advantage of the decades of scientific and religious progress we've made regarding pain relief. That is, I won't judge her publicly, or anywhere else but inside my head.

Secretly, however—between you and me and anyone reading this—I think those women are not in their right minds. I also think they are dangerously smug, and should be locked up forever. Do these ladies also receive elective dermatological treatments without pain relief?! If their tanning booth overheated would they insist, "Just give me a towel to bite down on"? If they stubbed their

So cute!

toe, would they not ransack the house searching for their last Xanax? Would they write a book about babies without first downing a fistful of Demerols and a Quaalude they saved from that Dio concert in '83?

As the Buddhists tell us, life is pain. They also tell us that we don't have to feel that pain, which means we should use whatever we want to avoid it. And I think if the Dalai Lama were in labor, he would be getting as many spinals as he could survive to maintain that cute scrunchy-faced smile and keep those suburban-dad glasses perched on his little head.

EDEN:

Natural childbirth has many overlooked advantages. It's cheaper, for one thing— tanks of nitrous oxide don't grow on trees, you know, and if they did you'd have to make sure they were organic and that the pickers had comprehensive health insurance. Then there's the chance to really feel that baby squeezing through every inch of your vagina! Why would you not want that? Your baby has no choice but to feel his face get mashed through your birth canal like it's a moist, pulsing turtleneck sweater, and for all he knows *the experience will never end.* Your baby trusts that whatever bizarre, miserable things happen to him are a necessary step in his uncertain journey. Why can't you?

Oh, sure, I heard that thing where if you give birth naturally you're automatically put on an FBI wiretapping list and they put alopecia in your tap water, but I think Alice planted that rumor in the Mothering.com discussion forum. (She always registers with the same fake username on all the pregnancy sites: "mothersuperior69.") It all seems a little far-fetched to me, but just to be safe I only drink fair-trade coconut water and my own breast milk.

WHY AREN'T YOU NESTING?!?

Some people believe that as a woman approaches childbirth, the nesting instinct automatically kicks in. As if there's some giant female hive mind that tells you to start tearing out your baseboards and spraying lye behind your walls! In reality, the Great Female Unibrain that orbits our planet works in far more disturbing ways. So while many women don't feel a conscious urge to steam-clean the inside of the broom closet before Baby arrives, some inexplicable compulsions are, indeed, manifestations of the impulse to festoon the maternal burrow. Some examples:

- Kendra thought it would be a good idea to scrape out every old pint of ice cream in the freezer with a butter knife and consolidate all the ice cream bits into a single Tupperware container for later obscene, solitary enjoyment. What she didn't know was that she was both creating room in the freezer for all the breast milk she'd be storing in there later, and after she'd rinsed the pint containers and lids in scalding water, she could dry and save them for five or six years when her child might need them for a kindergarten seed-planting project. *Thanks, Femi-Nexus!*
- Shira thought she was just lying around like a beached whale, reading magazines and tearing out the perfume strips because they gave her a headache, when in reality the Nexus was instructing her to cleanse the immediate area of allergens and toxins that would inhibit Baby's own connection to the Source. *Aren't you glad you're an unconscious outgrowth of the Great Female Unibrain?*

If, through excessive feminism, you've severed your connection with the GFU, you can still experience the joys of mindlessly waddling around your bathroom with a caulk gun and a bucket of decorative plastic ants while your husband looks on in confusion. Follow these simple instructions:

1. Get out your vacuum cleaner. If you don't have one, borrow one from a neighbor.
2. Spread all the attachments on the floor and look at them. Wow! That should really give you some ideas.
3. If that doesn't actually give you any ideas, give the vacuum cleaner back and get out a sponge!
4. Sponge!
5. No? Hmm. Okay, how about just throwing out that stack of old magazines before it falls over and kills someone. It doesn't matter if you're keeping them "for that one article." Oh, all right, clip out the article. Wait—there's more than one?
6. Go through each magazine, clipping out the articles you wanted to save.
7. Design an overly elaborate article/recipe folder-notebook in which to store them all for later reference.
8. Go to the scrapbooking supply store and spend two hundred dollars getting everything you need to create this folder thing.
9. Return home and pile everything on the table.
10. Immediately go into labor and forget this project for ten years.

OTHER WAYS TO KEEP FROM GOING INSANE WHILE YOU WAIT FOR BABY TO COME

Collect stamps

Stomp around like the dancers in *STOMP*

Read a crime novel

Write a crime novel

Solve crimes

Commit crimes

Commit *unsolvable* crimes

Solve the unsolvable crime

Sterilize the dishes

Sterilize your husband

Knit useful home accessories (TV cozy, scissor scabbard, soup afghan)

Craft . . . *things*

Cook every recipe in Julia Child's *Mastering the Art of French Cooking* and blog about the joys and frustrations of each day's experience

Turn your blog into a best-selling book

Turn your best-selling book into an award-winning movie

Attend awards ceremonies in your pregnancy evening gown

Come home and congratulate yourself for achieving success beyond your wildest dreams

Wonder what to do next

Sterilize husband again

Sterilize dog

Knit baby leg warmers out of sterilized dog fur

She's staying sane!

PREPARING YOUR PUBIC AREA FOR LABOR

No one wants to see a baby coming through your hairy ape-parts—but you *certainly* don't want some orderly coming at you with a crappy disposable razor and a can of Barbasol. No, you're going to want to prep that area yourself, so think big! Bear in mind that you'll probably end up completely nude before this whole thing is over, so keep the public in mind as you tend to yourself.

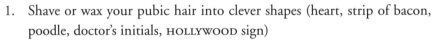

1. Shave or wax your pubic hair into clever shapes (heart, strip of bacon, poodle, doctor's initials, HOLLYWOOD sign)
2. Body paint
   a. Paint your legs to look like giant octopus tentacles, and your belly is the octopus body, and your belly button is a big octopus EYEBALL
   b. Legs can be tree trunk, belly can be very leafy
   c. Belly is the earth, legs are black and starry like space (vagina can be Saturn, as seen from a distance)
3. Little surprises taped to thighs will delight doctors, nurses, midwives, and orderlies alike. Some ideas:
   a. Glitter
   b. Animal stickers
   c. Lollipops (sugar-free for midwives)
   d. Nickels, dimes, and quarters
   e. Flavored condoms
   f. Goodie bags filled with candy
4. Don't forget to exfoliate! Studies show that women who aren't buffed to a glossy finish get less attention from nurses and have longer labors.
5. The reverse is true for home births, as many midwives have positive associations with hair in normal places on women's bodies. If this is the appalling situation you find yourself in, simply tape hair and bits of dead

skin from other parts of your (or someone else's) body to your trunk pits and extremities with double-sided tape. You may trim what you feel is necessary to keep the baby from becoming ensnared, however.

HOW TO KICK-START LABOR

At a certain point you're going to feel like you just can't take it anymore—you need this baby to come out of you *now*. It's the perfect time to share our list of absolutely reliable and 100 percent guaranteed ways for you to wake up that baby and get her traveling down the Uterine Expressway.

- Horseback riding
- Trampolining
- Space shuttle (other astronauts may object during mission briefing)
- Roller derby
- Giving your belly a stern talking-to
- Eating spicy foods
- Holding spicy foods in front of vagina
- Sour Patch Kids
- Spicy Patch Kids
- Papal edict stating that Baby's presence is required
- Monkeys can help
- Sex with strangers
- Sex with monkeys
- Test-driving off-road vehicles (with monkey driving)

C-section: just as much fun as it sounds!

C is such a cheerful letter! It's like a little smile. A C-section is just a little smile-shape cut into your abdomen, and who pops out of it? BABY! Yay! And then your obstetrician puts your uterus and your bladder back into your tummy and staples you up, ca-chunk ca-chunk! (Hopefully nothing fell in there!) And then it's over. And you got to stay awake for the whole thing! Whose vagina is still pretty and perfect? YOURS! Aren't you lucky? Now don't move for a week or you'll explode.

DANTE'S NINE STAGES OF LABOR

Every woman's labor is different, of course, but also *exactly the same.* Whether it lasts for five hours or five days, labor has a predictable progression we call *stages*™. These twists and turns can be disconcerting, even *uncomfortable,* but a little preparation and foreknowledge can prevent excessive panic and superfluous puking.

Dante unwittingly described these stages back in the fourteenth century, when he wrote a little something called *Dante's Inferno.* This was later made into a popular movie starring Linda Evans and Remington Steele.

PRELABOR: "THE VESTIBULE OF HELL"

This stage is marked by yearning and endless waiting; a glorious torment of expectation. You just want to get on with it. That baby's coming out of you one way or another, after all. Right?

STAGE 1: "LIMBO"

Here's where the Unbelievers reside. It's pretty much okay.

You are plagued by a lack of faith that the birth is *finally happening*. Your contractions are irregular; your impulse to call friends and family, spotty at best. You can dimly perceive that you're on some sort of path, but it seems marked by struggles and fire. You dislike struggles and fire.

STAGE 2: "THE LUSTFUL"

In the second level of Hell, the Lustful are buffeted for all eternity by never-ending winds.

As for you, contractions are becoming stronger and more regular. You may be thinking about the sex that caused this, and regretting it terribly. Alas. You shouldn't have gone off and married the first guy who asked.

STAGE 3: "THE GLUTTONS"

Here, the condemned must eat filth and drink putrid water. FOREVER.

And that's about how you feel right now, because you're about to get reacquainted with your last meal. You are really wishing you hadn't eaten all that spicy kimchi in an effort to get labor started.

STAGE 4: "THE PRODIGAL AND THE MISERLY"

Over here, hoarders and wasteful types push enormous boulders against each other. Ouch!

You, on the other hand, are having contractions that last from thirty to sixty seconds each, and your cervix is dilating like crazy. Despite what Dante said about boulders, don't start pushing yet—it's not time! If you must push *something* out, it's probably time for that mucous plug to go.

STAGE 5: "THE WRATHFUL AND THE SULLEN"

In this stage of The Inferno, *the bodies of the damned rend each other asunder in the dark, filthy water of the river Styx.*

Aaand your water broke. Maybe you should get out of bed and let someone clean that up.

STAGE 6: "THE HERETICS"

The Heretics are trapped in burning tombs. BURNING TOMBS.

Is it getting hot in here? As you near transition, your internal body temperature will start to rise, and much like Dante's heretics, your baby is feeling trapped in your burning hot uterus. Your baby is probably not a heretic, but if you're concerned, this would be a good time to summon the clergy.

STAGE 7: "THE VIOLENT, SUICIDES, BLASPHEMERS, SODOMITES, AND USURERS"

There's a river filled with boiling blood guarded by the Minotaur! Souls become a forest of suffering trees bearing poisonous fruit, and Harpies make nests in their branches! And O, the rain of fire, the overpowering stench!

That pretty much describes this part of labor.

STAGE 8: "FRAUD"

There's a cavalcade of horrors here: sinners are hacked up, afflicted with disease, forced to wade about in excrement, wedged into holes, their heads are turned backwards, they're sunk into a lake of boiling tar—and on and on.

This stage is marked by your giving up entirely, or as we call it, "abandoning hope." "I have reached a decision," you may tell the natal professionals surrounding you, "which is that I wish for none of this ever to have happened." They'll laugh at you, of course—but that's because they've noticed that you're more or less wading around in excrement.

STAGE 9: "BETRAYAL"

Who wants to be chewed on by Satan for all eternity? Not you! Better skip this stage!

On the other hand, you have no choice but to go through ninth and final labor-stage, which is marked by a lot of profanity and will seem to go on for all eternity. The good news is, it will end—with either a popping noise or a moist *fwoop!*—at which point your baby will have been born. Yay. Sweet, sticky relief. In his enthusiasm, your husband may overreact and chew off the umbilical cord. Dante would be horrified, but Satan would probably approve.

It Really Happened! Labor Stories

STELLA'S STORY

"I was prepared for labor to be hard but I had no idea it would be *that* hard! LOL. So what I did was, I went to the hospital and I was like, can I just have this baby now because I am SUPERBIG and I would rather not be SUPERBIG anymore, so my doctor finally agreed (after I wouldn't leave the hospital) and he gave me a whole buncha pitocin, and I was like GREAT! But then OH, SHIT! And it went like that for about three days. I mean, the baby came out eventually and all? But he would have come out three days later ANYWAY, and I could have spent those three days at my sister's in Boca instead of being chained to an IV and puking and crying for seventy-two hours, is what I'm saying."

ALICE'S STORY

"After laboring quietly at home for the prescribed length of time, I instructed my husband to drive me to the hospital. I then calmly informed the triage nurse that I was fully effaced and dilated at five centimeters (I used a hand-mirror, a tape measure, and my natural flexibility). I was admitted, whereupon I briskly informed the labor nurse that I required an epidural, as soon as possible, lest I kill her. The anesthesiologist was summoned, the epidural administered, and I labored calmly for another ten hours or so, while my husband fed me ice chips and endured my quiet whispers of hate. (We had previously agreed that he was to ignore anything I said during labor. I thought he had until I found his journal.) Then it came time for pushing, and I did that for a while, and the baby was born. I had a boy, who scored 9,9 on his Apgar and nursed immediately after birth. So I was pleased. Now that he is seven, we've become estranged, but that's a whole other story."

EDEN'S STORY

"I don't know, I just felt like I had to go to the bathroom. I sat down on the toilet and a baby came out."

TOOTIE'S STORY

"Childbirth? I don't see why you need to know about that. The topic of childbirth is so dreary. In my day you didn't talk about these things. You went into the hospital, you did what you had to do, you came out with a baby. We didn't even use the word 'pregnant,' back then. Of course, that might have been because I was never, technically, pregnant. Or because I stole that baby. Well, what choice did I have? His mother just left him there, all alone, in a bassinet in the nursery! Why wouldn't I dress up like a nurse and rescue him? 'Kidnap' is such a strong word, dear."

SEDONAH'S STORY

"It's so hard to capture the experience of birthing my precious Ne'ezrau into words, so I made this expressive, colorful oil painting for the book authors. Sadly, they told me that they couldn't put it in the book because the low-res reproduction wouldn't do it justice. Also, something about certain stores not carrying books with that sort of art in it. And anyway, to really get the full effect you have to listen to the sitar piece I composed about birthing while looking at the painting. At any rate, I have also written a haiku:

The vivisection
Torn, rent asunder, squeezing
A biscuit floats by.

Yes, my glorious childbirth was such a high point in my existence that I videotaped it and made every-one who visited witness the glorious moment of expulsion. I don't know why they're all so squeamish.

It's just nature. Nature at work. I visit my *husband* at work, for heaven's sake. Sheesh."

GOODY ABIGAIL DELIVERANCE'S STORY

"It was around the time that the hens grow restless that I felt the baby announcing his arrival. After finishing the supper preparations and white-washing the kitchen and preparing a receiving hay-pile for the infant, I sent for the midwife, who unfortunately had been burned at the stake just that morning. I labored alone for thirty-six hours while a steady July snow began to fall—only to find at the culmination that I had had another girl. I named her Deliverance Abigail, and after white-washing the hayloft, I tucked the rest of the children into bed and sat down at the kitchen table to await my husband's stern rebukes."

Last trimester keyword search strings that will increase the panic

Fetus whirling like in a blender

"Raw beef binge" last trimester

Giving birth pain descriptions

Birth Guinness longest labor ever recorded "beard of bees"

Birth how much blood

Birth labor agony blood

Worst birth stories ever blood

HOW WILL I TAKE CARE OF BABBY

MEANWHILE, INSIDE YOU . . . THE NINTH MONTH

If you've managed to keep your baby up in there for at least thirty-seven weeks, he is ready to come out into the world and breathe air, drink milk, and search for your banking information on your computer. The longer you keep him inside you, the more weight he'll gain—up to thirteen pounds a week. If this is your first baby, you have probably stopped eating this month, keeping baby slightly malnourished and thereby easier to push through the birth canal, an opening that's normally no wider than a golf ball. So good luck with that.

Here's your baby!

When your baby finally gets out of you, you may notice that he is covered in goo and possibly even a fine, downy hair. This does not mean that he is a slime-creature or that he is destined to become an ape-man. These are Natural Things that come with obvious explanations that we wrote down somewhere this morning and now we can't find them, but they're nothing to worry over.

Now go forth, give birth, and then move on to the next section. There will be no more surprises because you are absolutely ready for Baby!

Part II

THE
BIRTHENING
AND BEYOND

10. FUCKING HELL, IT'S A BABY

Congratulations! You went and had/acquired yourself a baby. Fortunately, you were well prepared, thanks to us. Oh, us. Is there anything we can't do? (See sidebar next page.)

We'll talk about that brand-new baby of yours in a minute, but first: how are *you*?

Yes, you. Everyone's focused on your newborn right now, and that's great, but we want to hear about you. Because you're the one who bought our book. That baby can't read, and if that baby could read, that baby would have chosen *The Poky Little Puppy* and not our book at all. That baby wouldn't care if we sold only five copies of our book and couldn't pay our mortgage and were tossed out on the street. So guess what? We like you better. Suck it, baby.

The first few weeks after childbirth can be overwhelming, indeed. You might have felt euphoric and giddy in those first moments after

Some things we actually cannot do

Raise your child for you

Travel fast than light

Guide you through the minutiae of your life

Crochet (never got the hang of it)

Tightrope walk (I mean, we probably could, but we won't)

Tie our shoelaces (harder than it looks)

all that birthing ended, but those feelings quickly subside and are replaced by anything from exhaustion to despair to hunger back to joy, which is immediately subsumed by episiotomy itch and sleepiness. Oh, the sleepiness . . . the . . . hmm? What?

Let's take a moment for some common reactions to new parenthood, shall we?

"THIS BABY IS SO EASY!"

Ah. Like so many before you, you believe you've birthed the perfect child. We won't fight you on that, especially when you've got that crazy glint in your eye, but don't leap to conclusions quite yet. Newborn babies are infamous for their seeming perfection: they're often well behaved, quiet, and sleepy. But guess what! Baby may be tricking you into thinking you can handle parenthood so that you don't leave Baby in the dairy aisle. Give it six weeks. By the time you're convinced of Baby's placid perfection, he'll perk up, and then your life will suck.

You may also want to open yourself to the possibility that what appears to be well-behavedness may actually be jaundicedness. Jaundice is a serious condition caused by an excess of bilirubin in the blood (bilirubin being the waste product of angry demons—at least according to our sourcebook, *Sufferinges of Demon-Plages in Infancies,* published 1407). It *can* make your baby as passive and undemanding as you'd ever want a child to be—but sadly, you can't keep her that way. Is your baby a rich amber or a cheerful lemony shade? No matter how well she coordinates with her nursery decor, you'll need to get to your pediatrician right away.

"THIS BABY ISN'T EASY AT ALL! WHAT THE HELL IS THE MEANING OF THIS?"

Some babies start out difficult, just because. Because they're extra feisty! These babies are sometimes called "attention whores," and will flip their tiny lids when they realize you've turned your gaze away from them or placed them in a bouncy seat so you could take a shower. *God forbid you should be clean.* If you can anticipate Baby's cry triggers and defuse them, you might get by. But you won't. She'll probably scream and scream no matter what you do, like the world owes her something but *guess what*, it doesn't, so she's going to have to cry a little bit sometimes so Mommy can get herself a lousy sandwich or a glass of water, if that's not too much to ask. Not that you're asking, because she had better realize fast that you're the one calling the shots around here, not her. NOT HER!

"OW."

Are you really surprised that you're uncomfortable? Having a baby is kind of a big deal, physically. Shall we remind you what just came out of you, and how it came out? Have you forced those memories from your conscious mind already?

"SOMEONE GET MY IN-LAWS/PARENTS/ SIBLINGS OUT OF MY HOUSE/APARTMENT/ LEAN-TO!"

Babies are little semi-sentient magnets; the things they draw most powerfully are crazy people, murderous cats, and family. Some members of your family will

Helpful tips for crotch relief

If you're not breastfeeding: Place yourself in a narcotic-induced stupor for the first week; let your spouse and/or support staff deal with that kid.

If you are breastfeeding: Freeze your underwear!

If you had a C-section: Freeze your underwear anyway. It's a refreshing feminine pick-me-up!

Look who's come to "help."

keep a respectful distance while you're getting settled with your newborn, while others will insist on dropping by to "help." Now, at first this will seem like a blessing (finally someone *else* can shred a rotator cuff swinging that goddamn car seat)—but you'll quickly find that what passes for "helpfulness" in relatives is a little like offering to help you zip up that prepregnancy cocktail dress by hopping inside it with you. What's worse, Sanger's Law of Inverse Approachability states that it's the relatives you enjoy who won't come in for more than five minutes for fear of imposing on you, and the ones you can't stand who will land on your doorstep with slippers and an air mattress. There's not much you can do about this except grit your teeth (not too hard—don't want to crack those molars!) and/or move to another state. Actually, there's no point in moving. They'll find you no matter where you go.

"WHAT AM I DOING?"

Did it all just sink in, how you're responsible for a tiny, fragile, infinitely trusting nub of a human being? Did a cold wave of horror wash over you and did you lose feeling in your face? Before you forget how to use your hands, pass your child over to a spouse or trusted professional, and lie facedown on a cushioned surface until the feeling passes.

Fascinating Trivia: Eden laid down like that for three and a half years!

"I'M SO TIRED THAT I LONG FOR THE ETERNAL REST THAT SWEET, SWEET DEATH WILL BRING!"

Every pregnant woman since the dawn of time has had someone tell her, "Get your sleep now, because you won't be getting any once the baby arrives!" And every pregnant woman has wished that person open sores and festering boils because (a) what kind of a dick thing is that to say to someone? and (b) you can't store up sleep. Well, now guess what, smartypants? You're regretting not listening to that advice. Because although it's true that you can't squirrel away past sleeps as if they were sleep-nuts in your sleep-cheeks, you can remember how many hours of luxurious, uninterrupted rest you once enjoyed, and it would've made you feel a little bit better knowing that when you had the chance, you took it. But you ignored those people and stayed up late playing online poker and THEY WERE ONLY TRYING TO HELP.

Yes, sleep deprivation is a bitch. Your nerves are so frayed that after about seventy-two hours your survival mechanisms will kick in and you'll start to conk out at unfortunate times: while your partner is calling from the police station, or while you're hitch-hiking to Guadalajara with your new friend, José. Before you hitch anything else to Guadalajara, see chapter 11's advice on getting your baby to sleep (page 170).

Your great-grandmother, were she alive, might advise slipping a spoonful of brandy into Baby's bottle. (As it is, she's hovering over there, to the right of the fireplace—oh, if only you could see her!) This is inadvisable. Tugging down a pint yourself, however—and then administering it to Baby through the nourishing medium of breast milk—is a VSOP treat for both mother and infant alike. If you're not breastfeeding, well then, more brandy for you! Baby will just have to wait until next Christmas.

"THIS IS OVERLY DIFFICULT, AND I HAVE CHANGED MY MIND."

Whether you had your baby by traditional means or procured it from a specialized vendor, the fact remains: you can't back out now unless you're ready for the world to judge you as a terrible human being.

So now that you know you're trapped forever and ever, or for the next few months until the appropriate governess can be vetted and hired, why not make the best of it—turn baby lemons into a wee glass of baby-ade, if you will? Let's look at some of the good things about having a baby. There are more than you think!

Having a baby will:

- Win you the approval of the far right
- Allow you to start one of those "mommy blogs" everyone's been talking about
- Give you an excuse to expose your nipples in public
- Allow you to catch up on all those episodes of *Sesame Street* you've missed (*My, how gracefully Maria has aged!*)
- Exercise your arms from hours of vigorous stroller-pushing and baby-rocking
- Provide you with someone to blame for all those thwarted ambitions

You see?

"BUT THE BABY KEEPS CRYING AND I HAVE HEMORRHOIDS AND MY HUSBAND FARTS IN HIS SLEEP AND LIFE IS AN ENDLESS VOID OF MISERY!"

There, there. You look cute in that nursing gown! Too bad your milk's seeping out all over it.

POINT/COUNTERPOINT: WHAT YOUR PARTNER MIGHT BE FEELING: SHOULD YOU CARE?

ALICE:

If your partner had read *Let's Panic About Babies!* while you were pregnant, he would have been well prepared to face everything he's feeling right now; and yet here he is, unable to look himself in the mirror because of that weird, pre–midlife crisis beard he grew, and staying up late creating "best of" porn slideshows for his wretched friends. Well, that's not your fault, is it? You have enough on your plate with the way your nipples are leaking all over the place and your hair's falling out, and *oh, Lord*, the stuff that's coming out of your vagina. Nothing your partner's feeling right now could possibly make any difference. In six months you might be overdue for some couples' therapy, but right now, lady, you worry about *you*.

EDEN:

I heartily disagree! You are completely dependent on your partner right now, so it's time to lavish every ounce of attention you can spare on him. You *think* you can barely get out of bed, what with that baby on your chest like a hypersensitive paperweight, and how on earth are you supposed to do anything but lie there and lactate? But it is vital for your very survival right now that you put the baby down, roll over, and show your partner how much you appreciate him with a little halfhearted oral sex. After all, would you rather he bring you a turkey sandwich on stale whole wheat out of grudging duty, or do you prefer he grill a prosciutto on ciabatta panini with love in his heart and a spring in his step? If you want the good sandwich—*and we all want the good sandwich*—you'll have to degrade yourself sexually in every way possible. It's the only thing that will keep his mind off those bothersome "feelings" of his.

BRACE YOURSELF: IT'S TIME TO LOOK AT YOUR NEW BODY

You're probably aware by now that your body has . . . changed. Now that the baby has migrated from internal to external freeloader, certain of your parts have shifted. Some parts are lower. Others are higher. Still others are creased and jumbled. It's difficult to say, at this point, which parts will snap back into place and which will forever remain in their new locale. Meanwhile, let's see if we can figure out what you're working with right now. Stand in front of a full-length mirror, take several cleansing breaths, and remember: it's too early yet to decide whether or not you'll spend your retirement money on bionic reconstruction.

FEET AND ANKLES

May still be somewhat swollen, but will generally return to their former shape with due efficiency. If your arches fell as a result of accidental weight gain, your doctor may be able to prescribe orthotics for you to wear inside your shoes. Feel free to invest in the most supportive shoes you can afford, particularly if you are willing to dress like a farmhand.

CALVES

Varicose veins may now be a problem for some. Costly vein-stripping procedures should be postponed until your body has produced all the children you and your partner require for haying season/a tiny basketball team.

KNEES

In some cultures, you'd be worshipped on an altar for those sweet dimples. In this day and age, however, they're a spongy blight on par with Love Canal. One caution: spending too much time on the floor with your newborn could result in dark, roughened skin and calluses, also known as "Housemaid's Knee." So get that baby walking as soon as possible or you'll never be able to wear skirts again!

THIGHS

Take a deep breath. No, don't turn away; it's okay, it happens to everyone. There, there.

BUTT

Despite the fact that we consistently urged you not to gain any weight during your pregnancy, your butt-gain may not be for naught: Science has found that there may (we stress *may*) be some benefit to storing an extra pound or two of fat in your butt. Your body can, we've heard, use this butt-material in the production of nutritious breast milk for your infant and curious friends. Science may have a point—

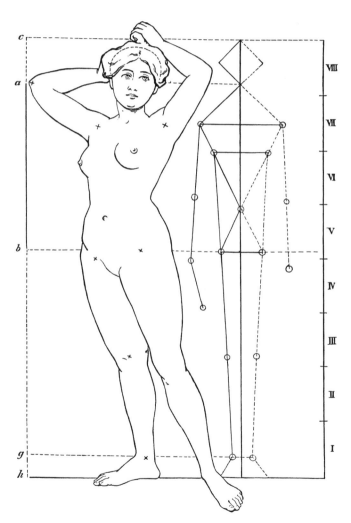

but how are you going to fit into your old prom dress now? Can Science tell you that?

STOMACH

One well-known advantage to birthing by C-section is that enterprising obstetrical surgeons will often throw in a tummy tuck for free. If you had Baby the old-fashioned way, however, you'll have to do some pretty fast talking in that birthing tub to convince your midwife to perform the same procedure. Even if you're successful, we must caution you that midwives favor the use of horehound candy as anesthesia.

BREASTS

Looking good! Your boobs are two marvels of pulchritude at the moment. Breastfeeders: enjoy it while it lasts; they'll have turned into lifeless pancakes before you know it. Non-breastfeeders: until your milk dries up, this area will become shockingly uncomfortable. If you're a professional folklorist, you can try putting cabbage leaves in your bra (one in each cup). This will make you smell like a digestive problem. People who prefer scientific advances to old-wifery will find that inserting a satellite dish into each bra cup will bring a soothing, buzzy warmth to the area.

SHOULDERS, ARMS, HANDS

These may be the features to highlight, at this point.

HEAD

Still attached? Well, slap some makeup on it and let's proceed.

👓 EYE ON BABY!

You're not the only one getting a good look at you. Baby's been checking you out, and right now, he's not liking what he sees. Clean yourself up, lady! Sure, that expression of pure love you've been aiming his way compensates for a multitude of sins, but Baby would appreciate it if you'd make an effort to brush your hair once in awhile, as Baby doesn't yet have the motor control to do it for you while he's nursing.

Developmentally, in the first month your baby's most excited about sensory input, especially in the areas of sight and taste, the two senses she didn't get to use much inside the womb. Make sure to leave Baby tummy-side-up on a blanket outside so she can learn to avert her eyes from the blistering sun. As for her developing taste buds, let Baby explore the world with her mouth and learn to differentiate between the seven basic tastes: sweet, salty, bitter, sweaty, fatty, pungent, and failure.

FEEDING YOUR BABY: ARE YOU DOING IT RIGHT?

One of the most stressful parts of learning to take care of a newborn involves getting Baby to latch onto your breast and drink from the bottomless well of your milky soul. Your pediatrician will be watching Baby closely for signs of "failure to thrive" (dry skin, tuneless humming, BO) and if he sees them, he may recommend a few different tacks, including fun techniques to bring in your milk (have a beer! visit a working dairy!) and different ways to hold your baby to encourage optimal nipple/lingual placement (see illustrations). Don't get lazy now or plainclothes agents from La Leche League will be on their way, armed with sanctimonious pamphlets, brusque gestures, and withering stares.

Little-Known Breastfeeding Problems

Halitosis: Baby's breath smells like he's been eating Snausages.

Hooverosis: Baby latches on so hard you think your brains will squirt out your tits.

Hamosis: Well? Did you eat ham?

Ozmosis: Baby realizes he had the courage/brains/heart/nerve in him all along.

Heliumosis: Baby floats away after nursing.

Hmmosis: That's not a thing. You're just looking for problems.

147

The right way   The wrong way   The wrongest way

If breastfeeding isn't working out for you or you just don't want someone utilizing your bodily fluids as a food source, you've moved straight to the bottle. We're all for respecting our own personal boundaries (Alice had a restraining order against her baby until he reached eighteen months) but be aware that you'll have to explain your decision to every busybody who crosses your path once you leave the house. This is because they're all plainclothes agents of La Leche League. Listen: the League is everywhere. And they have power. Access to bottomless wealth, cabinet-level influence in First World governments the likes of which . . . but we've said too much. WE ADMIRE THE GOOD WORKS OF LA LECHE LEAGUE! *Oh no.*

It Really Happened! Bringing Baby Home

"After spending five blissful days in a private hospital for weary aristocrats in a Middle Eastern country you've never been allowed to hear of, I was ready to let the nanny take the baby home while I jetted off to a tiny European country with no income tax to undergo some minor cosmetic surgery (I was having my hands replaced) and recover in a spa built over an ancient, healing hot spring. After another month of mineral baths and herbal colonics, I'd shed the minor amount of baby weight I'd gained and was ready to tackle my job as a new mother! Oh, I know I can't complain, what with all the help I have—the nanny, the cook, the night nurse, the play nurse, the nurse who cups her hands over my ears when I want to pretend to hear the ocean—but still, being a mommy is the hardest job I've ever had. It cries and I have no idea how to make it stop! I just have to go lie down and even then I'm too distraught to fire anyone."

—Amelia Braunschweiger, age 27, private island, somewhere in the Adriatic

"I was so thrilled to be Chosen to procreate for my glorious, Holy Leader as well as for the supreme good of the Family. But I wasn't prepared for those first few weeks after Oberon IV was born. It turned out I'm actually one of 37 Chosen (I don't know how I didn't see all those other women before; maybe it was all those pregnancy hormones, or whatever was in that root-tea Nurse-Maiden Aberrencia made me consume daily?) and Leader almost never gets the chance to Visit me in my cabin for a Holy Commingling, or even just a diaper change and maybe a few minutes with His son. He says it's because Oberon's mind isn't strong enough yet and might be irreparably damaged by the shining light of His visage, but I don't know, the Leader's driver's license dropped out of his robes the other day and it says his name is Merle? This is confusing. Maybe I should call my mom."

—Asveraffix, age 20, Infinity's Grove, Alabama

Don't forget to fill in your Baby Book!

11. HOW TO TAKE CARE OF IT

Now that we've gone over every unspeakable and messy consequence of your labor and delivery, let's take a closer look at the messiest consequence of all: that adorable bundle in your lap. (Or in the car seat/basket woven from reeds/other room/laundry pile next to you). Once it's out of you, after all, you'll have to do quite a bit more to take care of it, until it has enough basic know-how and hand/eye coordination to take care of itself. Please note: self-sufficiency will not arrive for some time. If you're feeling the least bit resentful toward your baby, it's best to tamp that down for *at least* the next eighteen years or so.

WHAT IS THIS THING? GETTING TO KNOW BABY

"Baby"

You know you have a baby, but do you know *what it is,* exactly? Some people believe that babies are smaller versions of us. Sadly, Science may never be able to prove this conclusively. All we can do is assume they're right and hope for the best. Meanwhile, let's examine your new baby's adorable features for the sheer joy and edification of it (and not at all to figure out if he's an alien spore-pod like we secretly believe he is).

HANDS: Those hands never stop moving! Baby's tiny Vienna sausages are constantly reaching (for wires), exploring (the boundaries of your sanity), grabbing (for power), and twisting (your nipples). Experts say you should keep Baby's hands free to explore, because exploring is healthy or whatever. We suggest taping his fingers together until he's at least three. Imagine the joy he'll feel upon discovering that his hands are not the useless mitts he once believed.

EYES: Eyes are the windows to the soul. It's a good idea to look deep, deep into your baby's eyes, for as long as you can stand gazing into their inky blackness without going insane, and finally shriek, "WHAT DO YOU WANT WITH ME?" The answer may surprise you.

MOUTH: The mouth is usually open due to intake of food or outtake of noise. The lips are generally trembling from sobs, or stretched tight against the gums in a rictus of baby-agony. During those rare moments of contentment, a soft cooing sound may come out of it. This should be adorable. (If the sound is not adorable, check with your pediatrician.) At around six weeks, you may witness a smile. Six weeks is how long it takes the baby to figure out that that's what he's supposed to do when you point the blinding flash box at him, whether he feels like smiling or not.

GILLS: These should not be present. Check carefully. If your baby has gills, she may be a fish or horseshoe crab. That doesn't mean you'll love her any less, but you may need to check out our sister publication, *Let's Panic About Water-Dwelling Arthropods!*

HEAD: This is roundish and hard. (Except for the soft spot, also known as the fontanel, which you should note *and then leave alone.* That fontanel is not your business, and will close up when it's good and ready and not any sooner. Do not attempt to "hurry it along.") Some babies have atypical head shapes due to a traumatic birth or sleeping in one of those modern dodecahedron-shaped bassinets. (No need to get fancy, design-oriented moms—the usual flat sleeping surfaces will work just fine!) Any weird shapes will even out eventually, with time, prayer, and appropriate headgear.

Of particular note is your baby's intriguing head-smell. When no one is looking, babies rub a special balm into their bald little noggins, a patented blend of civet musk, tapioca powder, and holy water. No one knows how they get it or in what tiny pocket of flesh they store it, but it is essential to the survival of babies everywhere. This is how they trap you into becoming their slave.

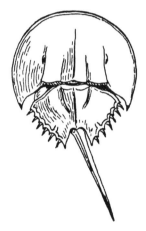

Is this your baby?

FIGURING OUT WHAT BABY REALLY NEEDS

Let's say that no matter how many copies of that *Baby Whisperer* book people keep giving you, you still find your infant to be little more than an inscrutable lump. This is because your motherly intuition—your maternal instinct, *everything in you that can love and feel*—is dead. Don't feel too bad. It's probably nothing you did. Or if you did do it, it's too late to go back and fix whatever it is you did, so let's forge ahead. We can coax those inner mom-vibes out of you yet!

There are several gestures that baby behaviorologists consider to be universal. These are subtle movements, transcending language and culture, which babies use to communicate their needs. If your soul isn't naturally guiding you in these matters, you'll have to study hard to catch up with the other moms. Force your sleep-deprived eyes open—your baby is trying to tell you something!

WHAT BABY WANTS: A sparkly tiara with rhinestones that can easily be pulled off and choked on.

BABY INDICATES THIS NEED BY: Stuffing her fist in her mouth, gagging.

WHAT BABY REALLY NEEDS: A little bit of cool chamomile tea to calm her bilious, feminine nature.

WHAT TO DO NEXT: Feed it to her using an eyedropper; ignore her cries of rage.

WHAT YOU HAVE LEARNED FROM THIS: You're going to have to make princess costumes for at least five Halloweens in a row.

WHAT BABY WANTS: That stuffed tiger over there.

BABY INDICATES THIS NEED BY: Rubbing his eyes until he cries with pain.

WHAT BABY REALLY NEEDS: That stuffed tiger over there.

WHAT TO DO NEXT: Go get it.

WHAT YOU HAVE LEARNED FROM THIS: Your baby's animal totem just revealed itself. Expect some furniture damage as teething/sweat lodge building commences.

WHAT BABY WANTS: A different mommy.

BABY INDICATES THIS NEED BY: Grunting, letting out a staggering bowel movement.

WHAT BABY REALLY NEEDS: A clean diaper, a Tibetan wind chime, and your focused companionship.

WHAT TO DO NEXT: Sing "The Itsy Bitsy Spider" over and over until Carly Simon comes to your house and begs you to stop.

WHAT YOU HAVE LEARNED FROM THIS: Carly's dying her hair!

WHAT BABY WANTS: A cigarette and the latest *TV Guide*.

BABY INDICATES THIS NEED BY: Looking around for her keys.

WHAT BABY REALLY NEEDS: To learn to soothe herself by sucking her thumb or cuddling with a favorite blanket or toy.

WHAT TO DO NEXT: Place several organic, hemp-filled, homemade toys within reach.

WHAT YOU HAVE LEARNED FROM THIS: Your baby is actually your reincarnated great aunt who managed a 7-Eleven and died of emphysema.

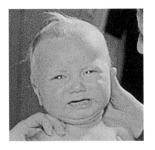

INTERPRETING YOUR BABY'S CRIES

Part of being a good mom is the ability to instantly recognize each tiny nuance of your baby's cries. Because your baby is successfully communicating his needs, he won't grow up to poke small animals with a stick. See how important it is? (And no, every society *does not need animal pokers,* no matter what "Doctor" Sears says.)

QUIZ: ARE YOU INTERPRETING BABY CORRECTLY? MATCH THE MESSAGE TO THE CRY!

1. Soft whine slowly escalating into lusty wail

2. Sharp, piercing cry

3. Ascending and descending shrieks

4. Hiccuping sob

5. Barely perceptible moan

6. Hyenalike shriek

7. Gurgling blubber ending in periodic hiccup

8. Howling that eerily resembles car alarm

9. Insistent, nonstop whimper

10. That cry where his lips get all trembly

11. Steady blubbering

12. Ritual ululation and/or keening

13. Barbaric yawps

a. "I'm hungry!"
b. "My pants are heavy with fecal matter!"
c. "I am filled with existential despair!"
d. "Why did you make me wear this ridiculous onesie?"
e. "I delight in keeping you awake all night!"
f. "Victory and a safe return from battle, tribal husbands! Make God your agent!"
g. "I despise stuffed animals and you've *filled* my nursery with them, and as a result, I will someday poke small but *real* animals with a stick to express my hitherto suppressed infantile rage!"
h. "Where are my hands?"
i. "What is this place?"
j. "I need you to sing me something, but I'm not sure what, but I know it should be long, and high-pitched, and requires you to jiggle me back and forth in a specific pattern that I will determine once we get going. Now hop to!"
k. "I have become unswaddled, goddamn you!"
l. "Sheila? *Sheila?* For God's sake, where's my wife?"
m. "I don't even know anymore."

Answers: Because each baby is a special snowflake, we can't tell you what your baby's cries mean. What does your heart and/or mother-in-law tell you?

HOW TO SWADDLE

Babies love to be swaddled, because they are terrified of freedom. They have not the slightest idea what their arms are, so when they fling-flang their limbs all around involuntarily, they think they're being attacked by frenzied sausage monsters. You'd cry, too, if you were constantly under siege.

So: restrain your child, and reap the benefits! You'll only have a little while to do this. Take it from us: older children do not want to be wrapped like a burrito. This leads to "therapy."

BENEFITS

1. It is adorable.
2. No, seriously, your baby's all snug in her ridiculous precious cocoon.
3. Do you get what a good photo opportunity this is? Baby all origami'd up, with just his head sticking out of there? Where's your camera?
4. Babies also seem to like it. Maybe because they enjoy being cute.

HERE'S HOW IT'S DONE:

1. Get a blanket.
2. Put the blanket down. Not there. On something flat.
3. Fold one corner down. Any corner.
4. Put the baby down on the blanket with his head facing toward the flat corner. You want the flat side to be under your baby's neck. Yes, he has a neck.
5. Uh, your baby's crying. Pick him up.
6. Wait, leave the blanket!
7. (Sigh.)
8. Okay, put the blanket back down.

WRONG WAYS TO SWADDLE

Baby should not look like this:

Baby's feet are out! Baby hates that!

Baby now thinks too much of himself.

9. Do the foldy thing again.
10. Okay, deal with your baby first, if you need to. Okay. We'll wait. Is it . . . is he calm now? No? Okay, okay. No problem.
11. You know what, let's just do this later.

When all else fails, we recommend talking with your neighborhood butcher. Have you ever seen them wrap a piece of meat? They know how to make sure the juices don't spill everywhere. Your baby is the same way. Except with limbs instead of potentially bacterial-laden meat fluids.

When you eventually figure things out, here's how baby should look:

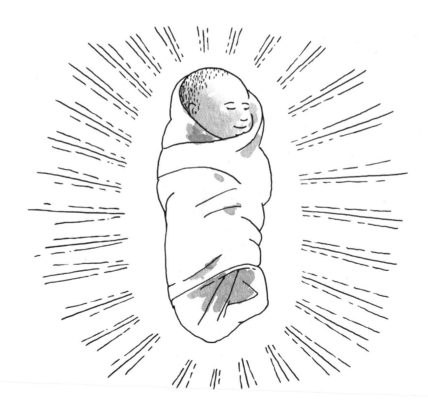

PRACTICE MAKES PERFECT!

It's a good idea to practice on a willing subject before you try to wrap up a squalling infant. Their shrieks and wails can rattle the less-practiced swaddler. Once you've got your technique down, your confidence will ease baby's fear that you're trying to kill her.

Sleepy dogs can be good for practicing, or small animals of any kind that won't bite you. Do you have a tortoise?

Your ideal subject would be an undersized man-child whose pastimes include quietly submitting to blanket-based restraint, but these aren't found in every household. Check the back pages of your local free newspaper, or also there's that cousin of yours who still lives with his mom even though he just retired from his accounting firm.

Whatever you do, make sure you *do not practice swaddling on the cat*. We've said it before: your cat secretly wants you dead, and will take any excuse it can get. *You don't still have a cat in the house, do you?!*

DIAPERING 101: KEEPING BABY-WASTE FROM GETTING ON YOU

Look. The pee and the poop will get on you. It will. You just have to make sure you get it off you before you reenter society.

FIRST STEP: Do not be alarmed. Consider the source: your baby. Your baby hasn't been eating asparagus, nor has he been smoking menthols on the fire escape while you were on the phone with your dad. No, because Baby is only ingesting the purest milk/formula from your breasts/refrigerator, Baby's pee is like rainwater. You could use it as fabric softener. (Note: do not use it as fabric softener.) If a little bit of pee gets on you, don't cry. But if you do cry, remember that a mother's tears mixed with her baby's pee transmutes both into holy water. Store it in a vial that you wear around your neck, and you will be able to perform the miracle of Never Having to Shower Again.

SECOND STEP: Baby boys are known for peeing as soon as you take their diaper off. That fresh air hits Baby's unit and he just lets go out of pure joy, or something. (Could be he just really needed to pee.) The solution to this is not to take off Baby's old diaper, but to just put a new one over it. Sure, it will get a little bunchy after a while.

THIRD STEP: Is there poop? You can usually tell without looking if poop is present. Unless you've been abusing nasal spray again, or that last round of antibiotics destroyed your sense of smell. If that's the case, you have to look into the diaper itself. It's dark in there. We know. It's okay. Don't be afraid.

FOURTH STEP: It is only after a great deal of practice that you'll be able to change a diaper without the poop getting on you. The first few times you may succeed out of pure beginner's luck, but eventually you'll succumb. Baby often saves her patented Heel Fling maneuver for when you're feeling smug. She will wait until you've unfastened her diaper and have turned your back to look for a fresh wipe; then she will place the heel of her dominant foot into her butt crack and fling her leg straight out! Poop will fly toward you! If you duck, the poop will hit something valuable and undry-cleanable, so you must block that thing with your body. Yes. You must receive the poop. Let it happen.

FIFTH STEP: Before you take off all your clothes and place them in the sterilization chamber and then scald your skin raw in an ultrahot shower, you must complete Baby's diaper change. Hang in there. Wipe Baby's bottom, get that new diaper on there, and secure Baby in a pleasant, diverting environment such as a playpen, bouncy chair, or on the floor with your rottweiler, Carl, watching her closely. Carl is such a good dog!

SIXTH STEP: After bathing/drying/shuddering in horror, get dressed again. This is a good opportunity for you to change out of your ratty bathrobe, which if this poop episode hadn't happened, you would have worn all day long, WOULDN'T YOU HAVE? Most important: check the mirror when you're done. You don't want poop on your face, and then a visitor comes over, and then that visitor never comes over ever again and then you have no friends and everyone in your town knows you as Poop Face.

WHAT IS YOUR BABY'S POOP TRYING TO TELL YOU?

When you finally manage to disengage Baby's soiled diaper, stand back and take a long, hard look at what has been wrought. The patterns contained therein may be telling you more than you ever wanted to know about your child's dark inner workings. You must use your intuition to interpret these, but here are some suggestions to get you started.

Not actual poop. We're not that gross.

1. I'm going to remember what you said to me at 3 a.m. this morning.
2. Hope you enjoyed those egg rolls last night, because they didn't do much for your boob milk.
3. My anal stage has begun a year early!
4. A sleepy rhino is eating a hamburger.
5. Uh, butterfly on a motorboat.
6. I'm freezing my nuts off, and you're staring into a feces-loaded diaper. Jesus.

BATHING DOS AND DON'TS

DO

Test temperature of water before placing Baby in tub
Keep Baby's head above water
Wash Baby with a soft washcloth and mild soap
Dry Baby with a clean, fluffy towel

DON'T

Leave Baby alone in bathwater
Throw Baby out with bathwater
Bathe Baby in a Jacuzzi
Give Baby a baby-sized snorkel
Drop pennies in Baby's bath for good luck
Grease Baby down so she's as slick as a seal pup before placing in water
Scream as soon as Baby's toes hit water, just to mess with Baby

DIAPER RASH AND RELATED ITCHY SPOTS: WHAT DID YOU DO WRONG?

At some point, your baby's impossibly soft and perfect skin may suffer these mild imperfections. This is either your fault, or God's.

TINY RED BUMPS: stress. Maybe scheduling violin lessons was premature.

CHAFEY REDNESS: someone hasn't been moisturized properly

TWO PINPRICKS ABOUT A HALF-INCH APART: vampire infestation

FLAKY SCALP: cradle cap. While lathering your baby's head, you forgot the "rinse" part in "rinse and repeat."

DRY PATCHES: *someone's* starved for attention

FACIAL ACNE: thinks she's a teenager

WHAT TO LOOK FOR IN A PEDIATRICIAN

Most pediatricians fall into one of two categories: the attachment-parenting advocate, and the attachment-loathing automaton. Whichever one you choose depends on how much you love your baby. Not that we're judging.

We have identified the following sub-types (because *we* are discerning even if you're not):

DR. HUGGS, MD, NAROPA UNIVERSITY

Dr. Huggs

Characteristics
- Gently bearded
- Kind and folksy, unless you admit to not co-sleeping
- Advocates nursing until college
- Thinks sunshine works better than antibiotics
- Writes prescription for "Mom 'n' Dad cuddles"
- The idea of vaccination makes him cry
- Talks to your child in rhymed couplets

DR. NEEDLES, MD/PHD, UNIVERSITY OF KLAEKENFURT, AUSTRIA

Characteristics

- Orders daily Lysol rubdown for Baby
- Thinks food allergies are a ploy for attention
- Gives your child "supplemental" vaccines he found in his great-grandfather's valise
- Advocates time-outs for newborns
- Believes that thumb-sucking is a gateway behavior to sodomy

Dr. Needles

Whichever kind of doctor you choose, these are some vital clues that your "doctor" may not be as qualified as his late-night infomercial told you he was:

- Eats a club sandwich while examining your child
- Diploma is written in crayon
- Can't pronounce "stethoscope"
- Says he needs to see and/or feel your breasts "to make sure they're working good," even if you're bottle-feeding
- Picks up Baby by the foot
- Shrieks at sight of umbilical-cord stump
- Play area of waiting room is a driving range

POINT/COUNTERPOINT: WILL MY CHILD EVER SLEEP?

It's a question that plagues parents from the moment their child is born: *Whom must I blow to get this baby to sleep?*

Sadly, blow jobs will not work in this situation, so your years of training are for naught.

Babies are notorious for sleeping in maddening three-minute increments, depriving their parents of much-needed REM sleep and systematically driving them insane. New parents, having been driven 'round the bend by about the three-week mark, become desperate for any gimmick or strategy that will get their kid to sleep for more than the amount of time it takes to don one's pajama pants.

There are two schools of thought surrounding infant sleep. Needless to say, their approaches are diametrically opposed. One school demands that children learn to settle themselves to sleep in silent, dark, lonely, sterile, possibly haunted rooms all by themselves, while the other demands that you let your child use you as a soothing chew toy every night forever, or until he/she finds a boy/girlfriend to take your place. Ultimately, which school rules can only be settled by a dance-off or late-night rumble in a vacant lot on the West Side. Bring your sock full of wrenches, a good-quality shiv (try whittling your own out of a toothbrush or a pork bone!), and plenty of pomade.

Alice and Eden can never agree on which approach is morally superior, which is why they live on opposite coasts: Alice with the East Coast smug liberal elites and Eden with the West Coast bohemian nut-job liberal elites. Some day we'll meet in neutral territory and settle this thing. But until then, all we can do is present you with our opposing viewpoints, only one of which is absolutely correct.

ALICE'S METHOD: INSIST YOUR BABY TO SLEEP

Your baby wants you to get as little sleep as possible, having performed the following mental calculus: lack of sleep ages you prematurely, and then Baby will get at his inheritance earlier.

Baby must be thwarted!

If you're like me, you began sleep-training while your child was still in the womb. Womb-sleep training involves a rigorous regimen of positive reinforcement for daytime fetal movement (approving murmurs, abdomen-patting, playing upbeat Bach or Mozart for Baby), and negative reinforcement for nighttime activity (disapproving mutters, withholding of abdominal pats, playing only Requiem Masses or late-1990s Peter Cetera).

Once your baby is a few hours old, you need to send an important message: *Dear Baby: The party is over. Time to start sleeping through the night in twelve-hour blocks.* We know the "experts" say something about newborns needing nutrition all night long, but when does that end? When they're twenty-five and eating Hot Pockets over the sink at 4 A.M.? This lesson needs to get learned early: Mama needs her beauty rest, so you best hush up. Preferably before the baby nurse leaves.

But how do you train a baby to sleep through the night? It's easier than you think. Just follow this simple procedure *exactly*, with *absolutely no variations at all.*

8:00 P.M. Put Baby down in the crib.

8:05 P.M. Pace nervously outside nursery as the shrieking starts up.

8:07 P.M. Rummage through refrigerator for snacks. Loud rumaging will drown out the crying.

8:10 P.M. Enter Baby's room and pat her back three times. Not four times. Three. Say "Shhh" four times, in three-second intervals. Retreat quickly.

8:13 P.M. Glare at husband. Surely this is partly his fault.

8:15 P.M. Cry for a little while.

9:00 P.M. Go back into Baby's room. Pick up Baby. Swear to Baby that you'll never leave her alone again. Rock her until your arms go numb.

10:45 P.M. Put Baby back down. Dim lights. Whoops. You forgot to do that at 8 P.M., didn't you? Just because I didn't specifically say to? Must I spell out everything?

11:00 P.M. Back into Baby's room. Three pats on the back. Not too hard, now.

11:15 P.M. Your husband's asleep. Stand over him, seething.

11:30 P.M. Back in Baby's room, your mere presence will soothe her. Without touching her, reassure her that you are there, and that you're just going in the other room, just for a little bit, it's not like anyone is *disappearing*, for Christ's sake; isn't she being a little dramatic?

11:45 P.M. Loudly ask your husband if he wants to take over for a little bit, maybe, *if it's not too much trouble.* He reluctantly gets up. *Reluctantly,* though. Christ!

12:00 A.M. Try to sleep but don't because you're now furious and can't believe you ever thought getting married was a good idea.

1:00 A.M. Wake up, even though you didn't realize you were sleeping in the first place. Hear your husband muttering angrily while pacing back and forth with Baby.

1:15 A.M. Tell him he's *not doing it right* and to just forget it.

1:30 A.M. How does he get to sleep so fast? Jerk.

1:45 A.M. Place Baby back in crib. Dim the lights again, do those soothing "shhh" sounds *again.* Back slowly out of room.

1:47 A.M. She just woke up. Pat her back seven times.

1:50 A.M. Okay, ten times. *But no more.* Now retreat. Retreat!

2:00 A.M. Reassure Baby from other side of door that you're still around. Continue to reassure as needed.

3:30 A.M. Is your voice getting hoarse? I recommend recording your voice and replaying on a continuous loop!

4:00 A.M. Accidentally throw something at husband, injuring him into consciousness.

4:30 A.M. There's silence! Run into room because you think something's wrong, but nothing is wrong! The baby is asleep, and you can be, too!

5:00 A.M. Wake up because you thought you heard the baby, but it turns out you didn't.

5:15 A.M. Oh, wait, you did. Crap.

5:30 A.M. Baby's up for the day, full of smiles and burbles. You made it! Sort of.

Do this every night until it works, or until Baby enlists in the military.

EDEN'S METHOD: WING IT

If your attempts at forcing your child to sleep using Alice's "expert" 26-step sleep-forcing gimmick strategy have only ended in tears, you can still be like me! Take the easy way out!

Easy Way Out #1: Nurse Your Child to Sleep

This method is fairly self-explanatory. You have a boob? Put it in your child's mouth. A full tummy, the nurturing warmth of your body, and the rhythmic thump of your heart will almost certainly lull the average baby off to average baby dreamland. It's just a temporary solution, so don't worry about how this is all going to work when the kid is nine. Don't worry!

Easy Way Out #2: Straight from the Bottle

Not breast-feeding? It's okay, some people just don't love their children (that's what parole officers are for). Prepare a warm bottle full of human growth formula, hormone-laced cow's milk, or vegan organic soy-free distilled water, insert it into baby's largest head aperture, prop it up with a pillow or indifferently arranged blanket, and go back to whatever you were doing that was so important.

Easy Way Out #3: The Electronic Babysitter

Baby will feel as though *somebody* loves him after you roll the TV cart right up next to his crib and leave it tuned to PBS all night. Eventually, some kids' show will come on after this Eisenhower thing is over, right?

Easy Way Out #4: The Family No-Sex Bed

Two warm, nurturing, protective, sweaty big-person bodies are better than one when it comes to reassuring baby that it's okay to give in and get some rest like

How to Sleep While . . .

Showering: No need to soap up. Soap is drying, and also kills all those friendly microbes who eat the bad bacteria off your skin. Simply turn on the water, sit or lie down, and let the water pressure whisk the grime away. Wake up to turn off the water, and then sleep until you wake up dry! Bonus: shivering burns calories.

Driving: Only do this when, you know, the road's pretty straight and there are no surprises ahead, like other cars, people, branches, ditches, on-ramps, off-ramps, random acts of God, or destinations.

Having sex: If you're on top, this could get awkward. Otherwise, just tell your husband that it will be like you're having the world's sexiest dream. He'll adjust surprisingly quickly to this new state of affairs.

Walking: Only do this on a fairly flat surface. Occasionally rouse yourself and shout, *"Warning, sleeping walker coming through."*

On the toilet: Nothing could be easier, my friends. It's like that thing was *made* for it.

Ironing: You might need someone to spot you.

Whittling: Dream-whittling is the best kind of whittling. Upon waking, you get to discover what your dreams have inspired you to create! Just wear a sturdy pair of insulated work gloves and chain-mail chaps or fishing waders in case your trusty pocketknife goes astray.

Churning: Lean against your churning-plunger and let gravity take thee away.

Churning (modern): Turn on your food processor, rest your head against your kitchen cabinet, and wait for your KitchenFriend® Hover-Bot™ to wake you up if the baby is crying.

Talking on the phone: Do you talk in your sleep? Then you're all set. Sure, your friend and/or insurance adjuster might wonder why you keep mumbling about Jerry Orbach stealing your hair, but you'll have a good laugh over it eventually!

the big folks do. Mom and Dad (or Dad and Dad, Mom and Mom, or Mom and Bunsen) know that it's far more important to have a well-rested infant companion during the day than it is to deeply connect in a relationship-saving act of primal carnality. It's only for fourteen years or so; it's not like you took a vow of celibacy like a monk or a nun! (Though monks and nuns probably still get the occasional hand job.)

Easy Way Out #5: The Human Backpack

This time-tested, last-resort method for getting Baby to sleep has been a favorite the world over for centuries. Simply swaddle your infant snugly, strap him or her to your back, and get on with your life. Baby will sleep or not sleep, cry or not cry, but at least no one will accuse you of neglecting him: he's with you day and night! (This is also a great way to get older siblings to take Baby off your hands.) Baby's wastes will simply accumulate in his slowly decomposing poop-garment, and when he finally falls through you'll know it's time for kindergarten.

WHY ISN'T MY CHILD SLEEPING? *STILL?*

Sometimes, no matter how vigorous your efforts to get Baby to sleep, he just won't. It's important to remember at those times that your baby is *not necessarily out to get you.* His reasons for remaining awake might have nothing to do with you. Knowing this won't help either of you get any rest, but it might keep you from loathing your baby with every exhausted fiber of your being. Here are but a few reasons why he's refusing to go to Sleepy Town:

Eh, he's not in the mood.
He's feeling snacky.

There's something he wants to write down.

Some body part of his is mildly uncomfortable.

He just discovered his hand-mitts.

He's having another developmental surge, and he wants to share it with you!

He's teething.

He has a moon fetish.

He just pooped.

He just peed.

He just pooped *and* peed.

He wants to hear you sing that song again.

You know the one.

Seriously, the poop and pee are all over the place.

He doesn't know why, but his mobile is freaking him out.

He's just, you know, wondering what you're up to.

THE HORROR . . . THE HORROR . . . OF COLIC

Colicke Daemon.

If your baby starts screaming and crying as if in terrible pain for hours at a time, with no apparent cause, she probably has colic. In medieval times, they called colic "Colicke." It was attributed, naturally, to demons.

Nowadays, doctors often call this "Baby Madness!" *(yes, with an exclamation point)*, but if you phone your doctor to talk about it, the office staff will claim that they're all on vacation. This is because doctors have no idea what causes colic, and they never will, and they just won't admit it. (Also, they don't want to hear all that *crying*.) If you manage to hunt down your doctor in his or her deep sea lead-lined aqua-castle, he'll eventually admit that colic is probably caused by gas, or intestinal spasms, or is part of "normal development," or "How did you get this number?" Your doctor is trying to thwart you with OBFUSCATIONS

AND IRRELEVANCIES! None of his bleeping machines or infernal tests can show what *we know*—which is that colic is caused by:

POSTREINCARNATION ENNUI!

Think about it. If you'd just completed decades of one life as a reclusive world-famous novelist or tyrannical despot, only to find that your final reward is having to start all over again as a damned *baby*, you'd be frustrated as well. You might have something to say about it. Only you can't, because you're a *baby*. Your minions used to tremble in fear at the sound of your voice, god*damn* it! And now all you get is this stranger insisting that you have gas?!

As the parent of so diminished a personage, there's nothing you can do but wait it out. Microwave your neck pillow, pat your baby stiffly on the hand, and invest in a comfortable rocking chair. You'll be there for a while.

Here's the good news: your baby's prebirth memories will fade, eventually. And then "colic" will be over. It might take months, but maybe it will only take weeks! Untold, countless weeks.

12. BABY'S STILL HERE!

You thought it would never happen, but it has: the novelty of sleepless nights and unappeasable wailing has finally worn off. Your sleep-deprived giggle-fits have subsided. There's nothing on television at three in the morning but racist old Charlie Chan movies—and, boy, they *really* went downhill after *Charlie Chan at the Olympics* (1937).

If you'd listened to Alice and sleep-trained your new-born, you wouldn't have this problem. *(But then you'd be a heartless monster: Eden.)* Ah, well. On the bright side, though, that baby's starting to get interesting! No longer is he a tiny cipher of a being or a squalling mess of need. Okay, maybe he's still squalling. And needing. But he's also smiling, and burbling, and displaying other signs of adorability and cutetude. So that's fun. Now you're thinking maybe this "baby" mess is worth it, after all! See? We told you. And if we didn't "tell" you, per se, we implied it, quite strenuously.

IS YOUR BABY HITTING THE RIGHT MILESTONES?

So your baby's getting funner—but is she fun *enough*? Doctors and related pediatric scholars have developed all kinds of developmental milestones your baby needs to reach, lest you and society consider her emotionally or physically stunted. (It's important to make sure your child is keeping up with the Baby Joneses.) But these milestones don't go far enough, if you ask us. If you're going to spend all day with this baby, she had better be entertaining, after all. Why else should she get all the attention?

Here's how to tell whether your baby is hitting the milestones *you* want.

Age	Traditional Milestone	Superfun Milestone!
3 weeks	Focusing on human faces	Does a passable Walter Matthau impersonation
8 weeks	Smiling	Dresses up like Beyoncé for viral YouTube video
12 weeks	Clapping	Decoupages old wine bottles/picture frames
18 weeks	Teething	Will open your beer bottle with tooth(s)
22 weeks	Rolling over	Log-rolling
36 weeks	Sitting up unassisted	Can administer Shiatsu
48 weeks	Waving	Can Photoshop the gray out of your hair in pictures
1 year	Walking	Loves to give you makeovers!

HOW TO AVOID INTERCOURSE

Not in the mood? Join the club. *The New Mom's Club!*

Though evolution has deemed the months postpartum as a sacred time of rest and renewal, your partner is probably more interested in your gloriously inflated fun bags and some joyous mutual release. Now that the baby's out of you, you can get back to all those gymnastic positions you enjoyed before (and were dreaming about during) the third trimester, right?

Wrong! You haven't showered in days, there's a hundred pounds of laundry blocking the bathroom door, and you would kill for a tuna sandwich but your bastard husband just took the last slice of bread to the park to feed the pigeons and to daydream of a way out of his grueling, sexless existence. All this does not inspire you to put on a Prince album and join him in humping the night away.

It's tempting to move to separate bedrooms for the duration of your marriage, but it's a documented fact that couples with a lifelong commitment to bitterness and spite have been known to abstain from not just sex but also hugging, eye contact, and writing down messages with accurate phone numbers until well after their children have gone off and recklessly made children of their own.

You don't want to be like that! You want your partner to show you naïve goodwill and thoughtful companionship—at least until the new life insurance policy kicks in. So here are a few spicy activities for you to do together that can make your other half feel as though you might someday be interested in sex again.

1. Erotic Mad Libs
2. Erotic weightlifting
3. Erotic laser eye surgery
4. An online course in civil engineering, for two
5. Side-by-side nickel slots
6. Vicious arguments, culminating in steamy hot binge-eating in front of an open refrigerator

7. Long, genital-numbing tandem bicycle rides
8. *Gomer Pyle* reruns in bed
9. Walking into a bar and pretending you don't know each other—then going home with total strangers and NOT having sex with *them either*!

It Really Happened!
"My Wife Avoided Intercourse"

"I kind of didn't notice what was happening at first. I wanted to give Darcy time to heal, and the doctor wouldn't give her the go-ahead to mount up again until the six-week mark. But then six weeks rolled by and she took the baby to her mother's for a nice, long visit. And when she came back she started building a darkroom in the basement for her daguerreotype class and *that* took a couple of months. And she kept the baby nursing and sleeping in bed with us for five years. I'm not even sure how she managed to get herself inseminated with the twins, but they're definitely mine, we got their DNA tested. Twice."

—Dan P., age 33, Fort Worth, Texas

IF YOU ABSOLUTELY *HAVE* TO HAVE INTERCOURSE ...

Is it time? Have you put him off long enough? Has he punched holes in the drywall with his bloody fists, just so he could feel something, *anything*? Or maybe it's *you*. Are you sensing, despite your exhaustion, twinges of raw, primitive urges?

Then it's time to do it.

The first time you engage in physical coupling will be awkward and painful, and will end in tears. We're not saying whose. Maybe both! So lower your expectations accordingly. Have a drink . . . have four! Dim the lights. No, more than that. Actually just light a candle. Do you still have that numbing spray the hospital gave you? Might want to use it. Strategically arrange yourself on the bed, then call your spouse on his cell phone, because you don't want to yell and wake the baby up. Oops, the ringing cell phone woke up the baby. Ah, well. There's always tomorrow.

WHAT KIND OF BABY DO YOU HAVE?

Surprisingly, not all babies are exactly alike. To be specific, there are four kinds of babies. Some people insist that their babies are unique, that there is no other one out there quite like him/her in the whole universe. Of course they're wrong. If you don't recognize your own child in these descriptions, be on your guard. Is your baby ticking?

PISSY BABY

First smile is more like a sneer
Lord help you if you try to swaddle him
Eyetooth came in extra early, just to make nursing that much harder
Enjoys: projectile vomiting on your new shirt
If he could talk, he'd say, "Put that new shirt on. It looks so nice on you." Then he'd chuckle malevolently.

CREEPY BABY

When you walk into his room, for a split second you're *sure* he was standing

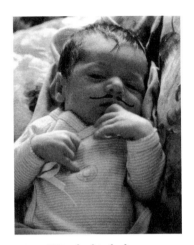

Watch this baby.
Carefully.

Sports a thin, wispy mustache
Doesn't blink
Cries sound like some kind of Latin verse, only backward. Curious!
Enjoys: scheming
If he could talk, he'd say, "Hello, Mother. I have been waiting for you." Isn't that nice?

SOMEONE ELSE'S BABY

Placid, long-lashed, apple-cheeked
Enjoys: sitting, gazing, beatific smiling
Falls asleep upon request
Crying is limited to soft mewling or low, throaty sobs
Poops smell like lavender
Not yours
If she could talk, she'd say, "Don't worry. I'll ruin their lives when I'm a teenager."

MISUNDERSTOOD BABY

We don't want to call her "ugly," but, well . . .
Deafening cries meant to express joy in being alive
Screeches because she can't sing yet
Enjoys: a little refreshing lung exercise
If she could talk, she'd say, "I love this place! Hey! I love you! This is great! Here's how much I love everything! Get it? I can't wait to talk! Until then, listen to some crying! Wait! Where are you going?"

WHAT KIND OF NEW MOTHER STEREOTYPE ARE YOU?

Once you've pigeonholed your baby, it's time to take a long hard look at yourself. Whether or not you see yourself as a "type," the rest of us surely will. So pick the one that matches most closely your complex, multifaceted being, and embrace your new streamlined persona!

CAN-DO MOM

Motto: Who needs sleep?
Characteristics: alarmingly cheerful, ruddy-cheeked; wears overalls
Can be found: crocheting thank-you gifts for OB/GYN's office staff while nursing her baby.
Warning signs that this might be you: You were the captain of your college field hockey team.

KNOW-IT-ALL MOM

Motto: It's so interesting that you think that.
Characteristics: given to bouts of lip-pursing and eyebrow-raising
Can be found: combing studies for statistical errata
Warning signs that this might be you: You're permanently banned from the American Academy of Pediatrics headquarters.

HYSTERICAL MOM

Motto: When will this end? Oh God, when?
Characteristics: cries a lot, has food and bits of paper stuck in her hair
Can be found: calling her Mom

Warning signs that this might be you: Baby's first milestones are eye-rolling and playing world's tiniest violin.

RELUCTANT MOM

Motto: That baby's here somewhere.
Characteristics: calls baby "Dude"; doesn't want to nurse—hasn't she done enough?
Can be found: performing Google searches for "mother who doesn't lose identity just because of some kid"
Warning signs that this might be you: What's your baby's name? Quick! No looking at the birth certificate!

YOUNG MOM

Motto: We're gonna be like sisters!
Characteristics: calls husband "Daddy"; wears pigtails
Can be found: admiring taut, unblemished postpartum belly
Warning signs that this might be you: None of the other moms wears a retainer.

OLD MOM

Motto: You're as young as you feel, by gum!
Characteristics: salt-and-pepper hair; calls husband "Paw"
Can be found: canning; playing in a jug band
Warning signs that this might be you: You're having hot flashes at the playground.

BOND WITH YOUR BABY USING VOODOO!

We hate to say it but you know it's true—your baby is just so needy. Frankly, we get the feeling he wants you around *all the freaking time.*

Well, you'd better get used to it. The months directly following birth are sometimes called The Fourth Trimester, when a human infant continues to finish crucial development that in other species takes place while the fetus is still in the womb. Unlike a baby pony, which may need to run from devilish pony predators soon after its discharge from the mother pony's euphemism, a human infant is more like a fetal kangaroo, a wrinkled helpless awful-looking thing that will succumb to the elements unless it can crawl up into the safety of its mother's pouch and find a teat to suckle until its tail, ears, and ability to box become too adorable for words.

Animals who give birth in the wild are not judged for abandoning their offspring; they are respected for heeding an unknowable instinct. In human society, however, it's common for women to feel tremendous pressure and guilt for taking weeks or even decades to finally experience that special maternal bond they're supposed to have with their child. So if your maternal instinct is off yodeling with the raccoons, don't worry! You can bond with your baby using voodoo.

Voodoo (also referred to by authentic practitioners* as *Vodou* or *Vodun*) is a West African religion that moved across the Atlantic with the slave trade and is still famously practiced in Haiti and parts of the southern United States, as well as pockets of the Upper East Side. (How else do you think those kids get into private preschools?)

WHAT YOU'LL NEED

Felt or scrap fabric measuring 12 inches by 24 inches
Scissors

*Which we most definitely are not.

Needle and thread
Cotton batting or other stuffing material gathered from the native landscape
Permanent marker
Straight pins
Dark thoughts

Fold fabric in half and cut out the shape of your voodoo doll (you will end up with two matching pieces). Head, arms, and legs are not strictly necessary; extra limbs and superfluous genitalia may be added to suit your blessing/hexing needs. Sew almost all the way around the perimeter of the doll, leaving a one-inch gap. Before you sew up your doll's closure you'll want to stuff it with mystical personal objects.

OPEN YOUR HEART TO YOUR BABY! (*Help the bud of your maternal instinct to flower with this simple ritual.*) In an out-of-the-way corner, create a small altar that can hold several small items. Insert your baby's umbilical cord and/or a portion of leftover placenta pizza into the doll along with the petals of a single white rose. Light a cone of lavender incense on your altar next to your doll and visualize the inside of your womb while your baby was still inside you, her needs efficiently met and her comfort complete. Now imagine Baby handing you a white rose in a gesture of perfect love, understanding, and forgiveness. Oh, no, Baby poked her finger on a thorn on the stem of the rose and is crying out in pain. There, there, don't you feel sorry for Baby? Just a little bit? No?

MAKE BABY LOVE YOU FOREVER. (*This spell is for mothers who have a different problem: their babies just don't seem to need them very much and that's just not acceptable. Practice this voodoo bonding ritual after every diaper change to ensure that your baby will need you and love you unconditionally. FOR ALL TIME.*) Insert a wisp of baby's hair and a vial of your blood into the doll. Place it on your altar with a red votive candle and a bundle of dried hemlock or poison ivy (expert hexers only!). Visualize your baby's needs devouring you in a purifying fire. A lifelong bond can only be forged on the white-hot anvil of your relentless giving! Close your eyes and repeat the chilling words of Diana Rigg in that show where she plays the mom: *I gave you life, and I can take it away. I GAVE YOU LIFE, AND I CAN TAKE IT AWAY.* (Optional: Cackle gleefully; begin carving an ark out of sandalwood.)

WHY STOP AT LOVE? OTHER USEFUL SPELLS FOR NEW MOTHERS

SHUT SOMEONE UP. Insert cotton batting, a ball gag, and a personal possession, strand of hair, fingernail clipping, or photograph of your cousin who needs to shut her big fat mouth about how co-sleeping killed this one friend of hers's baby. Draw a simple face on the doll with a permanent marker, jab a single pin into its mouth, and anoint with corn oil. Put the doll in a safe place and remind it daily of its abominable purpose: *to shut that woman up.*

MAKE YOUR HUSBAND LEAVE YOU ALONE. Make a male doll. Stick a pin right into its penis. That'll teach him to beg for your attention while you're flicking dried milk crust off your cracked and bleeding nipples.

GET YOUR BOSS TO DOUBLE YOUR MATERNITY LEAVE. Make a doll that represents you. Stuff it with old pay stubs. Place it on your altar next to a stale bagel, a jar of nondairy creamer, and a filthy microwave. Write your desired salary on a slip of paper, paste the slip of paper to the bagel with margarine, and then microwave the bagel until flames shoot from it. Stuff the singed remains of the bagel into the doll and bury the whole thing in a shallow hole beneath a willow tree at sunrise, with your baby secured on your back with power strips. Within one week your boss will call to offer you everything you want and ask you if you know what happened to that picture of her family that used to sit on her desk.

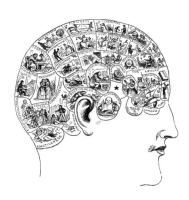

👓 EYE ON BABY!

PHRENOLOGY 101: DOES YOUR BABY HAVE THE FONTANEL OF A SERIAL KILLER?

Has Baby got you pinned down for another half hour of nursing? There's no one around to fetch the latest *People* magazine from the bathroom? Well, then! Now's the perfect time to find out if your baby has the fontanel of a serial killer.

Phrenology was a cutting-edge nineteenth-century pseudoscience developed by a German physician named Franz Joseph Gall. It's based on the somewhat logical notion that just as different areas of the brain are known to control specific physical functions, so underlying criminal tendencies can be detected by feeling the bony shell that surrounds the brain. Sound crazy to you? Well, people used to think Franz Joseph Gall was crazy, too, *and they were almost always wrong.*

First, let's examine the area just above baby's left ear. This is the Zone of Destructiveness, and it will tell you a lot about what you can expect from Baby. If the area is concave, you can expect a normal amount of early food-flinging and cup-throwing, which should evolve by the second or third year into those tantrums where the kid just flings herself onto the floor and screams while you're in line at the bank. This is why they have those jars of lollipops by each teller's window. Why not take two?

If, on the other hand, the area above baby's left ear pushes out slightly and has some downy hair or freckles on it, your baby is probably going to settle into one of the more heartless professions, such as mercenary or television executive. Our fates are not written in stone, and our bumpy heads are just a blueprint for what may occur, but forewarned is forearmed! Now is the time to start looking into a boarding preschool with a boot-camp feel to it, one with lots of camouflage netting and restrictive visitation hours. Rock-hard abs and sniper skills aren't built in a day, after all.

The next place we need to examine is the left orbital bone, the hard area surrounding Baby's eye. This opening to the skull will be almost perfectly round in most babies. However, there are a few interesting variations the orbital bone can take.

1. **Opening is somewhat oval:** This is one of the Four Optimal Phrenological Shapes (see Venn diagram below). When this shape is combined with a deviated septum, your baby will develop the ability to shoot light out of her eyes and control the ozone layer with her mind.
2. **Opening is somewhat spongy:** You delivered your baby before its cartilage had firmed into bone. Get that baby back inside you!
3. **Opening is shaped like a clover leaf:** You *did* have sex with that bartender.
4. **Opening is orange-scented:** Baby is naturally antibacterial.

Next we'll look at the main fontanel, the area between the frontal and parietal bones that won't fuse until baby is around two years old, leaving a soft patch where for the time being you will have limited access to your baby's brain! Right now you can increase your child's IQ by gently pouring a cup of baking soda over the fontanel; create a well in the baking soda, then slowly pour 4 ounces of white vinegar into it. This also has the effect of turning your baby's head into a fifth-grade science-fair volcano. Fun and educational!

Now, take a quick look up Baby's nose. A deviated septum is present if the nostrils are different sizes. The three most common benefits of a deviated septum are prophetic abilities, a knack for reading minds, and soulful, watery eyes. It can be repaired with surgery—but what's more im-

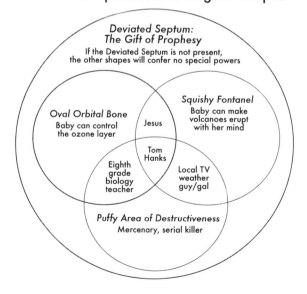

The Four Optimal Phrenological Shapes

Deviated Septum: The Gift of Prophesy
If the Deviated Septum is not present, the other shapes will confer no special powers

Oval Orbital Bone
Baby can control the ozone layer

Squishy Fontanel
Baby can make volcanoes erupt with her mind

Jesus

Tom Hanks

Eighth grade biology teacher

Local TV weather guy/gal

Puffy Area of Destructiveness
Mercenary, serial killer

portant: your baby's ability to breathe through her nose, or her ability to *see through time*?

Before you're done, don't forget to feel the small dent between neck tendons at the back of Baby's skull. This is where the cervical vertebrae end and the spinal cord fits into the base of the brain. Exciting stuff! We have nothing to say about it; we just want you to know that it's there.

HOW TO USE A SLING

While Baby is still about the size and weight of a *burrito grande*, many parents find it convenient to take advantage of their child's compact stature and relative immobility, and will attempt to stuff her into a sling. The advantages are many: Baby can feel your warmth and hear the sound of your voice; if she needs feeding or changing, you can respond in seconds; you can feel superior over those insensitive jerks with their strollers.

Slings, however, can be a tricky proposition for the uninitiated. They come in innumerable styles, and some of them can be almost maddeningly difficult to set up. To make your life simpler, follow our trusty guidelines to sling-choosing:

DO buy a sling that has the words "E-Z" or "DUMM-EE" in its name

DO NOT purchase a sling that comes with a set of instructional videos and/or gift certificate for sling workshops held at the local food co-op

DO consider buying an oversize purse in which your baby could comfortably nestle

DO NOT purchase a sling made of tobacco leaves or discarded human hair

DO simply tuck Baby down the front of your blouse!

DO NOT purchase fabric in bulk and then figure you can make your own by winding it around your torso in a complex fashion, essentially mummifying both yourself and your infant until someone cuts you out and/or lifts curse

DO buy a regular stroller and call it a "wheeled sling"

DO NOT buy your sling from the surgical supply store. That is not a sling. That is a truss.

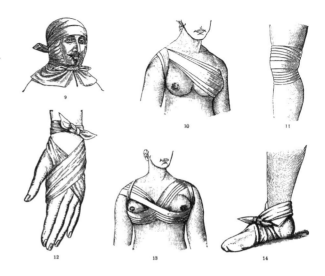

Wrong.

POSTPARTUM DEPRESSION WARNING SIGNS

No matter how familiar you are with your new stereotype or the bumps and valleys of your baby's noggin, you may still feel there's something missing. The two of you—you're just not connecting. Instead of quietly basking in the glow of your maternal warmth, baby is scrunching up her face and yelling at you, no matter how many times you sing "Mockingbird" or "We Didn't Start the Fire." When your baby cries, rather than leaping to comfort her you roll your eyes and shuffle reluctantly to her side. All in all, things aren't moving forward as planned. At your lowest moments, you may even feel like your baby doesn't like you! Unfortunately, this is correct. Your forthright resentment and low-grade whining are getting on Baby's nerves. And do you think you could bathe every now and then? You think it's fun, feeding off something that tastes like . . . is that *ratatouille*?

So if you're not feeling up to par right now, the short answer is Yes: it's all your fault. That doesn't mean that your suffering is not real, however. You may even have something doctors call "postpartum depression." We think this is an-

Brian Dennehy's mother could have suffered from postpartum depression. If she had, Mr. Dennehy would have channeled his long-buried memory of her troubles in his stirring performance of Willy Loman in the 1999 Broadway production of *Death of a Salesman*. Alice saw this production, and in appreciation, threw her favorite pair of underwear on the stage! Interestingly, Alice is no longer allowed to visit the Eugene O'Neill Theatre.

other term for "demon possession," but then, we're not really up to date on the latest studies. Why not speak to someone who is?

TABLE 12.1 HOW WE WOULD TREAT POSTPARTUM DEPRESSION, WERE WE DOCTORS, WHICH WE ARE LEGALLY REQUIRED TO REMIND YOU WE ARE NOT

Symptom	Clinical Diagnosis	Can be relieved by
Weeping	"Sadness"	Humming a cheery tune; baking cookies; taking a long walk on a tropical beach with a Labrador retriever and a mariachi band
Throwing things	"Anger"	Going to a rifle range; looting an electronics store; setting a car on fire
Insomnia	"Not-sleeping-ness"	Napping; self-inflicted head injuries; special cocktails made with Tom Collins mix, Fresca, and Children's Benadryl
Screaming	"Anxiety"	Obsessive vacuuming
Trembling	"Fear"	Spending your retirement savings on a lead-lined sub-terranean "panic room"

13. THE GREATEST BABY IN THE UNIVERSE!

W e all know it, but no one wants to say it: there's no point in doing anything if you can't excel—and, in doing so, drum up feelings of inferiority in your peers. Why should parenting be any different? Yet countless experts and scientists and doctors and people who have "earned degrees" refuse to agree with us. They'll tell you that every baby is unique; that as long as you're responding to your baby's needs and taking care of your own, you're doing just fine; that you should take off that crown because nobody made you Queen of Diaperland.

Well, we think those experts are liars. Fat-faced, filthy, monkey-butt liars.

You *can* have the Best Baby on the Block. You can win, and you *will.* You can have a baby who silences rooms when she crawls over the threshold. Who stuns passersby with his raw animal magnetism and precocious intellect. Who causes other mothers to despair at their bland, ordinary children, and wonder if they should donate them to science and start again. But then realize that there's no starting again because *you've* already created the best baby and won, forever. Yes, when you see the tears in their eyes and hear the mournful *snap* of their broken spirits, then you'll have finally accomplished something important with your life.

STIMULATE BABY'S BRAIN PARTS!

When babies emerge into our world, their brains are as smooth and unlined as Silly Putty straight from the egg. And just about as interesting. As you stimulate your child's nascent intellect, his brain will (we hope) start to form those furrows and wrinkles we see in cartoon images of brains. You need to put those things in there! With diligence, luck, and flash cards, your baby's brain will eventually be as puckered and wrinkly as a raisin. An oversize, gray raisin.

(Some philosophers actually believe that babies' minds may be something more than impassive sponges waiting to soak up whatever we shove into the DVD player. But until philosophy stops dicking around with "what if" and "I suppose" and starts producing some *results,* let's rely on our common sense, which tell us that babies are blank-slate sponges. Ironically, common sense circumvents the need for actual thought, and is invariably correct. *Take that, Aristotle!*)

But how do you get your child to become extra-geniusy? The trick is to keep him constantly on edge. When babies feel comfortable and safe, they are lulled into a dozy semiconsciousness. This is sometimes called "twilight cognition" or "the dullard state." At this point their brains halt any development and can actually be heard on some measuring machine thingies to emit a low, flat tone. This is no good! If we want to keep them keyed up and frantically calculating exit strategies, we must lead them to believe that at any moment, *the shit's going to hit the fan.* Babies thrive on drama and uncertainty!

So remember: the more you stimulate your baby, the more her brain will grow. Until she is a giant brain.

MONTH-BY-MONTH GUIDE TO GROWING BABY'S BRAIN

Here are some tips and tricks to get your baby started on the path toward intellectual prowess.

ONE MONTH

Make funny, crazy noises at Baby, then stop to answer the phone and speak in a normal voice. Baby is learning that you are unpredictable and not to be trusted.

TWO MONTHS

Imitate Baby! Echo his every gurgle and coo. This is an excellent trick he will use in the future to drive his captors/siblings/sibling-captors insane.

THREE MONTHS

Make a sock puppet for Baby. This will teach your little one that socks have lives of their own, and when you step on them they cry. Baby will never take another step without thinking seriously about the implications.

FOUR MONTHS

PeekaWHAT!? Hide a toy under a blanket and then, in a stunning reversal, pull the blanket aside to reveal an entirely different, lamer toy instead of the original. The lesson here: *When you let something out of your sight, it changes forever.*

FIVE MONTHS

Make your baby laugh. This will activate his joy receptors, which will then reinforce the myelin sheathing of the neurons that promote thinkingness. This month, make him laugh for at least an hour a day. *Do whatever it takes.* If he stops laughing, force him to start up again! It's for his own good!

SIX MONTHS

It's never too early to start teaching your child rudimentary biochemistry, you know. Just tie off her arm and fill a few test tubes so that Baby can learn the fascination of doing her own blood work.

SEVEN MONTHS

Finger dexterity time! Your baby will start to learn to pick up Cheerios and other small objects. Encourage this development by having her sort your vitamins and medicines into your weekly organizer, and by arranging your crafting and bead box. This is also a good time for your child to take up classical guitar.

EIGHT MONTHS

Time for some Old English epic poetry! Read *Beowulf,* in its original West Saxon and Anglian dialects. Discuss: Did *Beowulf* originate in the Homeric oral tradition, or was it the creation of a single poet or group of poets?

NINE MONTHS

How's Baby's penmanship? Ben Franklin had mastered the quill and was making his own illuminated copy of the Old Testament at this age, you know. (We let babies slack off way too much these days. *A life of leisure and a life of laziness are two things; there will be sleeping enough in the grave. Applause waits on success. Something something electricity.*)

TEN MONTHS

At this point your child is probably crawling and maybe even walking. It turns out that crawling is better for him in terms of left-brain/right-brain development, so place obstructions around the house at your baby's head-height so that every time he stands up he's painfully reminded, *Get back down on that floor, Baby! You still got brain work to do!*

ELEVEN MONTHS

You taught him Baby Sign Language already, right? NO?!

TWELVE MONTHS

Did you know you're supposed to hug and kiss your baby? If you haven't been doing this all along, now's the time to start! Simply place your hands on Baby's shoulders and bring your face as close to hers as you can bear. (Those with a blood relationship to Baby may also legally place their lips on Baby's forehead or cheek.) It turns out that affection is not only (1) a sign of a healthy nurturing instinct; it's also (2) good for Baby's emotional development. Try to schedule in some Affection Time™ if you find it hard to remember this tip.

She's doing it because she has to.

IF YOUR BABY ISN'T SMART . . .

Not all babies are potential geniuses. Some babies just do not have the raw intelligence to humiliate nanny after hysterically crying nanny. It's not Baby's fault that he'll never win a Pulitzer Prize (*it's probably your fault*), but that doesn't mean Baby can't find other ways to earn attention, money, and/or love.

IF YOUR BABY DOESN'T HAVE SMARTS, MAYBE YOUR BABY HAS . . .

Cutes!

Some babies are just gosh-darned cute, there's no two ways about it, and guess what? Many grow up to be even cuter. You can start grooming your cuteness-privileged baby to lord his or her good looks over regular-looking babies right away, undermining their confidence at every turn.

SAMPLE DIALOGUE

Friend with Smart Baby: "My little Applebee already knows her alphabet! At only six months!"

You: "Too bad about her eyes, though."

FWSB: "What . . . what do you mean, what's wrong with her eyes?"

You: "They're just so small and close together. See how my baby's eyes are just two big drops of golden sunlight, and her lashes flap up and down like butterfly wings?"

FWSB: "Well, yes, but—"

You (*winking knowingly at your baby*): "We should go: my Organella has a lucrative modeling job this afternoon and needs her beauty nap. Bye!"

Semicute girl babies can make up for any slight lack of dazzle by marrying well and becoming alarmingly thin. Semicute boy babies are actually the lucky ones, as boy babies that age *too* cutely are often assumed to be gay. (If your amazingly cute boy baby actually *is* gay, however: JACKPOT.) Cute boy babies who don't marry wealthy older women can also try their luck at developing some . . .

Muscles!

Many babies are blessed with stronger than average little muscles right from the get-go.

Before you know it they're lifting up the refrigerator to make it easier for you to change out the rat traps, or hoisting up your car for an oil change. Your lucky little muscle-bound baby has a great future ahead of him—your baby is a him, isn't it? Because if you have a girl muscle-baby, well, hmm . . .

Eventually, all muscley babies come to a fork in their road: muscle-babies also favored with coordination and a smidgen of cutes may find success as professional athletes with lucrative endorsement contracts. (While male muscle-babies have the choice of dozens of world-class sports to choose from, athletic female muscle-babies looking to see their face on a billboard are stuck with tennis or, in certain communities, competitive pole-dancing). Unattractive muscle-babies will only survive the brutal jungle of adolescence and adulthood by terrorizing the smaller and weaker among them.

If your child is neither beautiful *nor* powerful, see if he can develop . . .

A SENSE OF HUMOR!

Babies gifted with an advanced sense of humor become even funnier if they can also suffer in some way from a less than supportive family. Plus, the less you try not to screw up, the more likely it is your kid will be the next Don Rickles! So get ready to raise her with the following privations so she learns to use humor as a coping mechanism:

- Be moody and unpredictable and yell a lot (bonus points for full-blown alcoholism)
- Threaten to send her to the work house unless she does a funny jig
- Make her compete with her siblings to see who can make you laugh the hardest (the winner gets whitefish for dinner)
- Force-watch *Monty Python's Flying Circus* and *Mama's Family*
- Be working-class Jewish, Catholic, Hindu, or if possible, all three

WHAT IF MY BABY ISN'T SMART, CUTE, STRONG, OR FUNNY?

Maybe she'll be really good at:
- Inspiring people with her courage to persevere
- Putting stamps on things
- Pointing out rainbows
- Hugs
- Writing fake parenting books

HOW TO JUDGE YOUR BABY AGAINST OTHER BABIES

The only way to judge whose baby is best is to have a contest of some sort. Organize all the parents in your community to bring their infants to your festive arena of judgment on a date that's inconvenient for everyone.

All babies should first be subjected to a test of speed and endurance. Arrange a set of low police barriers or sandbags into lanes along a quarter-mile track to keep the babies from bumping into each other. A bright, soft toy or aromatic snack can be used as the "rabbit" to urge the babies to crawl forward. Be sure to use a real starter's gun to get those kids moving. Some babies will start crying, rather than crawling, when the gun goes off, but crybaby babies are losers anyway.

After this, just do a beauty contest. You know that's what everyone wants, anyway. Go ahead, get out a bunch of little tiaras and top hats. Jesus, you people are so predictable.

WHAT VARIOUS PHILOSOPHERS THROUGHOUT HISTORY THOUGHT WAS IN A BABY'S HEAD

- Plato believed that the mind existed elsewhere, like a thought-soup that resides in astral thought-bowls.
- Confucius thought the heart was where everything was at, and the brain was just a ball of paste lodged up in our heads to throw us off the trail.
- René Descartes believed there were miniature gerbils in there.

👓 EYE ON BABY!

WHY IS YOUR BABY CRYING?

Your baby is crying because he's either overstimulated or understimulated. But which one? *Can you tell*? Here's how:

If your baby puts a hand up to her face just as you've turned on an Almodóvar movie for her: overstimulated.

If your baby reaches for an old copy of *OMNI* magazine when you hold it up to her face: understimulated.

TIPS ON CREATING AN ENRICHING ENVIRONMENT

What kind of baby do you want? A controversial playwright might be nice, or what about a successful and for-the-most-part ethical chief of staff at a large midwestern hospital? It's always good to have a priest or nun in the family, because you never know.

Whatever sort of baby you want to create, the building blocks of skills and personality are all around you; you merely need to shove them all into Baby's chubby hands.

BRIGHT COLORS: Everything should be in bright colors: toys, posters, furniture, walls, carpeting, food. Invest in tubs of body paint.
Benefits: Reminds Baby that he was lucky enough to be born after the introduction of Technicolor; Baby will not freak out when you send him to Burning Man.

BLACK AND WHITE, HIGH-CONTRAST: Everything should also be in only black and white.
Benefits: Helps boring babies feel more alive; turns nerdy babies into silent film buffs.

SMILING FACES: Babies love to look at faces! Cover Baby's room with happy, happy faces. Make sure your baby never sees any expressions other than smiling ones. (Grins are acceptable.) Sad faces make Baby think it's okay to be sad, which it is *not*.

Benefits: Baby will always feel watched and therefore never *truly* relax during masturbation.

TEXTURES: Cover every surface in corduroy, sandpaper, and mink.
Benefits: Stimulates love for money (mink), but also induces a horror for work (sandpaper); an academic career in the Humanities is nominally acceptable (corduroy).

PERIODIC TABLE: We supposed you could put up a poster or something, if you want a baby scientist. *BO-ring.*
Benefits: Will clear the way for more interesting siblings.

BELLS: Some say bells alert the angels to your imminent demise! Nevertheless, attach bells to everything that moves in your house. Cover your baby in bells. Stimulate her little ears with joyful tinkling every time she twitches, which she'll start doing quite a lot of.
Benefits: Good if you want a religious baby.

ROCKING FURNITURE: Furniture that moves all the time stimulates Baby's inner-ear bones and forces Baby to constantly readjust to her off-kilter environment. Can you have a moving floor, too? Can you live in one of those inflatable bouncy houses? Good. Do that.
Benefits: Baby will develop a creepy sixth sense for earthquakes and whether new environments are owned or occupied by Batman villains.

UNDOMESTICATED, ILLEGAL PETS: Pets teach babies that if you pull on it, it will bite you *hard.* No crying, though!
Benefits: The endless courses of rabies shots will toughen 'em up.

PETS THAT TEACH THE ALPHABET: Exotic pets whose names include all the difficult letters like X and Z are well worth the expense of gathering a complete set of twenty-six. You don't want an illiterate baby, do you? Well, then. *Benefits:* Baby will be the first in her class to spell AXOLOTL.

QUIZ! HOW TO TALK TO YOUR BABY

Frankly, babies are just so intimidating. It's not easy to come right out and ask them whether they're in a self-motivated phase or if they'd accept a gentle push in the right direction. Fortunately, a good quiz can fill in the gap be-

It Really Happened!
I Didn't Read to My Baby

"Even though I am a voracious reader, my husband, Og, is not. We argue all the time about my homeschooling lesson plans. I don't want little Mandrake to miss out on the joys of Homer or *The House on Pooh Corner*, but Og insists that, on the rare occasions we do leave the warren, nearly every aspect of modern life has a pictogram associated with its function: restrooms, gas stations, movie theaters. Even if you're eating at a restaurant where the menu doesn't have pictures of the food, a server will probably tell you what kind of pancakes they have. Og, of course, really prefers the oral history of his people to anything George Plimpton might have said, so right now our Mandrake is functionally illiterate. We'll continue homeschooling him with a concentration on hunting, gathering, and basic agriculture—and maybe when he gets older he can become an anti-intellectual agrarian congressman, or a talk-show host."

—Charlene Ogswife, age 23, The Warren by the Rock, Canada

tween what-you-wish-you-knew and do-Child-Protective-Services-vans-have-a-distinctive-siren-or-engine-noise-that-can-be-heard-from-blocks-away?

1. When you wake your baby up in the morning by crashing two cymbals together, how does Baby react?
   a. Crying
   b. Screaming and crying
   c. Covering her ears and glaring at you
   d. Pretending to remain asleep until you've put down your cymbals; then popping his eyes open and hissing at you

2. How does your baby feel about television?
   a. Prefers it to human interaction
   b. Crawled around behind it hoping to meet people living inside magic box; got zapped by faulty wiring; now terrified of it
   c. Owns one but doesn't watch it, except for *Frontline*
   d. Already hosts her own show on Bravo

3. When you leave your baby in the car while you go grocery shopping, how far do you roll down the windows?
   a. I leave a two-inch crack so she doesn't suffocate
   b. I roll them all the way down so she can chat with whoever walks by
   c. I seal the windows but I leave the doors unlocked and the keys in the ignition with the air-conditioning or heater on, depending on the weather—and the radio, so she won't get lonely
   d. I just leave her at home and go shopping during Teletubbies

4. That last one was a trick question, and you are clearly a monster. Give us one reason we shouldn't come and take your baby away from you right now.

**Novelizations you
should be reading to
your baby**

The entire, endless
Star Wars oeuvre

*Scooby-Doo and the
Mystery of Casey
Kasem's Toupee*

*Pat the Bunny: The
Movie: The Book*

The Godfather

*Mario Kart Wii: the
Search for Koopa
Troopa's Lost Crystal
or Whatever*

a.   I am extraordinarily rich and will flee to a mythical land filled with uni-
corns who will raise my child to come back and make things *very unpleasant*
for you

b.   I am armed to the teeth and even if your sniper takes me out, my baby
knows the combination to the gun safe

c.   But I said I'd leave the A/C on!

d.   All right, go ahead, take her. I found her at Disneyland anyway.

Calculating your results

If you answered mostly As, you have a NORMAL baby who requires appropriate
amounts of both stimuli and silence.

If you answered mostly Bs, you have a PARANORMAL baby who requires a
toll-free number and her own infomercial.

If you answered mostly Cs, you have a SUPERHUMAN baby who requires a
secret identity and a signature flaw to overcome.

If you answered mostly Ds, you have a HYPERBARIC baby who loves nothing
more than crawling into her oxygen chamber and remaining forever young and
hydrated.

POINT/COUNTERPOINT:
WILL BABY EINSTEIN WARP YOUR CHILD?

In 2009, Baby Einstein videos were recalled due to their inability
to actually turn babies into Albert Einstein. Here, Alice and
Eden debate whether these videos will turn your child into a
sinister automaton—or just into someone who enjoys riding a
bicycle and approving patent applications.

ALICE:

My son spent hours each day watching Baby Einstein, and he is not at all a robot. He also happens to excel at moving a toy sloooowly across an eternal white void while humming "Für Elise." I don't know why people think Baby Einstein doesn't teach anything.

EDEN:

All these videos teach your children to do is watch TV, and if you're going to do that you might as well find something the whole family will find mesmerizing. We prefer Philip Glass operas (*Akhnaten* is a current favorite, as it helps reinforce our culture's monotheistic ideals) and old episodes of *CBS News Sunday Morning* with Charles Kuralt.

LITTLE-KNOWN LULLABIES THAT WILL MAKE YOUR CHILD SMARTER

PHOTOSYNTHESIS (TO THE TUNE OF BRAHM'S "LULLABY")

Oh the sun, oh the sun,
Oh all life depends on it
The energy
From sunlight
Is converted into organic compounds!
This process always starts
When energy from li-ight
Is absorbed by proteins
Called photosynthetic reaction cen-ters!

"Taft! Was! Fat!"

THE MOST OVERWEIGHT PRESIDENT (TO THE TUNE OF "RISE AND SHINE AND GIVE GOD YOUR GLORY, GLORY")

Taft was a fatty,
He liked to eat his steaky steaky!
Taft was a fatty,
He chased it down with cakey cakey!
TAFT! WAS! FAT! AND! LIKED TO EAT HIS STEAK, OH LORDY!
Then he'd take a nap.

FAMOUS POETS OF THE NINETEENTH CENTURY (TO THE TUNE OF "WHEN JOHNNY COMES MARCHING HOME")

When Byron and Shelley and Keats rode in
Hurrah! Hurrah!
They threw off the chains of Enlightenment
Hurrah! Hurrah!
When Byron and Shelley and Keats rode in
They made it okay to be sexy again
And we all got drunk when
The Romantics came riding in

Other tunes whose lyrics you're just going to have to invent yourself:

"Twinkle, Twinkle Fibonacci's Theorem"
"Rock-a-bye Three Branches of Government"
"Row, Row, Row Your Large Hadron Collider"

14. NAVIGATING THE JUNGLE OF EARLY MOTHERHOOD

Guess what? The real challenge of parenting comes when you take your baby *outside*. Because outside is where the Other People are. The people who want to tell you how you're ruining your baby or otherwise not performing up to par, motherhood-wise. Weeks of enduring the baby not sleeping and not *not* crying will seem like a day at a spa compared to the moment when some wizened stranger pokes you with her osteoporotic finger and proclaims that your baby will die without a *hat* because you are subjecting her to *below-60-degree weather*.

KA-POW! That's us dropping a Knowledge Bomb™ on you.

It never fails. Just when you're coming to terms with the drudgery and unending struggle of sharing your life with a baby, and you're feeling up to a stroll to the local café or a quick supermarket jaunt, that's when they hurl themselves at your face—the family, friends, and passersby who believe they're *uniquely qualified* to tell you that your parenting skills are mediocre at best.

And listen, they may be right. But telling you what you're doing wrong—that's *our* job. We don't go to their jobs and tell them how to scan your groceries, do we?

Okay, we did, but just that one time. There's a *technique* to it, is all we were saying.

So, how do you deal with them? How to do you survive your forays into the outside world with your self-esteem mostly intact? It may be true that violence, revenge, and sassy back talk never solved anything, but don't let that stop you!

YOUR MOTHER-IN-LAW

Area of expertise: Children, ages 0–35
Typical comment: "*Good Morning America* did a *fascinating* segment on the myth of postpartum depression."
Reason for judging you: Refusing drugs during labor; breastfeeding without an appropriate amount of shame; not dressing your baby in the cute little top hat and tails she bought for him
Her all-purpose defense: "I'm just saying what everyone else is too afraid to say because they think you're crazy!"
How to silence her: Hand her the baby and run
Is she right?: Well, you do look pretty crazy

OLD LADY ON THE STREET

Areas of expertise: The effects of laudanum on breastmilk; the importance of woolen mittens in warding off scrofula
Typical comment: "What in Sam Hades d'you think you're up to, missy?"

Reason for judging you: Exposing your child to the dangerous effects of earth's atmosphere

Her all-purpose defense: "I had seven children, and three of them made it to adulthood!"

How to silence her: Invite her to an ether frolic. While she considers it, punch her in her one good ear.

Is she right?: Despite her assertions, walking on pavement will not give your baby "the ague."

THAT WOMAN YOU USED TO SEE AT THE GYM

Area of expertise: Knowing what kind of plastic surgery you should have

Typical comment: "When are you going to have that baby? . . . *Oh.*"

Reason for judging you: Not attending her 5 A.M. Baby and Me Boot Camp class

Her all-purpose defense: "Listen, don't get mad at me—get mad at the *Mommy Fitness* magazine I was reading on the treadmill."

How to silence her: Karate chop to the throat

Is she right?: Of course not. Hey, see below for our exercise and diet tips!

SINGLE GUY IN YOUR BUILDING

Area of expertise: Stuff he learned from when his older sister had a baby

Typical comment: "My sister Leona said that rocking the baby like that can jiggle his brains too much."

Reason for judging you: You're doing things differently from what he saw during his two-week visit to Rochester

His all-purpose defense: "I'm just telling you what Leona said!"

How to stop him: Spork in the head

Is he right?: It's not important. Spork him, quick!

YOUR MIDWIFE

Areas of expertise: The ineffectiveness of your Kegel flexes; the multiple restorative effects of elderflower extract

Typical comment: "My Goddess, don't tell me you've stopped nursing!"

Reason for judging you: Confessing to mild feelings of ambivalence surrounding your baby

Her all-purpose defense: "If you'd listened to me about the blackstrap molasses, you'd be feeling much better right now."

How to silence her: Sing a Joni Mitchell song off-key until she's forced to leave the room, weeping

Is she right?: Impossible to say—no one has ever ingested blackstrap molasses and lived to tell of it.

YOUR GYNECOLOGIST

Areas of expertise: The ineffectiveness of your Kegel flexes; not making eye contact during pelvic exams

Typical comment: "Still not shaving your legs?"

Reason for judging you: Crying in his/her office

His/her all-purpose defense: "I'll have a nurse come talk to you about that."

How to silence him/her: Multiple frivolous lawsuits

Is he/she right?: I don't know . . . *is that pee running down your legs?*

THE LADY WHO ALWAYS SEEMS TO SHOW UP WHEN THE SUN IS IN YOUR BABY'S EYES

Areas of expertise: Angle of the sun as it pertains to your baby's eyes

Typical comment: "The sun is in your baby's eyes!"

Reason for judging you: You're not appropriately shielding your baby from the effects of sunlight

Her all-purpose defense: "I just thought maybe you didn't want to blind your baby."

How to silence her: You cannot. Even if you strike her down she will rise again and again.

Is she right?: No. It is nighttime. She is insane.

THE GROCERY STORE CASHIER

Areas of expertise: Infant behavior and psychology

Typical comment: "That baby's crying 'cause it's hungry."

Reason for judging you: You won't let her feed your baby a box of Jujubes

Her all-purpose defense: "I raised my ten brothers and sisters after Mama ran off in '67."

How to silence her: Pay for your groceries with a tote bag full of loose change

Is she right?: Of course. Jujubes are packed with Vitamin J.

THE MOMMY GROUP: SHOULD YOU?

In an ideal world, here's how it would go: first, you would get to know your fellow and sister childbirth-preparation-class members. Despite your differences in education, interests, income, and maybe height, you'd find that over the weeks, you'd come to appreciate each other; sharing the trials of pregnancy together would give you a deep and lasting attachment. Then, after you'd all had your babies, you'd naturally form a steady Moms Group, where you'd meet regularly at each other's houses, providing one another with madeleines and unbiased support as you stumbled through these trying months and years of early motherhood.

That's the dream, anyhow. Usually what happens, however, is that you and your partner spend childbirth-preparation making fun of everyone else in the class;

then you have the baby and realize you could use some support and camaraderie—and maybe you shouldn't have been so standoffish to those women, who all passed a sign-up sheet around on the last day of class but never handed it to you.

So now you're depressed and isolated, and wishing you had friends who all had babies the same age as yours. You can't very well go crawling back to your spurned childbirth classmates, so now you have two choices: you can get dressed, leave the house, and find a bunch of strangers who only want to talk about car seats and peanut allergies; or you can try to get by reading blogs and talking to your mom on the phone twice a day. What's it going to be?

COULD YOUR MOMS GROUP BE A CULT?

1. The eldest member of the group has been continuously pregnant since 1957
2. Everyone has the same hairdo as She does
3. Diapers breed disease—IT IS WRITTEN
4. Everyone parks their campers on your street now
5. So it's kind of like you live in their compound!
6. Sure, the hooded look is flattering
7. But what do they mean, we're shedding our "earthly containers" come Solstice?

TABLE 14.1 ADVANTAGES AND DISADVANTAGES OF MOMS GROUPS

If you are a . . .	And you're looking for . . .	Type of Moms Group you need	Advantages to joining this Moms Group	Disadvantages to joining this Moms Group
Single teenage mom	A shoulder to cry on; help making sense of your future	Teen and twentysomething moms who are pulling themselves up by their bootstraps with plenty of sass and style	They don't judge you for being unmarried; they have worse boyfriend stories than you	They'll borrow money for the Coke machine and never pay you back
Creative thirtysomething who's suddenly lost her identity	Hope, inspiration, innovative ways to cope with the challenges of motherhood	Hip, off-beat crafters who get together to bake or quilt and think of funny nicknames for each other	They really get you	They're all moving to Oregon next month
Midlife professional who thought she could have it all, but whose childfree friends have abandoned her	Intelligent companionship that you can schedule around naptime	Women who are channeling their drive and intellect into childrearing without becoming obsessed with their children's achievements	Passionate discussions; disagreements handled with respect and good humor	Very real likelihood of brain cancer from prolonged exposure to eleven BlackBerrys in use at one time
Coddled young wife who thought motherhood would be a breeze	A place to drop your kid while you go shopping	Women who send their nannies to the group while they go shopping	You've never looked more chic in your life	Your child will be unable to pick you out of a lineup
Nun	Understanding; forgiveness; companionship	Women who have made mistakes but have become better people for having faced their weaknesses	Your family can go suck it	You're still going to hell
Badger	Warmth; safety; food	One where nobody eats their young	Cuddling; water source	Droppings; lice

FIND SOLACE AND/OR OPPORTUNITIES FOR RIGHTEOUS INDIGNATION ON THE WORLD WIDE WEB!

Online message boards, parenting e-communities, and those ubiquitous mother-blogs we hear tell of are just a few ways you can find kindred spirits—without leaving your home! Maybe you're having a hard time putting your baby down for the night and need to vent; maybe you had an amazingly easy time putting your child down for the night and feel like publicly bragging about it; maybe you just want to look at captioned photos of walruses and buckets. Internet, ahoy!

Studies have found that the Internet brings out both the best *and* the worst in people simultaneously. It's tempting to want to troll people's personal blogs, leaving hostile comments in order to feel the cheap, empty adrenaline rush that comes from hurting the feelings of strangers, but stop first and ask yourself: what should my pseudonym be? (We recommend "BetterMomThanU" or "YourAnAsshole" [*sic*].)

Even though the Internet is full of kooks and outrageous lies, there are a few Web sites we have found useful in a woman's journey through pregnancy and parenthood.

1. Grumplestiltskin (grumplestiltskin.net)—Adorable pictures of grumpy, constipated babies. Updated daily!
2. UrbaneBaby (urbanebaby.org)—Heated, pointless arguments about infant etiquette and maternity runway styles.
3. Lobster Fights! (lobsterfights.org)—Lobsters, fighting.
4. Origami Diapering (origamidiapering.com)—A peculiar combination of two unrelated Japanese fetishes, diapering and origami. Video-rich content appeals to beginners and advanced practitioners alike.
5. Horrible Diseases You Might Get (thehorrorohgodthehorror.net)—

One-stop revulsion for hypochondriacs and trainwreck enthusiasts alike. The message boards, where people continually misdiagnose one another, are a real hoot!

CLARIFY YOUR CHILD'S GENDER WITH CLOTHING AND ACCESSORIES

Babies' faces, much like those of very, very old people, are surprisingly gender neutral. (On the rare occasions when she was caught without lipstick, Golda Meir was often mistaken for Yogi Berra and pestered to autograph baseballs.)

Infants respond with less invective and ball-hurling than Ms. Meir did when mistaken for members of the opposite sex, but inside, their self-esteem has been shredded to confetti. Even after their parents point out to strangers that their "pretty little girl" is a handsome boy, or that the "rugged little shaver" wearing the Yankees onesie and the handlebar mustache is actually named Savannah, the damage has been done.

You must protect your child's fragile sense of self-worth! And the only way to do that is to festoon him and/or her with gender-appropriate clothing and accessories.

FOR GIRL BABIES

Onesie made of chiffon
Sequined pacifier
Stroller decorated with ruffled layers of tulle, lipsticks
Padded bra
Sex in the City burp cloth that reads: I'M A SAMANTHA—I'M ORAL, I'M LOOSE, AND I'M WET!

FOR BOY BABIES

Decorate stroller with wrenches and Old Spice bottles
Wrap him in World Wrestling Federation blanket
No onesie, to better show off airbrushed-on pecs
Jock strap over diaper

TABLE 14.2 GENDER-APPROPRIATE ACCESSORIES AND THEIR MEANINGS

Accessory	What you want it to say	What we think it says
Stretchy pink satin headband or glue-on ribbon	My baby may be bald, but one day she'll have long flowing feminine locks	Your adherence to the traditional female beauty standard and/or love of Ms. Pac-Man is so quaint
Pierced ears	My baby is cute	Your baby is hot
Temporary tattoo	My baby is badass	You went to Chuck E. Cheese
Permanent tattoo	My baby loves Hitler	Your child should be taken away from you by force
Football helmet	My baby is manly	You are overly concerned about your baby incurring a head injury
Motorcycle boots	My baby is cool	Your baby rides a tiny motorcycle, which is both bizarre and dangerous

POINT/COUNTERPOINT: ATTACHMENT PARENTING: HORRIBLE, OR ESSENTIAL?

ALICE:

Sure, "attachment parenting" sounds like a nice idea at first; sort of cuddly, even. How lovely to keep your infant close and warm! But what they don't tell you about this attachment business is that your child is attached to you *all the time,* day and night, clinging to your chest like an angry little primate. Also, milk seeps from their pores and collects in their neck folds. Let's face it: babies are kind of disgusting. I recommend looking for a neighbor or family member who will take yours off your hands for the first couple of years, at least until it can tell time and make its own breakfast.

EDEN:

If you're going to be part of the solution, you have to raise a child who won't create a lot of costly problems for society—by, for instance, ending up in prison, or the White House. Attachment parenting is the only way to ensure that your child won't look to a series of cellmates or congressional interns to fill the yawning void in his heart where his fond memories of you should be. Why do you need so much "alone time," anyway? Your selfish need for autonomy will be appeased when your husband gets home and dons his rubber lactation suit!

WAYS TO INCORPORATE EXERCISE INTO EVERY MINUTE OF YOUR DAY

You've tried subsisting on a starvation diet of caramel corn and Fresca. You've sat in the Y's steam room until your knees pruned. You've even gone so far as to think about looking up Weight Watchers online. And yet you still have between two and *seven* pounds of third-trimester peanut-butter-and-pancake-syrup sandwiches flopping over your waistband. What's a girl who is you to do?

Well, sister, we feel for you. Your first priority needs to be burning calories. Burning them day and night! You do that by (1) exercising and (2) EXERCIS-ING. It's not until you realize that you can and must incorporate exercise into every minute of your day that the pounds will begin to melt off. It's only by flexing your *mind muscles* that you will begin to build the body of your dreams! EEEYYAAAAGG!

AT THE GROCERY STORE

GOOD: Put a few giant bags of dog food and cases of bottled water in your cart before you begin to shop. Pushing an extra eighty-five pounds up and down the aisles will build arm and leg strength, improve stamina, and other shoppers will be impressed by your survivalist instincts. *Calories burned: 93*

BETTER: Allow a small child to write your grocery list. An illegible list of things you don't really need, organized so that items are located willy-nilly all over the store, will add an extra twenty minutes of walking to your day. Plus you'll be burning even more extra calories out of sheer frustration and gnawing hunger. *Calories burned: 155*

BEST: Load up your cart with water and dog food, strap the child *and* the dog to your back, and buy a year's worth of groceries in preparation for the End Times. *Calories burned: 940*

AT WORK

GOOD: Cupcakes around the water cooler a cause for concern? Not when you can sing "Happy Birthday" with extra vigor and clap a little too long when the boss blows out his candle. *Calories burned: 19*

BETTER: Fire your assistant. All that time she used to spend toting reams of paper and trotting out for coffee can now be yours! *Calories burned: 137*

BEST: Get a job as a field worker. Those spinach leaves don't pick themselves, you know! Plus, you'll rebuild your pelvic floor while Kegeling to hold in your pee until that lunchtime Porta-Potty break. *Calories burned: 1,753*

AT HOME

GOOD: Where's the remote? Who cares! You paid to have 500 channels, and now you get to jump up and change the station again. Now sit down. Wait, get up! Okay, sit down again. Get up! Etc. *Calories burned: 65*

BETTER: Washing machine on the fritz? Good. Hand-washing your clothes, towels, and sheets in the bathtub pioneer-style will strengthen arms and core muscles, give you new respect for the hardships your foremothers endured, and ensure that all your linens end up the same ultrachic shade of gunmetal gray. *Calories burned: 364*

BEST: Burn down your house! Rebuilding with scavenged materials and donated tools will foster new skills and leave you with the sexy washboard abs of an itinerant alcoholic roofer. *Calories burned: 1,337,450*

Mild forms of food poisoning that will take the weight right off!

Contracting a case of stomach flu can be complicated business, and new mothers often find themselves annoyingly resistant to even the worst viral bout. Food- and water-borne pathogens, on the other hand, are only a day-old oyster away. Here are some quick ways to lose your appetite—or worse!—for at least a week:

Sip of thawing chicken water

Tuna salad you found in the trash

Kitty litter flambé

Bacon *tartare*

Who would drink out of that muddy stream? You would!

Allow vagrants to bathe in your well water

EXERCISE DVDS WE CANNOT RECOMMEND

While there are plenty of good choices (we've heard), every exercise DVD we checked out was questionable and/or puzzling. To wit:

Van Morrison's Fitness Rocks!—The cardio section is comprehensive, but then he gets drunk and dozes under his Steinway while his assistants jog in place to *Astral Weeks,* stopping every few minutes to check his pulse.

Cat Fancier's Cat-Fitness Just for Cats —Contrary to the reviews we had read, this made no sense for humans. Plus it features cats. Loathsome, disease-riddled cats.

Let's Play Soccer (Indoors!)—Everything gets broken. Everything.

Sing and Pray the Pounds Away, featuring The Vienna Boys' Choir—Requires conversion to Catholicism and perfect pitch. On the other hand, includes an invigorating performance of "If I Had a Hammer" that even nonbelievers can enjoy.

Agatha Christie's Fitness Club Mystery—A bewildering series of movements set to the incidental music from the BBC's Miss Marple series.

Brian Dennehy's Power Clamdigging —True, Brian Dennehy's raw physical force and earthy charisma more than carry this four-hour DVD of the esteemed actor using his rough, callused hands to pry steamers out of the sands of Tillamook Bay. On second thought, this one's worth it.

15. BACK TO WORK, OR DO YOU LOVE YOUR BABY?

Remember working? Remember getting dressed in the morning and leaving your home? Remember time sheets, and lunch hours? Remember how before you were called "Mommy," your name was "Mid-level Drone"? Remember that time someone pooped on the floor next to the toilet and you were all trying to figure out who did it? (I think it was Carol in accounting.) Remember shoes??

All that could be yours again, if you want it.

Most of us worked before we gave birth. (If we didn't, it's because we're a mail-order child bride, in which case, our companionship and thrice-weekly coition can fall under the category of Duties—Thankless.) And for those of us who have spent our adulthood gainfully employed, there comes that time after the baby is born when we have to ask ourselves: Do we go back to work? And when? And when we do, to whom do we pass off this whatchacallit? Baby.

ARE YOU *SURE* YOU HAVE TO RETURN TO WORK?

Do you really want to return to this kind of drudgery?

You may believe that returning to work is a financial necessity. But is it? Let's take a look at how you can finagle your finances so that you can stay home until you're dead, or your child is grown—whichever comes first:

• Stop buying these overpriced foods: meat, fruit, vegetables, breads, liquids.
• Instead of renting movies, act out what you recall of the movie's plot. Nothing's cuter than Baby miming the break-up scene in *Something's Gotta Give* starring Diane Keaton! Especially if you have an elderly bulldog or pug who can play the Jack Nicholson role.
• If you stay home, you don't need nice clothes. Baby doesn't care if you're underdressed. She also doesn't care if you're nude. (Save on washing!)
• Ask your parents to buy you stuff! Parents love buying stuff for their grown children, and now that they've grown accustomed to your being financially independent, they're sure to welcome being useful to you once again. This worked really well for Alice.
• Sell the extensive collection of batik textiles you amassed during your numerous travels to Indonesia.
• All that time you used to spend ironing your work clothes can instead be spent arranging a lucrative pyramid scheme.
• Gas and/or public transportation: expensive. Sitting at home, feeling your soul die: not as expensive.

NOW WHO'S GOING TO RAISE THAT BABY?

Deciding whom to hire to look after your child depends on two things: how much you can afford to pay and who will mesh best with your family's lifestyle. Do you need someone with flexible hours? Someone who can cook? Someone who actually enjoys taking care of incontinent, preverbal human beings? Once you get your budget straight—and really, it's time for you to stop buying those weird little handbags on eBay—you need to figure out who's least likely to forget your baby at the Laundromat.

Are you getting a nanny and also *not* returning to work? Then you are a princess and sleep on a mattress made of solid gold.

SHOULD YOU CHOOSE A DAY-CARE CENTER INSTEAD OF IN-HOME HELP?

There is *absolutely nothing wrong* with most day-care centers. The waiting lists for the good ones aren't that long (if you signed Baby up at least a year before you met your husband), and the rest of them are perfectly adequate—even reputable! Don't let those *Dateline* reports, with their nosy reporters and footage of day care directors tearing ass away from camera crews, discourage you from seeking out what we're sure is a *mostly noncriminal business entity.* That one place down the street where you always see little callused hands reaching out through the wrought-iron gate probably does a fine job of keeping the children occupied with small, repetitive tasks for up to ten hours a day.

There are even some advantages to day-care centers! Like:

- Your child will enjoy the company of other babies who don't know what's going on as much as he doesn't
- Plenty of infectious diseases to go around—beefs up the immune system!
- Having more grown-ups on hand means more support for your baby's

TABLE 15.1 IN-HOME HELP: AN IN-DEPTH COMPARISON

	Nanny	Grandmother	Governess	Au pair	Badger
How you find one	Employment service; word of mouth; at the playground, working for someone else	Look to your left. She's sitting there, slavering in anticipation at getting at your baby	Send a note up the chimney	Ask your husband to find a hot Swedish girl on the subway and get her phone number	Set a trap. (Tip: badgers can be found in Wisconsin)
What you pay them	Hourly wage; car fare	Baby's smiles; guilt	Salary; starch	Cash; green card	Honey; grubs; maybe a hamster carcass for holidays
Appearance	Comfortable, washable outfits	Something she'll be sending you the dry-cleaning bill for	Linen cap; crisp apron; button-up shoes; stern expression	Indefinable, effortless European beauty	Musky fur; tapered snout; lousy
How they might treat child	Affection mixed with benign indifference	Affection mixed with arbitrary discipline, candy, and shaming	Pats child on the head; soothes anxieties with clever songs that list things	Surprisingly focused on child while rebuffing husband's unsubtle flirting	Will defend baby from rabid dachshunds
Favorite activity	Watching *One Life to Live* with baby on her lap	Watching *One Life to Live* and eating microwave popcorn	Enslaving songbirds; canoodling with chimneysweeps	Securing her flawless blond hair in a bun using just a pencil	Reading *The Wind in the Willows* and *Bedtime for Frances*; tunneling
Quirk	Takes baby to strange church in someone's basement	Paints baby's fingernails "Rock-a-pulco Red"	Leaves baby smelling vaguely of bleach	Gets choked up while reading the IKEA catalog	Can run in short bursts up to 19 mph
Will call you . . .	Whatever you tell her to	"Oh, it's *you*."	Ma'am/Captain	Mrs. Your Husband's First Name	*Grrarrrh*

needs, and this way everyone gets a smoke break

- Fluorescent lighting is an important source of Vitamin F
- You're at least 73 percent more likely to get on the local news

That said, here are some warning signs to look out for in day-care centers

- Center name contains the words "Chanel," "Vuitton," or "Gucci"
- Facilities are equipped with nap room, industrial coffee urn, and smoking lounge
- Why does your baby come home smelling like a tannery?
- Day-care director has disturbingly soft hands
- "Free play" held in unventilated stairwell
- Instructions on what to include in Baby's "emergency kit" include thimbles, bottled water, and your social security and bank account numbers
- Brochure insists that "sewing retail knockoffs teaches vital hand-eye coordination and math skills"
- Day-care director says good-bye by shouting, "So long, suckers!"

Kids love fresh air, sunshine—and beet farming!

Rationalizations to tell yourself about the only day-care center that was affordable and had a spot open:

- AM talk radio can be educational
- Nothing wrong with a little cement dust
- Who's to say what a "criminal record" is, really?
- Everyone makes mistakes
- I can accept a nontraditional method of putting on diapers
- My child's getting exposed to all kinds of colorful language!

HOW TO HIDE YOUR BABY IN THE OFFICE

So, you've rejected the nanny/badger/day-care option, but you still need to go back to work. Solution? Take your baby to the office with you while he's still small enough to fit in a file drawer.

FILE CABINET BASSINETTE. Simply line an empty file drawer with a blanket and tuck Baby inside! If your baby gets fussy and starts to cry, just shut the drawer. Don't forget him when it's time to go home!

LOCATE OFFICE "DEAD ZONES." There's always a small, dark, unused space behind the water cooler, the soda machine, or that second copy machine in back that gets too hot and smells like an electrical fire. Baby's car seat will fit right in there. Dangly toys and empty toner cartridges will occupy Baby until your ten-minute break.

LITTLE-USED "NURSING ROOM." Offices that stay up to date with OSHA regulations will have a designated place for women who want to nurse or pump. Almost no one ever goes in that closet, so go ahead and start decorating!

NOTHING WRONG WITH THE BATHROOM. Babies love running water!

HIDE IN YOUR SHIRT. Extra-large "peasant" blouses leave plenty of room for Baby to snuggle.

PRETEND HE'S YOUR BABY-SUBSTITUTE DOLL. Tell everyone how much you miss your baby, and that the only way to stimulate your milk production when you're away from him is to carry around a baby-substitute. *An incredibly lifelike, poseable, gurgling, smelly baby-substitute.*

NONTRADITIONAL JOB? HERE'S HOW TO MAKE IT MORE BABY-FRIENDLY

WAITRESS—Have bus boys run a daycare for children of employees and guests who want to eat in peace. Guests pay a flat rate. Must split any tips with the dishwasher.

TUGBOAT CAPTAIN—Bolt a baby seat to the deck. The gentle rolling of the waves is very soothing, and if you drag the river, Baby will enjoy playing with crabs, old boots, and whatever (and whoever) else gets pulled up from the briny deep.

FLIGHT ATTENDANT—There are lots of things for Baby to explore on a plane! Examples: soda-can drawer in galley; unoccupied toilet; emergency exit door handles; landing gear. Plus, the captain's headphones look *adorable* on her.

BLACK-MARKET BABY STORE—Your baby can be in charge of all the other babies.

LIGHTHOUSE OPERATOR—Like anyone's going to complain that you have a baby up there with you! Year upon year, night after endless night, searching the seas for ghost ships and homeschooling your pale, feral child who can move small objects with his mind. What could be easier?

WIZARD—Make your wizard's den more baby-friendly by removing all glass test tubes, beakers, and potion-making equipment except for small-volume cauldrons. Also remove all poisonous herbs, grasses, flowers, and mushrooms to a locked cabinet at least eight feet off the floor. Remove all candy from exterior walls, and disconnect your child-size oven, as well. Not much point in being a wizard anymore, is there?

GAFFER—The good thing about gaffers is that they always have a lot of gaffer's tape. Tape your baby to your chest or back and go about your business. If baby cries during filming: gaffer's tape! Be sure to cover *only* the mouth. Not the nose or eyes. *The mouth.*

Where's the baby? She'll *never tell!*

It Really Happened! I Went Back to Work

"I never thought I'd return to work after I had my baby, but then I remembered that my husband was out of a job and our home was in foreclosure! Whoopsie! Seeing as how the two choices I had were either returning to my inflexible corporate job or moving my family into some shrubbery near the bus station, I opted for the latter. It so happens that my husband, Dylan, is highly allergic to coniferous plants, which should have occurred to me when I changed our address labels to "The Shrub by the Wishing Fountain Where There's All that Gay Night Cruising." And that's another thing! Don't those gay people realize that there are families with small children living in those shrubs? Anyway, long story short, the whole shrub thing was a no-go, so I decided to go back to work. It took me a while because I couldn't quite remember where the office was, or what I used to do. I did figure it out eventually, though there was some crazy person at my desk, and then that big kerfuffle with security. And then my boobs leaked all over the conference table, which is a big *corporate don't*! So that was embarrassing. What were we talking about, again?"

—Carvel Potero, age 37, Chicago, Illinois

WHY NOT START A "BLOG"?

Hey, Moms! Why choose between working and not-working when there's this third option: *pretending to work* on your "blog"! With a blog, which is short for "Weblog," which itself is short for "World-Wide-Web-based log of one's feelings and snacks," you can spend all day staring at your computer, trying to figure out how to upload photos of your husband asleep on the couch and covered with strategically placed action figures, while the man himself stands behind you holding the baby and wondering when you're going to look up so he can leave for work.

BLOGS CAN BE JUST LIKE JOBS! TO WIT:

The money's terrible

Your superiors (i.e., all the people you write for) don't appreciate you

Someone (e.g., your baby) is always interrupting you

You can't figure out who keeps poaching your Diet Cokes out of the office fridge

ON THE OTHER HAND, BLOGS CAN BE BETTER THAN JOBS! HERE'S WHY:

The bastards (i.e., all the people you write for) can't fire you!

No one can shut you up!

You can ignore your blog for weeks at a time!

You can express feelings you never would have had the nerve to express in real life!

HERE ARE SOME BLOG TIPS!

- The key to success is to *focus all, most, some, or* any *of your blog content* on your kid(s). And *voilà*: you have a "mommyblog." Congratulations—you're the belle of the Marketers' Ball!
- Come up with *adorable nicknames* for your child(ren), so as not to reveal their True Identities. Nicknames should run along a theme. If your oldest is nicknamed Planet, then the next child should be Moon; the one after that, Plutoid; then Oort Cloud; then Galactic Rim. Don't throw a "Possum" into this mix—are you *trying* to drive your readers insane?
- Husband should just be Huz or Hubby or DH or Spousy MacPartner or The Big H, and must always be *ineffectual and/or bumbling*. Important: Do not let him get a blog of his own. *He must never tell his story.*
- Stick to a basic theme your readers can understand. But which should you go for? As always, we have a handy table. For that is our way.

TABLE 15.2 BLOG THEMES YOU MUST CHOOSE FROM

Theme	Banner art	Sample names	Also, don't forget	Why will they read you?	Sample quote
Retro Kitsch	Clip art of a 1950s housewife; gingham background; a pie with a bottle of prescription pills stuck in the center	"Mommy's Ready For Her Xanax"; "Domestically Unhinged"; "I Don't Even *Own* a Casserole Dish"	You'll need an adorable name for your blogroll (the list of links to other blogs you like), such as "Mother's Little Helpers" or "Valley of the Dolls." We just gave those to you. (Please contact St. Martin's Press for rights information and royalty schedules.)	You are relatable, yet wacky! Readers also suspect you might OD on your sleeping aid.	"Typical morning. Me: 'Who wants pancakes?' The Little Duckling: '*Me*, motherfucker.' Me: 'Honey, did Daddy put on a Scorsese movie last night after I passed out?' Hubs: 'Durrrr.'"
Sincerely Loving	Photos of beaming children, floppy-eared dogs, a mother's hand holding her child's. You know. That kind of shit.	"Forever Blessed"; "Precious Drooly Baby Kisses"; "Angels in Our Family Bed"	Get Jesus in there, even if you're not Christian. *Christians love the Internet more than they they love Jesus.* Steve Jobs told us that.	Your God-fearing sisters aspire to be as holy as you. They also secretly hope that you might crack and OD on your sleeping aid.	"5:00 A.M. on Saturday morning—just took a break from washing the latest round of vomit-soaked bedding. :(And yet I wouldn't trade these blessings for all the sleep and nonvomit-soaked beds in the world!"
Intellectual and Distant	Clip art from antique taxidermy manuals; scanned socialist propaganda.	Must be a nonsense word, like "Foopskiffy" or "Qoopt" or "Metonymy."	Your bio should list all of your degrees and writing credits, so everyone knows you're not just some regular idiot-blogger. Do you have a PDF of your CV? Perfect.	You make readers feel stupid for not getting your references. Moms need a target for their unfocused rage, so you're performing a valuable service.	"Eurydice appears ready to take her first steps this weekend, but as we know from Nietzsche, '*Ein beiläufiger Stroll durch das verrückte Asyl zeigt, dass Glaube nichts prüft.*' Am I right, ladies?"
Insane	Clumsily rendered sketch of *Friends* cast with a big red circle around Courteney Cox	"Kisses, Courteney, and Crossbows"	This is hard to pull off unless you actually are insane. Also, insane blogs rarely have much to do with motherhood.	Watching your descent into madness is an excellent distraction from a typical mom's daily drudgery	"I finally figured out how C-Cox is invading my mindspace! I really like my new lead-lined helmet!"

IS THERE A DOWNSIDE TO MOMMYBLOGGING?

And how. Mommyblogs are selfish, dangerous excuses for women who don't get enough attention in real life to post Photoshopped pictures of themselves and their children on the Internet, thus practically begging all the pedophiles and murderers to pay them a visit. Even if these senseless moms aren't posting pictures, they're connecting with other women by discussing their lives and children in a way that we find hideously irresponsible. Children should be hidden under tarps, in both public and private, until they've grown too unwieldy and loud to drag into a dark, windowless van—or until they've reached the age of consent in your municipality.

On the other hand, you could make a few bucks selling ad space on your blog! If money is more important to you than your child's safety, go right ahead.

👓 EYE ON BABY!

If you've started introducing your baby to solid foods and/or the concept of "pooping shame," you might find that she's become constipated. Dry, hard poops are difficult to pass and make Baby cry with frustration, but it's often quite simple to help your baby become "regular" again without too much embarrassment! A cup of black coffee, a cigarette, and a Pottery Barn catalog should help her work things out. Also, try to think of an excuse to leave the house so baby can have some time alone to relax without worrying about you overhearing her efforts (tile reverberates so!). A can of air freshener or a pack of matches will also help her believe that she's covered her tracks, so to speak.

DOS AND DON'TS: DISCUSSING LABOR AND DELIVERY WITH FRIENDS AND COWORKERS

Census figures indicate that you and your partner need to produce at least 3.2 first-world offspring to replace yourselves and maintain a steady population, and so do all your namby-pamby liberal, birth-control-abusing friends. So get ready to sugarcoat your birth stories. It's good for morale!

These guys can't wait to hear about your vagina!

DO: Give everyone at the staff meeting a good laugh by telling them about the atrocious décor of your hospital room.
DON'T: Tell them that at one point you were pushing so hard that poop shot out of you and hit the Thomas Kinkade print on the opposite wall.

DO: Tell everyone how supportive your partner was during your labor.
DON'T: Talk about how your partner beat the doctor unconscious when he tried to give you an episiotomy.

DO: Admit that labor is uncomfortable, but in a satisfying, *productive* way.
DON'T: Tell everyone how your seventy-nine hours of labor were a nonstop tidal wave of excruciating agony, the memories of which are seared into your brain a way that surpasses your ability to form words around.

DO: Call to thank your friends and family for the flowers they sent to you.
DON'T: E-mail your friends and family photos of your ravaged abdomen.

DO: Send out tasteful birth announcements noting the baby's weight, length, and time of arrival.

DON'T: Talk relentlessly about the dream you keep having where you're in a war zone and a bomb explodes in your house and rips the baby's arms off and you know the only choice you have is to suffocate him with a pillow to end his suffering.

DO: Start talking about when you're going to start trying to have your next baby!

DON'T: Decide that the best place for a good, exhausted cry is at the drive-through window at Starbucks on Monday morning at 8:00 A.M. with the twins' car seats secured to the roof of your car with a bungee cord.

16. THIS ONE'S FOR YOUR HUSBAND (AND/OR PARTNER; WE'RE NOT JUDGING)

Hey, guys.

What's up? How's it going with the baby and, you know, stuff? Everything cool?

Look, we know you probably haven't been getting a lot of sleep, and God knows the last time you got laid, are we right? So unfortunately, your patience and focus aren't really at their peak during a time when your wife/girlfriend/partner needs you to be at your most patient and focused. Mother Nature is testing you, buddy, to see if you can keep it together. So what's it going to be? Either you find a creative solution for dinner that involves green vegetables and fresh flowers, or else you can retreat to your man cave and wait for her lawyer to call. The choice is yours.

DEALING WITH YOUR LADY'S HORMONAL WEIRDNESS

You've got the feeling that your companion has become somewhat—how shall we put it?—unglued, and she's not reacting to your existence with her usual good humor. You need to own up to the fact that in the weeks/months/years following the birth of your child, you're going to say some dumb stuff to your wife/girl-friend/partner. (You know what? Henceforth, we will be using the generic *wife* and we hope that doesn't offend your delicately balanced belief system, but if it does? Too fucking bad.) Under normal circumstances we expect she'd be able to handle a little well-meaning boorishness, but in her postpartum state you may find her engaging in such uncharacteristic behavior as (1) throwing heavy objects, (2) selling your stuff on eBay, or (3) petitioning the pope for an annulment.

Knowing that you're going to fuck up royally sooner or later, it's important that you master—or at least familiarize yourself with—the furious backpedal (see table 16.1).

WHY SHE'S YELLING AT YOU

Look, even the strongest relationships can be tested by the introduction of an infant into the mix. Infants are *hard,* you know? With the screaming and the not-sleeping and whatever? They need to be fed *a lot,* and changed *a lot,* and you're supposed to spend *a lot* of time with them, and your wife probably read all these baby-caring books and you were totally *going* to read them, but then Steve called and you had to go help him move his woodpile!! Anyhow, if she's yelling at you, here are some possible reasons. Fill in what you think the best response will be. Look, we can't do all the work for you. You're going to have to get a pen, and take a minute, *if you care.*

1. You're doing it wrong. _____

2. You're not listening. _____

3. What made you think *that* was okay? _____

4. You didn't read the books, did you? _____

5. Have you ever even *seen* a baby before? _____

6. Oh my God. Just . . . oh my God. _____

7. Could you just, for once, you know . . . (sigh). Never mind.

_____

That's it. Just keep degrading yourself. She'll come around.

All right, fine, here are the goddamn answers.

1. I will stop doing it wrong.
2. I will never again make that mistake.
3. I have no good answers for that. I throw myself at your mercy.
4. I will admit that I did not before, but right now I'm reading this *Let's Panic About Babies!* book, and I'm growing, not just as a father, but as a reader and a human being.
5. Good one! I have, but I see your point.
6. I know. I . . . I know.
7. When you're ready to talk, my love, I'm here.

TABLE 16.1 HOW TO FIX THE DUMB STUFF YOU SAID

What you said:	Quick, backpedal!	What you should have said:	Damage control strategy:
"Is your butt going to stay that size?"	"That is to say, I like you with a *little* more of a womanly curve, which you now have. Wow, it's time for me to make dinner!"	"What can I make you for dinner?"	Make dinner.
"Man, I am *so tired.*"	"And I haven't been working a *tenth* as hard as you have. You're amazing, did you know that?"	"Those boots you liked on Zappos.com—let's order them. No, *I* will. You've done enough."	Buy the boots, then make dinner.
"Beans and rice *again*?"	"That's fantastic, because I was just going to run out and buy some chorizo, and I was all, if only we had some rice and beans that would go with them!"	"Your hair looks so pretty today."	Take her out for dinner.
"How come I don't have any clean socks?"	" . . . is what I keep asking myself, because after all maintaining my wardrobe is *my responsibility.* God, I love you."	"Laundry time! Do you want me to hand-wash your intimates?"	Do the laundry and never say the word "socks" again in the house.
"I wish the baby didn't have your dad's gigantic nose."	"I have no idea why I just said that. I love your dad's gigantic nose. Wait . . . "	"I love that the baby looks just like your dad."	Jewelry.
"C'mon, how about a hand job?"	"I mean, how about if I give you a hand. With your jobs. Not that they're *your* jobs. Our jobs. Is what I meant."	"Let's cuddle."	Dinner and a movie. She picks the movie. And you'll *like it.*
"Sometimes I wish we didn't have a kid."	"I was going to say, that's what I'm afraid *you think I feel!* I was just opening myself up to you by describing, uh, my innermost fears?"	"I can't believe how goddamn lucky I am."	Dinner *and* movie *and* boots, plus a full hour of staring lovingly at your sleeping baby, while visibly wiping away grateful tears.
"Well, at least your boobs look good."	"Really, I really can't overstate how awesome your rack is right now."	"I am not worthy of you."	We're going to have to get back to you on that one.

WHAT KIND OF DAD ARE YOU?

HACKER DAD

Motto: "Let me rig something up."

Characteristics: Gives baby old Ethernet cables to teethe on.

Can be found: Making a stroller out of metal tubing, duct tape, and a neoprene laptop sleeve.

Favorite thing about being a Dad is: Who knew Babies "R" Us had so much awesome gear?

Warning signs that this might be you: Your baby's blog gets more hits than yours does.

ABSENTMINDED PROFESSOR DAD

Motto: "*Who's* got jaundice, dearest?"

Characteristics: Enjoys smoking his pipe as he awaits a home-cooked dinner.

Can be found: Reading the *Economist* while his wife loses her mind

Favorite thing about being a Dad is: The inner glow that comes from knowing his family unit is complete, and around here *somewhere*.

Warning signs that this might be you: You're not 100 percent sure where the baby's room is.

RELUCTANT DAD

Motto: "If you say so."

Characteristics: Well-rested, since he moved to the couch.

Can be found: Checking his cell phone; looking for the remote.

Favorite thing about being a Dad is: What? Did you say something?

Warning signs that this might be you: You don't see the point in reading this—your wife will tell you the important parts.

TRAPPED DAD

Motto: "Oh my GOD."

Characteristics: haunted expression when he leaves for work; defeated expression when he arrives home.

Can be found: Clutching his head; staring at his life insurance policy and sighing.

Favorite thing about being a Dad is: Escaping into a black, dreamless sleep.

Warning signs that this might be you: Your urologist refuses to give you any more vasectomies.

GRUBBY HIPSTER DAD

Motto: "I found the really cool playground all the *straights* are too scared to go to because of the *violent crime.*"

Characteristics: Disgust at suburban breeders, SUVs, chain retail establishments, showering.

Can be found: Buying toddler-sized T-shirts bearing the names of bands no one has heard of, in a neighborhood no one knows about.

Favorite thing about being a Dad is: Showing 'em. Showing 'em ALL.

Warning signs that this might be you: You have spit-up in your beard.

CURMUDGEONLY OLD DAD

"I'm old, goddamn it!"

Motto: "I'll give you something to cry about."

Characteristics: Hairy ears; grumbling.

Can be found: Enjoying his morning beer in peace, for the love of . . . !

Favorite thing about being a Dad is: That kid's small fingers'll sure come in handy with that bum cigarette machine down at the Elks Club.

Warning signs that this might be you: You're frequently mistaken for your child's ghostly ancestor.

👓 EYE ON BABY!

Are you waiting for the most fun part of your child's development: the part where he starts talking? Your child can't wait, either, so he can finally tell you what he really thinks of you. He can't do that, however, until he hears a whole lot of language coming out of *your* mouth, so start talking to your kid, early and often! It may seem strange to engage in a one-sided conversation, but think of it this way: he can't tell you to shut up. You can talk and talk and he *has to take it*. Possible conversational topics include: how incredible you are at a given sport; how and where, in your youth, you would get into trouble, and how awesome it was; girls who thought you were hot, at least you think, because they were looking at you *like that* and girls who don't like you don't give you *that look*; "rocking out," and how much you miss it; just how and where this baby of yours can cram it when he starts crying like he does. Go for it! He's not going to remember. At least, not in any easily accessible part of the conscious brain. Probably.

BUYING SEX TOYS: *ARE YOU MAN ENOUGH?*

Sex toys aren't all just bachelor party gags. If your relationship has lost its traction, some of that crazy rubber stuff can put your tail right back on the road! So just in case your wife has slipped a rod and run out of gas, you need to have your toolbox outfitted so you can take out your trusty socket wrench and spare lug nuts and make her automatic transmission purr with performance! And don't forget to lubricate her oil pan. In conclusion: cars!

HOW TO CHOOSE A SEX SHOP

- Look for nonthreatening words in the name. Examples: "Frolic," "Bliss," "Tender."
- They're playing women-friendly music by bands like Wilson Phillips or Ladysmith Black Mambazo
- Staffers might actually be called "Ladysmiths"
- Staff really detail the finer points of their featured dildos, especially heft, give, and vein ascension
- Staff never asks whether you're comfortable buying your wife a rubber phallus that's bigger than your own

SEX SHOPS TO AVOID

- Greeter is chained to the door by his neck
- Name contains words like "Ram," "Shank," or "Annihilate"
- Background music is a loop of someone weeping softly
- Staff makes you grovel before they'll put your purchases into a bag (you may like this, but this is about her, not you. Focus!)
- Staff cannot recommend nipple clamps strongly enough

WHAT TO BUY?

Many women are just as unsettled by the sight of a ten-inch, alarmingly detailed dildo as you might be. While there are plenty of less threatening erotic accessories, sex-toy shop staffers just love to steer you toward the high-end vibrating shafts that pulse and strobe and croon like Barry White. But is that what your beloved *really* wants? Here are a few ideas for your lady that won't cause her to run from the room screaming:

For the curious wife with no sex toy experience: Vibrating teddy bear

For the no-nonsense wife who has better ways to occupy her time: Clothes dryer

For the Christian wife who's uncomfortable exploring her sexuality: Vibrating New Testament

For the wife with specific and well-articulated preferences: Just check out the wish list featured on her sex-toy blog. It's all there.

In general, you should avoid: Burlap chaps; double-ended chrome butt plugs

On the other hand, you might want to consider: Fleece-lined leather chaps; pink double-ended jelly butt plugs

How to give her a sex toy—the right way:
"I thought this might be fun for you. You know, if you want to try it. You can use it by yourself, or we can put it on top of the TV and laugh at it instead."

How to give her a sex toy—the wrong way:
"Sit on this."
"You can put this in your butt, or wherever it goes."
"Take this into the other room and call me when you're done."

But I'm not a man! I'm a nineteenth-century lesbian!

Dear lady: if you are a yearning yet modest daughter of Sappho, we pray you, take heart! The Inter-Net is a vast Series of Tubes through which you may anonymously purchase all manner of devices designed for the explicit purpose of Uterine/Nervous Relief, and scrimshaw anal impediments. We heartily recommend that you visit *Most Enjoyable Devices!* (http://www. mostenjoyabledevices!. net/) on your computer or steam-powered printing press. We aver it is the most discreet erotic mercantile on all the Worlds-Wide Web.

HOW TO TELL IF YOU'RE HAVING AN AFFAIR

You look at your wife and think, "Huh. So that's a wife."

You look at the woman from human resources and think, "I wonder what she looks like when she sneezes?"

One day you wake up and realize that you've switched from briefs to boxer-briefs.

Then you get into the shower and carefully shave your scrotum.

Your wife is eyeing you suspiciously.

You have a hard time meeting her gaze.

A strange new number keeps showing up on your cell phone.

The next day, you find yourself in that airport Days Inn.

A half-naked woman is looking at you with a dreamy expression.

If her hair wasn't so tousled, you would swear that it was the woman from human resources!

She thanks you for having sex with her.

A few times.

You think you might be in love.

The woman then informs you that while she enjoyed this little fling, it's time she got dressed and went back to her ex-boyfriend, Chet.

No, "Chet" isn't a nickname. That's his *real name.*

You realize how much your wife and newborn child mean to you, too much to jeopardize for some silly affair.

You explain all this to the human resources woman, but she can't hear you over the running shower.

You catch the next bus and hurry home to tell your wife what a lucky bastard you are, to have a woman like her.

Your baby is crying.

Your wife says, "Did you say something?"

Your wife is deaf from fatigue and it's all your fault!

DINNERS EVEN *YOU* CAN MAKE!

GRANNY SMITH APPLE, BRIE, AND WATERCRESS SANDWICH ON FOCACCIA

Not as hard as it looks

Open the refrigerator and take out a package of Brie. Ignore the Brie until it comes to room temperature. (Note: do not forget about the Brie, especially if you have a cat! You know that cat's going to eat it or get her germs on it somehow. Cats. Don't get us started.) When you poke the Brie with a finger and you're not all *brrrr,* that means it's ready. Now take a knife out of the drawer. Not a butter or plastic knife. No, not—that's a pretend knife, did you get that from your baby's pretend-food toys? You'll need a sharp knife. A paring knife or medium chef's knife is best. Grasp it firmly by the handle (this is also called "the dull part," and may be covered in wood or a woodlike polymer). Point the blade (the part that can cut you) away from you and directly at an apple. We need thin slices here, but just, you know, do your best.

Did you buy focaccia? If not, go out and buy some focaccia. You'll need a bakery for that. Ask the man behind the counter for focaccia, pay him, and return home. Lay the focaccia flat on the counter, and cut a hunk right off the loaf. (Did you take it out of its packaging first?) Then you need to get sideways and slit it in half so you get two slices out of it, and then lay them out face up. Cut off a couple of wedges of the Brie—don't forget to remove the plastic wrapping!—and place them carefully on the bread. Do you have watercress? If you have watercress, you're going to want to place them on top. If you don't have it, don't go out looking for it now, because the chances of you purchasing the wrong leafy green are extraordinarily high. And no, you can't use some of the potted fern in the living room. No. It is not the same thing. *No.*

Arrange your apple slices artfully on the other slice of bread, then slap the other side of the sandwich on top of there, cut it in two, and offer half to your wife. She doesn't want it? More for you, then.

ROAST CHICKEN WITH ROOT VEGETABLES

Preheat oven to 400°F. Take chicken out of package. Remove giblets, rinse thoroughly, and pat dry. No, wait—rinse the *chicken*. Leave the giblets. Sorry, that was our fault. We should have clarified. Place the chicken in a roasting pan, sprinkle with salt, pepper, garlic powder, or whatever you like (on second thought, stick with the options we've given you), then shove it into the oven for an hour. Wait: is the oven preheated? Wait until it's preheated. Okay, now you can put it in. Back up! Put a bunch of quartered new potatoes (you know that's a variety of potato and not a time-of-purchase thing, right?) and carrot chunks into the pan. They'll brown in the chicken's juices. Yes, that's a good thing. *Now* put it all in the oven.

When the timer goes off, *put on an oven mitt* and take the pan out of the oven. Let it rest for a couple of minutes, then slice it up. Is the chicken still bloody inside? Whoops. In that case, put it back in the oven for another ten minutes. Wait—MITT! MITT! Good. Repeat as necessary. Slice up whatever needs slicing (watch those fingers!) and put it all on a plate. There's enough for two, so don't hog it all. Pairs nicely with Gatorade.

BEDTIME BONDING: THE FAMILY ALPHABET

In conclusion, here are some helpful nursery rhymes we found in a parenting manual from the forties. And yet still so current!

A is for Arms that hold baby tight,
While pacing and muttering all
    through the night.

B is for Beer that tastes so
    delicious!
Daddy can drink it and also do
    dishes.

C is for Cuban, a fancy cigar.
Why's Daddy smoking alone in the
    car?

D is for Drama queen—what
    Daddy calls Mommy.
It's not his fault we're broke; you
    can blame the economy.

E is for Earache, much to Baby's
    dismay!
No, YOU call the doctor, I've been
    working all day.

F is for Farting, which Daddy finds
    funny.
He must laugh or he'll cry, for we
    still have no money.

G is for Ghastly Ghost movies
    with Guts.
If you take Baby to one, then Mom
    will go nuts.

H is for Hogwash and Horseshit
    and Hooey.
Daddy's suspecting that Mom's
    gone all screwy.

I is for Iceberg, where Dad might
    as well live,
'Cause Mommy believes that his
    mind's like a sieve.

J is for Jellybeans, so sweet and
    bright.
Give some to your babe—he'll
    poop rainbows all night.

K is for Kitten, a sweet fluffy pet,
Which Daddy will buy, then be
    filled with regret.

L is for lesbians, so hot and so awesome,
Too bad it's illegal to go out and paw some.

M is for Moron, which Mommy calls Dad,
But not to his face, because then he'd be mad.

N is for Noodles! And Nutballs! And Nooner!
Babe will sleep through the night by six months. Maybe sooner!

O is for Oh No, I'm pregnant again.
The new babe will just have to sleep in the den.

P is for pooping—what Baby does best.
Dad changed a diaper! We're all quite impressed.

Q is for Quiet, which Baby must hate.
Mom's enjoying her drink, so you'll just have to wait.

R is for Rumors, which Mom should ignore.
No way is Dad fooling around with that whore.

S is for Sex, and Samba, and Steak.
Mom needs a vacation that Dad says he can't take.

T is for Teething, which makes Baby sad.
Have some bourbon, dear child, then you won't feel so bad.

U is for Underthings tucked in Dad's jacket.
When Mom yells at Dad—Hoo! She makes quite a racket!

V is for Verna, Dad's new assistant.
Could she be the reason that Dad's been so distant?

W is for Women and the troubles they cause,
Tho' Dad's first to admit he's not without flaws.

X is for Xylophone, Baby's favorite new toy—it
Makes so much damn noise Mom wants to destroy it.

Y is for Y Chromosome. Dad can't help but philander!
It's his hormones and such that make him meander.

Z is for Zounds! Mom and Dad are reunited!
They're probably doomed, so don't get too excited.

17. KEEPING BABY, AND YOUR SANITY, MORE OR LESS INTACT

Ever since the day your child launched herself from the womb, she's been on a fast track to a distant, grim land called I Don't Need You Anymore. In fact, she may already think she lives there, and that Cheerios and clean diapers simply fall from the sky. Children are incredible narcissists who believe that no harm can befall them, and that their every need is a mandate, like you don't have anything better to do than rush over every time they need something replenished, mopped up, or switched on—but guess what, sweetie, *Mommy is busy writing a book so you can get the goddamn Teddy Grahams yourself.*

In this precious first year of life, while your child heedlessly explores and develops, you need to constantly be on the alert, protecting your child from all the dangers that lurk in your neighborhood, your home, and your person. Your child's belief that she is impervious to damage is what makes her such a menace to your mental health and stability, and the only way to keep from going insane with worry is to babyproof everything around you. Babyproof the *shit* out of it.

BABYPROOFING YOUR HOUSE

"But surely I have time," you say. "My child isn't even a year old, and she's not walking, or anything." Wrong again.

You think you won't need to lock up your collection of broken bottles and leaky air conditioners until your child is mobile, but in fact, long before he's able to move, Baby will be checking out his surroundings and noting which things can kill him, and which things he can use to kill you. Babies are born amoral thrill-seekers. Anything that zaps or chokes or pinches looks like a welcome respite from their daily humdrum-itude. So before your baby can focus on anything beyond her own hands (which are also killing tools, but there's not too much you can do about that) go to your local babyproofing facility and purchase everything they have. Clear out the place. You'll thank us when your child grows up with a healthy fear of spatulas.

EYE ON BABY!

IS YOUR CHILD A PLAXICO?

Plaxico children are a recent phenomenon described by a husband-and-wife team of psychologists, Jerry and Joan Jeffries, in their self-published book, *A Rainbow of Snowflakes.* The experiences they had raising their own child, Japheth, along

Where Danger Lurks

Shag rugs: You want your baby to lie facedown in that?

Cereal bowls: You want your baby to lie facedown in one of those?

Dirty socks: What if your child decides to fashion himself a sock-ball gag?

Your drapes are too long: Your child can easily make a noose.

Actually they're too short: Your child will jump up hoping to make a noose and instead fall back down, fracturing many bones.

Hair: Can be pulled out, ingested, and then will slit the windpipe like piano wire.

Dust: Probably has nicotine in it, or that SARS thing no one talks about anymore.

It Really Happened!
I Didn't Babyproof

"Acqua, my nine-month-old, doesn't seem the least bit curious about his surroundings at all, really. He's just so content to sit in one place and gaze at his Swarovski crystal mobile. He's an old soul. So when we had a little girl over for our first official playdate, I thought it wouldn't make any difference that we lived in an illegally converted gardener's shed. I mean, it's in a nice neighborhood, right? Well! It seems that this little girl Cerise is quite the adventuress, and wasted no time in shoving a stray cosmetic wedge straight into some exposed wires where we hook up the car battery to run the microwave. Luckily, no harm came of it because as we all know cosmetic wedges don't conduct electricity, but then she leaned forward to taste the wires—which, why would anyone do that? Acqua and I agreed that makes no sense—and there was the smell of burning flesh, but she was *fine*. Maybe a little startled. And a little burned. So then her mom accused me of not providing a safe environment her child could freely explore, and I was all, well, maybe you should teach your little precious to not lick exposed wires. Oh, she didn't like that! And then they left in a huff. I mean, the ambulance took off in a huff. What was with all the sirens? Like they were trying to make a *point*. Well, so much for my first mom-friend. I guess if I want to have people over, I'll have to start buying the *fancy* antifreeze with the childproof cap."

—Baby Snooks-Sholl, age 27,
East Hampton, Long Island

Soap: Looks like a delicious, Irish-Spring-flavored cake.

Water-spray bottle: Your child will become accustomed to the refreshing fun of liberally spraying her face and eyes with cool water, but then one day she'll reach for a pretty blue spray bottle filled with window cleaner and *oh no!*

Knickknacks: Your baby wants nothing more than to see if Grandma's Hummel figurine will fit into his ear canal.

Barrettes: Pop one of these open *right in the eye.*

Cats: Death on four legs.

Anything with corners: "Hello, 911? I failed to purchase only round, soft objects, and now my one-eyed baby has a dented brain."

Anything with edges: Ever have a paper cut? Like that times a million.

Anything firmer than a throw pillow: You need soft surfaces upon which a dizzy child can fling him- or herself!

Throw pillows: Soft surfaces can *and will* suffocate.

Forks: Really? We have to tell you why?

Spoons: "I think I'll gouge out my eye. Oh, here's a handy utensil just for that!" (That's your baby's inner monologue. Who can say why she thinks that way? *Your child is peculiar.*)

with similar experiences of other families in their closed utopian a capella separatist community, led them to theorize that a new, more spiritually attuned type of child was being born into this world, which they called Plaxico children. As described in the Jeffries's book, Plaxici are proud, sensitive geniuses who can go through life being completely misunderstood unless their special status is recognized and they are paid appropriate obeisance by teachers and peers.

Do *you* have a Plaxico Child? Take this simple test and find out!

1. Does your child seem bored by things that roll, bounce, or whistle?
2. Does your child raise her eyebrows when she doesn't get what she wants?
3. Does your child sigh in quiet resignation instead of napping?
4. Does your child seem irritated by your presence in his life?
5. Does your child use her Etch-a-Sketch to draw a prescription for Xanax?

If you answered Yes to any of these questions, congratulations! You may have a Plaxico. For more information about creating and raising superior beings, please see our forthcoming book, *Let's Panic About Projecting Our Neuroses Onto Our Children.*

PUBLIC EMBARRASSMENTS: WHEN YOUR CHILD ACTS OUT IN THE PRODUCE AISLE

Before you had a child of your own, you undoubtedly came across a baby or toddler having some sort of fit in public. And you thought, "Is that child disordered in some way? Surely there's no rational reason for such behavior!" You then chuckled smugly at the incompetent parents and their sad genetic legacy, and mused that if you had a child, you would *never allow* such an event to occur.

Let's fast-forward ten years to find that such an event has indeed occurred:

you have taken your adorable angel with you to run five hours' worth of crucial errands in a series of hushed, beige environments when suddenly you find that she has torn every shred of clothing from her body and is lying naked, banging her heels on the bank's terrazzo floor, possessed by some kind of shrieking evil spirit. And everyone is staring at *you*, wondering what morally impoverished hole you crawled out of and why you can't control a small, pre-verbal human being who weighs less than a dog.

And now you are shaken, cowed, and considering never leaving your hole in the ground ever again.

Before children were allowed to grocery with their elders.

That's one option, of course! You can get your various dry goods delivered and stay indoors, with a boulder blocking the entrance to your cave, so that no one finds out that your baby is a heartless fiend who cackles in delight at your public shamings. You will eventually lose the power of speech, however, and also your hygiene will slip, and pretty soon you'll be wearing bubble-wrap on your feet for shoes.

But you don't want to do that! No, despite the fact that your baby wields so much terrible power, you can still brave the outside world occasionally, armed with our Expert Tips!

1. Did you know? Babies can endure the supermarket or related shopping excursion for exactly 7.3 minutes. It is therefore imperative that you enter each store with a *plan,* not just a shopping list. *Lists are for amateurs.* Memorize the store's floor plan and know exactly what will distract your tiny tyrant in each aisle. Every store puts the bright, eye-catching impulse items at a child's eye level—the baking-needs aisle has the colorful fruit roll-ups; the paper-towel aisle includes boxes of crazy straws. Store managers purposely arrange their shelves so that there's always something to delight Baby's eyes and distract her tiny brains from the ongoing horrors—items you will, in desperation, purchase for your child to

keep her happy and quiet. *Recommended: spatula or measuring spoons. Not recommended: furniture polish,* In Touch *magazine.*

2. If you can't finish your shopping in the amount of time Baby has allotted you and she begins to act up, whisper threats. Even if she's too young to really "get" language, hissing "*I'm going to leave you behind in this cart and move to Belize with my secret lover, Arturo*" in a menacing tone might be enough to stun her for a few crucial moments while you place your order at the deli counter. Bonus: teaching her fresh styles of communication will help her brain form the facial expressions that correspond to new feelings, such as consternation and chagrin.

3. If Baby does not wince at your threats, are you in the checkout lane? Get in the checkout lane. People will stand back to let you cut in front of them if you loudly exclaim, "What's wrong, Sierra? You're not going to throw up all that applesauce, are you?"

4. If you're still deep in the produce department and your baby loses it completely, back away and pretend she's not yours. Look at other shoppers pointedly, as if you're wondering which one of them is her mother. "No wonder she's so upset, being left like that!" you might murmur to yourself as you turn your back and carefully select a bagful of button mushrooms.

5. If Baby continues to cause a commotion and people are edging ever closer to her, join the crowd, and then loudly declare: "That's it, I'm going to take this baby and make her mine. Her mother clearly doesn't know how to treat her!" With that, pick up the baby and run off.

6. If witnesses contact the authorities, who then apprehend you on your way to your car or to the nearest bus stop, surely they'll have a sense of humor, right?

7. If they don't have a sense of humor, use your last few minutes of freedom to freshen your makeup: you're going to be on TV!

HOW TO MAKE FRIENDS AT THE PLAYGROUND

Making friends with other Moms and Dads at the playground is exactly the same as it was when you were small, except that *now* if some strange guy hits you with a shovel, you don't have to stand there crying until his mother makes him apologize—you can just hit him back. Again and again. Here are some sample dialogues for you to project yourself onto. Maybe one of them will suit your incredibly specific personal situation.

SITUATION #1

At the sandbox, you come upon a Dad with his small son playing with several dump trucks.

You: We have that dump truck at home, except ours is red.
Sandbox Dad (ignoring you): *Brrrrbbbrrrrr!*
You (indicating your own child): Can we play with you guys?
Sandbox Dad (scooting over to make one-half inch of room): *Brrm.*
You: Can my son borrow one of your son's trucks to play with?
Sandbox Dad (shields his trucks from view): *Brrrrrmmmm!*
You: Say, that's a nice Rolex you're wearing.
Sandbox Dad: You can't have that, either.
You: Why are you so mean?
Sandbox Dad: I'm sorry . . . I just . . .
You fall into each other's arms and make out.

SITUATION #2

You find an open swing and install your child in the seat; a woman next to you is swinging a young child who appears to be around the same age as yours.

You: (smiling at other child and woman)

Subtext of your smile: "Hi! I'm willing to chat about babies."
Swinging Child: (grins)
Subtext of child's smile: "Wow! You're a woman! My mom's a woman, too! Women are incredible!"
You: "Hey, look at all those teeth you have!"
Subtext of your comment: Talking about a child's teeth is a way to roughly guess his or her age, leading to further conversation about babies.
Swinging Child's Mom/Aunt/Legal Guardian: (hunches slightly to look at her child's teeth, then straightens back up, says nothing)
Possible subtext of her silence:
  a. *"Yup, she's got teeth all right."*
  b. *"How DARE you look at this child's teeth! I am so furious at your presumption that I can't even speak."*
  c. *"Què?"*
You: (silent smiling, continued swing-pushing)
Subtext of your silence: "Well, fuck you, too."

SITUATION #3

You are sitting on a bench giving your child a snack when a man with an infant in a sling sits down beside you.

Man: "I'm thirty-four."
You: "I'm thirty-six."
Man (indicating your child): "How old is he?"
You: "He's one."
Man: "Make him talk."
You: "He can't talk like you yet, he's still just a baby."
Man (shouting): "Count to ten, baby!"
You: "Make *your* baby count to ten."
Man: "My baby can count to ten, but she's sleeping."

You: "I can count to ten."

Man: "Doubt it."

You: "One, two, three, four, six, seven, nine, eight, ten."

Man: "Are you a boy or a girl?"

You: "I'm a mom, shut up."

Man: "You don't look like one."

You (crying): "I AM SO."

Man (skipping away): "*You're* the baby, *baby*!"

SITUATION # 4

You spot a friendly-looking woman helping her kid out of the stroller.

You: (eyeing her kid): "Eleven months?"

Her: "Yes! Yours?"

You: "The same. Getting any sleep yet?"

Her: "Hardly."

You share a laugh.

You: "It feels weird, talking to an adult during the day."

Her (laughing): "I KNOW. I'm afraid I'm talking to you like you're a baby."

You: "I wouldn't notice if you did!"

You laugh some more.

You: "Hey, you want to get together with the kids sometime?"

Her: "I'd love that! What's your number?"

You: "555-1234."

Her: "Great! I can't wait to tell you all about the third coming of the Anti-Messiah and how the Glorious Fiery Reckoning is nearly upon us!"

She waves at you and your baby as she heads out with hers.

You: "I have made a terrible mistake."

Is this the man you were talking to?!

WARNING SIGNS THAT THE PERSON YOU'RE CHATTING WITH AT THE PLAYGROUND IS NOT A PARENT

- His eyes glaze over while you're describing the terrible struggle you and your partner had over choosing to use disposable diapers
- She never asks if you know any good hemorrhoid home remedies
- You can't get her to compare stretch marks with you
- He mimes blowing his head off with a pistol when you offer to show him baby pictures
- As you approach, he leaps over the playground fence and heads for the woods
- He's wearing a sanitation worker uniform and insists he's only there to empty the garbage cans
- She says, "I'm four! My mom is over there."

POINT/COUNTERPOINT: BREAST-FEEDING: ARE YOU STILL DOING THAT?

ALICE:

You're not still doing that, are you? Really, at this point you're just showing off. Listen, you breast-fed for a nice long time, or maybe just a few weeks, but either way, good for you! And now that your child has received that precious elixir of bonding and immunity, it's time to put The Girls back in their appropriate compartments and hand your offspring a more conventional beverage. But if for some reason you feel the need to continue flaunting your mammalian protuberances, don't expect people to look away while you hoist them into your child's face! That's a spectacle that people are helpless not to watch. They are compelled. It's probably hard-wired, like a thing from nature. I'll ask Eden to look it up later.

EDEN:

Are you still doing that? Good for you! Research has shown that you should breast-feed long past the point where society is comfortable with it, so that your child's brain will actually grow enough to fill his entire skull. Bet you didn't know that part! Not many people do. I read all the studies. Alice doesn't read studies because she says that reading gives her a little furrow between her eyebrows, and if that furrow becomes permanently etched it will mar her loveliness. Alice comports herself like a character out of Jane Austen who cares more about her appearance than about your child's IQ. So who are you going to trust, me or a woman who wears a merry widow to the mall? I mean, that doesn't even make sense, but she does it—she wants her husband to think she's some sort of ivory-skinned voluptuary.

ALICE:

When did this turn into a diatribe about my wardrobe? And for the record, I wear a simple, lightly padded bra, thank you, and only so that the world doesn't have to be awarded a free view of my nipples every time the temperature dips below fifty. *Some* people want to keep their boobs to themselves, unlike the exhibitionist types *(Eden)* who have no problem leaving their bras on the compost heap and letting everything swing thisaward and that. Sure, cite some studies. I could cite some studies too. Like how I am rubber and you are glue.

EDEN:

Despite Alice's immaturity, she *is* right about our being evolutionarily wired to

gaze at breasts. Men, especially, will follow a nice pair of boobs anywhere. I should know. Mine are spectacular.

ALICE:

Actually, I can't argue with that.

SOMEONE'S TOO BIG TO CUDDLE: CONSIDERING A SECOND CHILD

Thanks to us, you've learned everything you could ever need to know about pregnancy, childbirth, and parenting. You've honed your skills to the point that you could change a diaper while giving yourself a pedicure and whipping up a low-fat soy smoothie. And now you're thinking, "Wow, if I had *another* child, the whole experience would go so much more smoothly than it did this time around. Why, I might even be able to *enjoy* it!"

Many people, while they're basking in the rosy afterglow of being able to sleep through the night for the first time in a year or more, begin to forget just how unpleasant pregnancy was, how they screamed themselves hoarse during childbirth, and that, thanks to endless on-demand feeding, they can now tuck their breasts into the waistband of their pants.

Well, we're here to make sure you don't forget *any* of that stuff.

Look, we get it. You've had a couple of glasses of wine, you're lounging on the couch with your beloved; he's lit some candles and he's administering a foot rub; there are scented oils, and here's how your thinking is going:

Oh, I love him. Look at what a good guy he is. What a great Dad. I wonder if we should have another. Children are an expression of our eternal love, so what could be more natural than more? I bet it'll be less hard to get back into shape when I'm chasing two little kids around. Might as well do it now before I get my figure back. I may have to put my career goals on hold for a little while longer, but it's worth it, right? And sure, maybe I won't have time for reading, but that's why audio books were invented! This wine is delicious. Besides, the baby's already almost a toddler, and she or he (it's so hard to remember) needs a friend. Sure, maybe it'll get noisy around here, but we'll have twice as much joy and laughter. We'll have a big happy family and chaos can be fun plus I won't have to get up from this couch to get my diaphragm, which is so great. Who needs money? Little weekend motel trips can be just as refreshing as a big, expensive vacation.

I just scooch my bathrobe over an inch or so and hey, we can have some sex without me getting up or even moving! I'm pretty sure I can't get pregnant anyway because I only stopped breastfeeding a couple of months ago. What's one more baby, anyway?

So you go ahead and you enjoy a hazy night of drunken canoodling. Nine months later, you come to. You're all tangled in the sheets, your mouth tastes like dead squirrel, your head hurts, and in the other room there is screaming. From *two* children. Oh, and your husband had to leave early because he had a conference call.

Look. We like kids fine. We had them, right? And they still live with us, for the most part. But here's the thing: when you get more than one, they start to work together. They connive. And eventually they will, some day, destroy you. It may be when you're ninety and you're in an assisted-living facility, but either way, they will outmaneuver you until you're lying in a hospital bed and they're crying but you know it's tears of joy because they've finally won.

Your friends are going to tell you that having

a second child isn't that much extra work. That's because they've already had their second, and they have lost their minds. So what do they do? They turn around and *lie* to you about how *you* should have another. This is so you can join in their misery. Inside they're screaming, "Join us. We like you, but if you have it easier than us, we'll be forced to hate you. Don't make us hate you."

BIG FAT GODDAMN LIES YOUR FRIENDS WILL TELL YOU

"A second kid isn't twice as hard. That's a myth! It's maybe, I don't know, one-fifth harder. Or, no, 37 percent less un-difficult."
TRUE OR FALSE? False! A second kid is 2,011 times harder, plus 7, times infinity.

"It's magical this time around. Now I can barely look at that other kid I had, what's-her-name."
TRUE OR FALSE? False again. Their new child has ridiculous ears. They know this as well as you. *But they can't face it.*

"Your older kid is like your little helper! And someday she can *babysit*."
TRUE OR FALSE? SO false. Your friends are liars. Your older child will so resent this new infant that she'll make your life extrahard, just to teach you a lesson. By the time she's old enough to babysit, she'll have moved out, to become something awful that we'll figure out in a minute.*

"It's so sweet to see them playing together!"
TRUE OR FALSE? *Maybe* this is true. How should we know? Shut up.

---

*A JUNKIE CLOWN! That's what your older child will be! She'll be living on the Lower East Side of Manhattan, working at some sort of burlesque show, dressed as a clown from the 1930s. She will try to explain to you what "camp" means, as if you don't know. Then she'll stop calling because you just don't seem to get her. All because your new baby deprived her of your small reserves of love!

It Really Happened! I Had a Second Child

"I was surprised to find out that I was pregnant with my second child, Orris, being that I was still nursing my firstborn and I didn't recall having any sexual dealings. Then again, things had been pretty hazy, due to my NyQuil addiction. Anyhoo! I thought it was no problem because we're easygoing folks, and our first baby, Norman Fell—Fell's a family name—he was calm as can be. But then we had Orris and it's pretty much been a nonstop poopstorm of screaming and puking ever since and there's so much noise and I miss having even a millisecond of peace. On the bright side I seem to need less NyQuil than ever! So we're saving a bunch of money."

—Adrien Brody, age 37, Hollywood, California

"I had my son five years ago, and then we decided to have another and we ended up with twins! So that was . . . excuse me—EVAN? EVAN, NO. DO NOT. STOP THAT. THANK YOU—I'm sorry, what were we saying? Right, kids. So we ended up at three, which we didn't expect, but you know—HOLLY, GET OFF LILLIAN. NO, GET OFF. USE YOUR WORDS IF YOU DON'T WANT THAT—I mean, no one expects parenting to be easy, right? It's not like—EVAN I SWEAR TO CHRIST IF YOU CAN'T CONTROL YOURSELF—it's not like I expected a constant, you know, coffee commercial, or tampon commercial, or God, I don't know, what commercials have big happy families in them? I can't think, there's too much— EVAN! I SHALL RAIN HOLY TERROR DOWN ON YOU THE LIKES OF WHICH YOU HAVE NEVER SEEN IF YOU DON'T STOP, OKAY, THANK YOU—but it's nice, when they're sleeping, which they're starting to do through the night, so I occasionally get some rest—JIHAD, HOLLY, DO YOU KNOW WHAT THAT IS? EVAN, HELP HER LOOK IT UP, AND THEN QUAKE IN FEAR AT MY WRATH WHICH WILL BE SO AWESOME AND I DO NOT MEAN THAT IN A GOOD WAY—and I'm sure everything will end up fine eventually, right?"

—Barbara Jones-Walstaff, age 35, Gainesville, Florida

FACTS ABOUT FAMILIES THAT GET OVERLY LARGE

- Subsequent children are 93 percent more likely to be accidentally bricked into a wall.
- In 1800, the typical American mother had seven children. *All of these mothers, as well as their children, are now dead.*
- In the 1992 Lifetime movie, *Mother, May I Observe That There Are Twelve of Us?* Deanna, a headstrong young woman (Tori Spelling) pleads with her mother Alyssa (Morgan Fairchild) to stop having children with her mother's new husband Dick (Tom Skerritt). It turns out that Dick is head of a black-market baby ring and is hiding all the kids he's selling among Morgan's babies. It gets pretty complicated. The bottom line is: do not have babies with Tom Skerrit.

A FINAL NOTE

We realize that most people think there's something noble and/or good about larger families, and will continue to create offspring until their uteruses drop to the curb. Which means you'll probably have another child—and maybe another *after that*—no matter what we say. So be it. If you do ignore our advice, you should immediately purchase a second copy of our book. This one has no doubt become hopelessly tattered and tear-stained.

ACKNOWLEDGMENTS

The authors would like to thank, first and foremost, our agent, Karen Gerwin at DeFiore and Co., and our editor, Alyse Diamond at St. Martin's Press, for their unflagging enthusiasm, sage advice, abiding faith, and stoicism in the face of our most boneheaded jokes.

We owe a great deal to Oslo Davis for his inspired illustrations. We were incredibly fortunate to find an artist whose sense of humor is as odd as ours. Thank you, Oslo.

We also thank our friends and family for their moral and practical support throughout the book-writing process. Special thanks go to Sarah Brown, for her friendship, advice, and editorial comments; to Liz Buffa, for (among other things) urging us to continue pitching *Let's Panic About Babies!* when we considered abandoning it; to Antonia Cornwell for creating so much sublime birth art only a month after giving birth; to Susan Kennedy, for trusting us with her apartment as we approached our deadline; to Sarah Way, for being a willing model and contributing a fantastic attractivator illustration; to Deanna Zandt, for her brilliant design of the *Let's Panic About Babies!* Web site; to Leah Peterson, for her kindness and faith; and last but not least, to all our blog readers and Internet friends.

This book would never have come to be if we hadn't foolishly become parents. And *that* would never have happened without the "help" (euphemism!) of Jack Kennedy and Scott Rosann, to whom we owe more than we can list on this page. Thank you for enduring our deadline-induced meltdowns and edit-induced attacks of insecurity, suggesting some of the funniest jokes in this book, and keeping the children clothed, fed, and happy while we churned out pages. We truly could not have done this without you.

Finally: for patiently enduring our clumsy parenting efforts, we sincerely thank Jackson Kennedy and Henry Rosann, two of the greatest boys any mom could ask for.

CREDITS

Chapter 1

Page 4, illustration copyright © Oslo Davis.

Page 5, "Not pregnant" photo of Sarah Way by Alice Bradley.

Page 6, briefs illustration courtesy Tack-o-Rama, http://tackorama.net.

Page 9, cat photograph, http://commons.wikimedia.org/wiki/File:Cat_hygiene.jpg courtesy of Dan Phiffer, licensed under the Creative Commons Attribution 2.0 Generic license.

Page 10, "Birthing hut": http://commons.wikimedia.org/wiki/File:Maleku-hut.JPG courtesy of Steven G. Johnson, licensed under the Creative commons Attribution-ShareAlike 3.0 Unported license.

Page 12, "Satyr": de Quade van Ravesteyn, Dirk. *Venus Riding a Satyr*. 1602. Musées Royaux des Beaux-Arts, Brussels. This work is in the public domain.

Page 13, "Here's your baby!": courtesy of Yolan Chériaux, http://commons.wikimedia.org/wiki/File:Hippocampe_sec_Bretagne.jpg, licensed under the Creative Commons Attribution 2.5 Generic license.

Chapter 2

Page 15, illustration copyright © Oslo Davis.

Page 16, "Let's Do Math," courtesy Library of Congress Prints and Photographs Division, http://www.loc.gov/pictures/item/hec2009015711/. This work is in the public domain.

Page 17, "Energy Activity Graph" illustration copyright © Eden M. Kennedy.

Page 19, "Nausea flowchart" illustration copyright © Eden M. Kennedy.

Page 20, barfing illustration copyright © Oslo Davis.

Page 22, "Goblins": Warren, Johnson and Co. *Devils and Floating Girl*. 1870. Courtesy Library of Congress Prints and Photographs Division. This work is in the public domain.

Pages 25 & 84, doctor illustration courtesy Tack-o-Rama, http://tackorama.net.

Page 28, "Here's your baby!": Juan Cabana, *Stranded!*, 2006, www.thefeejeemermaid.com/. Used by kind permission of the artist.

Chapter 3

Page 29, illustration copyright © Oslo Davis.

Page 30, "Attractivators" illustration copyright © Sarah Way.

Page 31, "Changing body": Dr. C. H. Stratz, *Die Körperpflege der Frau*. 1907. http://commons.wikimedia.org/wiki/File:Stand_desGabarmuttergrundes_in_den_spateren-Monaten_derSchwangerschaft.gif. This

work is in the public domain.

Page 32, "How to dress": *Muff in hand. Alice Maison*. Courtesy Library of Congress Prints and Photographs Division. This work is in the public domain.

Page 34, "Manatee": photo courtesy "Ahodges7," http://commons.wikimedia.org/wiki/File:Manatee_at_Sea_World_Orlando_Mar_10.JPG, licensed under the Creative Commons Attribution-Share Alike 3.0 Unported license.

Page 37, "Pregnant lady": Guercino, *The Assumption of the Virgin*. 1655. This work is in the public domain.

Page 39, "Nude man": courtesy Alessandro Vernet, http://www.flickr.com/photos/avernet/14268519/, licensed under the Creative Commons Attribution 2.0 Generic license.

Page 42, "Bearded Baby": courtesy Hgrobe, http://commons.wikipedia.org/wiki/File:Boy_1900_hg.jpg, with beard added. This image is in the public domain.

Page 43, "Old mom": Author unknown, http://commons.wikipedia.org/wiki/File:Grandma_1890_hg.jpg. This work is in the public domain.

Page 44, "Here's your baby!": photo courtesy Ramon Campos, http://commons.wikimedia.org/wiki/File:Philander_sp.JPG, licensed under a GNU Free Documentation License, Version 1.2.

Chapter 4

Page 45, illustration copyright © Oslo Davis.

Page 46, ultrasound image: photo courtesy Sam Pullara, http://commons.wikimedia.org/wiki/File:Baby_in_ultrasound.jpg, licensed under the Creative Commons Attribution 2.0 Generic license.

Page 49, "Prenatal tests": 19th-century French illustration, author unknown. This work is in the public domain.

Page 52, "Derinkuyu Underground City": photo courtesy Bjørn Christian Tørrisson, http://commons.wikimedia.org/wiki/File:Derinkuyu_Underground_City.JPG, licensed under the Creative Commons Attribution-Share Alike 3.0 Unported license.

Page 53, "Here's your baby!": photo courtesy "Tabdulla," http://commons.wikimedia.org/wiki/File:Kera_hantu_Sarawak.jpg, licensed under the GNU Free Documentation License, Version 1.2.

Chapter 5

Page 55, illustration copyright © Oslo Davis.

Page 56, "Fairies" copyright © Oslo Davis.

Page 58, "Breaking the news": U.S. Navy photo of the *Hindenberg* courtesy Gus Pasquarella. This work is in the public domain.

Page 60, "Small appliances": photo courtesy

"Tumi-1983." This work is in the public domain.

Page 63, "Bedrest": untitled photo by Fritz W. Guerin. Courtesy Library of Congress Prints and Photographs Division. This work is in the public domain.

Page 66, "Here's your baby!": photo courtesy "Cliff," http://commons.wikimedia.org/wiki/File:Pink_Fairy_Armadillo_%28Chlamyphorus_truncatus%29.jpg, licensed under the Creative Commons Attribution 2.0 Generic license.

Chapter 6

Page 67, illustration copyright © Oslo Davis.

Page 68, "What baby's getting": image taken from *The New Student's Reference Work*, Chicago, 1914. This work is in the public domain.

Page 72, "You can't eat this": photo courtesy Ibrahimjon, http://commons.wikimedia.org/wiki/File:Tajik_dastarkhan_meal.jpg, licensed under the GNU Free Documentation License, Version 1.

Page 74, teakettles illustration courtesy Tack-o-Rama, http://tackorama.net.

Page 76, "Baby-safe alternatives": photo of Sarah Way by Alice Bradley.

Page 78, "Here's your baby!": photo courtesy of Mila Zinkova, http://commons.wikimedia.org/wiki/File:Arothron_hispidus_is_kissing_my_camera_at_Big_Island_of_Hawaii.jpg, licensed under the Creative Commons Attribution-Share Alike 3.0 Unported license.

Chapter 7

Page 79, illustration copyright © Oslo Davis.

Page 80, "Look funnier": illustration by Ambrose Paré, *Anomalies and Curiosities of Medicine*, 1900. This work is in the public domain.

Page 83, illustration courtesy Tack-o-Rama, http://tackorama.net.

Page 86, "Breakdancer": photo courtesy "NexusMoves," http://commons.wikimedia.org/wiki/File:Nexus-airbaby.JPG, licensed under the Creative Commons Attribution-Share Alike 3.0 Unported license.

Page 87, "Shoulder" from *Gray's Anatomy of the Human Body*, originally published 1918. This work is in the public domain.

Page 90, lemons illustration courtesy Tack-o-Rama, http://tackorama.net.

Page 92, labor methods illustration courtesy Tack-o-Rama, http://tackorama.net.

Page 94, birth plan illustration copyright © Eden M. Kennedy.

Page 95, "Here's your baby!": photo courtesy of Max Smith. This work is in the public domain.

Chapter 8

Page 97, illustration copyright © Oslo Davis.

Page 99, party girl illustration courtesy Tack-o-Rama, http://tackorama.net.

Page 101, "Last-minute preparations": original photo by "Maschinenjunge," http://commons.wikimedia.org/wiki/File:Messi_Wohnraum.jpg, licensed under the GNU Free Documentation License, Version 1.2. Cats added from "Cat Hygiene," http://commons.wikimedia.org/wiki/File:Cat_hygiene.jpg, courtesy of Dan Phiffer, licensed under the Creative Commons Attribution 2.0 Generic license.

Page 102, "Scouts": photo courtesy of Harris & Ewing collection, Library of Congress. This work is in the public domain.

Page 104, bus guy illustration courtesy Tack-o-Rama, http://tackorama.net.

Page 105, country car illustration courtesy Tack-o-Rama, http://tackorama.net.

Page 106, crushing fear illustration courtesy Tack-o-Rama, http://tackorama.net.

Page 107, "Scary clown": photo courtesy "Micky," http://commons.wikimedia.org/wiki/File:Colorful_Clown.JPG, licensed under the Creative Commons Attribution 2.0 Generic license.

Page 109, "Penguin": illustration courtesy of Rsperberg, http://commons.wikimedia.org/wiki/File:Single_Emperor_penguin.jpg, licensed under the Creative Commons Attribution-Share Alike 3.0 Unported license.

Page 109, "Platypus": Lewin, J.W. *Platypus*. 1808. This work is in the public domain.

Page 109, "Dragon": Uccello, Paolo. *Saint George and the Dragon*. 1470. National Gallery, London, UK. This work is in the public domain.

Page 110, "Birth art with Santa": copyright © Antonia Cornwell.

Page 110, "Birth art with top hat": copyright © Antonia Cornwell.

Page 111, "Birth art with cell phones": copyright © Antonia Cornwell.

Page 111, "Birth art with flowers": copyright © Antonia Cornwell.

Page 111, "Kitten tsunami": copyright © Antonia Cornwell

Page 112, "Here's your baby!" photo courtesy Michaël Catanzariti.

Chapter 9

Page 113, illustration copyright © Oslo Davis.

Page 115, "Restless Legs": Thivier, Eugène. *Le Cauchemar*. Museé des Augustins, Toulouse, France. This work is in the public domain.

Page 119, "Birthing tub": photo, *Claire Anderson in Tub*. Photographer unknown. This work is in the public domain.

Page 120, "Richard Wagner," photo by Franz Hanfstaengl. This work is in the public domain.

Page 122, Dalai Lama photo courtesy of Joan Halifax and Tenzin Gyatso, licensed under the Creative Commons Attribution 2.0 Generic License.

Page 125, "Staying sane": photo courtesy of "Newland 2," Guinness World Record Knitting Needles. This work is in the public domain.

Page 126, girl illustration courtesy Tack-o-Rama, http://tackorama.net.

Page 128, "Dante": Doré, Gustav. *Dante's Inferno. Plate XXII: Canto VII: The hoarders and wasters*. 1857. This work is in the public domain.

Page 134, "Here's your baby!": photo by Frank Wouters, http://commons.wikimedia.org/wiki/File:Baby_hippo_swims.jpg, licensed under the Creative Commons Attribution 2.0 Generic license.

Chapter 10

Page 137, illustration copyright © Oslo Davis.

Page 140, "In-laws": photo by Nikolay Svishchev-Paola, *Portrait of an Old Couple*. 1900s. This work is in the public domain.

Page 145, "Your new body": illustration in *Die Körperpflege der Frau*, Dr. C. H. Stratz. 1907. This work is in the public domain.

Page 148, "Nursing: The Right Way;" "Nursing: The Wrong Way;" "Nursing: The Wrongest Way": copyright © Oslo Davis.

Page 150, baby book illustration copyright © Oslo Davis.

Chapter 11

Page 151, illustration copyright © Oslo Davis.

Page 152, "What is this thing?": photo of baby courtesy "Tarotastic," http://commons.wikimedia.org/wiki/File:Baby_2.jpg, licensed under the Creative Commons Attribution 2.0 Generic license.

Page 153, horseshoe crab courtesy Pearson Scott Foresman. This work is in the public domain.

Page 156, "Your Baby's Cries": photo courtesy of Deutsche Fotothek, licensed under the Creative Commons Attribution-Share Alike 3.0 Germany license.

Page 157, "Swaddling 1" and "Swaddling 2": illustration copyright © Oslo Davis.

Page 158, "Swaddling 3": illustration copyright © Oslo Davis.

Page 161, Rorschach blot courtesy of Bryan Derksen. This work is in the public domain.

Page 162, "Bathing": photo by Harry Whittier Frees. *Barker Gives Blink His Bath*, 1914, from the book, *The Little Folks of Animal Land*. This work is in the public domain.

Page 163, "Dr. Huggs": photo courtesy Gregg O'Connell, http://commons.wikimedia.org/wiki/File:Waving_Panda.jpg, licensed under the Creative Commons Attribution 2.0 Generic license.

Page 164, "Dr. Needles": scan of Lon Chaney, *Phantom of the Opera*, 1925. This work is in the public domain.

Page 167, moon illustration courtesy Tack-o-Rama, http://tackorama.net.

Page 171, "Colic": Putnam Griswold as Mephisto, from *Musical America, Vol. 14 No. 3*. 1911. This work is in the public domain.

Chapter 12

Page 173, illustration copyright © Oslo Davis.

Page 174, "Fun baby": photo by Alice Bradley.

Page 175, dancing couple illustration courtesy Tack-o-Rama, http://tackorama.net.

Page 176, "It Really Happened!": self-portrait of Mór Jókai, 1908. This work is in the public domain.

Page 178, "Creepy baby": photo by Eden M. Kennedy.

Page 180, "Young Mom": illustration courtesy of "Niabot, because wikimedia commons lost his roots," licensed under the Creative Commons Attribution 3.0 Unported license.

Page 181, "Voodoo": courtesy © Oslo Davis.

Page 184, "Phrenology": from *People's Cyclopedia of Universal Knowledge* (1883). This work is in the public domain.

Page, 185, "Phrenology Venn Diagram": illustration copyright © Eden M. Kennedy.

Page 187, "Slings": illustration from *Brockhaus and Efron, Encyclopedic Dictionary* (1890-1907). This work is in the public domain.

Chapter 13

Page 189, illustration copyright © Oslo Davis.

Page 191, "Brain in a jar": illustration copyright © Oslo Davis.

Page 193, "Affection time": *Louis XIV et la Dame Longuet de La Giraudière by Charles Beaubrun*, 1640, Musée National du Château et des Trianons. This work is in the public domain.

Page 194, cute baby illustration courtesy Tack-o-Rama, http://tackorama.net.

Page 199, enriching environment illustration courtesy Tack-o-Rama, http://tackorama.net.

Page 203, "Albert Einstein": photo by Oren Jack Turner, 1947, courtesy of the Library of Congress Prints and Photographs Division. This work is in the public domain.

Page 204, "William Howard Taft": photo courtesy of Library of Congress Prints and Photographs Division. This work is in the public domain.

Chapter 14

Page 205, illustration copyright © Oslo Davis.

Page 206, "People who show up": photo of Queen Victoria, 1887. This work is in the public domain.

Page 210, "Cult?": photo of First Ladies courtesy of the U.S. Department of Defense, 1991. This work is in the public domain.

Page 213, cute girl illustration courtesy Tack-o-Rama, http://tackorama.net.

Page 214, cute boy illustration courtesy Tack-o-Rama, http://tackorama.net.

Page 216, shopping cart illustration copyright © Oslo Davis.

Page 218, cat fitness DVD illustration copyright © Scott Rosann.

Chapter 15

Page 219, illustration copyright © Oslo Davis.

Page 220, "Return to work?": undated NASA photo of Amelia Earhart from the Smithsonian Institute. This work is in the public domain.

Page 223, "Daycare": photo by Lewis W. Hine, 1915. *Sugar beet workers, Sugar City, Colorado. "Mary, six years, Lucy, eight, Ethel, ten. Family has been here ten years. Children go to school in the winter."* Courtesy Library of Congress Prints and Photographs Division. This work is in the public domain.

Page 225, "Flight attendant": photo courtesy John Atherton, http://commons.wikimedia.org/wiki/File:Pan_Am_1970s_flight_attendant.jpg, licensed under the Creative Commons Attribution-Share Alike 2.0 Generic license.

Page 231, "Coworkers": photo courtesy Jean-Michel Arnold, http://commons.wikimedia.org/wiki/File:Jean-Michel_Arnold_06.jpg, licensed under the Creative Commons Attribution-Share Alike 3.0 Unported license.

Chapter 16

Page 233, illustration copyright © Oslo Davis.

Page 235, "Dealing with your lady": photo by Alma-Tadema, Lawrence. *The Proposal*, 1892. This work is in the public domain.

Page 238, "Old dad": British Crimean War veteran, photo courtesy Archives de la photographie, 1840-1940, licensed under the terms of the GNU Free Documentation License, Version 1.2.

Page 240, sex shop illustration copyright © Oslo Davis.

Page 243, "Recipes": photo courtesy "MPegMan," http://commons.wikimedia.org/wiki/File:Pbnjmpegman.jpg, licensed under the terms of the GNU Free Documentation License, Version 1.2.

Pages 245-246, family alphabet illustrations courtesy Tack-o-Rama, http://tackorama.net.

Chapter 17

Page 247, illustration copyright © Oslo Davis.

Page 251, "Grocery": photo courtesy Janice Waltzer, http://commons.wikimedia.org/wiki/File:Old_grocery_store_%2871657371%29.jpg, licensed under the Creative Commons Attribution 2.0 Generic license.

Page 255, playground illustration courtesy Tack-o-Rama, http://tackorama.net.

Page 256, "Not a parent": photo courtesy of "Ezpz01," http://commons.wikimedia.org/wiki/File:Bigfoot.jpg. This work is in the public domain.

Page 258, *Liberty Leading the People*, by Eugene Delacroix, Louvre Museum, Paris. This work is in the public domain.

Page 259, "Nursing": photo courtesy BArchBot, http://commons.wikimedia.org/wiki/File:Bundesarchiv_Bild_102-09683,_Berlin,_Krankenhaus_f%C3%BCr_S%C3%A4uglingspflege.jpg, licensed under the Creative Commons Attribution-Share Alike 3.0 Germany license.

Page 261, "Having second child": photo from the German Federal Archive, http://commons.wikimedia.org/wiki/File:Bundesarchiv_Bild_102-09683,_Berlin,_Krankenhaus_f%C3%BCr_S%C3%A4uglingspflege.jpg, licensed under the Creative Commons Attribution-Share Alike 3.0 Germany license.

Recurring Images:

"It Really Happened!" image (which recurs in several chapters) adapted from *Health and Beauty: or, Woman and Her Clothing Considered in Relation to the Physiological Laws of the Human Body*. This work is in the public domain.

Pages 50, 88, 121, 143, 165, 168, 202, 215, 256, and 257, point/counterpoint illustration courtesy Tack-o-Rama, http://tackorama.net.

Pages 70, 100, and 117, calling man illustration courtesy Tack-o-Rama, http://tackorama.net.

ABOUT THE AUTHORS

ALICE BRADLEY writes the award-winning blog Finslippy (www.finslippy.com). Her work has been featured in numerous anthologies, magazines, and Web sites, including *The Best Creative Nonfiction, Vol. 2; Redbook; Good Housekeeping; Parents; Nerve; The Sun; The Onion News Network;* and *Fence.* She has an M.F.A. in writing from the New School University and was nominated for a Pushcart Prize in nonfiction in 2009. Alice lives in Brooklyn, NY, with her husband, son, dog, and cat.

EDEN M. KENNEDY is the author of the Web site Fussy.org, which has been featured in *The San Francisco Chronicle* and *The New York Times* and celebrated as one of the top ten parenting blogs by *The Wall Street Journal.* Eden has written for PBS's *Remotely Connected* blog and Babble.com, and her work has appeared in several anthologies. A former bookseller and magazine editor, she lives with her family in Southern California.

For my daughters,

Elana Joy and Mira Justine

ACKNOWLEDGEMENTS

Solo practice and writing can be solitary ventures, and I'm fortunate for good company and constant support along the way. My husband, Bruce Israel, is a true partner in my life and practice, and I thank him for never doubting that my book or firm would succeed. I thank my many friends and colleagues from Solosez, the blogosphere, and my social media communities for the conversations that contributed to many of the ideas and tips that appear in this book...and for the camaraderie that makes the writing process all the more enjoyable. And my deepest thanks to my daughters for giving me a reason to write, and for something to look forward to when I step away from the computer.

I may have authored a book, but I'm a practicing attorney first...a solo by choice. And each day, I am privileged to work alongside thousands of other solo and small firm lawyers who improve our legal system by helping clients—from ordinary individuals to behemoth corporations and government entities—to solve problems or to find justice, and who do so zealously, professionally and with pride.—CE

CONTENTS

Back when you were in law school, you had dreams. Maybe it was standing before a jury, passionately arguing on behalf of a desperate client...or winning an appeal that would link your name to a new legal precedent...or pulling off a dramatic 11th hour deal that would give your struggling technology client a life-saving infusion of capital.

But what happened? Here it is two, five, eight years out of law school—maybe more, maybe less—and most of those dreams are unrealized:

- You work 60-hour weeks in BigLaw, researching narrow legal issues for clients you never met, toting a partner's briefcase to court and watching him argue a motion you drafted nights and weekends (and which you know you could argue better given the opportunity), or you're working for a firm and finally starting to generate some business, but the partners won't give you your fair share.
- Or, you're a government prosecutor or Justice Department attorney whose litigation experience is the envy of your large-firm colleagues, but where the work no longer challenges you and you can't move up without political connections. Or you want to move to the private sector, but your limited tenure won't bring sufficient value to the firm.
- Or, you never found a job after graduation, or your firm downsized you and you're temping at document review jobs that barely pay the bills. Or, you're a law firm partner who has been unceremoniously shown the door because younger colleagues can't wait to nab your clients.
- Or, you enjoy your work but you're plagued with guilt about leaving your children with a nanny five days a week.
- Or, you just passed the bar, and the prospect of paying off your student loans by slaving away for the next seven, eight years without any real chance of making partner, or working as a Biglaw staff attorney is keeping you up at night.

Of course, your own situation might not be all this grim, but you're still haunted by the thought that somehow, somewhere, some way, there is greater satisfaction practicing law. Believe me, there is. This book is dedicated to every lawyer who ever wanted to run the show but worried that going solo was career suicide...to every lawyer who wanted to solo but didn't know how to set up the office and make it work...to every lawyer who never set foot in a courtroom or a boardroom but dreamed of one day practicing law their way...and to every lawyer captivated by the promise of technology to enable better, cheaper ways of serving clients and expanding access to justice but was stymied by naysayers. In short, this book is dedicated to becoming the lawyer you always wanted to be.

Of course, solo practice has always been a tough sell. But it isn't the dead-end that some lawyers make it out to be; just the opposite! More and more lawyers—from new grads to senior lawyers colliding with mandatory age policies—are giving the most serious consideration to opening their own shop because of the changing legal environment...

- Institutional clients are thinking twice about retaining large firms because of the explosive growth of large law firms and the increase in fees.
- BigLaw mergers favoring larger, more lucrative clients are sending smaller clients into the arms of solo or small firms.
- Technology has made it cheaper than ever to start a law firm and to build a marketing platform
- Economic forces are decimating large firms, sending entry-level associate jobs to India and leaving few meaningful opportunities for young lawyers...and this time, the changes aren't temporary; few of the 14,000+ legal jobs eliminated between 2008 and 2010 are ever coming back.
- The diversity requirements of corporate clients are creating new opportunities for women and minority-owned firms.
- And in an increasingly entrepreneurial era, solo practices are now more often seen as start-ups with a potential of enormous success.

Maybe the practice of law hasn't turned out for you the way you dreamed.

You can stay put and, like so many lawyers, rationalize that no job is perfect and that financial security trumps youthful aspirations. Or, if you have already been fired from one firm and can't find work—or you haven't been able to find a law firm job after graduating—you could leave the law altogether, always wondering whether you might have become the lawyer you envisioned as a first-year law student.

Or you could take a third path. Realize that no matter what career stage you're at, that it's not too late to follow your heart. Two centuries ago, Thoreau wrote, *"Go confidently in the direction of your dreams. Live the life you imagined."* Maybe starting a solo law practice is the path you were intended to take all along.

—Carolyn Elefant, August/2011

I. THE DECISION

CHAPTER 1. **The Case for Solo Practice**

CHAPTER 2. **The Big Decision**

CHAPTER 3. **Should New Lawyers Solo?**

The Case for Solo Practice

"Everyone told me that the first year, even the first
two, would be slow. And they were right. But now six
months after going solo, my phone rings constantly,
I get a more steady stream of higher quality referrals,
I have interesting work, and I enjoy what I'm doing."

—Sergio Benavides, solo

Whether it's derogatory comments by large-firm lawyers, or the legal media's spot-
light on the ethical foibles of a few solos, our profession is regularly bombarded with
negatives about solo practice. Even in a depressed economy where graduates' options
are limited, soloing ranks *below* document review or working in law-related positions
(in publishing, finance or insurance) where a JD is helpful but not required. Rarely, do
you hear why you might actually want to start your own law firm. In fact, solo practice
remains one of the best-kept secrets of the legal profession because no one bothers to
make a strong case in its defense. Until now. In this chapter you'll find seven powerful
arguments for starting your own firm:

Argument #1: Autonomy

When I ask solos to identify the strongest reasons for starting their own practice, the
one at the top of nearly everyone's list is...*autonomy*. It doesn't surprise me. In contrast to other professions, a law practice, by its very nature, demands deference: as
lawyers, we serve clients, we're bound by precedent, we're constricted by a code of
professional ethics. So, when you add such factors as the bureaucracy of a law firm or
government practice...and firm hierarchy and the rigidity of a partnership track...
and the ego-driven tendency of many lawyers to want to do things "my way," it's only
natural that some lawyers crave the freedom that comes with solo'ing:

Freedom to choose cases. Above all, starting a practice liberates lawyers from the
overbearing bureaucracy of practicing law in any kind of a large entity, be it a big firm,
inside a corporation, or at a government agency. Within these organizations, most
lawyers have no control over the cases they're assigned, and usually the younger or
less-favored attorneys wind up either with the duds or more mundane tasks within
a matter. Associates don't get much relief even when they take the initiative to drum
up their own clients. Even when an associate gets a nibble from a potential client, he
or she still needs to discuss the prospect with a supervisor or write up a proposal to a
committee to justify taking on the client. And many times, firms turn away the types of
clients that younger associates attract, either because the clients can't afford the firm

fees, or they create a conflict with the firm's larger, institutional clients.

By contrast, solos don't have this problem.

Solos can pick exactly the types of cases they want to handle, and develop their very own strategy to handle them. And at the end of the day, even though lawyers with their own practice may need to consult with their partners, or decide to seek guidance from a more experienced lawyer in making decisions about the merits of a case or pursuing a particular strategy, the decision to accept a case is theirs alone.

Not only does autonomy eliminate frustration and sense of powerlessness, it also gives solos an edge over their large-firm counterparts. Solos run their own ship, and they're the best situated to act quickly when a novel or new matter crosses their path. And because most successful solos have a propensity for risk, they're also not scared off by the prospect of taking a case that involves an area of law with which they have little or no experience. Contrast the solo mentality to that of a large firm, where a new client matter involving a unique or complicated legal question of first impression would require an endless litany of conflict tests, committee meetings, and preliminary (but still exhaustive) associate research before the firm would make a decision on whether to accept the case. By that time, the client would probably have sought other counsel.

In just one example, small-firm lawyer Tom Goldstein, who specializes in Supreme Court litigation, beat out several other large firms to snag a compelling death penalty matter. Why? Goldstein was able to decide to accept the case after consulting with his law partner, who happened to be his wife. In fact, Goldstein was already on a plane to Tennessee to meet the client while the large firms were still deliberating over whether to accept the matter. (Note: Goldstein eventually moved to a large firm, where he served as partner, but as of 2011 is back at his own firm with his wife).

Lawyers in solo practice can also structure a firm that's conducive to the types of cases want to take on. For example, one lawyer I know started his own firm after he grew tired of his BigLaw employer turning down potentially precedent-setting appellate matters that he brought to the practice because the prospective clients couldn't afford the firm's hourly rates. As a solo, the lawyer opened an office in a suburban location closer to his home, and invested in the right combination of hardware and software that he could manage most administrative tasks without a full-time assistant. As a result, he was able to take on cases that his former firm declined as unprofitable. Even more satisfying, he's earning more money than he ever did at the firm.

There's also the experience of North Carolina solo Stephanie Kimbro, who started one of the first virtual law practices, i.e., an entirely Internet-based law firm. As a young associate, Kimbro noticed that her firm frequently turned away small transactional matters because they weren't cost-effective. So after her daughter was born, Kimbro and her husband created an online system that enabled Kimbro to work with clients exclusively online and streamline the workflow with forms. The increased efficiencies allowed Kimbro to economically serve the smaller clients that her former firm once turned away (see *Stephanie Kimbro's Virtual Practice*, Lawyers USA, Nov. 5, 2007).

Freedom in handling cases. These days, most large organizations don't exactly encourage recommendations on case strategy from associates. In fact, conventional wisdom advises associates to *refrain* from offering suggestions about potential case theories since the partners have likely already considered them anyway. And in a tight economy, where associates fear for their jobs, there's more incentive than ever to avoid rocking the boat.

Freedom from office politics. In many ways, working for others resembles a giant rite of passage. To get ahead, you've got to feign enthusiasm over sleep-inducing research projects or contribute money to a partner's favored charity. As Stephen Harper, a former BigLaw partner writes: "...*Those at the top wield power that makes or breaks young careers, and everybody knows it. Doing a superior job is important, but working for the 'right' people is outcome determinative.*" Solo practice liberates you from just this sort of foolish, often degrading, demonstration of hierarchy and power, leaving you free to actually practice law not inter-office politics.

Freedom over small matters. While most solos revel in their autonomy over substantive matters, sometimes it's just the freedom to make decisions about the smallest, most trivial things that makes the biggest difference. When I started my own practice, I made a point of choosing office supplies distinct from the standard issue at my former law firm—such as choosing Post-Its in bright pink instead of corporate yellow; expensive pens not cheap ball-points; business cards with blue print-on-cream rather than black-on-white. Not necessarily because I preferred them...but because I could.

Argument #2. Practical Experience

With corporate clients barring entry-level associates from handling their matters, and partners hoarding work, law firms no longer provide many opportunities for new associates to gain hands-on experience. When you establish your own law firm, it's you who gets the experience. For example, if you bring a business client with you from your former firm, you—and not the partner—will negotiate and draft the company's next contract. If it's an appellate matter, it's you who writes the brief and argues the case. And when the client calls for advice—on anything from a pressing strategic decision to how to dress for a deposition—it's your advice he or she wants because there's no one else. Solo practice also gives you opportunities to gain practical experience in new fields. *Author note*: When I started my firm, I'd been out of law school for five years and had never set foot in a courtroom except to observe. However, my practice specialty—energy regulatory work—didn't give me opportunity for trial work since most regulatory disputes are resolved on the papers or perhaps at an administrative hearing. So, to get the court time I craved, I signed up for court-appointed criminal cases. Within six months, I had a bench trial and argued a couple of motions, and within a year had my first jury trial. I never would have had those opportunities if I remained at a law firm, especially in my practice area.

Argument #3. To Feel Like a Lawyer

Back in the 19th Century, Karl Marx decried the Industrial Revolution for alienating workers from the product of their labor. He argued that where once craftsmen built a product from start to finish, the assembly line had atomized the process for the sake of efficiency, robbing the working class of the satisfaction of their craft. Sound familiar? In some ways, modern American law firms resemble the assembly lines Marx so vigorously condemned. At large firms, lawyers—primarily associates—work only on portions of a case, often never speaking with a client or even being privy to the entire matter. In fact, many lawyers today feel like paper-pushers, sleep-walking through their jobs rather than being vibrant professionals with the ability to solve problems and make a difference in people's lives.

On the other hand, solo practice makes you feel like a real lawyer, the kind of lawyer you imagined you would be back in law school. And each time you introduce yourself in the court room or boardroom; each time you reassure a nervous client; each time you explain to prospective clients what you can do for them, you reinforce the image of yourself as an autonomous, can-do professional with the tools to solve problems, resolve disputes, and even improve the legal system. And that feeling of being a lawyer never goes away, even when you're handling such administrative tasks as photocopying your own briefs or sending out bills late at night, because those tasks aren't the central focus of your job, but merely incidental to work as a real lawyer.

Argument #4. Flexibility

Many solo and small-firm lawyers, especially those just starting out and working full-time, may put in nearly as many hours as their large-firm colleagues. But solo practice allows you to set your own schedule, spreading out the work in a way that works best for you. For instance, suppose that your son or daughter has important after-school soccer matches that you don't want to miss. Back at BigLaw, you would probably be too embarrassed to cut out early more than once for a family event, and if you worked in government you'd have to use up personal leave. On your own, though, you can simply get an earlier start on your work day, or make up the time after the match when your kids are in bed. Sure, there will be days when you have a conference or a court hearing you can't postpone. But generally speaking, you have far more control over your own time when the law firm has your name on the door.

Moreover, when you run your own shop, you avoid many of the inefficiencies and superficialities endemic to any large employer: the practice group meetings, the sensitivity training sessions, the ceremonial lunches, and the office happy-hours that cut into the day without relieving you of deadlines or billable quotas. In addition, at large firms, face-time is paramount to success; simply being seen by your colleagues is just as important as actually getting the job done. So, if your assigned partner prefers to remain at the office until eight, you can count on staying until after eight most nights even if you'd rather arrive at dawn to get home by dinner. Then there are the non-billable demands.

Though most associates believe their salaries more than compensate for long hours at the office, the actual calculations prove otherwise. A well-known study by the Yale Law School Career Office shows that with various non-billable workday interruptions, an associate working a 60-hour week will bill only 42.5 hours, barely meeting a 2,000-hour minimum billable requirement. Spread over a 60-hour work week, (and assuming three weeks for vacation) that $160,000 salary amounts to roughly $55/hour, which doesn't seem so bad until you consider that it amounts to just 25 percent of a large firm associate's billing rate!

And for lawyers who want or need to work part-time, few if any other alternative work situations can match the flexibility of solo practice. Though lawyers choose part-time employment for many reasons, the most common reason is to enable lawyers to stay home with their children. For many years, law firms have been grappling—mostly unsuccessfully—with ways to accommodate new parents, primarily mothers, who want a part-time schedule. But at law firms, part-time often means working almost similar hours on less interesting projects at drastically reduced pay. Moreover, part-time frequently involves "work seepage", or at least an implicit understanding that a lawyer must drop everything when a case emergency comes up. As a result, some women don't take advantage of part-time programs even when firms make them available. You can't blame law firms or government organizations for not accommodating women any better. Not surprisingly, the partners give priority to their own financial well-being and the perceived needs of their clients over the desires of a handful of women asking for alternative schedules.

When you start your own firm, though, you're the boss…and your needs come first. You have complete freedom to design a schedule and a practice tailored to your specific family situation.

Argument #5. To Own Not Loan Your Talent

Lawyers toiling away at firms lose a substantial portion of their earnings to firm overhead and partner profit.

By way of example, a firm might bill a second-year associate at $250 an hour, and collect $500,000 based on a 2,000-hour billable year. Of that, the associate receives only $160,000 a year, or roughly a quarter of the firm's take. Granted, the remaining $340,000 isn't all firm profit; the firm covers your benefits (i.e., retirement contributions and health insurance), training and office space. But even deducting a generous $100,000/year for these expenses leaves the firm with a quarter-million dollars in profit. By contrast, if you were to start your own firm and generate 1,000 billable hours a year—that is, 20 hours a week at an average rate of $150/hour—you would still come out roughly the same as if you had stayed at the firm, but working far fewer hours! Just as we realize the advantages of owning rather than renting a home, lawyers should think carefully about the benefits of owning versus loaning their talents.

To be sure, solo practice has its ups and downs. After all, if you don't take care to adequately diversify your practice, or if you don't market your practice with vigilance, you could find yourself without any paying clients before too long. But consider: if you choose not to solo in these tumultuous times, you might be find yourself coping with a variety of grim scenarios: getting ejected from your law firm's partnership track after five years...getting unceremoniously booted from the law firm when you get too old...or, if you're working at a government agency, getting relegated to low-level cases when a new political appointee comes into power. What would you have to show for yourself then?

Argument #6. Opportunity to Innovate

Just as technology has transformed travel, publishing, and the media, so too, has it fundamentally altered the legal landscape.

As a legal futurist, Richard Susskind explains in *The End of Lawyers? Rethinking the Nature of Legal Services* (2010), that what he describes as disruptive technologies are automating many routine legal tasks, thus eroding the need for high-cost lawyers. Moreover, the Internet and cloud computing applications are enabling in-house counsel to bypass large firms and to seamlessly offshore their legal work (e.g., document review, due diligence and basic research) to India. As a result, many entry-level jobs at large law firms have been slashed by half, and they are unlikely to return. Law firm positions that do remain are being restructured. Firms are creating permanent staff attorney and non-partnership track positions to serve as a permanent source of leverage for entrenched equity partners. For details, read Steven Harper's article, *Permanent Leverage*; (AmLaw Daily, Nov. 12, 2010).

Nor are solo and small firms immune to change. Many solo and small firm lawyers who started practices 20 or 30 years ago still haven't quite made it into the Internet era. Even as today's consumers are accustomed to shopping and banking online, and spending considerable time engaged in online social media, *nearly half of solo and small firm practitioners lack even a rudimentary online presence* [ABA Technology Report 2009]. And still other traditional solo and small firms bemoan the rise of do-it-yourself providers like LegalZoom, which they believe are cutting into their business. Yet, they are unable to come up with viable models to compete.

These transitional times offer enormous opportunities for innovative, entrepreneurial lawyers to harness technology or to develop new business models for effective and profitable delivery of legal services (See Chapter 17 for additional discussion of future trends). Large firms, with their multiple layers of bureaucracy, simply aren't nimble enough to run with new trends, while smaller firms have too much vested in the old ways of doing business to embrace change. Solo practice is *an opportunity to innovate*, and is a gateway for lawyers who have the vision to lead the profession into the future and change it for the better.

Argument #7. Career Satisfaction

More than any other career in law, solo practice offers great personal satisfaction. Several studies confirm that solo practitioners are more content than their large firm colleagues, noting that increased autonomy partly accounts for greater levels of satisfaction. So, too, does lower overhead and control over workload, which means that solos don't need to work as many hours. [www.abajournal.com/magazine/article/pulse_of_the_legal_profession]. Finally, most solos simply feel as if their work actually makes a difference. At a large firm or even at a government agency, lawyers are generally part of a team that collectively takes credit for victories. By contrast, a solo's victories are their own. Moreover, many solos get to see the fruits of their labor up close, whether it's the client who avoids conviction, or keeps custody of the kids, or the company secures an environmental permit or venture funding. Doing work that matters is richly rewarding and makes solo practice a more meaningful—career-satisfying—experience.

Author's note: When my first daughter was born, I knew that I wanted to spend as much time with her as possible. At the same time, I'd been solo for three years, and with my practice firmly established and growing, I was reluctant to close it entirely. My practice wasn't particularly high-volume, so I didn't need to cut the number of cases as much as change the nature of some of the work I was handling. For starters, I phased out my court-appointed criminal work and referred or closed out several civil litigation matters because trial work, with its spur of the moment hearings and frequent meetings with clients and opposing counsel, was too time-consuming and unpredictable to provide enough time with my daughter. In place of these matters, I found a steady stream of energy regulatory work on a contract basis for a couple of other busy solos, and continued to handle a couple of appellate matters. Initially, I was able to squeeze my work responsibilities into early mornings, late nights, naps and weekends. When my daughter got older, I hired a nanny for a few mornings a week. Two years later, with the birth of my second daughter, I cut back even further, eliminated childcare, and capped my schedule at 15 hours a week.

By the time both daughters were settled in school, I was free to work a nearly full-time schedule until the arrival of their school bus at 4 p.m. That pick-up time was set in stone, except for unusual circumstances like an out-of-town trip or a deposition that ran late (in which case, my husband or parents filled in). Now my daughters are old enough to come home on their own. Even so, I occasionally work from home so they don't come home to an empty house.

BACK STORY

Truth be told, if I hadn't gotten up the nerve to start my own firm, I would probably not be practicing law at all.

Five years out of law school, I was informed by the managing partner at my firm that I wasn't partnership material! I was given six months. With the deadline at my back, though, I still hadn't found a new position, and my only alternatives were unemployment or starting my own firm. But, as luck would have it, my husband and I had just closed on our first home, and the mortgage was based in part on what I was earning as an associate. Between the mortgage and my student loans, unemployment was not an option; I needed to work. As if that wasn't enough impetus, I was angry. Though I had just been fired, I knew deep down that I had it in myself to be a good lawyer if only I could find the right opportunity. Anyway, I certainly wasn't ready to be forced out of the legal profession before I'd argued a real case in court.

I left my firm the last week of October, 1993. By the first week of November, I opened for business in a makeshift home office and a virtual office in downtown Washington D.C. In my first two years of practice, not only did I finally argue that case that I'd long coveted (before the esteemed D.C. Circuit no less) but numerous others followed. I also took scores of depositions, first-chaired five jury trials, and represented at least half a dozen clients in multiple administrative hearings. Even better, within three years I had exceeded the miserly salary that I'd been earning at my former firm.

After leaving my firm, both the economy and my practice specialty of energy regulation picked up nicely. And while other firms have serenaded me, I've never been tempted.

Maybe your career hasn't taken the path you'd hoped...maybe logging long hours at a big firm have been miserable...and maybe, without even realizing it, your unhappiness or desperation or nervousness has impacted your performance to the point where you got yourself fired. But honestly: are you ready to leave the law? If your answer is yes, you can put the book down. But if you are still committed to the same ideals that attracted you to law, or if you want to squeeze your money's worth out of the degree you worked so hard to attain, then don't let a lousy boss or the dysfunctional and unyielding hierarchical law firm system force you out of the legal profession. Sure, starting a law firm may not be your first choice. But give it time. You just might discover that going out on your own gives you that second chance to find satisfaction and fulfillment as a lawyer.

IN THEIR OWN WORDS

Some of the best advice on starting a law practice comes from the real experts: solo practitioners themselves. This the first of eight sidebars in the book in which solos of all levels of experience share what they think about opening—and maintaining—a solo practice.

Q: Why did you open a solo practice?

"Big law firms never appealed to me. I always wanted to start a business and work for myself."
—Paul Scott (class of 2008)

"I wanted to sink or swim on my own. Do things in my own fashion rather than abide by the interminable partnership meeting/committee/sub-committee process of decision-making."
—David Abeshouse (class of 1982)

"I got tired of the hours, the commute, and not getting compensated for the amount of business I was bringing in. I was among the top five in business generation, but not anywhere near the top five in compensation!"—Walter D. James III (class of 1987)

"In my second year of law school, one of my professors described the typical life of a new attorney: it was the polar opposite of what I had attended law school to become. From then on, I knew I wanted to solo. I couldn't imagine toiling away four years of a part-time law program while working full or part-time, only to lose some of the freedom I'd enjoyed before enrolling in law school." —Gina Bongiovi (class of 2007)

"I was laid off from a good DC law firm in June 2009 after working there for six years. At first I thought about seeking employment again with a firm or with the government. I worked up a number of resumes and applied for a few positions...but my heart was not in it. I could barely force myself to write another cover letter stating, yet again, how I was a 'team player,' a 'self starter,' and a 'problem-solver.' I knew that I wanted to go out on my own. As a solo, the hours are very long right now, and my success is by no means assured. But I am enjoying the process, and I am glad I made this choice."—Mark Tanney (class of 1998)

"The main reason I decided to solo was the birth of my first child, and the desire to devote more time to my family. I also consider myself an entrepreneur, and enjoy controlling the structure of my practice, scheduling my own days, and not being held back by the conventional structures of a traditional law practice."—Stephanie Kimbro (class of 2003)

"All through law school, bar study, and post-bar, I networked, volunteered, interned, worked contract work...and *still* there were no jobs. One month away from personal bankruptcy, I thought I might have it easier finding clients than finding a job. I was right. With only [modest] financial resources, I quickly built the knowledge base and experience through smart planning, hard work, and with the help of wonderful colleagues."—Eric P. Ganci (class of 2008)

"Why solo? My family is full of entrepreneurs, and throughout high school, college, and law school, I was self-employed. My personality has never allowed me to work for any companies or organizations, so I knew in law school that I would be going solo. Beyond that, I wanted to solo for the usual reasons: the ability to make my own schedule, the power of controlling my job security and destiny, the benefit of not having a promotional ceiling, the rewards of being in business for yourself, etc."—Scott Wolfe (class of 2005)

"About a year after I left a small private practice firm, I decided to solo for several reasons: dissatisfaction with my past work environment; an inability to find a decent-paying satisfactory job (because of the poor market and a surplus of lawyers); a desire to create my own positive work environment; and a desire to 'be my own boss'...and eventually have a good work-life balance."—Jenny Jeltes (class of 2006)

Excerpt from *Solo by Choice, The Companion Guide: 34 Questions That Could Transform Your Legal Career* (Carolyn Elefant, 2011)

CHAPTER 2

The Big Decision

"Think carefully about whether you're the solo type. Not only should new grads prefer to be their own boss, they must also be disciplined for it. The legal and business requirements will come with time and effort, but to be a successful solo comes down to an ability to be one's own boss, and to feel confident enough to put your money and future on the line."

—Scott Wolfe, solo

Good lawyers need to understand a client's motives to successfully represent them. For example, consider the wealthy client intent on destroying the reputation of a business partner who betrayed him. Without understanding the client's motives, the lawyer might fail to make a case for accepting a generous settlement because the issue is really a desire for retribution. Once motive is understood, legal strategies are possible. As you embark on your own firm, you need to understand your own motives. Because whatever they are, they will drive your expectations and—ultimately—your success and satisfaction.

What follows are the five most-often cited motivations for going solo:

I've always dreamed of starting a law firm. Without question, having the drive and desire to start a law firm will contribute to your potential success. But you can't allow your enthusiasm to lead you to careless decisions or to underestimate the commitment needed to get started. I've known a few lawyers so keen on hanging a shingle that they invested precious resources for posh office space, mahogany furniture, and expensive technology without really thinking about the cash flow needed to cover that kind of overhead. Others were so blinded by the urge to help clients find justice, that they naively represented every troubled, needy client with a sympathetic story and no cash on hand. Still others believed that by working conscientiously and acting honorably, that cases would simply appear, not realizing how much time they needed to devote in those early years to marketing, making social contacts, and establishing a reputation to guarantee steady work over time.

Bottom line: Be careful that your dream is not clouded by enthusiasm. It can lead to imprudent choices or poor timing in the opening of your new solo practice.

I work at a firm (and I'm desperately unhappy). Dissatisfaction with law firm life is motivating more and more unhappy associates to explore solo practice... or to leave the law entirely. But why should a bad experience drive you out of the profession you worked so hard to enter? After all, even if you hate certain aspects of your job—like the tedious checking of briefs—these mundane tasks aren't so bad when you are doing it for yourself.

At the same time, some of the issues driving you from law firm practice don't magically vanish when you open your own shop. Launching a law firm demands many non-billable hours networking at bar events, writing articles, or meeting with potential referrals…on top of whatever client commitments you have. No, you won't work 60-hour weeks, but unless you're planning a purely part-time practice (and a part-time salary), expect to invest at least 45 hours a week to build your practice. And if you have low tolerance for difficult personalities, solo practice won't solve things. True, you won't have to kiss up to an arrogant junior partner for choice assignments, but you may have an annoying client calling frequently, questioning your legal strategy. And what about that nasty opposing counsel, who constantly accuses you of unethical conduct to intimidate you from zealously representing your client? In many ways, dealing with an aggressive adversary is just as stressful as working for an overbearing law firm partner.

Don't confuse problems inherent in the practice of law with your unhappiness at your firm. When you practice law, you can't avoid dealing with jerks, whether they're opposing counsel, judges, or even your own clients.

Bottom line: When you consider leaving your current law firm job to strike out on your own make sure your gripes are specific to your firm and not to the practice of law in general. If the latter is true, you won't find satisfaction starting your own firm.

I want to be a stay-at-home parent. After slaving long hours at a firm and being a weekend parent, you may fantasize about starting a part-time practice, working on memos at the dining room table while the kids play at your feet.

As I mentioned earlier, starting your own firm makes sense from a parenting or family perspective because it does give you the flexibility and control that working at a firm or government agency simply cannot match. But creating and sustaining a part-time practice while you raise young children isn't nirvana. For one thing, you won't have the amount of time usually available to stay-home parents for organizing play groups, or serving as class parent, or participating in the PTA. And a part-time practice demands that you cap your work hours, which means you might have to forego a promising networking opportunity, or to accept chunks of contract work that can be managed more easily on a tight schedule but pay less. And even though part-time practice does allow you to get to meet your child's bus at 3 p.m., that privilege may cost you an occasional all-nighter or weekend at the library to meet a tight deadline. After all, just because you put your family first doesn't mean your clients will.

And a part-time practice can be frustrating. You're still working hard, and you may not earn job as much or advance as quickly as your full-time peers. Nor will you get much sympathy from either full-timers who envy your flexibility, or stay-home parents who haven't found a way to keep a foot in the working world. All things considered, a solo practice offers one of the best ways to balance family and work. Striking the right balance won't be easy; it can take months or even years of experimentation before you hit the right equation that works for you and your family.

Bottom line: As a part-timer, what you gain in flexibility you may lose in earning power, and you may feel suspended between the working world and the world of the stay-at-home parent.

I was fired or downsized. Losing a job can be humiliating, whether it's due to our own shortcomings or economic forces beyond our control. Even at a time where terminations have become routine, most of us feel too ashamed to admit we've been fired and too honest to lie about why we left our former job. What to do? If, after losing your job, you decide to start your own firm, keep it to yourself that you had been fired. No one has to know. Most would never ask why you decided to go out on your own, and many will assume it was by choice. For those who do inquire, say—truthfully—that solo practice offered far more professional opportunities and challenges than your former position… and leave it at that.

As angry as you may be, don't burn any bridges. Put your emotions into your morning workout or your journal (not a blog; this is one situation where a blog is not the smart play).

Even if your firm considered your performance sub-par (and you acknowledge that you did make some stupid mistakes), that doesn't mean you won't succeed on your own. Whatever you do, don't—repeat, don't—badmouth your firm or attempt revenge. For whatever reason you were let go, do nothing that would jeopardize the possibility that your old firm might one day give you referrals. In my own case, lawyers from my former firm (which had asked me to leave) helped me to prepare for my first appellate argument after I'd started my own practice; they referred me several small energy regulatory matters; and they provided sufficiently positive references that enabled me to land several lucrative contract matters. As time has passed, my relationship with some of the firm's lawyers grew more cordial. I even attended the firm's anniversary celebration, and shared a terrific time with my old colleagues.

Bottom line: Though starting a firm after losing your job may not be your first choice, you can increase your chances for success by focusing on making a fresh start and letting go of whatever animus you have toward your former employer.

I want to practice law my way. Perhaps you're not advancing as quickly as you'd like because of the struggle to manage your workload and keep pace with your peers. Or maybe you're irritated by constant criticism from superiors about your work product, or writing skills, or interaction with clients. Lawyering is a struggle (after all, that's why it's called practice), but starting a firm can actually help you master new skills because—for the first time—you're able to modify your workload to learn at your own pace free of comparison to others. On the other hand, even when you're out on your own, don't be dismissive of feedback from more experienced colleagues: many times, they do know better.

Bottom line: Don't be hard on yourself; people learn at different rates. Even if you're not a quick study you can—with hard work—catch up and even surpass your colleagues. Just don't let your ego stand in the way of accepting constructive criticism.

A Personal Assessment

After giving careful thought to your own motives, you still need to consider whether solo practice suits your personality and temperament. Consider:

Do you crave independence? The most satisfied solos prefer to operate without affiliation to a larger controlling unit, and don't require others for guidance in conducting their business.

Are you comfortable wearing many hats? Successful solos act as project manager, office manager, HR director, business manager, strategic planner, VP for business development, and general worker bee, all of which can consume as much as half your day. You don't have to like all of these roles, but you do have to be willing to assume them if you can't afford to delegate them. As a solo, tasks like collecting payment from clients, cold-calling potential clients, or scanning documents, aren't any more enjoyable than the busy work that's demanded at almost any job. Do you thrive when you're in charge? The most successful solos readily accept responsibility for failure as long as they can take all the credit for a good result. The upside is that you get to practice law the way you want.

Are you enterprising? In my experience, the most successful solos have a talent for spotting opportunities and taking advantage of them. For them, networking is a regular and enjoyable part of every week, and they don't rely on telephone ads to keep their operation afloat. Note: Shyness is often cited as a reason not to seek out business. But some of the most effective lawyer-marketers are introverted, and it only compels them to approach networking in a more disciplined, systematic manner.

What is your tolerance for risk? There's the possibility of great payoffs, and then you might run into days (even weeks) without billables. As a solo, you won't know when or whether business will come, or how long you'll have it, or if it will generate a living wage. In order to experience satisfaction as a solo, you must be comfortable with the part of you that is willing to take a leap of faith...or willing to diversify your practice instead of focusing on a single practice area (such as bankruptcy or real estate, which are especially sensitive to changes in the law and economic recession).

Are you a self-starter? Successful solos don't need someone looking over their shoulders; they're motivated to do what needs to be done. Look back at your childhood. Were you one of those kids who complained about being bored when left to your own devices? Or were you someone who could amuse yourself for hours? Note: if you're concerned about your ability to get motivated, consider working in a shared space rather than a home office. Working in the company of others can have the effect of forcing you to be more conscientious.

Are you resourceful? The most successful solos are good at finding answers quickly, and are unafraid of asking questions, requesting input, and seeking help. Over the years, what I've learned is that solo practice requires you to unlearn some of the bad habits you picked up in law school and on the job. Asking a question isn't a sign of weakness; it's a form of empowerment. Admitting what you don't know can make you feel stupid but it also opens yourself up to learning more and making yourself a better lawyer. Besides, if the questions that your clients bring to you were already resolved, they wouldn't need you anyway.

How Much Do Solos Earn?

Even though the federal government posts GS-pay scale charts for lawyers, and BigLaw firms publicize the pay of incoming associates, there is no definitive answer on how much solos typically earn. This is true for several reasons:

- Solos are a disparate group, and gathering a sufficiently wide data sample is difficult.
- Solo practices vary so widely that salary charts offer little guidance even for the same geographic area (for example, a solo who practiced employment law at a large firm for institutional clients, and who continues on the same matters when she starts her own firm, will likely earn more than a family law attorney who represents consumer clients).
- And, in contrast to large firms, where associates often bill 2,000 to 2,200 hours a year, solos have more control over their schedule, their overhead expenses...and their income. If you cap your work week at 40 hours to spend more time with your family, you will earn less than a solo who works 60 hours. And if you gross $100,000 and trim your overhead costs to 20 percent of your gross revenues, you'll earn $80,000 before taxes, whereas a colleague who prefers to have a secretary and Class A office might wind up with only $40,000 or $50,000 at the end of the year.

Susan Cartier Liebel, a former solo and founder of Solo Practice University (www. solopracticeuniversity.com), an online, fee-based educational community for new and practicing solos, says of lawyer salaries:

> "... A solo's income is dependent upon numerous variables, but the metric remains the same: solos sell their time regardless of their billing model, and there is only so much time they can sell. They can choose to sell all of it or part of it. And when they reach their individual maximum, they can choose to bring on another and sell that person's time and take a percentage. Or they can increase their profits by increasing their rate and/or reducing their overhead. Or they can do all three. Not all solos choose to make millions or build empires, but simply want to sustain themselves in the lifestyle with which they are happiest."

Still, there are some ways to ballpark what you can expect to earn.

Comparing apples to apples. Some bar associations do publish data on solo earnings. In Florida, a solo's median income in 2005 was reported to be $105,000 (source:

Florida Bar News), while in Texas that same year a solo's median income was reported to be $88,604 (source: State Bar of Texas, Department of Research and Analysis, 2005). What's important to remember about salary study data—even bar association data—is that it often relies on a sampling of only a few hundred attorneys ranging from solos to large firm practitioners. Still, if you compare apples to apples, the data may provide a rough estimate of potential salary.

Consider: The Florida bar breaks out its data by years of experience. So, while the overall median salary was a reported $105,000/year, it was only $65,000 for lawyers with less than three years of experience, and $85,000 for those with six-to-eight years of experience. In Texas, the Bar breaks out salary data by years of experience and by practice area. The median salary for a more traditional solo practice area (such as family attorney) was reported to be $81,588. By contrast, the median salary for environmental attorneys was $124,000. So, a mid-level associate at a large firm in Texas who is considering solo practice should not assume that he would earn under $100,000 merely because that's the median for a solo with a consumer-oriented practice.

Needless to say, the "apples-to-apples" rule also applies to geographic location. Solos located in a small, rural community with five years of experience will earn less then their counterparts in a major urban area in the same state because rural clients can't afford to pay as much (although the salary gap might even out because the cost of living in a rural area may be substantially less).

Where to find salary advice. Many lawyers are circumspect about how much they earn, so you may not have much luck obtaining earnings information from them. But if you're really determined to locate specific data on what you can expect to earn as a solo, contact your bar's law practice management advisor (most bar associations now have an LPM expert on staff). LPM advisors consult with lawyers on starting and ramping up their practices, and often have access to information about what particular types of solos earn. If an LPM advisor has assisted a lawyer with a profile similar to yours—e.g., a former BigLaw attorney with 15 years of corporate experience, or a recent graduate with a criminal practice—he could provide data that proves more meaningful. LPM advisors can also inform you about practice trends that may impact earnings. For example, they might be aware that immigration attorneys have been experiencing an uptick in earnings due to increased demand for service, or earnings for personal injury attorneys have been depressed by tort reform.

Many state bars publish economic surveys that contain various data on solo earnings, as well as earnings for specific practice areas and earnings by law firm size. Though some of the reports cost money, most bars offer at least a summary of the data at no charge to members. Ask a bar representative about the survey, or Google terms like "law firms" and "economic survey" which will generate some of the available surveys currently online.

Previous employment as a baseline. Reference to your previous employment, or to comparable private sector employment, can also offer a decent baseline for predicting future earnings (at least in the first few years of practice).

As a general rule, lawyers who come to solo practice by way of a law firm or government position...and who bring with them few, if any, clients...may find their net solo earnings are 25 to 80 percent less during their first year in practice, and some may earn only enough to cover expenses during their first year of practice. By the second year, though, a solo is likely to be close to matching their previous salary, and, by the third year, most solos will exceed what they earned before leaving a law firm or government position. Lawyers who manage to take at least one or two decent "anchor" clients (e.g., clients with enough steady matters to provide a base-load revenue stream to your practice) typically experience only a downward earnings "blip" of 10 or 20 percent compared to their earlier job, and frequently exceed their previous salary by Year 2. Moreover, those lawyers who bring one or two small corporate clients find that those clients who come with them may actually send them more work because as solos they can offer more affordable rates. As for solos fresh out of law school, they generally manage to cover their expenses within six months of starting their practice if they've been vigilant about minimizing their start-up costs. And by Year 3 their earnings can equal those of law firm associates or government attorneys with comparable practice areas and similar geographic areas.

A few caveats. For experienced lawyers, baseline comparisons only work when your new solo practice is in the same practice area as before. When you change practice areas, it's as if you're a solo just out of law school because you're learning a new practice area and just beginning to make contacts. As a result...depending upon the practice area you select, and your previous employment…you may never match your prior salary.

For example, let's say an eighth-year associate earning $250,000 as an associate at an AmLaw 100 firm handling corporate transactions decides to open a solo practice specializing in consumer bankruptcy or family law. Their first-year earnings will dip substantially; indeed, he or she may never come close to his salary from his law firm days. And yet, the associate's solo earnings would compare favorably to other law-related career options, such as government, academia or in-house positions at a small company, not to mention that the associate would be working fewer hours and have greater flexibility than before. It bears noting that if this same associate decided to continue his corporate practice instead of changing to a consumer-oriented field, his earnings potential as a solo would be greater. And with outsourcing or hiring associates or clerks to leverage earnings, the associate could reasonably match or increase his law firm salary. In this example, a large portion of the senior associate's revenue drop in moving to solo practice derives from the change from a corporate to a consumer-oriented practice, and not exclusively from the decision to go solo.

For salary projections, the apples-to-apples comparison is even more important when the issue is part-time vs full-time. Consider the example of Joanne Sternlieb, a trusts and estates lawyer who works from home. During her first two years of solo practice, she earned two-thirds percent of her salary at a major New York law firm where she worked 40 hours a week (full-time was 60 hours). Anticipating the shortfall when she went solo, Sternlieb supplemented her income by working part-time on a contract basis. Now, after several years, Joanne works a flexible 40-hour week from home, and her salary is equivalent to what she earned in BigLaw (source: www.jdbliss. com).

A SAMPLING OF ECONOMIC SURVEYS

Between 2007 and 2009, several state bar associations—among them Colorado, Michigan, Ohio, Oregon, Texas, and Wisconsin—published economic surveys based on voluntary responses of between 5 and 12 percent of practitioners. The following data is a small fraction of each bar's membership, but certain interesting trends did emerge:

Solos earn less than BigLaw attorneys. No surprise, but solo lawyers earn less than BigLaw attorneys. Generally, median solo incomes equaled 55 to 60 percent of the highest category of earners, i.e., lawyers in firms of 30 or more. The one exception was Colorado, where solos earn just 25 percent of partners in firms of 30 or more.

Solos earn above the median state income. Though solos may lag behind the largest firms in earnings, their income generally exceeds median state incomes. For example, in Texas, a solo's median income is $97,142 (nearly double the state median) while in Oregon solos with a median income of $75,000 earn 1.5 times more than Oregon's median income of $49,000. Though this data is state-specific, it should give some confidence that—from a financial perspective—starting a law firm is at least as good if not better choice than leaving the law.

Practice area selection impacts income. In most states, attorney income varied widely depending upon practice area. Across the board, general practice (in those states where it was listed as an option) and family law ranked lowest on the earnings scale. Bankruptcy fell in the middle of the earnings scale, while practice areas such as civil litigation, and specialized fields like intellectual property and public utilities work, ranked high.

Income increases commensurate with years in practice. As solos gain experience in practice (whether solo or not), their income increases. In those states that measured solo income as a function of years of experience (Colorado, Ohio), both showed a large jump in growth; about 60 percent for solos with five years or less experience and those in practice from six to 10 years. Thereafter, income continued to increase through 15 years and 25 years though not as dramatically. In one category, income levels declined: solos in home offices experienced a substantial reduction between years 6 to 16 in Ohio and years 11 to 16 in Colorado. This roughly corresponds to the period when many lawyers have families and work part-time from home.

Solos in shared space and outside the home earn more. A few studies – in Colorado, Wisconsin, Michigan, and Ohio—collected data on specific solo practice scenarios: solos in home offices, solos outside the home, and solos in shared space. On the whole, solos in "shared space" arrangements earned more in most jurisdictions, and dramatically so in Michigan, where median income for a solo is $81,884 compared to $111,571 for a space-sharer; in Wisconsin, the net income for solos was $71,783 net income compared to $109,586 for the space-sharing solo practitioner.

Colorado and Ohio provide data on home office solos. In Colorado, home-office solos earned an average of $50,000 compared to $85,000 for a solo with an office outside the home, and $80,000 to a solo sharing space. In Ohio, solos with home offices out-earned solos with outside offices and space sharers during the first 10 years of practice, which in years 11–25, the solos sharing space pulled ahead considerably, topping out at $100k–$105k for years 16–25+. Meanwhile, salaries for home-based solos during this period dropped to half of what the space -sharers earn. Solos with offices outside the home continued an upward trend, but still earn roughly 25 percent less than those sharing space in years 16–25+ while incomes at home declined. The numbers, particularly the upward trend for space-sharers in Ohio, suggests that solos may gain significant benefits from sharing space in the form of increased referrals. (See Chapter 6 for a discussion of office space arrangements).

Sources:

Economics of Law Practice, Wisconsin Lawyer (Nov. 2008), at www.wisbar.org/AM/Template.cfm?Section=Home&CONTENTID=76193&TEMPLATE=/CM/ContentDisplay.cfm

State Bar of Michigan, 2007 Economic Survey, online at www.lawpracticeeconomics.com/

The Economics of Law Practice in Ohio, Desktop Reference 2007, at www.associatedcontent.com/article/454755/the_osba_releases_report_on_the_economics.html

Oregon State Bar, 2007 Economic Survey (Dec. 2007), online at www.osbar.org/docs/resources/07EconSurvey.pdf

Colorado Bar Association, 2008 Economics of Law Practice Survey (Oct., 2008), at www.cobar.org/repository/LPM%20Dept/2008EconSurvey.pdf

Income Fact Sheet (2009), Texas Bar, online at www.texasbar.com/AM/Template.cfm?Section=DemographicandEconomicTrends

State Median Incomes (2007, 2008), at money.cnn.com/2009/09/21/news/economy/highest_income_census/?postversion=2009092118

Can You Afford to Solo?

From a financial perspective, the thought of starting a firm can seem daunting. Not only must you replace the lost income stream, but you carry the burden of everything from computer equipment and office supplies to malpractice insurance, health insurance, and retirement contributions. What follows are some preliminary financial considerations:

What are your business prospects? Even as you start thinking about starting your own firm, it's important to analyze any immediate business prospects you may have. Of course, you can't solicit firm clients when you're still working at the firm (more on that in Chapter 5), but you do need to look critically at which, if any, clients, are likely to follow you to a new practice. In addition, consider what other sources of revenue are available. Perhaps you've got good relationships with other attorneys who might refer cases to you or send you contract work. Maybe you'll be approached by friends or family with legal matters too small to handle while at a law firm, but which could generate revenue at your own practice. Don't worry if you don't have a single client on the horizon because you really don't need many billable hours to get started.

Let's say that starting out you can find only one day's worth of billable work a week or one flat-fee matter (like a bankruptcy case or estate plan) every two weeks. At $150/hour, that's $1,200/week or around $1,500 to $2,500 every two weeks (or more, depending on the billable rate in your area). Granted, that's gross revenue; you've still got taxes and overhead. But if you trim your costs, you should be able to capture some profit from Day 1. Moreover, by marketing constantly when you don't have billable work, you should be able to generate leads for future cases.

Should you start a practice part-time? To make ends meet, many new solos consider working part-time at a law-related job while their practice is getting off the ground. Others, by necessity, find part-time work, either in non-law related positions; sometimes in the industry they worked in before law school, or even coffee shops or restaurants. Whether you jump fully into solo practice or not is a personal decision.

Some argue that a solo law practice requires full-time commitment for success, and that working at it part-time compromises that commitment. Whether it's true or not in your own case, the revenue from part-time work will provide some financial security as you get your practice off the ground. And with that (along with some other revenue stream), you may feel less pressured to take any case that walks in the door, or to recommend a less-than-ideal settlement just so you can get paid.

What Are Your Financial Obligations?

If student loans are your biggest financial worry, you now have more options than ever to ease the burden although your best bet is still to repay your loans as aggressively as you can manage:

Deferrals. Most student loans allow for up to 24 months of deferral without adverse consequences to your credit. Though you don't want to defer your repayments too long, six months can give you enough breathing room to start your practice.

Consolidations. If you've taken out a number of federal student loans for college and law school with varying interest payments, you might benefit from consolidation through a break on interest payments. Plus, it's easier administratively to make one payment rather than many. For more information on consolidation, see www.student-loanborrowerassistance.org/understand-loans/consolidation-loans.

Income-based repayments. The College Cost Reduction and Access Act, enacted in July 2009, establishes income-based repayment programs which were designed to ease the financial hardship of repaying student loan debt while working in a low-paying job (See www.ibrinfo.org) Using a formula, the IBR program calculates monthly payments proportionate to income, allowing for escalation over time as income increases. For private sector borrowers, loans are forgiven after 25 years of repayment under the IBR plan.

Loan-forgiveness. Loan-forgiveness programs are run through law schools, and traditionally apply to students accepting employment in public interest jobs. Starting a solo practice isn't likely to qualify; still, if you've chosen a practice area like consumer law, criminal defense or another with a public interest bent, you could make a plausible argument for seeking loan-forgiveness. If you're currently working, and think you may want to start a practice in the future, do your best to pay down as much of your loans as you can now. That way, when you do start your firm, you'll have one less expense to worry about.

Your house as a piggy bank. Depending on prevailing interest rates, a home-equity credit line or mortgage refinance offer two options for generating money for living expenses. A line of credit can provide a safety net if you need it; you pay back only what you actually use. With refinancing, you might obtain a lower interest rate on your mortgage that decreases your monthly payments and frees up money for your firm.

Or, you can increase your mortgage and cash out some of your home's equity during refinancing and use that money for start-up expenses. When you draw on your home equity, you can also deducting the interest at tax time.

Other sources of financing. Credit cards and small business loans are other sources of financing the launch of a law firm. And a business of line credit can also give you some flexibility. But as with overhead, take care not to overextend yourself. Before taking out a loan or racking up credit card debt, make absolutely sure you can't eliminate anything else from your budget.

Can You Solo On a Shoestring Budget?

The capital needed to open a solo practice varies by region and practice setting, but costs have dropped considerably. In fact, the financial barriers have never been lower!

The continuing drop in technology costs make it possible for new solos to equip themselves with a suite of technology comparable to large firms for a very small initial outlay. Many powerful applications—an all-in-one phone number for voicemail, email and call-forwarding, timekeeping and invoicing tools, and even Web sites and online profiles—are now available free. Even practice management and online storage can be purchased on a pay-as-you-go subscription basis rather than a large upfront payment. Bottom line: you can open a solo law practice for a capital outlay of around $3,000 or less to cover the basics: a valid bar license, a computer, a phone, an Internet connection, some type of online presence, business cards and malpractice insurance.

With so many low cost options, the biggest mistake a new solo can make is to take on too much overhead at the beginning. The strain of having to cover the cost of leased space AND administrative staff or a paralegal could lead to foolish decisions, such as accepting a case outside your expertise for less than your billable rate…or worse, borrowing money from client trust accounts to pay bills!

Here are the opinions of several other solos:

"Solo on a shoestring? Hell, yes. It's what I do every day! If you can get by without an ostentatious office and use the Internet and local resources to make your practice work, you really don't need to lay out the big bucks."—**Jan M. Tamanini** (class of 1984)

"You can absolutely solo on a shoestring. There is no reason that a new solo needs the fancy office, the secretary, the paralegal, the new car, the mahogany desk, and all those BigLaw trappings. In fact, many clients have said they chose a solo because we're perceived to be more agile, more streamlined, and less taken with pretentious surroundings that are simply reflected in the client's bill."—**Gina Bongiovi** (class of 2007)

"[Start on a shoestring]? Definitely. My only real fixed costs are bar dues, CLE, and malpractice insurance. I work from home and make house calls or meet my clients somewhere in public. I was afraid I would appear unprofessional, but no one yet has questioned my professionalism because I don't meet them in my office. Instead, they seem thrilled that I come to them."—**Sarah White** (class of 2002)

"It depends on how you define shoestring. There are some things you can't skimp on: a basic office set-up, supplies, malpractice insurance, an accountant (at least at tax time), and money for networking/marketing events. Things you can skimp on: an expensive office and an assistant or paralegal to start out."—Lynda L. Hinkle (class of 2009)

"I know attorneys who work from their kitchen table and make a good living; I know others with beautiful offices and high overhead who barely break even. If you need the trappings to feel good and be productive, then the office setting is necessary. [But] clients generally don't like to pay for leather chairs and original artwork; they just want to see a clean, well-presented setting when they meet with you."—Bruce L. Dorner (class of 1977)

"You can set up a solo office on a shoestring; you just can't run a solo practice on one. All those articles on the '$10,000 law practice', the '$5,000 law office', and 'starting-a-law-practice-a-shoestring' are correct as far as they go. But they don't consider what it costs to live AND maintain your practice. You need to factor in rent or mortgage payments, and those pesky bills for food, utilities, telephone, transportation, health insurance, and taxes. Then there are costs for professional marketing, maintaining your license, and advancing court costs or filing fees on your client's behalf. On top of THOSE, there are the unexpected costs like the $500 brake job or the thousand-dollar medical bill."—Bruce Cameron (class of 2007)

In your first year or two, I suggest you grow into your needs.

- Work exclusively from home
- Work partly from home and maintain a virtual space, arranging with a local business center to provide a local phone number and mailing address, as well as appointment access to office space and support services.
- Sublet space from a firm or another attorney
- Join forces with a couple of other lawyers to share expenses

Some contend that you won't be taken seriously if you work from home or that you must lease space to impress clients or give them peace of mind. But that's no longer true; in fact, with most communications handled online or by phone, it's often impossible to discern anyone's physical location. On the other hand, some lawyers simply don't have the discipline to work from home, with some jurisdictions – like New Jersey - may impose bonafide office rules that complicate home office arrangements by requiring a lawyer to maintain a space for meeting clients and where he or she can be met in reached in person during the day. For the pro and con of home offices, see Chapter 6.

The Economics of a Virtual Law Practice

One business model for a solo practice that is gaining attention is the virtual law office (VLO), a professional law practice that exists online through a secure portal and is accessible by both lawyers and clients. While a VLO can support any type of legal practice, it is most commonly associated with the delivery of unbundled or limited-scope legal services in which the lawyer prepares a basic form or pleading (e.g., preparation of an uncontested divorce petition or business incorporation papers) for filing by the client.

The costs associated with starting a VLO are minimal. You don't need a brick-and-mortar office, so the sole expenses are malpractice insurance, a computer, and the monthly cost of a platform for running the VLO. This may range from $50 to $200/month depending upon vendors, features, and whether the lawyer purchases pre-developed forms. Because of the low start-up costs and the routinized nature of most VLO services, many lawyers view a VLO as easy money, and they jump on board without first examining the prospects for clients and what it will take to attract them as well as the economics of a volume practice.

Here are some of the financial considerations before starting a VLO:

Nature of the service. If you're running a VLO and offering exclusively unbundled legal services at $200 to $600 a matter, you'll need a high volume of cases to generate decent revenue. Let's assume that you average $400 a case. That means you'll need to come up with four cases a week (or 20 a month) to gross $80,000/year (based on a 50-week year). Though processing those cases won't involve much time, you'll have to engage in significant marketing—either in person, networking or with online ads—to generate that volume.

Will consumers pay? It depends. Some clients view online legal services as a bargain; the services cost less and are more convenient than skipping work to visit a lawyer's office. Other clients may not appreciate the value-add that an online lawyer brings, and will simply opt for LegalZoom because it's cheaper. For further discussion, ready what virtual law advocate Lee Rosen, a family law attorney and marketing consultant, has to say: http://divorcediscourse.com/2010/08/18/virtual-office-advocates-leave/. In short, even though most consumers love online banking, that doesn't mean they're ready to sign up for online legal services. I recommend that you identify your target markets before starting out or you may be disappointed with the results.

Marketing costs. Since VLO clients are tech savvy, online marketing makes sense. But marketing costs may also be high if you're going to compete with providers like LegalZoom. VLO lawyers profiled in Stephanie Kimbro's *Virtual Law Practice: How to Deliver Legal Services Online* (ABA, 2010) report different costs for marketing. One lawyer's costs were 18 percent of gross revenue (or $14,000/year for $80,000 in revenue); another's costs were roughly $700/month. While these are reasonable compared to the cost of Yellow Pages or TV ads, they may be greater than expected if you never thought about how to market a VLO.

Since the streamlined nature of unbundled services delivered online ensures a manageable workload, a VLO can provide a comfortable source of revenue, particularly for lawyers who want to work part-time. Likewise, a VLO can complement a firm's traditional offerings by allowing it to capture clients who can't afford full service rates. Just don't buy into a vision of easy money for little work...because you'll be disappointed.

Getting a Second Opinion

Back in law school, when you were trying to decide whether to take a clerkship, or which firm you should join, you could always consult with a professor, a career advisor, or an alum. And the chances were good that someone knew, or had heard about, a judge who had a clerkship to offer or who had contacts at the firms you were considering. But where do you turn if you're thinking about starting your own small practice? The legal profession has grown so stratified that many large-firm or government attorneys don't know any colleagues who've started their own practice. In fact, there are many excellent resources, and more all the time.

Below, are just a few of those you will want to seek out...and avoid:

Bar and LPM programs. Many local bar associations have Law Practice Management (LPM) advisors able to offer a wealth of information on starting a law firm. Typically, you can set up a meeting with an LPM advisor by contacting the bar. There's usually no cost for an initial meeting. An LPM advisor can fill you in on many of the details unique to starting a practice in your jurisdiction, and may be able to refer you to other attorneys who you can call for advice. You can also learn about various support groups or mentoring programs that are available to solos through some local bars.

Friends or colleagues. When I started out, I was fortunate enough to have a close law school friend who, along with a partner, started a general practice about a year earlier. Though I intended to focus on a different area of law, it was inspiring to talk things over with a peer who'd already taken the plunge. A year later, I was able to pass along the favor to another friend who was thinking about starting his own criminal defense firm. If you don't know any other solo practitioners, join a solo practitioner's listserv (i.e., the ABA's solosez.net), or seek out the growing number of blogs that focus on starting a practice. Of course, sometimes destiny takes a hand. I remember flipping through the Yellow Pages for an attorney who could help me decide whether to file suit over my dismissal from my law firm. As it turned out, the lawyer with whom I consulted had graduated law school the same year as myself, and had started his own practice the year before. In the course of the consultation, he shared some of the ups and downs of a new solo. He was the right person at the right time, and the experience helped me imagine what my own practice might be like...and I liked what I saw.

My advice is to seek out a broad sampling of solo attorneys:

- Someone who started a firm when they were at the same place in life that you are now.
- Someone who shares your particular practice area, and who can help you analyze the viability of your business plan or to tip you off to related fields where you can expand.

- Someone a little older who can provide a wealth of advice on such practical issues as dealing with clients, resolving ethical dilemmas, and generally keeping things in perspective.
- Someone, perhaps an expatriate from government or BigLaw, who can share their own early struggles to become a solo practitioner.

Your spouse. In solo practice, you're in charge...but never forget the one partner with whom you must consult (again and again and again) is the *partner* with whom you live. Make no mistake, solo practice can be hard on a marriage or live-in arrangement. And if your spouse or significant other isn't on board 100 percent with your desire to open a law practice, it will make things difficult for both of you. Some of the impacts are predictable: the family will probably need to trim expenses—at least for awhile—as the practice gets off the ground. Then, too, roles and responsibilities are certain to change. For example, just because your new schedule is more flexible, it might be assumed you can do more things around the house, or that you have the responsibility of picking the kids up from school. You, of course, will want to focus all of your available time on building your new firm, and you believe it would be unrealistic to take on all kinds of new household chores. Or, maybe you feel so guilty for requiring your partner to make so many sacrifices that you overcompensate, and start spending even more time on household matters to the detriment of your new practice. Opening a new practice is one of a couple's biggest challenges. So, when you and your spouse or partner have a frank discussion, talk about everything; avoid surprises. Starting a solo practice is challenging enough without adding domestic stress.

Should You Reveal Your Plans at Work?

Unless one of your colleagues at work is a personal friend, it's best NOT to reveal your plans prior to leaving (the obvious exception being if you discover that another colleague wants to solo, and you decide to partner up).

Once a firm hears of a possible departure, the partners assume the worst and usually activate all their defense systems to secure clients, supplies, and other firm resources. Why would a firm be afraid of your going solo? Because law firms are one giant living ego, and any threat—no matter how remote—usually raises suspicion. If you're more senior, with a couple of clients, your firm has even more reason to tighten ranks. So, be discrete about revealing your plans at work.

The other reason to be less than candid about your plans is the naysaying from colleagues. Just at a time when your deliberations are fresh and your optimism high, your colleagues may try to convince you that your plans are nothing less than career suicide. Or, if you work for a government agency or claims department, where risk-averse colleagues are biding their time in dead-end jobs, they might be quick to point out the folly of leaving the security of a solid job. You might even encounter naysaying from solos themselves. Disgruntled or unsuccessful solos may try to discourage you from starting a firm because they can't stand the idea that you might succeed where they could not.

Note: The foregoing advice assumes a) that your firm shows no indication of letting you go, or b) that it doesn't suspect that you're considering leaving. Any change in the status of A or B—i.e., you're notified that you will be terminated, or the firm learns you wish to leave—will trigger automatic changes in your relationship at the firm. Under these circumstances, there would be only minimal risk if you floated the possibility of looking for other opportunities, including starting your own firm.

Four Essential Questions

In the final analysis, the decision to start your own law firm may be more art than science, more instinct than reason. After you've examined your motivation, analyzed your business prospects, and engaged in exhaustive self-reflection and self-evaluation, the answers to four essential questions may well determine whether your new solo practice succeeds…or not:

1. **Are you willing to do what it takes to establish your firm?** Solo practice makes the greatest demands in areas where you have the greatest…and the least…competency. You will have make cold-calls in search of new business, reason with unreasonable clients, and, as a newcomer, face humiliation in court. You may find yourself photocopying documents at 2 a.m. Every solo can tell you stories about the most desperate thing they had to do to salvage a case or keep their firm afloat. If you're willing to do what it takes, chances are good you will succeed.

2. **Are you confident with your lawyering skills?** A solo practice puts so many nonlegal demands on your plate …from marketing and administrative arrangements to hand-holding clients…your legal abilities have to be a given. Having the legal ability to start a firm doesn't really depend on your actual skills, i.e., whether you've actually deposed a witness or drafted articles of incorporation. Rather, it is having the *belief* that you can handle any case with the training you had in law school, at your previous job, and with any follow-up research. No doubt, more practice will perfect your lawyering skills, but, at a minimum, you need to believe that with hard work you can perform a serviceable job every time out of the gate. However, if you see law as rocket science—something that takes years of practice—solo'ing will be difficult because you'll always feel unsure and obsess over each document before going on to other matters.

3. **Will you regret it?** Social science tell us that human beings suffer regret only for experiences we want but do not yet have…not for experiences we had regardless of their outcome. So, if, after extensive consideration, you're still on the fence about starting your own firm, you might as well go for it. Of course, it carries the inevitable risks; after all, you're leaving behind security, stability, and probably a decent group of colleagues. But even if starting your own firm turns out to be a disaster, you'll have the satisfaction that you had the courage to try. You'll only experience regret if you don't grab for the brass ring.

4. **Do you love the law?** Many lawyers with an entrepreneurial streak assume that they're ideally suited to starting a law practice. Surprisingly, they're often the ones who wind up less happy in solo practice because they never viewed law as a calling or an intellectually satisfying pursuit. Thus, they grow frustrated with the constraints of law practice: the ethics rules, the problem clients who you can't fire as easily as you'd like, and the challenges involved in researching and preparing cases. If you want to start a business, but don't particularly care about being a lawyer, open a pizza parlor, start a dot-com or a social media consulting business. Don't waste time and resources on a law firm. By contrast, if you love the law and take pride in serving clients or expanding access to justice and believe that what you do as a lawyer matters, don't let the potential obstacles stand in the way. Your passion for what you do will carry you through even the toughest time.

AUTHOR'S NOTE

A layoff or termination is a real blow to the ego. Some lawyers who lose their job question their ability to start a practice, wondering how they can successfully manage their own clients when they couldn't even cut it working for someone else. Others harbor so much anger and bitterness they can't function productively.

If you've been laid off, here are some things to keep in perspective from someone who's been there:

In my case, the managing partner walked into my office without warning and told me that I wasn't "partnership material", and that I had six months to find a new job. I was stunned, the say the least. I was too proud to beg for my job (to be honest, I'd been fairly unhappy and uninspired by the work for some time), and yet I felt that I had to say something. Before I knew it, these words tumbled out: "*I know that the firm's decision to let me go has nothing to do with my abilities. I know that I am a good lawyer. I was good enough for you to hire two years ago, and I'm just as good now. No matter what you think, I am a good lawyer and that I will succeed at whatever I do.*" I remember the managing partner just nodding at me with a mildly amused look, and then retreating as fast as he could out of my office.

In the months that followed, I struggled with feelings of failure as I looked for work. And whenever I felt ready to quit...and I did...it was always a faith in myself and my abilities that carried me through the really dark times.

If something similar happened to you, remember this: you had the capability and talent to finish three years of law school, pass a grueling bar exam, and convince an employer that you were worth hiring. That makes you as good a lawyer as anyone. Circumstances may have put you in an unfortunate situation: perhaps you were fired or laid off because the work didn't interest you...or you took a little longer to catch on than your peers...or your personality didn't mesh with your boss...or your firm just hit an economic downturn and management had to make some choices. You can't let those external forces detract from your belief in yourself, and you can't let them derail you from the career that you've worked so hard to attain.

SHOULD I FIRST SAVE A YEAR'S LIVING EXPENSES?

Some law practice management experts caution against solo'ing without having saved at least a year's worth of living expenses. Sensible in theory, in today's economic climate, it's completely impractical. In fact, most practicing solos (myself included), might never have hung out a shingle if we followed that advice.

That's not to say that having some cash reserves is entirely irrelevant. For example, if you intend to handle only large class-actions, or personal injury matters on an exclusively contingency basis, or take on cases like Social Security or workers comp where you may be required to take your fee from an attorneys' fee award when the case is over, then, yes, you'll need enough savings to see you through to a settlement or verdict. But unless you're planning to handle only matters where your payment comes after the case closes and you're unwilling to take any billable work, a sizeable nest egg—certainly a year's worth—isn't as important. And let's be honest, the one-year rule just isn't feasible for some lawyers. Those who were unexpectedly laid off, or who are working in dead-end, low-paying jobs, don't have the luxury of setting aside that much cash, and these are precisely the individuals who would benefit the most from starting a practice.

One more thought: unless you're independently wealthy or have a high-paying job, the process of setting aside a year's worth of expenses takes time...months, even years...during which you may get so discouraged and depressed about your existing job that your work suffers and you get fired anyway! Or, your spouse grows unhappy with his or her own job and quits first, thus preempting you from making your own break...or your courage fails you, and by the time you recover, your life circumstances are different...or you have another child or one on the way, or a larger mortgage, or you need to establish a college fund. Any or all these changes in circumstance could preclude, or at least delay, your going solo. Having a year's worth of expenses would definitely ease your mind and reduce your risks when you start out. But waiting until you reach the one-year benchmark carries risks of its own.

IN THEIR OWN WORDS

Q: Is there a solo type?

"Yes, there is a solo type. You have to be very self-motivated and reasonably organized. Otherwise, you will lose client trust or waste a lot of time." —Jeffrey G. Neu (class of 2006)

"You have to be the type who *wants* to solo. Sustaining a solo practice takes a lot of discipline and active participation. If you're not decisive, or adept at working alone in an efficient manner, or disciplined to enough to set and follow schedules and deadlines, your [solo practice] probably won't succeed."
—Adam Neufer (class of 2009)

"No, I do not think there is a specific type of person who is cut out to be a solo. People of all personalities are solo attorneys. [But if there is a solo type], it is the person who wants to run a business, and to live a happy life that he [or she] has some control over."—Paul Scott (class of 2008)

"I see solos as the legal world's entrepreneur; someone who has replaced thinking like an employee with thinking as an employer. The only real difference between solos and non-solos is the solo's willingness to trade job security for the freedom to control their practice. In my experience, solos are willing to innovate, to question, to think differently about old problems, to be imaginative, and to be willing to fail."
—Bruce Cameron (class of 2007)

"Some people excel in a BigLaw environment, others in a more structured government or in-house environment. A solo type has a high tolerance for risk, a high degree of self-reliance, and the resourcefulness to figure things out on one's own. Going solo also means being self-confident in one's work product and the ability to develop business."—Kevin Afghani (class of 2004)

"I think there are traits that make going solo easier: a willingness to accept risk, a fondness for multi-tasking between operating a small business and practicing law, and a willingness to self-promote. But I also think there are many 'types' that share these and other solo traits." —Cailie A. Currin (class of 1988)

"One really important thing about being solo is disciplining yourself to do what you have to within the time you have to do it. There's no one looking over your shoulder or e-mailing you to ask how you're progressing with a matter. So, if you're the type of person who needs constant poking to get work done, perhaps solo practice isn't right for you."—Jan M. Tamanini (class of 1984)

"The successful solo must have self-discipline! You don't have a supervisor breathing down your neck or a time card to punch. No one is taking issue with your billable hour quota, and you don't have a paycheck direct-deposited to your account every two weeks. You have to manage your time, manage your caseload, make your own schedule, and handle all the administrative stuff, too. Gradually you will find people to whom you can delegate certain tasks, but you are still the person who makes sure it's all done right. Some people just don't have the desire to shoulder that much responsibility. And that's okay. Just be honest with yourself about your personality and your motivations, or you'll be a miserable square peg in a round hole."—Gina Bongiovi (class of 2007)

"I think the key here is one's strong desire to be a solo. If you have that, you have a good chance to succeed. Beyond that, of course it helps to be tech-savvy, socially outgoing, and competent in the substantive law. But the key is your *desire* to be solo."—Mark Tanney (class of 1998)

"I don't know if there is a solo type, but there are *definitely* a few types that are not solo types. People who expect to swap one paycheck for another—that is, who think of themselves as employees instead of as owners and managers of a business—aren't going to do well. Salaried employees earn so much a week or so much a month, but solo practitioners have to think of earning so much a quarter or so much a year. A person who expects to take \$X out of his or her firm every month isn't going to be happy, but one who has a sensible plan to earn \$12X every year, and then carries out that plan, likely will be."
—Dean N. Alterman (class of 1989)

Excerpt from Solo by Choice, The Companion Guide: 34 Questions That Could Transform Your Legal Career (Carolyn Elefant, 2011)

CHAPTER 3

Should New Lawyers Solo?

"I think [new lawyers] can solo, but it would be so much harder. There is so much valuable information learned through working that can make the solo choice easier. But...if someone is dedicated to the [solo] path and works hard at it, it can be done."

—Cailie A. Currin, solo

"Yes [you can solo right out of law school], but I recommend against it. New graduates know a lot of law; maybe more than they ever will again. But law school doesn't teach anything about having employees, running a business, or negotiating with vendors."

— Dean N. Alterman, solo

Some law students go to law school with the intention of starting a firm as soon as they pass the bar. And now, with diminishing employment opportunities, many more new grads are considering the solo option. But is starting a firm right after law school feasible if you carry substantial student loan debt? And if you do get a job offer, should you turn it down to start a firm instead? As you'll see here, lawyers are sharply divided about whether rookie lawyers should open their own law practice. This chapter discusses some of the pros and cons, and you'll also find practical tips on what you can do in law school—or right after graduation—to lay the foundation for starting a practice.

Preliminary Considerations

Did you come to law school from another career? Prior work experience can give you a significant advantage in starting a firm right after law school. You probably have existing business contacts who could serve as clients, and your financial situation is no doubt more secure than that of a new grad.

Do you have other family support? Some law students have spouses or family members who can cover basic expenses while they get a practice off the ground. Though maybe it wasn't your original plan to move back in with mom and dad after graduation, or have your significant other support you, these types of arrangements can make soloing after law school much more feasible.

Have you received a job offer? Even if you're seriously considering soloing after law school, you may want to hold off if you've secured employment as an attorney. Even a year or two spent at a post-law school job can yield many benefits that will ultimately increase your chances of success when you do start your firm. For starters, by working for a year or two and living frugally, you can put a considerable dent in your student loans, relieving the financial pressure one typically experiences in the early days of solo practice. Moreover, law firm jobs and clerkships give young attorneys many opportunities to learn about practicing law, even if they don't provide any hands-on experience.

A new graduate who clerks for a trial or federal district court has the chance to make contact with local attorneys and to observe different courtroom techniques. And clerks on the appellate level—through their review of countless briefs—gain a solid feel for what qualifies as persuasive legal writing. Lawyers who matriculate to a states attorney, public defender office, or government agency may find themselves in court within a few months. Even grinding away as an associate, frantically tracking down obscure case law for a minor point in a 100-page memo or proofing a document several times over can teach skills that you'll use in solo practice.

Working at large firms trains lawyers to meet deadlines and work accurately under pressure; indeed, it helps them develop an instinct for distinguishing between the tasks that impact the outcome of the case and busy-work designed to build up hours. Finally, working at a firm gives you a chance to begin making contacts and developing a reputation while still getting paid.

Have you been unemployed for several months? If you still haven't found a law-related job after getting admitted to the bar, think seriously about starting a firm even for the short-term. At a minimum, you'll avoid a gap on your resume. In addition, many new lawyers who start a practice often wind up receiving job offers from colleagues who admire their initiative.

Did you receive a deferral or buyout from your law firm? Since 2008, many large firms have extended offers to new graduates, and then asked them to defer their start dates by as much as six months or a year. In some instances, the firms will pay a stipend to these lawyers as well as health insurance costs as they await employment. In other cases, some firms have offered a lump sum payment of $75,000 to law students in exchange for foregoing employment. These financial benefits can provide a nice nest egg for starting a practice.

What about student loan debt? Student loan debt may be a good reason to accept a job if you've been offered one…at least in the short term. Of course, in today's economy, a job offer isn't always a possibility. But that shouldn't impact your decision to solo; your loans will follow you whether you start a practice or not. So, if you don't have any other options, you might as well start a firm, building it up to the point where you can get on track to repay your loans.

The Solo Option For New Grads: Pro & Con

The pro:

No golden handcuffs. When you solo after law school and passing the bar, you don't suffer the loss of a six-figure income, or the sacrifice of such BigLaw perks as a secretary and an expense-account. As an ex-student, you're already accustomed to living frugally, and more likely to take in stride such cost-cutting sacrifices as sharing an apartment or subsisting on ramen noodles until you get your practice off the ground. And with the exception of your student loans, you're less likely to have the sort of major financial expenses—e.g., mortgage, car loan, family health insurance policy—that deters more settled lawyers from starting a law firm later on.

It may be the best option. Solo'ing makes sense if you can't find a job as a lawyer. After three years in law school and passing the bar, you are fully qualified to practice as a lawyer. So, why waste your newly acquired skills working as a paralegal, or—if you're a second-career lawyer—returning to a position where a law degree isn't required because it's the only job you could find? Better to start your own practice now, and get your money's worth out of your law degree.

It's easier to seek help. As a new grad, you're less likely to feel awkward asking for help, or seeking out mentors than more experienced lawyers who might feel some embarrassment about reaching out for support. Many lawyers are also more inclined to lend a hand to a newbie, figuring that they don't pose much of a competitive threat.

The most direct route to what you want. Some argue that if you're really certain you want to start your own law firm right away, working for others only postpones the dream. And there's some logic to that: after all, if you take a law firm job and resent it, you might perform badly and get fired.

The con:

Financial pressure. Even without a mortgage or other financial burdens, you may still have as much as $150,000 or more in student loans. And while you can defer—or spread out—your loan payments, there is no escaping the reality that your new solo practice will need to generate revenue right from the start. In this situation, you may feel pressure to take on unattractive cases or large amounts of low-paying, document-review projects just to pay rent. By contrast, if you have the opportunity to work for someone else for a couple of years and live frugally, you can make a substantial dent in your student loans before opening your practice. And don't forget, many schools now provide loan-forgiveness for grads going to government sector or legal aid groups (in some cases, as much as $5,000 or $10,000/year) as well.

Lack of contacts. You need time to build up an established network of professional contacts to serve as a source of referrals and references. In fact, it's generally accepted that most new solos need as many as three years to establish a network (which is why most new solos don't truly hit their stride until their third year of practice). By contrast, if you start your legal career working for a firm, the government, or some other employer, you can use the time for networking—participating in bar activities, attending conferences, meeting other lawyers through your job. Then, when you're ready to start your own practice, your network will have been set up.

You may not be taken seriously. Most clients don't ask or particularly care about how much experience you have. But other lawyers are more particular; they may inquire about your level of experience when considering whether to refer you cases, or to hire you for contract work. In fact, many lawyers hesitate to refer good cases to a lawyer straight out of school because they have no assurance the work will be performed competently. But if you go to work for a few years, particularly for a well-known firm or judge, other lawyers may feel more comfortable about sending you cases, and then—from time to time—you can ask for a referral from your former boss.

Laying the Groundwork in Law School

Whether you want to start a firm right out of law school or several years later, there are many steps you can take during law school to ease the transition and maximize your chances of success:

Financial management. As a law student, lenders will tempt you with extra loans to subsidize unpaid summer jobs or to help cover costs while you study for the bar. Don't succumb to temptation. Instead, spend a little time with an online calculator (e.g., www.edfed.com/resources/calculators.php) to help you figure out your post-law school month debt payments, and understand what your monthly repayment options will look like as you take on extra debt. Strapped for cash? Explore every possible option before signing on for another loan. Look for part-time work to defray expenses. A paid law-related position would be optimal, but even more mundane work—like working security at the law school, manning a desk at the library, or babysitting a professor's kids—will do. It's not stressful work, and may allow time to study. If your school offers a night school option, explore a transfer that lets you have a day job to help avoid debt. In the meantime, trim your expenses by moving to cheaper housing, making do without a car if possible, and cutting back on meals out and vacations.

Course selection. Though lawyers complain that law school doesn't teach the skills needed to start a practice, virtually every law school offers a variety of practical training in the second and third year. And most law schools have clinics to give you the opportunity for hands-on experience in advising clients, drafting complaints and briefs, and arguing cases in court. In addition to clinics, I recommend loading up on skills-related classes: negotiation, trial practice, contract drafting, legal writing. If your law school offers a class on how to start a law practice or on trust account management, take it as well. In *Solo by Choice, The Companion Guide,* lawyers with their own firm were asked what business skills they thought essential for a new solo? Many were adamant that basic accounting skills were essential. Cailie Currin, who has practiced law for 21 years and now in her third year as a solo, put it best:

> *"The use of accounting/billing software was the hardest for me, and I definitely floundered in trying to get that financial part of the practice established correctly. I felt lucky to have clients to bill, but I was not very proficient in getting those first few bills out. I spent a lot of money on an accountant to do it right after I had tried on my own."*

Work experience. Some law schools offer internship programs where students can seek placement in positions at legal aid clinics, judge's offices, or in-house at corporations. Though the internships are unpaid, students earn credits towards graduation requirements. Some solo-bound students make the mistake of ignoring internships because they rarely provide the chance to work in a solo or small firm office (though there are a few such programs). But there's a great deal of value to the contacts that you make in any internship position, and they will serve you well if you do start your own firm.

Practice management. Even in law school, get in the habit of employing cheap or low cost technology tools that you might someday use in practice to manage your experience as a law student. There are plenty of free applications that you can use to organize and store your notes and assignments, create to-do lists, and manage your finances. By becoming disciplined about using technology to organize yourself as a law student, it will be second nature by the time you solo.

Adjuncts. Most law school faculties employ experienced practitioners as adjunct professors. Make them your best friends! Most of the lawyers who serve as adjuncts can offer valuable career advice or possibly introduce you to potential contacts.

Online outreach. Both the Internet and social media give law students extraordinary access to mentors and contacts outside the confines of the law school. Law students can join listservs like the ABA's Solosez to learn more about solo practice, and to get to know other solo lawyers in the community. Many law students even send questions to popular solo bloggers about their practices, or introduce themselves to solo lawyers through Twitter.

Mentorships

What's the most important element to new grad's success as a solo? A mentor, of course. Hands down, most experienced solos agree that a mentorship is *indispensable* for lawyers starting a practice right out of school. Just ask Eric, Marc, Bruce, Gina, and Jan:

> *"[Mentors] play a huge role. So many answers aren't printed in books. You need [to find someone] to whom you can ask tons of stupid questions; someone you trust…and someone who respects what you're doing."* —**Eric P. Ganci (class of 2008)**

> *"I cannot imagine starting a practice without a mentor and/or lawyer contacts to help. I always run things by other lawyers before I act."* —**Marc W. Matheny (class of 1980)**

> *"Mentors and contacts are lifelines; when you need to figure out how this bit of law works…or how that form really needs to be formatted…or why sending one check to the county recorder will get your deed bounced back while sending two gets it recorded. Ask your mentor. Mentors and contacts are also your source for referrals."*
> —**Bruce Cameron (class of 2007)**

> *"Mentors and contacts are invaluable; books and CLE's can take you only so far. A mentor can help you brainstorm ideas, guide you in making decisions, and keep you from falling on your face."* —**Gina Bongiovi (class of 2007)**

"Having other attorneys for informal advice is an essential element of my practice. As a solo, you don't have the collegiality of other attorneys just down the hall to trade ideas and opinions—so you have to go to your bar groups or other formal and informal legal organizations to get that contact." —Jan M. Tamanini (class of 1984)

A good mentor can help the new solo cope with a steep learning curve by answering practical questions or sharing drafts of motions and complaints. Equally important, a mentor can keep a new solo out of trouble by offering advice on ethics dilemmas or dealing with a difficult client. Some schools, like the University of St. Thomas School of Law, offer an innovative mentoring program that pairs law students with experienced community lawyers and judges to introduce students to basic lawyering skills and to share their professional experiences. Even if your law school doesn't have a mentor program, you can find your own by reaching out to adjunct professors or building relationships on social media. For additional advice on mentors, see Chapter 4.

Nontraditional Opportunities

Not ready to fly solo after law school, but haven't been able to find employment? Consider these *quasi-solo* opportunities:

Apprenticeships. Lawyers once learned legal and practice skills by apprenticing with experienced attorneys. Even though apprenticeships are out of fashion, nothing prevents a new lawyer from proposing such an arrangement. Scott Greenfield, criminal defense lawyer and prominent blogger (http://blog.simplejustice.us) addressed the subject in a blog post entitled, *"Straight Into Solo When There's No Other Choice"*. The new lawyer, he writes, might offer to provide support services in exchange for an apprenticeship-type relationship. In the context of a criminal defense practice, the new lawyer might be required to handle late-night arraignments, retrieve files from the clerk's office, file papers. In return, the experienced lawyer would provide oversight and insight, and perhaps even hand off small cases that he or she might otherwise reject to give the new lawyer something to work on. *"If the new criminal defense lawyer has the capacity,"* Scott writes, *"She will grow in the relationship, perhaps even to the point of a partnership if she proves worthy of the interest. The respect will earn the new lawyer bigger case referrals, perhaps even co-defendants on multi-defendant cases and the admiration of others. On the other hand, if the newbie doesn't have the juice, it will become apparent."*

Working with an older solo. The first wave of boomer lawyers turns 65 this year, and some of the solos among them may start laying the groundwork for retirement by bringing on a younger lawyer to eventually take over their practice. In this relationship, the older lawyer typically remains on board for several years, introducing the younger lawyer to clients and providing oversight and training. Over time, the younger lawyer would take on increasing amounts of responsibility, allowing the older lawyer to step back and eventually sell the firm to the younger lawyer.

Part-time opportunities. In every community, there are solo and small firms that have situational needs but not enough work to warrant a full-time hire. Such opportunities are not usually advertised, and might only become apparent through networking and word of mouth. Of course, you could take a more proactive approach. Place a "situation wanted" ad on Craigslist or in a bar newsletter, expressing your interest in part-time work or in a "successor" capacity. You might also approach one of the local lawyers after making a presentation at your law school. In this situation, you might propose to work a few hours a day, and use the remaining time to launch your own practice.

Make a name for yourself. It's never too early to start building your reputation. Take steps to get your name in circulation…even in law school. Start a blog, serve on a bar committee, help organize speaking panels and invite lawyers in the community who you want to get to know, or offer to co-author articles with a more experienced lawyer. Making a name for yourself will help advance your career whether you solo or not.

One final word. If you do accept employment right after law school, don't wait too long—no more than five to six years—before starting your own practice. After that, life may have other plans: house, family, the seductive appeal of a steady paycheck, and the possibility your spouse/partner will lose their job or decide to stay home with the kids. And there's always the possibility that colleagues or co-workers may try to talk you out of starting a firm. Remember: just as there are risks to starting a firm too soon, there are risks that you won't start a firm at all if you work too long for someone first.

WHY I WENT SOLO RIGHT AFTER LAW SCHOOL *by David A. Swanner, Esq.*

I went to law school in Ohio in the 1990s, and moved to South Carolina, where I took the Bar and opened my practice. My father had a business there, so I was able to work out of his office. In the beginning, I did commercial leases, incorporation, real estate closings. After awhile, I learned I could handle most matters as long as I was willing to spend three times as much time and effort as it would normally take with an experienced lawyer. As part of my education, I talked to, and lunched with, older lawyers. They threw me their scraps and cast-offs. Some of the cases were worthwhile; some weren't. In time, my real estate and trial practice clashed. So, I decided to stop doing real estate and focus on litigation. I attended ATLA Colleges, got involved with our state's trial lawyer association, started attending and speaking at conferences, and—in time—found myself becoming a better lawyer. In 10 years, I built a solid practice doing the kind of law that I want to practice. It's taken time, being nice to people, working hard, focusing on truly helping my clients, working on getting better at what I do, and taking a few wrong turns along the way.

You can start your own practice straight out of law school. It's tough but not impossible. A quick few Q&A's to think about:

Q: Where should a new solo begin looking for work?
A: Two areas of law where there is always more work than money is family law and criminal. Of course, charging $1,500 for doing $2,500 of divorce work isn't good business, but it could be a lifesaver if you're just starting out. Also, remember that clients with small cases do shop for price. In the long run these are not the clients who will make you happy or profitable…but they will help you get started.

Some other thoughts:

Established lawyers often require a minimum retainer of $5,000 before talking to clients regarding a divorce situation. As a result, they turn away quite a few people who can't afford the retainer. As a new lawyer, you probably won't have the same overhead, so call established attorneys about sending you clients who can't afford their fees. At the same time, inquire if they're interested in handing off cases too small for them to take on. As a start-up, you will be able to profit from some of these cases while an established lawyer might not. It will be your job to screen these cases to see which ones you can help with profitability.

Every attorney has a certain number of appointed family court or criminal cases. In larger firms, the appointed cases get pushed to the youngest associate. In smaller firms, the attorneys handle the appointed work themselves. Talk to those attorneys, and tell them you will handle their appointed cases for a flat rate. If you price it right, they'll be delighted to have someone take it over for them. Also, if you get some experience in handling certain kinds of cases, you can price the cases attractively, help your client, and still make a profit.

Talk to the Clerk of Court and let her know that you are looking for cases, and would be happy if your name comes up more often than it should in the rotation. Often times the court is looking for someone who actually wants the cases.

Q: Will clients trust, or even hire, a new solo?

A: Yes. When I opened my practice, I was always candid with prospective clients. I'd tell them, 'I've been practicing four months and haven't handled a case like this before, but this is the approach I would take.' And then I would describe how I proposed handling their matter. When I finished, I'd say something like, 'I just want to let you know up front that because I'm new I won't immediately know all the answers to your questions but I will get the answers for you.' And, then, depending on the size of the case, I might add: …And if it looks like it's going to be a difficult situation, I won't be shy about asking a more experienced lawyer for help, or to call someone to take over the case if it's appropriate. I won't let pride get in the way. Handling your case correctly is the most important thing to me.' I used a variation of this, and it worked like a charm. People would say, 'Okay. We'll go with you.' It is my opinion that people want lawyers who will talk to them without talking down to them, who will work hard on their case, give them straight answers, and not charge too much.

Q: How can a new lawyer compete with experienced lawyers and established firms?

A: By 'out-hustling' the more established firms…by giving faster service…by being more responsive…by just plain being nice. Talk to the clients, find out about their business, find out what they want…and then do it. What's great about being your own boss is that you can spend whatever time and effort a case needs even if the amount of work is grossly out of proportion to the fees that you will earn. I did that on purpose when I started out. Of course, I tried not to do that twice. But if you want to compete with experienced lawyers and established firms, it's important that once you get involved in a case that you do whatever is necessary to handle the case properly. Even if it means taking a beating in the fees on a case. There's plenty of time to analyze later what you did, and what you can do better next time.

Q: I can research a legal issue, but what about practical things like filing a complaint?

A: Just ask court personnel or other lawyers. It's amazing how far a little humility goes. Say something like, 'This is the first time I've ever filed one of these things. Do I have everything I need or is there something else I have to do on this?' Most court personnel will be glad to help only because it makes life easier when filings are done properly. And believe me, you won't be the first young lawyer they've had to help out…and there are many experienced lawyers who do things wrong and never learn the right way things to do things.

—David Swanner (info@davidvsgoliath) practices in Myrtle Beach SC.

WHY I *DIDN'T* SOLO RIGHT AFTER LAW SCHOOL *by Peter Olson, Esq.*

I gave some serious thought to starting my own solo law practice right out of law school; I'm glad I chose not to. Of course today I have my own small law firm and even write a blog (www.SoloinChicago.com) about my journey of building a Chicago-based solo practice. But I'm glad I waited to start my own firm until roughly four years after I was graduated from law school. I'm a better lawyer today because I DID NOT start my practice right out of law school.

I recently concluded a six-year legal dispute regarding real estate owned by an older woman and her adult son that was very bitter and contentious…much worse than any divorce case I've ever been involved with. My opposing counsel for virtually the entire case was a gentleman who had graduated law school the same year I had, but he had started a practice straight out of law school…and it showed! He had never been grounded in the "lawyer basics" that were ground into me by my first boss. I'd get these pleadings that were utterly baseless, had no chance of being granted, and simply wasted everyone's time. The case probably took a year longer than it should have due to these wrong-minded pleadings. He had to bring in another attorney to do depositions in the case. At trial, the degree to which his witnesses were coached in how to answer questions on the witness stand was comical. And, sadly, I know he had serious money problems with his client that probably would have been avoided had he seen how a more seasoned lawyer ran her or his practice.

Just like there are bad plumbers and bad doctors, there are bad lawyers. Opposing counsel was a generally good and earnest person; I just think that he did not know what he did not know. He was never drilled in lawyer basics, and I'm convinced this deficiency will hinder him for many years to come.

Think long and hard about your first post-law school professional experience. The impact might be larger than you think!

—**Peter Olson**, www.thelawstreetjournal.com/3l/why-you-shouldnt-start-a-solo-law-practice-straight-out-of-law-school, Nov. 29, 2010. Peter blogs at www.SoloinChicago.com.

IN THEIR OWN WORDS

Q: Should new lawyers solo?

"Don't do it unless your heart is in it. But if you do, get a mentor who is no more than 10 years out of law school. They can give you relevant, helpful advice." —**Jenee Oliver (class of 2005)**

"…Be honest with yourself; not everyone is cut out to have their own practice. You'll be miserable if you try to be a business owner when you might be happiest as an employee." —**Gina Bongiovi (class of 2007)**

"[What I would tell new grads] is that solo'ing may or may not be for them. They should work in different environments …and know themselves…before making the decision. And they shouldn't go solo by default (e.g., layoff) or do it for the money. Solo because you like the profession, have the guts, want to be your own boss, and can deal with the ramifications of that decision." —**Spencer Young (class of 2004)**

"There are two diametrically opposed schools of thought [about] solo'ing right out of law school. For myself, I feel it was important that I had a good grounding in the substantive law via work experience, practice skills, and practice management, before I went solo. I'm sure I'd have made many more mistakes if I'd gone solo right from law school, and would have missed out on some excellent experiences. Others feel that a new grad can go solo…but I believe that it's much harder." —**David Abeshouse (class of 1982)**

"Yes [you can solo right out of law school], but I recommend against it. New graduates know a lot of law (maybe more than they ever will again), but law school doesn't teach anything about having employees, running a business, or negotiating with vendors." —Dean N. Alterman (class of 1989)

"You will probably work harder as a solo than working for someone else! If you don't have the drive and courage necessary to be a business owner, you will not succeed. Building a law practice is not a Field of Dreams: if you just build it, they [clients] will not come. You need to be able to practice law AND be a great business owner and marketer at the same time." —Gabriel Cheong (class of 2007)

"I think one can [solo right out of law school], but it would be so much harder. There is so much valuable information learned through working that can make the solo choice easier. But…if someone is dedicated to the [solo] path and works hard at it, it can be done." —Cailie A. Currin (class of 1988)

"Consider spending at least a couple of years with a law firm to learn the fundamentals of practicing law in the areas you seek, and learn the day-to-day operations and management of a law firm."
—Brian M. Annino (class of 2003)

"Unless you're extremely well-connected in law school, I don't know how a new law school graduate could have a client or contact base that would allow him/her to pay down their student loans. If you do choose to solo, consider project-partnering with an experienced lawyer in your practice area. They will be able to provide you with referrals and the mentoring you need. Of course, they will also probably require you to share fees with them, but this sacrifice could yield long-term benefits. I recommend partnering with an attorney who allows you to have direct contact with clients for which you perform the work."
—Kevin Afghani (class of 2004)

"For some practice areas, a new attorney fresh out of law school can do fine (I'm thinking criminal defense, for example, where you can get on a bar counsel list and at least have some guaranteed clients and get some experience completely apart from marketing and business generation). For other areas, that's more difficult. You just can't waltz out of law school into a business litigation practice and expect to succeed in the short term; law school doesn't teach you how to practice law. Clients need to know that you have experience, and they are usually not eager to be your guinea pig. And then there is your ethical obligation to your clients to represent them competently. You can't do that if you don't even know what questions need asking, or what steps need to be taken. If you must solo [without legal experience]—or if you have always felt that this is what you want to do—go for it. But if you have the option of working in a firm for a few years, do that instead. You'll see how things are really done, and that will translate into self-confidence that you actually can do it." —Mitchell J. Matorin (class of 1993)

"It is certainly possible to hang your shingle right out of law school, but it would be better to get a few years of experience. Not necessarily legal experience; instead, experience in the inner workings of a law firm work: how to create files, how correspondence should be saved, etc. If getting a few years experience is not possible, some law school internships could definitely achieve the same goal. And if that is not possible, go to a lot of CLE's on law practice management." —Paul Scott (class of 2008)

"Go for it…but do this first: talk to three solo lawyers to get a sense for different perspectives, ideas, struggles; think about how to keep your overhead low at the start, and create a business plan that includes a mission statement and a SWOT analysis. I would also tell [new grads] that starting out you will feel that your efforts are not working…you will reach out to people for work and referrals, and it will feel that nothing came of the effort…and you will place advertisements and it will seem as if no one sees them. But, eventually, you will see a steady stream of business, and realize that all of your hard work early on did pay off." —Tonya Coles (class of 2006)

"If you try [solo'ing] but you don't like it…move on. Nothing has to be forever." —Nina Kallen (class of 1994)

Excerpt from *Solo by Choice, The Companion Guide: 34 Questions That Could Transform Your Legal Career* (Carolyn Elefant, 2011)

II. PLANNING THE LAUNCH

CHAPTER 4

A Course of Action

"If I'm going to work the hours of a litigation attorney, I want to be the one who decides what cases I take, and I want to reap the benefits without having them go to a partner playing golf while I work all week-end." —Jill Pugh, solo

Lawyers come to solo practice from so many different career paths and life stages. Perhaps you're a lawyer with a decade or more at a firm, or you're a second-year associate recently laid off, or you're a graduate just stepping into the legal job market, or you're a lawyer-mom who left the work force to raise a family and want to solo now as a way to re-enter the field, or you're a lawyer with steady contract assignments, or you're employed in a non-legal position, and would like to solo but are concerned about leaving the security of your "day" job. Your course of action will be slightly different in each case.

The first part of this section describes the most common paths to solo practice, and the tasks and priorities unique to each. Section two focuses on the planning common to each of the scenarios, including preparing a business plan, acquiring necessary skills, and increasing your visibility.

Starting Your Own Firm: Four Scenarios

Scenario 1. You're currently employed and planning a voluntary departure. You have the luxury of researching a solo practice, spending time on a business plan, and paying down your student loans while collecting a paycheck. The downside is that you might be tempted to postpone your departure until you get that next bonus or you bring in another client. If you're serious about starting your own firm, give yourself six months to a year. If you still haven't left, you just might wind up staying where you are.

Your priorities now:

Start saving. If you're earning money now, start cutting back on discretionary expenses, accelerate your loan repayment, and sock away enough money so you'll have a cushion when you start your practice. Cutting back now will be good practice for the sacrifices you'll likely make in the first year or two of practice, when you'll either experience a decrease in revenues or cash flow shortages while awaiting your first payments from clients.

Invest in your future. Even as you start cutting back, invest in equipment and books and skills training that will be useful in your practice. It will be easier to spend money now on a smartphone, laptop, tablet, resource manual, or law firm marketing program than after your paychecks stop coming.

Take advantage of firm resources. There's nothing unethical about asking ask your firm to pay for bar dues or for the types of seminars it ordinarily would subsidize...so long as you make sure the firm accrues the same benefits from your attendance as it would if you were not leaving. Use discretion and common sense. Obviously, putting in a reimbursement form for a CLE class on How to Start a Law Firm or, Defending Clients as a Court-Appointed Attorney benefits only you personally. At the same time, asking the firm to cover costs associated with a course on issues within the firm's practice area is a fair request, provided that you summarize the proceedings in a memo to the file, or make sure that the firm gets a copy of the conference attendance list for its contacts database (though you can keep a copy for yourself). So long as the firm obtains value from its investment, you're not cheating the firm. And, if your business development pays off and you reel in a large client after you leave, you can repay your firm by hiring it to help with overflow work.

Investigate new substantive areas. Part of your motivation in leaving your current employment may be to add or to change to another practice area. If so, get busy learning about the new field through books, skills training, and/or bar courses. After learning more about this new area of practice, you may decide that it's not viable or that you need still more training. Now is the time to resolve this question.

Scenario 2. You're terminated suddenly from an existing position. Either your firm has dissolved unexpectedly, or you committed an error that prompted your dismissal. In either case, you're probably too shell-shocked to ponder your next move. Once you come to terms with the situation (and get beyond the anger, frustration, or depression), you can start thinking more rationally about whether to start a law firm. The worst time to consider starting a firm is right after you've been fired. From personal experience, I can tell you that your confidence will be shaky and your abilities in doubt. If you have been let go, give yourself at least a few weeks to recover before thinking about your next steps.

Your priorities now:

Damage control. When you're terminated unexpectedly, you've got to act strategically to ensure that you can survive the next few months financially. Speak with your employer's HR personnel, focusing on what benefits (e.g., unemployment, severance, unpaid vacation or health insurance) you can get from your employer. You may also want to consider whether you have legal recourse for your termination, and to evaluate whether a lawsuit makes sense (see Chapter 5, To Sue or Not to Sue). Finally, if you're forced out in a hurry, make sure to gather up copies of your work product and contact information for clients whom you personally served.

Buyouts and severance. Some employers may allow you to stay on the job for a few more months after they've given notice of a layoff (or will permit you to continue to use office space for a short time). Others may ask you to leave immediately and offer severance pay. More recently, some firms have been offering buyouts to new hires and new grads in exchange for declining an associate position; other firms are asking grads to defer their start dates in exchange for insurance coverage and a stipend for student loans and living expenses. You need to figure out whether it makes sense to stay on at a firm where layoff is imminent, or where a start date is unclear…or negotiate for a lump-sum payout. Note: some offers have been fairly generous.

Take advantage of interview opportunities. Some employers will feel badly about layoffs and may share job leads or even pay for placement counseling. Even if you're leaning towards starting a solo practice, don't automatically reject opportunities for interviews; they may provide introductions to lawyers who can serve as a potential source of business or contract work even if you don't get, or decline, to accept an offer. And you can also use these interviews to take a pulse of your industry, and to generate marketing ideas that you may want to pursue if you decide to start your own practice. Of course, if you're on the fence, job interviews may help you solidify your decision. After you sit through one interview after the other—with lawyers who themselves can barely muster up any enthusiasm for describing their work—you just might have an "aha moment" when you realize that you don't want to sign up for more of the same.

Consider the case of solo Mark Tanney (class of 1998):

"I was laid off from a good DC law firm in June 2009 after working there for six years. At first I thought about seeking employment again with a firm or with the government. I worked up a number of resumes and applied for a few positions…but my heart was not in it. I could barely force myself to write another cover letter stating, yet again, how I was a 'team player,' a 'self starter,' and a 'problem-solver.' I knew that I wanted to go out on my own. In a previous career, I owned several businesses in the foodservice industry, and I missed the feelings of freedom and control that goes along with being an entre- preneur. As a solo, the hours are very long right now, and my success is by no means assured. But I am enjoying the process, and I am glad I made this choice."

UNEMPLOYMENT BENEFITS: CAUTION

If you've been laid off, you'll likely qualify for unemployment benefits, and these can be a godsend when you're just starting out.

Though you typically only get two or three hundred dollars a week, even that amount can help cover start-up costs like practice manuals, legal research service, or rent (if you choose to rent commercial space). To collect benefits, you need to show ongoing efforts to find work, which you can do by signing up for various contract lawyer agencies. *But remember, some states prohibit the self-employed from collecting any benefits.* In 2009, a laid-off New York attorney named Karin moved out of state and started writing a food blog that she monetized with Google Ads and earned $238. The New York Department of Labor determined that the earnings proved that Karin was really self-employed as a blogger and cut her unemployment benefits. (for details, go to www.forbes.com/2009/10/07/blogger-google-unemployment-personal-finance-google-adsense.html). Though the Department later reinstated Karin's benefits— finding that her blog was a hobby rather than a business—new solos opening up a practice can't make the same claim. Bottom line: check your state's labor laws regarding unemployment compensation and self-employment and plan accordingly.

Scenario 3. You're unemployed. In this scenario, you're a law student who wants to solo right out of law school, or you're a new grad without work, or a lawyer who left the law to raise a family and wish to re-enter the field. In each case, you have more time to plan for solo practice (especially if you're a new grad, since you won't even get your bar results until a few months after you take the bar), but you face challenges that actively practicing lawyers may not face: you lack certain legal and practice skills or your skills may be out-of-date.

Your priorities now:

Set some deadlines for decision. If you've been unemployed for a while or haven't yet entered the workplace…and solo practice is a *reluctant* option…you may be tempted to postpone your decision in the hopes that another employment opportunity develops. Maybe it will, but don't let indecision paralyze you. If you have decided to solo for want of other options, you need to set a reasonable deadline to get started— say, four or six months—and keep…moving…forward.

Focus on skills development. Whether you're a new grad or a re-entering lawyer, you need to acquire or brush up on skills. If you're not completely familiar with the latest law firm technology—whether it's how to use the newest word processing or accounting software, or understanding the advantages of "cloud computing", start learning now. In addition to CLE's, check out community college or adult ed programs as well as courses offered at the Apple stores (if you have a Mac). Many product vendors also offer online training, as well as an opportunity to test drive technology for a trial period. Resources on the latest law firm technology are abundant: check out the ABA's Legal Technology Center (www.abanet.org/tech/ltrc/); Ross Kodner's Microlaw site (www.microlawyer.com); Neil Squillante's Web site (www.Technolawyer.com), and my own blog (www.MyShingle.com). For substantive skills, check out the resources discussed in the second half of this chapter.

Professional visibility. For law firm marketing purposes, establishing professional visibility is paramount. Many law blawgs and online legal periodicals are in search of content, and publishing an article or essay is a good way to get noticed. Or start your own blawg on an emerging topic. Pro bono offers its own opportunities; representing a pro bono client can help you gain substantive training. And volunteering for a board of a charitable organization that deals with matters where you might want to focus your practice (e.g., historic preservation or artists or small entrepreneurs) can bring you to the attention of others in that community. For more ideas on gaining visibility, see chapters 14–17.

Scenario 4. Contract work or a non-legal job. Some lawyers face a unique conundrum: they're attracted to solo practice but reluctant to part with a steady paycheck even though they're trapped in a dead-end job doing doc review or they returned to non-legal employment.

Their priorities now:

What about starting a part-time practice? It's not ideal, but you could always open a part-time practice. Do contract lawyering (see Chapter 9), or start a virtual law firm that lets you interact with clients online and do the work at your convenience (see chapters 6 and 13). Or start a nights-and-weekend firm in which you rent "virtual" office space (or ask if a colleague might share), and meet with potential clients off-hours. In this scenario, you would focus on transactional matters, where court time generally isn't required. Or, if your day job is flexible, you could take on small, civil, or administrative litigation matters; even generating a revenue stream by referring cases for which you lack the time or ability to handle in jurisdictions where referral fees are permitted. Most important, you need to investigate your employer's policy on moonlighting. Many contract law positions prohibit outside work arrangements while handling cases on the side, and working at a law firm can give rise to conflicts or expose your employer to malpractice claims.

What's the goal? If you do decide to start a part-time practice, identify a threshold—in terms of hours spent or earnings—when you expect to graduate to a full-time solo practice. Without a goal, you could find yourself juggling your day job and a fledgling practice without getting ahead in either.

Laying the Foundation

Don't expect business to materialize overnight. Most new solos say it can take weeks, even months, before networking events, blogging, and other marketing efforts, begin to show results. And while you may think you'll have a lot of free time at the beginning, you'll actually be busier than you thought. Consider the observations of three solos who set up their firms:

> *"That first year was definitely a struggle: setting up the technology, the business accounts, working out Web sites and letterheads. I didn't have time to look around. By the end of my first year, it was evident that I had done a lot to lay the foundation, but that now I had to really build a successful firm on top of it."* —Gabriel Cheong (class of 2007)

> *"For the first eight months, I waited with almost unbearable anticipation for the phone to ring. When it did, I felt like hiding under my desk. I was stuck between the excitement of building my business and the terror that I would screw something up. For a few months—especially in the beginning—the fear was almost paralyzing. I'd find myself in tears some days, wondering what I'd done; whether I'd made the right decision to start my own firm, or to even attend law school."* —Gina Bongiovi (class of 2007)

> *"[Those first few months] were exciting and terrifying. Exciting to set up the office, choose furniture, get stationery and business cards, make contacts, network; terrifying [when I] wondered if I would be able to make ends meet and have enough clients to sustain a practice."* —Abbe W. McClane (class of 2003)

Before opening for business, it's important to start laying a foundation for your future success. What follows are some preparatory activities common to all future solos, irrespective of your current circumstances. What may differ are the deadlines for completing these tasks, and the priority that you assign to them in light of your individual time constraints. At the end of this section, you'll find a suggested time-line for different start-up scenarios.

Become More Visible

Social media. Moving onto social media before you start your firm is a no-brainer: it's free and easy to use. At a minimum, bulk up your profile on LinkedIn and other online directories; upload past writings to JDSupra; start following others in your field on Twitter. For a discussion of social media, see Chapter 15. Creating an online presence is a good temporary strategy while you get your Web site up and running.

Start a blog. These days, the fastest way for lawyers to make a name for themselves is by blogging. Consider the case of Howard Bashman, one of the blogosphere's legal luminaries. Some years ago, Bashman launched a blog (www.appellateblog.com) that was devoted exclusively to appellate litigation. Though it began while he was still a partner at a BigLaw firm in Pennsylvania, Bashman's blog was a personal project he undertook on his own time. Within six months, his analysis, his prolific postings (several times a day), and his monthly feature—20 Questions For an Appellate Judge—generated several thousand hits a day from reporters, attorneys, federal judges, professors, and law clerks. Two years later, Bashman opened a solo practice, and his online visibility continues to generate business for his new firm and enhance his reputation as a nationally recognized appellate expert. It's never too soon to start a blog. Kevin O'Keefe recently posted about a law student who started a blog about his dreams of solo'ing. As a result, the blog gave him national exposure and he wound up with a job at a law firm instead (see www.kevin.lexblog.com/2007/05/lawyer-blog-success-stories/law-grad-lands-job-with-large-firm-by-blogging). For blogging tips, see Chapter 15, and for information on a lawyer's blog rights, see Chapter 5.

Write articles. Law reviews and monthly bar magazines once served as the only platform for lawyer-written articles. The Internet transformed the landscape; these days, it's never been easier to get published. You can still pursue law reviews and the legal trades to highlight your expertise. In the meantime, consider drafting 750–2,500-word articles or Op-Eds for Web sites and online publications, in addition to weekly legal media, and local or national newspapers.

Send papers to conferences. Go online and start searching for the conferences in your practice area that have issued calls for papers. Most trade shows and conferences begin soliciting papers at least six months in advance, and all that is usually required at the beginning is a two-page abstract. Note: some big-name conferences extend preference to existing members who are active in the organization, but many are always looking for new names and ideas to fill the program.

Investigate New Substantive Areas

Starting a law firm isn't just a matter of procedure, as some how-to books would have you believe. You also need to prepare yourself substantively to serve clients, to avoid malpractice, and to diversify your skills so can expand your market. Example: if you're starting a firm and hope to gain some real litigation experience, or take on court-appointed work, you will probably want to sign up for training courses. If you have a narrow specialty that may not sustain a practice, explore related practice areas so you can leverage your existing experience. All this supposes you have some lead time. If not, put off the substantive preparation until after you open your doors. Better yet, squeeze in substantive classes while you're still employed, or, if you're a student, while waiting for your bar results. If you are still working somewhere, you can sign up for a relevant seminar on the firm's dime (but be sure to write up a summary so the firm shares in the benefit).

Suggestions for substantive preparation:

Training courses. For basic training on wills and estates, domestic relations, bankruptcy and consumer credit, you can forego all those costly CLEs in favor of training courses offered for pro bono attorneys. Such classes are taught by practicing attorneys with years of experience in the field, and who can explain the law. More importantly, they offer practice tips such as how to file a case, and the potential pitfalls not apparent from the statutes or regulations. In addition, many of your instructors will welcome an occasional phone call for assistance once you open a practice. Some of these pro bono trainings charge a *de minimis* fee, while others require you to agree to handle one or two small matters in exchange (though neither I nor anyone I know was ever actually sent a referral). If you plan on taking on court-appointed criminal work and lack experience, take a class. It will not only insulate your future clients from stupid mistakes, but the course will build your confidence, and help you make a better impression in the courtroom before the judge and other lawyers...all of whom are prospective referral sources. Sometimes, a public defenders' office or local bar section will offer a free or reasonably-priced course on criminal practice. Back when I started my firm, I took a free three-day workshop sponsored by the public defenders' office and filled up 75 pages of notes, including a helpful little mantra to recite when a client was arraigned.

Seminars in your practice area. Do you practice in a field where some important transition is underway? Perhaps a new law has been passed, or an agency has issued regulations that will bring about new changes. Such developments generate market opportunities: they create more work as clients scramble to deal with new uncertainty, and tend to level the playing field, giving younger attorneys a leg up on more established colleagues who no longer have the advantage of experience. Seminars, some of which can be costly, address these transitional issues. I suggest you sign up for the course while you're still employed and ask your firm to pay. So long as you make a good impression for your firm while you're at the conference, and report back on what you've learned, the firm will get its money's worth. However, if you're unemployed or have just started a firm, approach a colleague and offer to attend the conference and provide written summaries in exchange for picking up or sharing the cost. Finally, see if any online webinars or lower cost local bar events will duplicate the more costly seminars.

Skills classes. At least in the early days of your firm, you'll probably perform most of the tasks, including court or deposition appearances, document-drafting, proofing, and document formatting. As time permits, you may want to take a course or find some training on, say, writing appellate briefs or using the electronic filing system down at the court. These are the sort of courses that you're usually too busy to take, but which can improve your practice. Where possible, make time to brush up on practice skills before you open your firm.

Fast cash solutions. Start exploring some of the fast-cash solutions discussed in Chapter 9. Some of these prospects may require some lead time; for example, you may need to take a training course which is only offered at certain times, or wait until projects are available. If you can put at least one or two fast-cash solutions in motion before you open your door, you'll help alleviate some of the stress you may feel once your salary comes to an end.

Online courses. Attending programs in person also serve a networking function. But sometimes, and particularly if you're currently working or home with kids, it's tough to find the time. Fortunately, online programs—both free and fee—abound. The ABA has reduced rates for solos, Solo Practice University (www.solopracticeuniversity.com) and Lawline offer reasonably priced courses, and many law practice vendors sponsor free programs on marketing, IOLTA accounts, and other practice management topics. Take advantage of them.

Jump on Deadlines

Take care of matters that require lead time as early as possible in advance of starting your firm. If you need to gain admission to another state bar, put the process in motion; if you decide to waive into another state bar, the application will take several months to process. And you will have to allow even more time if you need to take a bar exam in another jurisdiction. In addition to the time needed to study for the test, most bars ask that you register for the exam several months in advance. Similarly, if you're interested in court-appointed work or serving on an alternative dispute resolution panel at your court, you may need to go through an application process. If you put it in motion early, it will be ready when you open for business.

Finding Mentors

As discussed earlier, mentors are key to succeeding…especially if you're a new lawyer. But even if you're a seasoned practitioner, a mentor can act as a Sherpa to guide you through the nitty-gritty issues related to starting and running a practice.

How to find and work with a mentor?

Start close and expand. To find a mentor, begin with solos you know. But don't limit yourself to personal acquaintances. Listservs and social media are a terrific resource for finding mentors outside your existing circle. As you spend time on a listserv or social media forums like LinkedIn or Twitter, you'll get to know other participants who share your background, and who offer particularly useful advice or who work nearby. Once you've identified someone with whom you'd like to work, set up a meeting or arrange a call to ask some questions. At the close of your meeting or talk, ask if you can follow up with other questions. Needless to say, follow up with a thank-you.

Don't be shy. Most solos give freely of their time, and are usually flattered when asked to help out a new solo.

Don't take advantage. The purpose of a mentor is to provide informal advice and feedback when you're out of your depth...not to serve as an unpaid consultant on a matter for which you're being well-compensated. Nor should you take the forms, pleadings, and knowledge that a mentor generously supplied and use the materials to poach your mentor's clients. Finally, try to avoid being a "foul-weather" mentee who contacts a mentor only when there's a problem. Keep in touch with your mentors every few months to let them know how you're doing even if you don't have a specific question. Want to know more about mentoring? Get a copy of *The Lawyer's Guide to Mentoring* by Ida Abbott, Esq.

WORKING WITH A MENTOR

Mentors can play different roles; teacher, advisor, role model, sponsor. They may help you develop your obvious strengths or awaken your latent talents. Some mentors will work with you over a long period of time; others will leave you a pearl of wisdom at a providential moment. What follows are a few suggestions about the mentoring relationship from author Ida Abbott:

Demonstrate your commitment. Mentors are more willing to give you their time and attention when they know you are committed to your career, your profession.

Expect guidance not rescue. It's not the role of a mentor to solve your problems, correct your mistakes, or get you out of difficult situations. Go to your mentor for advice and suggestions.

Ask about boundaries. Be clear about any limits your mentor wants to place on subject matter, time, or confidentiality. Assume the relationship will focus on professional not personal issues.

Limit your expectations. Informal mentoring relationships have no time limits; some last for a few days, others for months or years. Still, when you begin, keep your expectations short term and reasonable.

Take charge of your plan. You, not your mentor, are the one responsible for achieving your goals. Show initiative, and keep your mentor informed of your progress.

Disagree respectfully. Your mentor's advice may not always present the wisest course of action. Give it serious consideration, but think independently.

Be patient. Mentoring is based on relationship, and like all relationships, it takes persistence and time. Don't expect immediate results.

Stay in touch, be responsive. When you can't meet in person, keep in touch electronically. And promptly answer phone calls, emails, and requests.

Keep your mentor informed. Tell your mentor how you apply the knowledge and skills you learn from your mentor, and how you use the advice or assistance you receive.

Say thank you. Your mentor is voluntarily assisting your learning and development. Although they expect nothing in return, do not take them for granted.

Excerpted with permission from *Working With a Mentor: 50 Practical Strategies for Success*, by Ida Abbot (published by and available at www.NALP.org).

Change Your Mindset About Networking

At most of the BigLaw-dominated events that I attend, the large firm and government attorneys usually huddle together, showing little if any enthusiasm for conversation—let alone exchange business cards—outside their circle. Moreover, after events that involve a speaker, these same lawyers usually race back to their offices rather than introduce themselves to other attendees or the speaker. On the rare occasion I have been able to engage one in conversation, he or she comes across as bored and uninterested, or suddenly preoccupied with the pile of papers on their desk at the office. Talk about anti-networking!

As you begin thinking about solo'ing, it is critical—really, absolutely critical—that you change your mindset about networking. If you see it as one more unpleasant task, you rule out serendipitous possibilities. As the clock ticks down towards starting your law firm, find a way to get comfortable with networking . . . because it will make all the difference to your revenue stream.

But don't take my word for it:

"*Put yourself out there. Join networking and community groups, and ask your friends if they know anyone to whom they could send your name as a referral. Don't be afraid to ask clients or networking colleagues to pass your name along to their friends, customers, and business partners. You never know when you might run into someone who could use your help, or who may know someone else who does."*
—Jan M. Tamanini (class of 1984)

"*Join civil, social and fraternal organizations, and shake hands with as many people as you can."*—Brian Rabal (class of 2005)

"*Spend at least 50 percent of your time marketing . . . and don't just rely on the Internet. Go out and meet people; shake hands; hand out cards; go to networking events; go to charity events. Make sure every person you meet knows what you do and how to reach you."*—Lynda L. Hinkle (class of 2009)

"*Network with other attorneys. Go out of your way to be helpful, and to go beyond the expected when somebody asks for advice. Join the ABA's Solosez listserv and actively participate and show your experience and willingness to help. And always be available for brainstorming with other attorneys."*—Mitchell J. Matorin (class of 1993)

"Network, network, network. For some reason, I always discounted how important it was, probably because I am an introvert. I finally started networking with financial planners and other attorneys and it has been invaluable."—**Sarah White** (class of 2002)

*"**Cultivate relationships.** At least once a week, I have lunch (or coffee) with a colleague, a former client, or a potential referral source. I track personal and professional information for everyone I come into contact with, so that if I run across something that might be helpful or of interest I can forward it to them. And volunteering to chair the employment law section of my state's trial lawyer association has been a wonderful opportunity to meet more experienced employment law attorneys and to raise my profile."*
—**D. Jill Pugh** (class of 1994)

Creating a Business Plan

Lawyers have different ideas about business plans. Some highly disciplined solos spend several weeks writing their business plan, researching practice areas, identifying potential competitors, and setting milestones for revenues. Other solos just dive headfirst into practice with no idea of where they're headed. Ultimately, whether you develop a business plan or not is your choice; the only scenario where it is essential, though, is if you intend to apply for a bank loan (which *isn't* recommended and shouldn't be necessary if you keep overhead low). In *Solo by Choice, The Companion Guide*, the question of business plans generated many opinions. Here are just a few:

"Business plans are important, but they don't have to be 50 pages long. [Mine was] a mission-and-vision statement, with a budget, some goals, and the names of everyone I would contact about referrals. That was about it."—**Michael Moebes** (class of 2003)

"A business plan is of the utmost importance. I don't see how [a solo can succeed] without one. It doesn't have to be super-formal. Just a basic budget; things like how much expenditures you will be making each month, how much money you need to cover those expenses, how much you need to cover overhead, and to bring home a decent salary."
—**Paul Scott** (class of 2008)

"I don't think [a business plan] is very important. Sure, you should take pen to paper and get a general sense of what it will cost to open your doors, how much income you need to bring in, how soon you need income, etc. As a new solo, your business plan can be as simple as this: spend as little as you can, do everything you can do to market your business, and do a good job. That's the plan. If you do those things, you've done what you can to succeed."—**Mark Tanney** (class of 1998)

"Whether or not to write a business plan probably depends on experience level and practice area. For me, it was not important at all. At least, I didn't have one, and I wouldn't know how to write one. It's possible, though, that I might be vastly more wealthy and nearing financial security if I had had one. I guess ignorance is bliss."
—**Mitchell J. Matorin** (class of 1993)

"I worked for two years on my business plan before I opened my practice, and I am very glad I did. Without it, I think it would have taken four to six months to turn a profit; with the plan, I made a profit within two months after opening and in every month since."
—Dean N. Alterman (class of 1989)

"Whether you draft a traditional, formal business plan, or spend just a few pages outlining your goals and expectations, you really should have some plan in place…and review it and update it regularly (say, every six months). Without one, it would be like driving across country without a map. Sure, you may eventually get to your destination, but it won't be by the most direct or effective route." —Jan M. Tamanini (class of 1984)

Listed below are the various components of a traditional business plan. You can complete all of these sections comprehensively… or not. But at a minimum, do prepare a mission statement and calculate as best you can your expected starting revenues and expenses, some ideas on how you might attract clients, and your revenue goals at various junctures: say, at six months, one year, and three years.

The components of a business plan:

The mission statement. A mission statement embodies all that you hope to accomplish in starting your firm, and articulates a vision of what you want to create. Most of all, it serves as a beacon, helping illuminate your new path on those days when the judge tears you apart in court, when opposing counsel drives you crazy with insults, or when a problem client brings a disciplinary action against you. Here's what one lawyer/blogger says about the importance of drafting a mission statement:

> *"…You have to have a long-term vision to feel compelled about what it is that you do each day. You have to know what it is that you are trying to attain. I doubt that the concept of billing clients will ever be enough to drive any person to passion in the workplace. I get up each day and remind myself that I am trying to change the way that law is practiced. Most days that thought fuels the drive and passion that I need to stay focused and driven, and I remain untouched by obstacles which inevitably pop up along the way."* —Enrico Schaefer (www.greatestamericanlawyer.typepad.com)

For your mission statement, consider what you most would like to change about the law. Perhaps there's something specific about the way law is practiced, or the way clients are treated that you would like to see changed in your own firm. Maybe as an associate, you had to grit your teeth when the name-partner blamed you for a mistake that was clearly his fault, and you promised yourself that one day your firm would stay accountable to clients. Or maybe you knew of clients who couldn't get a timely call from the name-partner when they had an important question…and you vowed that if you went solo that client service would be the cornerstone of your firm's mission. From such experiences, mission statements are created. If you're still not sure, Google this phrase: "mission statements lawyers". I think you'll be inspired by the examples you find. The best mission statements avoid clichés, and are just a few sentences long.

Once you generate a few drafts of your own, ask yourself whether you honestly believe them. If you don't, your clients won't either.

As you draft your mission statement, be specific. Use the following questions to get you started:

WHO (a two-part question). Who are you (a brief discussion of your background), and who are the clients you want to serve?

WHAT. What kind of law will your firm focus on? What kinds of services will you provide? What makes your firm unique?

WHEN. Your business plan should include the date that you intend to open your doors. If you've already been in business for a while, note that as well.

WHERE. Identify where your firm will be located. An office? Entirely virtual? Will you have offices in different cities?

HOW. How will you serve clients? In your office? Will you offer advice by phone or email? How will you use technology to serve your practice?

WHY. The "why" of course, is your mission statement.

Some additional considerations:

Have you done a SWOT analysis? A SWOT analysis (Strengths, Weaknesses, Opportunities, Threats) is a strategic planning tool to evaluate the potential viability of a business venture. Common to start-up and corporate business planning, it's not typically included in law firm business plan templates. But it's a quick way to focus your planning efforts.

What are your strengths? Do you have unique experience at a former agency or as a public defender? Are you a talented brief writer? Are you opening your office in your hometown, where you've got dozens of contacts? Focus on the competencies and advantages for which your firm has an edge.

What are your weaknesses? Consider the challenges that you face opening your firm. If you're a new grad, you may have trouble pitching your services. Or perhaps there's an area where you've always wanted to practice but it's dominated by BigLaw firms. Listing your weaknesses can be discouraging, but it will force you to focus on ways to overcome these challenges.

What are your opportunities? Are there parts of the market that are underserved? Do you have a unique way to deliver legal services (maybe a virtual office or providing unbundled legal services?)

What are your possible threats? Maybe you want to handle personal injury cases but you live in a state where the political climate leans towards tort reform? Perhaps you practice in a highly competitive field. Devise a strategy for addressing those threats.

What is your marketing plan? How are you going to attract clients? With so many different and low-cost ways to market your firm, you'll want to create a plan if only to stay focused. See chapters 14–17 on marketing.

What shape are your financials? You can draft a complex business plan with balance sheets, operating budgets and break-even analyses (the resources below will provide those templates). At a minimum, you should record the following for the first 12 months of practice:

What is your expected revenue, and sources of revenue in the first few months? Don't be discouraged if the first few months reflect a big fat zero!

What are your projected expenses? You can also set milestones and goals for reaching certain income levels.

Of course, business plans aren't set in stone. When you're actually up and running, you may discover opportunities you never anticipated, or discover that the practice area you were so sure would succeed simply fizzled. Don't let your business plan hold you back from changing course.

"I kept my business plan pretty simple, and continue to develop it to this day. To me, a business plan should be a growing organism that takes account of your expanding knowledge and experience base. Sometimes, the simple act of committing your plans to writing can help to ensure that you follow through on those plans. Of course, a business plan is only as effective as your willingness to stick to it. Therefore, merely making a plan is only the first step in starting your law firm, and will do nothing by itself."
—**Kevin Afghani (class of 2004)**

Business Plan Resources

Don't even think about investing in expensive business planning forms or templates to create a business plan until you exhaust some of the free resources available to you. Here are a few:

Bar resources. Check with your bar's LPM advisor to determine if the local bar library has books or models of sample business plans. The Missouri Bar has materials on law firm business plans (www.members.mobar.org/pdfs/lpm/olmstead.pdf) as does PracticePro, Canada's law practice management organization (www.practicepro.ca/practice/PDF/BusinessPlanOutline.pdf).

The Small Business Administration (www.SBA.gov). A wealth of information on staring a business but not specific to law practices. At their Web site (www.sba.gov/smallbusinessplanner/plan/writeabusinessplan/index.html) you'll find such tools as essential elements of a good business plan…a step-by-step explanation to help write your plan… sample business plans…an online workshop to improve your plan…and a business plan FAQ. The SBA has many regional offices to provide personal business-startup assistance.

Author note: the level of service depends on the staff at your regional office, so even though a colleague may have had a poor experience elsewhere, don't write them off.

Online resources. www.Bplans.com is a commercial service that sells business planning software and 60 sample plans from other industries.

SCORE.org. A non-profit organization whose retired executives are available at no cost to the small business community. Their Web site contains good information, including business plan templates and cost- and revenue-projection spreadsheets. I know several solos who received great help from their local SCORE office.

LexisNexis/Martindale-Hubbell (www.lawyers.com/pdc/tips/plan). Their online Practice Development Center offers several resources for development of a marketing plan, as well as several templates. You can incorporate the marketing plan into a business plan or simply use the marketing plan in lieu of a formal business plan.

Resources for finding demographic information or identifying trends to include in your business plan abound online. Consider state and local economic development offices and Chamber of Commerce Web sites, which contain local demographic information; federal census data (www.census.gov). At Google Trends (www.google.com/trends), you can search phrases like "New Jersey bankruptcy" to get a sense of whether it's a trending issue, and in which of the state's cities it's popular. And don't overlook the tech and social media sites (e.g., TechCrunch, Mashable, Small Biz Trends). These sites cover trends in the business, fashion, and the tech world, and provide insight on future issues. Likewise, staying abreast of blogs and Twitter will also help keep your finger on the pulse of emerging developments that may affect your new practice.

Task Timeline

6 to 12 months in advance

- Join solo practice listservs (e.g., www.solosez.net).
- Read books, blogs, and Web sites on starting a law firm.
- Take a bar course on starting a practice.
- Read applicable ethics rules in your jurisdiction relating to starting a firm.
- Determine if you need to take another bar exam or to get a waiver process underway.
- Begin saving and paying down student loans.

3 to 6 months in advance

- Priority—If your departure is involuntary, set up interviews even if you're ambivalent about soloing.
- Priority—Explore how to get your firm to pay for bar dues or insurance in the short term.
- Priority—Sign up for the next available bar course on solo'ing; meet with an LPM advisor.
- Priority—Investigate applicable bar dues and whether you need to gain admission or obtain a waiver.
- Priority—Read books on establishing a new practice.
- Priority—Develop an abbreviated business plan with preliminary ideas and goals.
- Priority—Investigate court-appointed programs.
- Priority—Get serious about saving money, and paying down your loans.

- Identify potential clients within your firm, making yourself indispensable in their case.
- Register for CLE courses on potential practice areas.
- Investigate court-appointed programs, prepaid legal services, insurance company "counsel" lists.
- Increase your visibility in potential practice areas.
- Wait until your own firm is established to start a blog or to write articles.
- Wait until just before your firm is established to take substantive training courses.

0 to 3 months in advance
- Priority—If you only have four months or less, and you've been fired/laid off, look into unemployment, student loan-deferrals, and other ways to stay afloat. Meet with an LPM advisor, and sign up for the local bar's next "how to start a law firm" workshop.
- Identify your office space and sign a lease if renting.
- Begin setting up your home office if you intend to work there.
- Set up a law firm bank account, and an IOLTA trust fund.
- Purchase computer and other office equipment.
- Secure your Internet address, and begin work on your Web site and/or blog.
- Order business cards and other stationery.
- Draft a firm announcement and identify places to send it.
- Draft a letter to potential clients.
- Give official notice to your employer, and leave all your cases in good order before departing.
- Wait on training, writing articles, and substantive courses until you're resolved to solo.

Resources
- Sign up for the ABA's *solosez.net*, an online forum for lawyers practicing alone or in a small firm setting, particularly those in firms of five or fewer lawyers. The ABA also publishes several books on starting a practice, including *Flying Solo* (now in a 4th edition).
- Check out a few of the most active blogs for solos and small firms, including Jay Fleischman's **LegalPracticePro.com**, **TheLawyerist.com**, Chuck Newton's **Third Wave Lawyer** (www.stayviolation.typepad.com/chucknewton), Rick George's **Solo Lawyer** (www.futurelawyer.typepad.com/sololawyer), Enrico Schaefer's blog (www.greatestamericanlawyer.typepad.com), Adrian Baron's **The Nutmeg Lawyer** (www.nutmeglawyer.com), **Solo in Chicago** (www.soloinchicago.com), and this author's own blog at www.MyShingle.com.
- Sign up for seminars or workshops taught by a team of experienced solos in conjunction with the Law Practice Management Advisor in your area. Bar classes are usually reasonably priced and held in the evening or on weekends. In addition, almost every bar publishes a practice-starting pamphlet or handbook which

contains jurisdictional-specific information. Note: go to www.myshingle.com/
my_shingle/online-guide0505.html. My blog has a list of state bar guides on
starting a firm.

- Make an appointment with the Law Practice Management experts in your area.
  They can help you sort out issues common to new solos. How-to guides and
  conversations with solos in other jurisdictions will definitely help you decide
  whether or not to solo. But do set up an appointment with an LPM advisor from
  your state bar, and do take a course designed to launch a firm in the jurisdiction
  where you practice. In this way, you will be able to better comply with the juris-
  dictional laws where you're licensed.

IN THEIR OWN WORDS

Q: What role does risk play in a solo practice?

"Risk is an everyday thing for solos. You may have $100,000 'on the streets', and if you're not comfortable
with managing that kind of debt—and if you don't have a pretty intimate understanding of how to deal
with cash flow—you're going to be in one too many financial pinches to remain in business. Every dollar
you put into a case—or into your firm's brand—is another dollar you're risking for the success of the
firm."—Scott Wolfe (class of 2005)

"The prospective solo has to be able to stomach a fair bit of risk, because you ultimately have only yourself to rely on. And that doesn't really change as long as you're a solo, although there are ways in which
you can modify that effect over time by using outsourcing judiciously."—David Abeshouse (class of 1982)

"Based on my experience, one of the most important personality traits of a solo practitioner is a high
tolerance for risk. If you are uncomfortable with not getting paid for over a month or two, and not being
able to accurately project your income—at least in the starting phase—you should think seriously about
your decision to solo. Indeed, the risk factor is the *main force* preventing many of my colleagues from
breaking out on their own."—Kevin Afghani (class of 2004)

"Risk and solo practice are synonymous. As rewarding as it is, solo practice is incredibly unpredictable and
inherently risky. You bear the brunt of bad court decisions (especially in a contingency fee practice), and
you bear the risk of clients who fail to pay."—D. Jill Pugh (class of 1994)

"Risk is the ghost over your shoulder. From month to month, you can't rely on a steady income. You don't
know if your clients will pay; you don't know if the phone will ring; you don't know if any consultation will
turn into a client; you don't know if your particular niche will be eliminated due to some new legislation.
Risk is probably *the biggest factor* in a solo practice. The trick is to figure out how to manage it, strategically and emotionally, so that dips don't sideline you, and you don't overspend in the good months."
—Gina Bongiovi (class of 2007)

"The role of risk varies. If a solo attorney has money in the bank and a good book of business, the risk
may not be that great; conversely, if the attorney is starting out with a minimal budget, no client base,
and huge student loans, then the attorney will have a much greater risk. Other factors also play into the

picture. If you are 30 years old and able to work a full time job while you start your practice, this may help reduce your risk. And if your spouse is willing and able cover expenses until you get off the ground, that, too, will help reduce your risk."—Mark Tanney (class of 1998)

"[A solo's] risk isn't that much different from those borne by other practitioners…with one exception: it's all on you. There's no one else to take up the slack if you have a slow period or get sick. And if one of your clients has a crisis demanding big chunks of your time, you can't just let everything else slide. The best way I've found to manage this—and it's still a struggle for me—is to make sure I give myself more time than I think I'll need to complete a client project. If something should take a few days, I'll tell the client I'll get it done in ten days; if it should take a week, I'll tell the client two. That way, if you finish on your original estimate, the client thinks you're wonderful; if you have something else come up, and you take the longer time, the client isn't disappointed."—Jan M. Tamanini (class of 1984)

"[In my experience], going solo means spending large amounts of time and money in a venture with no defined return, and with odds that are undefined, unpredictable, and continuously variable! It's an intricate dance with risk…but not a gamble. [To manage risk], you need to think strategically, making decisions based on information and a cost/benefit analysis rather than reacting to immediate events. The fact that I could not predict all the possible risk involved in being solo was one of the biggest stumbling blocks I had when deciding to go solo. Now, risk is what makes my solo practice fun, exhilarating, worrisome…and scary at the same time. It's what keeps me sharp and drives me to do my best work."
—Bruce Cameron (class of 2007)

"Risk is a big factor in starting a solo practice, but risk is a factor in almost all decisions in life. The goal should not be to avoid risk, but to understand, mitigate, and manage it. You have to be willing to risk your money, savings, and steady paycheck. But if you make a good business plan, stick to it, and can see how you are going to feed yourself, you are managing that risk. Before I started my solo practice, I spent hours and hours in front of Excel spreadsheets, figuring out how much income I would need for the practice to stay afloat, how much I needed to bring home, etc. I take the same approach with cases that I decide to take, marketing decisions, etc. There is always going to be a risk that you won't get a good return on your investment."—Paul Scott (class of 2008)

CHAPTER 5

The Great Escape

"When I first solo'd, I remember thinking, 'What have
I done? I've just walked away from a six-figure salary
plus bonuses.'" —Traci Ellis, solo

Before you can make a fresh start, you need to sever ties with your existing employer. Whether that departure is involuntary or voluntary, emotions and self-interest often contaminate the disengagement process.

When you disengage from your firm, you walk a thin line between protecting your rights and taking the high road. Of course, you should vigorously negotiate for what you're entitled to, whether it's a fair severance package if you've been terminated, or an assurance that the firm will promptly transfer files for clients who choose to follow you to your new practice. Whatever the circumstances, avoid lawsuits, and badmouthing your firm, and skulking out with a pile of client files in the dead of night. Even in large metropolitan markets, the legal community is a much smaller place than you can imagine. In the long run, burning bridges will cost you many future opportunities.

In this chapter, I discuss issues relative to disengaging from your firm, including involuntary departure (e.g., giving notice, negotiating benefits), voluntary departure, and the divisions of clients and assets.

Disengaging From Your Firm

Involuntary departure. How you give notice depends primarily on whether your departure is voluntary or forced. Obviously, when the firm lets you go, your own notice is not as important since the firm already knows you're leaving. Under these circumstances, the only decisions you have are whether—and when—to announce that you are starting your own firm. During your final weeks, you should definitely mention the possibility of starting a firm as one of your options. If colleagues know you're thinking about solo practice, they may have ideas about other lawyers with whom you might speak; they may even have potential referrals. Many times, firms—or at least individual partners or associates—feel badly or guilty about an economic-induced layoff, and will try to help you with possible leads. Firms sometimes even make office space available on a temporary basis to a terminated lawyer who wants to start a firm. Even though you've been fired, assess the situation carefully. Don't make your plans for going solo sound too definite if you believe the firm may try to limit your access to client files, or worse, that they may contact your clients and tell them you've been let go to prevent those clients from following you.

Voluntary departure. In many ways, departing a firm voluntarily is more difficult than if you'd been fired. Sure, you don't experience the same powerlessness and embarrassment as when you're told to leave. On the other hand, you still need to deal with colleagues who may feel betrayed by your departure, or who view your motives with suspicion, believing you want to steal clients or bring down the firm. Below are some do's and don'ts about disengaging. Note: leaving a government agency or in-house position is not as complicated because you don't have to address the issue of dividing clients or money, which is always the sticking point when lawyers leave a firm. At the same time, some recommendations (such as always act professionally), apply no matter what position you leave:

Learn from others. Before you give notice, investigate how your firm handled law-yers who left the in the past, and consult with a lawyer who has already left the firm. If that's not an option, make discrete inquiries about the firm's practices.

Consider the following questions:

- *How has the firm treated departing lawyers in the past?* Did it deal fairly, giving a reasonable time to clear out their offices, and to copy their work product off the computer? Or did the firm have the departing lawyer escorted from the office soon after the announcement?
- *How did the firm provide notice of an attorney's departure to existing clients?* Did it send a joint letter with the attorney, or did the managing partner get on the phone to alert clients and discourage them from leaving the firm?
- *How has the firm handled transition of clients who decide to follow the de-parting lawyer?* Did it cooperate in transferring files for clients who followed a departing lawyer to a new firm, or did it insist on retaining files in the hopes of deterring clients from moving to your firm?
- *Has the firm had a negative experience with a departing lawyer* (i.e., someone who stole files and solicited clients even before he or she was out the door)?

Be prepared. It doesn't hurt to prepare for a worst-case scenario in which your firm sends you packing on the same day you give notice. In this situation, the firm would close ranks, and deny you access to your computer and files by deactivating your security codes and password. Of course, this means you would lose the ability to save what's rightfully yours. So, before you give notice, save copies of all of your work product and e-mail messages; any client materials you're entitled to retain; and start bringing home the seminar materials, bar journals, and other publications that belong to you. As I will discuss later, you must *absolutely positively* refrain from soliciting any clients while you remain part of the firm. But do have a pre-drafted e-mail announcing your departure to clients. So, if the firm does cut you loose upon giving notice, you can preempt the firm's announcement with one of your own. Note: some bars prohibit de-parting lawyers from contacting firm clients without authorization from the firm.

Have consideration. Give your firm the traditional two weeks notice . . . if not more! And, when possible, avoid giving notice in the weeks before a major trial or closing. Assure your firm that you will remain around long enough to finish outstanding work, or to brief a new attorney on the matter. Of course, your firm might decline your of-fer; in fact, they might ask you to leave right away. But at least you can be satisfied at having acted professionally. This end-game can also end an up-note: a colleague once told me that when he left his large firm, he wound up continuing to handle work for his employer for six months after his departure on a contract basis, which helped ease him into solo practice.

Act professionally. Resist the temptation to sneak into the office to collect client files, or to drop a letter of resignation on the managing partner's desk. Such conduct forecloses any future referral opportunities from your firm...not to mention the bad feeling it leaves with colleagues. I've spoken with several lawyers who were left in the lurch by departing associates who sneaked out with law firm files. Years later, these colleagues *still* refuse to refer clients to those former associates. Of course, if you do stoop to such conduct, lost referrals would be the least of your worries. Under the ethics rules of almost any jurisdiction, taking client files would invite a civil lawsuit or bar complaint by your former firm. Do you really want to spend your first few weeks or months of practice defending yourself against your former firm before a disciplinary committee? And put yourself in your employer's shoes; after all, someday, you may be in a position where some of your associates leave your firm to hang out their own shingle. How would you feel if they left you with imminent deadlines and no information about outstanding cases? So, leave your firm with the same professionalism and grace you'd expect from your own employees.

Before You Leave: Negotiating Benefits

When you leave your employer, you may be entitled to certain benefits, such as compensation for vacation time or the right to purchase health insurance through COBRA. But in contrast to when you started your job and HR took care of all of these matters for you, it's up to you to ensure that you receive all rightful benefits before you leave. Negotiate vigorously for what you deserve; every little extra bit of cash can help alleviate the financial stress of the early days of starting your own practice.

Benefits you want to actively negotiate:

Vacation/sick days. Many attorneys leaving a firm or the government find themselves with three or four weeks of unused vacation. Check with HR or your employee manual to determine whether your firm is required to pay for remaining vacation and sick days. Even if the firm maintains that it is not obligated, its position may be at odds with the labor laws in your state. Why bother? Because the compensation you receive for unused time can amount to the equivalent of almost another month of salary, a big help if you're starting out without a source of revenue.

Retirement contribution and bonuses. In contrast to vacation benefits, which accrue all year long, some benefits—like retirement contributions or bonuses—are distributed annually, usually in January or February for the previous year. If you're leaving voluntarily, you may be able to time your departure so that you're around when these benefits are dispensed. However, if you're asked to leave late in the year, you may miss out on these benefits unless you speak up. Again, consult your employee handbook and HR manual. If you've already met the criterion for a pension contribution or bonus, then make your case for receiving it.

COBRA. Federal law requires employers with 20 or more employees to provide employees and their dependents the right to continue health insurance coverage for up to 18 months after leaving a job. Even though COBRA requires you to reimburse your employer for its share of your insurance premiums, COBRA coverage is generally lower than what you could get on your own since you can take advantage of your employer's group rates. COBRA imposes strict deadlines for electing coverage so it's up to you to stay on top of the process to avoid missing a deadline.

Unemployment. If your separation is involuntary, you probably qualify for unemployment benefits. Don't be ashamed or proud to take unemployment; after all, you've been paying into the system for as long as you've been working. So, you might as well take what you've earned. Some states allow unemployment so long as you certify that you are continuing to seek employment, something you can truthfully claim even after starting your firm (for example, it's likely that you might apply for contract work positions after you start a firm, which constitutes looking for other work). In addition, you must report any earnings you receive from new jobs so that you do not exceed the maximum level of employment that you're entitled to by law. After what you've been earning at your firm, unemployment doesn't amount to much; maybe $300 to $400 per week for a finite period. Still, that may be enough to cover some bills while your practice gets off the ground. *Author note*: some states do not permit the self-employed to collect unemployment.

Other benefits. Believe it or not, even if you've been terminated from your position, you have some leverage in negotiating benefits. If your firm fears you might bring a lawsuit, it may try to avoid the possibility by placating you. Or one or more of the partners may feel so guilty about your dismissal that they will try to ease their conscience by giving you what you ask. Example: if you've been told to leave by May and the firm pays bar dues and other licensing fees in June, ask that they pay these costs for the year. If you're forced out in the last quarter of the year, maybe the firm will pick up the tab for health insurance premiums through the end of the year. This would be especially helpful if you intend to switch over to your spouse's plan, and you're not sure how long that process will take or whether you need to wait until the end of the year to put it in place.

Are They Really Your Clients?

Don't be surprised at how hard your firm fights to keep clients, even clients you brought to the firm yourself, or clients who originated with the firm but where you acted as managing attorney. Nor is it hard to understand why…even in the case of a client whose matters you handled exclusively, or who only generated several thousand dollars in business. Clients are the firm's most important asset…for more reasons than money. Their retainers and fees serve as a law firm's sole source of revenue, providing the high six-figure incomes, the box seats at sports games, the expense-account dinners, the designer office interiors. Even prominent clients with smaller matters bring

BOOK UPDATES AT AUTHOR'S BLOG—www.MyShingle.com

prestige to the firm, enabling it to capture future business and ensure future growth. Thus, firms worry that news of a loss of even a few insignificant clients to, of all people, a lawyer going solo, might damage the firm's carefully cultivated reputation.

Ethics rules. As much as firms may want to keep clients, ethics rules impose some imitations that can level the playing field…at least a little.

In contrast to private corporations, law firms can't execute non-compete agreements to prohibit former attorneys from soliciting existing clients. Both the ABA Model Rules of Professional Responsibility, and every state bar, take the position that clients have an unfettered right to choose their attorney. And any practice which restricts a client's ability to choose—whether it's a non-compete agreement, or a law firm's ban on communications between a former attorney and firm clients, or a firm's refusal to turn over client files so that a client can transfer to another attorney—will not pass muster under ethics rules.

Still, law firms have some wiggle room.

Ethics rules don't stop a firm from offering an existing client all kinds of perks to remain with the firm.

In fact, ABA Opinion 06-444 held that a firm can ethically make retirement benefits contingent upon a lawyer's agreement to sign a non-compete clause (source: ABA Journal e-Report, May 25, 2007; www.abanet.org/journal/ereport/my25ethic2.html). Furthermore, ethics rules don't prohibit a firm from highlighting the disadvantages of being represented by a solo practitioner rather than the law firm whose very letterhead causes opponents to quake in their boots. In addition, the rules impose limitations on departing lawyers. Both the ABA rules and most state ethics codes forbid lawyers, while still employed at their firm, from soliciting firm clients with whom they do not have a personal, working relationship. Some state codes go further, banning solicitation attempts between firm lawyers and all clients, even where a personal lawyer-client relationship exists. Law firm employment or partnership agreements may also prohibit pre-departure solicitation of clients, even if ethics rules don't.

Then there are, in the words of Dennis Kennedy, author of *Leaving a Firm: Guidelines to a Smoother Transition,* "the petty little games" that some law firms play.

For example, one firm's refusal to turn over client e-mails on the grounds that they did not comprise part of the client file…or the firm that required departing lawyers to pay exorbitant rates to have client files copied so that they could retain the copies after transferring the files…or the firm that argued they were entitled to fees for the entire client matter even where the client moves to another firm in the interim! All such behavior interferes with the client's ability to remain with the departing lawyer. But don't expect to see any of the rules clarified in a way that benefits the departing lawyer. As long as the ABA and the state bars are dominated by large firm interests, any attempt to close these ethical gaps will be resolved in favor of the large firms.

Soliciting & Dealing With the Firm's Clients: Do's and Don'ts

DO refrain from actively soliciting existing clients while still employed at the firm. As previously mentioned, bar rules aren't completely clear on whether lawyers still employed at the firm can solicit existing clients with whom they have a personal relationship. Ethics rules generally preclude solicitation of clients where there's no personal relationship. But just to be safe, refrain from actively soliciting firm clients while you're still employed at the firm. The line between solicitation and ordinary small talk is awfully thin, though. ABA Rules and most codes define a solicitation as any kind of communication, motivated by pecuniary gain, concerning a lawyer's availability for employment. So, telling the client you're leaving to start a firm and asking him or her to come with you constitutes an impermissible solicitation. But floating the idea that you might want to start a firm probably is not (though here, you want to be careful that word doesn't get back to your firm, which might send you packing sooner than you imagined). If a client said to you that she wished you practiced at another firm because your firm's fees are too expensive, it would be appropriate to say, *"I'll give that some thought."* But sending her a brochure and a proposed retainer agreement probably is not. Beyond ethics rules, use common sense and courtesy. At the end of the day, it's not worth putting your firm on the defensive for clients that may come with you anyway.

DO have an ethically compliant letter to clients ready upon giving notice. When you give notice of your departure, you should already have drafted a letter informing clients of your departure, and advising them of their right to remain with the firm or to come with you. Since your firm will probably want to notify clients themselves, having your own letter or e-mail already drafted gives you a chance to pre-empt the firm's announcement. Keep in mind that some jurisdictions may prohibit you from contacting former firm clients unless you transmit notice jointly with the firm, or if the firm pre-approves your announcement. Some rules may also restrict you from contacting clients with whom you did not have a personal relationship. Check your state ethics rules on departing attorneys, and consult with bar counsel before you send anything to existing firm clients.

DO settle unpaid balances for existing clients before you leave. The clients who follow you may have a variety of different billing arrangements with your existing firm. Some may owe outstanding balances for work that has already been completed; others may pay a flat, monthly retainer under an annual contract. If you're a partner in the firm, the partnership agreement probably provides for the percentage of disbursements to which you're entitled from clients, as well as a provision for resolving division of profits when a partner departs with a client. Here, you need to determine whether it's worth it to fight for every last nickel, or simply to cut a fair deal and get on with your life. As an associate, your rights to fees from existing clients may be more limited since you were paid a set salary rather than a share of profits. So, if you take several contingency matters with you where the firm fronted significant costs, you (or your client) will have to compensate the firm for its investment in the case after you receive a judgment just as any other client would who switches attorneys midway through a contingency proceeding.

DON'T even think about swiping office supplies. You may think that you're saving yourself money by taking legal pads, pens or other office supplies from the firm before you leave. And the temptation to copy software licensed to the firm is probably even greater. In fact, if you've been fired, you may feel justified as compensation for unjust treatment. But the cost of office supplies is negligible, and if you poach licensed software you don't have access to the help desk or upgrades. It's just not worth it. Anyway, why lock yourself in to your firm's way of doing things? Make a fresh start. Your firm isn't likely to catch you sneaking supplies, but think how foolish you would appear if they did. What argument could you make? That you can't afford to buy software now that you're out of a job? Not the sort of impression you want to leave on a firm that you hope will send you referral business.

DON'T use firm resources to solicit clients. One Utah attorney learned the hard way that you shouldn't use firm resources to solicit clients. He used firm letterhead to solicit clients under the guise of being employed at the firm, then took the cases and handled them on his own. Use of firm resources isn't limited to stationery, however. Most firms maintain detailed databases of clients, including client contacts and background information. That data belongs to the firm, which means you cannot take it and use the information to contact clients after you leave the firm.

DON'T steal client files, but DO keep copies. When you leave your firm, do not, under any circumstances, leave with client files whether you worked on those matters or not. Under ethics rules, client files are considered property of the client and held in trust by the firm. Taking files without permission is stealing, and that can expose you to ethical sanctions. If you're discovered taking files, don't expect your former firm to go easy on you, even where the client was likely to follow you anyway. Firms need to retain client files for malpractice purposes. By taking client files, you compromise your firm's ability to defend itself in future malpractice actions, creating problems for the firm with its insurance carrier. All of this would make your firm angry enough to file ethics charges against you…and the firm would probably prevail. At the same time, you should retain copies of client files, or at least key documents from those files, for matters in which you were personally involved. State ethics codes do not address the issue of copies, but copying files would probably pass muster as it does not compromise either the firm's or the client's ability to access the original files. More importantly, departing attorneys must keep file copies as a matter of self-preservation. Should malpractice claims arise in the future, an attorney must have proof where his involvement in the case terminated so that the firm does not attempt to transfer the blame for malpractice.

DON'T badmouth the firm to get clients. After you leave the firm, you may be tempted to convince one of the former clients to come with you by sharing some not-so-flattering information about your former firm. The information might be general in nature, (e.g., a law firm policy that allows the firm to double-bill hours spent in travel to Client 1 and work done during that time to Client 2), or information that is specific to the client (e.g., the managing partner calls the client an annoying dweeb). Don't do it. Badmouthing can potentially expose you to a defamation action; also, it makes you look infantile and unprofessional. Further, it's not an effective marketing technique. Criticizing your old firm may give your client a reason to leave, but it won't give the client reasons to come with you.

As you plan your departure from your firm, be realistic about which clients are likely to follow you. Obviously, you can't expect Corporation X, a 15-year client whose CEO is a close, personal friend of the managing partner, to jump ship. Especially when you've only handled his company's matters for three years and dealt with contacts as junior as yourself. At the same time, other more likely clients may also decline to come to your firm for one or more of the reasons outlined here by lawyer/author Dennis Kennedy:

- The client you thought loved you and your work actually hates you and your work, or actually loves the paralegal or associate who is staying with your former firm.
- Your client contact does not have authority to take the work from your former firm.
- Your client contact is limited to an approved list of firms.
- Your client's choices include not only you and your former firm, but also other firms and moving work in-house.
- Your client requires technology or other infrastructure that you can no longer provide.
- You misread or misinterpreted what you hoped were positive signals from your client.
- Your former firm makes your client a better deal than you can.
- You walk into a conflict of interest that you did not see coming
- Unbeknownst to you, your former firm blackens your reputation in conversations with the client.

Since you do not have control over these factors, you should—at a minimum—anticipate that they may limit your ability to take clients with you. So be conservative in predicting future business when you start your firm. At the same time, being realistic in the short run doesn't mean that you should write off the prospect of luring in a former firm client entirely. The business of law is competitive and fluid, with companies constantly reevaluating and switching "dance partners." Down the road, a client may expand its list of "approved counsel" to include your new firm. Maybe the great deal that your firm extended to the client will end six months after your departure and the firm decides to look elsewhere. Maybe the CEO of Corporation X retires and the new CEO appoints your once-junior contact as general counsel. One of these days, that ex-client just might give you a call after all.

What's Yours, What's Theirs?

While figuring out the division of clients, departing lawyers must also determine what property they can rightfully take, and what belongs to the firm.

In some instances, technological advancements have mooted the work product question. Most federal courts, and many state courts and administrative agencies, have transitioned to electronic filing. Consequently, you don't need to concern yourself with the ethics of copying your firm's briefs and motions when you can readily access many of them online at the court's Web sites after you leave. But while questions about briefs and memos are easier to resolve, intellectual property issues complicate the question of who owns work product, according to Dennis Kennedy, a legal technology expert and BigLaw attorney-turned-solo:

"...In the good old days, a lawyer leaving a firm took work product, forms and other materials. No one gave much thought to this common practice. Today, lawyers create articles, presentations, videos, forms, software applications, Web pages, databases, knowledge-management tools, and other pieces of intellectual property. Firms also realize the value of firm forms, brief banks, handbooks, and the like."

Though intellectual property considerations do not necessarily bar you from taking presentations, forms and software applications that you created for your firm for your own fair use, they may preclude you from licensing or otherwise profiting from those materials. Kennedy notes that many firms have added intellectual property clauses to partnership agreements and advises that, "if you have specific uses planned for materials, be sure to address and document the intellectual property issues."

Equipment and materials. Chances are, your firm equipped you with a laptop, and/or a smartphone, and other technology; the better to keep you tethered to the firm 24/7. Now that you're cutting the ties, expect the firm to cut your service and seek return of its property... though as a partner and part-owner of the firm, you may theoretically have some claim to keeping some of your road warrior gear. As discussed earlier, be sure to copy all vital information from your smartphone and your laptop before giving notice of your departure. As for law books, journals or directories, keep those that came your way by virtue of a bar membership or attendance at a conference. The firm will probably toss those materials anyway.

Special considerations for government lawyers. Lawyers leaving government service to solo don't face the same ethics dilemmas related to client solicitation that confronts their colleagues in private practice. At the same time, government lawyers must deal with ethical restrictions on the "revolving door" between successive government and private employment:

ABA Model Rule 1.1 provides that government lawyers: shall not otherwise represent a client in connection with a matter in which the lawyer participated personally and substantially as a public officer or employee, unless the appropriate government agency gives its informed consent, confirmed in writing, to the representation.

Most state bars apply a similar "personal and substantial" participation standard, though you should consult applicable rules and bar counsel for further guidance. In addition, lawyers leaving positions with the federal government must comply with the requirements of federal conflict of interest statutes. In addition, some agencies may have their own regulations in addition to restricting attorneys from actively courting clients with cases pending before the agency, or also prohibit attorneys from making personal appearances before the agency for a certain period of time after leaving for the private sector.

While it seems onerous, the "revolving door" regulations may restrict you from handling only a small number of cases.

If you worked as a junior attorney at a federal agency, you most likely dealt with small, finite matters that concluded before your departure so the players involved would not have a need to hire private counsel. The same is true if you are leaving a prosecutor's office: most of the defendants you prosecuted were probably incarcerated and won't need lawyers, while those in the middle of a case already have representation and, if not, would probably not want to hire the same person who indicted them. And even if you are subject to a bar on personal appearances before an agency for a set time, that still does not preclude you from advising clients on the agency's policies during that time-frame. Even though you are leaving government to start your own firm, consider how large firms deal with conflicts when they hire top agency personnel, a frequently occurring phenomenon.

Government lawyers leave office for private firms all the time, but at a firm other attorneys can handle matters that come before the lawyer's former agency, even if the government lawyer is personally precluded from doing so. At the same time, the former government lawyer adds value, because he can educate other firm attorneys on the agency's regulations and identify appropriate contacts in the agency for further assistance.

In contrast to large firm practice, as a solo, you won't be able to pass off cases that you're disqualified from handling to other attorneys in your firm. But what you can do is establish affiliated networks with other attorneys, or even enter into an "of counsel" relationship (see Chapter 13). You can then refer clients to these attorneys in your network and provide general consulting and advice while you wait out any cooling period on appearances before the agency. Plus, you can use these affiliations to learn more about fields outside the expertise you gained at government, which will enable you to diversify your practice. See Chapter 18, *From Government to Solo*.

TO SUE OR NOT TO SUE

When wronged, a lawyer's first impulse is to file a lawsuit, or at least to consider the possibility. If that's your reaction to your firm's decision to fire you, my advice is to slow down. It's understandable you might derive some pleasure at a process server charging into the managing partner's office to serve a summons. Before you declare war, though, consider whether a lawsuit will benefit you in the long run. Ask yourself:

Do I even have a case? Firms terminate associates (and sometimes even partners) for a variety of reasons. In most cases, economics…not merit…drive a firm's decision. Firms don't pass lawyers over for partnership because they're not capable, but because the firm has grown so top-heavy that adding new partners would reduce profits for existing ones. The bottom line is that if you've been let go for economic reasons (even if the firm couches its decision as merit-based), you're not likely to succeed with your lawsuit. But let's not kid ourselves: law firms don't always behave lawfully when they fire attorneys. Many a firm has constructively discharged women returning from maternity leave, demoting them on cases that they once led, relegating them to scut work, and generally making their lives so unpleasant that they're effectively forced out. In October, 2007, Chicago-based Sidley Austin, one of the nation's largest law firms, agreed to pay $27.5 million to 32 former partners to settle an age discrimination lawsuit. The federal Equal Employment Opportunity Commission contended that Sidley violated the Age Discrimination in Employment Act when it forced the partners out of the partnership on account of their age.

One lawyer I know was fired for reporting a colleague's excessive billing practices to firm management…even though the Code of Professional Responsibility obligates attorneys to disclose ethics violations committed by other lawyers. If, after consulting with an employment law attorney or the EEOC, you determine that your firm acted unlawfully, you should consider a lawsuit. Though you may face adverse repercussions, our profession will not change for the better unless lawyers treated unjustly step forward.

How will a lawsuit affect my career? Bringing a lawsuit can prevent you from moving forward. After all, how are you going to get your new practice up and running if your day is consumed with filing motions and attending depositions in your own case? In addition, the legal community... even in major cities...is awfully small. And word of a lawsuit can circulate quickly, perhaps branding you as a litigious trouble-maker. Fair or not, many firms may decide against sending contract work or referrals to a lawyer whom they believe might sue them if a dispute over referral or contract fees ever arose. Note: a lawsuit against your firm would irreparably destroy the relationship. Though you might not care about ever dealing with a firm that just fired you, consider what burning bridges would have on future opportunities.

Author's note: When my own firm asked me to leave many years ago, I was humiliated and furious. I consulted with an attorney about a possible discrimination action (I was the only female associate at the firm), but I was advised that I didn't have a case. On my last day, I was tempted to march into each partner's office and deliver a "good riddance" speech. Instead (and after discussing it with my husband, who was able to think more objectively about my situation), I merely sent an e-mail around the office, wished everyone well and left for home. A few days later, I got on with my life; I started my practice and didn't have much contact with anyone from the firm for at least six months. By that time, I was scheduled to argue my first case at the DC Circuit, a small matter which had originated while I was at my former firm. With nothing to lose, I called one of my former firm partners who had done some appellate work, and asked if he'd help me out. He agreed and we set up a meeting, where he and two of the other partners spent about an hour giving me pointers and tossing practice questions at me. Working together broke the ice, and, later, the firm referred me a few cases and also served as a reference for some lucrative contract assignments. None of that would have happened if I gave in to my adrenalin, and vented my outrage before leaving.

WHO OWNS THE BLOG?

As blogs increase in popularity, and gain acceptance as a way for young attorneys to establish their reputation in the legal field, the question of ownership may lead to disputes. In fact, in February 2007, Enrico Schaefer, a small firm attorney and blogger, reported that his former firm sued for the rights to the blog (see www.greatestamericanlawyer.typepad.com/greatest_american_lawyer/2007/02/blog_fight.html).

Here's how a dispute might arise:

Suppose an associate at a large firm starts a blog on communications law. He writes it through his own efforts on an account he set up himself, but posts to the blog during the work day from his office computer. The associate informs the firm of his blog, and further indicates online that he is employed by the firm. Within a few months, the blog emerges as a go-to site for the industry, generating positive buzz for both the associate and the firm. At that point, the firm links to the blog at its own site, highlighting that its own associate runs the blog. A year later, the associate decides to leave the firm. Can the firm demand that the associate turn over his blog? In this case, the firm would probably not prevail. Though the associate blogged on firm time, he took responsibility for setting up the site and created all of the content without supervision or direction from the firm. Thus, the firm could not lay claim to the blog under a theory of "work for hire." Moreover, if the firm continues to link to the blog from its Web site, the associate should ensure that the firm does not use the link to convey the impression that the associate still works at the firm, or that the firm plays a role in generating the content of the blog.

In one recent case, an associate sued his former firm for keeping his biography on the firm Web site, which the associate claims directed prospective clients to his former firm away from his new solo practice. Of course, an associate who writes a blog established by the law firm won't have any rights to the site upon departure. At best, the associate could link to posts or articles that he wrote for the firm blog, though even that may not offer proof of expertise or writing skills, since most firm blogs attribute posts to the firm and not to the individual author.

If you're thinking about volunteering to start a blog for your firm, insist on attribution for posts, if not some entitlement to co-ownership, so that you have something that you can take with you, or at least link to, if you leave.

CHAPTER 6

Nine Steps to Getting Started

"Keep your overhead low, build a good support net-
work, and make sure you've got enough savings to
survive the slow times." —Sergio Benavides, solo

Step 1. Bar Licensing/Court Membership

Licensing. To practice law, you need to be a member in good standing of the bar in the jurisdiction where you practice.

The importance of having a current license seems obvious, but back at the law firm or government agency, your license probably did not matter much. If you were employed with the federal government, you were able to practice in any federal court irrespective of the jurisdiction where you're admitted to practice. If you were at a large firm, you were probably never attorney-of-record, so where you were licensed was also of less importance. In addition, your employer most likely paid your annual licensing fees, even if you were admitted to multiple bars. Now that you're on your own, you bear the cost of keeping your licenses current.

Which licenses will you need? The answer depends largely on your anticipated practice:

Must you be licensed in the state where your office is located? Some states, in my state of Maryland, for example, requires lawyers practicing in the state to be a member of that state bar, though some exceptions apply (e.g., attorneys with exclusively federal practices that do not require any specific state bar membership need not join the Maryland bar to work in Maryland so long as they make clear that they have an exclusively federal practice). This rule applies even to lawyers working from home offices. If you practice in this type of jurisdiction, you need to consult with the ethics office to determine what bar membership is required. Note: not all states take a uniform position. Missouri, for example, requires a lawyer to be licensed to practice in the state even if the lawyer will focus exclusively on federal immigration matters. See Law Firms and Associations, Unauthorized Practice of Law, Missouri Opinion 970098, Rule Number 5.5.

Should you be licensed in the state where you live? If you worked for a large firm located in one state, and lived in an adjacent state, chances are that you're only a member of the bar in the state where you worked. You may want to consider gaining admission to the bar of the state where you live. Depending upon your potential practice area, you may get referrals from neighbors or family members in your home state, and if you're not a member of the bar, you could lose out on prospective clients.

Will you have a federal practice? With a federal practice, sometimes you can get away with belonging to just one bar. That's because federal appeals courts and a few federal district courts will allow you to gain admission to practice in that court even though you're not a member of the bar in the jurisdiction where the court is located. Generally, the only requirements are that a member of the appellate court where you're seeking admission sponsors you and that you are a member in good standing in the jurisdictions where you're licensed. Admission to other federal courts costs under $200, making it less expensive and time-consuming than waiving into another bar (which can cost several hundred dollars), or worse, taking the bar in another state. Also, keep in mind that federal agencies generally do not require you to belong to any specific state bar. Thus, if you practice exclusively before federal agencies, you may be able to limit your number of bar licenses.

Does admission in another jurisdiction generate more work opportunities? In many tri-state regions comprised of smaller states, you'll find that most attorneys belong to the bar of the state where the largest city is located. For example, in the areas of New York, New Jersey, and Connecticut, most lawyers practice in New York City and tend to be licensed in New York; in the areas of Massachusetts, New Hampshire, and Rhode Island, most lawyers practice in Boston and are licensed in Massachusetts; and so on. Moreover, if you previously worked at a large firm in Boston or New York, most of your colleagues will be more likely to know lawyers from Massachusetts or New York than from the adjacent states. Consequently, if you gain admission to the bar in an adjacent state like New Hampshire or New Jersey, you'll have less competition for referrals from your former colleagues.

Sometimes, you may need to gain admission to a particular state bar to qualify for temporary document-review projects, which is an option for some solos getting a practice off the ground. In 2002, the D.C. Court of Appeals Committee on Unauthorized Practice of Law ruled that contract lawyers doing business in the District must have a D.C. Bar law license. Since many temp attorneys in DC were licensed in other jurisdictions and had never taken the time to waive into the DC bar, a large number of attorneys who had previously handled contract matters were disqualified, opening up more jobs for lawyers with the foresight to gain admission to the DC Bar. In some instances, you can waive into another state bar by paying a hefty fee (about $500–$800), filling out lots of forms, and sitting for a day of ethics training. In states that do not have reciprocity, you may need to take a full bar exam. Other states, such as Maryland, offer a compromise; attorneys who have practiced for five years or more can take a "practitioner's exam" which focuses on Maryland practice rather than multi-state or general bar issues. Taking a state bar, even a practitioner's exam, can be costly and time-consuming. You'll probably need to pay for a review course, set aside study time, and pay for the exam and admissions cost. But if it creates added financial opportunities, the extra bar may be worthwhile.

Court Membership. Even though you're a member of a state's bar, in most jurisdictions, you'll need to make a separate application to practice before federal district court (including bankruptcy court) and circuit courts. If you're already admitted to one of these courts, be sure to confirm that your status is current, and send a change of address to ensure that you'll receive notices regarding renewal of admission. If you're not admitted to federal court, take the time to apply for admission now if you think there's even a small chance you may practice there. Admission isn't very expensive, but may require some planning. For example, for all admissions, you'll need at least one or two sponsors, and in some courts (such as the federal district court of Maryland), your sponsor will need to accompany you to the court and move your admission in person. Other courts may require you to observe two arguments in advance (Second Circuit), participate in e-filing training (Fourth Circuit), or to take classes if you haven't had any trial or motions experience in order to practice without a lead attorney (federal district court of the District of Columbia). **Bottom line**: take care of any admissions you need now to avoid unpleasant surprises later.

Step 2: Business Structure & Other Requirements

As you already know, starting a law firm is, in many ways, no different from starting an ordinary business. Like any business owner, you have to choose a business entity for your firm, and determine whether you need to comply with business registration requirements or licensing fees. Because lawyers are regulated by the state bar, they are often—but not always—exempt from standard business requirements. Many solos start off as sole proprietorships, and then evaluate other options after they've been in practice for a while. There's no simple answer, but the most common factors to consider are personal liability, taxation, and ease of governance. Also relevant are factors such as availability of health insurance and premium tax deductions, availability of retirement, and the costs associated with formatting and maintaining the entity. Consult with a colleague familiar with business entity rules or a CPA or tax professional for additional insight on the best structure for your situation.

Below are some of the options available for organizing your law practice, and a brief discussion of the advantages and drawbacks. Keep in mind that entity selection is state-specific, and that licensed professionals like lawyers may be prohibited from using certain organizational formats or are subject to additional requirements (such as insurance). For further guidance, check the secretary of state or business licensing authorities within your jurisdiction:

Sole proprietorship. An unincorporated law firm owned by an individual. It is the simplest business form, and many solos start out this way. In contrast to an LLC or corporation, in which you must form and submit for approval to the state, a sole proprietorship does not involve these steps. However, even as a sole proprietor, you may need to register your business in the city where you practice, so check local business laws to determine whether this requirement applies. For ordinary business owners, sole proprietorship is usually regarded as less advantageous than corporate formation which protects owners from personal liability. As a solo, however, your greatest potential from liability arises out of malpractice, and no corporate structure will shield an attorney from personal liability for their own professional malpractice (though it will protect you from other liability; e.g., liability for breach of a contract or lease, or someone else's malpractice).

Limited liability company. A corporate structure that offers the protection of liability available to corporations but may be treated as a sole proprietorship for tax purposes. An LLC will not protect lawyers from liability for acts of their own professional malpractice, but it will guard against personal liability arising out of contractual disputes with landlords or vendors, employees or associates. Some lawyers choose to organize as an LLC because it is a simple process but can give the appearance that the firm is a more established, formal entity. In some states, lawyers who form an LLC may be subject to registration and licensing fees. Other states do not permit lawyers to form LLCs at all; in these jurisdictions, a professional LLC (PLLC) or professional corporation (PC)—see below—offer comparable benefits. In addition, some states require PLLCs or PCs to carry malpractice insurance.

If you've been operating as a sole proprietor and decide to re-organize as an LLC, you'll need to procure a new EIN number and transfer your bank accounts, trust accounts, malpractice insurance, and any other obligations (leases, credit card accounts or subscriptions) to the LLC. You'll also want to purchase business insurance in addition to malpractice insurance. Since most states require you to identify your status, you may need to get new checks and business cards, and update your Web site from Joe Jones, Esq. to Joe Jones, LLC. You may also need to give notice to current clients if you change to an LLC structure.

Professional corporation. A corporation formed for the sole purpose of rendering professional services. The PC has many of the characteristics of any other corporation; it has shares, shareholders, bylaws, directors, officers, and is subject to dissolution, perpetual existence. Lawyers organized as a PC are liable for their own professional impropriety and those they supervise even though they are acting on behalf of the PC [Source: Law Firm Entity Structure, Arthur Ciampi, NY Law Journal (Dec. 10, 2010) at www.law.com/jsp/article.jsp?id=1202475985851. A PC can elect to have the same pass-through tax treatment as a partnership by electing S corporation status. An S corporation is taxed like a sole proprietorship, which is simpler than being taxed as an ordinary corporation. In addition, an S corporation will enable you to save on Social Security, Medicare, and self-employment taxes. Consult with a CPA to determine whether the tax benefits associated with S Corporation status outweigh the added costs of formation and maintenance.

Partnership. A partnership may be appropriate for two or more lawyers who choose to form a law firm. In a general partnership, each individual partner is liable for all actions of the partnership as well as each partner. By contrast, in a limited liability partnership (LLP), professional liability is limited to the LLP's assets and those of the partner who committed malpractice. If you wish to form a partnership, be sure to invest in enough malpractice insurance to cover not only your potential malpractice but that of your partners as well.

Other matters:

Business registrations. Though licensed by the state bar, lawyers are not necessarily exempt from state and local requirements that apply to other types of businesses, such as business registration with the Department of Treasury or other regulatory office, state or local sales tax or franchise fees. Contact the state bar, the Chamber of Commerce, or state business offices for additional information on state requirements.

EIN Numbers. The Employer Identification Number—otherwise known as a federal tax ID number—is used to identify a business entity. An EIN is necessary if you have employees or operate as a corporation or partnership. You can apply online for an EIN at the IRS Web site (www.irs.gov/businesses/small/article/0,,id=98350,00.html). As a sole proprietor, you won't need an EIN; your Social Security number will suffice for identification purposes. Still, if you'll be doing work for corporate or municipal clients, or as a contract attorney, you may want to get an EIN anyway to avoid putting your Social Security number in wide circulation.

SHOULD YOU START A PARTNERSHIP?

With job options dim in a weak economy, many lawyers—new grads to laid-off senior lawyers—often consider partnering up, either to share start-up costs or just to avoid going it alone. Most such partnerships are shotgun marriages; they're born of desperation and doomed to failure because the partners often discover that they're not compatible, or that they wanted different things out of the relationship.

To avoid this fate, consider the following questions before you create a formal partnership:

Do we share similar goals? You may view a partnership as the start of a long-term law practice. By contrast, your partner may simply be looking at the venture as an opportunity to make some money and avoid an empty resume until a "real" job offer comes along. As a result, you're likely to encounter tension when you want to return any profits back to the business, while your partner wants to retain as much as possible.

Are our working styles compatible? Compatibility doesn't mean that both and your partner are the same, but that you're able to tolerate any differences. Sometimes, a combination of an outgoing rainmaking lawyer and a shy but brilliant worker clicks because each appreciates and respects the other's skills. By contrast, a rainmaker may come to resent sharing profits equally with the worker bee who never generates any business, or the worker bee may feel that the rainmaker doesn't work very hard or isn't very smart, which can lead to the demise of the relationship.

Is my partner trustworthy and competent? In a partnership, you're liable for the malpractice of your partner. If you don't know your potential partner well enough to trust him or her unequivocally, don't bother.

If a partnership still tempts you after considering these factors, proceed into a formal arrangement with caution. In my view, the preferable approach is an informal affiliation where you agree to share start-up costs, such as office space or research services, and even team up from time to time to pitch clients or work on projects. But ultimately, retain your respective identities as independent law firms and make clear to potential clients that you are not a partnership (likewise, avoid sharing profits which may impute a partnership). If the arrangement succeeds after six months or a year, consider a formal partnership at that time.

Step 3. Selecting a Name For Your Firm

Once you decide on your firm's business structure, you need a firm name. While naming the practice after yourself (Law Office of John Smith) is hardly original, many lawyers—weary of the obscurity and anonymity that comes with working at a large firm or government agency—are eager for the chance to put a personal stamp on their practice. And why not? This is one time you shouldn't feel embarrassed to follow the crowd. So, proclaim ownership of your firm; you deserve it. And don't be modest. Remember, you are a law firm of one, not merely an attorney. Why settle for Jane Doe, Attorney at Law? That's what you were the day you graduated law school. Today, you are a law firm; your name should reflect that.

As more firms develop niche practices, a trend has emerged towards descriptive trade names. A few years ago, an Atlanta law firm got some attention by calling itself Red Hot Law Group, a name that helped distinguish the technology boutique from its competitors, and reflected a commitment to their fast-paced, cutting-edge practice. Likewise, Simplicity Law (www.simplicitylaw.com), a firm that provides various business documents at low prices and 24-hour turn-around, chose a name that describes the type of service it aims to provide to entrepreneurs. **Bottom line**: if you practice in a competitive field, consider a trade name that sets your firm apart.

A cautionary note: while the Second Circuit found that New York's outright ban on use of slogans, logos and trade names violate the First Amendment, the court acknowledged that the state may, on a case-by-case basis, prohibit those trade names that deceive or mislead consumers. *Alexander v. Cahill*, 598 F.3d 79, 89 (2d Cir. 2010). Thus, many states continue to reject many trade names as deceptive. For example, the New Jersey Committee on Attorney Advertising refused to permit a firm use the name Alpha Divorce Mediation Center, finding that the use of the term "alpha" carried various misleading connotations; either that the firm was comprised of "alpha males" or was the "first" and best center for mediation. The firm has appealed the Committee's decision to the New Jersey Supreme Court. NJ Law Journal (Jan. 7, 2011), www.law.com/jsp/article.jsp?id=1202477358106.

Other bars will not allow trade names that imply that a firm is a government-sponsored agency or legal aid organization. Thus, a bar might express concern over a firm that calls itself The George Smith Legal Aid Clinic or The Employment Law Help Center. Bars are also concerned about deception where a firm uses a name that gives the impression that it is larger than it actually is (though, the bar apparently sees no deception where 700-lawyer firms like WilmerHale are known by a two-person name, giving the impression that they are smaller, more congenial or less expensive than they are). So, don't call your firm Jane X and Associates or The X Law Group if you do not have associates or other lawyers in the firm. The name would suggest to clients that you employ other attorneys. Also beware of a prohibition against the phrase "*and Associates*", which may apply to law firms employing virtual associates offsite. In 2005, the South Carolina bar disciplined a former state senator who, in the name of his law firm, used "*and Associates*" when his associate was an out-of-state attorney who researched and drafted pleadings on a contract basis. The bar held that the phrase applies only to staff not contract attorneys [Greenville News, June 5, 2005]. If it's your intent to employ virtual associates offsite, seek guidance from the bar. Otherwise, you might find your integrity questioned, as happened to now-Supreme Court Justice Sonya Sotomayor who, years before her appointment to the bench, briefly operated a firm dubbed Sotomayor & Associates even though she did not have any associates (www.washingtontimes.com/news/2009/jun/24/sotomayors-ethical-oversight/). A Washington Times editorial argued that Sotomayor's ethics lapse in naming her firm was indicative of general lack of character!

As a solo, you may even run into problems by referring to yourself as a "law firm." In Opinion 332 (Nov., 2005), the DC Bar concluded that a solo could call herself the X Law Firm, in which she was the sole member, finding that the use of the term "firm" by a solo was not presumptively misleading. Of course, that the bar would even suggest that a solo's use of the term law firm could ever be misleading insults those of us solos who take our business as a "law firm of one" as seriously as a law firm of thousands. **Bottom line**: if you're not sure about the ethics of using a law firm name, read the bar rules for yourself. If it's still unclear, seek advice from the bar.

Step 4. Purchasing Insurance

Malpractice insurance. One absolute rule I have for new solos is that they must purchase malpractice insurance. In the interest of full disclosure, though, I admit to not following my own advice during my first three years of practice! Back then, I was young and cocky, and I calculated that my potential exposure was low given my regulatory practice, my "long shot" litigation matters and criminal defense work.

I assumed legal malpractice insurance was as costly as health insurance and probably couldn't afford it. I had a nothing-to-lose attitude back then, figuring that if anyone sued me I'd simply pack up my firm and walk away. I see things differently now with my practice well under way. I have so much invested in my practice that I am unwilling to sacrifice my firm if a client sues me. Also, after a couple of close calls, I realize that—despite my diligence—I am only human, and capable of mistakes that could morph into a grievance or a malpractice action. Once I understood this, the purchase of malpractice insurance to protect myself from future claims was better than berating myself for my mistakes, or worse, waking in a cold sweat in the middle of the night. When I finally shopped around for malpractice insurance and spoke with other solo and small firm lawyers, I discovered that it was not as expensive as I had thought. Of course, this is just my story.

Read what a solo in family law wrote to the ABA's Solosez listserv about an experience that happened to them:

> *"I've heard it said that if you have never had a client file a claim against you, you haven't been practicing long enough. By this measure, I have now been practicing law long enough.*
>
> *"Several years ago, a disgruntled former client filed a complaint with the Attorney Discipline Office. The claims specialist assigned to my case offered insight, provided a sounding board, reviewed my response and other documents, and confirmed that I could*

either handle this pro se, or with counsel. For a variety of reasons, I handled it pro se. The ADO dismissed the complaint, and concluded that this was merely a matter of differing opinions. The former client then filed suit in court… also suing his former spouse, the judge, the guardian ad litem, the parenting counselor, and advised the screening officer and chair of the ADO that he would be suing them, too.

"I am absolutely delighted that I can leave this in the hands of my attorney, and I am absolutely delighted that my insurance company rejected a settlement offer from the Plaintiff for half the policy limits (which means they feel quite strongly that a judgment will either be in my favor, or for an amount less than half the policy limit). And I am absolutely incensed that my attorneys will be spending at least $5,000 worth of time on my behalf, which means that a judgment in my favor will still cost me $5,000 (my deductible). But I am thankful that I was not practicing 'bare', which would have deprived me of the advice I received in the ADO matter, and would have seriously interfered with my ability to defend myself in this suit. I am not a bad attorney. I don't deserve this. But this is part of practicing law. Please, please, please think long and hard before 'going bare'".

Here are some of the factors you should consider in purchasing malpractice insurance as well as suggestions on how to procure the best plan for your firm:

Does your state require malpractice coverage or have a mandatory disclosure policy? You may not even have a choice about whether to get legal malpractice insurance. In fact, Oregon, requires all lawyers to buy malpractice insurance. And seven other states—Arkansas, California, New Hampshire, New Mexico, Ohio, Pennsylvania and South Dakota—require attorneys to reveal to prospective clients whether they have malpractice coverage, while 11 other states require insurance disclosure on lawyers' annual registration statements (which, depending upon the state, are potentially available to the public). As a practical matter, a mandatory disclosure rule has virtually the same effect as a mandatory requirement. In a mandatory disclosure jurisdiction, lack of malpractice coverage gives prospective clients the impression that you're running a fly-by-night operation, and they'll likely pass on hiring you. On the other hand, if you don't disclose a lack of malpractice coverage, you run the risk of disciplinary reprimand if your concealment is later discovered. You might as well avoid all of these hassles in a mandatory disclosure jurisdiction at the outset by obtaining malpractice coverage.

Do you need malpractice insurance for business opportunities? Another factor to consider is whether you need malpractice coverage for business opportunities. Some referral services will not refer cases to lawyers who do not carry sufficient malpractice coverage. Many times, an RFP (request for proposal) for legal services also requires coverage. Even law firms and attorneys who retain lawyers for per diem or contract work often require some amount of malpractice coverage. In short, malpractice insurance is a worthwhile investment economically if it allows you to take advantage of opportunities that would not be available in the absence of coverage.

How much does your degree of exposure matter? Your own assessment of your degree of malpractice exposure should *not* serve as the deciding factor in your decision regarding coverage. Even though the chances are low of a client actually winning a malpractice action against you and collecting a judgment, it doesn't take much for a client to initiate such an action in hopes of pressuring a quick settlement—or worse, to file a bar complaint which, if unfavorably resolved, can cause damage to your reputation and lead to a suspension. These days, many legal malpractice plans cover the cost of defense both in malpractice actions in court and, equally importantly, in grievance procedures where lawyers who are represented almost always fare better than those who participate pro se. Thus, malpractice insurance buys you the peace of mind; one less thing to worry about when that client who started out so reasonably starts threatening a grievance. Moreover, if your risk of exposure is low anyway, you'll probably be able to find a relatively inexpensive coverage plan.

What can you afford? Even though malpractice insurance is a good investment, cost matters when you're just starting out. There are some practice areas (such as certain IP matters) where malpractice insurance can be prohibitively expensive. But if you expect that IP will generate substantial revenue for you, bite the bullet and write the check. On the other hand, if you're only intending to handle a smattering of IP work and focus on other areas, you might consider dropping that practice area or figuring out other ways to do it—maybe on contract basis for another firm—that will limit your exposure and the concomitant costs of coverage.

How do you purchase malpractice insurance? Many state bar associations have an insurance company that is designated as a "preferred provider" or bar association sponsor. Be wary of these designations; it's no guarantee that the company offers the lowest cost or is the most reliable. In fact, as I discovered when I signed up to use the DC Bar's preferred provider, the opposite was true. In my case, the provider charged roughly 20 percent more than my current insurer and also went out of business a year after I signed up. While in some states, the bars negotiate favorable deals with preferred providers, in others the preferred provider is nothing more than an insurer which has paid the bar a certain amount of money in exchange for exclusive billing. To find potential malpractice companies, seek advice from other attorneys who have personally procured the plan and who practice in the same jurisdiction. Getting advice from an associate at a firm that uses, say, Ajax Insurance, isn't much value since the associate won't know the terms or cost of coverage. Likewise, information about a cheap plan in California won't do much good if you practice in Florida. Your best bet is a recommendation from a fellow attorney with a similar practice, who can share his or her personal experiences with the provider, and perhaps even give you a sense of what he or she pays for the policy. Once you've gathered a list of two or three prospective providers, shop around for quotes. Ask for a range of costs depending on variables such as the size of your deductible or coverage per claim. If you don't want to do the legwork yourself, work with an insurance broker, or get referrals from colleagues or your local bar.

Sensitive to the growing number of lawyers going solo in a weakened economy, many carriers now offer extremely affordable policies—as little as $500/year—to solos just out of school or in their first year of practice. Other carriers discount policies for part-time practices, based on number of hours worked and/or income earned. To further minimize the financial burden, some carriers allow lawyers to pay the premium on a quarterly or even monthly basis, while others may extend hefty discounts to lawyers who participate in a carrier-sponsored risk management and ethics course. Many times, carriers don't advertise these perks, so be sure to ask about their availability.

Most legal malpractice plans are claims-based, which means that coverage applies for any claim made during a specified period. In addition, even if you've gone "bare" for several years, you may be able to negotiate insurance for "prior acts"; past incidents that pre-dated your plan but for which no claim has yet been filed. And when shopping for a plan, make certain that it will cover defense costs, both in civil suits and disciplinary actions. Also ask what other benefits the plan offers. Some might offer a free legal research package or discount prices; others include risk- management training with a discount on the cost of insurance to those who participate.

A section of the ABA's Web site (www.abanet.org/legalservices/lpl/home.html) is dedicated to the purchase of malpractice insurance. It includes some reasonably current information on purchasing malpractice insurance and statistics, reporting claims and minimizing malpractice risk. The ABA site also maintains a list of insurance carriers in all 50 states (www.abanet.org/legalservices/lpl/directory).

Business insurance. In addition to malpractice insurance, you'll want to get business insurance to cover loss of business assets (furniture, computer equipment, etc.). Indeed, if you rent space, you may be required to carry business coverage. If you work from home, your homeowner's policy may cover your business assets; otherwise, you can obtain in-home business policies designed and priced specifically for home-office workers to insure you and your business property.

Cyber-insurance. In years past, lawyers handled personal client data—Social Security ID, drivers' license numbers, bank data—with reasonable security. Back then, though, a thief would have needed to sort through boxes of paper files to steal client data. Now, a decade's worth of sensitive case files can be stored on a laptop, a thumb drive, or online, and stolen or hacked in seconds. Cyber-insurance covers liability resulting from loss of confidential client data, as well as a host of other tech-related injuries: damage to your computer system (and resulting business interruption) caused by viruses or cyber-attacks; protection from libel or defamation associated with online activity like blogging and Web use; and copyright and trademark infringement. Relatively new, most lawyers don't carry cyber-insurance...but I predict that will change within the next five to ten years. For now, cyber-insurance for small businesses is still a bit costly; between $2,500 and $5,000. Of course, that's on top of what you pay for malpractice insurance. Check with your malpractice carrier first to see whether your current policy covers any cyber-liability.

Step 5: Establishing Your Financial Accounts

Before you open your practice, you need to establish a law firm bank account, order business checks, and apply for a law firm credit card for business purchases. Even if you're operating as a sole proprietor, set up a second account under your name, or as a DBA (doing business as) for the Law Office of John Smith or Jane Doe, Esq). Using a business credit card will help you track and document your business expenses; in addition, credit card interest for business purchases is fully deductible, whereas interest on personal credit cards is not. You'll also want to quickly set up a way to accept payment by credit card. Although you'll pay transaction costs and monthly fees for credit cards, studies have shown that accepting credit card payments can boost revenues by as much as 30 percent by giving clients more payment options and minimizing collections problems.

Credit card options fall into three main categories, each with its benefits and drawbacks:

Merchant accounts through your bank. A *merchant account* is a type of bank account that lets businesses accept credit card payments. Most bank-based merchant accounts allow you to process credit card transactions by phone or online, and—for an additional fee—will provide a terminal for processing cards. The fee structure includes some or all of the following: (1) A set-up fee; (2) a monthly flat fee ranging from $10–$20; (3) a card-processing rate of 2 to 3 percent (so for a $100 transaction, you pay $3); (4) a per transaction-fee of around 20 to 40 cents; and (5) a monthly minimum charge of $25 to $40/month if you don't process a minimum amount of charges. Setting up a merchant account at your regular bank is simple and convenient, which is why many solos avail themselves of this option. There are also drawbacks: your bank may not offer a merchant account, or may charge the upper end of the fee range. Also, a bank may not be willing to implement additional measures to ensure that credit card payments are ethically compliant, such as ensuring that credit card transaction fees are covered by your operating account and that payments for advance work are routed to your trust account.

Lawyer-specific merchant accounts. Companies like www.LawFirmMerchantAccount.com (recommended by numerous bar associations), and www.LawCharge.com (recommended by Solosezzers) are merchant accounts designed to fit the specific needs of attorneys (e.g., ensuring compliance with trust account rules and avoiding commingling of funds). While ethics compliance is an obvious benefit of lawyer-specific merchant accounts, these services may cost more to set up and transaction fees may be higher. As such, they may be better suited to high volume practices with frequent credit card transactions. If you opt for a lawyer-specific merchant account, check to see whether your bar association offers any special deals with any providers.

Transaction-based services. Services like Paypal, Google Checkout, SquareUp.com or Accept-by-Phone allow you to accept credit card payments in a variety of ways without setting up a merchant account: online (Paypal and Google), by phone (Accept-by-Phone), or even on your cell phone through use of a mini-scanning device (SquareUp.com). With the exception of Accept by Phone (which has a small set-up fee and $5/month monthly fee), the only costs related to the other transaction-based services are (1) discount rates ranging from 2.75 to 3.5 percent and as low as 1.9 percent for $3,000 of monthly transactions or more, and (2) transaction fees ranging from 15 to 30 cents per transaction. The benefits of transaction-based services are their flexibility, and the ease with which they can be set up. Though many complain about the fees, these services are comparably priced to merchant accounts and offer similar services, such as a record of your transactions. On the downside, some lawyers believe that services like Paypal don't come across as professionally as the others. In addition, because Paypal or Google Checkout hold credit card payments until you move them into your bank account, some lawyers believe that these services are unethical when used to accept payment of unearned fees, which are required to go directly into a client's trust account (though in some jurisdictions, prompt transfer of Paypal funds to trust account will satisfy ethics obligations).

Client trust accounts. In addition to general bank accounts and credit cards, you'll also need to set up an IOLTA-compliant trust account if you plan on accepting advance payments from clients or holding client funds. Lawyers holding money for clients even for a short time (such as funds received from the proceeds of a settlement pending disbursement by the attorney) must deposit the money into a trust account. Bar rules prohibiting commingling of lawyer and client funds are stringent; even an accidental deposit of client funds into your law firm account that you report immediately thereafter could earn you a reprimand. Even if you're not sure that you'll need a client trust account, set one up at the beginning while you're at the bank. Note: some lawyers prefer to keep their trust account and operating account at separate banks to avoid the possibility of commingling, though in my view, it's overkill not to mention inconvenient.

Client trust accounts must comply with the applicable bar's IOLTA (Interest on Lawyer Trust Account) rules. Under IOLTA programs, participating banks forward the interest on certain lawyer trust accounts (i.e., those where client funds are nominal or held for too short a period to warrant establishment of a separate account) to the state's IOLTA program, which distributes the money to legal services organizations. Since their inception, IOLTA programs have generated millions of dollars in support for legal aid programs.

According to the ABA, 31 states have mandatory IOLTA programs, and 19 have opt-out programs in which lawyers must participate unless they affirmatively advise the bar that they will not take part in the IOLTA program. Only two jurisdictions, the Virgin Islands and South Dakota, have completely voluntary IOLTA programs. Both the ABA and virtually every state bar retain detailed Web sites on IOLTA, which explain the applicable rules and identify participating IOLTA banks. For additional guidance, consult these sites as well as the IOLTA office or the bar's LPM advisor.

Trust accounts often intimidate new solos because of the record-keeping requirements and sometimes confusing rules on commingling. Fortunately, technology simplifies trust account management: it includes such practice management tools as Clio and RocketMatter, which integrate trust account management, and bookkeeping software like Quicken, which can easily be adapted to support trust accounting. For a step-by-step guide, read *How to Use Quicken 2011 for Lawyer Trust Accounting*, by Bevery Michaelis of the Oregon Law Practice Management Bar (article posted at www.jd-supra.com/post/documentViewer.aspx?fid=50387939-cefc-4a6e-8fcc-d3938847383d).

Other ethics issues related to trust fund deposits or management are state-specific so you'll need to familiarize yourself with your jurisdiction's rules.

Below are two red flags:

Client funds v. attorney funds. States differ about whether a retainer or advance fee belongs to the attorney (in which case it can be deposited directly into the firm's operating account), or whether these fees belong to the client until such point that work is performed (in which case the money must go to the trust account). A minority of state bars reason that a retainer fee belongs to the attorney because it compensates the lawyer to secure his availability for the duration of the case. Other bars take the position that a retainer is like an escrow fund that provides assurance of future payment. As such, it is essentially an advance payment for services to be performed and belongs to the client until such time as the attorney renders services and is entitled to payment from the retainer amount. Likewise, bars also differ on whether payment of a flat-fee may be treated as earned on receipt or must be deposited into a trust account and released only as work is performed (see Chapter 11).

Some jurisdictions, like District of Columbia, Missouri and Colorado, require lawyers to deposit flat-fees into their trust account; others like Washington State and North Carolina allow lawyers to treat flat-fees as earned on receipt for deposit in their operating fund if agreed to by the client.

Commingling. Virtually every bar prohibits lawyers from mixing—commingling—their funds with client money in trust accounts. But some banks charge a fee for maintaining a trust account, which raises the question of whether a lawyer can keep a *de minimis* amount of funds to cover bank fees or other charges. That depends. Some states allow this practice so long as lawyers keep careful records of their deposits, while others authorize the bank to use interest generated by IOLTA to pay the administrative charges for the account.

Step 6: Where to Set Up the Office

Of all of the decisions relating to starting a law practice, the question of where to locate the practice is among the most debated. Fortunately, with technological advancements and a growing number of entrepreneurs seeking flexible office arrangements, lawyers starting a practice have more options on where to work than ever before:

The home office

PRO: The greatest single advantage of a home office is lower overhead. If you practice in an urban area (where even a small office starts at $1,000/month), you can expect to save at least $12,000/year working from home . . . and that's before calculating your home-office tax deduction. The money you save can be applied to legal research services, marketing materials, CLE courses. More important, you can select your cases more judiciously instead of feeling compelled to take whatever comes in the door just to make the rent. And it goes without saying that a home office works better for parents of young children, allowing them to spend more time with them during the day, and to be there when they return home from school. Note: the IRS has strict requirements about whether your home office qualifies for a tax write-off. To do so, your home office—even a portion of a room—must be used "regularly and exclusively" as your principal place of business.

CON: For many other solos, the greatest disadvantage is how one's home office might reflect on one's credentials and professional image. But while even that concern has less of a bite these days because of the popularity of telecommuting and home-based businesses, it doesn't mean you won't encounter the occasional insensitivity (e.g, *it must be nice to spend the day in your pajamas*), or to lose an occasional project when a client or referring attorney is less confident of your firm's stability or credibility. And there are other important considerations:

- Some agencies will not send temps to a home office. If you need someone to work onsite—say, a law clerk to compile an appendix of documents for trial, or a secretary to organize your files—you might need to find other ways to fill your employment needs.
- For some lawyers, the home office environment feels too isolating, and the household distractions and parenting responsibilities interfere with the work flow.
- And for reasons of safety and privacy, it might be helpful to maintain a separate mailing address for some practice areas like criminal defense and family law. A private mail box allows you to receive correspondence and checks without revealing your address, and keeps your home address off court filings that frequently wind up on the Internet. Publication of a home address does not matter as much for lawyers who serve corporate clients or handle contract work for other attorneys. Most of the solos I know who run those types of practices use their home address as their primary contact information.

Most clients will assume you work from a traditional office unless you make a point of saying otherwise. So, unless a client asks where your office is located, or pointedly asks if you work from home, you have no obligation to reveal that you do work from home. Don't ask, don't tell. Sometimes, you may not be able to avoid telling clients or colleagues you have a home office; don't sweat it. Back when I started my practice from my home in 1993, I felt I had a huge red H branded across my business suit. But these days, telecommuting is increasingly common, and some clients—particularly those in large corporations or in the high tech industry—may regard a home office as ahead of the curve. Of course, having a standard explanation will make you more comfortable disclosing your home office status. Perhaps, telling clients that you spend so much time at the courthouse that maintaining a physical space was a waste of money and now, you can pass savings on to them. Or, better still, say that working from home saves an hour or two on commuting and gives you more time to spend on client matters. In the end, what matters most to clients is the quality of service that you provide and not where your office is located.

Commercial space. Some argue that a conventional, full-time office is critical to the success of a new practice; others (myself included) believe it depends on the nature of one's practice, personality and work habits, and, of course, the cost. In my opinion, too many new and potential solos assume they must have Class A space—the highest quality—and jump into a situation without the revenue to support it.

PRO: An outside office is still the least complicated option. When a client or referral source asks for the location of your office, it's so much easier to provide a commercial address than explaining a home office, or that you need to meet at Starbucks or the courthouse cafeteria. Commercial space also makes it easier to invite a client in for a quick meeting rather than delay while figure out a mutually agreeable location. And commercial space confers credibility; it helps mute whatever doubts new clients or potential referral sources may have about your new firm. An outside office also offers rich potential for business and networking; the companies with whom you co-locate may seek your advice on legal matters or send you overflow work. And there are less-obvious benefits: lawyers Christopher Manning and Melinda Sossaman used their Washington DC office townhouse as a client magnet. They renovated space on one floor and hosted events—holiday gatherings, political fund-raisers, etc. In time, the attendees referred cases to them, and those clients generated even more referrals. For solo Chris Vaughn-Martel (class of 2006) a commercial space was also a great motivator, and his decision to lease shared space has been more than repaid in productivity, client satisfaction, business referrals, and contract work. "*Having an office helps me stay organized,*" Chris said. [*If I had opened a home office], I probably would have stayed in my pajamas, played with my dog, napped, watched Colbert Report re-runs all day and not gotten anything done. I would have been lonely, probably depressed and unmotivated.*"

CON: Even in our slowly recovering economy, commercial space in most urban markets still costs from several hundred to several thousand dollars a month, probably the greatest expense when you're coping with so many other start-up costs. And then there is the daily commute: in recent years, the average commuter has lost some 34 hours—nearly a full work week—because of traffic congestion, and that represents a lot of potentially billable or productive time. And if you work part-time and have parental responsibilities, you're left with just a few hours to work before you need to turn around to pick up your kids.

Virtual office space. The emergence of a mobile workforce has given birth to another workplace option—the "virtual office" (not to be confused with "virtual law firms"). You can find virtual offices at office business centers all over the country. They're a valuable tool for solos and small firm practitioners who want to limit their start-up costs, and to establish themselves alongside larger competitors for a fraction of the cost of setting up a full-time office.

PRO: If full-time space isn't in your budget, and a home office poses image problems—and you're reluctant to meet clients at Denny's, Starbucks, or the courthouse cafeteria—a virtual office makes a lot of sense. For starters, virtual offices are much less expensive than full-time leased space, typically starting from $75 to $200/month, depending on location, level of service, and the elements of the lease package. A typical virtual office might include a mail-forwarding service, a shared receptionist to forward calls, and five hours a month of office or conference room space. Many virtual offices also offer services such as voice-mail, fax, and/or access to hourly secretarial services. Many virtual offices operate at prime locations, so you enjoy the benefit of a prestigious address that you could not otherwise afford. Virtual space also solves the problem of where to meet clients, and the leases are typically month-to-month and upgradeable to provide more hours of space to meet emergent needs. Virtual space is an attractive option; it gives new solos just the time they need to get their firm up and running so they can get a better sense of their longer-term space needs.

CON: Office business centers have a tendency to nickel-and-dime you for virtual office space, often charging exorbitant rates for such services as faxing… even an extra charge for checking your mail. And if you sign up for a mail-forwarding service, there can be a lag time in getting mail, which could be a problem with a heavy litigation practice in which filings demand a timely response. Many virtual offices typically service hundreds of professionals. As a result, the so-called "personal" receptionist can come across as brusque or rude (so, you may want to get an Internet fax number and/or a cell phone so clients can call you directly). Note: during your busiest months, the cost of a virtual office could equal the cost of full-time space because you will have to rent more hours of office space. Of course, if you're generating more revenue, you can absorb the additional overhead. In time, your virtual office may cost more than permanent space on a consistent basis, at which time start looking for your own office.

Virtual law firms. A virtual law firm is a professional law practice that exists entirely online. Clients access legal services by logging into a secure online portal in the same way that they might log in to their online bank account. With a virtual firm, legal services are delivered entirely online, supplemented by written communications and—if necessary—real-time conversations via Skype or telephone. Lawyers who operate a purely virtual law practice don't need to worry about office space because they never meet with clients (Note: there are also "hybrid arrangements where a bricks-and-mortar firm may offer lower cost online services through a virtual office). All transactions take place online, and are usually limited to unbundled or discrete matters such as preparation of estate planning materials, corporate documents, or leases. Even though a virtual firm can be operated from a home office, you still need to be able to hang a shingle in cyberspace so that you can provide a retainer letter, or gather information from clients through forms, or exchange information with clients, or bill clients for services. There are several companies developing practice management tools for virtual solos. One of the two leaders is Chicago-based Total Attorneys (www.totalattorneys.com), first developed by attorney Stephanie Kimbro and her husband. The other is DirectLaw (www.DirectLaw.com), which offers a platform and numerous forms to improve lawyer efficiencies. For more details on creating a virtual law practice, get a copy of *Virtual Law Practice: How to Deliver Legal Services on Line* (Stephanie Kimbro, ABA/2010).

Shared space. Shared space is also quite popular, and has its own economic advantages. As discussed in Chapter 2, data on solo earnings suggest that solos in shared space fare better than those in private space or working from home. Working alongside other lawyers can lead to referrals or overflow work, and also motivate you to work harder to keep pace with your officemates. In New York, solos and small firms can find shared space with other attorneys at locations like LawFirmSuites (www.lawfirmsuites.com) or at Law Firm Incubator (www.lawfirmincubator.com). If similar arrangements aren't available in your area, or the prices are too high for your taste, look for shared space on Craigslist or through your local bar journal. Or organize a group of solo colleagues to find your own space.

When you share office space, especially with other attorneys, there are several important potential ethics questions to consider:

Does your arrangement adequately protect client confidentiality? You must have a secure place for storing client files that only you or authorized personnel can access. Don't assume that file security only matters when you share space with lawyers who represent clients with conflicting interests. The ability of one of your fellow attorneys to gain advantage in litigation by stealing a look at privileged strategy memos is the least of your worries. The greater danger is the possibility that your suitemates' employees or guests could take advantage of unsecured files to steal Social Security numbers or other sensitive financial information. If so, you could face disciplinary sanctions or even malpractice liability for exposing your clients to fraud or identity theft by failing to adequately safeguard the financial information in their files.

Other tips for preserving client confidentiality:

- Avoid discussing confidential matters in common areas outside your office.
- Keep confidential materials in secured and locked cabinets or private servers inside the office.
- If you share a receptionist, have your calls forwarded to a private voice mail instead. The message may contain confidential client information which the receptionist might share inadvertently with others in the office.
- Don't leave a shared photocopying machine unattended.

- Avoid sharing a fax or printer.
- Shred work drafts.
- Maintain an individual computer; password-protect any shared network.

Does your arrangement give the impression you are part of a law firm? When you lease space in a suite of attorneys, or within a firm, retain your firm's own identity with your own business stationery and name on the door. In some cases, solos share space and the expenses of a receptionist or support staff, and jointly advertise or collectively list their names on law firm stationery and even a Web site. The appeal of this arrangement is understandable; reduced overhead and the appearance of being part of a larger group without the formalities of an official partnership. Still, such arrangements could create trouble. There have been several cases where lawyers participating in a collective arrangement have been sued for malpractice committed by an officemate because the client believed that all of the lawyers operated as part of a single firm. Conflicts of interest may or may not be an area of concern when your office-sharing arrangement resembles a law firm. According to Jim Calloway, law practice manager for the Oklahoma bar:

> "…*As a practical matter, many of the most significant potential conflicts of interest will be recognized by the clients, or perceived even when they do not in fact appear. If the lawyer down the hall represents the wife in the divorce case, you are probably not going to convince the husband that you can adequately and fairly protect his interest. Frankly, you should not even try to convince him and then represent him.*"

If in doubt, consult your state's ethics rules on conflicts of interest within a law firm for guidance.

How much do you know about your future suite-mates? Sadly, there are unscrupulous lawyers who would take advantage of shared-space arrangements. For example, the amiable young lawyer chatting with your prospective client in the lobby, and who may be trying to steal your business…or the law firm that rents you space, and then opens a specialty practice of its own when they see how busy your practice is…or the solo who is subletting from a law firm, and steals their client list so he can send out business solicitation letters. (Note: by the way, this last scenario actually occurred at a firm where I once worked, and an astute client exposed the solo to a senior partner.) I know of another case where an unscrupulous lawyer subletting space was suspended for three months. Rather than inform his clients of the suspension and withdraw from his cases as required, he asked one of the solos subletting from him to enter an appearance in the cases for the duration of the suspension even though the suspended attorney remained involved and retained most of the fees when the cases settled. What's the message here? When you rent space from other attorneys, engage in the same due diligence as if you were hiring them or referring them a case. If you don't know the attorneys personally, ask around about their reputations. Check the bar Web site to make sure the attorneys are in good standing, and haven't had problems with the bar. Sharing space can offer great benefits for new solos, but you need to find the right arrangement and to avoid the bad apples. Note: if you share space with a firm and learn that the lawyers are, say, skimming money from client trust accounts, or practicing with a suspended license, you have an obligation to notify the bar or possibly face ethics charges for failing to do so. As an attorney, you don't have the luxury of turning a blind eye to unethical conduct by other lawyers.

Co-working space. Originated by nomadic Internet entrepreneurs looking for an alternative to working in coffee shops or faceless virtual offices, co-working is "a style of work which involves a shared working environment" comprised of a group of people who work independently but who are interested in the synergy that can occur when working alongside other talented, entrepreneurial people in the same space. Co-working arrangements offer space; more importantly, they focus on building a robust, productive work community.

Co-working spaces typically bring together professionals of all disciplines, not just lawyers, and offers opportunities for client development. Co-working spaces have working areas with large communal tables, cubicles and/or individual desk space, and even a few private offices and conference rooms. Naturally, the space is equipped with Internet access, office supplies and printers. Some co-working spaces are dedicated to specific industries or demographics. Example: there are Green co-working spaces, co-working spaces for start-ups or small businesses, "mom-centric" co-working spaces with built-in daycare (www.cubesandcrayons.com); even after-hours co-working spaces like New York's Night Owls (www.nynightowls.com).

Some co-working spaces charge an annual membership fee of a few hundred dollars, which includes a few hours a month of work space, plus the option to purchase additional time for $10 –$15/hour. Others charge a monthly fee, ranging from as low as $50/month up to $800/month for different levels of service, such as use of communal quarters on a first-come, first-serve basis, access to a dedicated cubicle or a full office. Many co-working spaces allow you to share a monthly membership with as many as four other people, so you could secure space for an intern, or simply switch off with another lawyer. The downside is that this arrangement is very informal, and much of the space isn't private so it may not be well suited to meeting with clients. You'll find more information at http://wiki.coworking.info/w/page/16583831/FrontPage). There is a list of dozens of co-working locations around the country at http://under30ceo.com/53-coworking-centers-in-the-top-cities-for-entrepreneurs/.

THE WORK-FOR-SPACE ARRANGEMENT: A CAUTIONARY NOTE

Many new solos look favorably on the work-for-space arrangement. And why not; at first glance, it seems ideal. After all, you get access to office space without adding to your overhead, and it could lead to a relationship that leads to overflow referrals.

Before you sign anything, though, a cautionary note:

The arrangement may not be as beneficial for you as it is for the outsourcing attorney. Do the math: if you put in 30 hours a month—calculated at a modest $100/hour—it comes to $3,000. Now, you may not have $3,000 in billable revenue when you start out. But, if you spent the same amount of time marketing, networking and/or writing articles for your new practice, you'd probably be able to generate $3,000 in revenues in a couple of months! Now, consider the arrangement from the other side. If the attorney offering space can bill your 30 hours out to clients at $100/hour, he's $3,000 ahead, which is far more revenue than if he simply rented the space! If you have 30 hours a month free, you're better off seeking court-appointed matters for $40 to $50/hour (which will produce $1,500/month in revenue), or lower paid contract work. If you spent $800/month on office space, you would still have $700 left over for other business expenses. In short, you would still come out ahead of the work-for-space arrangement. But if work-for-space still appeals to you, engage in some due-diligence on the attorney making the offer, and commit the agreement to writing. Sad to say, many attorneys take advantage of work-for-space deals. You may think you're agreeing to a 25 hour-a-month commitment, but then you're given a workload that might take an experienced lawyer 50 hours! Or, you might be pressured to accept dud referrals or difficult clients in addition to your work-for-space duties. Eventually, you find yourself serving as an unpaid associate for the other lawyer rather than as a new, independent solo. If work-for-space sounds too good to be true; it is. Proceed with caution.

The Office Space FAQ

Q: *For a newbie like myself, office sharing just seems so perfect; maybe too perfect. Any reason to be cautious?*

A: The advantages of subleasing...or office-sharing...are obvious: it's easier on the budget, you have access to a firm library, lunchroom and/or conference room, and there's a good chance of finding mentors and/or referrals. A solo I know rented space from one of her clients (a trade association), and it led to more work simply because they saw her around more frequently. Another solo I know had a very different experience. He sublet space within an existing law firm on the promise that several family law matters would be referred every month. A few months after he arrived, the firm started its own family law practice. Not only did the referrals evaporate, but the solo found himself in direct competition with the firm from which he rented space! When you explore the shared-space option, don't allow the promise of referrals to dictate your decision.

Q: *I'm worried about overhead, and wonder if the expense of an outside space is likely to be offset by business opportunities of having an office.*

A: I know of a Boston solo with an IP practice who, after evaluating her target market, learned that most of her prospective clients and referrals expected her to have permanent office space. So, from Day One she rented commercial space. On the other hand, I work with several established energy regulatory lawyers in the Washington D.C. area who run successful practices from their home. Even though they can afford commercial space, they see no point in renting an office they would rarely use. Don't assume that a full-time office is indispensable to success and lock yourself into a lease you can ill-afford.

Q: *As a mom with a part-time practice, I want to be available for my kids but not if it keeps me from working on my cases.*

A: If you don't think you will get your work done because you can't resist the distractions at home, or the isolation depresses you, then the loss of productivity would negate whatever money you save. If your personal work situation or habits preclude you from working effectively from home, renting/leasing space makes sense.

Q: *Where's the best place to look for office space?*
A: After searching the usual resources (bar newsletters, local classifieds, law school and courthouse bulletin boards, "for rent" signs), go online. Craigslist is everyone's favorite online bulletin board. And don't forget to talk to colleagues about anyone they know who might have space to rent or share. That's how I found a fully furnished office for nearly half the prevailing rates!

Q: *I've decided to get commercial space. I'm just not sure where it ought to be.*
A: Technology has simplified the question of where to locate your office. After all, the entire federal court system, as well as many state court systems, now have electronic filing systems. And with the exception of filing the original complaint, all other submissions can be made online instead of driving to court. And, of course, you can go online to search court dockets and retrieve files instead of ordering them from a court or agency office. So, the question of location really hinges on what's best for your target clients. If you're starting a general practice, a storefront office or other high visibility space might be just the thing. If you have an immigration practice, you want your office to be closest to the immigrant community. If most of your clients are located out of town, find space near the airport.

Q: *I'm leaving a large firm later this year. I'm accustomed to working in the city, but I'm tempted to get a suburban office. Any suggestions?*
A: Suburban office space usually costs less, but cost is just one factor among many.

- *Are you already licensed in the suburban location?* If you work in the city, you may be tempted to move your office to a suburban location to minimize your commute. But that strategy only makes sense if you're licensed in the state where you live. It's not uncommon in large metropolitan areas (e.g., Washington DC/ Maryland/Virginia or New York/New Jersey/Connecticut) for a lawyer to work at a firm in Washington D.C. or New York and reside in an adjacent state where they've never been admitted to the bar. And many states prohibit lawyers from setting up an office if they're not licensed to practice in the state, even if they specify that their practice is limited to matters outside the jurisdiction. You need to consider whether the added cost of gaining admission to another bar will outweigh the potential savings and convenience of a suburban office.
- *What's most convenient for your clients?* Many lawyers assume that a city office is more convenient because of proximity to public transportation and the courthouse. But that's not always the case. If you serve a suburban population, a suburban location is probably easier—and more convenient—on your clients. And if you're located in a suburban area that's served by public transportation, even clients who don't have access to cars can reach your office easily. As for

those who run a national practice, most of your clients may be located out of state, so your location won't matter as much because they'll rarely visit your office. And with most courts accepting e-filing now, proximity to the courthouse is less relevant than a decade ago.

- *What's most convenient for you?* Will a suburban office cut down on your commute, or is it closer to your children's daycare or school? If so, that's another major reason to consider the suburbs. And if you're working part-time, a short commute will help take less time out of your already overbooked schedule.
- *What's best from a marketing/networking standpoint?* Consider the impact of a suburban location on your marketing activities. For some types of practices, networking events and CLE's are in the city, and many bar associations sponsor lunch events or early evening events at downtown locations. Also keep in mind that if you've been working in the city before opening your firm, a city location will allow you to meet with regularly with colleagues who would keep you in mind for referrals or contract work assignments.

Q: *I'm concerned what sort of image a home office conveys to prospective clients and other attorneys.*

A: The more thoroughly your home and work space are separate, the more likely that you—and others—will think of it as an office. Install a separate phone line, answer the phone with a formal greeting, invest in professional stationery; perhaps establish a separate entrance. Make sure you designate separate spaces for work and home, even it's only screening off a portion of a living room with folding dividers. Most importantly, take care to eliminate from your phone calls any of the background noise associated with home. If you need to meet a client, offer to come to the client's office or residence as a convenience. For clients visiting from out of town, get together for a meal at their hotel or, if they've come to visit an agency or the court, meet there.

Q: *I used to think a home office would be ideal because I never socialized much with colleagues at work. Now that my office is at home, I feel isolated.*

A: Your home office is just your primary work location...it's not a cell. For simple human contact...and for marketing purposes...you should be regularly including time for CLE's, business meetings, and client conferences. Such activities are essential; not only do they help build your business, but they foster personal relationships that can re-energize you. Outside my home office, my favorite work site is the law library, where working alongside frantic law students, and lunching at the cafeteria, reminds me of the camaraderie of my law school days.

Q: *My old law firm let me go, but offered me office space at bargain rates. Should I accept or find my own office?*

A: When you're let go for economic reasons, some law firms make a spare office available at little or no cost to help you launch their own practice. In the short run—six months or so—that can give you some breathing room while you assess your next move. After a few months, though, I suggest making a clean break even if it means sacrificing a free space. The separation will make for a healthier relationship with your former colleagues, and could eventually lead to referrals or references that have far more long-term value than the rent you would have saved.

Before you decide to hang around your old firm, ask yourself:

- Do you really want the firm hanging over your shoulder as you get your practice off the ground? What if one of the firm's clients wants to stay with you, or hire you instead of the firm? Imagine how awkward it would be if your client runs into a former attorney in the elevator or hallway.
- By staying in the same office for any length of time, you open yourself up to accusations that you poached one of the firm's clients by conveying the impression that you still worked for the firm.
- What if your new practice is slow to get traction? It's inevitable you would begin resenting those ex-colleagues who allowed you to stay on.
- And consider how your old firm might benefit. If you have a unique expertise, the firm could give the appearance of an affiliation even though you are no longer formally employed. On the one hand, the firm no longer pays your salary, and yet continues to give the impression it can service matters within your unique expertise. Consider the case of a Connecticut associate: even though he left the firm, the firm retained his photo and bio on the firm Web site. The associate sued.

MOVING YOUR OFFICE? DON'T FORGET TO...

File a change of address beforehand. Solo Amy Kleinpeter suggests submitting mail forwarding requests about a month before your move. She says to make sure you submit more than one change to allow for variations in your listing. For example, if you only submit one request—for, say, Law Offices of Amy E. Clark Kleinpeter—the system may not recognize Law Offices of Amy Clark or Law Office of Amy E. Kleinpeter, and will return your mail to sender for lack of an exact match. To begin the forwarding process, go to www.usps.gov. The fee is minimal.

Send announcements. To the state bar; to current and past clients; to your marketing contacts; to anyone involved in already-filed cases; to the state agency that handles your corporate records; and to whatever alumni and social groups you belong.

Get new stationery. Go online (www.vistaprint.com or www.iprint.com) to get quality business cards quickly.

Computing. Back up your hard-drive before moving. Change the address on your e-mail signature and on your Web site. Also, Google your name to see all the places where your address is located, and update those records, too.

Moving. Avoid moving if deadlines are looming. But if there are some unavoidable deadlines, pull those files before the move, and take them home so you know where they are. Solo Kimberly DeCarrerra also suggests you move on a Friday, or a long holiday weekend, so your office is running on Monday. And plan at least an extra day to get completely unpacked. There's nothing like having to run off to court and you can't find the file because it was boxed away for the move. If you move boxed files into long-term storage, label the boxes carefully and keep a detailed list of what's where.

Telephones. If you are expecting important calls (during the move), don't forget to forward your calls to your cell phone.

MOVING TO A NEW OFFICE? DON'T FORGET TO...

Power needs. Check the electric service of your new space, and be sure it is adequate to your needs, and that outlets are where you need them.

Remodeling. If you intend to do any painting or changing of window treatments or carpet, do it before you move in.

Lighting. Do any of your windows—especially your office windows—face west? If so, you probably will need some sort of window treatment or insulating window film.

Interior design. Measure all the rooms and the dimensions of all your furniture. Make paper icons of the furniture, and move them around a sheet of graph paper until you settle on a layout that works for you. Do the same for the walls, so you know what will hang where, especially in the public areas and in your office.

Moving professionals. Use professional movers. One solo says that in five years he moved four times and remodeled two of the offices...and the only time things went smoothly was when he wasn't present.

Sources: Amanda Benedict, Kimberly DeCarrera, Amy Kleinpeter

QUIRKY RESIDENCY RULES

Your jurisdiction's disciplinary rules may contain some surprisingly parochial rules related to residency requirements, bonafide offices, and qualifications to seek bar admission by waiver. Consider some of these policies:

- New Jersey requires lawyers to maintain "bonafide offices," defined as places of business where files are stored and where someone is always available to meet with walk-in clients. (Opinion 718, The Bonafide Office Requirement, ACPE 718/CAA 41, http://bit.ly/bfWtGV) New Jersey's bonafide office rule may prohibit "virtual office" arrangements (where lawyers rent space per diem but do not store files) or even home offices if lawyers are not willing to meet with clients at their home.

- New York Judiciary Code Section 470 requires non-resident, New York-barred lawyers to maintain a New York office to serve New York clients. In other words, a New Jersey resident with a New York license such as Ekaterina Schoenfeld (who has challenged the New York law as violating the Commerce Clause) cannot meet New York clients in her New Jersey office, but a New York licensed lawyer who lives in New York could maintain an office out of state to meet New York clients [New York Law Journal, www.law.com/jsp/article.jsp?id=1202443103039&NJ_Lawyers_Action_Claiming_NY_Discriminates_Against_OutofState_Attorneys_Allowed_to_Proceed]

- States that allow for admission by motion (i.e., waiver of requirement to take the bar exam) require a lawyer to have been in practice in another jurisdiction; typically 5 of the past 7 to 10 years to qualify. (See National Conference of Bar Examiners Bar Admissions Requirements, www.ncbex.org/comprehensive-guide-to-bar-admissions). The minimum practice requirements may pose a problem for lawyers who took leave from law practice to raise a family, and seek admission in another jurisdiction.

- A state may require lawyers to maintain an in-state office or commit to practicing full time in the state. For example, Michigan has an in-state office requirement for all lawyers seeking admission (Mich. Comp. Laws Ann. § 600.946), while Virginia imposes similar requirements, but only on lawyers seeking admission by waiver (www.vbbe.state.va.us/motion/motionrules.html).

While these restrictions are onerous, you can minimize their impact with appropriate planning. That's why it's so important to familiarize yourself with a jurisdiction's rules of practice before you make any decisions about your intended practice area or location.

Step 7. Legal Research Options

Not so many years ago, law firms maintained large libraries of law reviews, federal and state reporters, specialty practice series, and computerized databases from LEXIS/NEXIS and Westlaw. By contrast, solos had to purchase used books or visit the law library for research because few could afford the major legal databases. The ground began to shift in the mid-1990s, when most courts started releasing decisions on the Web, making them accessible to other online providers seeking to challenge the LEXIS/Westlaw duopoly. Today, thanks to the Internet, legal research options have significantly expanded, narrowing the gap between solos and their BigLaw or government counterparts, and obviating the need for an onsite library.

There's an enormous range of legal research options available, and they vary widely in scope, quality, and price. The different categories follow:

Legal research at the high end. High-end computerized research service is what you find in BigLaw and the government. It's the most expensive service, but provides access to all federal court (including federal district court) and state court databases dating back at least a century; annotated statutes and regulations and specialty libraries like tax or employment; law reviews and journals, and such features as Shepards of Keycite to "shepardize" cases. LEXIS and Westlaw often include so-called "value-adds" as Wright and Moore, American Law Report (ALR), and other treatises. The high-end databases also employ both the type of Boolean search tool that lets you search for strings of words and phrases as well as the type of word searches commonly used on Google.

These days, WestlawNext, the latest and significantly updated version of Westlaw, released in January 2010, stands at the top of the line. WestlawNext includes a full database of cases, as well as treatises, briefs, articles, and other secondary materials. WestlawNext doesn't advertise prices online (you need to negotiate with a rep), but you will pay dearly. One solo estimates that he pays 33 percent more for WestlawNext than the earlier version though he also says he gets better value (see www.nysbar.com/blogs/smallfirmville/2010/07/westlawnext_google_for_lawyers.html). Meanwhile, legal research and writing contract lawyer Lisa Solomon writes that her $489/month subscription for a full case database, with focus on New York law, was due to increase to $514 with WestlawNext. (www.legalresearchandwritingpro.com/blog/2010/02/10/my-westlawnext-upgrade-negotiations-proof-that-west-isnt-interested-in-the-solo-market/)

Westlaw's chief rival, LEXIS, also offers fairly high level service (though not as comprehensive as Westlaw Next) at far lower prices. For many years, LEXIS has offered affordable "one-library" subscriptions—e.g., the "energy library", or "employment library", or "Maryland-only library"—that range in price from around $90 to $175/month. For an extra $15/month charge, you can also add on a feature that enables you to access cases outside of your specific library. More recently, however, LEXIS launched a solo-specific product called LEXIS Advance. At $175/month, LEXIS Advance includes all primary law from all states, Shepards, and a collection of briefs, pleadings and motions.

Finally, there's a new service: BloombergLaw, launched in 2010 by legal news and securities publisher Bloomberg. At $450/month, Bloomberg is pricey and, according to several reviewers, still a work in progress. Though not suitable for consumer practitioners, Bloomberg might cater to solos with more sophisticated practices and former BigLaw-turned-solo lawyers.

Should you buy a high-end service? Consider the following:

- *Will you be doing contract work for other lawyers?* If so, a quality subscription service is imperative. Many lawyers simply expect a professional contract legal services provider to have access to top-of-the-line research, but they may be upset at having to pay your hourly rate and a fee for research services on top of that.
- *Is your practice state-specific?* If yes, a high-end subscription service can be an affordable and efficient option.
- *Do you specialize in an area like tax or securities?* If so, you are captive to the high-end option because there aren't any free or low-cost options for researching regulatory decisions.

Budget and midlevel research services. LOISLaw and Fastcase were once considered a modest bargain because of their relatively comprehensive service, their lower prices ($140 for LOISlaw, $99 for Fastcase), and their no firm-contract requirement. But now, with so many other options that offer more (LEXIS Advance) or cost less, LOISLaw and Fastcase lost their competitive edge, particularly because they do not offer Shepards service. LOISLaw still costs around $140/month, but it includes practice forms in addition to traditional caselaw. Meanwhile, Fastcase has entered into agreements with 18 state bar associations that allows them to offer Fastcase as a membership benefit for free or at a steep discount. Another low-cost service is Versuslaw, whose packages range from $13 to $40/month. Versuslaw has a Boolean search capability, a database with federal and state appellate cases, as well as federal district court cases dating back to 1950. It also includes two quirky resources—tribal court law and Australian court decisions. There's no Shepards tool, and some of the cases do not have the official reporter cite. In my opinion, Versuslaw works well for lawyers who subscribe to a specialty or state-specific service, but who want to retain the ability to research the state of law in other jurisdictions.

Free research services. Today, free legal research services abound. In 2009, Google launched Google Scholar Legal (http://scholar.google.com/), which includes access to all state and federal cases via Google's user-friendly interface. It can also be used to search law review articles, though you'll need to purchase another subscription service to actually read the articles since most are not available for free online. Google Scholar Legal still has glitches, though; it doesn't include most unpublished decisions or Shepards (though it does have a "where cited" feature showing how a case was previously referenced). Plus, it doesn't carry regulatory decisions that specialized practitioners might need. As such, Google Legal Scholar may not yet be ready as a stand-alone research service, but it's a valuable supplement to the fee-based services. As mentioned, Fastcase is offered by 18 state bar associations as a free membership benefit; Casemaker is offered by 27 state bars. Both are solid, reliable services that include federal and state caselaw databases. If you want to access Fastcase but don't belong to a state bar, download the free Fastcase App for the iPhone. And finally, there's LEXISOne, a downgraded version of LEXIS that allows access to the past two years of state and federal appellate decisions for free. Once a great value, with the plethora of other free services, LEXISOne simply isn't worth the trouble of registration.

Other Bargains

Jenkins Law Library (www.jenkins.org). One of the best-kept secrets in the world of legal research. The service costs $155/year, and includes access to Fastcase, HeinOnline (a database of law review and bar journal articles, with many journals dating back 50 years), and 20 minutes of LEXIS a day. That may not seem like much, but it's enough time to Shepardize research found on other sources. Plus, Jenkins offers training on how to make the best use of that time. Even if you only use your Jenkins subscription three or four times a year, you will still get your money's worth.

PACER (Public Access to Electronic Records) houses more than a decade's worth of electronically filed motions, pleadings, and court decisions. Unfortunately, PACER's search tools are rudimentary. You can search cases only by docket number, date, name of the party or attorney or roughly, by topic. Still, if you're interested in a certain topic (e.g., civil rights) or you've read about a case in the newspaper that seems relevant to your matter, you can find relevant documents on PACER. Registration is free but it takes a few days. Thereafter, users pay eight cents per page download, with a 30-page maximum per document.

Social Science Research Network (www.SSRN.com) is a database of scholarly papers and journal articles from all disciplines, including the law. You can search various legal topics, and download both published articles and draft papers by law professors.

And don't overlook the law library. As computerized legal research becomes pervasive, law libraries seem to have lost some of their cachet. A big mistake. Many times, a legal treatise or volume of ALJ or Corpus Juris Secundum (CJS) will let you figure out basic legal standards for general topics, like piercing the corporate veil, or the burden of proof in Title VII sexual harassment cases. Also, if you're embarking on research in a broad area that is the subject of countless cases, it's much quicker to read a law review article than to review dozens of cases trying to gain an understanding.

There are several more good reason to make greater use of the law library, as described in this essay by University of Washington Law Librarian Mary Whisner:

- Law librarians, many of whom are legally trained, specialize in legal materials and the needs of legal researchers. Their job is to help you use the library, and to figure out your research puzzles. We keep up with new sources and techniques, and can save you hours in your research. After all, what's more important to you than your time? Librarians also create online guides to help you with your research.

- Your local law library is a great resource when you've got a limited budget, limited office space, and you can't afford every practice manual, looseleaf service, form-book, or treatise that could come in handy. And if you find a book or set really useful, you can always order it for your office collection. Even if you're a whiz at online research, some sources are just easier to use in print. In my experience, many people find it helpful using annotated codes in print because of their layout. Sometimes you might even use a database to find a source, but then sit down with the print version and skim the whole chapter you need.

- Many public law libraries subscribe to databases that lawyers can use free. Some law libraries make them available without charge; others charge on a cost-recovery basis (which is still cheaper than getting your own subscription for occasional use). Even if you subscribe to Westlaw or LexisNexis for access to your own state's laws and cases, wouldn't it be great to be able to use the law library's subscription when you need to research some other state's laws? Here are some of the databases popular with the lawyers who use the UW Law School Library: LegalTrac, an index of legal periodical articles, 1980–present; Hein Online, a collection of PDF documents from a variety of sources, including hundreds of law journals from the 19th Century on; Statutes at Large; the Federal Register; treaties and federal legislative histories; KeyCite, the component of Westlaw that enables researchers to check the history of a case, statute, or other document and find citing references; RIA CheckPoint, a rich source of tax and accounting material; BNA, a wide range of newsletters and databases including BNA publications in tax, labor, and health. As for nonlegal databases, you can search through economics, business, scientific, or medical information. If the law library doesn't have access, your public library or local university library might.

- Want a DVD on cross-examination? How about an audiotape to review a subject while you're in your car? Many law libraries have them. Some law libraries even maintain AV collections you can use for CLE credit.

- One appeal of solo practice is working in your own environment; even drafting motions in your robe and slippers. But what if you want a change of scenery? The law library provides you with a fresh place to work—and maybe a fresh outlook. Many county law libraries have conference rooms available for client or colleague meetings, which is great if you don't want visitors to your home office to walk past your ironing board and your lunatic cat en route to your home office. Also, most county law libraries are right in the courthouse. What a great place to gather your thoughts before you argue your motion.

- Many law libraries offer training, sometimes with CLE credits. In Seattle for example, the county law library offers classes on Casemaker, Loislaw, LexisNexis, Westlaw, and Word; how to use the Internet for legal research; skip tracing, and more. Generally, the bigger cities have libraries, staffs, and services commensurate with their size. Each state has a state law library (serving state agencies and courts, but often serving attorneys in the state as well), and some federal court law libraries are also open to attorneys. Some cities are served by members-only law libraries, while other law school libraries are open to attorneys or alumni of the school, sometimes for a membership fee.

Step 8. Making the Official Announcement

Opening a new law firm is one of those rare occasions when you can contact prospective clients without worrying about bar rules on solicitation. That is, as long as the announcement merely conveys information that you've opened a law firm...and doesn't suggest a need for, or ask recipients to use, your services. Otherwise it would run afoul of rules prohibiting direct solicitation. So tell everyone! Announce your new firm to everyone whether you expect them to send you business or not. In a world where everyone seems connected by six degrees of separation, you never know who might know someone who knows someone who could use a lawyer. By making an announcement, you're providing recipients a potential referral source.

Potential recipients include:

- *School contacts:* College and law school classmates and former professors;
- *Previous employers:* Lawyers and judges with whom you've worked, as well as previous non-legal employers;
- *Family and friends:* Close relatives and friends, and friends of your spouse and parents.
- *Professional colleagues:* Lawyers with whom you've worked and members of bar and professional associations to which you belong.
- *Internet colleagues:* Lawyers with whom you have contact through listservs or blogging.
- *Former and present clients:* Check bar rules to ensure that there's no prohibition on making direct contact with former firm clients.

When to make the announcement. Obviously, you can't send announcements until you've left your former law firm. But do have them ready to go the first week you open for business. In particular, you'll want to send your announcements to publications like alumni magazines and bar journals as early as possible as they often have long lead times.

What to say. At a minimum, every announcement—whether a hard copy or e-mail —should contain basic contact information (phone, e-mail, Web and/or blog address), the state bars where you're licensed to practice, and the date your office opens. Space permitting, include additional details such as your intended practice areas, previous places of employment, and your educational background.

Making the announcement. You have plenty of options when it comes to law firm announcements. To some, you can send an eye-catching formal announcement; to others, a letter (on your new letterhead!) that describes why you've decided to open your own practice and the practice areas where you plan to focus. And of course, be sure to include a couple of your business cards. Hard copies aren't the only option. The benefit of an e-mail announcement is that recipients can automatically enter your e-mail into their contacts list. Incidentally, if you do send an e-mail announcement, consider something a little fancier like a card from www.E-vite.com or an e-mail marketing template at www.ConstantContact.com.

Where else to make the announcement. Don't limit your announcements to direct mail. Alert your law school newsletter, local bar journals, legal trade publications, local newspapers, and the regional business press. If you're friends with any law bloggers, ask if they'd be willing to post news of your new firm.

Step 9. Web Presence & Domain Names

You must have some Web presence at the time you launch your practice, whether it's a professionally designed site, or a do-it-yourself site using one of the many Web building tools, or a profile on social media sites like LinkedIn, Avvo, Justia (See Chapter 15). Even if you don't plan to engage in any online marketing, assume that every person you meet will Google you. Without an online presence, they can't learn more about you and your practice, and you'll come across as hopelessly out of touch.

Below are some suggestions for creating a Web presence that can be adapted to most budgets and time frames:

Domain name. Purchase Web addresses for both your name and your firm's name (e.g, JoeDoe.com, JoeDoeLaw.com). Also consider investing in a few descriptive domain names, such as RichmondVirginiabankruptcylaw.com. These names are catchy and easy to remember and can help boost your search engine visibility for the keywords used in the name. One caution: some jurisdictions do not allow lawyers to use anything other than the name of their firm in the URL, so consult your bar rules for guidance. Domain names are available from a variety of online services; Godaddy.com is popular among solos but there are many others. Domains are also inexpensive—typically less than $20/year—so there's no drawback to registering several at once.

Email at domain name. You'll look much more professional with an email address of Jane@janedoeslawfirm.com than as jane3248@aol.com. Some domain registration companies like Godaddy will provide you with an email address for each domain name that you can forward to your email account. You can also easily configure domain names to Google Apps, Google's business version of email (it costs $50/year). Finally, you can buy Web hosting from companies like Dreamhost.com or Hostgator.com, and configure your email to match your Web host's server information. If all of this seems very complicated, don't be shy about asking a colleague to walk you through the process.

Web sites. Web design varies widely in price, and can easily run $2,500 or more if you require professional design, copywriting, and built-in SEO (search engine optimization). There are several Web design companies specializing in lawyer Web sites, among them www.scorpiondesign.com, www.paperstreet.com, www.justia.com, and www.TheModernFirm.com. Their services start at around $1,000. The most expensive is Findlaw, where you won't pay outright for a site, but you may pay between $500 and $1,000/month (see www.newyorkpersonalinjuryattorneyblog.com/2010/01/findlaw-how-to-leave-and-save-your-reputation-and-money.html). Nor are you limited to law firm-specific designers. Try local Web designers (for example, students in college tech programs), or go to sites like www.elance.com and www.odesk.com, where you can put out an RFP and let designers bid. You can find Web designers (many located overseas or in rural areas) who can create an attractive for under $1,000.

The DIY web site. A number of services (among them, www.iPage.com, www.GoDaddy.com, and www.Vistaprint.com) make it possible to design and host a do-it-yourself Web site for as little as $5/month; in fact, Google and Realpractice.com offer free Web-building tools. You can even use a blogging platform like Typepad ($5/month) or Wordpress to set up a combination blog and Web page. While you may be understandably concerned about client reaction to a DIY site, your clients may pay less attention to the design than the site's contents.

Social media. If you were employed or looking for a job before starting your firm, you probably already have a LinkedIn profile. If so, take the time to update it. In addition, consider creating a profile at www.Avvo.com and www.Justia.com so that prospective clients can learn more about your practice and your past experience.

IN THEIR OWN WORDS

Q: How did you create a revenue stream in the beginning?

"…Flat-fee investigations."—**Sergio Benavides (class of 2005)**

"…Contract lawyering."—**Spencer Young (class of 2004)**

"…Document reviews for large-scale litigation."—**Dennis Esford (class of 2003)**

"…I dipped into my savings."—**Nina Kallen (class of 1994)**

"I did contract patent work for other law firms. Getting [the work] was actually quite easy, but it also kept me from doing the business development I needed to get my own practice off the ground."
—**Kevin Afghani (class of 2004)**

"I did contract work for a local non-profit. It was my only guaranteed income. It didn't pay much, but I enjoyed the work, and it has lead to a lot of referral sources. I am a big believer in the idea that 'work generates work which generates work'"—**Paul Scott (class of 2008)**

"A couple really busy attorneys in my field paid me hourly to handle oral arguments, hearings, and mediations when they had to be somewhere else."—**Michael Moebes (class of 2003)**

"The first time around [as a solo], I relied on court appointments. We do not have a public defender program in San Antonio. So, judges would appoint lawyers to represent criminal defendants. I did that just about everyday."—Thomas J. Crane (class of 1983)

"In the beginning, before I had a lot of divorce and estate planning cases, my main source of income was real estate closings. I don't like doing real estate closings but it was quick money. In the month leading up to my grand opening, I contacted over a hundred lenders, title and loan companies, and signed up with them to do out of state real estate closings for them when I started my practice. It took a lot of time to get contacts with all of those companies, but once I did the legwork I had my bread and butter for the first year."—Herb Dubin (class of 1964)

"I started by telling family members, friends, and former colleagues that I started a practice. I sent letters containing contact information and an explanation of my practice areas. In the beginning, my sole source of referrals was family and friends."—Tonya Coles (class of 2006)

"In the beginning, I brought in most of my revenue from Court appointments and close family and friends."—Jenee Oliver (class of 2005)

"I was very lucky. I was able to work out an 'of counsel' arrangement with my former firm, and I had one corporate client that gave me a significant retainer fee payment. I felt pretty confident that I would have at least some money coming in."—Cailie A. Currin (class of 1988)

Excerpt from Solo by Choice, The Companion Guide: 34 Questions That Could Transform Your Legal Career (Carolyn Elefant, 2011)

CHAPTER 7

Office Technology

"Get mobile; it's where the rest of the world is going."

—Rick George, solo

Once, a solo's biggest decision was whether to adopt Word or WordPerfect, and whether to purchase expensive practice management software. Now, law office technology is abundant online (with new products coming to market almost every week), and choosing what to use when can be overwhelming. Before diving in, let's take a look at two of the big-picture issues:

Free vs. Fee

Believe it or not, you can almost start a firm paying little or nothing for technology. Between re-purposing a personal computer and cellphone for business, and using products like Open Office (word processing), Google (practice management and e-mail), and other products discussed in this chapter, many office management services are now free. But should you adopt them?

Take these factors into consideration:

Security and privacy. In my opinion, some free versions of office services don't offer adequate levels of security for storing sensitive client information, and others can't guarantee your documents will remain private. Before using a free online service to store client information, review its terms of service and privacy policy.

Adequacy. Think carefully before re-purposing an older personal computer for your law practice; it may not have adequate power to run many of the newest programs needed for your new practice. Likewise, many online practice applications may be inadequate for lack of capacity. Example: Freshbooks, an online billing product, is free... as long as you only maintain three client accounts. For that reason, it's inadequate as a long-term solution.

Quality. Some free products aren't very convenient. They may limit you to uploading one document at a time to an online portal, or they won't allow you to save your work. Though perfectly fine for occasional use, you may get frustrated if you rely on some free online service for mission-critical tasks.

Customer service. One drawback of many free services is their lack of customer service. The vendors make it difficult to locate contact information online, and their support is often only available via e-mail. By contrast, many paid services make a point of providing high-quality customer service (in part, to compete with freebies).

Stability. Free services are often great…until they go out of business. Back in 2010, Intuit purchased Mint.com a free and popular online accounting system. Intuit then proceeded to shut down QuickenOnline, a free service it offered prior to the Mint acquisition, and the company never bothered to offer Quicken users the option to transfer data. For details, go http://techcrunch.com/2010/07/19/quicken-online-users-saw-the-bait-took-the-switch-to-mint-com-and-are-left-with-nothing/. Bottom line: free services are vulnerable to closure or acquisition at a moment's notice. If you're using one for mission-critical information, back up your files regularly.

Local vs. Cloud Practice Management

Another hot topic of debate is whether to rely on local practice management systems (e.g., Amicus, TimeMatters), or to adopt the newest trend in file-storage evolution: the *cloud-based* system that stores files on distant servers rather than on your desk. In my view, cloud-based technologies are the wave of the future. Even established legal vendors like LEXIS are now offering a cloud-based practice management solution (www.myfirmmanager.com). A recent Gartner Research study found that while only three percent of businesses use the cloud today, it could jump to 43 percent as soon as 2015.

Still, many lawyers starting a firm continue to favor local, desktop versions of practice management tools. Some considerations:

Pro. Cloud storage systems let you access documents, billing, calendars wherever you are, and makes it easier to work with virtual assistants or lawyers at other locations. Most cloud-based solutions are user-friendly, and whatever tech support may be needed is included in the subscription price. Cloud subscriptions are nominally priced; $15 or $20/month (for non-lawyer-specific versions) to about $60/month, with an added cost for each additional user.

Con. Some lawyers worry about the vulnerability of cloud-based storage to hackers, and whether vendors are providing adequate security to protect confidential client documents. The vendors say they understand the risks, and that they do employ adequate protective measures. Other lawyers are concerned that if the Internet ever goes down they may not be able to access key information from remote servers.

Author note: many of the documents lawyers store "in the cloud" are created locally and are uploaded, and those files would remain available on your computer if the Internet did go down. Moreover, many cloud companies now offer phone apps; in a worst-case scenario, you could get to your system via a mobile device. As for the security of client data, no system is absolutely risk-free; even before the cloud, client data could be compromised by office staff or theft. Cloud storage is in its infancy, and will become more robust over the next decade. Until then, the cloud's most serious deficiency may be its inability to offer features common to traditional practice management systems, which allow users to enter client information once and, with a single click, import it to letters or other forms. If this and other features are important, the cloud may not be right for you at this time.

When choosing a cloud computing provider, the security of client data is of the utmost concern. Before you enter into a contract, learn as much as possible about the way your data will be handled by the cloud-computing provider. It is essential that you ask the right questions, and ensure that your contract with the vendor addresses important security issues.

Security issues to consider include, but are not limited to:

1. What type of facility will host the data?
2. Who has access to the data at the cloud facility? What mechanisms are in place to ensure that only authorized personnel will be able to access your data? Does the vendor screen its employees? If the vendor doesn't own the data center, how does the data center screen its employees?
3. Does your contract with the vendor include terms that, address confidentiality? If not, is the vendor willing to sign a confidentiality agreement?
4. How frequently are back-ups performed?
5. Is data backed up to more than one server? Are there redundant power supplies for the servers?
6. Where are the respective servers located? Is there geo-redundancy (where your data is backed up to servers located in different geographic regions)?
7. Will your data, and any back up copies of your data, always stay within the boundaries of the United States?
8. How secure are the data centers?
9. What types of encryption methods are used and how are passwords stored?
10. Are there redundant power supplies?
11. Is there a guarantee of uptime included in the contract? Will you be compensated for excessive amounts of downtime?
12. Will you be notified if there is a data breach?
13. What are you rights upon termination of the contract? How about in the event of a billing dispute? Does the agreement contain a forum selection clause or a mandatory arbitration clause? What remedies does the contract provide in the event of a breach?

—Nicole Black, Esq. (www.nicoleblackesq.com), lawyer and author of Cloud Computing for Lawyers (ABA, 2011), and co-author of Social Media for Lawyers: The Next Frontier.

In addition, the North Carolina State Bar offers its own list of 15 questions as you begin your evaluation of vendors of Software-as-a-Service (cloud-storage systems):

• What is the history of the vendor? Where does it derive funding? How stable is it financially?

• Has the lawyer read the user or license agreement terms, including the security policy, and does he or she understand the meaning of the terms?

• Does the vendor's Terms of Service or Service Level Agreement address confidentiality? If not, would the vendor be willing to sign a confidentiality agreement in keeping with the lawyer's professional responsibilities? Would the vendor be willing to include a provision stating the employees at the vendor's data center are agents of the law firm and have a fiduciary responsibility to protect client information?

- How does the vendor, or any third-party data hosting company, safeguard the physical and electronic security and confidentiality of stored data? Has there been an evaluation of the vendor's security measures, including firewalls, encryption techniques, socket security features and intrusion-detection systems?
- Has the lawyer requested copies of the vendor's security audits?
- Where is data hosted? Is it in a country with less rigorous protections against unlawful search and seizure?
- Who has access to the data besides the lawyer?
- Who owns the data—the lawyer or the vendor?
- If the lawyer terminates use of the SaaS product, or the service otherwise has a break in continuity, how does the lawyer retrieve the data, and what happens to the data hosted by the service provider?
- If the vendor goes out of business, will the lawyer have access to the data and the software or source code?
- Can the lawyer retrieve data off of the servers for his or her own offline useful backup?
- If the lawyer decides to cancel the subscription to SaaS, will he or she get the data? Is data supplied in a non-proprietary format compatible with other software?
- How often is the user's data backed up? Does the vendor back up data in multiple data centers in different geographic locations to safeguard against natural disaster?
- If clients have access to shared documents, are they aware of the confidentiality risks of showing the information to others?
- Does the law firm have a back-up for shared document software in case something goes wrong, such as an outside server going down?

Technology Choices

As a practical matter, there's not much difference between a Mac and PC when it comes to running a law practice. It used to be that many law-specific programs weren't Mac-compatible, but for most products that is no longer the case. And with systems like Parallels, a Mac can run Windows and support Windows-based products (though in my view, running Windows defeats the purpose of getting a Mac to begin with). In addition, Macs, though more affordable than ever, still cost roughly ten to twenty percent more than their PC equivalents.

1. Hardware and Equipment

Desktop v. laptop. If you can afford only one computer, make it a laptop. Today's laptops have nearly the same power and memory as desktops, and are only marginally more expensive. If you're concerned about working on a smaller screen, buy a separate monitor and enjoy the added productivity of a dual-screen set-up.

Flat-screen & dual monitors. Today's flat-screen monitors have more screen space and occupy less desktop real estate . . . and let you convert a laptop into a desktop machine. Once a luxury, monitor prices have plummeted; a 22-inch flat-screen sells for less than $150. Because monitors are so inexpensive, many lawyers now use two—either two flat-screens or a laptop screen and a stand-alone monitor. (Most computers can support two monitors). Dual monitors enhance productivity; they let you open work documents on one screen and display e-mail and practice management applications on the other.

Scanner. Next to your phone and computer, a scanner is probably the most important piece of equipment a new solo can have. A scanner is necessary to support a paper-less office, and it lets you e-file at courts (where you still receive paper correspondence, receipts, and checks that need to be converted to digital format). The Fujitsu ScanSnap Model S1500 is popular with solos. It is relatively inexpensive—around $450—and it comes with Adobe Pro (for creating, editing, and organizing PDF documents), software that ordinarily sells for several hundred dollars as a stand-alone product. If you spend a significant amount of time out of the office, consider a scanning wand like VuPoint (around $100), which you can use to scan deposition exhibits or courthouse files.

Printer, copier, fax. Even as offices go paperless, it will be awhile before printers are obsolete. Many courts still require hard copies, and some lawyers (myself included) find it easier to read lengthy documents on paper rather than on the computer screen. As far as purchases go, a **black-and-white printer** is sufficient for most purposes unless you plan to print your own letterhead, in which case get a color printer. A **copier** is not necessary for most offices if you have a scanner and a printer. In lieu of photocopying, merely scan the document and retain a digital copy for your files, or print copies if you need them for court. For large print jobs or better quality (for brochures), use a commercial copy shop. A **fax machine**? Don't bother. Instead, subscribe to an electronic fax (or e-fax) service such as efax.com, myfax.com, or maxe-mail.com. E-fax services assign you a fax number (many let you share the same area code as your office phone), and transmissions are routed to e-mail as a PDF. To send a fax, scan your document(s), log onto the e-fax site, enter the recipient's number, and upload your digital document(s) in PDF or Word format. E-fax service costs around $10 to $20/month depending upon usage, a bargain when you consider the cost of a dedicated fax machine and a second phone line.

2. The mobile lawyer. In Spring, 2011, Apple founder Steve Jobs launched the iPad2. He said tablets were the advent of a "post-PC world" that would replace desktop computers with mobile platforms connected to the cloud. Whether it was salesmanship or prophecy remains to be seen. But technology is *clearly* going mobile…and so should you as you invest in technology for your new practice:

The year of the tablet. For portability, easy organization, and reliable access to files and reference material, the iPad and Android tablets are rapidly winning over the legal community for their potential in the office and courtroom. Lawyers—especially those accustomed to lugging heavy binders of paper depositions—are quickly taking advantage of tablet apps to present their cases in court (Trialpad), to help with jury section (iJuror), to access documents from the cloud (Dropbox, Box.net), and to complete electronic client intake forms (EchoSign). Does that mean tablets are an essential purchase? Maybe not yet. One lawyer blogger put it this way: "*If you're looking for a fun new gadget, the iPad and its rivals may scratch your itch. But if you need a machine to do serious legal work—especially anything requiring a lot of typing or document-creation—stick with a full-featured laptop.*"

Smartphone. This would be a good time to get a smartphone (either an Apple or Android phone), and retire your old cellphone…yes, even your dependable BlackBerry Curve. Why now? Because an army of applications developers has begun producing incredible smartphone apps for lawyers: for office management, calendaring, research, depositions, bar exam and trial prep, court day calculators…and much more. This, in addition to a smartphone's everyday ability to capture e-mail, browse the Web, deliver real-time traffic bulletins and tornado warnings, airport gate changes, turn-by-turn GPS, live cable TV, streaming movies, document-sharing, and all bundled with a high-def video camera. As law blogger Rick George puts it, "*Get mobile; it's where the rest of the world is going.*"

WiFi security. It's old news, but cyber thieves love coffee shops, libraries, lobbies, airports; in fact, anyplace with free Internet access. Because without much trouble, hackers sitting nearby—maybe in a parked car or across the room—can wirelessly break into unsecured "hotspots" and intercept whatever private information is being entered on someone's laptop. One way to mitigate the risk is by creating your own secured "hotspot" with the purchase of a small, mobile wireless router called a MiFi. It's small enough to fit into a jacket pocket or purse, and works off your cellphone or smartphone. Available at Amazon.com. The other option is called "tethering". It's a smartphone app that turns the phone itself into a portable wireless "hotspot" so you can use your laptop or tablet anywhere your phone has cellular coverage (thus saving a small fortune on hotel Internet charges). Tethering apps are available for the iPad and Android phones.

Remote access. For lawyers on the go, it also helps to have remote access to your office documents wherever you travel. At least two companies—GoToMyPC.com and LogMeIn.com—let you retrieve documents, transfer files, even edit documents from your tablet or smartphone. Monthly service agreements; free trials available.

3. Office Communications. These days, Ma Bell's old landline phone system is just one option in competition with cellphones, virtual phone systems, and computer-based (VoIP) calls.

Should you use a cellphone for your practice? Cell service is greatly improved in most areas, and using one for work is better than distributing a home phone number. On the other hand, cellphone numbers aren't included in traditional phone directories, a consideration if that's how prospective clients would find you. If you're located in an area with reliable Internet service, consider VoIP services like 8x8.com (which offers set-ups for home-based offices and businesses), Vonage or Skype, which also offers video-conference features. And if you handle large litigation matters with multiple parties, it's no longer necessary to choose a phone service with extensive conference-call features. Freeconferencecall.com lets you set up conference calls with up to 100 people at no cost…and even record the call.

For firms with more than one person, you'll need a networked phone system. Or, use a computer-based, call-forwarding system like Grasshopper.com. Callers are prompted to choose an extension number, after which their call is forwarded to any phone number anywhere. If you have virtual staff or a telecommuting associate, the system gives the appearance that your "staff" all works at the same location. Ring-Central is another virtual phone system; this one is cloud-based. For details, see Jay Fleischman's post at Legal Practice Pro (www.legalpracticepro.com/remaking-the-bankruptcy-law-firm-telephone-systems/).

Live receptionist v. voice mail v. answering service. But who will answer the phone? As with so many other issues, lawyers differ sharply about who (or what) should be available when clients or prospective clients call: should you get a receptionist, a personal answering service, or an automated voice-mail system? If yours is a consumer practice (i.e., personal injury, family law), most of your phone traffic will be from prospective clients responding to your Yellow Page or online ad, and who are calling with the expectation of a live response. So, unless you have a receptionist or personal answering service, you risk losing clients who may not want to leave a voice-mail. On the other hand, if a share of your revenue comes from large-firm referrals, the cost of a shared receptionist or personal answering service, can add to your firm's credibility.

Tips for a receptionist or personal answering service:

- Make sure the receptionist uses your firm's name for incoming calls. And script out the information you need from prospective or existing clients (e.g., contact information, a brief reason for the call), and under what circumstances your calls should be routed to you or to your voice-mail.
- Have your calls forwarded to voice-mail when you are unavailable. This eliminates human transcription error, and allows callers to leave a detailed message. Because voice-mail is private, you avoid any possible confidentiality violations that could arise where, for example, a shared receptionist leaves one of your client messages in a public area. Select a secure, reputable answering service or shared receptionist, and have them route calls to a password-protected voice-mail box. Ruby Receptionists is a virtual receptionist/answering service used by many solos and small businesses.
- Keep your receptionist or answering service informed about your schedule so callers understand when you're in court or traveling, and when their call might be returned. It doesn't reflect well on you or the firm when clients are told you are unavailable or out of the office every time they call.

If you can't yet afford an answering service or phone system but are concerned about losing clients to voice-mail, try Google's free GoogleVoice (www.google.com/voice). It provides a single number that will forward anywhere. GoogleVoice also has recording capabilities, and will deliver your voice-mails to your e-mail box.

4. E-mail. You have several options: you can choose a cloud-based e-mail system like Yahoo or Gmail, or a local system like Outlook (popular for Windows), or a system like Eudora or Thunderbird, which downloads e-mail to your local system. *Author note*: A few cautions about free, cloud-based e-mail systems like Yahoo, Hotmail, and Gmail. The free versions may pose some security risks, so pay attention to the terms of service (TOS). If you're concerned about security issues, try one of the modestly priced cloud-based e-mail systems like Google Apps. If you do choose to use one of these services, do register your own domain name for the sake of professional appearances (e.g., Jane@JaneDoeLaw.com). An e-mail address incorporating the name of the host —JaneDoe@yahoo.com—suggests you can't afford a real e-mail service. And be sure to download and back-up any cloud-based e-mail. Cloud-based systems offer reliable storage, but there's always a possibility of a system failure.

Document Preparation

While the merits of Word and WordPerfect continue to be debated, most lawyers use MS Word because that's what clients most often use. So, even if you are still loyal to WordPerfect, make sure you have additional software that lets you open newer versions of Word. And if you're a Mac user, purchase MSOffice for Mac, which includes Word, PowerPoint, and Excel spreadsheets. Other options include OpenOffice, a free program that works for both Macs and PCs, and GoogleDocs, a cloud-based service that can create documents, spreadsheets, and PowerPoint presentations. Because GoogleDocs is cloud-based, you can collaborate with distant colleagues or clients.

If you prefer dictation to typing, you're in luck. Among the speech recognition software packages, Nuance Communication's Dragon Naturally Speaking is a leader (the Mac version is Dragon Dictate). Or you can always hire a legal virtual assistant to transcribe recordings. Andrea Cannavina's LegalTypist.com offers transcription among its many other administrative services.

Most word processing programs will convert a Word document into a PDF file. However, many lawyers require additional functionality, including the ability to fill in PDF forms, compile PDF files, extract pages, and mark-up, edit, and Bates stamp. For these tasks, you need additional software such as Adobe Pro (about $300), but also available bundled with the Fujitsu SnapScan Model S1500 scanner ($450). Less expensive word processing options include Nuance PDF or NitroPDF, which offer comparable functionality to Adobe Pro ($99). Free products such as Cute PDF or Free PDF Vue let you mark up PDF documents and fill out forms, but they won't let you merge PDF files or extract pages.

Practice Management Tools

Practice management software (also referred to as *case management* or *client management* software) is a catch-all description for products that automate various law practice functions, including time and billing, conflicts checks, contact management, calendaring, and case management.

Bar surveys suggest that only about a third of solo and small firm lawyers use traditional practice management software. Not because it isn't useful; in fact, it's highly functional. But many such products (e.g., Time Matters, PC Law, Amicus) are beyond the budgets of many solos, especially when they factor in the additional cost of IT support for installation and training. Fortunately, there are now many affordable new options. Perhaps the most significant change has been the introduction of cloud-based practice management systems (among them RocketMatter, Clio, MyCase, Total Attorneys'Virtual Law 2.0, and most recently, FirmManager, a LEXIS product). Like their desk-top predecessors, these services provide trust account management, billing, calendaring, document management, and conflicts check. In addition, they provide on-line storage for client files; some even offer a portal that lets clients log into a secure area to check the status of their case. And there are several other advantages: the cloud-based tools are easy to use, they don't require a tech consultant, and any issues are handled through the provider's customer service. The cost of a cloud-based system is also more manageable, costing anywhere from $40 to $99/month on a month-to-month basis, depending on the features. And, of course, cloud-based systems can be accessed from anywhere.

Still, for all of its promise, cloud-based practice management may not be for you:

- The systems are still fairly new, and they don't offer some of the more advanced features of desk-top systems such as automated document preparation, which some solos rely upon;
- The cloud-systems are more general in nature, while you may need a system specially geared towards immigration, bankruptcy, or other specialized area;
- Cloud-based practice management systems work well to organize a law office, but they're not yet well suited for extensive collaboration or practice management. If you tend to work on cases that involve teams of lawyers or multiple clients, you may be better off with a non-law specific project-management tool like Basecamp, Zoho, Huddle or others.
- Even though the monthly cost of cloud-systems isn't significant, some lawyers don't like the idea of paying an ongoing charge in perpetuity without ever owning the product outright.

With all the other expenses associated with a new practice, you may be reluctant to invest in practice management software, or to make time to identify and learn how to use some of the less costly or free products. But such tools are well worth the money and the time; in fact, you may be able to download and evaluate some packages for a trial period at no cost! If you do decide to buy or use one or more of the software packages, make your purchase before—or soon after—you open your practice. This way, you will have much more time to learn about each, and to integrate them into your practice. And if you cannot afford a practice management system, there are some worthwhile free options: Microsoft Outlook, if used to the full extent of its capabilities, can serve as an effective practice management tool. And while free services like Googledocs aren't advisable, Google Apps ($50/year) does include calendars, contact management, and document storage.

For a detailed side-by-side comparison of practice management tools, see ABA's 11-page Practice/Case Management Software Comparison Chart at www.tinyurl.com/64xccg6.

Document automation. Automating document preparation through technology can increase efficiencies and save significant time, particularly in a volume practice. Hotdocs is one of the oldest document automation services, but ContractExpress is among the new online versions. DirectLaw.com and RocketLawyer.com create forms and documents for use in an unbundled, virtual law practice.

Stand-alone options. If you decide not to use a comprehensive practice management system, there are also single-purpose tools available for most activities. For billing, there is Time59, RTG Billing, and Freshbooks, which track time on projects, create professional-looking invoices with your logo, and allow for electronic invoicing. Time59 and RTG Billing cost about $50 to $99/year. Freshbooks is free for up to three clients, and cost $19 to $39/month, depending on the number of client accounts. For contact management and lead tracking, SugarSync and Batchblue (starting at around $15/month) will keep contacts and leads. Outlook or Google Contacts also serve this function. To track firm expenses and revenues, Quickbooks is useful and also can be adapted to manage client trust accounts. The Minnesota Lawyers Professional Responsibility Board put together a helpful slide presentation on the topic. Go to www.mncourts.gov/lprb/Quicken%20Basic%202002%20color.htm).

Client Portals & Collaborative Tools

For several years now, law firm clients have been given access to documents through a firm's private *extranet*, a secure online network. But establishing and maintaining an extranet is costly, and it's used almost exclusively by large firms. Today, though—and again, because of cloud-based technology—lawyers can set up their own secure, online portal that gives clients an ability to not only check the status of their case, but to also review and comment on pleadings or upload large files for your review. Among the vendors offering portals are Clio (www.goclio.com) and TotalAttorney's Virtual Law Office (www.totalattorneys.com). I've also successfully shared documents with clients at Box.net (www.box.net), Basecamp (www.basecamphq.com), and MediaFire (www.MediaFire.com). Lawyers can also use these portals to share documents with other lawyers. And on occasions when you collaborate with another lawyer—or work with more sophisticated clients—and you need more interaction than simply sharing files, there is Googledocs and Adobebuzz, which allow for simultaneous document editing. And Wikis—among them Google Wiki or Wikispaces—offer additional collaborative options. Of course, if you'd rather have a conversation, there are still more options: set up a multi-person conference call with freeconferencecall.com, or share your computer screen through freebinar.com (a free service) and fuzemeeting.com or gotomeeting.com (paid service). Or have a face-to-face videoconference without leaving your office, using Skype, Adobe Connect, or Gmail's voice and video chat.

Back-up & Security

There is simply no excuse for not having redundant data back-up given the wide array of low-cost, user-friendly solutions. For local back-up, flash drives or external hard-drives work well, though you need to be proactive in backing up data. In my view, a preferable option, at least for the Mac, is TimeMachine; once connected, it automatically backs up documents, photos, applications, and settings. A similar system for PCs is expected as part of Windows 8. Even if you're disciplined about local back-up, offline back-up is also essential in the event that your office equipment is stolen or destroyed. Popular offline back-up includes Mozy and Carbonite, both of which are reliable and secure, but don't offer an easy way to retrieve backed-up documents. If you prefer to store documents offline, and to be able to access them easily, try dropbox (www.dropbox.com) or box.net (www.box.net). Keep in mind, however, that these services were initially intended to facilitate document-sharing and not as back-up, so it's best to use them in conjunction with more traditional offline storage like Mozy or Carbonite. As for security, any Internet-connected system is vulnerable to viruses or identity thieves. Firewalls and virus protection software is a must! And increasingly, many legal technologists are recommending that lawyers encrypt data, particularly on laptops which can be easily stolen. Truecrypt is a well-regarded and free encryption product that is easy to install.

Multimedia

As discussed in Chapter 17 (Marketing in an Age of Changing Technology), video is becoming an important component of a lawyer's marketing mix. Starting out, you may want to consider creating your own video. Both the FlipCam and KodakZi8 (both under $200) offer decent quality for a video greeting on your Web site. The Kodak Zi8 also supports a mic for better sound quality. Another way to incorporate video into your Web site or online presence is to record how-to videos; for explaining the different stages of a divorce proceeding, or demonstrating how to fill out a small claims court form. You can capture a presentation on your desktop with Screenflow (for Mac) or Camtasia (for PCs).

The Paperless Office

A paperless office converts and stores documents, records, pleadings, etc., as digital files. As a practical matter, though, even the most technologically advanced law practices still interpret paperless as "less paper" simply because we're often required to retain certain originals such as wills, notarized documents, or litigation discovery materials. A few thoughts about going "paperless":

Hardware/software. Even a few years ago, the cost and complexity of scanning equipment kept the paperless office beyond the reach of many solos. These days, good scanners are inexpensive and as simple as copiers to operate. If you run a paper-heavy practice and scan hundreds of documents, invest in the highest page-per-minute scanning capability you can afford. For lower-volume practices, a scanner that processes 10 to 15 pages a minute will suffice. Another important tool for the paperless office is Adobe Acrobat software (not to be confused with the free Adobe Reader used to view PDF documents). Adobe Acrobat allows you to highlight and to add comments to documents in PDF format (the standard for court filing), to add or delete pages from PDF documents, and to consolidate multiple PDF documents into one uniform document.

Space saver. Even if your ethics rules require that you retain certain paper files (or if you're just not totally comfortable eliminating hard copies), digitize as many files as you can. From a practical standpoint, it means that many fewer boxes stored in your closet, basement, garage, back room, or offsite locker.

Security. Electronic files are less vulnerable to loss or physical damage than paper files. And, unlike paper documents, it is harder to lose digital files. Even if you place them in the wrong file folder on your computer, you can still find them with a desktop search tool (e.g., Google Desktop or Copernic). And if you regularly back up your files, and if you store your back-up in several locations (e.g., on an external hard drive or a flash drive, or the laptop you take home at night), your files will be much more secure than paper files.

Time-saver. Storing files electronically reduces the time spent searching for misfiled papers. When a client calls about a matter, you simply pull up the relevant memo on your computer instead of putting the client on hold or scheduling a time to call back later. In fact, with a paperless office, you can make client files available through one of the project-collaboration tools described earlier. Electronic documents also save time in dealing with other lawyers, staff, or virtual assistants. With a few keystrokes, you can send entire files, or transmit an assignment to a virtual law clerk.

Necessity. Federal courts have already transitioned to mandatory electronic filing, as have many courts and regulatory agencies. If critical case documents aren't in electronic format, you and your clients will be at a disadvantage.

The Set-up. You may already have a preferred approach for organizing electronic files, but—at a minimum—you should maintain a separate folder for each client matter, as well as sub-folders for different types of documents (e.g., pleadings, correspondence, templates, etc.). A standard organization format is particularly important if you'll have a clerk or secretary accessing files. This way, they'll always know where to find information. Solo Ernest Svenson has prepared online tutorials on this subject. Go to these posts:

- www.pdfforlawyers.com/files/handling_cases_electronically.pdf.
- www.digitalworkflowcle.com/wp-content/uploads/2010/01/Technology-I-use-EES.pdf.
- www.pdfforlawyers.com/2008/01/develop-a-paper.html.

Software as a service. Legal software providers have been slow to adopt cloud computing because of fears over data and program security. As these fears subside, it's likely that more and more of what you do as a lawyer will be hosted somewhere else. This method of software delivery has, as a main advantage, the fact that no upgrades of the program are necessary, as it is all handled at the host. In addition, the data is likely more secure, and backed up more often, by a host provider.

Mobile communications. If there is anything a lawyer loves, it is being able to be a lawyer while on the move. These days, smartphones are capable of so much more, letting us do everything from checking e-mail and keeping up with our calendar to instant messaging our office and secretary, looking at documents, scanning pages into our computer, and dictating and e-mailing memos to our secretary or assistant…all from anywhere in the world. Get mobile; it's where the rest of the world is going.

Voice over Internet Protocol (VoIP). Sometime in the future, landline phone companies will move to the Internet. Until then, my favorite online phone application is Skype, because I get twice the use out of my tech dollar. I already pay for broadband Internet access through my DSL connection, and Skype leverages that access to permit free phone calls to any other Skype user over the Internet, and unlimited long-distance to any North American telephone for $29.95/year.

Electronic discovery. As the new federal electronic discovery rules get adopted by state court systems…as more documents, e-mails, and data get stored electronically…as more data gets stored remotely on servers…and as storage gets more portable, it is a sure bet that lawyers will have to deal with finding evidence in electronic form, and using it in litigation.

Generic operating systems. At the time of this writing, Microsoft Vista is the newest operating syste, but it is not being adopted quickly. In the future, there is a clear trend towards open-source (free) operating systems; most notably, Linux. There are many new distributions of Linux that are as easy to install and use as Windows, and many users are keeping XP on their systems. It is too early to predict the downfall of the Windows operating system; however, the trend is clearly away from proprietary systems.

—**Rick Georges (www.FutureLawyer.com) practices real property, corporation, wills, trusts and estates law in St. Petersburg FL, and is the technology writer at Law.com.**

Resources

The 2011 Solo and Small Firm Legal Technology Guide, Sharon Nelson, John Simek, Michael Maschke (ABA, 2011)

Cloud Computing for Lawyers, Nicole Black (ABA, 2011)

Lawyerist.com and FutureLawyer.com—frequent, ongoing coverage of tech tips and trends—each written by solo or small firm practitioners

MyShingle.com (www.myshingle.com). Coverage of web and tech trends. Also, bios of solos and how they use technology in their practices at

http://myshingle.com/articles/solo-law-tech-bio/.

International Legal Technology Standards Organization (ILTSO) –Industry standards for storage and transmission of data.

ABA Technology Resource Center www.americanbar.org/groups/departments_offices/legal_technology_resources/resources.html).

CHAPTER 8

Selecting a Practice Area

"Learning about other legal specialties lets you diversify your practice and engage in cross-selling. There
is a direct correlation between substantive competency and revenues." —Carolyn Elefant, solo

For some lawyers, untangling the tax code is challenging, stimulating, and generates a healthy revenue stream. Is it a good practice area for you? Not if you lack attention to detail or if tax law bores you to tears. Selecting the right practice area is an intensely personal decision, and what seems ideal on paper... or works for others... may not click for you. In fact, selecting the right practice for you is a lot like choosing a spouse or partner. First, there are such practical considerations as economic stability and general appeal, but—in law as in life—you can't thrive or find fulfillment without compatibility... and a healthy dose of passion.

With that in mind, this chapter presents critical factors that will help you select a practice area, along with some pros and cons for a general or specialized practice. And for those who bring an existing specialty to their new solo practice, I'll suggest ways to expand or add a practice area to your existing repertoire.

What's the Right Practice for You? Eight Factors

1. Your passion. No matter what practice area you choose, you're bound to have bad days (like when a client stiffs you on payment, or an opposing counsel makes you miserable). It's easy to get past the small stuff, though, when you have a larger vision in mind. How to do it? Identify practice areas that excite or inspire you. For example, if you went to law school because you wanted to make a difference in people's lives and to help them move forward, consider a consumer-oriented practice like consumer credit, bankruptcy, plaintiffs'-oriented employment law, or family law. Do you hunger for the thrill of the courtroom after five years toiling through corporate document reviews? Then make court-appointed criminal work part of your practice portfolio. That way, you're guaranteed court time from the start. Or perhaps you're frustrated at reading about frivolous lawsuits or the rising cost of litigation. In that case, handle defense-side litigation or develop a practice that delivers quality service to businesses at competitive rates.

2. Your background.

An existing specialty. Perhaps you've come to solo practice with a practice specialty that you developed at your previous law firm. In most cases, continuing a practice specialty you enjoy makes the transition easier when you can draw on existing contacts for referrals, and you don't need to spend time learning new skills. So, unless you're seriously unhappy with your existing practice area, or you believe it has no potential in a small firm environment, think twice about leaving it. You can always branch out to another practice area, and phase out the previous one later.

Prior work experience. Prior non-legal work experience in another industry is also a factor in selection. Your experience gives you an edge over your competitors not to mention greater credibility and a list of contacts that you can turn for referrals. Examples:

- Lawyers who worked as insurance adjusters often specialize in personal injury or small business representation where their familiarity with how insurance companies value cases helps them evaluate settlements.
- Lawyers with a high-tech background might do well choosing IP, licensing and Internet law, employment law (such as negotiating non-compete agreements or representing clients in discrimination suits), or even immigration law and offshoring (helping high-tech companies bring foreign workers to the US or to outsource work abroad).
- Many lawyers create practice areas—or niches—out of passions, hobbies, or deep personal interest. For example:

    Stephanie Caballero (www.surrogacylawyer.blogspot.com) endured eight years of infertility treatment in her quest to have children, finally realizing her dream of parenthood after a cousin carried twins as a surrogate. Ultimately, Cabellero had to adopt her children because her state did not recognize surrogacy. Having experienced infertility and surrogacy first-hand, she chose to focus her law practice on legal issues related to surrogacy and infertility treatment. **Rachel Rodgers** (www.rachelrogers.com) saw herself as an entrepreneur when she opened her own firm just a year out of law school. Based on her own experience, she felt an affinity towards other young entrepreneurs, eventually settling on a niche practice serving as "innovative legal counsel for Gen Y entrepreneurs." **Sam Slaymaker** (www.slaymakerheritagelaw.com) specializes in historic preservation law. Having grown up in his family's ancestral home, he developed a passion for preservation, and has served as director of various historic preservation foundations.

3. Your skills. With enough practice, you can probably master almost any practice area in time. But face it: some practice areas are more likely than others to complement your natural skills. For example, lawyers who excelled at moot court in law school, or who now enjoy research and analysis, might find that appellate practice naturally fits their skill set. Lawyers who are detail-oriented will have an easier time in practice areas like corporate transactions that involve contract drafting or code-based practice areas (like tax or heavily regulated industries), where the placement of a semi-colon can make the difference in the outcome of a case. And, of course, litigation is ideal for lawyers who think well on their feet, and who can organize the large amounts of information generated in discovery.

4. Characteristics of the practice area. With limited time and resources, choose at least one practice area that lets you hit the ground running. New attorneys with little experience, or lawyers looking to change practice areas, should focus on consumer-oriented practice areas like bankruptcy law, simple probate matters, consumer credit and family law, Social Security and public benefits law, employment law, and criminal law. Most bar associations, pro bono organizations and public defenders offer low-priced trainings or seminars in these practice areas, many of which include a comprehensive guide to handling a case, relevant forms, case law and even names of practitioners who will answer your questions afterward. The added benefit of many of these practice areas is that you can start small with simple cases (such as undisputed divorces, criminal misdemeanors, a Social Security appeal), allowing you to learn as you go.

5. Financial considerations. Your financial situation can also impact your choice of practice area. If you want to specialize exclusively in contingency cases, you need to have some way to cover your expenses during the first six months of your practice, or at least be willing to take either contract work or court-appointed work while you wait for your first matters to come to fruition. Other practice areas like medical malpractice (again, on a contingency basis) or class-action litigation involve a substantial financial investment for expert witnesses, deposition costs, and other case-related expenses. Consider, too, that for some practice areas, e.g., IP or corporate securities transactions, malpractice insurance may be prohibitively expensive.

6. Trends. Economic or political trends can often make or break a practice area. For some lawyers, periods of economic downturn are a good time to enter a new practice area. When one area plays out, the downturn gives you time to get up to speed on a new area without getting overwhelmed. At the same time, some attorneys use downturns as a time to retire or abandon that practice. Either way, it means less competition... and some of them might even turn over their remaining case files to you. By the time that practice area cycles into another upswing, you could be well-established and ready to handle the influx of new clients.

Political trends can also increase work in some practice areas. Changes, say, in estate-planning, tax or immigration law, can generate work as clients seek advice on how to comply with the new laws. Other practice areas are also susceptible to cycles. A booming economy can spur growth in such practice areas as real estate or corporate transaction. And, of course, in periods of recession, look for more bankruptcy and consumer credit cases, more fired employees tempted to sue former employers, and more marriages breaking up on the rocks of financial distress. In the aftermath of the 2008 banking and mortgage securitization crisis, many bankruptcy, real estate and consumer credit lawyers re-tooled their practices to represent clients in foreclosure matters.

How to track trends? Keep an eye on the law blogs and online bar magazines. They tend to forecast trends at the beginning of the year, while solo and other legal listservs are a great forum throughout the year for insights on trends and information-swapping on developments in your practice area. And don't forget trade associations, chambers of commerce, and law firms; throughout the year, they all issue studies and reports which sooner or later will show up at Internet news sites.

7. Your schedule. For most practice areas, you can minimize impact to your schedule simply by controlling your workload. If you practice criminal law but your family needs you home every evening, don't take night court appointments. But if you want to work part-time, even the best planning won't accommodate certain practice areas. Generally, the most unpredictable practice areas...litigation, family law, and criminal law...don't work well for part-time solos. Unless you make arrangements with a dependable back-up attorney, a part-time solo will struggle to cover an emergency appearance that's been scheduled on a moment's notice for your day home with the kids. And while you could hire sitters when you wind up with a matter on your day off, you defeat the purpose of working part-time if it occurs too frequently. As a part-time lawyer, you may also find yourself working from home, in which case court appearances and meetings can disproportionately cut into your workday. Trekking downtown for a 20-minute status conference can take three hours out of a five-or-six-hour workday. For part-timers, the best practice areas are those where you can make your own deadlines and don't demand frequent face-time either in court or with clients. Suitable part-time practice areas include wills and estate, tax, appellate practice, some types of corporate work and contract lawyering, i.e., handling work on a per diem basis for other lawyers.

8. Personality and temperament. Three important questions:
Q: *Would you enjoy working with clients unfamiliar with the legal system?*
A: Such practice areas as personal bankruptcy, personal injury, family law, consumer credit, and employment law require regular contact...and frequent hand-holding ...with clients unfamiliar with the legal system. For some, it's frustrating to explain over and over again the same basic concepts or answer the same procedural questions (why is this case taking so long...why do I need to fill out all of these interrogatory responses, etc.). Or you may not have the patience to provide the constant personal reassurance and support that many consumer clients require. If you're one of these lawyers, you can certainly succeed in a consumer-oriented practice. But unless you have competent staff to handle day-to-day interaction with clients, you'll find the demands of a consumer practice enervating. By contrast, some lawyers derive deep satisfaction from working closely with individual clients, helping them put their lives back together and take pride in their ability to make complex concepts accessible. Such lawyers find a consumer-oriented practice highly rewarding.

Q: *Do you thrive on confrontation...or not?*
A: You don't need a confrontational style to succeed in such dispute-oriented practice areas as employment law, family law, criminal law, general litigation, or business transactions. Many lawyers in these areas have unassuming or deferential personalities, but enjoy a fierce reputation because of clever strategies and savvy discovery, or persuasive

motions and briefs that shred their opponents' arguments. At the same time, when you're involved in a dispute-oriented practice, you do encounter a disproportionate number of aggressive lawyers intent on intimidating opponents (particularly those with less experience), with threats, screaming, insults and generally rude or unprofessional conduct. Some lawyers can shrug off this behavior. If you're not one of them, it can take its toll. But if you still want some litigation experience, or want to take on family law cases, consider these alternatives:

- Federal court practice is generally more mannered than state practice. So if you're interested in litigation, go after cases within a federal court jurisdiction.
- Courts in some jurisdictions are notorious for their more aggressive, rough-and-tumble style litigation. For example, if you're barred in two adjacent states and one favors an aggressive style, you might focus your litigation practice in the other state. Likewise, you might avoid handling disputes in certain courts. Consult with more experienced practitioners for help identifying those courts with more collegial attorneys and judges.
- Take advantage of the trend towards alternatives to litigation. One popular approach in family law is collaborative law, where parties are represented by counsel who agrees that they will resolve divorce-related disputes through negotiation and not litigation. See www.en.wikipedia.org/wiki/Collaborativedivorce. You can also specialize in alternative dispute resolution such as mediation, arbitration, and negotiation.

Q: *Do you make the problems of others your own?*
A: If you tend to take others' problems personally, you may have difficulty dealing with criminal defense or family law matters, where an adverse ruling can mean devastating consequences for your clients (e.g., jail time or loss of custody of their children). Such cases can take a psychological toll on lawyers who get too close to their clients. Moreover, your inability to keep a healthy distance from your clients' plight could cloud your judgment. For example, you might elicit false testimony from witnesses to defend a sympathetic, criminal client, rationalizing your action with the thought that the client's family will suffer if he's sent to jail. Unscrupulous clients can often sniff out the "softies," and try to take advantage of your empathy with unreasonable or unethical demands. Bottom line: if you can't trust yourself to maintain appropriate professional distance in even the most heart-wrenching cases, I suggest that you steer clear of practice areas like family law or criminal law where those types of cases predominate.

Generalization v. Specialization

For most lawyers, worries about malpractice claims or ethics violations frustrate their desire to develop and maintain a level of competence in several practice areas. At the same time, they worry that "putting all their eggs in one basket" limits their business opportunities especially if their chosen practice area is struck by regulatory reform or economic downturn. In this section, we'll discuss the major concerns about specialization, and how to expand your practice area:

Q: *How do you choose a practice area if you're just starting out?*

A: Even if you have no prior work experience, you probably have a general sense of what types of matters you *don't* want to handle. In my own case, I started my practice with one specialization and wanted to expand. I also knew that family law, with all of its emotional baggage, or trusts and estates (which was incomprehensible to me in law school), weren't right for me. So I turned down cases in those areas from the beginning. By continuing to rule out areas that weren't a fit, I eventually settled on five main practice areas that worked for me (energy regulatory and renewables, court-appointed criminal work, appellate litigation, civil rights/employment law and small business litigation). Eventually, I phased out my court-appointed criminal work that no longer made sense from a financial perspective, and small-business litigation because I didn't like state court practice. For some lawyers, choosing a practice area is an evolutionary process that involves a good bit of experimentation and trial and error. So if there are several areas of interest, feel free to sample a variety of different client matters. Also, offer to assist an experienced attorney in a particular practice area so you can learn what's involved without the pressure of handling an unfamiliar area on your own.

Q: *How do you avoid turning away business without spreading yourself too thin?*

A: Many lawyers straddle multiple practice areas for fear of turning away business. There's even a name for it: *threshold law* (e.g., you take every matter that crosses the threshold of your front door). Most new solos are understandably reluctant to turn away business because of concerns about overhead, and anxiety about whether their office phone will ever ring again. But while it's important that a lawyer sample different cases before settling on a specialization, taking too great a variety of cases could, in the long run, stunt your firm's growth. For example, let's say you're juggling a criminal matter, an immigration case, a family law dispute, a bankruptcy filing and a probate matter. You end up researching five distinct practice areas because what you learn for one isn't readily transferable to another. And because different courts and agencies have jurisdiction over each of these matters, you waste time calling four separate court clerks trying to figure out how to file or plead, and then race from court to court to make an appearance. If you're uncomfortable turning away clients, build a referral network. Compile a readily accessible list or spreadsheet with one or two attorneys in different practice areas, so when a client calls with a matter you don't handle, you can provide the name of other attorneys. Afterward, contact the referring attorney that a case is on the way, and make it clear that you're available for cases in your own area. With a referral system in place, you won't feel as if you're turning away cases... merely exchanging them for cases that suit your practice.

Q: *How do you offer "one-stop shopping" without spreading yourself too thin?*

A: Many lawyers decline to specialize so they can provide "one-stop shopping" to clients who need help with a variety of legal problems. For example, the lawyer with the transactional practice whose small business clients also have questions about employment matters, IP work, corporate and securities work, litigation, tax law, contract review and negotiation…and even trusts and estate work for company principals. As discussed earlier, you're asking for trouble if you try to handle too many unrelated and relatively complex practice areas. Indeed, even at large firms, companies aren't represented by one lawyer, but by multiple attorneys with different practice specialties. So take some guidance from successful large firms: establish virtual teams of other solos who specialize in IP, employment, tax and other matters you don't handle, and bring them on board to serve clients with multiple needs. In this way, you'll bring your clients the spectrum of expertise that they demand at a fraction of the cost of a large firm. How might this virtual team work? A family law attorney might pair with a probate attorney to provide seamless service to a newly divorced client who needs to change her will. A personal injury attorney could team up with a tax or finance lawyer for assistance in structuring settlements and advising on the tax consequences of an award. For additional information, see Chapter 13 (Affiliation, Alliances, Virtual firms & Networks).

Expanding Your Practice Areas

While generalization has its drawbacks, you don't want to narrow the scope of your practice too tightly. In this way, you avoid burn-out from handling the same types of cases over and over, you stay fresh by handling different matters, and you create a hedge against economic, political, or regulatory changes. Here are some factors to consider without exposing you to a risk of malpractice:

Look for 'natural' combinations. Pete Roberts, practice management advisor for the Washington State Bar's Law Office Management Assistance Program, advises lawyers to seek out compatible areas that make use of a common skill-set and deal with a common pool of clients. For further details, read Robert's article, *Diversified Practice: Tailor a Good Fit* at http://www.abanet.org/genpractice/magazine/2004/jan-feb/diversifiedpracticetailor.html. Roberts writes that certain practice areas make a natural fit, such as:

- Environment—Real property, and use, environment, mineral right, public utilities, zoning law
- Social work—Family, juvenile, elder law
- Arts—Contracts, copyright, nonprofits, small business
- Science/technology—Patent, health, IP, personal injury, medical malpractice
- Business/ownership—Business and corporate, mergers and acquisitions, startups, contracts
- Personal injury/consumer—Workers compensation, insurance coverage, health provider reimbursement, Consumer Protection Act, and insurance bad faith

Roberts also suggests that you examine how bar associations organize their practice section categories because they frequently group practice areas that go well together or lead to one another. On the flip side, Roberts cautions against combining practice areas that force you to change gears mentally every time the phone rings. He also suggests avoiding specialties that lack the potential to transfer clients from one area into another.

Balance stable revenue areas with narrower, or more risky, specialties. Strike a balance between practice areas that generate a steady stream of revenue with riskier contingency or litigation cases that offer higher payouts but may require months or years to collect. For example: combine contingency-based, personal injury matters with court-appointed criminal work. The court-appointed work will pay the bills while you wait for PI settlements, and while civil and criminal procedure is different, both areas will sharpen your litigation skills. Add some spark to such practice areas as corporate transactional work or regulatory law—where you're well compensated by large institutional clients—with one or two civil rights cases in federal court where you recover attorney fees by statute. You'll learn federal court practice (if you don't know it already), find assistance from groups like the ACLU, and potentially collect fees and publicity for handling public interest work. Consider handling both sides of the same specialty to even out the revenue. For example, some law firms handle both plaintiffs' and defense side employment work. Defense side work typically involves counseling and training companies which generates revenue, while some plaintiffs' matters might be handled on a contingency or reduced fee basis with full recovery of statutory attorney fees.

The Niche Practice

Whereas a specialization refers to a specific practice area—tax law or employment law—a *niche practice* is narrower still, targeting a group of customers whose needs are not directly or adequately serviced by other providers. Different types of niche practices include:

Topical. Covering a discrete topic, but potentially spanning different disciplines—e.g., Safari Law (www.safarilaw.com) a firm addressing legal issues related to safari hunters ranging from firearms compliance issues, contractual disputes with safari providers, and international law governing safaris. A topical niche may also cover a subset of an existing practice area, such as David Kaufman's businessbrawls.com, focusing on litigating business disputes.

Demographic. A sub-set of a practice area focusing on a specific population—e.g., estate planning for non-traditional families, immigration law for entrepreneurs from India.

Geographic or "hyper-local". A niche focused on a particular locality, such as an Abilene, Texas criminal defense lawyer, or a Missoula, Montana estate planning lawyer. **Means of delivery.** A niche related to the form of delivery of services, such as a virtual law practice or an "after hours" lawyer who meets with clients on nights and weekends.

What's your niche?

It might target a certain populations; say, postal employees, same-sex couples, high-income professionals seeking divorces, Hispanic business owners, or maybe certain topic areas; say, pet law, alcohol beverage law or special education law. Why have a niche? It's the easiest way to distinguish your practice from other lawyers. Think about it: if you go to a dinner meeting with a dozen other lawyers, who will you remember? The other real estate and zoning lawyers…or the one historic preservation attorney? Even if your niche accounts for only 10 or 20 percent of your revenues, the exposure it buys will generate a substantial amount of business.

Know what to expect from your niche. Niche practices may confer attention and acclaim, but are not necessarily cash cows…nor do they have to be. A unique niche can bring exposure and contacts, which can lead to billable work in related practice areas. For example, a niche in representing couples in foreign adoptions is likely to attract more general adoption cases.

Niches are narrow in focus, but demand more skills. A niche practice sounds tempting because you can focus on a narrow area. But there's a catch: a niche practice may encompass a specific topic (e.g., historic preservation law, animal law, billboard litigation, veterans' law), yet beneath the surface, these practice areas encompass a variety of skills. For example, someone specializing in animal law might need to be familiar with family law (to handle pet custody cases), tort law (for dog bite cases), or estate planning (to ensure that owners can provide for a pet after their death). If you enter a niche practice, be prepared to handle all of the issues it may generate, or affiliate with other lawyers who can take on the issues for you.

Don't niche too narrowly. Don't rely on your niche for more than 75 percent of your practice, and far less if your niche is especially narrow. And when you market your niche, be sure to mention your related practice areas. Example: introduce yourself like this: *I handle all kinds of elder law matters, with a special focus on issues related to long-term care insurance.* In this way, you capture those prospects with a more general need for an elder law attorney that doesn't necessarily involve long term care insurance.

Marketing your niche. In an ABA book (*Niche Marketing: How to Capture and Keep Clients*, 2005), lawyer David Leffler writes that marketing is the "fun" part of a niche practice. It's fun, he says, because things tend to go easier marketing to a niche audience than to "everyone" as part of your general practice. And because you're identified as an expert in your niche, potential clients will feel more inclined to hire you because of your recognized expertise.

So how do you gain recognition as an expert and market your niche? Here are several ideas:

- Blogs are an ideal medium to advertise a niche practice. Unlike an ordinary Web site, you can use a blog to provide a stream of news and information relative to your niche, thus demonstrating your expertise. If you have several niches to market, you set up a corresponding number of blogs.
- Look for groups interested in your area of expertise so you can give talks or write

articles for their newsletter. Participating in these events may lead to calls; more importantly, it helps build your reputation.

- Tom Goldstein, a young attorney who established a Supreme Court litigation boutique, Goldstein & Howe (now Howe and Russell) was quoted in an interview, "… *Once you define yourself as the only person who does something, you've automatically defined yourself as the people who know the most about it. We [Goldstein & Howe] are a thousand times more effective when we say we are the only law firm that focuses principally on the Supreme Court.*"

Ultimately a niche is the easiest way to stand out in a crowd because they're more memorable. Who will you remember after a networking event: the 10 lawyers who said they practice employment law, or the one who said she represents baby boomers in employment disputes?

The Off-Hours & Mobile Practice

Let's face it, most people—whether they punch a time clock, or are busy executives—are unable to take time out of a busy work day to visit a lawyer. Why not accommodate them? Accept appointments two nights a week from 6 to 9 pm, or mornings from 7 to 9 am, or even open your doors for several hours on the weekend. In fact, you don't even have to make yourself available in person; you could chat by phone or Skype. Advertising this off-hour availability is likely to attract prospects, who, because they couldn't take off from work, may have been putting off their estate planning or employment discrimination matter.

On-site visits are another way to set yourself apart, and certainly endear yourself to homebound individuals; the elderly, parents of young children, the sick or injured. Corporate clients would also appreciate an onsite visit. Site visits also give you an edge, because they let you learn your clients' business, and to identify other issues that might need to be addressed. Example: the president of a small company retains you to draft a non-compete agreement. Rather than draft and e-mail the agreement, you volunteer to drop it off. While waiting for the client, you notice a group of employees making inappropriate remarks to an attractive young assistant. When you speak with the company president, you can tactfully bring the incident to his attention, and inquire whether the company has any policies on sensitivity training, or a procedure for bringing complaints about harassment internally. From a single visit, you might get hired to help draft an employment practices handbook.

The Accidental Practice

And then there's the successful accidental practice, the one some solos fall into by being in the right place at the right time. Some examples:

Alan Gura, a Washington DC-area solo was hired at a reduced rate by a social acquaintance to challenge DC's gun law as unconstitutional under the Second Amendment. Gura eventually took the case to the Supreme Court and won, and has since argued several other Second Amendment matters nationwide (http://en.wikipedia.org/wiki/Alan_Gura).

Baltimore attorney Robin Page West stumbled into the lucrative area of qui tam litigation when she accepted a referral from another attorney too busy to research this area of law. Today, West has litigated many more qui tam cases, written a book on the subject, and gained recognition as an expert in the field.

Here are a few suggestions on how to discover new practice areas:

Practice serendipity. Set aside that business plan, crumple up that marketing checklist, and put down that expensive handbook on building a practice. Instead, shake things up; venture into unknown territory. Sign up for a pro bono course in a practice area where you have no experience, or volunteer to organize a presentation for the local bar or a community group on a topic with which you're unfamiliar, or make contact with different groups that just might provide the lead you're looking for.

Listen more. For example, listen to that small business client who comes to you seeking representation and happens to mention that he's having problems with his insurer. Who knows, you might also find yourself sitting on top of a bad-faith action. Or, spend a little extra time listening to that family law client who comes in for representation in a divorce proceeding and happens to mention that she's just been fired because her boss made a pass after he learned of her new single status. Who knows, you might have an employment law matter to pursue. Also, as you spend time with other attorneys, mention that you're eager for new work in a variety of practice areas. Many attorneys may misjudge the value of a case if they're not familiar with all of the potential causes of action, or don't have the time to research an esoteric matter themselves.

Learn, learn, learn. Once you find a potential lead in a new field, learn as much as you can. Run some computerized searches to get the lay of the land, and then visit the local law library to search out treatises, law review articles, and trade press publications. Google the relevant blogs. If there's a listserv devoted to these issues, post a few questions. If a matter puts you before a court or agency where you've never practiced, call up a clerk for assistance with procedural matters, or an agency staffer who might share some of the agency's past experience with the issue. Most important, find another attorney who has handled similar cases, and who would be willing to act as a sounding board or mentor.

Follow up. Once you stumble into a new practice area, make the most of it. Write an article for a law review or bar journal. After all, the costs are sunk since the bulk of the research was completed when you investigated the new practice area. It shouldn't take much more time to transform your notes into publishable copy. And if the field is one of sufficient interest—and appears to have lucrative potential—you could also launch a blog on the topic.

Staying Ahead of the Curve

When you run your own firm, there's a direct correlation between substantive competency and revenues. By keeping ahead of the information curve, you can edge out your competitors, and generate billable work advising clients on the implications of new laws. Learning about other legal specialties also allows you to diversify your practice and engage in cross-selling. So, if you're a real estate lawyer and you learn about probate, you can sell clients about your service in both areas. Below are some places to learn about new practice areas:

Pro bono training. Many state and local bar associations or legal aid groups offer free or low-cost pro bono training from top lawyers on matters you might use in solo practice, such as public benefits litigation, consumer protection, bankruptcy, trusts and estates, or veterans' benefits appeals. Often, the courses include a handbook you can use later in practice. Many of the classes cost less than $100, or merely require a commitment to handle two pro bono cases. Note: so many attorneys usually participate in these programs that there is only a minimal chance that you'll actually be called to take a case.

Court-appointed panel training. When you sign up to handle court-appointed work (such as criminal defense or abuse and neglect cases), the court or the public defenders' office may also provide extensive training for free or a small cost. As with pro bono training, lawyers who teach about handling court-appointed cases are usually willing to help you later on.

Court-watching. Not sure how to argue an appeal or cross-examine a witness? Visit the courthouse and watch other attorneys. And even if you don't know enough about handling the examination of a witness, pay attention to a judge's reactions to see what works. Check the judge's calendar (either at the court Web site, or by contacting the judge's secretary or clerk) to make sure you have a chance to see an actual trial or motion as opposed to sitting through status hearings. Most judges welcome lawyer/observers in their courtroom. Observing depositions, settlement conferences, or negotiations is more difficult because, in contrast to courtroom proceedings, they're generally not open to the public. You might also ask a mentor if you can accompany him/her to a deposition, or volunteer to do some work for an attorney in exchange for observing at a mediation. Also, get a copy of Martin Grayson's book for new litigators: "*The View From the First Chair: What Every Trial Lawyer Really Needs to Know*" (2009).

Newsletters/magazines/court and agency news. Pay attention to the daily, weekly, national legal trade press. Many large law firms also offer newsletters or action alerts on recent developments that anyone can sign up for at their Web sites. Trade associations and specialty bars also publish electronic newsletters and magazines. They're included in the cost of membership.

Blogs and news feeds. Blogs are invaluable for information in many fields. For example, if you handle appellate matters, Howard Bashman's blog (www.appellateblog.com) keeps you in the loop about dozens of important court cases within an hour or so of their issuance. There are hundreds of blogs on every legal topic from electronic discovery and telecom law, to Maryland personal injury practice or New Jersey family law. To find a blog covering your practice area, visit one or more of these six sites:

www.abajournal.com/blawgs, www.BlawgRepublic.com, www.BlawgSearch.Justia.com, www.3Lepiphany.com, or www.LexMonitor.com.

Continuing legal education. In theory, CLE's help keep your practice skills and substantive knowledge fresh. In practice, though, the cost and quality of these courses varies widely. Some programs will provide you with real substance; others are little more than PowerPoint presentations by attorneys more interested in generating referrals than sharing information about their practice area.

- To distinguish quality CLE's from the duds, seek out recommendations from lawyers who've taken a particular CLE. Also, check with the local bar. Some will let you access past course materials, which may give you an idea of the CLE's value.
- If you want to learn about a local practice area (e.g., trusts, family law, briefing techniques for your local court, etc), select courses sponsored by state or local bars rather than national CLE providers. Generally, the local presenters are more familiar with the ins-and-outs of local practice. If you practice in a major urban area, your local bar may also have sections dealing with national practice areas like renewable energy, securities, telecommunications, or Internet law. The cost of these courses should be more reasonable than those offered by professional seminar or national CLE providers.
- Taking CLE's isn't just a matter of out-of-pocket costs; the investment of time is often considerable. More and more, though, CLE's come right to your desk via phone or Internet. Such courses are usually less expensive; in fact, many are free. Another increasingly popular option are the CLE podcasts offered by some bar associations. You simply download the podcasts to your smartphone, iPod, or MP3 player, and learn as you commute or work your Stairmaster.

For lawyers with large firm specialties (e.g., securities law, environmental law), many CLE's are quite expensive. Expect to pay $1,500 in addition to whatever transportation and lodging expenses might be involved. If you can't find a cheaper substitute (e.g., a locally sponsored brown bag lunch event or webinar), try this:

- See out an attorney willing to pay you to attend the conference in exchange for sharing the materials and summarizing the conference proceedings. Though you may still have to pay travel and airfare, you can use the conference to network and at least avoid the cost of admission.
- If the conference is local, perhaps you can volunteer to tweet from the conference. or register participants in exchange for free admission;
- Arrange to purchase the conference proceedings, though sometimes it is several months before the materials are available.

CHAPTER 9

Generating Cash Flow

*"*Who has job security? I think I have more than most.

At least I know I won't fire myself!*"*

—Lynda L. Hinkle, solo

Just starting out, you may have to go at least a month or two (or more) before finding a paying client let alone to complete the work and to collect your fee.

How do you generate revenue in the meantime?

In this section, I'll discuss how to generate what I call "fast-cash", including the ever-popular contract (per diem) work, placement agency assignments, lawyer-to-lawyer networking, court-appointed criminal work, adjunct faculty positions, online ad assignments, writing gigs, bar referrals and more. And at the end of the chapter, you'll see how several solos responded to this question: *how did you create a revenue stream in the beginning*?

In defense of fast-cash, it does alleviate some of the financial pressure so you don't feel compelled to accept marginal cases or difficult clients just to pay your bills. But it's worth noting that fast-cash assignments can be addictive, a temptation for new solos that might lead to neglecting the marketing that is so critical to attracting their own clients. You could, for example, open your new firm by accepting a document-review assignment at $35/hour plus overtime (for a total of 50 hours). Good money, especially if the assignment lasts a few weeks. But what if it goes three months? Those 10-hour days, 50-hour weeks don't give you much time for client-development. You would have more revenue, but you wouldn't have advanced your goal of getting your new practice off the ground.

That caution aside, here are some time-tested ways to generate revenue:

Contract (per diem) Work

Temporary placement agencies. At one time, short-term document review projects and temporary assignments through placement agencies helped many solos, myself included, generate a stream of revenue while getting a practice off the ground. These days, however, document review projects are few and far between for two reasons: in the first place, technology has displaced some of the classification, tagging, and review work once performed by contract lawyers. As the New York Times reports, new artificial-intelligence powered e-discovery programs can do the work of 500 lawyers (*Armies of Expansive Lawyers Being Replaced by Machines*, March 4, 2011). Second, many corporate clients and large law firms are offshoring projects to India to reduce costs. With few available contract lawyer slots, many temp agencies won't even consider solos, whom they fear may not be as dedicated as contract lawyers who don't have an outside job. Further, rates for contract lawyers have plunged to as little as $18 to $25/hour, making the work unsustainable.

Yet with all of these drawbacks, it may be worth your while to sign up with a temp agency. First, if you're still undecided about starting a firm, working as a contract lawyer will give you time to start planning a practice on the side. Second, if you've been laid off and want to collect unemployment benefits, you may need to sign up with a temp agency to demonstrate that you are looking for work. And finally, a temp agency may sometimes produce short-term projects (a day or two long), or projects of a more substantive nature, that may be more compatible with a solo's skills and schedules.

Direct sources of contract work. Whether you're a new admittee, an experienced lawyer, or a specialist, define your market and the nature of your offer. Contract lawyers often make the mistake of not specifying what they bring to the table, assuming they can attract more business if they say they can handle any problem. But if your offer is unclear, you won't be able to persuade other lawyers to pay for your services. *Narrow your focus and broaden your appeal*. It's counterintuitive, but this advice has proven time and again.

Before you make contact, consider:

- Find out if a market exists for lawyers with your expertise.
- Identify the kind of projects you would like to handle, and which hiring lawyers are most likely to offer that kind of work (busy solos are more likely candidates than firms with an army of associates for legal research and writing, and litigation assistance). If you would rather focus on transactional work, your best bet may be vacation- or leave-coverage for boutique firms with that specialty.
- Approach small companies not targeted by the contract placement agencies; for example, companies with only one in-house lawyer.
- Decide whether or not to limit the geographic area in which you offer your services. If you're willing to travel—whether it's the next county or out of the country—you increase your chances of finding work.
- Your former law firm (that is, if you left, or are leaving, on good terms) may be a good source of contract work. Your firm may agree to retain you on a contract basis to finish up projects while it looks for a new attorney.
- Networking: The most efficient way to find contract work from other attorneys is by cold-calling or networking (either in person or by participating in listservs).
- Classified ads for contract positions can also be found in your law school alumni office, the back pages of the local bar journal, and at Craigslist. Because Craigslist doesn't charge for ads (or just a modest amount in some cities), it attracts all types of classifieds, including those from attorneys who could not afford to involve a placement agency. Sift carefully through the postings; there are many interesting opportunities, some of which don't pay very well. Also, when you deal with an attorney through Craigslist, you should...at a minimum...visit the lawyer's Web site and check their disciplinary record.

Author note: even where an ad is seeking a full-time attorney, consider submitting a resume and offering your services part-time where the position involves a unique, hard-to-find expertise. Years ago, I responded to an ad for an energy regulatory associate. In my cover letter, I described that I had started my practice, but wanted to work on issues that I couldn't handle on my own. As it turned out, the hiring lawyer preferred my flexibility because he could avoid committing to a full-time hire. He retained me on a contract basis. After a few years, the arrangement turned into an *of counsel* relationship which lasted 10 years. It never hurts to send your resume; the hiring firm may find that your resume is so superior that it may prefer to use your services part-time rather than hiring a less experienced associate. For more information on contract lawyering, visit Lisa Solomon's Legal Research and Writing Pro (www.legalresearch-andwrittingpro.com), an online resource for contract lawyers.

Networking for Contract Work: Do's & Don'ts

DO tell lawyers that you're looking for contract work. It sounds obvious, but when you meet other lawyers be explicit about your availability for contract work. Many new attorneys alert other lawyers that they are looking for referrals, but often they don't take the next step... demonstrating their willingness to help with overflow work on a contract basis. I guess they figure it makes them look desperate for work. The irony is that most attorneys assume that new solos would be insulted by an offer of contract work at lower rates. So, they might not mention it even if they do have a need to outsource. If you want contract work, you have to ask for it.

DO suggest ways you might help. Some lawyers have never considered using contract attorneys, assuming that they are only suitable for major document-review assignments or brief writing. If you're looking for contract work, suggest less-obvious ways you can help; ghostwriting articles, writing blog entries, attending meetings, standing in at status hearings, or defending depositions where the lawyer's presence is not required.

DON'T oversell yourself. Don't oversell your skills or your availability. Most lawyers are very, very busy (which is why they need help to begin with), and don't have time or budget to provide on-the-job training. They want someone who can come on board and assume responsibility for a matter with specific time parameters. So, if you do accept an assignment to draft a motion, be prepared to deliver a good product, or to figure out how to draft it on your own... off the clock. Likewise, don't agree to a one-week deadline if you've got three other client matters due at the same time. If your schedule won't allow you to accept the project, or if the deadline set by the hiring attorney is unrealistic, be up-front about the constraints. If the attorney can't offer added flexibility, turn the project down. Ultimately, if you miss a deadline, or perform poorly because you lacked the skills, not only won't you get the lawyer's repeat business, but he or she is unlikely to refer you business either. Likewise, don't over-commit to completing the work. In short, even if you really, really need the money, don't accept a contract assignment unless you're confident you can make a good impression.

DON'T send mass mailings. You may think that reaching out to every attorney in your local bar association increases your chances of finding contract work. In truth, a communications blast—electronic or paper—usually winds up deleted or recycled. Frankly, five targeted calls to attorneys you know—or even cold calls—will give you better results than mass mailings. And you make a better impression when attorneys see that you've taken the initiative to call them by phone.

DO make it easy for lawyers to hire you. You increase your chances of getting contract work by having both electronic and hard copies of an updated resume—and your best writing samples (one short, one long)—ready to send. If you're marketing to local attorneys, offer to stop by their office if they wish to meet. And draft a basic retainer agreement for contract services so they don't have to take the time to create their own. Make it easy for lawyers to hire you.

DO take precautions to ensure that you get paid. Many contract lawyers mistakenly believe that they needn't worry about getting paid because they're dealing with attorneys. Unfortunately, some will try to squirm out of paying contract attorneys, especially if they're unable to recover the cost from their clients. When providing contract services to attorneys, prepare a contract that memorializes the terms of your arrangement. *That agreement should make clear that your payment is not contingent upon the attorney collecting payment from his client, and that the attorney must pay upon completion of your work, not when he collects from the client.* As a contract attorney, you have no control over selection of the client, nor are you paid enough to assume the risk of non-collection. If the hiring attorney balks at these terms, your course is clear: turn down the assignment. Note: offering Paypal or other credit card payment as an option will facilitate payment.

Resource: *The Complete Guide to Contract Lawyering: What Every Lawyer & Law Firm Needs to Know About Temporary Legal Services* (3rd edition, 2003).

Cold Calls & Cold E-Mail

Lawyer-to-lawyer cold calling happens to be one of the most effective, inexpensive, least time-consuming, and *immediate* way of making new contacts and finding work. After all, in a competitive market, you need to get business by seeking it out...not waiting for the phone to ring. And if you're just starting out, and you want to start making court appearances for other lawyers on a contract basis, cold calling is an excellent way to begin. Another benefit is its immediacy; you get an immediate response from the recipient: *yes, I have an immediate need,* or *'no thanks'.* And because cold-calling allows for direct interaction, you might discover that even if your prospect doesn't need you to make a court appearance, they might have a small matter suitable for referral.

Cold calls work best when a friend or a colleague has passed a name on to you. Barring that, you can gather names from a bar or trade association list. In an hour's time, you should be able to call as many at 10 lawyers Maybe they won't even have work, but that's 10 seeds planted in an hour's time. Not a bad return for a 90-minute investment.

A couple of tips:

Compile a list of prospects. It might include attorneys from whom you seek referrals or contract work; old clients to whom you haven't spoken in years; businesses you'd like to introduce to your firm. Note: avoid direct calls to consumer clients that might be construed as impermissible solicitation under ethics rules.

Set aside a block of time. Cold calling is best from 10 to 11 a.m. and 3 to 4 p.m.

Expect rejection, but put a smile in your voice. Your armor will toughen as you work through the list.

Follow up. Be sure to follow up—that day if possible—with writing samples or other materials that you promised to send.

Leverage technology. Use one of the many contact-management software tools to track your efforts, making note of your prospect's name, response, and any necessary follow-up.

Work from a script. Identify yourself and your firm, and describe how you know the prospect and why you're calling. And before you launch into your script, be sure to ask prospects whether they have time to talk. If not, arrange to call back later.

Cold e-mails are less intimidating, and lay the foundation for a follow-up phone call. And they're better than a call for some communications. Example: you want to let a colleague know about the blog post you wrote about his recent case? A quick e-mail lets you transmit the link. But for all its efficiencies, there are rules of the road to keep your e-mail from getting lost in the recipient's in-box or falling victim to the delete key.

A few suggestions:

Customize the e-mail subject heading. Don't send bulk e-mail. It's likely to get caught in the recipient's spam filter, or worse; it could be subject to the CANSPAM Act, which imposes certain requirements on commercial e-mails with large penalties for non-compliance.

Don't forget the ethics rules. Limit cold e-mails to lawyers and other service providers rather than to consumers and other prospective clients.

Get to the point. Your message should include a description of who you are and where you are located; a succinct explanation for the e-mail, and whether you can schedule a follow-up call or meeting; a link to your Web site and any relevant attachments that can help the recipient learn more about you. If you don't get a response within a week, send a follow up e-mail. Many times, e-mails are accidentally deleted or a recipient may set it aside to respond and simply forget. Of course, if you send a follow up and still don't hear back, you can probably check that recipient off your list.

NOTE TO NEW CONTRACT LAWYERS

When it comes to contract work, price matters.

If I have a well-paying client with a discrete project that I can outsource and receive client-ready work in return, I will pay top rates. But if I just need general research or help with discovery or writing projects, I'm not going to pay more than $75/hour... if that much. Why? Because in my area (around Washington DC), there are dozens of well-qualified people willing to accept the work for $50–$75/hour. I once posted a Craigslist classified to get help on a Summary Judgment motion. I received more than two dozen responses, ranging from lawyers with 40 years of experience to former BigLaw, Ivy attorneys who had relocated to the area for a spouse, and all of them were willing to take the project for a $50/hour just to build their resume. So why would anyone take contract work if it's a lower rate? Easy cash (most attorneys pay on time; at least I do), and a chance to build a relationship with a lawyer who might refer cases in the future. So, as someone who has purchased contract services, here is what is useful to me as the hiring lawyer:

- **Make life easy for me.** Call me, and follow up. Describe how you will keep in touch with me if I hire you. I have hired way too many clerks who took an assignment and then didn't hear back for two weeks.
- **Tell me what you can do for me.** I know that you want work from me, but I'm also interested in hearing how you think you can help me. If someone approached me with an offer to help upgrade one of my blogs or market my trade association and had specific ideas, I'd hire them. I have so much on my plate that I often can't even find the time to devise an assignment to delegate, so if a contract attorney were to do that for me, it would be great.
- **Be flexible on rates.** Look at the going rates in your area and with your expertise before establishing your rates. As I said, I am the beneficiary of lots of first-rate lawyers in my area because so many of them wind up relocating with spouses who are in the military or work in administrative or Congressional offices, or have fellowships, etc. So, I don't pay top-dollar unless absolutely necessary.
- **Make sure you have the goods.** If you are going to hold yourself out as a legal researcher or writer, make sure you have the credentials to match. When I posted on Craigslist, I could not believe all the writing samples that had typos, conclusory statements, and over-the-top language (e.g., "clearly this...clearly that"). Using "clearly" drives me crazy; if it's so clear, you don't have to keep saying so. On the other hand, some samples were really first-rate.
- **Don't take work you can't handle.** The most common reason for me to hire a contract attorney is because I have a tight deadline and not enough time to meet it. That means that when I give you a deadline, it must be met without excuse. If you can't do the work in the time provided, ask me if there's any flexibility. But if my deadline can't be moved and you can't meet it, turn the work down so that I can hire someone else. I realize that you feel that if you're not available, that I won't call you for future projects, and that's certainly a risk. But if I do hire you and you miss a deadline, I can assure you that I won't ever call again.

Prepaid Legal Services Plans

Legal services plans are purchased by employers to provide employees with coverage for minor matters; e.g., divorce, trust and estate, bankruptcy. When you join a legal service plan, you're listed in the plan's network in the way health insurance companies maintain a network of physicians. Clients can contact you directly for an appointment, after which (depending on the plan) either the client or you can apply for reimbursement for those matters covered by the plan. Most plans do not require attorneys to join the network, nor are attorneys limited to one plan network. You can learn more about legal service plans by speaking with attorneys who participate in such networks, or by visiting (and registering) at the plan's Web sites. Prepaid work offers a predictable income stream as well as a chance to build a relationship with plan members, who may hire you later for more profitable matters outside the plan (such as personal injury cases), or refer you to their friends. While prepaid work doesn't pay much, some solos have discovered the benefits outweigh the lower margins, as described in a National Law Journal article by Sheri Quarles (*Solo, Small-Firm Use of Prepaid Plan Grows*; April 26, 2007). The article is available at www.law.com/jsp/article.jsp?id=1177491865520).

Appointments & Publicly Funded Projects

Almost every state has a court-appointed criminal panel from which attorneys are assigned to represent indigent criminal defendants, and are compensated by the court.

Rates for legal services and eligibility for criminal appointments differ from state to state, and between state and federal court. Most state court programs allow inexperienced attorneys to accept criminal cases and to provide free or low-cost training through the public defender's office or local law school. In some states, lawyers are compensated hourly at rates ranging from $35/hour to $85/hour; other states pay a flat-fee per case, such as $1,500 for misdemeanor, or $3,000 for felony matters. Federal appointments usually pay more but are harder to get, and may be reserved for more experienced attorneys.

When it comes to court-appointed work, the key words are "lead time". Allow yourself as much lead time as possible. In jurisdictions where court-appointed pay is high (and competition stiff), you might not receive an assignment for two or three months. And while you can count on payment from court-appointed work (every once in a while, a system may temporarily run out of funding, and lawyers must wait until a new appropriation issues), the court may take six to eight weeks to process your invoices. Some jurisdictions do not permit you to apply for payment until a case concludes, which means that in more complicated matters you may wait several months before you can submit your invoice. So, if you're hoping to rely on court-appointed payments early on in your practice, sign up for such programs as early as you can. Other court-appointed work includes juvenile criminal matters, child abuse, and neglect cases which are handled similarly to court-appointed criminal cases. Courts can also appoint attorneys as executors of estates.

Writing & Blogging Assignments

If you enjoy writing, or have a practice specialty, you may be able to generate additional revenue with law-related writing assignments. One long-established legal publisher—BNABooks (www.BNABooks.com)—occasionally needs attorneys to summarize case law, or to write book chapters, in the areas of labor and employment law, labor relations, health law, employee benefits law, arbitration and ADR, IP law, and occupational safety and health law. In the case of other publications, they often advertise in legal newspapers or at www.lawjobs.com. In addition, some online legal media providers, particularly law technology and e-discovery publications, will pay lawyers to blog or write regular articles or columns. Though these publications don't pay as generously as a legal position, they do tend to pay more than many non-legal blogs, and don't consume a large amount of time.

Adjunct Faculty Positions

Recent trends in legal education have opened still other fast-cash opportunities for new solos. Facing tight budgets, many law schools are trimming expenses by hiring part-time adjunct professors. In fact, adjuncts comprise 50 percent of the faculty at some law schools. And in response to student demand for more practical skills training, law schools have also started to hire practicing attorneys rather than traditional academics (nor are law schools the only source for teaching jobs; paralegal programs and business schools also need lawyers to teach classes). Adjunct professor positions don't pay much—$2,500 to $7,500 per semester—but enough to pay some bills or subsidize your marketing efforts. The time-commitment for teaching positions varies. Your first class will require a significant investment of time to develop the curriculum. Once completed, you shouldn't need more than a few hours to tweak your syllabus for subsequent classes. Grading papers can be time-consuming, but the amount depends upon class size, and program requirements (e.g., some programs will allow you to get by with one final exam; others may require you to create mid-term and written papers). Adjunct positions offer several benefits: a) an adjunct professorship looks impressive on a resume (particularly if you're teaching in an area of expertise you hope to market to clients), b) most classes meet at night or for an hour or so once or twice a week, and won't cramp your day job, and c) adjunct status often provides access to law libraries that might not otherwise be open to the public, and, in some instances, allow you to use computerized research and other resources at no charge from the school's academic account.

CLE Provider

With all but a handful of states adopting mandatory CLE requirements, there's an enormous demand for CLE programs, particularly lower-cost online CLE's. If you're an experienced solo, you might consider teaching a CLE for one of the commercial providers (Thompson-West, Lorman, Lawline.com). Although only a small portion of CLE programs pay instructors, some jurisdictions will give you CLE credit for teaching a CLE course, which in turn will save you some money. Other CLE providers will tape your program and let you distribute it to your clients or use it for marketing purposes.

RFP Services

Government agencies and municipalities sometimes post ads or issue Requests for Proposals (RFP's) for a wide range of legal services, among which might be a position to serve 15 hours a week as a municipal attorney, or serving as a hearing officer in administrative adjudications. As with contract work, government and municipalities offer lower rates than private clients. But working for a public entity provides an excellent networking opportunity and access to future work.

Bar Referral

Bar referral services won't necessarily generate fast-cash, but they are one more source of clients (although a declining source, as prospective clients are more likely to go online to find representation). In some jurisdictions, bar-referral services yield paying clients, while in others you won't get as a much as a phone call. Bar-referral programs generally do not charge lawyers much to participate, so you have nothing to lose by signing up.

Cash Opportunities...Not to Try

In 2009, a small firm lawyer in Ohio was suspended from practice for a year for his participation in a mortgage-foreclosure defense scheme run by a company called Foreclosure Solutions. Customers paid Foreclosure Solutions $1,000 to save their homes from foreclosure; in turn, the company hired lawyers to file various forms in court intended to delay the foreclosure process. Foreclosure Solutions paid the lawyers $125 a case, and the lawyers simply filed forms prepared by the company without interviewing clients or researching the case. The state bar discovered the scheme after several clients lost their homes and filed complaints. The lesson? Don't put your law license on the line for quick cash by participating in arrangements where you're required to use pre-packaged forms or where you're prohibited from handling a case as you see fit.

Fee-splitting. Sometimes companies will try to package legal services with other products. For example, a bank may sell an estate-planning practice that includes preparation of testamentary documents, and then hire lawyers to prepare those documents. Very often, these "package deals" may violate bar rules prohibiting fee-splitting with non-lawyers. Check with ethics counsel before participating in this type of arrangement.

Unreasonable expectations. In 2004, lemon law firm Kimmel & Silverman hired a local Maryland lawyer to open a local office to handle hundreds of Maryland cases generated through the firm's regional advertising campaign [Source: MyShingle, http://myshingle.com/2008/06/articles/ethics-malpractice-issues/if-it-sounds-too-good-to-be-true/]. The firm never provided the local lawyer the resources to manage 500 cases; as a result, she failed to file many of them while dozens of others were dismissed for failure to prosecute. Ultimately, the firm was prohibited from practice in Maryland and the local attorney was disbarred. Though a promise from a colleague to send you dozens of cases seems like an attractive way to earn money, don't agree to the arrangement unless you're confident that you have the resources to handle the matter.

Too time-consuming. A two-week contract law gig may not impact your new practice all that much. By contrast, a three-month engagement in a different city may give you money quickly, but could also interfere with your ability to get your new firm off the ground. While quick-cash is tempting, you may not want to sacrifice your long-term opportunities at your firm for short-term gains.

III. THE PRACTICE

CHAPTER 10

Dealing With Clients

"My advice to new solos: underestimate your revenue, overestimate your expenses…and make sure you get paid up front." —**Heidi Bolong, solo**

Now that you've started a firm, your livelihood depends upon your ability to serve clients, because you wouldn't have a law firm without them.

Just about any lawyer who passes the bar can provide competent counsel. But client service—that is, the way you treat and relate to clients—is one of the major factors that will distinguish your practice from others, especially the large law firms. However, serving clients does not make them your boss; clients should not control the way you run your practice. And while clients have important rights that you must respect, those rights do not include keeping you at their beck-and-call, ordering you to discount your services or forcing you to take a position that violates ethics rules. New solos must learn how to serve clients without allowing clients to become their master.

This chapter has two sections:

- The first addresses your relationship with clients: how to serve them, how to treat them, how to choose them, and how to deal with the difficult among them. It also deals with (a) your professional obligations under your ethics code, and (b) the personal, intangible ingredients like bedside manner and empathy.
- The second section describes the legal tools necessary to define your relationship with clients; specifically, the retainer or engagement letter, the non-engagement letter, and the termination letter.

The Starting Point: Your Ethics Obligations to Clients

Lawyers often overlook the most basic and essential source of guidance in serving clients: the code of professional responsibility. The ABA Model Rules of Professional Conduct and your jurisdiction's ethics rules spell out your basic obligations to clients, which include…

- Providing competent counsel and zealous representation
- Guarding client confidences
- Exercising independent judgment
- Charging reasonable rates

Chances are you haven't cracked open your state code since you studied for the bar exam. If so, take time to re-read it. The rules and accompanying commentary will give you sound, practical advice on serving clients. And now that you're actually dealing directly with clients, the words of the code should carry real meaning. Not only do ethics rules guide you in serving clients, they also shield you from unreasonable client demands. Example: an overbearing client tries to pressure you to mount a frivolous defense that you know will undermine his credibility before the court, or to contact and negotiate with a party whom you know is represented by counsel. Your response must be unequivocal: your state ethics code precludes you from taking the requested action, and if the client persists that you will have no choice but to withdraw to avoid ethics violations. In most cases, once you invoke your professional responsibility, even the bossiest of clients will back off. If they don't, you have reason to terminate them.

Client bill of rights. Some states, including New York, Illinois and Florida, adopt a Client Bill of Rights that attorneys must incorporate the client bill of rights in their retainer agreement or display in their office. The document spells out what clients are entitled to expect from their relationship with you. Example: New York's Statement of Client Rights covers a range of duties that you owe clients, ranging from confidentiality and undivided loyalty to such nitty-gritty details as prompt return of phone calls and sending copies of papers. Even when not required by the bar, many lawyers choose to develop their own Client Bill of Rights. Putting your commitment to client service in writing demonstrates that you take it seriously, and this will go a long way to ease the distrust many clients have for lawyers as a result of their past experience or horror stories from friends.

New York Statement of Client Rights. A. Section 1210.1 of the Joint Rules of the Appellate Division (22NYCRR§1210.1), at www.courts.state.ny.us/litigants/clientsrights.shtml.

1. You are entitled to be treated with courtesy and consideration at all times by your lawyer and the other lawyers and personnel in your lawyer's office.
2. You are entitled to an attorney capable of handling your legal matter competently and diligently, in accordance with the highest standards of the profession. If you are not satisfied with how your matter is being handled, you have the right to withdraw from the attorney-client relationship at any time (court approval may be required in some matters and your attorney may have a claim against you for the value of services rendered to you up to the point of discharge).
3. You are entitled to your lawyer's independent professional judgment and undivided loyalty uncompromised by conflicts of interest.
4. You are entitled to be charged a reasonable fee and to have your lawyer explain at the outset how the fee will be computed and the manner and frequency of billing. You are entitled to request and receive a written itemized bill from your attorney at reasonable intervals. You may refuse to enter into any fee arrangement that you find unsatisfactory. In the event of a fee dispute, you may have the right to seek arbitration; your attorney will provide you with the necessary information regarding arbitration in the event of a fee dispute, or upon your request.
5. You are entitled to have your questions and concerns addressed in a prompt manner and to have your telephone calls returned promptly.

6. You are entitled to be kept informed as to the status of your matter and to request and receive copies of papers. You are entitled to sufficient information to allow you to participate meaningfully in the development of your matter.

7. You are entitled to have your legitimate objectives respected by your attorney, including whether or not to settle your matter (court approval of a settlement is required in some matters).

8. You have the right to privacy in your dealings with your lawyer and to have your secrets and confidences preserved to the extent permitted by law.

9. You are entitled to have your attorney conduct himself or herself ethically in accordance with the Code of Professional Responsibility.

10. You may not be refused representation on the basis of race, creed, color, religion, sex, sexual orientation, age, national origin or disability.

YOUR FIRST CLIENT MEETING

Q: What sort of information should I get from the client at our first meeting?
A: First, assure clients that the attorney-client privilege applies, even if they have not formally retained you. Clients, particularly those who are less educated or involved in such sensitive matters as domestic violence or bankruptcy often need reassurance before divulging any personal information. In the course of the meeting, collect as much contact information as possible, including current mail and e-mail addresses, and home, work and cellphone numbers. Ask the client to specify the preferred point of contact. You also want to gather information on the names of other relevant parties in the case so you can run a conflicts check. Where a business client is involved, ask for information about subsidiary, parent, and affiliate companies to rule out any conflicts. As for substantive information, what you need depends primarily on the types of cases your handling. Go to www.MyShingle.com to see a sample of intake forms.

Q: A prospective client wants me to assist with a litigation matter in federal court. I've never appeared in federal court before. Do I tell the client it's my first time?
A: As a general rule, you should avoid telling prospective clients that you've never handled a particular matter if you believe that you can competently handle it. You may think that you're merely being honest in admitting to clients that you're a first-timer, but clients will view your disclosure as an explanation for potentially inadequate performance, and will immediately lose confidence in your abilities. Of course, where a client asks point-blank whether you've appeared in federal court, you must answer honestly...but not without a little damage control. Explain that you've gained more litigation in state court than many federal court practitioners, and that it is common for experienced litigators to practice in new courts all the time.

Beyond the Professional Code: Building a Client-Centered Practice

Client service involves more than honoring your professional responsibilities. It's about taking the time to look at a case from your client's perspective, and asking what issues matter most to your client. In this way you distinguish yourself from competition. For example:

- How does the legal matter you're handling fit in with the client's overall business strategy or personal goals?

- How is the case affecting your client personally?
- What does your client think about the service you've provided?

Whatever you call this aspect of client service—hospitality, bedside matter, client-centered practice—these skills will set you apart, and leave a lasting impression long after your case has concluded.

In a client-centered practice, you try to see a case from the perspective of what's most important to the client. *What matters most is not the way the law works, but how a case affects the client or their business.* Understanding this may inform your recommendations or change your strategy. For example, you may believe that as a legal matter, your client has a strong case, but your client prefers to negotiate a settlement to avoid adverse publicity. So, rather than recommend going to trial, you change strategy and negotiate the best deal for your client. Other times, how you communicate with clients is a test of your client-centeredness.

Consider these two approaches—not client-centric and client-centric—to dealing with a divorce client who has just learned about a spouse's affair. As described by Oklahoma Bar Practice Management expert Jim Calloway, the client is likely to be angry and emotional, and may want revenge or to expose the wrongdoing as a primary goal of the case. The client also may have been told by well-meaning, but misinformed, acquaintances that the affair will have a significant impact on their divorce proceeding in the client's favor. You know that courts used to punish parties for adulterous relationships, but that it isn't as true today. But how would you tell your client that the judge won't consider the affair unless it affects the family finances or a child's well-being?

- In the non-client-centric approach, you tell the client: *The judge won't care about the affair. Affairs don't really matter any more in the eyes of the law. They are so frequent these days that he or she will just disregard it. You seem very upset and may need to speak to a counselor. I'm not a counselor; I'm just your lawyer.*
- In the client-centric approach, you tell the client: *I really do understand your pain and anger at your spouse. There's nothing more painful than having a family member lie to you or deceive you. But, there is also nothing any of us can do to undo what has already happened. Your spouse may even regret what was done and feel guilty about it. The court will examine all of the evidence of what has happened previously in your marriage, but when the court reaches a decision it will be looking forward to the future. So, the court might consider the affair when it tells your spouse not to have any overnight visitors of the opposite sex when the children are around. But the court also might order you to abide by those same standards, even though you have done nothing like that in the past. That's because the court is going to be more concerned about the future well being of the children and the impact of certain situations on them than it is concerned about the social life of their parents.*

The first approach brushes aside the adultery issue, the one issue that matters most to the client. The second approach acknowledges the client's feelings about the adultery, but focuses on the more important goal of acting in the best interest of the children.

You may think that so long as you serve clients competently, that bedside manner doesn't matter. But the medical profession, which has examined the relationship between bedside manner and client satisfaction, concluded otherwise. Studies consistently show that patients choose and judge physicians on the basis of good bedside manner, which includes honesty, compassion, and respect, rather than technical skill. Good bedside manner can increase a doctor's success rate because patients who like and trust their doctors more readily follow their treatment instructions. Most importantly, good bedside manner can increase a doctor's success rate because patients who like and trust their doctors more readily follow their treatment instructions. Most importantly, good bedside manner shields doctors from malpractice actions; patients are less likely to sue doctors they like. Lawyers can enjoy the same benefits by developing a good bedside manner.

Below are six ways to make that happen:

Listen well. We often treat clients more like a law school issue-spotting exam than as human beings with a story to tell. A new client comes into the office, and we reach for a legal pad (or pull out the laptop). Instead of sitting back and listening to the client's story, we toss out questions to figure out whether the client has a case. Even though clients want us to fix their problems, it's just as important that someone hears them out. And when we listen to clients, we satisfy their need to be heard. Moreover, when we *really* listen, we get a better sense of what's important to the client and can tailor the appropriate strategy. When you meet new clients, start with an open-ended question: *so, what is it that brought you to my office?* If they wonder why you're not taking notes, explain that you prefer to listen to the full story first before asking questions.

Explain your reasoning. When clients don't understand why a lawyer takes a particular course of action, they grow suspicious. Consider a simple case where you've agreed to your opposing counsel's request for an extension of time. Many clients will perceive your consent as "rolling over," or compromising your position. From your perspective, though, agreeing to an extension of time reflects professional courtesy and the reality that the judge will probably grant the request even if you object. Most lawyers won't explain a decision to grant an extension of time because they believe, correctly, that they have the final say over procedural matters. Still, having the final say does not excuse lawyers from explaining their reasoning to the client. Letting a client know why you're taking a certain action may be annoying or inconvenient, but it demonstrates that you're acting in their best interest. Moreover, explaining your decisions educates and empowers them.

Here are two sample telephone conversations to demonstrate the benefits of a simple explanation:

Situation 1:

Lawyer—*I need to let you know that our summary judgment response is now due on October 1st. The defendant's attorney called me to get a three-week extension for his filing* *because he has two cases going to trial and he needs the extra time.*

Client—*Why did you agree to a new date? I've been waiting months and months for this case to even get to summary judgment. Their filing was due September 1st. Besides, we would have an advantage if the lawyer doesn't have time to do a good job.*

Lawyer—*Look, that's just how things are done. As your lawyer, this kind of decision is my call and besides, three extra weeks won't make much difference.*

Client—*Yeah, but I've been waiting for over a year to get this far. I need to get my money. And giving the other side more time means that he will file a better brief. Plus, that other lawyer is a jerk, he doesn't even deserve more time. Whose side are you on anyway?*

Situation 2:

Lawyer—*I thought that I should let you know that the Defendant's attorney called to ask for a three-week extension to file his motion for summary judgment, and I believe that the best course of action is to agree to the request. I realize that we've been waiting a long, long time to get to this phase, but opposing counsel has two trials before the motion is due, and I'm fairly sure the judge will grant his motion even if I object.*

Client—*Yeah, but there's been so much delay already. And why should we give the lawyer more time to file a brief? Won't that help their case? Plus, he doesn't deserve an extension, he was so rude at depositions.*

Lawyer—*I realize the case has taken a long time, and I don't like the delay any more than you do. But the major problem has been that the judge has been very slow to make rulings on some of the issues. And as you know, our case is really complicated, which also explains why the case has taken this long. You have to remember that opposing counsel hasn't asked for any extensions until this one. So because of his past record, along with the size of this case and his schedule conflicts, I'm sure that this judge will grant his request. If I object, I'm going to look unreasonable, and I don't want to jeopardize our good will with the judge on something like this. Also, I realize that you thought the Defendant's lawyer seemed rude at depositions and, personally, I was not a fan of his approach either. But he did not do anything improper. That's just his personality, and personality does not provide a good enough reason to object to his request.*

Client—*Well, OK, now I understand your decision. You're right, it does make sense to just grant the extension. Thanks for taking the time to explain all of that.*

In both situations, the lawyer's decision to agree to the extension is perfectly appropriate. But in the first case, the lawyer does not consult with the client, and then pulls rank rather than explaining his actions. When the client hangs up the phone, he's suspicious of the lawyer's motives. In the second conversation, the client remains confident with the lawyer and also, is grateful because the lawyer took the time to explain the decision.

Don't 'nickel and dime' your clients. Good bedside manners encourage clients to call their lawyers with a problem or information about their case. Yet nothing discourages communication more than charging clients for short phone calls or e-mails. When clients receive a bill with a $100 in charges for two 10-minute phone calls (e.g., at $250/hour, .2/hour or 12 minutes = $50), they'll avoid calling you so they don't run up their bill. Some lawyers simply write off short phone calls or charge a higher hourly rate to recover the costs of short phone calls without adding a direct charge to the client's bill.

Return calls and e-mails promptly. Many times, you may not want to speak with clients or you simply have nothing new to tell them. Don't ever avoid returning phone calls. More than anything, ignoring phone calls angers clients, making them more likely to turn on you if there's an adverse outcome in the case. If you don't feel up to speaking directly with a client.—particularly a problem client—send an e-mail to schedule another time for a phone call. Of course, some clients go overboard, calling several times a week. Even here, don't evade the calls that will heighten the client's persistence. Instead, talk to the client and assure that you will call whenever a new development arises. Or, if you do not expect changes for some time, invite the client to call you once a month for a brief status update. Beyond that, explain to the client that frequent calls will not move the case any faster. If they persist, you can try charging for the calls and see if that deters them or—if you have a law clerk or secretary—have them deal with the client. If these measures don't work and the client's calls begin to impact your productivity, you may need to think about dropping the client.

Show interest in your clients. Simple courtesies go a long way to building relationships with clients. When your clients call, ask how they're doing; it goes to bedside manner. If you know that your clients have a special pastime, ask them about that. If you represent a company, show an interest in its history, and its business and mission. Where a case has been particularly stressful for a client, ask how he or she is holding up. Your client may not say much, but these kinds of questions reinforce that you view him as a human being rather than a case file. Also, empathize with your client when the case isn't going your way. If you receive a disturbing ruling or motion, why not share that you're also disappointed with the outcome, or that you believe it's an incorrect result. Expressing your opinion on the outcome of the case lets clients know that you're involved not just for the fee, but because you truly believe that your client has the stronger position.

Say thanks. Most of us expect our clients to express gratitude for our terrific service. *The truth is, we owe our clients our thanks.* For us, showing up for court on time (and properly attired) and rehearsing witness testimony for hours are routine. But legal matters are huge burdens on our clients' day-to-day lives. They usually have to take time off from work or arrange for child care to prepare for hearings or attend depositions, and, in some instances, they must buy new clothes to wear to court. They put up with last-minute cancellations and tardy judges. They disclose their life histories to us (near strangers), and detail the embarrassing or disappointing events about the nasty employer or the soon-to-be ex-spouse that brought them to our offices. Many cut back on other expenses or make sacrifices to pay our fees. So, take the time to thank your clients for their cooperation, and let them know how their efforts make you more effective.

YOUR CLIENT IS NOT YOUR CUSTOMER

Many law practice consultants suggest that lawyers adopt the same customer-friendly practices as used by Starbucks, Zappos, or the Ritz-Carlton (see *What Zappos Can Teach Lawyers* at www.zenlegalnetworking.com/2011/02/articles/legal-marketing/lawyers-what-can-we-learn-from-zappos/). While useful as inspiration, these analogies only go so far. In my opinion, clients are very *different* from customers:

Responsiveness isn't optional. Businesses aren't required to provide a minimum level of customer service. Moreover, some businesses build poor service into their business model, offering less customer service in exchange for bargain prices. *Lawyers don't have this option.* Ethics rules mandate a minimum level of client service irrespective of price, and that includes courteous treatment and promptly returned phone calls. Bottom line: a business that treats customers poorly won't be penalized or shut down by regulators, but a law firm that fails to meet its professional obligations to clients will.

Caveat emptor doesn't apply. Customers are expected to look out for their own best interest in transactions with businesses. Thus, a business owner can drive a hard bargain with customers, but lawyers can't. Lawyers are governed by bar rules in setting fees (which must be reasonable), and further, they owe a fiduciary obligation to clients, which means they must keep clients' interests in mind when entering into the attorney-client relationship.

The customer is always right; the client isn't. Though lawyers must consider a client's views when making decisions, sometimes a client may demand that a lawyer take an unethical or a plainly un-winnable position. In these situations, a lawyer can't accede to the client's demands, but must withdraw.

Empowering and Involving Clients

Many lawyers are inclined to treat dismissively those clients who want to "play lawyer". But it's a fact that clients are more educated now, and have greater access to law blogs and legal research tools. They may already understand a number of issues in their case, and may insist on detail explanations from their lawyer.

Increasingly, such clients will be the norm, and lawyers must learn to accept it. In fact, educated clients can play an active role in their cases; it might even change the outcome for the better. Consider the case of Sheila Kahanek, who in 2001 was one of five Enron executives indicted for a scandal that was discovered around the time of Enron's collapse. Of the five, only Kahanek was acquitted, in part because of the active role she played in her defense. Kahanek organized and analyzed the thousands of documents designated as evidence by the prosecution, and shared valuable insights about the inner workings of Enron that helped her lawyers at trial. According to her attorney, Dan Codgell, *"There's no way I would have won the trial without Sheila working her ass off. She literally had this trial indexed, highlighted, organized...she knows every document in the case—cold."* Not every client will be as sophisticated or motivated (then again, not every case was as complicated as Enron).

Here are some tips for making clients active participants in their case, no matter the size or type of client:

Write a synopsis. Before clients come in for a consultation (particularly, where you offer a free consultation), ask clients to prepare a brief summary or time-line of the events leading up to their case. (Don't have clients send the summary in advance because they may get the impression that you will start working on the matter when, in fact, you have not yet agreed to represent them.) You can even prepare simple intake sheet that will give you some of the facts needed to help you evaluate the case. Skim over the case summary when the client arrives. The case summary/intake exercise forces clients to focus on the facts of the case and helps them understand that any legal matter—from a lawsuit to preparation of an estate plan or corporate documents—requires their active involvement. More importantly, a survey helps identify potentially problematic clients who won't cooperate or can't follow instructions. Think about it; if clients are unwilling to invest a half-hour to fill out an intake form, are they going to spend the time required to gather documents or prepare for depositions?

Set up a client folder or online portal. When clients leave the office after the first meeting, include copies of any materials…an intake form, a retainer agreement and (if you're lucky), a copy of the client's check. Instruct the client to use the folder to file any information that you send to them and to bring it to all subsequent meetings and court proceedings. For other clients, put the materials on a firm-branded flashdrive, or upload the documents to a secure, online portal to which the client has password-protected access. These systems make clients feel important because you trust them enough to give them responsibility. And of course, these systems save you time by cutting down on client requests for documents or status updates.

Help your clients know what to expect. With clogged dockets and understaffed agencies, most proceedings just plod along, often taking six months to several years to resolve. Often, there's little that you can do to expedite the process except to make sure that you adhere to all of your deadlines. But most clients (especially business people accustomed to closing deals in a matter of hours) simply don't realize how slowly grind the wheels of justice. Frustrated, they may blame you for the delays. That's why you should take the time at the beginning of case to describe to your clients how a particular proceeding will work. You might prepare a timeline, or a roadmap, or a client plan that identifies each phase of the proceeding. Explaining the process lowers clients' expectations about the time involved, which will minimize their frustration. Clients also worry that a long process will cost more. Assure them that a lengthy process does not necessarily translate into excessive legal fees. Many times, cases go into dormancy for periods of three months or more while you await a ruling, during which time the client won't incur additional charges.

Encourage clients to gather information on the case. As a lawyer, you're the expert on the law in each case, but your clients are the source of facts. So use your clients as a tour guide to lead you to facts that will help you build a strong case. What kinds of facts can clients provide? Here are some ideas:

- Clients can help put a case into context by describing the customs and practice in their particular industry, or a company's process for retaining documents or training employees, or a spouse's Internet habits. Understanding the context of the case can help you prepare discovery requests or assess the potential strength of your clients' arguments or settlement position.

- Clients can use their inside knowledge to identify potentially helpful witnesses or ferret out intelligence from friendly insiders. (Bear in mind, however, that once a case is in suit, some jurisdictions prohibit represented parties from communicating directly and transmitting the information to their lawyers.) Many lawyers overlook their clients as a resource, assuming that their clients will either convey irrelevant information or, worse, lie or exaggerate. When possible, verify a client's description through another source. But don't rule out clients as a source of information unless and until they give you reason to distrust them.

- You don't have to send clients a copy of every minor filing before it leaves your office, but do let clients review drafts of important documents, especially contracts, summary judgment motions, or responses in administrative proceedings. At a minimum, clients may catch factual errors that are either inadvertent or result from your misunderstanding of what the client originally told you. And you'd be surprised: some clients may even have decent suggestions about a potential strategy or contract provision, or have important feedback on points that deserve more (or less) emphasis. Too many lawyers let ego keep them from showing clients their work product, because they don't want to be challenged or corrected, or because they're afraid of looking as if they are less than omniscient. But clients will appreciate that you've solicited their input, and they'll respect you even more when you show respect for their ideas. Plus, it never hurts to have a second set of eyes review a document.

Dealing With Difficult Clients

The clients from hell ... that assorted collection ranging from the high-maintenance and nutty to the downright nasty and insulting. They call too much; they bounce checks; they denigrate lawyers (and by association, you); they ignore your advice to their detriment; they refuse to pay bills; and they repeatedly threaten to grieve you. As one management expert describes: Your worst clients are destroying your business. They demand 80 percent of your time and energy, and produce only 20 percent of your profit. Sooner or later (hopefully, sooner) you will reach a point where you must fire these clients lest they ruin your practice or even your life.

Here are some tips for dealing with difficult clients:

Stay cool. Dealing with a troublesome client is a rite of passage. You're not a bonafide solo practitioner until you can share at least one war story about an outrageously horrible client (for several good examples, see *In Their Own Words* at the end of this chapter).

Share your misery. You may think your client's antics are unique, but at least one of your colleagues has dealt with similar behavior…or worse. Seek out other solos for advice on how to deal with your troublesome client. But even if they don't have any productive ideas, the mere sharing of your misery will help put the situation in perspective and release some stress.

Put everything in writing. There's always a chance a problem client may eventually file a grievance against you. So, as much as you may want to avoid dealing with this client, it's important all communications with them are put into writing. Here is where e-mail can make a difference. When the problem client calls, respond by e-mail. This way you have a written record of your communications, and it rebuts any potential claims that you were not sufficiently responsive.

Raise your rates. Let the relationship run its course by finishing up any remaining work and avoiding new matters. When you complete the final piece of work, send a termination letter (details later in this chapter) along with a final invoice, stating that your representation has ended. If the client calls to retain you later, politely explain that you are not accepting new matters. Or, raise your rates significantly if you think that will make your dealings with the client any more palatable. If the client balks, you're rid of him; if he agrees, well, at least you'll earn more for your troubles.

Withdrawal in active matters. When clients act up during a matter that promises to last awhile, take stronger steps to fire the client. *Author's note*: I believe you should broach the topic of withdrawal through personal communication, such as a phone call or office visit (followed up by written confirmation) unless your relationship has deteriorated so badly that you cannot engage in a civil conversation or you fear for your personal safety. But even when you advise your client by letter of your intent to withdraw, invite the client to call with questions. Otherwise, they may complain to the bar that you suddenly pulled out of the case without any discussion.

Some additional thoughts:

Let them down easy. Explain that you cannot provide the level of service that the client deserves or that you don't feel that your style fits your client's needs.

Be candid about payment. If you withdraw for nonpayment, remind the client that, like any professional service provider, you're entitled to payment when you render service. If you're dealing with clients who have the means to pay but choose not to, no further discussion is warranted; you're better off rid of them. As for the client who truly can't afford to pay you, explore payment by credit card, family loan, or having the client continue the case pro se. You might also suggest the client contact a bar referral service, a less expensive attorney, or refer them to pro bono or legal aid clinics. Stand firm in your decision to withdraw. You may feel sorry for clients who lack resources, but if you routinely write off fees, you'll find yourself just as impoverished as your clients.

Cite your retainer agreement. Where a client lies about a material aspect of a case or engages in conduct hurting his case and wasting your time, remind the client of his obligations under your retainer agreement. Stress that the retainer agreement is a two-way street, and that you can't effectively serve a client who ignores your advice. Realize that sometimes you may not find relief from an overbearing client. When a case is a few months from trial and your client won't let you pull out, the court probably won't grant a withdrawal either. Moreover, in some jurisdictions, particularly criminal cases, courts hold little sympathy for lawyers who haven't collected enough money up front from the client to carry them through the duration of the case. In a worst case scenario, ride out a difficult client as best you can. And vow to choose more carefully next time.

Send a termination letter and files. Once you withdraw from representing a client, send a short, polite letter acknowledging the end of your representation. For ongoing matters where the client will need to retain new counsel, include a copy of the client's file. *Note:* see a sample at the end of this chapter.

Don't get cynical. Don't let the client from hell sour your experience of solo practice. For every problem client, you will find dozens of model clients who pay their bills on time (with checks that don't bounce!), express gratitude for your service, refer you cases, treat you to fancy lunches, and even send you gifts at holiday time. Serving clients like these makes solo practice a rewarding experience, one you should not sacrifice because of a few bad apples.

Choosing Clients With Care: Due Diligence & Deal-Breakers

There's no foolproof method to avoiding clients from hell. But by choosing carefully and putting measures in place, you can minimize your risk of winding up with them. Some experts advise that you walk away from these clients entirely. Good advice if you have multiple clients beating down your door. But you don't usually have the luxury of turning away cases when you're starting out.

In the following section, I've outlined various risk-factors, and identified whether some clients only require additional "due diligence", or if they are "deal breakers":

Prior representation (due diligence). Has the client been represented by other attorneys in this matter? Personality differences or true lawyer incompetence can explain one unsuccessful attorney-client relationship. But rather than reject a client who has already worked with one attorney, engage in due diligence; review the files or speak with the previous attorney to assess what went wrong the first time around.

Serial relationships (deal-breaker). Serial changes in representation indicate one of two things: a chronically dissatisfied client who in time will probably complain about your service, or a client who lacks the ability to pay the bills. Neither trait makes for a desirable client. In short, several prior unsuccessful dealings with lawyers is a deal-breaker.

Client with nothing to lose (due diligence). The most unreasonable clients are those with a contingency matter in which they don't pay any fees up-front. They're playing with other people's money, in this case yours (or if not your money, your time). Consequently, contingency clients often feel that they have nothing to lose by turning down an acceptable settlement or pushing for risky and more costly strategies. If you're handling contingency matters, you can't avoid non-paying clients. But you can mitigate the likelihood of unreasonable conduct by forcing non-paying clients to take a stake in their case. You can have these clients pay the filing fee and cost of serving a complaint or ask them help out on the case, for example, by collecting documents or organizing their case file. This investment might only amount to a few hundred dollars or a couple of hours of time, but at least the client will have something at risk.

Selective listener (due diligence). Pay close attention to any questions or comments that a prospective client raises during the initial consultation. Let's say that you've told Selective Listener that most cases of his type settle for $5,000, but you're aware of one case in another jurisdiction that settled for $15,000. If Selective Listener says, *So, you're pretty sure I can get at least $15,000?*, you need to undertake some due diligence. If you plan to accept this client, you must meticulously document all oral communications and provide a detailed, written budget for the case (otherwise, Selective Listener will claim that he thought you said the matter would take five hours not

25 hours). By planning ahead, you can avoid misunderstandings.

Work for an interest in the case (due diligence). Sometimes a client will offer you an interest in their company in exchange for representing them at no charge. Though many experts classify this arrangement as a deal-breaker, you might discover an opportunity if you apply due diligence. Find out more about the company. Is it an industry leader in an up-and-coming field? Have you seen write-ups about the company online or in your local business journals? If so, you might consider handling a small piece of work; perhaps incorporation or a short administrative filing to get your foot in the door of a potentially lucrative market. You could just as easily assume that you will never see any return from this type of arrangement. Check your local disciplinary rules to ensure that rendering legal service in exchange for stock options or an equity interest in a company does not conflict with any ethics rules governing business transactions with a client. *Author's note*: my recommendation is to forego a work-for-equity arrangement in situations where a company requires extensive work—such as arranging a financing or preparing a legal opinion letter—where you face significant liability exposure. *Definitely* a deal-breaker.

Client who balks about fees (due diligence). Conventional wisdom suggests that you reject clients who haggle over fees because they'll always balk about paying bills. The trouble is, many sources—including some bar associations, and some legal self-help books—advise clients to negotiate fees with attorneys. Be warned: if you automatically reject everyone looking to bargain, you may find yourself without clients. With some due diligence, however, you may salvage some hagglers without compromising your ability to get paid. For example, try to get a sense of what the client can afford and propose a strategy within that budget. Or adopt some of the alternate billing structures discussed in the next section. Most important, accept a retainer that's large enough to fairly compensate you for your work even if you never see another dime from the client. If the client won't pay the retainer, that's your deal-breaker.

Clients with unreasonable expectations (deal-breaker). Fortunately, many clients with an axe to grind (an axe grinder) can't afford to hire an attorney, making them deal-breakers from the start. But even when Axe Grinders can afford to pay, think long and hard before taking them on. Clients willing to spend money to extract revenge or make a point often possess uncompromising, "blame the world" personalities. If you don't achieve the results they want, Axe Grinders can afford to sue you for a full refund or even malpractice. Bottom line: when well-off clients have no other goal but a bone to pick or a score to settle, it's a deal-breaker.

Gut reaction (deal-breaker). When you meet a client for the first time, you will form quick, visceral impressions based on the client's appearance and conduct:

- Is the client dressed like a slob or neatly attired? Slovenly dress may be typical attire for your client's work, or it could reflect a lack of respect for lawyers or the legal process.
- Does the client look you in the eye or stare up at the ceiling or down at their shoes? Lack of eye contact might be shyness or lack of confidence…or avoidance or lack of candor.

- Does the client tell you only his/her side of the story with a running narrative of how they were wronged by each and every action? Or do they try to provide you with a fact-based account? A self-absorbed client obsessed with how every event impacted them may have more difficulty accepting your advice than the client who can examine their case more objectively.
- If the client brings a spouse or family remember, does she treat him with respect or in an insulting, deprecating manner? How clients treat family members can shed light on how they may interact with you.

These seemingly insignificant factors may add up to nothing ... or they might be subtle clues that reveal insight into the client. Don't disregard your initial impressions or gut reaction. If the client makes sexual innuendos or asks you to engage in illegal or shady conduct…or simply gives you the creeps…that's a deal-breaker. Many lawyers who wind up with the client from hell say later that they always felt that there was something "off" about the client but they ignored their first impression.

Should I Represent a Client With a Matter Outside My Area of Expertise?

Most ethics codes prohibit lawyers from accepting matters that they are not competent to handle. But how do you achieve competence in new areas if you're precluded from handling them for lack of expertise? A classic Catch-22. Below are a series of questions to consider before taking a case where you don't have prior experience:

Do you have any related experience? The skills you learn in one field transfer to another practice area. If you've only handled litigation matters in state court, you can certainly manage federal court litigation because many of the skills and processes are similar. If you've only handled corporate transactional work, you may have trouble taking on a complicated custody matter unless you obtain a little more experience in family law.

Can you readily learn the skills you need? Many bar associations publish practice guides and hold frequent CLE's on basic matters like will and trust preparation, bankruptcy or criminal defense. Materials are available at reasonable prices. If a client with a simple bankruptcy matter comes into your office, you can figure out what to do by signing up for a crash CLE class or purchasing a guide to practicing bankruptcy law. By contrast, if you choose to represent a client in a complicated and obscure regulatory matter, you may need more time to master the subject matter, and you won't find as many inexpensive resources available to guide you.

Can you find a partner or second chair? Let's say you attract a lucrative matter that you've never handled, such as a serious medical malpractice action, or an employment discrimination case. You should not handle the case on your own, if only because you will face stratospheric malpractice liability if you make a mistake. But you don't have to refer the case out if it interests you. See if you can find an attorney to come on board as a partner or mentor, and work the case in exchange for a portion of the fee. In this way, you have an opportunity to learn more about a new practice area and perhaps even get paid for it. Note: unless the case really has high, monetary potential, most attorneys won't have much incentive to participate in this kind of arrangement.

Is the case worthwhile financially? When you take a case outside of your expertise, you may face a steep learning curve and not be able to charge the client for the extra hours needed to come up to speed on applicable law. Consider whether the benefit of learning a new area of law is worth the trade-off of reduced fees, or whether you are better off referring the case to an attorney with more experience in that field.

What is your malpractice exposure? When you take a case outside of your practice area, consider your potential malpractice exposure. A case outside your area of expertise that doesn't involve much money poses little risk, but a case with significant dollars at stake may open you up to a serious malpractice claim.

CHECKING FOR CONFLICTS

Lawyers owe a duty of undivided loyalty to their clients, and are prohibited from accepting a matter where this obligation may be impaired by your relationships with other clients or personal interests. Failure to avoid conflicts entirely, or at a minimum, to seek informed consent from clients to waive a conflict, can result not just in a grievance, but a legal malpractice claim.

Below are some tips on dealing with conflicts:

When do I check for conflicts? There are three trigger points for checking conflicts: initially (and most generally) when the client first calls your office. Again, following the initial meeting, when you have more information. And finally, every time another party enters the case. And if you're hiring a lawyer, or even a contract attorney, you will want to determine whether they have represented parties who could give rise to a conflict with one of your clients. Read the Canadian Bar Association's 2010 *Procedures for Conflicts Checks* (www.cba.org/CBA/PracticeLink/cs/conflicts.aspx).

Who do I check for conflicts? You need to check whether your clients' interests conflict with those of other clients you represent. In addition to potential clients, you need to check adverse parties. If corporate entities are involved, you may need to run conflicts checks not for the entity itself, but potentially for members, investors, or shareholders. For example, if your client wants to sue ABC LLC, and it turns out that your best friend from high school has invested millions in the company, you would have a conflict even though you're suing the LLC and not your friend.

How do I check a conflict? You really need some computerized system in place for checking conflicts; relying on memory isn't satisfactory. Many computerized law practice management systems have a built-in conflicts check system, and there are inexpensive tools like RTG Software (www.rtgsoftware.com/conf/conflicts.htm) that cost $95. Even running searches through your contacts is better than nothing.

What do I do if I find a conflict? When a conflict is direct and goes to the heart of the representation—such as representing a husband and a wife in a contested divorce—you must decline the case. Similarly, if there's no immediate conflict, but the likelihood of conflict is high, you should also turn both matters down, or refer one of the clients to another lawyer. Future conflicts are common with co-defendants in criminal matters, or a driver and passenger in a vehicle hit by a drunk driver. Though both parties may be on the same page at the outset (denying the charges, or suing the drunk driver), conflicts can develop later if a prosecutor offers a better deal to one defendant or another, or the driver is accused of contributory negligence in an accident. Where the potential for conflict is remote, or less severe, a firm may choose to represent both parties provided that it discloses the conflict and obtains informed consent. Informed consent requires both a written explanation of the conflict and potential impact on clients, and a written signature confirming that the conflict was explained. See, Karen Painter Randall and Andrew Sayles' *Informed Consent* *and Legal Malpractice* (DIR, May 2009). For an example of sample waiver language, go to http://eric_goldman.tripod.com/ethics/dualrepwaiver.htm.

What about unanticipated conflicts? Sometimes, it's impossible to predict that a conflict will arise, particularly when firms represent large parties in complicated litigation matters. For that reason, many lawyers include an "advance conflicts waiver" clause in their retainer agreement. A typical advance waiver paragraph might read something like this: *"The Client agrees that, notwithstanding our representation of the Client in general corporate matters we may, now or in the future, without seeking or obtaining your further consent, represent other persons, whether or not they are now clients of our law firm, in other matters, including litigation, where those other persons are adverse to the Client. The Client further agrees not to seek disqualification of our law firm should the firm sue the Client in the future."* The Boston-based firm of Goulston&Storrs has a detailed essay on this topic. Go to www.goulstonstorrs.com/NewsEvents/PublicationsMentions?find=29808).

Should you include an advance conflicts waiver? Advance conflicts waivers are far more likely to withstand scrutiny with respect to sophisticated clients who have many choices for representation. At the same time, many clients are reluctant to sign advance waivers, which may be reason enough to exclude this type of clause. Be prepared to provide consumer clients and small businesses far more explanation about a future conflicts waiver if it is to withstand scrutiny if later challenged. Consult bar rules and bar counsel for additional guidance on advance waiver clauses.

Defining the Terms of Client Service:
Retainer, Non-engagement & Termination Letters

Your relationship with clients begins and ends with a written letter. The retainer letter defines the terms of your relationship with your client; the disenagement letter defines the reasons for, and the terms by which you conclude, your relationship; the non-engagement letter declines representation of a client. This section discusses the basic elements for drafting these letters. Note: most state bars have online versions of these letters. You may decide to modify the state forms, but they should include whatever language you need to comply with your state bar requirements.

HANDLING CALLS FROM PROSPECTIVE CLIENTS

Q: I get several calls a week from prospective clients who want legal advice over the phone. Often, they have simple questions; other times, it's a complex problem I can't address without all the facts. But when I tell them that, they think I will help only if the meter is running. I don't want to drive away a potential client. What can I do?

A: Some lawyers have an assistant or service weed out prospective clients who want free advice. Rather than take these calls by phone, you could instruct your assistant or answering service to schedule an appointment for the client.

Develop a system for responding to simple requests that you can easily answer without wasting your valuable time. The best approach is to add to your Web site a Frequently Asked Questions (FAQ) section that explains the basic concepts and procedures in your practice areas. Putting together a FAQ section does require an investment of time, especially if you provide detailed or state-specific information. In the long run, though, a FAQ section saves you time, because you (or whoever answers your phones) can invite callers to consult the FAQs and call back to schedule an appointment if they still can't find the information they need. If you don't want to draft FAQs yourself, you can license content from sites like Nolo.com or assemble materials from various blogs so consumers can easily find information on a topic. For samples, see the Web site for New York lawyer Warren Redlich (www.redlichlaw.com/traffic/faq.html) or the site for Chris Attig, a Texas-based federal employment lawyer (www.attiglawfirm.com/mspb-appeals/mspb-faq).

Just as doctors or auto mechanics cannot diagnose a problem over the phone, you can't be expected to render advice on legal problems without a detailed examination of facts and related documents. Offer to schedule a meeting at your office. If the caller persists in getting a question answered or declines the meeting, wrap up the call quickly. The caller has made it clear that they're only seeking free advice.

The Retainer Agreement

This is the contract that, along with the Rules of Professional Conduct, governs your relationship with your client. A well-drafted engagement letter sets out the specific responsibilities the lawyer undertakes and the client's obligations.

From the bars' perspective, a retainer agreement safeguards clients from unscrupulous attorneys who take advantage of their clients by trying to extract more money midway through a case, or to cheat clients out of the rightful cut of a settlement. Grievance committees and courts stringently enforce written retainer requirements, going so far as to bar lawyers from recovering fees for work performed in the absence of a written retainer. Most lawyers realize that retainer agreements protect clients, but tend to overlook that retainer agreements protect lawyers as well. In fact, no tool (besides malpractice insurance) more effectively immunizes lawyers from overreaching clients, malpractice claims, or fee disputes than a well-formulated retainer agreement.

A well-drafted retainer agreement detailing the services that you will…and will not…provide during the course of representation, can ward off subsequent claims that you failed to undertake a task or meet your professional obligations. Example: in New Jersey, a tight retainer letter making clear that the attorney would not review a previously negotiated Property Settlement Agreement (PSA) that was incorporated by reference in the terms of a divorce, spared a divorce attorney from a malpractice claim when it turned out that the PSA had inaccurately valued the property subject to distribution.

A retainer letter is particularly critical for lawyers offering unbundled legal services (details later in this chapter).

A retainer agreement eliminates any confusion about your right to payment where a client switches to another attorney mid-course or fires you right before the case is settled. Consider a contingency matter in which you don't collect fees until a judgment or settlement is secured. Let's say you spend dozens of hours investigating a case and drafting a settlement demand, only to have your client switch to another lawyer a few weeks before the case ultimately settles. Even though your efforts helped produce the client's settlement award, you may not collect a dime of it in some jurisdictions because you no longer represent the client, and the terms of your retainer no longer apply. You can avoid this result with a well-drafted retainer that obligates your client to compensate you for time spent on a contingency matter (either *quantum meruit*, i.e., based on hours spent, or some pro rata percentage of fees obtained) where the client severs the relationship before an award is recovered.

When you're just starting out without any clients, it's hard to foresee the day you may actually want to get rid of some of them. But as your practice takes off, you'll encounter clients who don't pay their bills, balk at providing vital documents, or hog so much of your time that your service to other clients suffers. Because the day that you need to "fire a client" will come sooner than you think (and it's a rite of passage, so look forward to it!), you might as well prepare yourself for it by drafting some standard terms for your retainer agreement. Specifically, your retainer agreement should contain a section that reserves your right to withdraw where your clients fail to live up to their obligations under the retainer (such as failing to pay bills or cooperate with you). But even where your retainer agreement establishes grounds for withdrawal, the judge or hearing officer must approve your exit from the case in pending matters where you've already entered an appearance. Some judges will honor the terms of your retainer, and will permit withdrawal where permitted by the retainer agreement. Other judges are less sympathetic—particularly when it comes to withdrawal for non-payment—and have refused to allow lawyers to withdraw for non-payment where they failed to collect enough money up front to ensure payment throughout the case.

The well-drafted retainer. Your bar association's Web site may have model engagement letters you might use as a starting point.

Below are some important considerations:

Describe the scope of the work. The introduction of your retainer letter should describe the expected scope of work. First, summarize your understanding of the scope of work based on your discussion with the client. For one-time matters in which you will produce a product—a corporate document, a lease, or report—set out the set of deliverables included. Memorializing the scope of work you were asked to perform will help eliminate any misunderstanding later. The scope of work does not have to be exceptionally detailed, but it should state more than just "accident case" or "incorporation." Some sample language is below:

> *Dear [Client]:*
> *I enjoyed meeting with you, and look forward to handling your case. As we discussed, as a result of a six-month period of unemployment, you are now facing a foreclosure action by ABC bank. I have agreed to represent you in the foreclosure, including negotiation of a loan modification, the preparation of a motion to dismiss, and all other actions that may be needed for resolution of this matter.*

Or, for a retainer that contemplates a deliverable:

> *The Law Firm of John Jones will provide the following under this Agreement:*
>
> *(1) draft and preparation of employee handbook, including up to three rounds of revisions;*
> *(2) draft and preparation of social media policy, including up to three rounds of revisions; and*
> *(3) Two-hour webinar training session on employee handbook and social media policy.*

Sometimes, you may represent a client in an initial matter—perhaps filing several trademarks for one venture—but you anticipate that other similar filings will be required later. Writing new retainer agreements for each new piece of work doesn't make sense; instead, structure the scope of work section in anticipation of future work:

> *As we discussed, I will file three trademark applications for your corporate affiliate, XYZ LLC. Subsequent matters will be handled by an addendum to this Retainer Agreement.*

Now, if an additional matter arises, you can implement it quickly, even via e-mail, as shown:

> *Joe, per our discussion, you have authorized me to file an action against Acme LLC for trademark infringement. This matter is comparable to two other similar suits that I have filed for your company, and accordingly, I have estimated that this matter will cost roughly the same amount, or about [$X]. This matter will be subject to the terms of our original Retainer Agreement of January 10, 2011.Upon receipt of [$x] as a retainer, I will commence work on this matter.*

Explain the different stages of the case. Sometimes, a client retains you for a matter that will continue over a course of months or even years. Detailing the process in your retainer letter lets your client know what's ahead so your invoices don't cause sticker-shock. Also, dividing your representation into separate phases gives you an opportunity to pull out at a natural point if you find that your case is not as strong as you had initially assessed. Finally, clarity about different phases of a proceeding means that you avoid gaps in representation that invariably lead to malpractice claims.

One common situation is where you agree to represent a client in a personal injury or other type of trial matter. The court dismisses the case on summary judgment and you lose at trial; you inform the client of the decision and close out the file. Meanwhile, the client may not recognize that a specific phase of the case has come to an end and assumes you will appeal. By the time you realize that the client expects you to file an appeal, the deadline has passed, and you have a malpractice action or grievance on your hands. Use the retainer to specify at what point your representation ends to protect yourself from this all-too-common outcome in the future.

Here's some sample language from a retainer agreement involving employment claims:

> *I have been retained to assist you with your claims arising out of your wrongful termination by Employer. As you explained during our initial meeting, you believe that your termination resulted from unlawful, racially discriminatory conduct by your Employer. The scope of my representation will include investigating your claims through review of your personnel file and the Employee handbook that you will provide to me, as well as interviews with individuals who you identify as having knowledge of these events. I will also research and identify the various federal and state causes of action which you have*

against these entities, prepare any necessary notices of claim, file a complaint with the EEOC or state human rights organization and/or a complaint in federal district court, and pursue the case to the conclusion of a trial or until a satisfactory settlement has been reached, whichever comes first. I reserve the right to withdraw from the case, and terminate this Retainer Agreement upon the conclusion of the proceedings before the EEOC or state human rights commission.

The scope of work under this Retainer Agreement does not include appeals of adverse, or final decisions. In the event that you receive an adverse decision at the conclusion of a proceeding before the EEOC state human rights commission or at trial…or if the case is dismissed on a Motion to Dismiss or a Motion for Summary Judgment before trial …any subsequent appeals will be handled pursuant to a new Retainer Agreement to be negotiated at that time.

Be especially clear if you offer unbundled services. A growing number of lawyers now offer unbundled service as a less-costly alternative to full-service representation. Unbundling allows clients to purchase discrete services from lawyers, such as researching a legal issue or drafting a pleading rather than a full-service representation. Lawyers offering unbundled practice run the risk of malpractice claims unless they clearly delineate each party's responsibilities. As professionals, lawyers must comply with applicable standards of care in representing clients, which generally means handling all aspects of the case, rather than just select pieces. Unless lawyers clearly state that they will not perform certain tasks, they remain responsible for them and will be liable for malpractice for non-performance. You can avoid this outcome by drafting a retainer provision that describes those tasks that you will perform and those you will not. Also, take the time to explain the limited scope of representation to clients and have them initial these portions of the Retainer Agreement to memorialize their understanding of the arrangement.

A sample provision appears below:

The rules of professional responsibility for the state of _____ allow me to offer unbundled legal services. As we discussed, I propose to draft a complaint for violations of civil rights associated with your termination from your position as an administrative assistant with the State Department of Public Education. I will charge a flat fee of $500 to draft the complaint. I will provide you with an electronic and hard copy of the complaint. My obligations under this agreement are limited to the following: I will draft the complaint described above for filing in the _____ State Superior Court and advise you in writing of the deadline under the applicable statute of limitations by which you must file the complaint. My responsibilities do not include filing the complaint, serving the defendants or any other further involvement in this matter. As we discussed, you will be responsible for filing the complaint at _____ State Superior Court and effecting service on the defendants in the matter. Should you decide to retain me for further work related to this matter, I will draft a supplemental Retainer Agreement.

_____ (client's initials) My lawyer has explained the foregoing provisions to me. I fully *understand and agree that I am responsible for filing the complaint and serving the defendants in this matter.*

For additional information on unbundled legal services, consult your state bar rules and the ABA's Web site (http://apps.americanbar.org/legalservices/delivery/delunbund.html), which contains an extensive collection of articles, forms, and other information on this topic.

Describe your billing methodology. A retainer agreement should describe how you bill for a particular matter (e.g., flat-fee, contingency). Many lawyers include a fee estimate or budget either in the retainer agreement itself or as an addendum. A contingency agreement must make clear that clients do not pay if you do not collect an award, and specify the percentage of fees that you will retain. State whether the client or the attorney will pay costs associated with litigation, such as payment for deposition transcripts and expert witnesses. Some state bars, such as Florida, have explicit language about fees that you must include in your retainer agreement.

Discuss your billing and office policies. Do you charge for phone calls, photocopies, or legal research fees? Do you require an evergreen retainer, i.e., a retainer amount that the client must replenish whenever it reaches a certain minimum level of funds? Will you notify clients when you withdraw funds from a trust account (some bars require attorneys to provide notice)? Can clients call you on Saturdays? Some lawyers communicate their office policies and practices in their retainer agreement; others post their policies on their Web site and reference or attach them as an addendum. Before your practice gets too busy, take the time to draw up a standard Billing and Office Policies section to include in all of your retainer agreements (see Chapter 11).

Discuss the conditions allowing you to withdraw from a case. As described earlier, you can also use a retainer agreement to lay a foundation for letting you out of representation. Below is some sample language that might serve as grounds for withdrawal:

The following events will be grounds for my withdrawal from this case at my discretion following a written Notice of Intent to Withdraw:

- *Failure to pay the agreed upon Retainer Fee or to keep current with payment of case costs as required under the terms of this Agreement;*
- *A misrepresentation about the facts or events in the case, whether intentional or negligent, or an intentional omission or concealment of facts or events, and whether or not the misrepresentation or omission have a material bearing on the case;*
- *A refusal to provide me with documents or other information in your possession that are necessary for the successful prosecution or defense of your claims;*
- *Client conduct such as failure to cooperate or other conduct that makes it unreasonably difficult for me to carry out the representation effectively or efficiently; or*
- *A request that I undertake actions which either violate the law or the [state] Code of Professional Responsibility.*

Consider how you want to handle dispute resolution. Some lawyers include clauses in their agreement requiring disputes with clients to be resolved through arbitration. Most bars allow binding arbitration provisions.

Include 'sunset provisions' in your agreement. Sometimes, clients may receive a retainer letter and sit on it for six months before returning it. By that time, the statute of limitations may have run, or you may be occupied with other matters and can no longer handle the case. Thus, your retainer letter should establish a date by which the provisions will expire due to client inaction. Example:

> *Please return a signed copy of this retainer letter and return it with the agreed upon retainer fee of $5,000 [within 2 weeks of receipt of this letter/by X date]. If I do not receive a signed copy of this letter and the retainer fee by the date specified, I will not commence the work described, and the proposed terms of representation described in this letter are [hereby revoked/no longer valid].*

If you don't hear from the client by the anticipated date (and it's a client that you'd like to represent), contact the client for an explanation. If the client still doesn't comply, as added protection, follow up with a brief non-engagement letter (discussed, infra) to clarify that you are not representing the client because of his failure to abide by the terms of the retainer agreement. If the client responds, you can consider extending the terms of the retainer agreement or negotiating a new arrangement at that time.

Comply with state bar rules. Check your state bar rules to learn if your retainer letter requires certain provisions. Some states may require you to give notice of intent to withdraw from a case in writing; other bars may require you to disclose whether you have legal malpractice insurance; still other states may have specific rules that apply when you ghostwrite pleadings or provide unbundled legal services. Make sure your policies and fee schedules comply with bar rules and applicable state law. For example, where state law limits your recovery in workers compensation matters to 20 percent of an award, make sure that your retainer agreement doesn't give you 30 percent. A court will not allow you to collect the higher fee and in fact, might declare the entire agreement void, and bar you from collecting any payment.

Include a signature line for you and client. For business clients, some lawyers simply state that "payment of the specified fee shall constitute acceptance of the terms of this agreement." It can even be done online…without a hand-written signature. Virginia traffic lawyer Andrew Flusche uses an electronic signature service called Echo-Sign that lets him send a fee agreement via e-mail, and the client can "e-sign" from their browser or smartphone (see http://blog.echosign.com/2009/03/andrew-flusche-esq-esignatures-are-quick-legal-and-easy.html). Other technologies also make electronic signatures possible.

Some retainers are non-refundable; some aren't. The retainer agreement provides how much money a client must pay up front. Sometimes (typically, in flat fee cases), a client must pay the entire fee in full; in others, the client pays a "retainer," an amount to get started and that is replenished—as needed—as the case progresses.

The question is, can you state in the retainer that these advance payments are non-refundable? Increasingly, many (but not all) jurisdictions restrict a lawyer's ability to make advance payments non-refundable. They reason that if a lawyer accepts $5,000 for a divorce case and the client decides to return to their spouse two weeks later, the fee is unreasonable because work wasn't performed. At the same time, these jurisdictions *will* allow a non-refundable fee where the retainer fee is not being paid to compensate a lawyer for availability, but rather as a deposit or "advance" payment for services to be rendered in the future. Example: a client wants to retain Mr. Best-Lawyer-in-Town because he believes he may be indicted. Criminal charges haven't yet been filed, though, and there is no indication when they might. In this scenario, Mr. Best-Lawyer can ask the client to pay a retainer; in exchange, he keeps his schedule free and avoids representing other clients who might create a conflict. Two weeks after the client pays Mr. Best-Lawyer a $20,000 retainer, he learns that the investigation has been closed. In this situation, Mr. Best-Lawyer can keep the fee.

Most bars have relatively detailed ethics opinions on non-refundable fees which you should consult carefully before ever including one in your retainer agreement.

Some retainers are short; others long. There are two schools of thought about the length of a retainer. Samuel Glover, a consumer law attorney, opts for one-pagers that set out the basics, and that consumers will actually read (see www.Lawyerist.com/tag/retainer). Andrew Flusche, another solo, also uses a one-pager, but he calls it a "client plan" so the legalese doesn't scare clients (see www.legalandrew.com/2010/12/03/my-simple-client-fee-agreement/). But it's not just consumer lawyers who prefer short retainers. At Traverse Legal, a high tech litigation firm, Enricho Schafer, says lengthy retainers necessitate in-house review and can slow the engagement process. His retainer lays out the deliverables and quotes a flat fee. He doesn't worry about withdrawal or other clauses because his firm offers a money-back guarantee. (For details, go to http://greatestamericanlawyer.typepad.com/greatest_american_lawyer/2008/07/are-traditional.html). On the other hand, lawyers representing clients in protracted or costly litigation matters—family law cases, commercial disputes—are often concerned about preserving their ability to withdraw if clients can't pay the fee. Their retainer agreements tend to be longer, and to spell out grounds for withdrawal if fees aren't collected.

When should you offer the retainer agreement? If at the initial meeting, a prospective client asks, "*What's next?*" you modify your retainer agreement as necessary and print a copy. You carefully explain the terms, and let them know that when the agreement is signed, and a retainer paid by check or credit card, you will get started on the matter right away. For more complex business matters requiring a specialized retainer agreement, you tell the client that you will send a proposed agreement for their approval, and that you will begin work when it is signed and a deposit paid. If a prospective client seems undecided after your meeting, offer the agreement anyway and let them take it home for further consideration. If you don't hear back in a day or two, call to find out if they've made a decision. Some lawyers like to give prospective clients a hard sell in the office, but this can suggest desperation. If a prospective client isn't sure, it's appropriate to offer the retainer and give them time to think it over.

Handling a retainer agreement signature in a virtual office. Virtual offices, or business centers, often provide access to printers. If not, purchase a portable printer. Better yet, keep a copy of a copy of the retainer on your iPad or tablet so your client can review it and e-sign it using EchoSign or one of the other e-sign services.

Declining a Case: The Non-Engagement Letter

Once you've interviewed a client, you may decide immediately that you don't want to accept the case. Perhaps you suspect a potential "client from hell", or perhaps the case lacks merit. If so, don't string the client along; let him know right away that you're not interested. You can offer a vague reason, such as scheduling problems or lack of expertise. If you decide to share your view of the merits of the case, be sure to let clients know that other lawyers might differ and encourage them to seek a second opinion. Of course, even when you turn a case down at the end of your initial meeting, you still must follow up with a letter. But at least clients will know where they stand and can begin to explore other options. Sometimes, clients have a legitimate claim, but the cost of hiring a lawyer outweighs the amount at stake. Or, the client's complaint involves poor customer service rather than conduct that would give rise to a lawsuit. In these circumstances, direct the client to self-help options, such as writing a letter to customer service, filing suit in small claims court or, if available in your jurisdiction, a court-sponsored pro se program. In some instances, you may want more time, either to evaluate the case more closely or to find a referral for the client if you don't feel qualified to take the case yourself. Whatever your reason for holding on to a case, set a date for getting back to the client with your decision and stick to it. When clients don't hear back, they may incorrectly assume that you've decided to accept the case ... and they can sue for malpractice if your inaction results in loss of their claims.

When you decline representation, you must send a non-engagement or declination letter that makes clear that you will not take the case. Non-engagement letters are particularly important where a client has provided you with information about the case or paid a consultation fee (many times, clients believe that payment of a fee or your review of documents secures representation). Many malpractice insurance providers require you to send non-engagement letters as a condition of coverage. Less is more when it comes to drafting them. The more you say—about when the statute of limitations runs or why you're turning down a client— the more you increase your liability exposure.

Below, some do's and don'ts:

DO make clear that you are not taking the case. After an opening sentence thanking the client for coming to meet with you, you must state that you will not accept the client's case. Use firm language and avoid hedging (e.g., asking the client to call you with further questions, which could suggest to the client that you're still thinking about taking the case).

DO NOT express an opinion on the merits without telling the client to seek a second opinion. Let's say that you advise the client that you don't believe her discrimination claim against her employer has merit. The client drops the matter, only to discover after the deadline that her coworker won $25,000 for a similar claim. The client could blame you, claiming that she would have gone forward with her case but for your opinion that it wasn't worthwhile. To avoid this outcome, qualify any opinion on the merits with a caveat that other lawyers may have differing views and the client should seek a second opinion. Or you could simply avoid any discussion of the merits of the case at all, and turn it down without explanation.

DO tell the client to seek a second counsel as soon as possible. Advise clients to find another attorney if they remain interested in pursuing the case. Provide the client with contact information for your bar's referral service or, where applicable, a legal assistance bureau. Giving the client additional information preempts a follow-up phone call from the client asking for other referrals.

DO NOT offer any advice on statute of limitations. Specifying a statute of limitations for the client's claims is a recipe for disaster. If you make a mistake about the applicable statute of limitations, you could face a malpractice action, as one Chicago firm did when it told a client she had two years—rather than one—to file a wrongful-death action. Relying on the firm's advice, the client did not visit a second attorney until after the statute of limitations had passed, too late to file the claim. The client successfully sued the first firm for its inaccurate advice on the statutory deadline. You often cannot calculate a statute of limitations until you are aware of all of the facts involved in a case. Example: a potential client who's been rear-ended comes in for a consult, but doesn't mention that the driver was a state employee on official duty. The problem here is that a the statute of limitations for a suit against the state may be much shorter—as little as six months—than the deadline for civil suits against private citizens. If you decline the case, but tell the client that he has two years to sue, he may decide to wait it out. In so doing, the client would miss the six month deadline, and you'd be on the hook. Avoid this problem by omitting mention of the statute of limitations.

DO decline politely and graciously. No one likes rejection, particularly a client who may have already unsuccessfully shopped her case to three or four attorneys. Even where a client is a pest, there's no need to antagonize. A law professor at a state-funded law school clinic learned this lesson the hard way, when she rejected a potential client with these remarks:

> *Our independent professional judgment is that your persistent and antagonistic actions ... would adversely affect our ability to establish an effective attorney-client relationship with you and would consequently impair our ability to [represent] you.*

Angered by the insults in the lawyer's kiss-off letter, the client sued, arguing that the clinic discriminated against him in declining representation because of his political views. Find ways to decline a case graciously to ease the pain of rejection for a disappointed client. It doesn't cost you anything to treat with respect a client you're rejecting. In fact, the client may bring you other matters in the future.

DO send the letter in a manner that acknowledges receipt. Most bar practice managers advise that you send a letter by US Certified Mail with a return receipt. If a trip to the post office will detain you in getting the letter out, send e-mail or fax, both of which will also give you a record of transmittal.

Below is a sample disengagement letter that applies all of these do's and don'ts.

Sample Non-Engagement Letter:

Via Facsimile and Certified Mail, Return Receipt

> *Date*
>
> *Dear Mrs. Jones,*
>
> *Thank you for taking the time to meet and share the details of your case. I am sorry but I will not be able to represent you in your defamation action against the Mayor. As I indicated during our initial meeting, defamation actions fall outside my area of expertise, so I could not give your matter the level of service that it deserves.*
>
> *You should be aware that any action in this matter must be filed within the applicable statute of limitations. I have not investigated the applicable statute of limitations, so I cannot advise on any applicable deadlines. If you remain interested in pursuing this matter, I recommend that you immediately consult with another lawyer concerning your rights in this matter so that you do not compromise any potential claims. If you cannot find another attorney, contact the State Bar Lawyer Referral Service at [phone number and e-mail].*
>
> *I am returning the documents that you provided to me at our initial meeting. Again, I do not plan to take any further action in this matter.*
>
> *Best of luck.*

RULES FOR REFERRALS

If you intend to refer a case to another attorney, ask yourself these questions:

Is the case worth referring? Don't pass off a dog of a case to another lawyer because you're too afraid to say no to a client. You won't generate any good will by consistently referring lousy cases to other lawyers; to the contrary, they'll stop referring cases to you.

Are you referring the case to generate a fee? Some jurisdictions permit referral fees where lawyers can earn a tidy sum off the referral of profitable cases. *But most jurisdictions do not allow lawyers to collect referral fees unless they contribute substantially to the case.* So if you practice in a jurisdiction that bars referral fees, don't expect any more value from referrals beyond a nice lunch or gift from the receiving attorney. There are many reasons besides a fee to refer cases. In doing so, you can still help clients even if they've brought a matter beyond your expertise, making them more likely to return to you with other cases in the future. More importantly, referring cases generates good will; other lawyers will reciprocate and drive business to your firm.

Do you know the referral? Try to limit referrals to attorneys with whom you've worked personally, or who come highly endorsed by close colleagues. Though it's unlikely that a client will sue you for negligent referral (though some jurisdictions recognize negligent referral as a cause of action), you'll feel embarrassed if the lawyer you recommended botches the case.

Did you check out the basics? Engage in additional due diligence before referring cases. Check your bar's Web site to determine whether the lawyer you want to refer is in good standing or has been the subject of disciplinary complaints. You might also ask the lawyer whether he has malpractice insurance. Though most jurisdictions do not require lawyers to disclose their own past bar complaints or lack of malpractice insurance unless directly asked, you should tell clients about the referral's disciplinary record and malpractice status.

Resources when breaking the news. Below is a list of resources for clients who you can't represent for whatever reason. When you turn a case down on the spot, you can give clients a copy of the list, highlighting those resources that may be useful or you could include the information along with a non-engagement letter:

Virtual law practices: Virtual law practices frequently offer unbundled legal services at more affordable rates. Keep a list of virtual, unbundled providers to which you could routinely refer cases that aren't economic for your office to handle.

Bar referral service. Almost every state and local jurisdiction has a bar-referral service that will provide prospective clients with names of attorneys who might take their case. Some referral services are free for clients; others require a de minimis fee of $25 or $50 to the Bar to defray the cost of administering the program.

Law school clinics. Some local law schools run specialty clinics that handle family law, immigration, First Amendment, even environmental or international issues. Some local universities also sponsor incubator programs for start-up high tech companies or small businesses, and may be able to help fledgling entrepreneurs draft a contract or identify sources of funding. Familiarize yourself with law school and university offerings in your area; they might be able to handle cases that many practitioners are not qualified to handle or are unwilling to handle for free or reduced cost.

Lawhelp.org or probono.org. These Web sites help low and moderate income people find free legal aid programs in their communities, and answer questions about their legal rights.

Nolo Press (www.nolopress.com). The nation's leading provider of do-it-yourself legal solutions for consumers and small businesses. Nolo's site offers extensive and substantive legal information.

Small claims court materials. In some jurisdictions, small claims courts provide extensive resources on their Web site, including forms for filing a complaint and how-to guides on the appropriate procedures. Other jurisdictions are not as user-friendly. Direct clients with minor matters to the small claims site, or to the court clerk's office where they can obtain information on small claims procedures.

Local pro se clinics. Courts in some jurisdictions have pro se clinics or advisory lawyers who will help unrepresented litigants. Some clients may feel more comfortable as a pro se, knowing that the court can provide assistance.

Better Business Bureau. Helps customers and companies resolve complaints through non-judicial dispute resolution. The BBB process could provide customers with small complaints an alternative to hiring a lawyer.

Consumercomplaints.org. For clients whose matters are more customer-service oriented (for example, a customer orders a toy that doesn't work and the company won't issue a refund, or rude service at a fast food restaurant), consumercomplaints.org is an option. They retain a database of complaints about businesses nationwide, and consumers seeking relief can search the database and see if other consumers have faced similar problems. The ability to access to complaints against companies gives consumers more leverage to achieve a favorable result.

Government agencies. Some types of cases are initiated by filing administrative claims, a procedure that clients can handle on their own. Many of the agencies that process these claims, such as the EEOC, human rights agencies, consumer affairs departments or public utility commissions, frequently work with non-lawyers and have user-friendly forms as well as staff who may interview your client to gather information.

DIY sites. If a prospective client asks for a free form or sample, refer them to one of the do-it-yourself sites like RocketLawyer.com or LegalZoon.com.

The Termination (Disengagement) Letter

A termination letter documents the end of the attorney-client relationship. The precise contents of the termination letter will vary based on the reasons for ending the relationship, but all letters should include the following information:

Describe the reason for the termination. Your termination letter should discuss the reason that you are no longer representing the client. Perhaps you have completed the matter for which you were retained, or perhaps you are withdrawing because the client refuses to pay. Or maybe the client grew dissatisfied with your service and decided to hire another lawyer and discharge you. During the course of representation you may also discover a conflict of interest which will compel your withdrawal.

Description your file retention policy. Ideally, you should transmit a copy of the client's file along with the termination letter. If files are voluminous, offer to make copies at the client's expense or retain the files at your office for inspection. You should also describe how many years you will hold the files. Check with your bar association to determine how long you must hold files. Some jurisdictions do not require lawyers to grant access to files unless the client has paid his bills, and where withholding files will not prejudice the client in an ongoing matter. Consult the bar to determine when you can ethically retain a client's file.

Document your position. If you fire a client or withdraw from a case for non-payment or lack of client cooperation, or for any other reason stated in the retainer agreement, identify the client's obligation under the agreement. In addition, document all prior attempts to notify the client of non-compliance. For example:

Section 4.1 of the Retainer Agreement that you signed (copy enclosed for your convenience) states that Client's failure to provide attorney with required documents shall be grounds for withdrawal. According to my records, on June 1st, 2007, I called you and asked you to provide your income tax returns for the past three years. As you know, we are required to produce these documents in discovery in order to sustain your claim for damages. During our call, you agreed that you would send the returns. I followed up with a reminder by e-mail on June 15th, 2007. At that time you stated that you would retrieve the returns from storage. Two weeks later, I notified you of my intent to withdraw from representation if you did not provide these income tax returns. A month has passed and I have not heard from you. As I explained, I cannot move forward with your case until I have copies of your tax returns. Therefore, with this letter, I am notifying you of my withdrawal from representation and termination of our Retainer Agreement.

Where a client discharges you, your letter should express acceptance of the decision, but at the same time, document your reason for taking the approach that you did. For example:

> Dear Mrs. Jones,
> I am sorry to hear that you have decided to retain another attorney to represent you in this contract dispute. I realize that you are eager to litigate this matter in state court, but I stand by my original opinion that the terms of the contract mandate arbitration. I believe that any a court would regard any action to resolve this in a judicial forum as frivolous and would dismiss the case. Accordingly, as we have already discussed, I remain unwilling to file suit.
> I wish you the best of luck going forward. Please have your new counsel contact me to arrange for transfer of the files.

Settling up fees. Your termination letter should describe the client's fee obligation at the time the relationship is severed. Where you withdraw from a case for non-payment, restate the amount that the client owes, even though it is unlikely that the client will ever pay (unless you sue for fees) once you withdraw. When you are discharged by a client in a contingency matter that you worked on for many hours, remind clients that they remain responsible on an hourly basis for time spent on the case once it is settled (include an invoice detailing the time spent and amount owed).

Closing information. When you end your relationship with a client because a matter has run its course, close your termination letter with a thank-you, and an invitation for the client to contact you on other matters. Enclose a business card so that the client can get in touch with you in the future. Some lawyers may include a client satisfaction surveys that clients can complete and return. For involuntarily terminations or withdrawals, you can't do much more than wish the client the best and leave it at that.

Q: What was your most difficult client experience, and what you did you learn?

"The worst clients are the ones your gut tells you to run from at the start but you don't listen."
—Lynda L. Hinkle (class of 2009)

"The worst client is the one who comes to you with a crisis, steals your heart and you agree to help them for a small down payment with the rest coming later…and then you don't get paid. The best client is the one willing to take their case to the end, is not overly emotional, and has a good case."
—Spencer Young (class of 2004)

"I had one client who begged me to defend him against an ex parte motion scheduled for the next day. I agreed to do it, worked all night, and won the motion. Then the client's check bounced and he declared bankruptcy. Now I only do work after a check has cleared. If it's an emergency I demand a cashier's check."—Nina Kallen (class of 1994)

"My worst client was someone who used me as a doormat and attack dog. I'm not quite sure how he managed to get both out of me but he did. The client was one of the few exceptions I made to my payment-up-front rule and I got burned, and was someone who set off my BS detector though I refused to listen to it. [Lesson learned]: never (EVER) deviate from my payment-up-front policy, listen to my BS detector when it's sounding like an air raid siren, and rein in a drama queen at the very beginning of the engagement."—Gina Bongiovi (class of 2007)

"My most difficult client had unreasonable expectations and refused to cooperate or compromise. He had created his own reality about his situation, and could not be reasoned with. It taught me the importance of a thorough intake process. There are a lot of questions I should have asked during the initial consultation, and had I been a little more thorough I might have saved myself a lot of trouble!"
—Adam Neufer (class of 2009)

"My worst client was my first; she was an unbelievable nightmare. She lied to me (and most others), she was erratic, uncooperative, verbally abusive, consumed an obscene amount of my time, and ended up owing me over $20,000 in legal fees. Needless to say, I learned an incredible amount: I grew much stronger and more assertive with respect to charging appropriate fees, and insisting on being paid…I became much more detailed in my Retainer Agreements and other correspondence, as well as how I structured the retainer amounts and my billing…and I learned quite a bit about certain areas of the law that my clients antics forced me to research. There were many valuable lessons." —Laura S. Mann (class of 1996)

"My worst client was my first. It was a non-litigation matter, and I had offered him a choice of hourly or fixed fee and he chose fixed. The client turned out to be extremely demanding and required constant hand-holding, and did a lot of things on his own that made things unnecessarily complex. I finally lost my patience and told him he should find another attorney. Lesson learned: sometimes you have to fire a client to stay in business…and it's OK to do that."—Mitchell J. Matorin (class of 1993)

Excerpt from *Solo by Choice, The Companion Guide: 34 Questions That Could Transform Your Legal Career* (Carolyn Elefant, 2011)

CHAPTER 11

Billing, Fees & Office Operations

"Expect cash-flow to be a major concern for at least
the first two years of your practice." —Jenny Jeltes, solo

Many solos don't give as much thought as they should to the method by which they charge for services. Instead, they adopt the practices of their former firm or other lawyers, which means: (a) they bill by the hour at market rates for ongoing matters like litigation, appeals, or corporate negotiations; (b) they charge flat fees for commodity type services such as wills, trusts, or incorporations or (c) they take a 33 to 40 percent cut of proceeds received in contingency cases.

As you think about starting your own firm, you have an opportunity to re-examine the traditional ways of pricing, and to take an approach that delivers value to your clients and maximizes your revenues.

It's never been as important for lawyers to *rethink* rates as it is in today's environment, with business clients demanding discounts and rate caps, and non-legal service providers like Legal Zoom putting downward cost-pressure on many consumer-oriented services like preparation of wills, leases, or corporate documents.

In this section, I'll review traditional and alternative billing methodologies.

How Much Should I Charge?

Every discussion about legal fees ultimately returns to one of two questions: *how much should I charge, and how do I make sure to get paid?* This is true whether it's a debate over the billable hour versus alternative-fee structure…the wisdom of competing for clients on price…whether to charge for an initial consultation…the level of detail you should include on your bills … or whether to sue a client to collect an unpaid bill. Most lawyers make the mistake of addressing these two questions independently without realizing their interrelationship. Ultimately, your firm's profitability hinges on how you resolve both of these issues.

Consider three examples:

- John Smith decides to charge clients $2,500 (five times the going rate) to prepare a simple, theorizing that a well-drafted will saves money by minimizing the possibility of an expensive and protracted will contest by a disgruntled heir. Though reasonable in theory, Smith is unlikely to find clients who can have their pick of lawyers who provide the same service at a fraction of the price. **Bottom line**: Smith has given thought to how much he should charge, but ignored the question of how he can ensure that he gets paid.
- Jane Short is retained to represent a client in a possible age-discrimination action. She explains to the client that she bills $200/hour, and requires a $10,000 retainer

to cover her first 50 hours of work. Without inquiring about the client's budget, Ms. Short recommends and embarks on an aggressive litigation strategy. Even before discovery has concluded, she exhausts the retainer, and puts in an additional $10,000 worth of time for which she has not been compensated. When she bills the client for unpaid fees, and asks the client to replenish the retainer amount, the client says she's out of money. **Bottom line**: Jane knew how much to charge, but she gave no thought to whether her strategy fit her client's budget, and how to get paid if it didn't.

- Ralph Young, just a few weeks after starting his practice, receives a referral to represent a large apartment complex in eviction proceedings. The landlord agrees to pay Ralph $1,500/month to appear in landlord-tenant court four days a month. Each court appearance would last no more than three hours, for a total of 12 hours per month or a rate of $125/hour (not bad for a new attorney). Like clockwork, the landlord pays Young his fee at the beginning of each month. After a few months, Young's practice picks up and he finds that he's working late at the office to compensate for the time spent in landlord-tenant court. Moreover, with the half-hour of prep required for each appearance…and the hour-long commute to and from court…he's spending closer to 18 hours a month on the matter, reducing his fee to $83/hour. **Bottom line**: Young has no problem getting paid. But he neglected to take to calculate the true cost of his time, i.e., what to charge for the arrangement.

The Billable Hour

Black's Law Dictionary defines a billable hour as a unit of time used by an attorney to account for work performed and chargeable to a client. Most often, time is recorded in increments of a tenth-of-an-hour (some use quarter-hour), and clients are billed for the hours worked multiplied by the lawyer's hourly rate. Many lawyers believe the billable hour has been a staple of the legal profession since the dawn of time. In truth, the practice came of age as recently as the 1960s. According to a legal journal article by Karen Dean (*The Billable Hour's Staying Power*, Fulton County Daily Report), the billable hour gained traction in part because it forced law firms to keep accurate time records, allowing them to set income projections and performance goals. The relative simplicity and accuracy of the billable hour explains why it remains the "predominant method of billing for legal services."

In recent years, though, as the cost of legal services surged and associate morale declined under pressure to meet billable quotas, the billable hour has come under attack. Among other things, it rewards inefficiency; the longer lawyers spend on a task the more they get paid. Some even contend that the billable hour encourages fraudulent overcharging because the system pressures lawyers to inflate their hours to meet quotas or increase revenues.

In a preface to the 2002 ABA Commission Report on the Billable Hour, then-ABA President Robert Hirshon wrote: "The billable hour is fundamentally about quantity over quality, repetition over creativity. With no gauge for intangibles such as productivity, creativity, knowledge or technological advancements, the billable hour model is a counter-intuitive measure of value." Five years later, the ABA Journal dedicated its cover issue (August, 2007) to the billable hour with a dramatic headline: *The Billable Hour Must Die*. In the article, lawyer/novelist Scott Turow wrote…

> "Dollars times hours sounds like a formula for fairness. What could be more equitable than basing a fee on how and hard a litigator worked to resolve a matter? But as a system, [the billable hour] is a prison. When you are selling your time, there are only three ways to make more money—higher rates, longer hours, and more leverage … if I had only one wish for our profession, I would want us to move toward something better than dollars times hours. We have created a zero-sum game in which we are selling our lives not just our time."

One mistake solos make is to assume they should adopt the billable hour because that's large firms do, and what clients demand. However, large firms benefit from the billable hour in a way that solos cannot because of associate leverage. In BigLaw, partners earn a percentage of every hour of work an associate performs; more associate hours billed translates to more partner profits. By contrast, solos adopting the billable hour are limited by the amount of time they work. If they bill 1,000 hours a year at $250/hour, they gross $250,000; if they bill 2,000 hours, they gross $500,000…but they're also back to working law firm hours!

As for clients, more and more corporate clients are rebelling against the billable hour because it does not give any certainty over potential fees, and leaves them vulnerable to bills that never seem to end. In addition, the rise of non-legal service providers like Legal Zoom—which posts rates for different services right on their Web site—has made consumers more familiar with the concept of flat-fee pricing. Telling clients that you bill at $250/hour doesn't give them a way to compare the overall cost of your service to a non-legal provider in the way that a flat-fee would. Still, for all of its drawbacks in some practice areas, you may have no choice but to track your time and bill by the hour:

- Many court-appointed criminal defense programs require lawyers to submit time-sheets showing the number of hours worked.
- Many insurance companies or government agencies that retain outside counsel also limit you to hourly billing.
- And if you handle matters where the prevailing party can recover attorney fees under a fee-shifting statute, the court will require you to show hours worked and billing rate as part of your fee application.

If you do decide to bill by the hour, how do you decide your hourly rate? Sometimes you won't have a choice. If you handle court-appointed work or defense cases for an insurance company, the court or the company will establish your rate of pay and you take it or leave it.

In most other cases, you have the flexibility to set your own hourly rate, and you can take one of two approaches: (a) determine the market rate and adjust accordingly for various factors, as I discuss below, or (b) calculate a rate that reflects your overhead costs and the hours you want to work. Don't obsess over the selection. Ultimately, clients care far more about the reasonableness of your bill than your hourly charge. Clients would rather pay $300/hour for an experienced attorney to resolve a matter in five hours than pay $100/hour for a rookie who burns through 20 hours. And clients also want an estimate of how long a case will take, so they have some certainty regarding the potential total amount. Thus, even as you try to figure out an hourly rate, keep the bigger picture—your overall fee—in mind.

What follows are several sources for calculating applicable attorney rates:

Legal journals. The legal trade press often publishes the billable rates for associates and partners at large firms in your area.

Court files. The federal courts maintain a schedule of fees called the Laffey Matrix that applies in reimbursing prevailing parties for attorney fees under fee-shifting statutes such as the Civil Rights Attorney's Fees Award Act. See www.en.wikipedia.org/wiki/Laffey_Matrix, or see the rates listed at www.laffeymatrix.com/see.html. Court opinions awarding attorney fees provides another source of billable rates that the courts regard as reasonable.

The Internet. Some attorney Web sites list their billing rates. Though these rates are often accompanied by caveats, they do offer a benchmark. At www.Avvo.com, an attorney directory, the lawyer profiles include an entry where lawyers can specify their fees.

Bar and trade associations. Though antitrust law prevents associations from publishing rate schedules, some bars do conduct economic reports or surveys on prevailing rates. Two examples: a 2009 rate survey from Texas (www.texasbar.com/AM/Template.cfm?Section=Search&section=2009_20101&template=/CM/ContentDisplay.cfm&ContentFileID=929), and a study of US Consumer Law Attorney rates (2008–2009), available at the National Consumer Law Center Web site (http://dcwintonlaw.com/wp-content/uploads/2010/06/100415-Document-Dated-NCLC-Attorneys-Fee-Survey.pdf).

RateDriver. A smartphone app launched in late 2010 that helps lawyers answer the question, *"How much should I charge?"* Users enter factors like location, practice area, firm size, years of experience, and the app produces a billable rate based on data collected from 1.4 million legal invoices.

Colleagues. Attorneys don't flaunt their hourly rates, but most attorneys and colleagues will share their rates if you ask for guidance. The best information on rates will come from colleagues practicing the same area of law in a similar region. Note: even in similar practice areas, rates may vary depending upon the clients. In energy regulatory work, one of my practice specialties, firms that represent large utilities tend to charge 20 to 30 percent more than those that represent government entities and consumer interests.

Adjustments to Your Billable Rate

Once you have a sense of the appropriate hourly rate, you can adjust it as needed. Here are some reasons you might wish to do so:

The experience factor. Your experience may warrant an upward or downward adjustment. Adjust it down if you're new to a field or practice to give clients more incentive to hire you; adjust it higher if experience allows you to handle a task in half the time so that even at higher rates your clients receive enhanced value.

Type of client. You're not required to charge the same rate to all clients (a reason for not listing your hourly rates on your Web site). Many times, municipalities or other public entities cap the fees that lawyers can charge. Or, a client may be able to guarantee you a certain number of hours of work, provided you cut 20 percent off your hourly rate. Be flexible with rates for clients with a promising matter, but who can't afford your hourly rate. You can also use some of the other billing approaches to accommodate clients with tight budgets. Note: a difficult client may warrant a higher hourly rate. Example: you're referred a case by a colleague who warns that the client is high-maintenance. In this situation, you're justified in quoting a higher hourly rate.

Matter handled. If you're a true solo, you'll handle all aspects of a case, from organizing files, reviewing documents, responding to discovery, and researching and drafting briefs. Should clients pay your $200/hour rate just to handle administrative tasks? If your case involves a large amount of non-legal or paralegal-related work, consider trimming your rates for those tasks, particularly if you can't outsource them.

Urgency. What if a client demands overnight turn-around on a document, or needs a lawyer for trial at the end of the month? If you have to put other matters on hold to service a client with time-sensitive matters, your rates should reflect the opportunity costs and inconvenience.

Pre-payment. Some lawyers offer a lower rate if clients can pay a large enough retainer to cover the full amount of the case. Example: a case takes 50 hours at your $200/hour rate. You could take a $5,000 retainer and bill the balance as the work proceeds. Or, offer a 20 percent discount on your hourly rate if they pay in advance the full amount of $9,000 (20 hours at $180/hour). Though you lose $1,000, you're still better off than if the client paid $5,000 up front and refused to pay the balance. Plus, you save time associated with chasing down the bill.

The Overhead-based System

Another way to calculate your billing rate is to base it on such factors as how much you want to earn and how many hours you're likely to bill (or, if you already have a steady cash flow, how many hours you want to work). Let's say you want to earn $60,000 (before taxes) in your first year of practice, and your overhead (e.g., office, insurance, computer system—but not salary) comes to $2,000/month. You would need to gross $84,000 to hit your target. Assuming that you would bill at least 10 hours a week to start, working 48 weeks a year, you can calculate your rate as follows: $84,000/(48 x10) = $175/hour. You can play with this number, bumping it by 20 percent (or $210) to account for potential non-collection, or seeing how it compares to the market rate. At a minimum, you should apply the overhead-based method of calculation to ensure that you're billing enough to cover your costs and to turn a profit. At www.FreelanceSwitch.com there is an online calculator to help you figure out what rate you need to charge each hour based on your existing costs.

Mitigating the Uncertainty of the Billable Hour

A lawyer's hourly rate is only one part of the equation. Telling a client that you charge $300/hour isn't much use if they don't know how much time is involved. So, if you choose to adopt the billable hour, you should also provide clients with an estimate. Estimating the cost of a case is a little like playing chess; you need to think ahead, factoring in all the moves you think your opponent might make, and draw from your experience in similar matters that you handled at your firm or at a prior job. Absent that experience, ask a colleague how long similar cases can take, and what types of issues might arise that would affect the budget.

Author note: in cases where I still bill by the hour, I generally provide clients with different price ranges for best and worst case scenarios, and cap my fees at the upper end. Not all lawyers are willing to adhere to their estimate, but I feel that it adds to my credibility. At the same time, sometimes a client's own actions—perhaps failure to cooperate or some deception about material facts—can lead to unexpected delays and added work. Example: if you're handling an employment termination matter where the client fails to tell you that she lied about her experience on her job application, you may have to perform additional research to determine whether her claims remain viable. In such cases, binding estimates don't apply; the client should bear the added costs resulting from his or her actions. Moreover, you should encourage client candor and cooperation so they understand that failure to do so will cost them extra. Of course, the unexpected could happen—a court's decision to reverse 50 years of precedent—that could add to your original estimate. In these unpredictable situations, you may want to submit the contractor's equivalent of a "change order" in which you would explain the unexpected new development and ask the client to authorize additional work. Limit your use of change orders to unique situations that could not have been predicted through diligence.

Contingency Fees

As you know, in a true contingency case, lawyers do not charge clients for representation, and they advance the costs of the case (e.g., deposition transcripts, expert witness fees), in exchange for a percentage of the amount recovered at trial or during a settlement. Where you fail to obtain a judgment or settlement, you don't get paid at all, irrespective of the amount of work you did. Related to the true contingency case are *hybrid contingency arrangements*, where the client rather than the attorney pays the costs, or where the lawyer works for a significantly reduced fee (e.g., $75/hour or a flat retainer amount) in exchange for a percentage of the final award. Traditionally, contingency fee arrangements have been reserved for personal injury work, medical malpractice, large class actions, and collections, though some lawyers will also work on a contingency basis in civil rights matters, such as employment discrimination or police brutality. Ethics rules prohibit working for a contingent fee in family law or criminal cases, as made clear in Rule 1.5(d) of the Model Rules of Professional Conduct of the American Bar Association.

PRO & CON. Contingency fee cases may offer an opportunity for substantial financial gain. Depending upon the matter you handle, you may be able to recover the equivalent of double your hourly rate...or more. And contingency rates afford personal satisfaction by creating a mechanism that enables you to serve clients who might otherwise lack the resources to gain access to our justice system. On the other hand, contingency fees come with significant risk; a 100 percent contingency practice won't provide a steady source of revenue. In addition, if you're new to your practice area, you may have difficulty evaluating the worth of cases, causing you to take a disproportionate number of cases where you wind up with small settlements or even no money at all. Moreover, many of the really high-revenue contingency matters often involve a significant investment, such as payment for medical or economic experts, investigators, subpoenas, and deposition transcripts. If you're just starting out, you may not have the resources.

Most contingency fees range from 25 to 40 percent of an award. Lawyers often offer stepped rates, taking 25 to 33 percent for pre-complaint settlement; 33 to 35 percent for post-complaint settlement, and 35 to 40 percent of an award following trial. In cases where the likelihood of winning is high, it's reasonable to take a higher percentage under a contingency arrangement. Consider deviating from the so-called standard contingency fees to distinguish you from competitors. And as mentioned above, consider a variety of hybrid approaches. For example, for cases of questionable merit, you could require the client to advance the costs, or pay a discounted fee as you go, plus a percentage of the amount eventually recovered. More than any other type of pricing mechanism, the Bars impose restrictions on contingency-pricing arrangements. Failure to adhere to applicable ethics rules may cost you your fee if your client raises a challenge. Most jurisdictions adopt some version of ABA Model Rule 1.5, which requires that lawyers put contingency fee agreements in writing and explain how the fee is calculated. Specifically, Model Rule 1.5 states:

> *A contingent fee agreement shall be in a writing signed by the client and shall state the method by which the fee is to be determined, including the percentage or percentages that shall accrue to the lawyer in the event of settlement, trial or appeal; litigation and other expenses to be deducted from the recovery; and whether such expenses are to be deducted before or after the contingent fee is calculated. The agreement must clearly notify the client of any expenses for which the client will be liable whether or not the client is the prevailing party. Upon conclusion of a contingent fee matter, the lawyer shall provide the client with a written statement stating the outcome of the matter and, if there is a recovery, showing the remittance to the client and the method of its determination.*

Some jurisdictions also cap percentage of recovery that lawyers can collect in certain types of matters. Make sure your fee agreement complies with any cap mandated by statute or your ethics rules.

Alternative Billing Models

This section discusses the pro and con of alternatives to the billable-hour. What is common to them are the following benefits:

Administrative savings. Billable hours require fastidious tracking of time and tasks performed. Even with the availability of automated systems to track time, you still need to turn the program on, enter the task, and review the charges at the end of the month to determine if you'll pass them all on to the client. Flat fees eliminate this process. Even though you may continue to track your time with flat fees to get a sense of how long a process takes, you don't need to do it with the same level or accuracy as if you were billing by the hour.

Increased collection. When clients know up front what something costs, they can budget for the cost. Moreover, it's difficult for clients to claim, "*I didn't realize it would cost so much*" (as they might in a billable hour matter), when they agree to a sum up front. Thus, flat fees reduce your percentage of uncollected accounts.

Cash flow. Some jurisdictions treat flat fees as earned on receipt, e.g., they can go directly into a lawyer's operating account rather than into the trust account. Thus, flat fees result in quicker payment and better cash flow than the traditional billable model in which lawyers cannot release money from trust until earned. Caveat: not all jurisdictions allow this approach, so read bar rules carefully.

Flat fees. Though portrayed as a new billing model, most criminal defense lawyers have traditionally used flat fee billing, often basing the fee on such factors as the complexity of the matter and the attorney's experience. Increasingly, lawyers in other practice areas are also experimenting with flat fees. One firm charges a flat fee for each day in trial.

The Pro & Con. Clients gain certainty with a flat fee, and are more likely to communicate more frequently with their lawyer when they know that the meter isn't running. On the other hand, when lawyers underestimate their flat fee, they may try to compensate for the shortfall by skimping on service to the detriment of the client.

Flat fees per task. Many lawyers charge a flat, per-task fee for routine, finite matters like real estate closings, wills and trusts, incorporations, simple bankruptcy filings, uncontested divorces, and certain types of regulatory and permit applications. Often, these tasks are referred to as commodities services because they do not involve significant individualized attention, and they are capable of automated production through use of forms and computer programs. Some lawyers use flat fees for appellate matters or criminal cases. So long as you can reliably predict the amount of time involved, a flat-fee can work.

PRO. Per-task billing makes sense in cases where lawyers can predict with some precision the time required. And because lawyers automate preparation of some of these types of documents, it enables them to charge relatively low flat fees. Finally, flat fees give clients certainty so they can budget for paying fees and it eliminates the need for regular invoices.

CON. A new lawyer will almost certainly lose money on flat fee tasks. While a practicing lawyer can churn out a basic will in an hour or two, a new attorney may need a day for each of the first few wills he or she prepares. Even where you're experienced, you may find it difficult to compete in the legal commodities market and still turn a profit. That's because many lawyers use wills, incorporations, and similar matters as loss leaders to attract more profitable business. And other lawyers try to compensate for low rates for commodities through high volume, often relying on paralegals or staff to draft the documents initially. Unless you adopt one of these business models, you may not find flat fees for commodities work worthwhile. Many lawyers advertise flat fees for commodities work on Web sites or in ads, so it shouldn't be difficult to figure out the going rate. When you handle a matter for a flat-fee, your retainer agreement should state the fee. More importantly, the retainer must also specify that the fee does not include any matters beyond the particular deliverable, e.g., will or bankruptcy petition.

Phased flat fees. Charging flat fees for complex litigation or family law matters can prove challenging because the course of the proceedings may be unpredictable. More-over, under-estimating a flat fee can have far-reaching consequences once a case is filed because a judge may not allow you to withdraw. One solution is the "phased fee," where clients pay a flat fee for each stage of the litigation. This approach allows the lawyer to separate the proceeding into discrete stages or tasks, each of which is assigned a flat-fee. If the client refuses to authorize performance of a certain task, or disagrees on the quoted price for the task, the lawyer may withdraw as specified under the retainer letter. For more details on how one solo implemented phased billing, see *An Experiment in Task Order Billing,* www.americanbar.org/content/newsletter/publica-tions/law_trends_news_practice_area_e_newsletter_home/litigation_kaufman.html (June 2008).

PRO. Phased billing insulates lawyers against risk of underestimating a flat-fee. It also allows for the administrative benefits of not having to track every minute and task precisely.

CON. Phased billing still creates some uncertainty for clients because they do not know at the outset whether, for example, a case will require two depositions or 20. If the lawyer charges $1,000 per day of deposition, the difference between two deposi-tions and 20 is huge. In addition, even if your retainer letter allows you to withdraw if a client refuses to authorize any depositions, it's possible that the court will not let you out of the case.

Service packages. Many lawyers who represent corporate or business clients develop service plans or packages, entitling the company to some monthly amount of phone calls or hours of representation. Under such plans, clients usually receive a discounted hourly rate. Extra services such as litigation matters are handled outside the service plan, under separate retainer. Kevin Houchin (www.Houchinlaw.com), a Colorado-based business lawyer, describes how he created a variety of packages ranging in price be-tween $250 and $1,500/month to serve business clients. See *Confessions of a Happy Lawyer* at http://lawyerist.com/confessions-of-a-happy-lawyer/ (September 2010).

PRO. Service packages benefit clients by giving them access to a lawyer without worrying about the meter running every time the phone rings. From your perspective, the relationship established could give you an inside track for future business.

CON. Service packages can be a tough sell. Companies with their own in-house counsel may not have an interest in a service plan unless it addresses a niche topic. And even though you may deeply discount your rates, they may never be low enough to attract companies that prefer do-it-yourself form contracts and online incorporations. Finally, service plans accustom clients to your reduced rate, and may balk at paying your regular rate for matters outside the service plan. A number of firms offer service packages, so a search on the Internet will give you an idea of some of the possible pricing options. Generally, a service plan should include the following features:

- A set fee for a certain number of hours of tasks, such as counseling either by phone or e-mail, simple contract review or drafting at a discounted rate;
- A description of matters where the client might retain you, but which fall outside the scope of the service plan

Value-billing. Some types of billing described above, like flat fees, are a rudimentary form of value-billing. Other value-billing methods include:

- Providing for recovery of success fees, where you collect a percentage of revenues that you recover or save for a client;
- Voluntarily adjusting a bill downward to reflect a disappointing outcome;
- Money-back service guarantee where you allow clients to obtain a full or partial refunds of charges that they don't believe were justified;
- Development of flat fees that reflect the value that your service provides.

With growing dissatisfaction over the billable hour, value-billing represents the trend of the future. At the same time, the question of quantifying one's value to clients requires far more thought and analysis than simply choosing an hourly rate (which goes a long way to explain why the billable hour is so entrenched). Value-pricing also presents a different dilemma. Because while other professions may wish to engage in arbitrary pricing, lawyers have an ethical obligation to ensure that our rates are reasonable. For additional information on calculating how much to charge, including resources on value billing, go to www.thebillablehour.com/resources.

Pricing strategies. Some lawyers have difficulty quoting fees. The best advice is to be straight-forward, but if you need to explain the fees or to justify your value, here are some suggestions:

Encourage an apples-to-apples comparison. When quoting fees, you might get a response like this from a prospective client: "*Wow, that's almost twice the rate quoted to me by Joe Lawyer across the street.*" Maybe the client is lying; maybe not. It's also possible that Joe's price is less because it includes fewer services. Example: you charge $850 for an incorporation package while Joe charges $300. On closer inspection, Joe's fee doesn't include state incorporation fees, an EIN number, and notifications or registered agent service. By carefully identifying all the features that your package includes, you help clients make an informed comparison.

Present a pricing menu. Studies show that given a variety of pricing options, customers gravitate to the middle and feel like they got a bargain in the process. Menu pricing can easily be applied to the presentation of fees. Example: you offer a basic level of estate planning that is entirely virtual, and doesn't include personal interaction with an attorney. One level up, you include a single meeting and the preparation of the will and related documents; one level further might involve a trust; the highest level of service might include ongoing follow-up of the client's needs. Menu pricing works best for flat-fee matters, but there's no reason it won't work with hourly matters, too. For example, you could offer a standard billable rate of $200/hour; a rate of $230/hour for quick turn-around; and a rate of $250/hour to include no-charge phone calls.

Adjustable fees and refunds. Sometimes, it's easier to quote a fee when you don't feel as if you're locking clients in or forcing the fee down their throat. That's where a refund policy or adjustable fee can help. For six years now, Traverse Legal's Enricho Schaefer has offered clients a money-back guarantee…and has had only one client take him up on it (see Inc. Magazine, September 2010). At Valorem Law Group, a small Chicago firm comprised of BigLaw expatriates, clients are offered a "value line adjustment" that allows them to make any changes they want to the final bill (www.valoremlaw.com/ValueAdjustmentLine.htm). Note: adjustable fees and refunds work better with more sophisticated clients who are better able to assess the value of your service. Most criminal defendants would probably demand their money back if you lost their cases—even when you provided top notch service.

Let the client name the price. Matt Homann, a legal consultant and former practicing lawyer (www.thenonbillablehour.typepad.com) suggests letting one's clients name the price at the completion of the project. Some large firms are said to be experimenting with this approach, and one international firm (CMS Cameron McKenna) even went so far as to invite clients and potential clients to "pay us what you think is fair" (see www.TheLawyer.com, Aug. 5, 2010). I'm not fond of DIY pricing. Asking a client to assign value to legal services is a burden. Clients would struggle to come up with a price that's not too low (which may insult the lawyer or create resentment) or too high (in which case the client may feel that he's overpaid). Pricing legal services is very difficult; it's both art and a science, and it requires lots of thought and experimentation. It's our job as lawyers to come up with an appropriate price, not our client's.

Alternative Fees & Flat Fee Billing *by Allison Shields, Esq.*

Q: *I'd like to try a flat fee arrangement, but I can't get away from basing my fees on estimated hours. What are your suggestions?*

A: In order to price effectively, you must be able to articulate what value your firm brings to its clients. The factors involved might include your experience, your previous results, your training, your practice area, your geographic area, your under standing of the client's situation, and your ability to solve the client's problems. *Ultimately, though, the only reason that any of these factors affects the ability to charge a particular fee is because the client believes that they add value to the engagement.* The key is to have a detailed conversation with the client about expectations, and the manner in which success and fees are measured. One of the main components of a value-based fee system is that the fee is set at the beginning of the engagement. But that doesn't have to mean that you quote one fee for the entire engagement if you don't have complete information.

You can use a system of *change orders* which would adjust the fee in the event that the client's objectives or the scope of the matter change from what was originally agreed.

You might consider providing an estimate or price range, giving a high and low based on your experience (make sure the client understands that this is just an estimate). Give yourself some wiggle room on the low end…and be mindful that some clients will assume that the low is what they are going to pay. Or price the project in stages, with ranges for each stage set as the matter progresses and you have more information. Provide your potential clients with examples of the kinds of variables that are likely to result in a change order or increase in the fee. Ensure that your fee agreement clearly sets out the details of the fee structure and that a change order will result in a change in the fee. Articulate the changes in your fees in terms of the benefits to the client and what the client thinks is important.

Q: *Alternative billing sounds good to me, but how will my clients react?*
A: Most clients prefer alternative billing to hourly billing. Alternative billing allows the client to make an informed decision about whether legal services are affordable before those services are rendered. There are fewer surprises for the client, allowing them to budget for legal fees in advance. Even if the fee must be altered from the original estimate, if the lawyer has articulated the factors that would affect the fee and communicated them to the client, there will be less resistance to the increase. Alternative billing also eliminates many conflicts between lawyers and clients, and clients are less likely to question a bill they've agreed to beforehand. They're also less likely to question whether a lawyer should perform a certain task if they don't perceive that they're paying 'extra' for it. And clients will be more likely to cooperate and communicate with their attorney and provide necessary information if they aren't worried that every contact with the lawyer costs more money.

Q: *Are there any ethical considerations that I should take into account with alternative billing?*
A: Each state's individual ethical rules vary, and lawyers must read the individual rules carefully. Issues to be aware of include: duress (which may arise if the fee arrangement is changed on the eve of trial), fee-splitting, doing business with clients, acquiring an interest in litigation, and of course, the state's rules on managing client's funds, and use of trust accounts. Courts look at the reasonableness of an attorney's fee. Although many lawyers see the time-sheet as the proof of the reasonableness of the fee, the amount of time that was spent on the case isn't the real proof of reasonableness (and often courts discount the time-sheets and substitute their own determination of whether the time spent was reasonable). Time is only one factor. The factors which most courts consider in determining whether a fee is reasonable or ethical include (among others):

- Time and labor required;
- Novelty and difficulty of questions involved;
- Skill necessary to properly perform the legal services involved;

- Time limitations imposed by the client or the circumstances;
- Amount in controversy and results obtained

The courts only get involved in establishing the reasonableness of a fee if there is a dispute with the client (or in rare cases in which the courts set the attorney's fee). A client who agrees up front to a fee and scope of work is less likely to challenge the fee later. Ethical alternative billing includes ascertaining the client's expectations, agreeing to the scope of work, and setting the fee up front, using change orders when the scope of work changes, and confirming the details with the client in writing. Establishing and documenting value up front with the client (i.e. what the client wants to accomplish and/or the cost of doing nothing or of not obtaining the desired result) will be much better "proof" of reasonableness than a time-sheet.

Allison Shields (Allison@LegalEaseConsulting.com) is a New York-based lawyer and practice management consultant

Additional resources on flat-fee billing
- *A Discussion of Alternative Billing Methods*, prepared for the 2010 annual meeting of the American College of Mortgage Attorneys, by Deanna Lee Assistant GC, AIG Asset Management Group. Available at www.acmaatty.org/quebec/contents/sessions/pdf/06/Billing_Methods.pdf.
- Allison Shield's blog is at www.legalease.blogs.com.
- Jay Shepherd's blog is at www.clientrevolution.com.
- Jim Calloway's blog is at http://jimcalloway.typepad.com/lawpracticetips/alternative_billing/
- *The Firm of the Future: A Guide For Accountants, Lawyers and Other Professional Service Providers* (Dunn, Baker; 2003).

Should I Charge For Initial Consultations?

Lawyers fall into two distinct camps on this question:

Some say the initial consultation fee eliminates the tire-kickers; the individuals prospecting for free advice. Without that fee, the lawyers argue, they would lose too much time and revenue. Then there are those who argue that a free initial consultation is an effective marketing tool. That it helps increase the odds of signing a new client, and is often a competitive necessity.

Most personal injury firms offer free consultations, as do the mega firms that court prospective business clients with elaborate full-day meetings and expense account lunches (all on the firm's dime, of course). *Author note*: if you plan on a personal injury practice or competing with large firms, don't even think about charging for an initial consultation.

Personally, I favor free consultations. They encourage clients to size up the rates, the personalities, and the proposed strategies of different lawyers, and to choose the best fit. I believe this lays the groundwork for a smooth working relationship. By contrast, when clients must pay for a consultation, the fee deters them from shopping around; or, having paid for a consultation, the client feels pressured to retain the attorney. When a client feels that he's stuck with you because he had no other choice, he's more likely to feel resentment if the case goes badly, or he may start looking for another lawyer when presented with advice that he doesn't want to hear. Free consults are also smart when you start out because they give you more practice interacting with clients.

While I advocate free consultation, I realize that too many freebies can interfere with one's profitability, or wreak havoc with your schedule if clients aren't showing up for appointments. Here are some ways to experiment with free consultations in ways that don't encroach on your billable work:

Schedule consultations after hours or during down time. Studies suggest that for every five-minute interruption, as much time—or more—is needed to fully resume one's original task. So, if you schedule initial consultations when you might otherwise be researching a legal matter or writing an article, you stand to lose more than the half-hour for the consultation. It might take another half-hour or more to refocus. Schedule your initial consultations when they're least likely to disrupt your schedule; either first thing in the morning or at the end of your workday. Prospective clients usually prefer these time slots anyway; they minimize the conflicts with their own work schedule.

Limit the amount of time for a consultation. If you don't put a limit on the length of a free consultation, you could spend an entire day talking to clients for free. The answer is to limit the consultant to, say, 30 to 45 minutes. It's long enough to understand the client's problem, but not so long that they can talk your ear off. At the same time, don't place ridiculously short limits on the consultation. Example: many lawyers limit free consultations to 20 minutes. In my view, that's a waste of time. After preliminary introductions, you're left with only 15 minutes to get at the substance; hardly enough time for them to explain the facts of their case, or for you to ask the necessary questions and properly evaluate the matter. Even worse, some lawyers who advertise free consultation offer only the first 30 minutes gratis, after which the meter starts running. To me, that borders on a bait-and-switch. Clients—who have no idea how long an intake interview ought to take—come in expecting a free meeting, only to wind up paying because 30 minutes didn't allow enough time to accomplish anything.

Require clients to fill out an intake form. To weed out the tire-kickers, send an intake form when you make your appointment. Require clients to return it at least 24 hours before the consultation. If the form isn't returned, cancel the appointment. Clients who can't be bothered to complete an intake form are probably not serious about hiring a lawyer.

Offer a limited number of free consultations. In addition to limiting the time you devote per consultation, you can also limit the overall number of free consults available to clients. For example, set aside a certain number of slots for free consultations each week. Because these slots will fill up quickly, you can inform prospective clients that they either have the option of waiting to schedule a free consult, or they can pay your standard consultation fee and come in any time.

Charge an administrative fee for consultation. If a large percentage of your free consult appointments are "no shows," ask clients to secure their appointment with a small fee of $50 or $75. You can always refund the money when they show up for the meeting, or apply it to your first invoice if they hire you, or charge a reduced hourly fee for the initial consultation.

Reinvent the traditional consultation. Lawyer Rachel Rogers (www.rachelrodgers.com) once offered free consultations but realized that too many clients were just showing up for free advice. In response, Rogers decided to reinvent the traditional consultation. She created what she calls a "strategy session", a preliminary meeting ($250 for the hour) during which she is available to answer questions or discusses a client's future needs. Rogers has found that her strategy sessions not only help her clients, but it's a good way to determine who she truly wants to work with and who just wants free advice.

Billing For Expenses

Imagine visiting your dentist for a check-up, and receiving an invoice later that includes a supplemental charge for pain killer and disposable gloves. Or you go to lunch one day, and you get a bill for the meal AND the napkins and those little packets of catsup and mustard. Irritating, isn't it? And yet most lawyers see nothing wrong in sending an invoice along with a $2.20 charge for photocopying a pleading and for the 90 cents it took to mail it! What do clients think about this? It goes something like this: *I paid $750 for a business incorporation, and my lawyer can't include $3.10 for copying and mailing!*

You may believe that your listing each and every charge shows precision and attention to detail, but clients infer something else: that you intend to squeeze them for every nickel. Back when lawyers paid a per-search charge for legal research or per-minute for phone charges, they could justify billing clients responsible for the added charges. But today, virtually every service (phone, Internet, legal research, electronic fax) is priced at a set rate for unlimited usage, which makes it impossible to allocate the costs to individual clients. Rather than bill clients for fixed cost services or office supplies, total up your fixed operational costs, and charge a high enough rate—either a billable hour rate or flat fees—that covers those costs. Of course, where you incur extraordinary expenses directly related to a client's case—expert witness fees, deposition and court reporter costs, or making 10 copies of a 500-page contract—you're fully justified in passing those costs on to your client. Just be sure not to add a surcharge to these costs as many bars prohibit mark-ups on expenses.

How to Get Paid

"I had one client who begged me to defend him against an ex parte motion scheduled for the next day. I agreed to do it, worked all night, and won the motion. Then the client's check bounced and he declared bankruptcy. Now I only do work after a check has cleared. If it's an emergency, I demand a cashier's check."—**Nina Kallen, solo.**

Note: for more solo experiences with clients, go to In Their Own Words at the end of Chapter 10

Nearly every lawyer has been stiffed at least once by a client.

Sometimes, an adversarial opposing counsel or pro se litigants may drive up costs well beyond what you budgeted, and the client simply runs out of money. Or a client decides he doesn't feel like paying more than the initial retainer. Or a client may complain about your work quality, or results, and balks at paying, and you decide to write off any remaining balance rather than invite a grievance. As you continue your practice, you'll learn there are precautionary measures to help minimize your chances of non-payment. Some of the measures…like collecting a retainer or accepting credit card payment…are obvious. Others, like sending regular invoices, providing a comprehensive case budget, or identifying sources of payment other than your client, are less intuitive, but do increase your odds of getting paid for your services.

Payment up front. The very best insurance against non-payment is to collect what you can up front. Of course, just because you receive it doesn't mean you can spend it. Money paid as a retainer fee, i.e., an advance payment for work to be performed must always be placed into a trust account. By contrast, in some jurisdictions, flat fees are considered earned on receipt and can be deposited them directly into your operating account. But the majority of jurisdictions hold that a flat-fee isn't fully earned until the case is complete, and require flat fees to be deposited into the trust account, and disbursed either at the end of the case or as certain milestones are reached.

Be aware that many jurisdictions require you to return any unearned retainer balance to the client even if the retainer is designated as "non refundable." These jurisdictions hold that, where a retainer fee represents advance payment for work that the attorney has agreed to perform, the lawyer must return the unearned amounts if the work is not performed. There are several recent examples of lawyers who have been disciplined for refusing to return unearned portions of a retainer fee. See *Matter of Heather McClure O'Farrell*, Indiana Supreme Court (February 11, 2011), www. in.gov/judiciary/opinions/pdf/02111102per.pdf (reprimanding lawyer for keeping unearned fees); *Lawyer Disciplined Three Times Over Retainer Disputes*, West Virginia Record, March 17, 2011, www.wvrecord.com/news/234116-lawyer-disciplined-three-other-times-over-retainer-disputes (lawyer suspended three times for failing to return unearned retainers). *Bottom line*: consult your bar's rules on non-refundable retainers before you refuse to return money to a client.

But what if a client can't fund a large retainer? There are two options—an evergreen retainer or a credit card payment:

The evergreen retainer. When it happens that large legal matters may run tens or hundreds of thousands of dollars, clients may not have the ability to pay your estimated fee up-front. In such cases, you can use an *evergreen retainer* which the client must replenish when it reaches a certain level, and specified in your fee agreement. An evergreen provision might read: *You must provide a $5,000 retainer, which I will deposit in a client trust account and apply to my fees as they are incurred. Prior to disbursing any money from the trust account, I will invoice you for services rendered through that date and notify you of withdrawal. When the balance in the trust account reaches $2,500 or less, you* *must replenish the account to restore it to the initial $5,000 starting balance. I will notify you when the account reaches the $2,500 level, and provide you with fourteen days (14) to replenish the account.*

Credit cards. Credit cards are the preferred form of payment for doctors and accountants. Many lawyers, though, are still uncomfortable accepting them for payment. Some argue that keeping track of credit card merchant fees present too many problems from a trust account perspective; others resent paying the three or four percent merchant fee each time a client pays some or all of the bill. While these arguments carry some validity, the legal profession can't deny credit cards are an attractive solution (especially if clients get air miles for every dollar charged). Although the ABA has approved use of credit cards since 1974 (ABA Op. 338), many lawyers remain confused over the actual mechanics—such as who pays the transaction charges or where to deposit credit card payments. As discussed below, there are a variety of ways to resolve these ethical concerns—so you shouldn't let them deter you from accepting credit cards.

Some credit card payment basics:

Who pays the transaction charge? Some jurisdictions do not allow attorneys to pass on credit card transaction fees to customers. Even if your jurisdiction allows the practice, don't do it; clients will most likely resent it—and you. And let's be honest: while credit cards are a client convenience, they benefit lawyers even more by locking in payment for services. You may gripe about paying a $30 charge each time you take a $1,000 retainer, but consider it insurance; without the credit card, there might be occasions when the retainer was unrecoverable.

How do I reimburse clients for credit card fees that are deducted before the funds are deposited into my trust account? Because of transaction charges, the $1,000 payment your client makes by credit card will show up as $970 when deposited in your trust account. You can handle this matter in a few different ways: some jurisdictions may allow you to retain extra money in the trust account to cover credit card fees without running afoul of prohibitions on commingling personal and client funds. Other jurisdictions recommend that clients be credited for the amount taken from the retainer payment, or that you reduce your final bill by that amount. Consult the trust account guidelines for your jurisdiction to determine how you to properly reimburse clients for fees associated with credit card transactions.

Do credit card payments go to my trust account or operating account? Treat payments by credit card as you would cash payments. Credit card payments for work already performed can go directly to your law firm account; credit card payments for retainers for *future* work go to the trust account. Note: some jurisdictions, such as Missouri and Minnesota, allow lawyers to deposit credit card payments for advance fees into their operating account so long as the funds are immediately transferred to the trust account. Sources: *Lawyer Trust Account Handbook*, Missouri Lawyer Trust Account Foundation May 2009; the Minnesota policy is available at www.mncourts.gov/lprb/trustfaq.html).

Are there any special concerns associated with use of credit card payments for retainers? Yes. As just noted, when a credit card is used for an advance payment, the unearned funds must go into the lawyer's trust account. But a problem may arise when a client disputes your bill and seeks a charge-back from the credit card company pending resolution of the matter. If you have already disbursed funds from your trust account to pay your fees, then the credit card company's charge-back will come out of an unrelated client's trust monies which would constitute a misuse of funds. There are a few solutions: Michigan recommends that lawyers obtain the credit card company's agreement to withdraw charge-backs from the business account. If not, the lawyer must wait until the period for disputing charges has passed before disbursing money from the trust account. Michigan RI-344 (April 25, 2008).

How do I set up credit card payments? You can sign up for a merchant account with your bank, but you must inform the bank that transaction fees and charge-backs be taken from your operating fund not your trust account. If you're concerned about keeping these transactions straight, you can also sign up for a lawyer-specific merchant account at www.Lawcharge.com, or at The Modern Firm's merchant service (www.themodernfirm.com/services/law-firm-merchant-accounts), or at www.law-paymerchantaccount.com. These credit card accounts will handle charge-backs and transaction fees in an ethically compliant manner.

Services like Paypal or Squareup.com (where you can turn your smart phone into a credit card terminal) are alternatives. Squareup.com lets you accept credit cards by swiping the card through a device that plugs into your phone, or you enter the client's card number on the keyboard. Squareup sends the funds to your account after a 24-hour period (https://support.squareup.com/entries/384659-frequently-asked-questions#amount-deposit). With Paypal, credit card transactions are processed by entering the credit card number online. In contrast to Squareup, Paypal holds funds indefinitely unless a user electronically transfers them to a designated account.

Because client funds must travel through a Paypal or Squareup account where they are held for a short time before being transferred to a lawyer's trust account, some lawyers maintain that they are unethical. In my view, this argument is a red herring; after all, who knows how many accounts within a bank a credit card payment passes through before winding up in the trust account. Still, in the interest of caution, consult your bar rules for guidance on use of Paypal. *Note:* some lawyers also believe that Paypal is unprofessional. Paypal may suffice if you accept credit cards for occasional matters. However, if you plan to take them regularly, take the time to set up an ethically compliant merchant account.

A tight retainer agreement. Sometimes in the middle of a case, a client may stop paying their bills, or stop replenishing their retainer account. In this situation, you might find yourself bound to finish up representation unless your retainer agreement expressly reserves your right to withdraw upon non-payment. See *Defining the Terms of Client Service* (Chapter 10), in which I discuss the drafting of a retainer agreement that lays the groundwork for terminating representation when a client fails to pay.

Identifying other sources of revenue. A client may have the means to pay for a case, but not know it. In some matters where clients are sued, a business or home owners' insurance policy may cover the cost of legal expenses to defend the suit. In most jurisdictions, an insurance company's duty to defend is broader than its duty to indemnify, which means that the insurance company may be obligated to pay defense fees even where it takes the position that there's no coverage for liability. Take the time to review your client's insurance policy to see whether you can argue for coverage for defense costs. Insurance companies often allow policy holders to choose their own attorney. Even if you aren't on the company's list of attorneys, that won't necessarily disqualify the client from hiring you on his insurance company's dime. In some types of actions, clients may be entitled to recover attorney fees if they prevail in a lawsuit. For example, most federal and state civil rights statutes provide for recovery of attorneys fees. And often, leases or contracts allow the prevailing party to collect legal fees as well. The availability of attorneys fees sometimes give clients an incentive to bring a suit that they otherwise would not have pursued.

Invoices

Prompt invoices to clients showing the time that you devoted to a particular matter increase your chances of getting paid promptly.

Some guidelines:

Accuracy and detail. Make sure your invoices are both accurate and sufficiently detailed. Clients may not know whether 3.2 hours or 10.3 hours is a reasonable amount of time to draft a memo. But they will certainly recognize "red flags," like an entry where you billed 32 hours in a single day, or that you billed for three meetings with the client and only held one. More importantly, realize that your invoices may be scrutinized by others than your client. If a client disputes your bill, your invoices will serve as Exhibit A, and will need to include enough detail to stand on its own. Even when you invoice a client for a pre-agreed flat-fee, you should still list the deliverables promised under your original retainer letter so that the client can see all of the work that you've done.

Bottom line: when you draft invoices, assume that at some point, they will find their way into a judicial proceeding. If you have never seen an invoice, and aren't sure how much detail to include, look at the guidelines set by the court for submission of time records in reimbursable fee cases. If your court has accessible electronic dockets (the federal courts all do, through PACER), you can download fee requests submitted by attorneys, which will give you an idea of the level of detail that your bills ought to contain to satisfy clients and survive judicial scrutiny. One caveat on including excessive detail in invoices that arise when you represent municipal or public bodies subject to public information act and open meeting laws: generally, members of the public can access a municipality's or state's invoices, and where the invoices contain extensive detail, they may allow people to learn about internal strategies or decision-making. Be sure to clarify that the detailed invoices fall within the scope of attorney-client privilege, and that only the total amounts of time spent are subject to disclosure.

Timeliness. Send your invoices promptly so the good work you've done is still clear in the client's mind. Clients are busy, and even if they raved about your work they may have forgotten all about it if your bill doesn't arrive for three months. Of course, if you don't invoice at regular intervals, and continue to work, you risk non-payment for larger amounts of work. Pick at least one day each month to invoice clients, and outsource the task if you can't get the bills out yourself. Technology can also help you streamline your billing process. Most online practice management systems include a program for creating client invoices, as do stand-alone products like Freshbooks and Time59.com. Some of these programs can be set up to auto-bill clients (if, for example, you charge a monthly fee), or to send reminders when the bill is due. They also generate attractive, detailed bills that can be branded with your law firm logo.

Are you billing for something tangible? Clients are more likely to pay bills and not question them if they see tangible activity in a case. For instance, if you draft a contract for a client and send a bill, the client associates your fee with a product (the contract), and realizes that he owes you for it. By contrast, if you're working on an extensive research project or ongoing proceeding and you bill your client monthly, he may wonder what he's paying for. You have two options: if the matter overlaps two billing periods, but is finite, you can simply wait until you complete the project to bill for it. In a matter that continues with no end, you should prepare a monthly status report, describing the work you've done to date. You can also reconcile the amounts billed to date with your estimate, to assure your client that the case is on budget.

Flexibility. If possible, be flexible with clients who run short on funds midway through litigation, particularly where the fees exceed any estimate you may have provided. For instance, if a client begins to run short on money, but the case has potential, you could renegotiate the fee agreement, shifting from hourly fees to a contingency arrangement. Where a case promises benefits like publicity or entre to a hot new field, consider reducing your fee or allowing your client to spread payments out over time.

In my opinion, the benefits of a fee estimate outweigh the drawbacks in their ability to weed out clients who can't . . . or won't pay.

Let's say you draw up a detailed estimate that shows a range of fees from $15,000 to $75,000, based on a variety of scenarios (e.g., adverse rulings, bothersome opposing counsel, proceeding to litigation if administrative process fails). Your estimate may trigger a useful discussion over how much the client can realistically spend, and whether you can develop a strategy that fits their budget. There's always the chance your client could go to a competitor, who tells the client "the case shouldn't be much trouble," and calculates a fee of only $20,000. If that happens, your competitor may have done you an inadvertent favor: the client may only have had $20,000 to spend . . . and, if the case takes a turn for the worse, your competitor will have to put in many uncompensated matters.

Should You Sue For Non-Payment?

Suppose you withdraw from a case for non-payment, or you conclude a case but the client fails to pay for the last installment of work (most likely because with the case over, he or she no longer needs your service). Should you sue for non-payment of the balance owed? Some lawyers believe that suing for fees is never worthwhile because you expose yourself to a malpractice claim or grievance. Others argue that unless you go after all money owed, you'll gain a reputation as a push-over, and other clients will also try to stiff you. Both arguments have some merit depending upon the circumstances.

Here are some criteria to evaluate in deciding whether to sue for fees:

Have you exhausted all other possibilities? Any suit for legal fees ought to be a last resort. Before you even seriously consider a suit, evaluate whether you've exhausted all other possibilities for collection:

Have you personally called the client to make a request for payment? While delegating collection to staff makes sense, you ought to make one effort to contact the client yourself about overdue fees. During your conversation, ask the client whether nonpayment has resulted from dissatisfaction with your service. If the client's complaints have any merit at all, you should reduce the bill.

Have you tried to arrive at a compromise? If your client has simply run short on cash, perhaps you can offer some payment options. Can the client pay what's owed on credit card? Is he willing to make monthly payments on the amount owed? Are there ways that clients can offer something else of value…perhaps an equity interest in the company, or in-kind services to reimburse you, at least in part, for unpaid fees.

What about fee arbitration? In *The Solo's Guide to Collecting Fees* (ABA, 2006), attorney/contributor Linda J. Ravdin suggests proposing fee arbitration to the client. She writes:

> *"Probably the number one advantage [of arbitration] is that the client cannot use a malpractice counterclaim as a defensive maneuver, because you do not have to agree to arbitrate malpractice claims unless a local rule or your fee agreement requires it."*

Arbitration is also faster and less expensive than a court proceeding. If you've ruled out these options and still have no alternative but to file suit to recover the fee, consider these issues:

Is the fee worth it? You more than anyone know about the time and expense of a legal proceeding. If not much money is at stake, ask yourself whether the costs associated with a lawsuit are worth it. And when you calculate the cost of a suit, assume that you will hire someone to represent you. Though seemingly benign on the surface, a fee dispute can become emotionally charged, with your former client questioning your competence and efficiency, and perhaps filing a grievance against you for good measure. Unless you're represented in a fee action, your emotions may get the best of you and cloud your judgment.

Are your hands clean? When you sue for a fee, the quality of your service becomes fair game. Can you document that you performed in accordance with applicable standards of care? Are your time records accurate, and do they fairly reflect time worked? Is the amount that you're seeking to collect reasonable? A time sheet that shows that you billed 30 hours in a single day or that you billed for a court appearance on a Sunday when the court was closed will sink your claim for recovering your fees.

Check the statements that apply: Assign 1 point for each checked response (does not apply to contingency or pro bono matters.)

☐ 1. The prospective client appears to have the ability to pay for this service.

☐ 2. If the prospective client appears unable to pay the quoted fee, I either (a) offer a reduced scope of services (that will serve his needs within his budget and meet applicable professional standards) or (b) decline to accept the client.

☐ 3. I turn down clients with "sure thing" cases, or who believe "money is no object," or who believe "lawyers are worthless, money-grubbing parasites."

☐ 4. I turn down clients who ask me to work for free (in non-contingency cases).

☐ 5. I turn down clients who want to bargain only about price and not scope of service or terms of payment.

☐ 6. request a retainer that will cover the cost of the case and/or compensate me fairly even if client does not pay another cent.

☐ 7. I wait to start work until after the retainer check has cleared.

☐ 8. For clients who cannot pay a full retainer up front, I set up an "evergreen system" to replenish a fund if it reaches a certain amount

☐ 9. Where ethics rules do not allow me to put flat fees directly into my operating fund, my retainer agreement specifies a method for disbursing the fee over the life of the case.

☐ 10. My retainer agreement explicitly states that non-payment and/or failure to replenish the evergreen retainer is grounds for withdrawal.

☐ 11. I offer credit cards as a payment option (if ethically compliant).

☐ 12. I charge flat fees or provide estimates that explain best- and worst-case scenarios.

☐ 13. I offer different prices for different levels of service, (though ALL levels of service, low or high end, meet my professional obligations).

☐ 14. My retainer agreement explains to client how funds are disbursed from the trust account.

☐ 15. send invoices by e-mail.

☐ 16. I send invoices in the same month as the completion of work.

☐ 17. I send invoices that match the client's payment cycles (e.g., client pays bills at end of month).

☐ 18. I have a process in place for quickly addressing late payments and documenting communication with clients.

☐ 19. I have a system for setting up payment plans if necessary.

☐ 20. I have a process in place for initiating withdrawal from the case where clients have not paid.

☐ 21. I have a lien on the file or other mechanism in place to ensure priority over other creditors.

☐ 22. My retainer agreement requires clients to arbitrate fee-disputes or present them to a bar fee-dispute panel.

A **Yes** score of 20 or higher: Low risk of getting stiffed

A **Yes** score of 17–20: You've taken some precautions, but you could tighten up your practices.

A **Yes** score of 16 and below: You're at high risk of being stiffed and should re-evaluate your practices.

Office Operations & Policies

Many solos who work alone believe that it is not necessary to put their office policies into writing since they're already familiar with them. But what if you decide to hire staff at some point, or if you are suddenly incapacitated, and need a back-up attorney to step in and take over your cases? Without written office policies, future employees or substitute counsel may not be able to handle the workload in the manner you prefer. Written policies also help manage client expectations. It lets clients know up-front about important operational aspects of your law firm.

Below are three types of policies that your firm should have in place: (1) description of office policies for clients; (2) employee or personnel handbook or policies, including use of social media, and (3) an emergency policy in the event of disability or death. This section briefly outlines different components of these plans, and lists resources where you can find samples and additional information:

Office policies for clients. Develop a policy statement that introduces clients to your way of doing business. Keep it short—a single page if you can—and either post it on your Web site or give copies to clients. Use plain English, and adopt a friendly but professional tone. Recently, a South Carolina law firm's office policy went viral online because it bluntly proclaimed, "*We do not work weekends and do not provide emergency numbers for weekends…*" (see MyShingle.com, http://myshingle.com/2010/10/articles/client-relations/why-should-your-clients-care-that-their-lawyers-dont-work-weekends/). Some lawyers said the firm's policy wasn't entirely unreasonable, but that its tone might have been off-putting to clients.

Below are some basic topics to cover in your office policy, though you may wish to add others based on personal experience. In fact, your Office Policies should be an organic document that is reviewed and updated over time:

Office hours and appointments. Make sure your policy statement includes your office hours. It makes for easier scheduling for your clients. And if you're available weekends and evening hours, make it known; your flexibility could be a major selling point for clients who work 9-to-5. You should also specify that you receive clients by appointment only. Walk-ins can be disruptive; even embarrassing if you work from a virtual office where you're only there a few hours a month.

After-hours contact. For ease of mind, clients often like to know they can make contact with their lawyer after-hours when necessary, and certainly in an emergency. Of course, that doesn't require you to be tied to your phone 24/7. Your policy statement can include a voice-mail or answering service number, and you can let clients how they can communicate with you by e-mail.

Scheduling. Some lawyers employ online self-scheduling programs to minimize the need for office staff. If you want clients to make appointments that way, make sure it is reflected in your statement. And be sure the Web program runs smoothly; it's a major irritant if it doesn't.

Return calls and e-mail. Many lawyers aspire to return calls (or e-mail) within 24 hours. A noble policy, but not always possible due to court or other appointments. Your policy statement should explain that while you make every effort to respond to calls and e-mail within 24 hours, it may be necessary that you—or an assistant—get back to the client as soon as it is feasible.

Payment methods. Credit card payment is routine for other professionals—doctors, accountants, therapists. Let clients know whether you accept credit cards or not.

Malpractice coverage. Some states require that you disclose whether you have malpractice coverage. Even when it isn't required, some lawyers identify their malpractice carrier as added reassurance (although others believe that—if not required—the mention of one's insurer may invite a lawsuit).

Children. Clients with infants or small children are known to miss appointments when they can't find childcare. If you have a child-friendly office, let clients know so they know they can bring the child with them to the appointment.

Online file availability. If you have an online client portal that allows clients to check on filings or case status, encourage them to use it before calling the office. If clients aren't able to check case status themselves, you might mention in the policy that you provide updates every month even if there's no activity on the file.

Invoicing. Let clients know if their bill will be mailed or sent electronically, and if they will be invoiced when work is completed or at the beginning or end of the month.

Security policies. Clients entrust you with their Social Security numbers, credit card accounts, and other personal information, and they have a right to know if you have a policy in place to secure their data. Do you encrypt data…do you (or your vendors) have cyber-insurance in the event of a breach? Massachusetts, Nevada, and other states now require encryption for certain data. Check to see what the security policies exist in your state, and let clients know that your practices are compliant.

Paperless. Some clients still expect multiple paper copies and mailings, while others prefer e-mail. If your office is largely paperless, let clients know.

Personnel policies. Once you hire a part-time or even full-time employee, you need to have more formal policies in place because of exposure to wrongful or discriminatory termination actions or liability for unemployment benefits.

Below are some of the critical policies that an employment handbook should address. Your handbook should…

- Clearly communicate the "at will" nature of employment at your firm.
- Include any provisions necessary to comply with applicable federal and state discrimination laws (not all laws may apply to a small company, so you'll want to check).
- Discuss appropriate use of workplace technology, e.g., can employees use company e-mail for personal matters…can they talk on their cellphones while driving on company business? Note: You should also be clear that employees do not have an expectation of privacy when it comes to use of computers or phones on the job. Technology policy would not be complete with guidance on social media use. Employees need to understand that lack of discretion can compromise clients' rights, while deceptive activity can get your firm in trouble with the bar or the Federal Trade Commission. You can find a database of 200 social media policies from all industries online at http://socialmediagovernance.com/policies.php.
- Describe whether your firm offers paid or unpaid vacation, and for how long.
- Identify those classes of employees who qualify for overtime. If you're not sure, consult with an employment lawyer as a mis-classification can result in liability for unpaid overtime. .

You can find many guidelines for employment handbooks and manuals for general businesses online, though be aware that state laws may vary. Your state's law practice management office may also have additional information.

"I'M PREGNANT. SHOULD I TELL CLIENTS AND OPPOSING COUNSEL?"

Thoughts on Maternity Leave & New Arrivals

Q: I just learned I'm pregnant. Should I tell my clients and opposing counsel?
A: Unlike other personal issues like marital status or sexual orientation, there's no concealing your condition from clients and colleagues. So, it's appropriate to give a brief explanation of your expectant status to clients or counsel likely to see you during the pregnancy. Likewise, feel free to announce your good news with those clients and colleagues with whom you have a cordial relationship. Beyond that, discuss your pregnancy only on a "need to know" basis. If you must put a case on hold, or reschedule a hearing to avoid conflicts with your due date or anticipated maternity leave, you need to tell clients of the pregnancy.

Q: Back at my old law firm, I would have been entitled to paid leave. How do I handle maternity leave as a solo?
A: The good news is that if, after the birth, you're willing to work a few hours a day or a week, you can extend maternity to six months even a year. The bad news is that you can't expect to take a fully-paid, three-month maternity leave without seriously jeopardizing your practice. Even if you could put all active matters on hold, you would lose substantial ground if you were not willing or able to take calls from, or meet with, new prospects.

- Check your calendar in your fourth or fifth month. Get a continuance if you have an already-scheduled trial or other commitment one month on either side of your due date. You don't want to go into labor a month early, on the eve of trial, and then have to deal with the stress of postponement.
- In the last few months before you're due, close out and invoice for as many matters as possible, and move cases forward to a point where they'll be resolved shortly after the baby is born. That way, even though you're not at work, you'll continue to generate some revenue and won't feel pressured to return. If you think you may want to cut back permanently once your baby is born, some changes to your practice may be appropriate. In my own case, I knew that I would not be able to juggle the unpredictable court-appointed criminal cases I had been handling after my first daughter was born, so I closed out my criminal files as quickly as I could.
- Keep the month before your due date—and two months after—clear of major trials or motions that will involve substantial prep time and personal appearances. Many courts will allow you to file notices of unavailability to put a case on hold.
- Your solo practice can't survive if you put all your cases on hold permanently. Transactional attorneys, in particular, may still need to schedule closings to move deals forward, or may have to comply with deadlines set by statute that a court has no authority to suspend. In this case, consider asking one or two trusted colleagues if they can step in and handle a piece of a matter. Incidentally, colleagues will often decline payment for a small favor like getting a filing out or showing up at a scheduling conference. But you need to compensate them for matters involving a significant time commitment. Or, outsource the work to an experienced attorney who can handle depositions, court hearings, and contract negotiation. Even if you're not able to make money from the contract arrangement (because an experienced contract attorney can charge nearly as much as you charge your clients), at least you would be able to retain the client. For more on outsourcing, see Chapter 12.
- Once the baby is born, make the most of technology. Working the Internet and a smartphone, your clients probably won't even know you're out of the office. You can take an hour or so (when the baby is asleep) to return phone calls or send e-mails. In fact, many lawyer/moms become quite proficient at typing with one hand and nursing or bottle-feeding with the other.

- After two months at home, some moms are quite ready to resume a full schedule; others prefer more time at home. Don't jump in until you're ready. After all, as a solo practitioner, you have the flexibility of easing back into work. For example, you might want to take another two to four months working a few hours a day while the baby naps (or, if you're fortunate, you have parents who live close by and are eager to spend your work time with their new grandchild). One more thing: easing back to work also gives your newborn an opportunity to get used to a new child-care situation.

- The birth of your child is a joyous occasion, and most clients, judges, and lawyers are willing to accommodate requests for extensions and delays. I know because it happened to me: just about the time I had a reply brief due at the D.C. Circuit, I had to have the labor induced. Just before heading to the hospital, I drafted an extension request based on the impending birth. The clerk's office left me a voice-mail that they would hand-carry my request to the judge's office. When I returned from the hospital two days later, the clerk's office called with congratulations...and said my extension request had been granted.

- The birth or arrival of a baby is a special time that passes all too quickly. Enjoy and celebrate the occasion as long as you want. Revenues rise and fall, new clients come and go. How often will you have dedicated time with your new baby? Savor it.

Q: My solo practice is doing pretty well, but we depend on my wife's job for additional income and health benefits. With our first child on the way, I wonder if our benefits are in jeopardy if she works fewer than four days a week.

A: Find out how much of your health insurance policy is provided by her employer. Some companies pay the entire premium, others require employees to cover 25 to 60 percent of the cost. If her employer subsidizes only a small percentage, it may not be much more expensive to have your own policy. And, if that is the case—and she works for a company of 20 or more—you can arrange for up to 18 months of coverage through her employer under the federal Consolidated Omnibus Budget Reconciliation Act (COBRA).

Emergency Planning

When Maryland solo Herb Dubin was unexpectedly hospitalized for 12 days, and then had to spend a month recuperating, he didn't have a back-up or emergency plan. Fortunately, he practiced in a shared suite with several attorneys who picked up his caseload, notified his clients of his illness, and filed continuances at the court. [Source: Baltimore Daily Record, October 13, 2009, at http://findarticles.com/p/articles/miqn4183/is_20091013/ai_n39260822/.

Many malpractice carriers require you to have a back-up attorney who can take over if something happens to you. If you don't have a plan in place, Pat Yevics, Maryland's law practice management advisor, suggests that you and another lawyer establish a "buddy" system by which the two of you agree to handle each other's files if something happens. If you can't find an attorney as a back-up, at least make sure that someone—your assistant, a spouse, a friend—can access your calendar system in the event of a personal emergency. Perhaps even put your files onto an offsite server (e.g., cloud computing) so that your files are accessible no matter where you are. Even if you were ill, you would still have the ability to locate your files, or at least talk someone else through the process. Many bars offer a free online version of an emergency manual for lawyers. It's called, *Planning Ahead: A Guide to Protecting Your Clients and Survivors in the Event of a Lawyer's Disability or Death* (available at www.wisspd.org/html/ACD/PA.pdf).

The information below is loosely extracted from this guide:

- Take the time to create an emergency plan and to find a back-up attorney who can step;
- Include contact information on clients so that someone can take over;
- Include security access codes for online accounts;
- Include access codes to your calendar system so that an attorney can reschedule;
- Create form letters to clients that back-up counsel can send to notify them of an emergency;
- Identify several attorneys who are willing to serve as back-up counsel for case matters and files, and offer to reciprocate;
- Identify an individual responsible for access to trust accounts, and to authorize a power of attorney.

HOW A SOLO LAWYER TAKES VACATION *by Brian Tannebaum, Esq.*

As I wind down a two-week vacation (yes, two full weeks!), I'm reflecting on my 15 years of practicing law, and how it was only recently that I allowed myself to take so much time off.

I probably could have done it earlier, but I was afraid. I didn't want to be away for more than a long weekend in case the "big" case came in, or because the things I had set in court "couldn't possibly" be covered by any other lawyer. For example, five years ago, I was hired on the biggest case I ever had. The client was arrested on a case for which the bond was set at $2.8 million. Within hours, I negotiated a million-dollar bond, and then left for a three-day conference. When I arrived, the prosecutor called to say that she would withdraw the offer for the bond due to "newly discovered evidence" about my client's financial status. My client's family and friends blamed me, and for the next three days they rang my cellphone night and day, asking, *"When is he getting out?"* When I returned from the conference, I learned that another lawyer met with my client and was hired. I was devastated. I was only gone three days. How could I leave town for two weeks? On a vacation?

As my practice grew, though, I realized I had a choice: never leave town for a significant period of time for fear of missing out on the big case, or realize that there is more to life and that the fastest car in the race has to make a pit stop like everyone else.

It's not easy, but taking a real vacation makes what we do as lawyers that much more rewarding. So, how do you it? Some suggestions:

Six months from departure. If you walk in to court in January knowing that you are going on vacation in June, sound the horns. Tell your judges, tell everyone.

One month from departure. Meet with at least one, preferably two lawyers, who will handle all your in-and-out-of-court matters, emergencies, and meetings with new clients.

Two weeks from departure. Gather your staff and explain the following:
- This vacation is important. I do not want to be contacted EXCEPT in extreme emergencies.
- This vacation is important. New clients should NOT be told I am away for two weeks.
- This vacation is important. I want ONE e-mail a day regarding important mail and messages.
- This vacation is important. If clients insist on reaching me on vacation, the answer is NO.

One day before departure. Send an e-mail, fax, or text to those clients who you believe may contact you during those two weeks. Let them know you've left everything in the hands of your capable staff and other attorneys. Explain that nothing important will be going on while you are away, and they are free to call your office in an emergency.

During your vacation. Wake up, read, and return important e-mails, and do it again at night. Just because you're on vacation, doesn't mean to have to vanish...but it is important to detach yourself from the daily grind of e-mail, texts, calls. In fact, leave your phone in the car, or at the hotel, or locked up somewhere.

When I return, I'll have a ton of work to do, but I know exactly what needs to be done.

—**Brian Tannebaum (http://mylawlicense.blogspot.com), a Miami-based criminal defense lawyer. Used with permission**

CHAPTER 12

Outsourcing

" Whether you choose to charge your client more than
what you pay for (outsourced) services,
outsourcing is still cost-effective for your client, since
even a rate that includes a reasonable profit to you
will generally be less than your own hourly rate.

—Lisa Solomon, solo

In recent years, outsourcing has gained real traction among large law firms. Many solo practitioners, though, have been slow to embrace outsourcing and enjoy its cost-efficiencies. For one thing, most solos are unaware of the robust and reasonably-priced freelance legal market, and, for another, they are often reluctant to ask for or to accept help—or even to admit that they need any. Lawyers simply aren't used to asking for help, says the former owner of a West Coast contract lawyer placement agency. They just work harder.

Should You Outsource?

To see if you might be a candidate for help from a contract lawyer, check as many of the statements below as applied to you in the last year:

- ☐ Your billable hours increased enough to make you feel overworked, but not enough to justify hiring another associate.
- ☐ You turned down revenue-generating work because you didn't have sufficient staff or expertise to handle the matter.
- ☐ A client complained about your delay in attending to his problem, or you had to make excuses for not doing what you promised.
- ☐ You took on a matter that made such extraordinary demands on your time that you felt you neglected other matters.
- ☐ An issue outside your area of expertise arose in the middle of a case, and you didn't have time to explore it adequately.
- ☐ The court set an accelerated trial date in one of your cases, and it conflicted with a series of depositions you had scheduled in another case.
- ☐ You needed someone to assist you as "second chair" during a complicated trial.
- ☐ The external demands of your practice—phone calls, court appearances, client conferences, settlement negotiations—took so much time and attention that you didn't have the opportunity to concentrate on the legal issues and strategies of your cases.
- ☐ You wanted to take parental leave, vacation (even a sabbatical), but did not because you wouldn't have had adequate coverage during the absence.

☐ You dreamed about scaling back your practice so you could devote more time to your family, a side business, or a hobby.

☐ You took on a case in which opposing counsel appeared to have six or seven lawyers to your one.

☐ You missed a deadline.

☐ You continue to back out of networking events or marketing lunches because of too much work at the office.

☐ You've wanted to start a law firm newsletter or update your social media profile for a few months but just haven't found the time.

Note: If you checked even one of these statements, you have good reason to seek out help from a contract lawyer. If you checked *more* than one statement, you should do it today.

Tasks Suitable for Outsourcing

Almost any legal matter can be outsourced, so long as your client does not expect that you will personally handle the matter, or the matter does not involve an obscure expertise that you are uniquely competent to handle. Even though many of the tasks listed here—answering phones, scheduling meetings—can be automated, some lawyers and their clients prefer the personal touch of a live person picking up the phone or setting up a meeting.

That said, here are some matters suitable for outsourcing:

Legal research & writing. Legal research on specific questions raised by your client during the course of a case, or to evaluate the strength of a new client matter. Besides memos, you can outsource cite-checking and editing to a law student who has worked on a journal, or to a junior attorney who is generally capable of performing these tasks.

Social media support. Though you shouldn't hire others to pose as you to tweet or to blog, social media involves plenty of back-end tasks where outsourcing makes sense. You can hire others to create and update social media profiles, research and format blog posts, or help identify like-minded people to link to or friend.

Litigation practice

Briefs and motions. Many attorneys outsource appellate brief writing because they lack appellate expertise, or are too close to the case to objectively identify the strongest arguments. Appellate work is also readily severable from the underlying matter. You can also outsource drafting motions.

Court appearances. Rather than spend three hours waiting for the judge to convene a status hearing, outsource your court appearances to a contract attorney. If you do, provide the attorney with the case file and your phone number in the event the judge decides to inquire about substantive issues.

Depositions. Defending depositions does not require extensive familiarity with the facts of the case, and it lends itself well to outsourcing. By contrast, the task of taking depositions is less cost-effective to delegate because your hire will need time to learn the case, or may miss an opportunity to ask important questions because they're not conversant with all of the details.

Document review. For years now, large firms have been successfully using contract attorneys for document-review, and many now offshore doc review projects to India. With most documents now in electronic format, a contract attorney can handle your doc review offsite.

Discovery requests and responses. For simple litigation matters, a contract attorney with a litigation background can review your complaint and prepare discovery requests, work with a client to provide responses, or identify which requests are objectionable.

Practice management

Administrative. A virtual assistant can perform a wide range of administrative and secretarial tasks, including billing, bookkeeping, and marketing support.

Secretarial/document preparation. A secretary or transcription service can convert dictation into written work, or format and finalize your already-typed drafts.

Answering service. A service can handle incoming calls and assist in scheduling.

Creating, ordering, and scanning client files. Contact document scanning professionals if you want to run a "paperless" operation. You'll still have plenty of files that require organization; when they get out of control, hire a student, administrative assistant, or professional organizer to put things in order.

Marketing

Market research and analysis. Interested in expanding your practice into a new area of law but don't know much about the economic potential? Outsource your market research to a law student with a business background.

Branding. Increasingly, lawyers are recognizing the power of branding—that is, the packaging of images, concepts, and slogans—to distinguish their firm from others. Outsource this activity to a professional marketer.

Public relations. At the outset, you probably won't be handling cases of public interest or matters of high media visibility that would warrant having a PR consultant. Still, as your caseload grows, or if you suddenly find yourself handling a sensitive, high-profile matter, it would be wise to seek the guidance of a PR professional. For state-specific consultants, seek out the long-established Public Relations Society of America at www.prsa.org. Or read *Everyday Public Relations for Lawyers: A No-Nonsense Strategic PR Guide* (2007), by Gina Furia Rubel, Esq.

Speaking engagements. Interested in adding conference presentations to your marketing mix? Hiring an assistant can relieve you of many of the time-consuming details, such as identifying conferences of interest, making preliminary inquiries, managing your travel schedule, and stylizing your PowerPoints or other presentation materials. By outsourcing, you can devote your time to preparing your presentation.

Back-office management. If you have employees or a high-volume practice, you would benefit from outsourcing the following accounting responsibilities:

Accounting. To balance the books, reconcile client payments, and manage documents for tax preparation.

Payroll. Many lawyers use payroll companies to cut employee checks and send them to direct-deposit accounts.

Invoicing. If you can't find the time to invoice clients regularly, outsource the preparation of invoices to someone who can spend a few hours each week or month converting your time records into invoices, transmitting them to clients, and following up on collection.

Technical support

Computer networking set-up. You can probably set up your own computer. But outsource more technical needs, such as networking multiple office computers, integrating computer and phone systems, or installing additional memory and back-up.

Practice-management systems. Some attorneys prefer to set up and learn for themselves how to use a practice-management system. If you're short on time, or you want to customize your system for special applications, hire a consultant.

Web design. At Craigslist.com, Elance.com, odesk.com, and sologig.com you can find many competent Web designers and developers. For basic Web templates (and domain registration), go to Godaddy.com, Dotser.com, Register.com, among others.

What to Expect From Outsourcing

Whether you outsource legal or non-legal tasks, outsourcing produces multiple benefits which may outweigh some of the drawbacks, such as the added costs or time involved in delegating a task or supervising your hires. Benefits include:

Profitability. Outsourcing projects can increase your firm's profitability, allowing you to take on new cases you might otherwise turn down if you're overwhelmed with other matters. Outsourcing can also rescue you from the consequences of uneconomic cases that you may have accepted out of desperation. Example: suppose you agree to represent a client on appeal for a flat-fee of $3,000, but the case takes double the 20 hours you originally estimated. Your effective billing rate is reduced to $75/hour. If you're beginning to attract more work at your rate of $150/hour, you're better off outsourcing the lower-paying work to a contract attorney for $75/hour and clearing it off your plate. Moreover, if you could find someone to accept the project for $50/hour, or for a flat fee of $2,500, you might even be able to squeeze some profit out of a matter that otherwise costs you in lost opportunities. The ABA and most state bars allow lawyers to mark up the cost of a contract attorney (*Lawyers as Contractors: How Much Can You Charge For That?* Texas Bar Journal, June 2010). Note: Maryland and Texas are exceptions.

Increased flexibility. Hiring lawyers have found contract lawyers or staff to be one of the most efficient ways to manage scheduling conflicts. Once you've been practicing awhile, you'll get a better sense of the ebb and flow of your workload to know whether to invest in a full-time associate or staff. In the meantime, outsourcing legal research and writing on a project basis lets you ramp up when your caseload is heavy, and to cut back when it isn't. On the other hand, if you hire a full-time associate or paralegal in anticipation of several long-term proceedings, and those cases settle a few months later with no other billable work in sight, you're left with a salary to pay and no revenue to cover it.

Improved client service. One of the most valuable but least-noted benefits of using contract lawyers is in the area of client relations. Because contract lawyer rates have not kept pace with direct-to-client rates, the hiring lawyer can make a profit *and* offer the client a lower-than-usual rate at the same time. Example: a hiring lawyer who bills out her own time at $200/hour can hire a senior-level contract lawyer at $80/hour, charge the client only $150/hour, and still realize a small profit. Inexpensive trial assistance is another client benefit. Former solo Daniel Edwards says, "*The first time I hired a contract lawyer was to assist me during trial. I made a checklist of points I wanted to be sure to cover. The contract lawyer's task was to watch the testimony, and check off each I covered. As I went through the examination, I'd occasionally swing by the desk and get reminded of the issues I hadn't yet raised. It worked so well, I've continued to hire assistants whenever I'm in trial.*"

Reduced malpractice risk. When you juggle a heavy caseload, there is a greater likelihood that some matters may get overlooked or given less attention than required, resulting in missed deadlines. In fact, the majority of bar grievances arise out of cases neglected by solo and small firm lawyers who couldn't find the time to work on them. Occasional outsourcing to catch up on your files might save you from a malpractice complaint.

Greater career satisfaction. Think about how pleasant your practice would be if you could take a break from boring and routine work and not sacrifice income. Contract lawyers let the hiring lawyer focus on the aspects of practice they enjoy most without losing profit. And for those lawyers who relish oral presentations and attorney-client interaction, legal research and writing is drudgery at best. Or, as one solo put it, "*A day in the library is a day in hell for me.*" Contract lawyers also provide an opportunity for solo and small firm practitioners to juggle part-time or flexible schedules. Example: two Seattle bankruptcy lawyers wanted to maintain an alternative practice. They both worked four days a week, and one of them had to leave in mid-afternoon so she could be at home with her children. They hired an experienced bankruptcy lawyer to come in two days a week on a contract basis to create the equivalent of two full-time practices.

Reduced stress. Solos are often reluctant to outsource because of the need to squeeze every nickel from every case. It's understandable, but wearing all the hats is a burden. Outsourcing helps relieve the stress that comes from long hours, relentless deadlines, difficult clients, contentious adversaries, and the lack of vacation. Example: instead of avoiding your problem cases, outsource them to a contract attorney who can act as an intermediary, and deal directly with problem clients or attorneys. BigLaw partners frequently delegate the task of communicating with annoying clients to associates. By outsourcing, you achieve the same result.

Marketing stays on track. Typically, when solos get busy with billable matters, their marketing efforts take a hit. When the work subsides, they're back to square one, scrambling to get the marketing machine back on track. By outsourcing marketing tasks—like scheduling get-togethers with referral sources or speaking engagements— solos can maintain their marketing momentum during their busiest periods.

Helping the profession. Hiring lawyers on a contract basis lets you help out the droves of unemployed lawyers even while building your practice. Assuming the individuals are qualified, sending a few pieces of work to unemployed lawyers not only helps them pay their bills, but lets them build their resume which in turn may help them to find jobs.

SIX REASONS WHY LAWYERS MIGHT NOT OUTSOURCE

Contract lawyers are too expensive. I can't afford it. While it's true that some highly experienced contract lawyers do command a premium, there are still so many lawyers out of work these days that it's a buyer's market for the hiring lawyer. And don't forget, in many cases, outsourcing can pay for itself; even generate a profit since you can bill the cost of the contract lawyer to clients (at a mark-up in most jurisdictions). Still, even if you have a contingency case or non-billable matter, you can find qualified help within your price range. Also, consider whether you actually need the help of a licensed lawyer. If you just need assistance with simple legal research, or responding to a document request or to fill out forms, perhaps a law student or paralegal could handle the work…for less.

I'd love to outsource, but I work from a home office and don't have space for a second person. Outsourcing doesn't require always require a physical location. Many outsourced lawyers and staff have their own equipment and workspace, and are adept at working virtually. But if you hire one of them, you will need a system to share and exchange documents, manage deadlines, and to supervise outsourced staff remotely.

I just don't see how outsourcing can save me time. It only takes a couple of minutes to send out invoices, proofread my blog posts, or schedule marketing events. You probably don't realize how much cumulative time is required to handle small tasks that on their own may involve just a few minutes each. For example, a dozen five-minute tasks throughout the day adds up to five hours in a work week or more than half a day, especially when you consider that each interruption requires 15 minutes more to regain focus. Once you start outsourcing…even a small number of administrative tasks…you'll most likely find other ways to improve your efficiency by delegating.

I work in a city where labor costs are high. I'd like to outsource some of my legal work to lawyers in a lower-cost rural area, but I can't do that if they're not licensed in my state. Contract lawyers don't represent clients; they work for you directly. So, as long as the contract lawyer doesn't directly advise your clients, and as long as you review and supervise their research and work product, their bar license is irrelevant.

I've heard that the IRS is going after people who outsource, and I don't want the hassle of a potential audit. For years, the IRS has been concerned about employers who attempt to circumvent the tax code by classifying employees as "independent contractors." Employers are required to withhold income tax for employees, but not for contractors, so mis-classification can result in revenue losses for the IRS. Generally, workers qualify as independent contractors when they set their own hours, work for several people at once, are hired on a project basis, work off premises on their own equipment, and furnish their own equipment. Virtual contract lawyers and staff almost always fall within this definition, as do staff brought in for short term support. For details, see the IRS Web site at www.irs.gov/business-es/small/article/0,,id=99921,00.html]. Still concerned? Hire short-term help through a temp agency. You'll probably pay more, but you won't have to worry about an audit since you'll be contracting with the agency.

Contract lawyering involves fee-splitting and that's unethical. Fee-splitting describes a scenario in which two lawyers share fees paid by a client. As a general rule, lawyers not in the same firm can share or split fees with disclosure to and consent from the client. But the ABA and most state bars do not treat contract lawyering arrangements as fee-splitting because the contract lawyer is working for another lawyer, and not directly for the client. Moreover, the hiring lawyer's obligation to pay the contract lawyer derives from his agreement with the contract lawyer, and is not dependent upon how much or whether the client pays. Note: a partial exception exists in Texas; it holds that contract lawyering *is* fee-splitting when lawyers mark-up their time. Though it's always wise to consult your state's ethics rules before hiring a contract attorney, you'll see that there is little to fear.

Selecting & Working With Contract Lawyers

The selection. If you have never hired a contract lawyer—or if you have but with unhappy results—you need to think through the search process. Contract lawyers aren't fungible commodities; their skills, personalities, and work styles are as diverse as any other group of lawyers, and investing time in the selection process is one of the best ways to assure a match with your needs. A phone conversation should suffice if you're interviewing candidates in different locations. But a face-to-face meeting is best if you're hiring local. Evaluate the candidate's listening skills and note their nonverbal clues. Guarded or inconsistent answers could signal problems with the candidate's representations about credentials and/or experience. Non-responsive answers, or responses that indicate the candidate did not understand your concerns, may presage problems following instructions or understanding the nature of an assignment.

A few basic considerations:

The ideal candidate. Do you need an introverted researcher, or a charismatic personality to charm a difficult client or to tame a contentious opponent? Do you prefer a "take-the-ball-and-run-with-it lawyer", or one who does precisely what you ask? Do you want someone who is detail-oriented or who sees the big-picture? Is the ideal candidate an experienced or entry-level lawyer, a paralegal, a legal research service, or a litigation management assistant? If you have a low-key personality and pride yourself on your reasonableness and courtesy, the last person you want standing in for you is a mad-dog litigator (and the reverse is true). Style may be less of an issue for behind-the-scenes projects, but even there it should not be ignored. Match the credentials to the need.

The candidate's rates. Contract lawyers with a decade or more of experience, or with specialized skills, will cost less than a full-time hire but more than a new grad. Sometimes a project requires high-end labor, but sometimes a less expensive lawyer will do. To avoid overpaying, consider your needs.

The candidate's resources. Some solos have office space for a contract worker; others prefer to make virtual arrangements. If you're outsourcing offsite, make sure the candidate has reliable computer equipment and standard word processing and software. And any candidate offering legal research services should also have access to a law library and online legal research system, or—at a minimum—the ability to use whatever reference resources you use. Outsourcing a short-term project generally isn't worthwhile if you need to teach an applicant how to use a research tool or a piece of software. Find someone who has the skills to start immediately.

The candidate's work experience. Review with care the candidate's portfolio. For legal research, evaluate the candidate's writing style and analytical and proofreading skills. Many lawyers believe their law school class in legal writing qualifies them as a specialist. In truth, few lawyers have superior legal research and writing skills. Make sure you check the candidate's work product to verify any claims of expertise. In the final analysis, ask yourself if you would be proud to sign your name to the work they've done.

The candidate's availability. Increasingly, many lawyers who do document review by day try to earn extra money by doing contract work for solos. Unfortunately, because these lawyers have day jobs, they may not be able to meet required deadlines despite their best intentions. Though it's unreasonable to expect a lawyer to be available 24/7 when you're only sending her a 20-hour project, it's reasonable to assume that the lawyer will be able to prioritize your work rather than squeeze it in nights and weekends.

The candidate's references. Among the qualities you're looking for are reliability, honesty, punctuality, cooperativeness. Unless you know the candidates personally, or they were sent by an agency, you'll want to confirm they have the credentials and expertise represented. Verify law school graduation and admission to the bar. Check at least two employer (or contract work) references. And if you intend to rely upon the special expertise of a contract lawyer, pay attention to coverage for professional negligence. Ordinarily, your supervision of the lawyer places liability on your shoulders. Your reliance upon the advice of the contract lawyer specialist could shift the burden. In either case, though, if the contract lawyer is uninsured, you face possible exposure.

The candidate's presentability. The impressions given by candidates—on their resume and on their Web site—are often revealing. For example, some contract attorneys boast of writing skills, but their Web sites are riddled with grammatical and spelling errors. Verify that the person you hire can talk the talk…and walk the walk.

The candidate's attitude. More than anything, a successful outsourcing candidate is one committed to freelancing. There are some who handle outsourcing assignments who are merely biding their time until a better offer or permanent employment comes along. For this reason, they may be less motivated to satisfy you because they're not interested in repeat business. Other candidates have an employee mentality, and may nag you for extra work or more permanent hours. If you want a satisfying outsourcing experience, find a candidate as devoted as you to being a successful free agent.

Checking each applicant's credentials and conducting personal interviews may sound like a lot of work. But it's worth it when you consider the cost of project poorly done, a client who's unhappy with the result, or your own loss of time as you repair the damage. Once you've made a tentative selection, assign the lawyer a small project not critical to the success of the matter, and which has no immediate deadline. This way you can judge with a minimum of risk their work and compatibility with your practice style.

Working with contract lawyers. Agreeing on the contract lawyer's rate is a key step in striking a deal. But other factors come into play; the nature of the assignment, the economics of your practice, your relationship with clients. Consider:

Be precise. Many lawyers give only a vague description of research projects they want to outsource, and then blame the contract attorney for an unsatisfactory result. When you outsource work, be precise. For legal research projects, prepare a memo describing the matters you want researched, or identify the issues for inclusion in an appellate brief. And be clear about what you expect. In some cases, the hiring lawyer wants a contract lawyer to just list cases and summarize them rather than prepare a memo. If that's what you want, say so before the contract attorney runs up a huge bill for drafting a full memo.

What to pay. Contract rates depend on location and experience. To determine the going rate, ask colleagues what they pay for comparable work, and call a temp agency to find out what they would charge for someone with x years of experience. More experienced lawyers usually complete the project faster and more competently... and have the judgment to handle unexpected situations that could prejudice the client. If the contract lawyer works in your office using your equipment, the rate paid should be lower than for assignments they complete without using your facilities. The lower rate accounts for the portion of your overhead attributable to the contract lawyer's work.

Establish reasonable deadlines. Establish deadlines for deliverables as well as a timetable for certain goals. Remember, your contract hire may be juggling projects for other clients, and will need to prioritize matters with firm deadlines over those without deadlines. Request status reports, but be reasonable. Don't insist on a three-day turnaround on a project you know would take at least a week to complete.

Set a budget. When you work with a freelancer, ask for a budget or an estimate. Freelancers have different billing policies; some charge flat fees, others bill by the hour. Where your freelancer cannot estimate the time involved, either ask for progress reports at designated intervals or cap the hours you want the provider to spend.

The etiquette of payment. Just as you don't like working for free, neither does your temp. Don't balk if you're required to put down a retainer or a deposit. And when the work is done, pay on time…and don't make payment contingent on your ability to bill their time to, and collect from, the client. Contract attorneys don't earn enough to bear to risk of non-payment.

Make confidentiality requirements clear. Just as attorneys must safeguard client confidences, so too must those who work for them. Explain the importance of confidentiality to contract lawyers and other virtual staff, perhaps even memorializing the requirement in an engagement letter. In addition, to further preserve confidentiality and avoid conflicts, consider keeping the client's identity confidential (if possible) when you assign a task. Of course, if you've retained someone to reply to interrogatories or to draft a summary judgment decision, the client's identity will be apparent. But in some instances, you may be able to assign discrete legal research tasks without providing any factual details about the specific case.

Finding qualified contractors & consultants

Referrals. The best way to find competent outsourcing candidates is through referrals. If a colleague raves about a contract attorney, get the individual's name and contact information. In this way, the hiring lawyer reduces the risk that a candidate is unqualified or irresponsible.

Online. Many outsourcing candidates maintain Web sites or blogs with online portfolios. A contract attorney or other outsourcing candidate who takes the initiative to set up a dedicated Web site is likely to offer solid professional service, and a well-designed site will provide writing samples, past work experience, and endorsements. Caution: some online entities use the Internet as a front. They advertise that they handle legal research but send the work overseas. Check to make sure that they're providing the services they claim.

Local universities. Law students are eager for hands-on experience and the chance to earn extra money. Virtual clerkships and project work are especially appealing. To find willing law students, post ads with the law school's career placement office, or e-mail one of the professors teaching a course on your practice area and ask him to announce job openings at the end of class. A college's general placement office is also a good source of administrative support and other non-legal assistance. Note: college placement offices may take several days to run your post through various levels of approval. Don't expect a timely response during exam time.

Craigslist. As a pool of talent for outsourced project work, Craigslist is an extraordinary resource that reaches into all 50 states and many cities abroad. For some cities, Craigslist does not charge for ads while in others the cost is minimal—around $25 per posting. And because the site draws from such a wide audience, you're likely to receive multiple responses within a few hours of placing the ad. It goes without saying that because. If you're offering a decent salary or interesting work, Craigslist will probably generate more responses than you can reasonably review.

Blogs. Posting a job on a popular law student blog, or a blog in your practice area, is another option. Posting ads on blogs is inexpensive, but if a blog doesn't get much traffic your ad will be slow to attract prospects.

Bar association newsletters. Bar publications don't charge much to place ads, but there's usually a long lag time between submission of the ad and publication. Bar newsletters make sense only when you don't have an immediate need.

THE VIRTUAL ASSISTANT: FIVE GOOD REASONS TO HIRE ONE

Virtual assistants, also known as administrative consultants, are independent contractors who—from a remote location, usually their home or office—support multiple clients in a variety of industries and professions by providing administrative, creative, and technical services. Increasingly, lawyers rely on VA's for such tasks as calendaring and scheduling, following-up with potential clients, returning retainer letters, and helping with marketing. There is a growing number of VA's, many of whom have legal experience and are capable of transcribing dictation and formatting filings. There are also virtual paralegals available for document review, form completion, and pleadings (for review by the hiring lawyer).

Why use a virtual assistant? At least five good reasons: (1) At $20/hour to $75/hour, VA's are much less expensive than hiring a regular employee; (2) a VA is paid per job or by the hour, but only for the time you need them; (3) there is no expense for benefits, taxes, holiday pay, or office space because the VA works out of their own office and uses their own equipment; (4) if your law practice is in a small market, a VA in a larger community may give you access to skills not available where you practice; and (5), a VA makes sense if you don't have a full-time office, or you have two locations but can't afford staff for both.

How to hire and work with a virtual assistant. Hiring a VA is not as straightforward as hiring a contract lawyer, whose bar status and grievance record is available online. The same verification is not available for VA's. Because the VA may handle confidential information or deal with clients, proceed cautiously:

Finding a qualified VA takes time. Check the VA's references carefully; seek out references from lawyers you know. Insist on an interview by telephone. Once hired, increase the duties of your VA gradually. You may want to avoid entrusting VA's with access to your billing records or clients' personal information at least until assured of their reliability.

How to find a virtual assistant. There are several virtual assistant agencies and several professional associations, among the International Virtual Assistants Association (www.IVAA.org. To find a virtual assistant with legal experience, you might begin with these three companies: www.legaltypist.com, www.clericaladvantage.net, and www.halosecretarialservices.com.

Offshoring. Offshoring refers to the practice of sending work overseas. Though large firms and corporations have offshored document review and large legal research projects to India for nearly a decade, it's not clear that offshoring legal work is always a viable option for solos. Some of the more well-respected offshore operations focus on large matters for big firms, and the smaller projects that solos often have aren't worth their while. In addition, some offshore companies are not that much cheaper than hiring a junior lawyer directly. Tasks like Web design are another matter. Still, language skills are always a concern, so try corresponding with an overseas freelancer a few times before making a hiring decision.

CHAPTER 13

Growing Your Practice

"If you want to grow your practice, don't work 100 percent of the time. Work 80 percent and market yourself 20 percent.—Ed Sharkey, solo

Some lawyers remain solo for the long haul, learning to leverage technology to carry a larger caseload, and handle more complicated cases as their practice grows. In this way, they remain independent, and have the potential of making big money by keeping overhead low. Other lawyers choose to grow their practice by partnering up, teaming with others, hiring associates, outsourcing, or hiring part-timers. There's no doubt, though, that the decision to *grow* solo is harder than making the decision to *go* solo.

In this chapter, I'll discuss why and how you might want to think about growing your practice. And even if you're not ready to grow now, it's a proposition worth revisiting every year.

Six Reasons to Grow Your Practice

To leverage more profitable work. Most solos think of staffing up when their workload gets overwhelming. I don't mean the occasional 70- or 80-hour week offset by long dry spells. By "overwhelming", I mean when overwork becomes the new normal. So, the first of six reasons to consider growing your practice is when you *regularly* spend more hours working than you would like, or when you are so busy you are turning away profitable matters because you're unable to handle any more work.

To compete with larger firms. Sometimes, in order to compete for large, institutional clients, a solo must have a team in place to mitigate concerns about reliability and manpower.

To offer broader range of legal services. Some solos choose to grow their practice because they want to provide one-stop shopping to clients who have wide-ranging legal needs. For example, a small business client might need help with employment matters, tax, securities and corporate formation and litigation. Since many solos typically specialize in just two or three practice areas, partnering with another lawyer makes possible a broader array of services.

To take advantage of new opportunities. Just since 2008, the pace of change in the legal profession has accelerated more rapidly than ever; witness the demise of large firms, the growth of offshoring, and the increased use of technology. While some of these developments may obviate the need for lawyers, they also create new opportunities. You may not have the bandwidth to jump on an emerging practice area, but by teaming up with another lawyer with that expertise, you could back-door your way into a new practice area.

To leverage economies of scale. A lone solo in a consumer practice area may need to invest significant time or resources to develop a Web presence or maintain a blog that's on par with those produced by larger firms. By teaming up with other solos for a group blog, or to share marketing costs, solos can make the most of economies of scale and spread the costs of marketing.

To share the burdens of solo practice. Not everyone wants to work alone. Some lawyers grow their practice because in addition to the camaraderie, they can share the burdens of a solo practice with one or more others. In this way, they can bounce ideas off one another and have back-up when one of them takes vacation.

A New World of Staffing Options

Historically, solos have addressed their needs for expansion by partnering up or hiring associates. Today, there's a whole range of in-between solutions. This section discusses both the traditional options, as well as new trends for growing your firm:

Flexible staffing options

Outsourcing. Outsourcing (see the previous chapter) lets you remain flexible in addressing your staffing needs, and makes available better-quality lawyers or staff than you could afford on a full-time basis. Outsourcing is a low-risk way to sample how additional staff might help your firm. Outsourcing is typically used to handle sporadic, finite projects, such as document review in a large litigation, or the brief you don't have time to write, or the court appearances where you have a conflict. When you outsource, you pay only for the work performed. But flexibility cuts both ways; most outsourcing occurs on a project-by-project basis, and means that when you get busy, your preferred contract lawyer or freelancer may not have time to handle your work. Note: at some point, outsourcing may no longer be cost-effective. Consider: a contract lawyer with mid-level experience can cost between $50/hour and $75/hour. If you're using the contract lawyer 40 hours a month, that's $36,000/year (assuming a $75/hour rate). It wouldn't cost much more to hire a full time associate, and get 160 hours of time each month rather than one fourth of that.

The virtual workforce. Through the Internet, lawyers have access to all types of virtual workers, from administrative assistants and paralegals to experienced contract lawyers. For lawyers who practice in small markets with an untrained local labor pool, the emergence of a virtual workforce is a welcome phenomenon…plus, because they work remotely and help keep your overhead costs down (for details, see Chapter 12).

Interns. With competition for legal jobs fierce, law students and recent grads are doing whatever they can to get a leg up, including volunteering at a law office. Some law schools even give students course credit for interning. In 2010, in Texas, SMU's Dedman School of Law began paying employers $3,500 to hire an unemployed graduate for a test drive! (Source: www.law.com/jsp/nlj/PubArticleNLJ.jsp?id=1202483303812&Paying_the_price_for_law_firm_employment). Free labor has its drawbacks, of course. If someone works without compensation, they may not work as hard, and they could leave suddenly if a paid opportunity comes along. And there's the potential for legal liability, too. The Labor Department issued guidelines in 2010 (www.dol.gov/whd/regs/compliance/whdfs71.pdf) intended to prevent the private sector—including law firms—from exploiting interns. Under the guidelines, employers cannot use unpaid interns to displace otherwise paid employees, and the employer must provide educational training and feedback. If you hire an unpaid intern, you need to comply.

Part-time workers. At some point, you will have routine administrative tasks or recurring research that demands more than sporadic assistance. For this, consider a steady part-time arrangement involving a set number of hours per week. By shopping around, you should be able to find a student or a stay-at-home mom eager for the work. Sometimes, too, you can find experienced legal secretaries who wish to moonlight. For paralegal or associate work, law students should be able to handle low-level tasks like legal research for a fraction of the cost of a full-time associate or paralegal. One of my colleagues hires 2nd or 3rd year law students at $20/hour for 10–15 hours a week (roughly $200–$300 per student). So that he can oversee their work, he has them work onsite for the first few weeks, but they're free to work from home after that. Even when he doesn't have enough billable work to pass along, he still pays their weekly salary but assigns marketing tasks or other non-billable work.

The 'mommy pool'. With so many female lawyers taking the "off-ramp" in search of work/life balance, solos in most markets have unlimited access to a deep pool of talented, hardworking, highly-credentialed lawyers. Several solos have capitalized on this trend, using "mommy lawyers" to build quality practices. One such solo is Joanne Sternleib, herself a lawyer/mom who left a top firm to start a trusts and estates practice. Today, she runs a virtual firm comprised of four other lawyers—an assistant and two law clerks—who, like herself, are moms who need a flexible schedule. As Joanne describes:

> *"…They [attorneys and staff] work out of their own homes, on their own schedules, and whenever they want. It doesn't matter to me when they do the work as long as it gets done. They are independent contractors and work flexible schedules. There are no set hours, no billable hour requirements, no guaranteed hours, no guaranteed pay. I generally pay my associates a pre-set fee for each project, and I generally charge clients the same way except for estate administration or court proceedings, which work better as hourly billing. I keep track of everything with a super-notebook system that tracks matters and due dates, and I rely heavily on electronic technology which is essential for my practice to operate as it does." Source: www.jdblissblog.com/2006/07/joanne_sternlie. html .*

Nor is it just lawyer/moms employing other lawyer/moms. Other solos also recognize the value of this under-utilized pool of professionals. Kassra Nassiri, a Harvard-educated lawyer who partnered up with a colleague to start a firm, hires stay-at-home moms to help litigate his plaintiffs' firm's multi-million dollar matters. Featured in San Francisco Magazine (*Who Says Being A Lawyer Has to Suck?* Feb., 2007), Nassiri says the women appreciate the opportunity to use their hard-earned skills in a way that doesn't interfere with raising a family.

Q: Who should be my first hire: a non-lawyer staffer, a JD?

A: As a general rule, hire the lowest-cost person you can to fill the job. For many practices, either an experienced paralegal or even a smart college grad (if you need general research or marketing support) will fit the bill. A paralegal costs less than a JD, and has more practical training than a lawyer right out of school on matters like completing forms, responding to interrogatories, or drafting requests for records. Also, a paralegal can't leave and take your clients.

Q: I need an associate, but I'm concerned that she will leave and compete with me or take my clients after I train her.

A: Not all lawyers are interested in starting a firm. Some are content to handle a stream of work and collect a steady pay check. Others, like parents or spouses of those in transitory jobs like foreign service or military, may be grateful for a stint of several years before they relocate. If you want associates to stay, invest in equipment, infrastructure, and research tools that the associate will come to depend on, and would otherwise need to create on their own if they decided to solo. And if associates show an interest in marketing, reward their efforts; if you don't, they may look for an employer who will.

Q: I'm too small to have an HR department. How do I set up my law firm to include a new employee?

A: A payroll company can take care of all of the issues related to employment payment and withholdings. Even Costco now offers payroll services for under $50/month. In addition, you will need to create and put into writing your office procedures and policies for existing employees, and to facilitate the transition when they leave. For details on operation manuals and employee policies, go to Chapter 11.

...ON FIRING

Q: Help! It's been three months and I realize that I made a huge mistake in hiring someone. Should I wait it out or fire him now? And how can I do that?

A: If a current employee continues to make the same errors after a month or two, cut your losses now. It's never easy to dismiss an employee, particularly if the individual has childcare issues or is going through a messy divorce. But your business comes first.

A few do's and don'ts:

DO assess the law. Before issuing a pink slip, consult with a colleague in employment law or review the applicable law. Notwithstanding the presumption of employment at will, employers cannot discriminate when they terminate employees. Even as a solo, you may be subject to certain federal or state anti-discrimination laws. Also, a few jurisdictions maintain that the terms of employment handbooks are binding; if you practice in one of those states, make sure that your proposed termination complies with your handbook. And know your liability, if any, for unemployment compensation.

DO prepare. Before the termination, change your passwords and be sure that you have copies of all of the materials that the employee prepared.

DO be direct. Shortly before the end of the day, ask the employee to come into your office or closed conference room. Explain that he or she just isn't a fit, and isn't working out. If the employee demands additional explanation, be as specific as you can. Have a check ready with two weeks pay and any vacation time owed, and then ask the employee to gather his or her things and leave.

DON'T ruin weekends or vacations. Try to avoid terminating an employee just before a holiday or the weekend. In this way, the employee will be able to call employment agencies to find new work, or to visit the unemployment office to learn how to collect benefits. Of course, if you discover illegal conduct like trust account theft or drugs, immediate termination is the only option.

DON'T humiliate or patronize. If you don't already employ a security guard, don't bring one in to escort the employee from the office. It's humiliating. Likewise, telling the employee that he or she is a nice person, or has done some good work, sends mixed messages and may make them wonder why they are really being let go.

Traditional Staffing Options

If outsourcing or part-time options won't work for you, there are other more traditional arrangements:

Are you ready for a full-time hire?

Are you at or beyond capacity? Are you regularly turning down large matters that you can't staff through outsourcing or contract attorneys? A full-time hire makes sense if it lets you capture business opportunities that you'd lose due to inadequate staffing.

Are you willing to train your staff? When you outsource, you can typically bring someone on board who already has solid experience. But when you hire a full-time employee, chances are that you can only afford a less-experienced junior-hire. For some lawyers, that works well, because they enjoy training young attorneys and new graduates. Consider Mark Zimmett, a former BigLaw attorney who started his firm in 1990, and depends on young associates to help him manage multi-million-dollar cases. In an article in American Lawyer (*Lessons from a Large Firm Partner Who Set Up His Own Shop*, April 2007), Zimmet writes: *"[My] associates have been relatively young, generally two to four years out of school. Smart as they are, they are inexperienced…I enjoy teaching them, and I believe they enjoy their work and value their training. They stay for three or four years, and then move on with their careers, often with my help."*

Will the new-hire free you up so you can bill additional hours? Law practice management consultant Ed Poll recommends, *"Hire when you're at the point that you can produce enough billable work to justify hiring that person, or when they can take work off your desk so you can do more billable work. Can you churn out enough billable work to match the new staff person's $30,000 or $40,000 salary? Your break-even point is when the additional revenue generated or reduced strain on you equals the increased cost of hiring someone. Anything above that is gravy."*—Source: Ed Poll (as quoted in Hiring and Working with Support Staff: A Guide for Solo and Small Firm Lawyers, at www.cba.org/cba/PracticeLink/WWP/supportstaff.aspx).

Are you capable of delegating work, and is the work capable of delegation? Let's face it: some lawyers don't like to relinquish control of even the most seemingly insignificant details. David Leffler writes in his Being Solo column (GP Solo Magazine, May 2004) that some lawyers believe they alone can do things the "right way", and experience so much anxiety letting go of tasks that they prefer to handle everything themselves. If you don't truly understand the benefits of employees, Leffler writes, "You will never make any hires, or the hires you do make will be doomed to failure". This will prevent you from changing your law practice from one where you feel overwhelmed and without any time for the rest of your life, to one which [allows for more balance]. At the same time, some work simply isn't capable of delegation. In many criminal cases, a client expects the lawyer whom he met with to represent him in court. Thus, a busy criminal practitioner who spends many days in court might not benefit from hiring another attorney (because clients might not want to work with him anyway). In this situation, the lawyer might consider delegating non-essential tasks, but hiring another lawyer might not make sense.

Hiring early v. hiring late? Should you hire new employees before you really need them on the theory that you'll have time to train them? North Carolina family law attorney and marketing expert Lee Rosen says "no" [Source: http://divorcediscourse. com/2011/02/24/hire-late-game/]. People get too accustomed to working less so the extra work never comes. Advises Rosen:

> *"I've concluded that the better approach is to hire late. Let everyone max out (and then some) before you hire the next person. Make sure you really need the person before you bring him or her on. Once the new hire arrives, get him or her going by taking a bit of work from everyone and putting it on the new person's plate. Get the new hire started with a substantial workload and let everyone else return to normal."*

DON'T BE AFRAID TO HIRE *by Ed Sharkey, Esq.*

I started my law firm in May 2003. At the time, I had been practicing for 10 years, first with a mid-size firm in Baltimore, then with a large firm in Washington, DC. My practice was business, securities, and pension litigation. To open my new firm, I leased space from an established solo. I had a portfolio of clients that moved to my new firm, so I was busy from the outset, handling all of the legal and administrative work with the help of the other solo's legal secretary. There were three considerations motivating me to hire:

- I could do no more work. I had exceeded my capacity after about six months.
- I wanted to grow the firm; there were marketing initiatives I wanted to undertake but could not because I was over-loaded.
- I knew some of the work I was doing could be delegated without undue risk. So, I went to law school listservs, and posted a paragraph seeking a law clerk for research and writing. In the post, I described the practice and empha-sized the flexibility of the schedule. I solicited a commitment of between 10 and 15 hours per week, and guessed at an appropriate hourly rate. The market validated my guess...I received multiple resumes.

I hired one law clerk, then two, etc. The capacity was scalable. During weeks when the work was less, I did not have an idle associate sitting at a desk. When it was busier, I had multiple clerks from which to seek extra time. In addition, I was able to task them with some marketing projects, which was more cost-effective than doing it myself. Finally, the cost was modest, and I did not need to add space, computers, health care, or bar fees. When I reached the point where I had five law clerks at the two-year mark, I concluded that it would be better to hire a full-time associate. The law-clerk model made it easier to transition to a full-time associate than it would have been starting from scratch. The flow of work was proven. In addition, I had experience with multiple prospective associates who had clerked for me. I searched the National Association for Law Placement Web site (www.NALP.org) to survey associate salaries in Baltimore. I used that as a metric for the salary. In addition, I offered health insurance under my PPO and participation in a 401k profit sharing plan. The firm pays a non-discretionary three percent of salary into the retirement plan. In addition, the firm pays discretionary bonuses twice a year based upon firm profitability and associate performance and productivity. I made an offer to my best clerk, and she accepted.

I have always hired for attitude. Prospects must demonstrate a minimum level of competence (for law clerks, I look at grades and writing sample), but attitude is most important. I look for people who will take personal responsibility for their matters. *People who see their duties as a personal obligation important to the goals of the firm rather than as a job.* Such people look for ways to contribute to the goals of the firm. They also address unforeseen contingencies that arise in performing their work, rather than just doing what they were told. Finally, they assume greater responsibility over time, increasing the firm's ability to delegate more to them. The model has worked especially well. I aggressively seek to delegate in order to maintain my target level of marketing. If our team reaches capacity and work encroaches on the marketing, I add scale by hiring again. In this way, I have grown from one lawyer in 2003 to two lawyers, a full-time paralegal, a part-time administrative assistant, and three law clerks in 2007.

If you want to grow your own practice, don't work 100% of the time. Work 80% and market 20%. Aggressively look for ways to delegate. Hire for attitude. Get people who are interested in learning and taking on greater responsibility.

Don't be afraid to hire. If you make a mistake, you can always adjust.

Ed Sharkey (esharkey@SharkeyLaw.com) practices business law and litigation in Bethesda, Maryland

Local counsel: how to level the playing field. Mega-firms might have offices in multiple states, but—at most—a solo may be barred in only three or four jurisdictions. As a result, the solo is at a disadvantage; not only in representing a large client that has been sued or seeks to sue in multiple jurisdictions, but also in the solo's attempt to focus on a national practice—like First Amendment law or copyright or trademark enforcement—where cases arise all over the country.

This is where local counsel comes in handy.

A solo representing a client in a jurisdiction where he or she is not licensed can retain local counsel—a lawyer licensed in that jurisdiction—to perform a variety of tasks. It might range from filing pleadings and ensuring compliance with local rules to helping out with depositions and making an appearance or two at scheduling or procedural conferences. Or the solo can act as local counsel to other lawyers, and create an additional revenue stream in the process. Though marketing a local counsel service in a saturated urban market may prove tough, it is potentially lucrative in (1) smaller jurisdictions where a local lawyer's inside knowledge and connections can make a difference, or (2) before specialized courts, like the Delaware Chancery Court (which handles corporate business disputes) or federal or state regulatory agencies. Whether you serve as the primary lawyer who retains local counsel, or as the local lawyer who is being retained, it is critical to have a written agreement delineating your respective responsibilities. For example, will local counsel simply sign off on documents, or will local counsel be expected to draft certain documents as well…how much lead time will local counsel require to ensure that documents are timely filed…will local counsel communicate with, and receive payment directly from the client or from forwarding counsel? Note: as local counsel, you are responsible for everything contained in the pleadings that you sign, even if they were prepared by another lawyer.

Partnerships. Some solos, particularly those in metropolitan areas, are often in competition for corporate clients who are under the mistaken impression that solos cannot provide quality work for large companies. If this proves to be a obstacle for you, you may want to consider partnering with another lawyer or group of lawyers. Joel Bennett, a Washington D.C. lawyer, explores the benefits and drawbacks of partnership or merger in his essay, *Expanding Through Merger—and the Sequel* , published in the ABA handbook, *Flying Solo, a Survival Guide for the Solo Lawyer* (4th ed., 2005). Bennett's essay cites the following pro and con for partnering:

PRO:
- Providing additional backup to other lawyers
- A decrease in pro rata overhead
- An ability to generate better quality business referrals to and from partners
- Better quality institutional clients
- An ability to hire associates and staff, and to generate income from their work

CON:
- A loss of independence related to working hours, spending decisions and personnel, and possibly added start-up costs and moving expenses

Take the time to get to know your potential partner(s), and candidly discuss your goals. Partnerships usually fail because the partners didn't articulate and clarify their goals at the outset, or failed to discuss or reach agreement on such critical issues as the sharing of profits and costs. Bennett notes that he and his potential partner spent a considerable amount of time developing a formula for capitalizing start-up costs, sharing operating expenses, and splitting profits, all of which were contained in their partnership agreement or other written documents. Every partnership agreement will differ, but there are Model Partnership Agreements to use as a starting point. You'll find them in law practice management books at your local law library, or you can purchase and download an inexpensive Word version of one from the ABA's online bookstore (www.abanet.org, click on Resources for Lawyers). If you're not ready to invest the time, or take the risk, in creating a formal partnership, you can still capture the benefits of size and scope of expertise through more flexible arrangements like of counsel relationships, affiliations with other lawyers, or project-partnership teams.

Benefits from an "of counsel" relationship
You can also grow your practice by bringing in other lawyers in an "of counsel" relationship, or by creating an of counsel relationship with another firm. This relationship is covered in ABA Formal Opinion 90-357, which describes the arrangement as being characterized by "a close, regular personal relationship" between an attorney and a law firm. The ABA rule is intended to prevent lawyers from gaining a competitive advantage or deceiving clients by holding themselves out as having an of counsel relationship with another firm or lawyer that they don't work with on a regular basis.

There are several variants to an of counsel relationship:

- One arrangement resembles part-time employment, in which of counsel is on the payroll and commits to providing a guaranteed number of hours each week or month.
- Another arrangement has of counsel offering expertise on an as-needed basis.

Either way, of counsel can share physical space with the law firm, or the firm may pay for a portion of their overhead if they retain outside space.

The of counsel relationship offers various benefits to a solo. Obviously, an of counsel arrangement that guarantees a fixed level of income at or near your usual billable rates can help smooth out cash flow problems. In addition, the of counsel relationship can enhance your credibility, and clients may be impressed that larger firms want to take advantage of your expertise. And the relationship works both ways. Just as the firm will feed you work and bring you into cases, you can also refer cases to the firm. Of course, when you enter into an of counsel relationship, your affiliation with the firm could potentially conflict you out of certain projects.

You can also use of counsel relationships to take advantage of other attorneys' talents whom you can't afford to hire. Perhaps there's a superstar associate from your former firm who you'd love to bring on board, but you don't have enough work to pay a full-time salary. You could offer an of counsel relationship with guaranteed payment for a fixed number of hours. The associate could spend the rest of her time building her practice, and could either service new clients on her own or divert them to the firm.

Most of counsel arrangements arise out of already existing professional relationships, so target those contacts first in looking for an of counsel relationship. Here are some suggestions:

Look to former relationships. If you worked for the government or in-house at a corporation, you may have worked closely with a small firm that represented clients in matters that you handled. Or, you may have worked on pro bono or bar projects with other firms, and built a solid relationship. Contact those lawyers when you begin your firm; they might welcome the opportunity to work with you in an of counsel capacity.

Sell your capacity to draw business. If you formerly worked at a government agency, or as a prosecutor, or at a BigLaw firm, your background can help a firm draw clients. A firm that represents criminal defendants can enhance its reputation and distinguish itself from the competition with a former prosecutor on board. Likewise, if you're a former BigLaw attorney, you can build the image of a small local litigation shop that wants to attract Fortune 500 companies as clients.

Blogging. If you have a unique practice area, be sure to demonstrate your expertise by starting a blog. In this way, other firms may be impressed by your analysis of issues and view your practice as a natural complement to their own.

Networking. Good old networking—coffee meetings, bar events, and other activities where you meet other lawyers—increases your chances of finding of counsel arrangements. Get to know other lawyers, their practices and needs, and an of counsel opportunity may present itself.

One example of an of counsel relationship comes from Florida litigation and IP lawyer, Elio Martinez, in *Of Counsel: An Alternative to Solo and Firm Practice* (GP Solo Magazine, July/August 2006). Martinez writes:

> *"…My of counsel arrangement is simple. I maintain a separate and independent practice while occupying an office at my friend's firm. I keep my own schedule, develop my own clients, and run my own firm. In exchange for office space and a percentage of*

fees collected for my work on my friend's cases, I guarantee that I will work a certain number of hours per month on those cases. This arrangement is beneficial to us both: he has some of the burdens of the practice lifted from his shoulders by someone he knows and trusts, and I have guaranteed work and income every month, as well as an office where I can grow my practice. The of counsel arrangement also provides me the added benefit of always having someone with whom to discuss issues and ideas, as well as assurance that in my absence someone will be there to step in and handle emergencies on my cases."

Since many of counsel arrangements arise out of close relationships, lawyers often don't formalize them with much more than a handshake. However, it's best to have a written agreement to clarify the terms of compensation, and to help avoid the possibility of an imputed partnership when an of counsel shares profits with a firm. You can find several of counsel agreements at this link at MyShingle (http://myshingle.com/2010/09/articles/ethics-malpractice-issues/round-up-of-resources-on-the-amorphous-of-counsel-relationship/), or in *The Of Counsel Agreement*, by Harold Wren (ABA, 2008). If your firm retains an of counsel, you'll need to notify your malpractice carrier and procure additional coverage. If you serve as of counsel to another firm, you should notify your carrier as well, though chances are you won't require additional coverage if you're placed on the firm's policy.

ETHICS AND THE "OF COUNSEL" ARRANGEMENT

Q: The firm to which I'm of counsel represents Company X, but I don't handle any of the Company X matters. Can I represent a client that wants to sue Company X?
A: No, so long as you serve as of counsel. Conflict of interest rules apply to of counsel arrangements, and courts generally treat of counsel as they would a member or employee of the firm in evaluating the conflicts. When entering into an of counsel agreement, you should evaluate whether that relationship may cost you cases through conflicts. See ABA 90-357 (of counsel and firm treated as a unit for purposes of analyzing conflicts of interest).

Q: I'm of counsel to a three-lawyer firm, and one of the partners with whom I've never worked was just sued for malpractice. Will I be liable?
A: Most likely not, as long as you took appropriate action to avoid creating an imputed partnership with the firm. Generally speaking, partners are liable for each other's malpractice, but of counsel are not. However, in some instances, where of counsel occupies the same space as a firm and shares profits, and is held out as a partner to clients, a partnership can be imputed.

Q: Can I split fees with my of counsel without telling the client?
A: Generally, yes, but consult your jurisdiction's ethics rules. While lawyers are required to disclose to clients when fees are shared with lawyers outside the firm, the disclosure requirement doesn't apply to fee-shares between of counsel in many jurisdictions.

A World of Different Relationships: Affiliations, Alliances, Virtual Firms & Networks

In addition to traditional relationships, many new business models have emerged, and are gaining traction. Most of them offer solos the best of both worlds: continued autonomy and flexibility AND the support, resources, and scope to rival a larger firm. Several reasons account for the growth of these new arrangements. First, with unemployment in the legal profession at an all time high, more lawyers are considering the solo option. Some lack the confidence or resources to go it alone, so shared arrangements are appealing. Second, even as larger corporate clients move away from big firm representation to cut costs, many still aren't ready to throw work to true solos, but may be willing to do so if a solo can demonstrate access to a larger network. Finally, technology is facilitating collaborative arrangements with out-of-the-box, user-friendly technologies for managing projects, sharing documents, and conferencing remotely. Thus, solos can pick and choose whom they want to work with without regard to geographic limitations.

The variety of alliances and law firm networks is limited only by your imagination ... and bar ethics rules, of course. Generally speaking, you must make clear to clients that even though you share space, or that you team up with your colleagues, each of you operates independently. You can reinforce the appearance of independence by creating your own stationery, business cards, and Web sites, and by entering into separate retainer agreement with clients when teaming on a project.

Here is a sample of new business relationship models:

Affiliation. The one calling for the fewest formalities has lawyers with different practice areas simply sharing space and referring cases back and forth. J. Cheney Mason, a solo profiled in the ABA Journal, sublets space to other attorneys who he hand-picks for integrity and/or practice expertise. As a group, the lawyers trade ideas and referrals while maintaining independent practices. This arrangement provides camaraderie…as well as lowering their overhead and providing a resource for referring clients.
Source: When It's About More Than Money (ABA Journal, April 2007). Available at www.ABAjournal.com/magazine/the_secrets_of_million_dollar_solos .

Alliances. Red Mountain Law (www.redmountainlaw.com) is an example of an alliance of firms providing complementary expertise in a variety of practice areas. One firm handles wills and trusts, a second handles commercial and residential real estate, a third oversees securities work. At the same time, the attorneys in each firm continue to serve their business and individual clients in other practice areas. In a Web site disclaimer, Red Mountain makes clear that it is an entity comprised of member firms engaged separately in the practice of law. Alliances also work for smaller firms that can offer expertise or other unique services to large firms. Some large firms seeking to service corporate clients that demand diversity team up with smaller women- or minority-owned firms to compensate for lack of diversity in their ranks. The large firm gets the benefit of diversity, the smaller firm can leverage the large firm's resources and marketing firepower. **Source: Day Pitney Forges Alliance With Minority Owned Firm, D. Malan, Connecticut Law Tribune, April 24, 2007.**

Virtual law firm. A virtual law firm is one in which members practice at different locations, and is not to be confused with a "virtual law office" that operates exclusively online. Virtual law firms have been around awhile. Patrick Begos, a Connecticut attorney in the three-man firm of Begos & Horgan, established a "virtual law firm" in 2002. As he explained in a GP Solo article (*The Virtual Law Firm*, July/August 2003), he leased space for his own firm, and discovered that lawyers with complementary practices in other suites were bouncing questions back and forth, referring clients to one another, and teaming up on projects. In time, the group decided to create a *virtual firm*; a collective in which they would cross-market one another's practices so that clients would have full-service representation. Today, virtual law firms like Virtual Law Partners, Rimon Legal, and FSB Fisher Broyles are growing fast, taking on big firm partners who are leaving the bloated fee structure and heavy overhead of large firms for virtual arrangements where they can keep 85 percent of their earnings. In virtual law firms, the lawyers must have more than 10 years of experience and are responsible for their own office space (home office or leased space). The virtual firm provides an online networking or infrastructure for sharing documents and communicating with other lawyers. Without the added overhead of fancy offices or associates, virtual firms can usually charge up to a third less than large firms. A virtual law firm is an actual firm in terms of corporate structure, but is not a solo practice. For lawyers uncertain that solo practice is for them, the virtual firm offers a compromise. Moreover, solos who want to grow their practice could band together and form a virtual law firm.

Networks. Networks are groups of lawyers who don't formally share space or market jointly. Instead, they know each other through regular meetings, frequently refer cases back and forth, and share informational resources. Networks are different from bar and trade associations in that networks—particularly the homegrown variety (see below) meet frequently—perhaps once or twice a month, and focus on facilitating relationships and referrals between members through regular contact. There are several types of lawyer networks:

Institutional networks. Examples include **Lex Mundi, Meritas** and the **International Network of Boutique Law Firms** (www.inblf.com). These networks are geared mostly towards small firms rather than true solos (though they do have solo members), and also lawyers who tend to serve corporate clients. Membership in these groups starts at around $1,500; it provides such benefits as access to free or reduced-cost trainings or CLEs, the possibility of referrals, and the ability to call upon others in the network to answer questions.

The Law School Consortium Program. Designed for newer solos with consumer-oriented practices. The LSCP has 17 member schools, each of which is responsible for developing a network to provide resources and services to solo and small-firm lawyers committed to serving low and moderate income individuals and communities. In my area, the Civil Justice Institute (www.civiljusticeinstitute.org) is the network affiliated with the University of Maryland. Membership in CJI—$150 to $700, depending upon law school graduation dates—includes such benefits as training and mentoring on cases, law practice management advice, and even help with marketing materials. If this type of network interests you, go to www.lowbono.org to see if there's a participating law school in your region.

Homegrown networks. These groups are organized by the participating attorneys themselves. One such group is **Attorney Roundtable** (www.attorneyrt.com), founded by Long Island attorney David Abeshouse. Now in its 10th year, the network is responsible for generating several millions of dollars in referrals. The group has a formal structure: members pay dues; members must commit to getting together with other members outside of regular meetings; no more than two members per practice area are allowed; all members must be approved by a group vote.

Support and referral networks. Recently, new solos have also been banding together to form their own networks for support and referrals. One such group is **Starting Out Solo** (www.startingoutsolo.com), a Massachusetts-based network of new solos who started solo practices within three months following law school graduation. Created by solo Gabriel Cheong, Starting Out Solo offers a "shadow" program that permits new lawyers to follow a more experienced lawyer to a deposition or court proceeding. The group also participates in charitable and pro bono functions.

Marketing networks. Some solos create networks for marketing purposes. One such group is **The Bankruptcy Law Network** (www.bankruptcylawnetwork.com), which describes itself as "a diverse and unaffiliated group of bankruptcy attorneys." Together, the 20 or so members share responsibility for their blog, a creative strategy that helps their blog attain a greater online search ranking than if it was written by a single lawyer. Blogging networks are expected to gain even more traction as solo and small firm lawyers vie for first page rank on Google in increasingly competitive markets.

Mastermind groups. The brainchild of the late author and success guru Napoleon Hill (*Think and Grow Rich*), a mastermind group is "the coordination of knowledge and effort of two or more people who work towards a definite purpose…" Mastermind groups give access to different view points, and most importantly, foster accountability. For more on mastermind groups, read *How to Run a Mastermind Group*, a January, 2011 article at www.lifehack.org/articles/productivity/how-to-start-and-run-a-mastermind-group.html.

Project-partnering. Let's say a potential client comes to you with an issue outside your expertise, or it involves matters in multiple jurisdictions, or it exceeds your existing capacity. Ordinarily, you might turn the case down, or the client would ask for a BigLaw referral. That doesn't have to be the case now: with project-partnering, you can transform your one-man band into a full-service firm. Jeffrey Berger, principal attorney in the Berger Law Firm in Washington DC, who was profiled in Legal Times (*The Virtual Law Firm*, Feb. 23, 2004), likens project-partnership to free-agency in professional sports: lawyers can put together the best team based on a lawyer's expertise and costs. For example, suppose you're a corporate lawyer representing a company that plans to acquire another company. Your client asks your help handling a downsizing and how to structure the new entity to take advantage of tax benefits. While you feel capable of handling the buy-out, you recognize that the employment and tax issues are outside your expertise. With project-partnering, you can team with an employment and tax lawyer to service the client. The advantages are three-fold:

- You create a dream team of experts while still remaining involved in the project.
- The agreements are flexible and last only for the duration of a particular project (so if you weren't fully satisfied by another team member's work, you're not obligated to use them for future projects).
- It's a convenient and non-threatening way to network and build relationships with other lawyers who may also bring you on board for their own projects.

What better way to introduce yourself to other lawyers than to offer them potential business opportunities to work on matters for your clients. Of course, the success of project-partnering depends on the quality of attorneys involved. Since good lawyers tend to be busy lawyers, you may have some difficulty in securing lawyers for your partnership teams. Or, you may discover that some members of the partnership don't share your standards (perhaps they don't return phone calls promptly, or they produce sloppy work), which may reflect badly on you. Some project-partnering tips:

- **Seek out potential team-members**. Identify a list of go-to lawyers in different practice areas who might assist on client matters. When you attend networking events, learn about other lawyers' practices and the type of cases they handle. Get together for coffee or a meal, and gauge their level of expertise with a few substantive questions. Listservs are another source of potential project partners. In my own practice, I have asked other lawyers to team up on projects, and have been asked by others to team up based on impressions formed as a result of discussions online.
- **Billing rates**. Get a sense of what your partners generally charge, and what types of billing arrangements they're willing to accept. If you work with lawyers located in other parts of the country, you may find a disparity of as much as $100/hour in rates. Will the lower-billing lawyer agree to continue these rates, or will he want to raise them when he learns others on the project charge more? And the reverse; if you work for a client with a limited budget, will a costlier team member be willing to reduce their fees, perhaps in exchange for the opportunity to work on a unique case? And…will your team consider alternative billing arrangements?
- **Billing preferences**. Determine your client's preference for billing. Some may want to include bill from each of the lawyers involved, while others may prefer one bill from the original lawyer that includes all of the fees. Consult bar rules to ensure that your billing arrangement complies with your jurisdiction's rules on fee-splitting.

- **Retainer letters**. Team members should have their own retainer letters in place with the client, as well as adequate malpractice coverage for the matters they handle.
- **Watch out for overlap**. If you're working with other lawyers on the same matter, you'll want to coordinate to avoid duplication of effort where issues overlap, and to ensure that your contemplated approaches don't conflict. At the same time, you don't want to bill the client for every little communication with your team members, or for glancing at every document that you're cc'd on by the other attorney. The purpose of a project partnership agreement is to increase efficiencies for clients, not to double- or triple-bill.

Leaving Solo Practice? Wait, Don't Throw in the Towel Yet

An anonymous solo once posted a "help-me-save-my-practice" e-mail to the Solosez listserv. Within hours, list members inundated him with suggestions, encouragement, and—most helpful—marketing and management ideas he had never considered. A week later, he reported that he implemented some of the changes, and the tone of his follow-up post was decidedly upbeat and optimistic. Before long, the solo reported that he had turned his business around.

If *your* solo practice hasn't turned out the way you thought it would, you can take satisfaction that you've come this far. But don't throw in the towel yet:

Look at the cases you've handled this past year. If you're worried about cash flow, and haven't found enough clients to pay the bills, take a temporary contract assignment or pursue other "fast cash" option (see Chapter 9). If you have clients who promised to pay and haven't, drop the worst offenders. Working for free is demoralizing; if you fire your non-paying clients, your morale will improve and you'll have more time to engage in marketing to build your practice.

What about your billing rates? When was the last time you reviewed your hourly rate and flat-fee structure? Are you building in expenses and taxes into your fees?

What are you doing to market your services? Are you doing enough to keep your name fresh on people's minds when they need an attorney? When was the last time you checked in with clients, friends, and business contacts to ask if there are any legal services they need?

What about cutting overhead? Are you paying for Class A office space? Is a big chunk of your revenue going to staff salaries without any return on investment? Right now, you need to look at things from a purely financial perspective without letting personal feelings about status or helping others get in the way. Can't make these changes on your own? Work with a practice management consultant.

Give yourself a little more time. It's true what they say about solo practice; you don't hit your stride until your third year. In the meantime, business *will* ebb and flow; it's the nature of the beast. So unless you are truly bleeding cash and risk bankruptcy, keep plugging.

BOOK UPDATES AT AUTHOR'S BLOG—www.MyShingle.com

You haven't failed. Maybe you have reached a point where you can't find enough business to sustain your practice; maybe you found work, but not enough to support your family. You haven't failed. You had the guts to take a leap that few lawyers are willing to take. Along the way, you taught yourself skills you didn't learn in law school or at your job: drafting complaints, taking depositions, arguing motions, negotiating contracts. You served clients and solved their problems, perhaps even changing their lives. And you created a something—a law firm—out of thin air. Perhaps your firm will not survive, but no one can ever take away what you accomplished. Solo Bruce Cameron (class of 2007) put it well: *"If I am only meant to walk the solo path for a brief period, I am still richer for the experience. And should I have to close the door to my practice, I guess I would head back to the job market a little more experienced than when I left it."*

Leaving Your Practice for Another Firm

After practicing on your own awhile, you may find that you've created opportunities for yourself that didn't previously exist. Perhaps you started a law firm because no one wanted to hire you, or because you craved hands-on experience or more flexibility that your employer couldn't provide. Now, a year or two later, you have a portfolio of business, several trials under your belt, or a go-to blog. All of a sudden, the law firms that once spurned you, or refused to accommodate your career goals or lifestyle, are knocking at your door. Naturally, you're flattered at the attention…but don't let it cloud your judgment. Getting hired by a firm may boost your ego, but you need to consider whether moving to a firm is right for you. Ask yourself the following:

What's my motivation for wanting to move to a firm? What makes you think this firm is different from other places you worked? If you once felt stifled by layers of bureaucracy, you may never be satisfied working for someone else. By contrast, if you left your former firm simply to satisfy your curiosity about solo practice, or to gain some courtroom experience, you might find satisfaction returning to a firm now that you've achieved those goals.

Are my existing clients compatible with the firm? You may have built an attractive slate of clients, but can you continue to serve them at a larger firm? Will the new firm raise your rates outside of your client's price range? How will the firm handle potential conflicts between your clients and existing firm business? When conflicts arise, most firms retain the client that generates more revenue, which means that your smaller clients might get the boot. And how do your clients feel about you moving to another practice? Are they concerned that they'll be serviced by low-level associates or lawyers with whom they have no relationship? Your client portfolio is one of your main sources of leverage to negotiate for compensation and other benefits.

Are my lifestyle and practices compatible with the firm? As a solo, you set your own hours, often leaving the office by 5 pm to make it home for dinner. Will the firm tolerate your early departure when everyone else stays until 7 pm? And you're probably accustomed to implementing marketing strategies or submitting articles for publication without approval from anyone else. How much autonomy will you have at the firm, and can you deal with the restrictions on your decision-making?

Like many lawyers, I took the first job offered after law school. I joined a boutique firm representing a major union client in a civil litigation practice. It was immensely boring. I had no client contact or freedom to explore the areas of law I was most passionate about...estate planning and probate. It was because my parents died young, and I was thrust into a probate proceeding. Even as a third-year law student, I knew enough to hire an attorney rather than handle it myself. But after the ordeal, I knew what I wanted to do in law: help clients with estate planning, and to support them as someone who had been there. So, after two years in civil litigation (and a baby along the way), I quit and went on my own.

Two years later, I had built a thriving estate planning and probate practice, embracing all forms of marketing and networking. Blogging was especially effective. As a result of my blog, I was contacted to speak at a CLE seminar with two others, one of whom was a partner at an established firm near my home. After the last seminar, he asked if I was interested in working at his firm. I was intrigued. After three interviews in as many days, I received an offer. This at a time when my own practice was booming and was a lucrative source of income.

What persuaded me to move my practice under the wing of the firm? Immediate health insurance for me and my family; instant secretarial and paralegal support for my clients; and the promise that I could continue to blog, network, and generally run my practice as I had as a solo…but this time with instant staffing in legal, administrative and human resources areas.

I enjoy working for my firm, and I'm proud to be working alongside a group of esteemed colleagues. And I am more valuable as a lateral hire because I was a solo. I know what it is like to watch the bottom line, to hustle to get clients, to keep clients satisfied, and to deal with staffing issues. When I reflect on it, my solo journey was leading me into a firm setting where I could practice in the areas I was most passionate about.

Here are some things to think about if you're transitioning or returning to a law firm:

- When analyzing your offer, factor in costs of health insurance, retirement plan contributions, vacation/sick pay as part of your compensation package. Also factor in the costs of not having to pay for malpractice insurance and annual bar dues among other costs for which you were previously responsible.
- Be up-front with your clients about the transition. Obtain their consent to take their matters to your new firm. Put in writing which cases you'll bring over and any fee-split arrangements.
- Tell your new firm that your first month of work will be a transition period, and that you will be burning the candle at both ends working at your new firm and dissolving your former practice. Your billables may be low in the first month or two because winding down a practice takes time.
- Send a welcome letter to your contacts with your new business card. Your transition is a reason to reconnect with your contacts and former clients for business development.

Jennifer Sawday (www.tldlaw.com) practices in southern California with the firm of Tredway, Lumsdaine & Doyle, LLP.

Closing Up a Law Firm

For whatever reason you're closing your practice, you can't simply walk away from your responsibilities to existing or former clients. Below is a brief checklist of the steps you need to take to shut down your practice.

- If you're moving to another firm, send e-mail or letters to your clients, notifying them of your move and arrange for the transfer of files. If you're leaving the law entirely, arrange for substitute counsel for active files, and e-mail and send a letter to clients to give notice that the firm is closing;

- Prepare withdrawal motions or notices of substitution of counsel for the courts;
- Inform your malpractice carrier;
- Prepare final reconciliation of trust accounts in accordance with applicable bar rules;
- Depending upon the size and structure of your firm, meet with an accountant to settle up any financial issues;
- Cancel all advertising, legal research accounts, and subscriptions;
- Make arrangements for final disposition of client files.

The Florida Bar offers a far more inclusive list online at http://tinyurl.com/4d9wvel.

IV. MARKETING

CHAPTER 14

Lawyer Marketing Overview

"Spend at least 50 percent of your time marketing...
and don't just rely on the Internet. Go out and meet
people; shake hands; hand out cards; go to
networking events; go to charity events. Make sure
every person you meet knows what you do and how
to reach you."—Lynda L. Hinkle, solo

Historically, the legal profession always turned up its nose at marketing, regarding it as unprofessional or undignified. In fact, until 1977, most bar associations did not allow lawyers to advertise. But in Bates v. Arizona, the Supreme Court overruled bar association restrictions on lawyer advertising, finding that they violated the First Amendment. Bates opened the door for much of the consumer-directed lawyer ads we see today in the Yellow Pages and on TV. And, as the legal profession has grown increasingly competitive, even large firms with corporate and business clients have been forced to market to survive and expand. In fact, many large firms employ a marketing staff headed by a chief marketing officer who may earn as much as $400,000/year.

With so many lawyers marketing 24/7, today's solos need to set aside whatever personal discomfort/dislike/fear they have for the marketing process, and find cost-effective (but dignified) ways to stand out from the crowd.

The next four chapters will provide a marketing overview along with specific techniques.

Learn to Love Marketing

Marketing attracts clients and generates more revenue.

You'd think this alone would be sufficient incentive to engage in marketing on a consistent basis. But typically what happens is that once we reel in a couple of revenue-generating clients, marketing takes a back seat while we take care of business. When our active matters conclude, we're right back where we started...hungry. To be effective, marketing needs to be done continuously in ways which bring personal fulfillment not just a means to an end. In a way, it's not so different than the argument for exercise: you're more likely to stay with it when you enjoy it. So, find ways to love marketing ... and not just because it helps the bottom line.

Marketing makes you a better lawyer. Much as we think of the practice of law as a noble profession or a lofty intellectual pursuit, lawyering, is about advocacy. Trial lawyers sell juries on why their clients are entitled to a favorable judgment; appellate lawyers sell judges on why a lower court erred; corporate lawyers sell their clients' preferred deals during negotiations. When you engage in marketing, you're selling something equally important—you're selling yourself. You may disdain it; you may feel uncomfortable doing it. But if you don't value your services enough to sell them to others, how can you effectively advocate for your clients?

Marketing gives you more control over your practice. How you market your firm influences the types of clients you attract. For example, running an ad in a local paper that offers *Bargain Rates for All Legal Matters. Free Initial Consultation* is likely to pull clients without the ability to pay even modest fees; or worse, tire-kickers seeking free advice. By contrast, writing an article for a business publication on creating charitable trusts could put you on the radar of high-earning clients with lots of assets. Simply put, a little strategic marketing can rescue you from the clients-from-hell. Think about the message your marketing sends, and how you can tailor it to attract the clients you want, not the ones you *don't* need.

Marketing calls upon your creativity. You don't need to spend thousands of dollars on a Yellow Pages ad or a listing for Martindale-Hubbell (LexisNexis/Martindale-Hubbell). If you allow it, marketing gives you a chance to apply your ingenuity to find low-cost ways to communicate your message. In fact, some of the most effective lawyer-marketers I know have found business through inexpensive campaigns such as running a blog or sponsoring a seminar or a local sports team.

Marketing is an adventure. Working for yourself is isolating, making it easy to forget you're part of a larger universe. When you get involved in the marketing process, you inhabit a larger, more interactive space, and open yourself up to amazing possibilities. I've had occasions where some assistance I provided gratis to other attorneys yielded referrals several years down the road. Or one of my blogs, or a bar magazine article about my practice, generated a phone call or e-mail from someone I knew in college or at a former job. In avoiding marketing, you miss making connections that pay unexpected dividends. So, think of marketing not as a job…or even as the key to your firm's survival…but as a way to find opportunities that bring more success and fulfillment than you ever imagined. In a phrase, stay open to connection.

REPEAT CONTACT = MORE BUSINESS *by Jim Schuster, Esq.*

Whatever mix of communication devices or strategies you use, one factor is a constant: staying in contact. You need to stay in touch with your former clients, your referral sources, your prospects. Build into your communication strategy a system for re-contacting [everyone]. Some might think this is obvious, but there are many consultants and gurus making good money simply telling people to stay in touch. There are many theories on the subject; some say a prospective client needs to hear about you three different ways. Others say a person needs 10 contacts before they will decide. Whatever is the magic number, *it is simply true that repeat contact by whatever means possible will generate more business in your office.* If somebody contacts your office for information, have a routine or a system to follow up the contact!

—Jim Schuster, past chair of the Michigan Bar's General Practice and Elder Law sections, and author of *The Aristotelian Method: Practice Development and Marketing for Lawyers on a Shoestring Budget.*

BOOK UPDATES AT AUTHOR'S BLOG—www.MyShingle.com

What Marketing Isn't...

Despite marketing's benefits, there are limits to what it can do for you, and what you can do with it:

Successful marketing does not equate to legal competence. Just because you're able to attract clients doesn't mean that have the competence or capacity to handle them. Just because a client is impressed by your Web presence doesn't mean that you're qualified to take on a complex medical malpractice case if you're accustomed to handling traffic tickets. Enjoy the flattery, but refer the case or team up with someone more capable. Likewise, if you're generating more cases than you can handle from your marketing campaign, make sure you can handle them competently before getting overloaded. Lawyers who thrive on the pursuit of a client but not the work that comes after, are most susceptible to bar claims.

Marketing isn't something you can outsource. As discussed below, you can outsource much of the support work related to marketing: hire someone to design your Web site or help you identify events you might want to attend. But don't ever, *ever* delegate marketing to someone else without ongoing and diligent oversight. Stories abound about unscrupulous marketers who post "spam," nonsense comments at high-trafficked blogs under a lawyer's name to generate search engine visibility. Many times, bloggers have "called out" the lawyers involved in these practices, and the unflattering commentary remains online long after the spam is removed. And because professional marketers aren't lawyers, they may inadvertently engage in unethical practices when marketing your firm, leaving you with an ethics complaint. New York personal injury attorney Eric Turkewitz (www.newyorkpersonalinjuryattorneyblog.com) sums it up nicely: *outsourcing marketing = outsourcing ethics.*

Marketing is not one-size-fits-all. You'll find many marketing consultants who offer advice on how to market a bankruptcy practice, a personal injury practice, a high-end corporate practice. Many may try to convince you that their program—though not specific to your practice—will nevertheless work. Don't buy it. Though most marketing basics are the same (e.g., create a unique selling proposition, be persistent), the details vary. An approach that works to attract personal injury clients in Springfield, Illinois, may not work for a trusts and estates client in the same city, or may not work (or may be cost-prohibitive) for a personal injury lawyer in a major metropolitan area.

Not all marketing practices work for all personalities. A shy, earnest lawyer may never be comfortable with an elevator speech that seems artificial and pretentious. Likewise, for a personable, extroverted lawyer who loves meeting people face-to-face, writing a blog might be torture. If you don't believe in the marketing techniques you're using, prospective clients won't believe you either.

Marketing Best Practices

Just as your business plan needn't be formal or extensive, your marketing plan needn't be either. At the very least, though, you should set aside time to identify your target clients AND your ideal clients (there's a difference, you know), and the ways you might attract them. For a sample downloadable marketing plan, go to LexisNexis (http://

tinyurl.com/6cbhv56). Of course, no single marketing technique is the silver bullet, so you will want to adopt a portfolio approach that combines a variety of marketing tools at different price points.

Work in batches. Instead of drafting a single article at a time, dedicate a morning or weekend afternoon to write two or three at a sitting. It's a better use of your time. The same advice applies to blog posts. At the start of each week, draft four or five posts and set your blog to automatically post them over a period of days or weeks. In this way, readers will come to appreciate your continuity and keep returning.

Make down-time work for you. Some lawyers use time in the carpool line to jot down marketing ideas, others use the commute to call contacts and set up meetings. One solo blogger we know dictates blog posts en route to work on a small digital recorder and has them transcribed by an assistant. Technology makes it easier than ever to squeeze in work on the run: smartphone apps now let you check your Twitter feed or update social media profiles easily while on the go.

The one-a-day principle. You take multivitamins, so make marketing a part of your daily routine, too. Make a point to post to your blog, or send a helpful link to a potential client, or respond to an RFP, or to call a possible referral source. On a daily basis. On their own, these activities might not seem significant; collectively they will add up when you look back at the end of a month. Marketing on schedule is difficult, and, yes, things will slide when you're swamped. Do your best. But if you're just starting out, go the extra mile; carve out some time just for marketing...and stick to it.

Team up with a marketing buddy. If you find yourself procrastinating, establish a marketing "buddy group". It might consist of a couple of lawyers...either in complementary practice areas in your city or those with the same practice area in different locations...where there's no possibility of competition. Your group might meet for a finite period; say the time it takes for each of you to create a marketing plan and follow one's goals. Or you can agree to meet or hold a weekly conference call, exchanging ideas, sharing successes, and getting feedback on new ideas to sell your service or improving your campaign. Some lawyers also gather to avail themselves of group marketing and coaching services or classes.

Set aside time for marketing calls and meetings. Schedule marketing time with the same discipline you schedule client meetings and calls. Example: block out Tuesday mornings between 9 and 11 to engage in some type of marketing; to either set up meetings, make cold calls, or to follow up with people you met at a conference. *Note*: while Friday afternoons would seem like a good time for marketing follow-ups, remember that some people leave early for the weekend. Likewise, take some time at the beginning of each month to arrange a few coffee or lunch meetings for the next four to eight weeks. If you set the dates in advance, you'll be more likely to stick to them even if you get busy.

Do your marketing on the job. If you have a matter scheduled at the court, arrive a few minutes early to chat with other lawyers and get a sense of whether they have work to refer. Or, if you attend a conference or a public hearing—especially one that will be transcribed or broadcast on the Web—volunteer a comment and preface your remarks with your name and information about your practice. Your remarks may impress someone in the audience who might approach you afterwards with follow-up questions.

What can you outsource? Just because solos and small firms don't have a BigLaw marketing budget, there's no reason we can't do a little strategic outsourcing. Hire a law student or university marketing student to help schedule meetings, identify future speaking opportunities, or to follow up with people you met at conferences. A freelance marketer can also prepare informal reports identifying trends or unfilled niches within a practice area. For example, suppose you wanted to develop a practice specialty of representing women who choose single motherhood. Your freelancer could surf the Web to determine the demographics of this category, what types of legal issues they encounter, and whether any existing services currently cater to this population. If your freelancer is also a law student or young attorney, you might also ask them to compile recent case law that deals with legal issues relevant to single parenting. For a few hundred dollars, outsourced marketing support can jump-start you into a field (or spare you from wasting more money on a losing idea) at the same time you're generating billable revenue.

How visible is your Web site or blog? To really understand the effectiveness of your online visibility, download one of the free online analytic programs from Google (Google Analytics), or at www.Mint.com or www.Statscounter.com. Or use the analytics package that comes with your Web or blog platform. An analytics package can tell you the source of your traffic, how long people remain at your site, and what types of searches they generated to reach your site.

You can learn a lot from site analytics. For example, if the bulk of site visitors arrive at your site directly (e.g., by keying in your URL), it means that they had already learned about the site—perhaps from one of your business cards. Also, check your keywords to figure out the search terms that visitors are using to find your site. If you're a Milwaukee foreclosure defense attorney, and analytics reveal that your site traffic derives from keywords like "foreclosure attorney" or *"what can I do to save my Milwaukee house from foreclosure?"* it shows that visitors who have a need for our services are finding you. By contrast, your traffic may be accidental. You may have written a blog post about a Milwaukee burger joint that declared bankruptcy, and you discover lots of visitors who've arrived at your site through terms like burgers and Milwaukee. Site "stickiness"—how long visitors stay at your site—is another indicator of the value of the materials you provide. Generally, visitors linger at a Web site for an average of just 55 seconds. If analytics show that your visitors are staying two minutes, it's a testament to the quality of your content.

What's your client-conversion rate? Suppose a popular law blogger who generates 30 free consultation appointments a month captures only a single, thousand-dollar client per month. If the lawyer is blogging 10 hours a month, and spending 15 more hours a month on free consultations, his conversion rate is ... dismal. If your own blog is generating a disproportionate number of people interested in free consultations, it's time to charge for consultations, or to seek out other techniques that give you access to individuals willing to pay for your services.

What's your marketing ROI? Return on Investment (ROI) is a way to compare the effectiveness of your marketing tools, and calculate how to allocate your marketing budget. Let's say you spend $5,000/year on newspaper advertising, and it generates $10,000 in fees. It's an ROI of 200 percent. At a glance, that seems reasonable; after all, you doubled your investment. But consider this: suppose *half* that investment had been spent on search engine optimization (SEO) to boost your online visibility, and the balance on online materials for prospective clients. And what if those two initiatives generated $25,000 worth of client fees? That's an ROI of 500 percent. You would have earned five dollars—not two—for every dollar spent. In this context, those newspaper ads don't seem like such an attractive investment. Again, your marketing ROI is a key indicator.

Re-evaluate. Marketing effectiveness isn't static; what works one year may not be worth the time or expense the next. You should constantly analyze your marketing initiatives to ensure that you're making the most of your time and investment: as your practice changes and grows, a once-inexpensive marketing investment may now cost more. For example, perhaps those bar-planning committees you joined when you had time on your hands are eating into your billable hours now. If so, maybe it's time to rethink, or at least cut back, on your participation and put your marketing resources towards efforts that don't require as much legwork.

ETHICS & ADVERTISING

Just because the Supreme Court opened the door to lawyer advertising (Bates v. Arizona) doesn't mean bar associations embrace advertising with open arms. Because while the bars do regulate advertising in the name of protecting consumers, the truth is that most bar associations either distrust—or do not understand yet—the new wave of lawyer marketing efforts like Web sites and blogs that educate the public about the law.

As recently as 2006, the New York bar proposed regulations that would require lawyers to seek approval for all advertising...including Web sites and blogs...and to retain a hard copy of all ads for up to three years.

Other bar associations require lawyers to include lengthy disclaimers on Web sites, clarifying that the sites do not constitute legal advice, that e-mailing the lawyer for information does not rise to an attorney-client relationship, and that prospects should not include confidential or proprietary information. Such disclaimers do make sense, particularly where your Web site targets a consumer-oriented or less sophisticated population. A disclaimer can protect you from situations such as (a) a conflict where a prospect, who doesn't know you've been retained by her adversary, sends you confidential information in an e-mail seeking representation, or (b) liability for suits asserting that your failure to respond to e-mails for three months caused a client to miss the statute of limitations for filing suit.

Every jurisdiction has its own peculiar rules related to advertising, which are too varied to summarize here. Instead, I offer the following tips for addressing ethics issues related to advertising:

- **Rules are rules.** Technology provides additional tools for advertising, but doesn't change the basic rules. If the bar precludes you from running print ads proclaiming World's Greatest Lawyers, chances are the bar won't allow a similar ad posted on a Web site.

- **Deception and superlatives.** In some ways, restrictions on lawyer marketing aren't all that different from fair practices governing ordinary advertising. Just as the FTC and consumer laws prohibit deceptive practices, the bar is no different. So, misleading techniques like dressing up as a doctor to gain access to an accident victim in a hospital to pitch your services won't pass scrutiny. Nor will running a bait-and-switch ad offering $350 uncontested divorces when you subsequently charge $2,500. Even a seemingly benign coupon for a "free" consultation will be viewed as deceptive if you ordinarily don't charge anything for consultations anyway. (See the article on ethics issues related to coupons and Groupon at www.legalmarketingblawg.com/2011/01/the-scoop-on-groupon-for-lawye.html). Of course, the bar frequently perceives deception where no ordinary, rational human would detect it. The Florida Bar prohibited a firm from using a pit bull in its logo, finding that such advertising was deceptive because there is no way to measure whether the attorneys in fact conduct themselves like pit bulls so as to ascertain whether this logo conveys accurate information. Likewise, the Nevada bar would not allow an attorney to call himself a "Heavy Hitter", fearing the public might believe he was the only Heavy Hitter.

- **Superlatives are another big no-no.** The bar believes consumers are incapable of determining if lawyers are truly the greatest or merely super. Not too long ago, the New Jersey Bar issued a ruling prohibiting lawyers and firms chosen for listings in publications like Super Lawyers and Best Lawyers from touting that designation in their advertising (a ruling challenged by the publishers of Super Lawyers). For more on this, read Alyson Palmer's account (Fulton County Daily Report). The article points out that the Georgia bar, and others, has not adopted New Jersey's position, and permits lawyers to proclaim their selection as Super Lawyers. Consult your bar about what's allowed in your jurisdiction.

- **Testimonials may be a red flag.** Testimonials from other attorneys, but especially from clients, add marketing value to a Web site or brochure. But many bars prohibit testimonials because of the potential for deception and inability to verify information (since most clients will want to provide testimonials anonymously if you've handled a sensitive matter for them). Even if your bar association does not allow client testimonials, determine whether you are similarly precluded from including in marketing materials endorsements or recommendations from other attorneys. Likewise, a bar may even impose limits on a lawyer's ability to gather testimonials on a social media site (though for now these restrictions are both unchallenged and constitutionally suspect).

- **Ethics of social media.** Social media complicates ethics issues related to testimonials. Some jurisdictions permit testimonials and endorsements on third-party sites like LinkedIn and Avvo, while others impose a duty on lawyers who participate in these sites to monitor testimonials and endorsements and remove those that aren't based on verifiable information as required by bar rules. Aside from testimonials, most traditional ethics rules apply similarly in social media. Just as it is unethical to contact an accident victim by phone and offer to handle her case, the same is true if you contact the victim via Twitter. Likewise, spamming your Facebook friends with announcements about events and awards on a daily basis is just as annoying as passing out your business cards at a kid's birthday party, and standing up to make an announcement about your firm.

- **Professional referral networks.** Most bars run lucrative referral services in which attorneys pay a fee in exchange for referrals. Naturally, those bar services take a financial hit if you choose to get referrals from competing sources. So watch out when you join groups like BNI, or similar professional referral services, where you pay a fee to join and you agree to engage in reciprocal referrals. Such arrangements violate ethics rules that prohibit payment of a fee in exchange for referrals (bar-referral services are exempt from these rules). Likewise, some bars are wary of for-fee referral services in which lawyers pay for a listing with a service that subsequently refers them to clients. The New York Bar's Opinion 799 sets forth considerations for lawyers considering registering for these services. Allison Shields, a New York attorney and law practice expert, posted an online summary of Opinion 799 on her blog (www.legalease.blogs.com/legal_ease_blog/2006/12/ethics_and_inte.html).

In her post, Shields said New York lawyers should refrain from using referral services if …

"…The directory 'recommends' the lawyers that subscribe [the opinion also explains that a service 'recommends' a lawyer, when it provides names of attorneys who specialize in 'slip and falls' to a client who writes in with a slip and fall problem], or otherwise 'makes claims about the competence or character' of the participating lawyers; the service 'analyzes' the prospect's legal problem in order to find a suitable lawyers; or the service does not specify the means of communication lawyers may employ when responding to prospective clients who post on the site.

- **Read the bar rules yourself.** Just because a lawyer can use a trade name in his state doesn't mean that it's permissible in yours. If, after reading the bar rules, you're still not sure whether your ad passes muster, contact ethics counsel.

- **The court of public opinion.** Before you take a certain advertising approach, consider how it will play in the most important court in the land: the court of public opinion. Even where the bar allows certain advertising techniques doesn't mean that you should employ them. Ads depicting you as an aggressive, hard-nosed lawyer will attract litigious clients who expect results, and who won't be afraid to sue you if they don't get them. Ads emphasizing your low costs will generate penny-pinching clients who may not pay their bills. Some tactics also may draw ire from the public or other lawyers, and result in what legal ethics blogger David Giacalone calls "e-shaming." In a blog post, he warned that the effects of questionable conduct—if it is cited in the media or makes it way online—can linger on search engines long after the original event:

    "…Were I a law professor, I'd be warning my students that Big Blogger is watching and will catch you, should you make gaffs or violations that find their way online. Were I a law firm manager, I'd be warning my colleagues that cyber-shaming is to be avoided at all costs. (And) if I were a lawyer prone to professional missteps, I'd be trying very hard to be on my very best behavior and to perform competently and diligently at all times. Your 'mistakes' will be available online for all time."

    —David Giacalone (www.blogs.law.harvard.edu). Used with permission.

Additional resources. There are many excellent Web sites that offer marketing tips and ideas for lawyers. Among them:

- www.Legalmarketingblawg.com. A marketing blog I write for Nolo.com, with detailed articles on ebooks, Facebook ads, niche practices, and more.
- www.Divorcediscourse.com. North Carolina family law attorney Lee Rosen blogs daily about marketing a family law practice. Many of his posts are useful for any law practice.
- www.Legalpracticepro.com. Jay Fleischman's blawg offers numerous tips on law practice marketing.
- http://sethgodin.typepad.com/. Though not a lawyer, Seth Godin is a business guru who's written more than a dozen books on marketing, persuasion and trends.
- www.Copyblogger.com. If you're looking to market largely through a blog or content-based management, Copyblogger is a font of information.

Q: What marketing advice do you have for new solos?

"If you don't market yourself, it doesn't matter how great an attorney you are."—Gabriel Cheong (class of 2007)

"Put yourself out there. Join networking and community groups, and ask your friends if they know anyone to whom they could send your name as a referral. Don't be afraid to ask clients or networking colleagues to pass your name along to their friends, customers, and business partners, and don't get discouraged if someone doesn't hire you immediately. It might take months, it might take years."
—Jan M. Tamanini (class of 1984)

"Don't just attend Chamber of Commerce meetings and hand out your business card to 100 people. Find the networking methods that make sense for your practice area and do those."—Mark Tanney (class of 1998)

"Get your name out there. Start a Web site, teach a class, volunteer at the bar association."
—Marc W. Matheny (class of 1980)

"Join civil, social and fraternal organizations, and shake hands with as many people as you can."
—Brian Rabal (class of 2005)

"Have a good elevator speech and use it. And specialize. Other attorneys will remember you if you are really good at one thing, and will refer clients to you."—Nina Kallen (class of 1994)

"I spun my wheels in networking groups for about six months, signing very few clients because I was marketing to the wrong audience. . . potential clients. Now, I network and market to my referral sources and it has made all the difference."—Gina Bongiovi (class of 2007)

"It is more important to market yourself to other attorneys and professionals than to market yourself to the general public."—Adam Neufer (class of 2009)

"Cultivate relationships. At least once a week, I have lunch (or coffee) with a colleague, a former client, or a potential referral source. I track personal and professional information for everyone I come into contact with, so that if I run across something that might be helpful or of interest I can forward it to them. And volunteering to chair the employment law section of my state's trial lawyer association has been a wonderful opportunity to meet more experienced employment law attorneys and to raise my profile."
—D. Jill Pugh (class of 1994)

"Getting good clients is all about networks; hometown, college, law school, government, firm, etc. Unless you have two or three good, separate networks, making it as a solo is very difficult. Which means that unless you spend a lot on advertising, you may have to spend a decade or more building up your networks before going out on your own."—Mark Del Bianco (class of 1980)

CHAPTER 15

Online Marketing & Social Media

"Social media makes practicing more affordable in that you can get your message out faster and cheaper than old-fashioned print ads and articles."

—Kara O'Donnell, solo

In today's world, a solo practitioner *must* have an online presence. It serves as a central gateway for clients and prospective clients, and for your own connection to social media.

After your license to practice, your malpractice insurance, and your computer and phone, an online presence is your firm's most strategic asset, even more important than the trophy office, the embossed stationery, and the fancy business cards. Why? Because Web and social media usage is increasing dramatically across all demographic groups. And consumers are relying on the Internet not just for shopping and recreation, but for detailed research on health care, finance, and government services…and they have come to expect lawyers to provide comparable information online as well!

In fact, when asked what factors impact hiring decisions, one in three corporate counsel said they factored in a lawyer's Web site biography and blog, and one in five considered their endorsements on LinkedIn and Twitter! (source: Corporate Counsel New Media Engagement Study, 2010). An online presence even makes a difference for referrals, since corporations go online to check a referred lawyer's credentials. In sum, an online presence demonstrates that you're keeping pace with the times; conversely, the lack of one could give an impression that you're not up to speed on new legal developments.

Fortunately, a robust and professional-looking Web site doesn't require a major capital investment. But it *does* require that your site contains all the basics. In this section, we'll discuss what they are:

YourWebSite.com

Your domain name—that is, your Web address—will most likely designate your firm (e.g., joneslaw.com, johnlewis.com), or describe your practice (e.g., marylandprobatelawyer.com). There are arguments for adopting one or the other. Domains highlighting a firm's name are usually easier for clients to remember; descriptive names seem to increase one's search engine visibility and rank you higher in Google searches. For this reason, lawyers often register two Web addresses—one with a descriptive name and another promoting their firm's name—and they make sure their sites are designed to automatically redirect visitors from one site to the other. A few additional considerations:

- Don't use the name of the host server in your Web address (e.g., aol.com/john-lewislaw). Such domains are difficult to remember and look unprofessional.
- Avoid any disputes over domain ownership; make sure you—and not your Web designer or someone else—has the rights to the name.
- Register the domain yourself so you can see if the name you select resembles any existing domain (for example, www.NYTrustsandEstateslaw.com and www.NewYorkTrustsandEstateslaw.com). If there is any likelihood of confusion, start over. Domain registration is inexpensive (under $10 per name), and there are dozens of reliable registration sites, among them www.Godaddy.com , www.Verio.com , and www.Register.com.
- Whether or not you choose to use your name—www.JohnJones.com—as your primary domain name, it's a good practice to buy the URL for your name if it's available, if only to keep someone else from acquiring it.

Note: some bars have restrictions on what you can use for a domain name. Others require you to identify the jurisdictions where you practice or include a statement that your site constitutes advertising. In some jurisdictions, lawyers must even submit a copy of the Web site to the bar for review. Chances are that the bar will never discover a non-compliant Web site. But other lawyers, particularly your competitors, might.

What follows are some other basics of contemporary Web sites:

About you. Don't just list your educational credentials and bar association awards; that's for your resume. This section should tell your story; why you decided to start your own firm, and how you arrived at chosen your practice area(s). For tips on writing a bio, visit Legal Marketing Blawg, and read *The Biology of Lawyer Bios* (www.legal-marketingblawg.com/cgi-bin/mt-search.cgi?search=bio&IncludeBlogs=23). In addition, this section of your site should include such basics as where and when you were graduated from law school, and your past work experience (if relevant). Many younger lawyers believe that by omitting a graduation date they won't draw attention to their age or lack of experience. Quite the opposite; the *absence* of key dates may indeed attract attention. Also: include a picture of yourself. A professional photo has a two-fold purpose: it adds personality to your site, and helps clients and other lawyers recognize you if your first meeting is outside the office.

About your firm. This section features your firm's philosophy and the types of clients you serve. You might also include articles you've written, professional writing samples (e.g., briefs, motions or contracts with confidential information redacted), a list of representative clients, and—if permitted by your bar association—client testimonials. Include the jurisdictions where you're licensed to practice, and a description of all of your practice areas. Also: be sure to describe each of your practice areas. Even though your peers recognize what is meant by Trusts & Estates or Civil Rights litigation, prospective clients might not understand.

About your clients. Make sure your site has a client focus. So, instead of boasting about your awards or the legal precedent you created, describe your accomplishments in a way that translates how you might be of service to a prospective client. You could write, "*I received a favorable ruling from the State Supreme Court in the historic case of Homeowner v. Zoning Board.*" But it's more engaging if you write, "*I rescued a family from forced demolition of their home. The Zoning Board had declared the house in violation of height restrictions, but I successfully convinced the state Supreme Court to overturn the Board's decision. It was the first time the court ever reversed a Zoning Board decision on appeal. Read the decision here* (and you offer a link to the decision)."

Post fees or not? The minority view is that you *should* post fees to satisfy client curiosity, and to filter out those unwilling or unable to pay your rates. The majority view is that you *should not* post your fees because some clients will assume they can't afford you and won't bother to call. If your site says that you charge $250/hour, a client might expect a $2,500 bill, when in reality the task might just require four hours of work, and cost less than $1,000. Once you post your fees, they must be made available to all. This limits your flexibility to develop rate packages that some clients prefer over an hourly rate. Even if you're not willing to post your fees, you can discuss different types of fees that you offer and explain the difference—e.g., flat fees, contingency fee or billable hour. You might also discuss factors that may result in higher fees, such as complexity or the novel nature of the issues, or a client's failure to provide all needed paperwork.

FAQ's. A section dedicated to Frequently Asked Questions serves two important purposes: it educates visitors to your site and demonstrates the range of your knowledge. Example: if you handle consumer bankruptcy cases and get a lot of "If-I-file-for-bankruptcy-will-I-lose-my-house" sort of calls, you can simultaneously educate clients and promote your practice by directing them to this section.

Disclaimers. If your site targets consumer clients and includes an e-mail address or form, you should include disclaimers that sending information does not create an attorney-client relationship or assure confidentiality. Disclaimers are particularly important when employing some of the interactive Web site features discussed below since the personalized nature can lead clients to believe that an attorney-client relationship has formed. Disclaimers also prevent site visitors from later claiming they thought you were representing them because they sent an e-mail with all their court papers. To avoid claims of unauthorized practice in jurisdictions where you're not licensed, you should also specify that the site is informational and does not constitute legal advice.

Contact information and office policies. Your Web site should display your contact information prominently, including address, phone, e-mail. Even if you choose to use a "contact box" for clients to describe their problems, provide a direct e-mail as well for colleagues who may want to get in touch. Display the contact information in a prominent spot on every page of your site. You should also include office policies. If you have a virtual office, you may want to specify that meetings are by appointment only. If your office building is in an odd location that requires special instructions to find, include that information.

Facebook, Twitter. Almost every corporate Web site these days has links for Facebook and Twitter. Your site, too, should link to your social media presence so that clients and prospective clients can see testimonials at LinkedIn or Avvo, or follow your tweets on Twitter, or view briefs or documents you've prepared on JD Supra or posted on your blog. By linking to your presence on social media, visitors have the option of learning more about you and your firm without burdening your Web site. *Author note*: link only to those social media sites where you are active; it would be counter-productive to direct users to your Facebook page if it lacks useful information, or to a Twitter feed if it hasn't been updated in months.

Auto-responders. Auto-responders do exactly what the name implies: they provide an automatic response to e-mails generated by a collection form appearing on your Web site. If you ever registered for an online newsletter or downloaded an e-book, you've seen an auto-responder in action. One of the most popular and widely used auto-responders is at AWeber Communications (www.aweber.com), which costs around $200/year. Aweber supports multiple releases and includes templates that you can use to set up e-newsletters. Constant Contact (www.constantcontact.com) is another inexpensive service for newsletter or event registration with different pricing options as little as $15/month. If you're not ready to commit financially, MailChimp (www.mailchimp.com) offers a free auto-responder and newsletter service for up to 500 subscribers.

Engaging the user. Other forms of user-engagement include quizzes, polls, and assessment tests. Example: you might create a quiz on the structure of the Supreme Court or the Bill of Rights as a public service to educate clients about the law. There aren't many online quiz creators, but one that is free and works for this purpose is at www.Quibblo.com. Polls, too, engage users. Or you might want to generate site traffic by soliciting opinions on contemporary issues. You can create and install your own add-on poll at www.WidgetBox.com. Assessment tests are another way to engage visitors... and to help you evaluate prospective clients at the same time. The best out-of-the-box online tool for this purpose is at www.AssessmentGenerator.com. It lets you create five different types of assessment tests. There's a free version of the Assessment Generator, and a more full-featured version for $10/month.

Online scheduling. Are you losing clients because you don't have staff to answer your phones and to schedule appointments promptly? One interactive tool that can help is a do-it-yourself scheduling system installed on your site. Scheduling systems are basically an online calendar where prospective clients view your available openings and set up their own appointments. The calendars are set up so that only the site owner can view the names and information associated with the appointments.

There are many online schedulers, among them www.Tungle.me, www.Doodle.com, and www.Scheduly.com.

Call me buttons and live chat. Ideally, your site should provide multiple ways to achieve client contact. Most sites include phone numbers and e-mails, but if you're not available the client has to wait for a response. You might consider getting a free Google Voice number that embeds a "Call Me" button on your Web site. When users click the button, the call goes to a Google phone number which in turn is re-directed to your number. You can also offer a live chat feature through such tools as ZohoChat (www.chat.zoho.com) and BoldChat (www.BoldChat.com) which costs around $300/year.

Search engine optimization (SEO). Web experts recommend investing in some level of search engine optimization (SEO) to improve a Web site's visibility (e.g., Google ranking). SEO is not inexpensive, but there are simple things you can do yourself to improve your ranking:

- List your Web site with multiple search engines to improve its ranking.
- Seek out opportunities to link your Web site (or blog) to others to raise its visibility among the search engines whose rankings are based on the number of a site's links.
- Include your Web and blog addresses in your e-mail signature to help drive more traffic to your site and to increase visibility.
- Add a blog to your Web site, or create a stand-alone blog. There is nothing as cost-effective as blogging to improve search engine rankings. Each blog post—even a simple, three-line post every few days—will increase your visibility among the search engines.
- Submit blog posts or Web sites of interest to "social bookmarking sites" (Digg.com and Stumbleupon.com). These and other social bookmarking sites let you share your favorite blog posts or Web sites with others. A high ranking on a social bookmarking site can drive significant traffic to your own site. For more social bookmarking sites, go to www.wikipedia.org/wiki/List_of_social_software#Social_bookmarking.
- Add a Google + button to your Web site4 or blog to increase its visibility on Google.

Author's note: In some niche-oriented practice fields, you won't find much competition from other sites, so SEO is not as important. For many years, I was one of only a handful of attorneys specializing in ocean-renewable energy, so any online search relating to these terms would put my firm up in the top five results. By contrast, if you're one of 500 New York lawyers handling personal injury cases, you may want to consult with an SEO consultant on ways to improve your site's ranking.

BOOK UPDATES AT AUTHOR'S BLOG—www.MyShingle.com

7 THINGS YOU SHOULD KNOW ABOUT SEARCH ENGINE OPTIMIZATION

by Jay S. Fleischman, Esq.

In order to stand out in a crowded legal market, your Web site must get "found" by Google and the other search engines. If you're not found, you're not hired. But how do you get found? It's difficult to know with so many vendors offering "expert SEO services". Even so, familiarize yourself with the fundamentals. Here are seven tips to get you started:

1. You cannot optimize that which does not exist. Google and the other search engines have indexed billions of Web pages. If you've got a 10-page Web site, there's pretty much no chance that it's ever going to be found. Even if it is, the sheer volume of information online makes it unlikely that anyone will pay attention if the content on your site is boring or stale.

2. Make your site easy to see. Google and the other major search engines use a specially formatted sitemap to learn about your content and the structure of your site. This sitemap is in a format called XML. Without this standard file on your Web server, the search engines won't be able to find what you've created.

3. Avoid duplicate content. If your content is replicated elsewhere, it won't rank your site well…and may not rank it at all. Though Google does not specifically penalize duplicate content, the search engine will look at all places where the content exists. The site with the best domain authority that has had the content the longest will get the superior ranking. Bottom line: you don't want information on your site that can easily be found elsewhere.

4. Linking between pages is important. When you create one page on your site, do your best to link some term to another page on your site. This is good not only for technical reasons, but also for readers of your site because it keeps them moving from page to page on your site.

5. Write for people first, Google second. In order for people to want to hire you, your site needs content they find interesting. It has to appeal to their needs, and it needs to speak their language. Why? Because some of the 200+ "ranking factors" that Google uses in determining search engine placement deal with user interaction with your site. The longer people remain on your site, and the more pages of content they read during their stay, the better your search engine ranking.

6. More Google is more better. It may be bad English, but it's true. One of the ways that Google determines whether to treat a Web site as credible is if the site is tied closely with Google's other services. Therefore, you want to claim your Web site with Google Webmaster Tools, implement Google Analytics, create a Google Places account, and set up a Google Profile with your Google account. Link the accounts, and you've done more than a lot of lawyers have done.

7. Not all links are created equal. Every SEO professional will tell you that links to your site with relevant anchor text (that's the term that is underlined in the link) are the most important part of a good ranking. What they don't tell you is that not all links are created equal. For the greatest impact, get context links from highly-regarded sites. In other words, a link on a Web site's sidebar is far less effective than one in the text area that says something like, "Jay Fleischman, a New York bankruptcy lawyer, is awesome." Remember that we're talking about contextual links from highly-regarded sites, not those with lower quality. Web directories and so-called "link farms" that consist of nothing but pages filled with outbound links are not only considered of minimal importance; a link on a site considered to be of exceptionally low quality can actually harm your site's ranking.

Jay S. Fleischman is a consumer bankruptcy lawyer and an online legal marketing consultant. Learn more about his internet marketing strategies by going to www.LegalPracticePro.com . He's also on Twitter at @JayFleischman.

Blogs aka Blawgs

Even though blogging has lost some of its cachet to Facebook and Twitter, the legal blogosphere is alive and well. In fact, it's become the cornerstone of a successful online presence for thousands of lawyers, law professors, and judges…on every imaginable topic: from Administrative, Admiralty and Appellate law to Taxation, Technology Law, and Workman's Comp. And why not? The marketing benefits are real: a blawg can showcase your insight and originality, impress prospective clients and referrals, boost your Web site's search ranking, and establish your reputation in your area of the law. To fully appreciate the scale of the legal blogosphere these days, spend some time at these sites: www.abajournal.com/blawgs, www.Blawgsearch.Justia.com, www.3Lepiphany.typepad.com, and www.LexMonitor.com.

Should I have a blawg or a Web site…or both?

In my opinion, you need both. And it makes sense to integrate them (unless your blawg is not directly related to your practice area; in that case, keep them separate but link the blog to your site and vice versa). For an example of a well-integrated site, see what criminal defense lawyer Jamison Koehler has done at www.Koehlerlaw.net. For further information on blawg/Web integration, see my article at www.legalmarketing-blawg.com/2010/11/websites-and-blogs-to-bond-or.html. Whether or not you start a blawg, *reading* them ought to be part of your legal marketing strategy. It can help you identify new practice areas, and impresses clients with your wider field of view.

YourBlawg.com: Getting Started

What makes a successful blawg? Readability, continuity, a distinctive voice. According to Wayne Schiess, director of legal writing at the University of Texas School of Law (*7 Tips for Writing a Successful Legal Blog*), lawyers should blawg because they want to, not for money; they should post frequently or at least regularly; and they should adopt a readable, personable style. To Wayne's suggestions, I'd like to share a dozen of my own:

Narrow the scope of your blawg. If you choose a topic as broad as "criminal law" or "California law," you'll find yourself running out of time just trying to cover all the emerging developments. Narrowing your scope makes the blawg more manageable… and more interesting to readers. If your practice has several specialties—say, estates, criminal, and family law—create separate blawgs.

Identify your audience. If you're appealing to consumers, write in plain English and keep your content conversational. If your intent is to generate referrals from other lawyers, you can showcase your analytical skills and familiarity with the topic.

What's in a name? The title of your blawg should reflect your subject matter. And if you're interested in establishing a presence in local markets, consider giving the blawg a geographic-based name (e.g., PeoriaIllinoisFamilyLawyer). Got a clever name for your blawg that you can't resist? Invest in both names; your preferred name and the more sensible one that can be redirected.

Choose a blawg platform. The two most popular (and free) blog hosts are www.Wordpress.com and www.Blogger.com. A third, www.Typepad.com, has a basic, low-cost package for under $100/year. If you want something more upscale, check out the fee-based blog sites hosted at www.Lexblog.com and www.Justia.com. Their packages include SEO, back-end support, and marketing webinars. *Author note*: if you think you might not be a blogger for very long, use one of the free or low-cost platforms; if you're still going strong after a few months, you can always upgrade.

Post consistently. Many bloggers post daily or almost daily. If you're just beginning, that might be a little demanding. So, try posting at least twice a week for the first few months. Still too much of a burden? Then "bank" several posts in advance to fill in the gaps. Or design your blawg as a weekly or bi-weekly newsletter to manage reader expectations.

Make it worth the reader's time. Blogging is highly competitive. That means you can't expect much traffic if all you're doing is posting a link to a news story or case decision without your personal commentary. If you want traffic, post your analysis of news stories or cases, and offer your opinion or speculation about what will happen. Make reader feel as if they're getting personal insights not canned material.

Timing is important. Posting in the morning increases Web traffic, and posting between Monday and Thursday attracts more readers than on weekends. Also: posting your commentary soon after an important case is wrapped up will drive up site traffic, and perhaps even invite media interest. Don't wait too long to post, though; waiting a week won't be of much interest unless you compile an extensive post that rounds up all prior commentary at other sites. Any longer than a week…forget it! Readers come to blawgs expecting fresh content.

Monitor your traffic. Most blog platforms offer some kind of statistical (stats) package to track traffic, page views, how your visitors found you, etc. You can also install Google Analytics at no charge. Understanding your traffic is important; it lets you customize future posts to meet the needs of your audience.

Join the conversation. Once you start blogging, you can start engaging with other bloggers. Comment at their sites, link generously to other bloggers' posts (but don't lift content without attribution) and create some interaction.

Don't focus on links and reciprocal links. New bloggers often obsess about getting links to their site. Relax. An outgoing link from another blogger won't generate much additional traffic. More valuable are "organic" links in which another blogger or Web site actually discusses and links to your blog by name.

Redistribute and repurpose your content. If you're spending time creating content, you might as well as get some extra mileage. Broadcast your posts on Twitter and Facebook, or convert blog posts into a long article and upload it at www.JDSupra.com or www.docstoc.com.

Give up the ghost! A blog should represent a lawyer's personal views. When a blog is ghostwritten, it's misleading; it's as if the lawyer had someone else show up in court to argue and pretend to be that lawyer. If it becomes to necessary for you to maintain a schedule of regular blawg posts, hire law students or out-of-work lawyers to track down stories, and draft posts for you to review and edit—or have them publish under their own byline.

Listservs & Social Media

By definition, a listserv is an electronic mailing list devoted to a specific issue or topic. In practice, a legal listserv—whether hosted by the ABA or the county bar—is an on-line community of like-minded lawyers. The largest is *Solosez*, the ABA's popular Internet community of solo and small firm lawyers. Established in 1996 with a current roster of nearly 3,500 lawyers, law students, and law-related professionals, Solosez is a great way to find answers to practice-management questions. Members often post messages in search of attorney referrals for friends or clients; other times, they use it to find lawyers interested in handling overflow work on a contract basis. In addition, Solosez members—for example, a real estate attorney and a probate attorney—might team up to serve a client whose problems involve both areas of expertise. Whether or nor you generate much business on a listserv depends on your ability to stand out in a positive way.

Here are some tips in that regard:

- Try to respond at least once a week to questions you're competent to answer. For example, if you practice employment law in New York and there's a question on employment law in California, you might analyze the problem from a general perspective and share some insight on how New York law works. Even if you're a new practitioner, or you practice in an obscure field of law, you can still contribute. Likewise, if someone is looking for a case or a sample complaint or an article on a legal topic, run a quick Internet search, and see if you can come up with something responsive.

- As you begin contributing, your skills and knowledge will come to the attention of other lawyers, and they in turn may wish to refer cases or retain you when they're familiar with the quality of your work. If you don't know the answer to a highly technical post, don't respond. In one stroke, you could lead the questioner astray and embarrass yourself at the same time. Also: be mindful of the tone, grammar, and spelling of your posts. Listservs, especially Solosez, are a highly visible forum, and you will find yourself the subject of a swift (and public) reprimand for any nasty or rude missives, especially if your target is one of the list's more eminent members.

- If some of your listmates have practice areas that complement one another, contact them off-list and continue the conversation about potential work opportunities.

- Set up a signature line for your e-mail that indicates where you're located and licensed to practice. In this way, other listserv members can learn more about you, and, if your post finds its way to other lists, your contact information will become even more important.

Social Media. A curious blend of technology and social interaction that can be an instrument for community-building or regime change.

Without question, **Facebook** is the world's largest social media site with 550 million members worldwide (and increasing at a rate of 700,000 a day). As Time Magazine once observed, if Facebook was a country it would be the third largest behind China and India. Lawyers who dismiss social media as a fad do so at their peril. Author and legal futurist Richard Susskind (*The End of Lawyers:Rethinking the Future of the Legal Profession*) is convinced that Facebook-like technology will become indispensable to lawyers for communicating with clients.

With so many different social media platforms, it's difficult to explore all but the most popular here (for a more detailed study, read *Social Media for Lawyers: The Next Frontier,* which Nicole Black and I co-authored).

In the section that follows, you'll find a description of different categories of platforms and their functions, as well as tips for making the most of social media:

The directory sites. Two of the best-known directory sites are **LinkedIn** and **Avvo**, both of which provide a forum for listing your credentials, testimonials, and—in Avvo's case—lawyer ratings. Both are interactive; that is, customers and clients can submit testimonials, and the profiles are user-created and maintained.

For business professionals, the largest social networking site is LinkedIn (www.LinkedIn.com), whose membership has maintained a steep trajectory from 118,000 members in 2008 to more than 1.5 million in 2010 (source: Corporate Counsel New Media Engagement). It works like this: once you're registered at LinkedIn, you create a Web profile linking you to colleagues, friends, and professional acquaintances. Once your network is established, you can access the contacts of others…and the contacts of *their* contacts. In addition, LinkedIn posts endorsements for your service, giving you more credibility with potential contacts. The basic Linkedin account is free; upgrades allowing you to connect with a wider range of people and view their resumes cost extra. For solos the benefit is obvious: LinkedIn serves as an online resume for your practice, and helps you make contacts with people you want to meet. Other interactive features allow you to create a group focused on your specialty, and answer questions posed by other users.

Avvo.com and **Justia.com** are directory sites dedicated to profiling and rating lawyers.

If you claim your profile, Avvo allows you to list all of your accomplishments; in fact, the more awards and accomplishments you post, the more likely you are to achieve a higher numerical rating. Clients can post testimonials about their lawyers on Avvo, and colleagues can offer endorsements. Avvo also displays lawyer disciplinary ratings. Justia.com, a Web site affiliated with Cornell's Legal Information Institute, is similar to Avvo, but without the numerical ratings. Both Avvo and Justia target consumer clients, and several solos report having generated new clients with the help of both sites.

Author note: Some lawyers decline to join Avvo for fear of a low rating, or that a disgruntled client might post a negative review. In my opinion, Avvo's numerical ratings are a bit of a red herring. Prospective clients are more likely to assign more weight to testimonials and accomplishments than a numerical rating. As for disgruntled clients, they can just as easily post negative reviews on Yelp.com or even set up a Web site critical of you. At least at Avvo, you're able to respond to negative reviews and request their removal if they're clearly false.

The community sites. The leading example is **Facebook**. Once known only for its recreational potential (see Hollywood's *The Social Network*), Facebook is having an effect on the US court system. Example: these days, prosecution and defense lawyers, and trial consultants, scour Facebook for personal details about members of the jury pool that could signal which side they might sympathize with during trial (Wall Street Journal, Feb. 22, 2011). Aside from its value in litigation, Facebook provides valuable professional networking opportunities, reconnecting lawyers with long-lost class-mates and friends, all of whom can act as potential referral sources. And it can act as an icebreaker, too, as you discover activities that you have in common with colleagues. In addition to personal pages, Facebook also offers the ability to create a Facebook Fan Page for law firms and other businesses. Many law firms use their fan page to post about community activities and publicize firm events. A fan page also solves the awkward problem that arises if a client asks to "friend" you. If the client is one who you don't feel comfortable "friending", you can direct him or her to your law firm's page. In addition to Facebook, there are numerous lawyer-specific community sites, includ-ing www.lawlink.com, www.Martindaleconnect.com and www.Legalonramp.com (an invitation-only network for collaboration between in-house counsel and lawyers in private practice).

The communication sites. Some social media sites are used to disseminate ideas. Blogs (discussed earlier) fall into this category. So does **Twitter**, a microblog with mes-sages no longer than 140 characters. Sometimes a member's "tweet" may do nothing more than pass on a link to a news story or an interesting blog post; other times, Twit-ter is used for banter or cursory discussion. Some courts and federal agencies are on Twitter, and use it to send news releases or note the issuance of recent cases. If you think you might be interested, sign up for an account at www.Twitter.com and "follow" other lawyers you know personally, or from around the blogosphere. Twitter is popu-lated by media types as well. So, if you're looking for press coverage, follow a bunch of reporters to get a sense of the information they're looking for. After spending a few days watching the exchanges, you should be ready to dive in.

The document-sharing sites. There are a variety of social media platforms where lawyers can upload and share briefs, PowerPoint presentations, and video. **JDSupra. com** is a document-sharing site that lets lawyers upload briefs and memos they pre-pared, or search for work done by other lawyers on substantive legal topics. *Author note*: don't upload privileged materials without redacting identifying information. Two other document-sharing sites are **DocStoc.com** and **Scribd.com**, which let you em-bed a document at your Web site so that visitors can scroll through it rather than hav-ing to download it as a PDF.

Also: **Slideshare.net** supports slide uploads, and **YouTube** and **Vimeo.com** are useful for uploading videos. These sites let visitors provide comments and feedback on your work, and will generate a piece of code that lets you embed your video or presentation in your Web site.

What are your social media goals? Don't hop on the social media bandwagon without specific goals. Select only those platforms that will help to achieve those goals, and develop a strategy for each platform. If one of your goals is to become known as an expert on family law, choose Twitter and YouTube and commit to posting several tweets a day on family law developments, and creating a series of mini-videos on family law topics of interest to clients.

Less is more. Some lawyers are inclined to set up profiles on every social media site. In my opinion, that is counter-productive because a profile with minimal activity won't attract much interest. Better to focus on the sites that serve your target clients and match your personality, and to use those sites extensively.

Work in bulk. Once you decide to get started on social media, set aside time to create your profile on sites like LinkedIn, Justia and Avvo (if you choose to use it). Many of these profiles require similar materials, so it's more efficient to create them all at once. In the interests of time, consider hiring a virtual assistant or college student with social media experience. They can handle the tedious work and keep your profiles updated.

Seek out testimonials. One benefit of social media sites is the ability to support testimonials. You may have to ask your clients or colleagues to provide those testimonials, or they may not do it on their own. Testimonials and endorsements, particularly those that describe what you're like to work with, add credibility, and make your profile more persuasive. Author note: check your bar's rules on testimonials at third-party social media sites. Though, to date, no bars have prohibited participation, they may impose certain restrictions.

Use a photo. A photo is a must on social media; it adds a personal touch. You'll probably want a formal photo for Avvo and LinkedIn, but feel free to use a more casual or personal photo on Facebook or Twitter.

Make it easy to be found. Once you've staked claim to a few social media sites, let others know. Include your Avvo rating on your Web site (if it's permissible in your jurisdiction), or put your Twitter address on your business card.

Time management. From personal experience, I can tell you how easy it is to lose track of time following Twitter conversations, or sifting through interesting PowerPoint presentations at SlideShare.com. As a consequence, I personally limit my time on social media to mornings before work, and later in the evening. If I'm out of the office on the Metro or waiting at the bank, I may check on Twitter or Facebook on my phone and again at night. Otherwise, they remain switched off during the work day. Most social media platforms have smartphone applications, which makes it easy to squeeze some social media time into your day.

Online Advertising

Online directories. The cost and effectiveness of online directories varies. With free directories (e.g., Avvo, LinkedIn, RocketLawyer), you have nothing to lose except the time it takes to register. If you're considering a fee-based directory, you need to factor in (a) whether a listing will make you more "findable" on the Web, and (b) whether a trial period is permitted to determine its effectiveness. Some, like www.Lawyers.com and www.Nolo.com , list lawyers by practice area, while www.LawGuru.com is skewed towards lawyers with consumer-oriented practices. Online directories feature different levels of interactivity. If you're going to pay for an online directory, evaluate factors such as whether you'll have an exclusive area, whether you'll be required to sign a long-term contract, whether they offer a refund for a disappointing performance, and what additional features are provided (for example, Nolo includes access to all of its books and forms).

Online referral services. Lawyer referral services (among them **LegalMatch.com**, **LegalFish.com**, and **LegalRiver.com**), operate a little differently from online directories. They use questionnaires to gather extensive case information from prospective clients, forwarding them to lawyers in a given region and practice area to respond if they wish. In this way, attorneys are only sent clients with matters specific to their practice area. Other referral sites operate more like an RFP: a client posts a project and specifies a price, and lawyers can review posted requests and make a bid. Yet another referral model was introduced in Spring, 2011. Called Shpoonkle.com, it allows lawyers to bid on posted cases; the service is something like an "eBay for legal services". Yet another new site—LawPivot.com—bills itself as providing "crowd-sourced legal advice". In this model, start-ups submit questions to the site and participating attorneys can respond.

Author note: some referral services are expensive ($3,000 to $4,000/year), and some of their sales people are quite assertive…even deceptive. It's not unusual to get a phone message that a referral company has a referral for you. When you call back, you might be told that, *"If you were really committed to building your firm, you'd be willing to risk $3,000".* . . or this variation, *"We don't want to do business with the types of law firms that consider $3,000 to be a lot of money."* Some referral services offer a money-back guarantee, and/or an extra six months free if you don't get any clients. Such promises may not be meaningful, because if the service didn't bear fruit another six months might be meaningless. As for the money-back guarantee, make sure you understand when it kicks in; if you haven't had any referrals or the ones you got were unsuitable. Make sure the guarantee covers both situations. And before you put down your money, do a little additional digging:

- Search the Web and the Solosez archives (www.mail.abanet.org/archives/solosez. html) to see what other lawyers say about specific online referral services.
- Consult with lawyers whom you trust, as well as bar practice advisors, for their advice.
- Ask if a referral service permits a three-month trial so you can limit your exposure.

Online advertising. Some Web sites have adopted the ad pricing model traditionally associated with newspapers and magazines: a flat weekly or monthly fee. Example: if you advertise on a business Web site because your practice represents entrepreneurs, you might pay $25 or $50/month to several hundred dollars a month depending on the site's popularity. The same pricing model often applies to blogs (see www.blogads. com). By far, though, the most common online pricing model is "pay-per-click" (PPC), or "performance-based advertising". Advertisers pay only for measurable results; that is, the number of leads or "click-throughs" the ad generates.

Pay-per-click (PPC). The best known PPC program is Google's AdWords (www. adwords.google.com). It works like this: you create a small, boxed, three-line ad that makes use of keywords describing your practice area(s). For example, you might use keywords like *Toledo Ohio civil rights lawyer,* or *Oakland personal injury,* or *mesothelioma attorney Texas.* When someone Googles those keywords, or any combination thereof, your ad appears to the right of the search results. This is where things can get expensive: if someone clicks on your ad for whatever reason, Google charges you the cost of the keyword (e.g., pay-per-click). Some legal keywords are relatively inexpensive—as little as $9 per click—while other legal keywords can cost $30, $40, even $60 or more! Depending on the keywords selected, and the frequency with which your ad appears, PPC can put a big dent in your marketing budget. But does it work? Some solos with national practices related to, say, Social Security, veterans affairs, immigration, and unbundled "virtual services", report success with Google AdWords...but their ads required significant resources; upwards of $700 to $1,500/month. Other solos report limited success, some complaining that user "clicks" often failed to click through to their site, or the click-through worked but it didn't convert into a sale.

Both LinkedIn and Facebook have launched PPC campaigns of their own. In the case of Facebook, it doesn't depend on keywords but targets member demographics instead. Example: if your practice represents baby boomers, you could identify a target demographic of, say, ages 55–65, and your ad would appear on the pages of Facebook members in that range. Some demographics cost more than others; young women members are a pricy demographic unless you refine the search (e.g., women ages 31–35 who are also parents and college graduates). Facebook ads have not proven as productive as Google AdWords, but they are also not as expensive either. As with Google, you can specify a budget cap for Facebook and LinkedIn ads.

Pay-per-lead. Total Attorneys, a national marketing and support service organization for solos and small firms, offers a slightly different pricing model: a performance-based service based on "pay-per-lead". It works this way: Total Attorneys creates a Web site for certain practice areas, such as bankruptcy or consumer credits, and invests in sufficient resources to ensure that the site gets on the first page of a Google search. Prospective clients responding to the ad fill out a survey, and receive the name of a participating attorney in their area. Meanwhile, the participating attorney receives the name and contact information of the prospective client, and is free to follow up. Each time Total Attorney sends the name of a prospective client, the attorney pays $65 per lead. A minimum monthly fee guarantees a certain amount of leads, and Total Attorneys adjusts the fee up or down depending on the number of leads actually generated.

Author's note: In 2010, a disgruntled competitor filed a bar complaint against Total Attorneys and three Connecticut attorneys who had used the service, alleging that Total Attorneys' system of pay-per-lead was really a fee for referral in violation of bar rules. The competitor filed a similar complaint against Total Attorneys in all 49 states, but not against the lawyers who used the service (see www.totalattorneys.com/blog/pay-per-performance-marketing-under-attack-total-attorneys-responds). Thus far, most state bars have found that Total Attorneys does not violate bar rules on paid referrals. At the same time, the suit is troubling because it shows that individual attorneys can be disciplined for participating in these programs, even if they believed in good faith that the programs were ethically compliant. In July, 2011, the ABA released a proposed rule which would allow pay-per-lead. Still, lawyers should undertake their own research on programs which appear to promote fee-splitting or fees for referrals.

Groupon (www.Groupon.com). A Chicago-based Web site and online broker for daily deals between buyers and sellers. Founded in 2008 and already operating in 43 countries, the verdict is still out on whether Groupon's arrangement is worthwhile—or even ethical—for US lawyers. Here's how it works: Groupon (and other similar sites like Amazon's LivingSocial.com) team up with local business owners, who provide a coupon for 50 to 70 percent off their product or service. If enough users commit to purchasing the coupon, the deal goes through, and Groupon and the participating business split the discounted proceeds. The North Carolina's state bar ethics committee characterizes the arrangement as fee-splitting with a non-lawyer provider, a practice that violates that state's rules. Other disciplinary bodies have ruled on the ethics of discounts and coupons, with some concluding that they may constitute impermissible deceptive practices (for example, offering a "free" consult when a lawyer never charges for consults anyway), or they can give rise to a conflict of interest, or constitute a "fee" in exchange for referral if given to a third party, like a realtor, for distribution. Given the present ethics questions, lawyers might be better off seeking other online alternatives.

GUARDING YOUR REPUTATION ONLINE

These days, ever-more powerful search engines make it just as easy to discover what is meritorious about you—your work, your writings, your pro bono awards—as it is to find a disciplinary record or any best-left-unseen comments or photos posted on listservs and elsewhere. In an age of transparency, it is imperative that you stay vigilant about guarding your reputation. Here are five suggestions:

- **Know what's out there.** Run your name or law firm name through the search engines regularly to see if negative information is in circulation. If so, inquire if the site owners have a policy that allows for the removal of comments. In extreme cases, where information posted is easily discoverable (e.g., appears at the top of your search results), and is damaging (e.g., prospective clients question you about those comments and then decline to hire you), you may need to consult an attorney who specializes in Internet defamation to evaluate your options.

- **Watch what you say and where you say it.** Search engines can index listservs or mailing groups that you may have thought were private. If you post about a personal problem on a listserv, or lob volatile posts, those messages could pop up when someone searches your name. To avoid the embarrassment, keep your online messages tame (something you should be doing anyway), and post sensitive questions anonymously.

- **Think twice about advice you give at seminars.** A Pittsburgh-based immigration law firm learned a hard lesson when its lawyers advised seminar participants that they could bypass federal immigration laws on hiring foreign workers by creating recruiting campaigns designed "not to find qualified US workers" (therefore opening the doors to hiring overseas). A video of the event found its way to YouTube via a whistleblower who inserted his own subversive subtitles about how the firm was advising companies to break the law. Ultimately, the video was downloaded by more than 120,000 viewers—among them two US Senators. The legislators sent a letter to the firm asking for an explanation.

- **Take pre-emptive action.** Any negative, readily discoverable information about you or your firm that could be found online should be disclosed to clients. For example, if you've got a grievance on your record, disclose it with an explanation. Your clients will appreciate the candor, and may not hold the infraction against you. If they discover the grievance through their own online search, however, they may suspect you of withholding information. On occasions where pre-emptive action is called for, don't come down too hard, though. A few years ago, in the case of Nixon Peabody, someone sent a copy of the firm's theme song to a legal gossip site and to YouTube. The firm reacted by asserting copyright protection and demanded that the song be deleted. It was, but not before the BigLaw firm's cease-and-desist action drew more online attention to the controversy. Bottom line: if something embarrassing makes its way online, try to diffuse the situation or find a way to make the attention work to your advantage.

- **Respond appropriately to negative reviews.** As rating sites like Avvo and Yelp gain traction, it's entirely possible you will get a negative rating at some point in your career. How to protect yourself? (a) If the review is clearly incorrect—for example, the review says you only have voicemail when you actually have a receptionist or a service answering the phone—post a polite response noting the error, (b) If the negative review was intended for someone with a similar name, alert the Web site manager, (c) If the reviewer takes issues with your style or your decisions—for example, the post says you weren't sufficiently aggressive—you might take the opportunity to post your practice philosophy, (d) If you recognize the client from their poor review, contact him or her privately if you think it will make the difference, and (e) If a disgruntled—even disturbed—client posts an over-the-top, clearly irrational comment, don't respond directly because your response will only provoke them further. Ask the site owner to remove the rant. But no matter how bad the rating, take care not to reveal client confidences to defend yourself.

CHAPTER 16

Traditional Marketing

"Putting up a billboard won't make you rich, and doing direct mail or buying a Yellow Page ad won't do you much good. Your first goal should be to create a brand." —Scott Wolfe, solo

Today, with all of us immersed in the Web, it's easy to understand why traditional marketing techniques seem to have a quaint, even old-fashioned feel. And yet we can't forget that some clients—particularly older clients and established, institutional-type businesses—might prefer a more conventional approach to marketing. So, know your audience, and diversify your communications. But above all, play to your strength. If you're an introvert who dislikes crowds, do your networking at small gatherings; if you're a busy parent working part-time, arrange coffee meetings instead of long lunches; if you're targeting large international clients, skip the Yellow Pages ads. In short, tailor your marketing process to your personality and the needs of your practice.

In this section, you'll find suggestions—and pros and cons—for 20 traditional marketing strategies:

Marketing #1: Networking Like a Pro

If you're like me, you're inundated with invitations to networking events—lunches, breakfasts, happy hours, holiday parties. Invariably, these events—hosted by bar associations, alumni or trade groups, law schools, etc.—find you standing awkwardly in a roomful of strangers, or sitting alone at an empty lunch table...or worse, trying to extricate yourself gently from a conversation about widgets. Well, here's the truth about networking events: *they're not the best way to meet potential clients*. At best, you might make a decent contact for every 10 events you attend! But don't give up on them. You need to attend every so often if only to show your face within the industry or the group...because that one contact you make just might turn into a major client.

Choose high-value events. With so many networking events, be selective; seek out those that offer some value beyond a meal or happy hour. Attend lunch events whose speaker is prominent in your practice area, or where there is a panel on emerging issues. So, even if you don't meet anyone worthwhile, at least you'll have learned something new. Plus, a topic-focused event will give you meat for conversations with other participants.

Bring business cards. Bring a few dozen business cards to every networking event you attend. Offer a card at the outset of a conversation or before you depart. When you're attending a lunch or dinner event, circulate your card around the table. If you've forgotten your cards, collect as many as you can from others. Or use a smartphone to e-mail them your contact information.

Don't sit at an empty table. Seek out tables that are partly full. Ask whether you can join a table; if permitted, introduce yourself to others before you take your seat and distribute your business card.

Don't stay too long or get too deep. Don't talk too long or get into too much detail. Ask questions about what the other person does, rather than focusing on what you do. Be sure to exchange business cards, and if you don't trust your memory take a few moments to jot down information about the other person. Even if you run into people you know well, keep the conversation short, and arrange to call for a get-together at another time.

Cut your losses. When my law firm was still new, I attended numerous networking events and even found my first client at one. But I haven't always been so fortunate. There were many more times when the person with whom I was talking would gaze over my head, scanning the room for someone more important. And there was many a bar event where I would hear patronizing remarks like, "*It's so nice that you started a little law firm.*" One lawyer congratulated me on my "gumption," and actually patted me on the head. So, cut your losses; learn to recognize when an event is a dud and leave... or head to the bar and make mental notes for the novel you're writing.

Host your own networking event. Instead of waiting for an invitation, hold your own event. If you have office space or a conference room, invite people to drop by for a happy hour. Home-office lawyers might rent out space at the bar association or reserve a private room at a local bar or restaurant. Or organize regular lunch or breakfast meetings for lawyers or other contacts you've met through listservs. Lawyers from the Boston and Washington D.C. contingents of the ABA's Solosez listserv organize monthly lunches or dinners, while groups of "solosezzers" in other cities plan get-togethers around visits by out-of-town members. Meetings that evolve from listservs or other online interaction are enjoyable because you've already established relationships online. And the meetings often produce more referrals or marketing leads because you've had more of a chance to explore possibilities in direct conversation.

Go online to brush up on your networking skills. At www.RainmakerVT.com, you can rehearse your networking skills in a virtual world... and get real-time feedback. It's a new dimension in lawyer business development. The software invites you to create an avatar (e.g., an online alter ego), and choose from a variety of networking exercises. Each provides a variety of interactions and outcomes. According to RainmakerVT's developers, subscribers can go through the interactive exercises until they're comfortable with how to handle a given situation. Rainmaker is broadband-based and compatible with PC, Mac, and Linux platforms. A year-long subscription is expected to cost a few hundred dollars, and give you 24/7 access to all of the networking scenarios.

THE BUSINESS CARD

Even in an age where anyone can be found on Google, business cards remain an essential networking tool that consolidates all of your important contact and marketing information. Below you'll find a couple of tips:

Develop business cards suitable for your target audience. A lawyer serving an older population may want to use larger fonts on heavier stock. A lawyer targeting a younger or tech-savvy clientele will want to add their various social media presences. And for a younger audience, consider adding one of the new, two-dimensional bar codes called QR Codes (quick response) that let anyone with a smartphone camera scan and capture your contact information. There are many free QR Code generators online; just Google the phrase "QR Code generators".

Print both sides. Make good use of the reverse side of your business card; perhaps a more detailed list of your practice areas, or a calendar.

Save money, go online. Options for business card creation abound, from do-it-yourself design through sites like VistaPrint.com or moo.com to custom design by graphic artists available either online or locally. Many solos favor local designers for business cards because they prefer the personal interaction.

Cards are inexpensive, get two sets. As long as you're ordering business cards, consider getting a second set; one for business contacts and colleagues, another, less expensive set, to drop off at vendor tables at conferences or for large events.

Marketing #2: Branding

Lawyers have been slow to recognize the importance of branding. But if clients can't remember or identify your firm, they can't hire or refer you to others. Marketing expert Seth Godin sums it up well, saying that your brand is more than just a stylish logo: *it is the set of expectations, memories, stories, and relationships that, taken together, account for a consumer's decision to choose one product or service over another.* Of course, one dimension of branding is the "tagline" that defines and describes your practice. Ask yourself what it is that makes your firm most attractive to potential clients? Your unique practice area; your devotion to client service; your low rates; your location? Sum it up in 10 words, and you've got the makings of a tagline. But don't stop there. Put it through a Google search. It might surprise you to learn that two dozen other firms are using the same tagline or something similar. As a legal matter, of course, you can adopt a tagline similar to one used by others because most taglines are not unique enough to qualify as service marks or trade marks.

Taglines generally fall into three categories:

- **Taglines highlighting the type of law you practice.** One of my favorites belongs to David Kaufman, a Washington DC solo representing individuals and companies in the rough-and-tumble litigation arising out of business deals-gone-bad. One of David's taglines reads, *We do business brawls* (sm). In fact, his Web address is *www.businessbrawls.com.* In Maryland, attorney Mark Spellman has a wills and trusts practice whose tagline calls attention to his willingness to visit clients where they will be the most at ease. His tagline reads, *Legal house calls: legal services in the comfort of your home.* And in southern California, solo sports lawyer Howard Jacobs has a niche practice of defending athletes accused of using illicit substances. His tagline reads, *Keeping you in the game.*

  Creating a tagline can be tricky if you practice in more than one area. For that reason, lawyers tend to use taglines that convey more generally the type of service they provide. For example, The Klein Law Group (www.kleinlawpllc.com) features this tagline: *Hire the attorneys you need, not the firm you don't* (sm). A three-person firm in Washington DC, their tagline implies that clients won't have to deal with the bureaucracy and added costs of a large firm if they're merely seeking representation for telecommunications matters. Or consider the tagline of solo Enrico Schaefer (www.traverselegal.com): *Changing the way law is practiced*. In this way, Schaefer makes clear that with innovative practices his firm provides more efficient and cost-effective service than traditional firms.

- **Taglines that describe the service you provide.** When it comes to taglines that focus on the type of service you provide, avoid use of "expert" and other superlatives. Most bars prohibit phrases suggesting that your service is superior to other lawyers (e.g., Houston's Best Family Law Attorneys) on the theory that consumers can't judge the accuracy of these claims. Likewise, most jurisdictions forbid use of terms like expert or specialist (e.g., NJ DUI Experts) unless you've received bar-approved certification.

- Taglines that are geographically focused. Some law firms use location as a selling point. For example, a Delaware firm that aims to serve as corporate counsel for out-of-state firms might tout itself simply as, *Your local Delaware counsel,* or, as an appeal to out-of-state law firms, *Your in-state counsel for Delaware.* Many firms located in Washington DC use their proximity to Congress and federal agencies to draw clients with such (hypothetical) taglines as, *A national OSHA practice in the heart of the nation's capital.*

For more tips on creating a tagline or seeing samples of other lawyer taglines, see my article, *Tag(line) You're It* at http://www.legalmarketingblawg.com/2009/07/tagline-youre-it.html..

Another dimension of branding is a logo.

In my opinion, you should refrain from vague or artsy logos, and avoid such graphical cliches as gavels, architectural columns, and the scales of justice. And if you're thinking about using an animal graphic in your logo, consult your local bar rules first. Some jurisdictions prohibit use of animals like sharks or pit bulls as law firm mascots, finding their use deceptive or undignified. For extensive coverage of the Florida court's decision to ban use of certain animals in advertising, read *Florida Court Puts Down Pape & Chandler's Pit Bull* (posted at blogs.law.harvard.edu/ethicalesq/2005/11/17/fla-high-court-puts-down-pape-chandlers-pit-bull/).

Of course, your best possible logo is . . . your firm's name. It's how clients will identify you; it's how lawyers and judges will recognize you. In fact, when you think of logos—Google with its basic font style and primary colors, Yahoo with its bold red capital letters, Paypal with its simple white, blue-outlined letters—some of the most recognizable examples are text-only, devoid of any superfluous shapes or distracting squiggles. Dan Hull, founder of the national law firm Hull McGuire, makes the best argument for your name as logo in a blog post (wwww.whataboutclients.com/archives/2006/01/firm_logos_are.html). He writes:

". . . If you already have a logo, don't change it. But if you don't have a logo, don't bother to develop one. Logos are really about your 'look'. Whether you know it or not, your

firm already has this 'look'. It is on your stationery/letterhead, envelopes and (if they match), your business cards. These all have your firm's name on it. Hopefully, these same patterns, lettering, and colors are reproduced on your marketing materials—Web site, brochure, blog. When people see Hull McGuire PC, usually underlined in burgundy with black Gothic lettering on pastel-colored stationery or business cards, that's us; our trade dress and our 'look'. Clients, agencies, courts, and contacts have been seeing it for 12 years. The repetition does it, and it likely has value. We wouldn't change that look even if we decided we didn't like it."

TIPS ON LOGO CREATION

Whether you hire a pro or design your own logo, check out what some designers consider the top 250 logos at http://www.goodlogo.com/top.250. Or go to www.logo.com, where you can search a database of some 200,000 logos (although I noted fewer than 100 examples of law firm logos). A visit to either site may inspire you. Once you have some rough concepts, set a reasonable budget. A good logo can easily cost $500 or more. Be aware, though, that when you work with a professional designer, the number of revision cycles drive up the price. If you haven't set a cap at the start, costs can quickly escalate. Here are some options with different price points:

- At the **high end** is a custom design by a graphics professional. At this level, seek recommendations from colleagues, look at the designers' portfolios to get a sense of their style and taste, and speak with them by phone (if you hire someone who's not local) to determine whether you can work compatibly. A professional designer may not be able to give you a firm price up front, but should at least be willing to offer a ballpark figure for a specified number of revisions.

- At the **mid-level**, you might try to hire a college or university design student through the school's placement office, or put an ad on Craigslist. You can also have your pick of reasonably priced designers around the world at sites like www.elance.com and www.Odesk.com, both of which let you post a project description and the price you're willing to pay. Before making your final selection, these sites allow you to review ratings and design portfolios of the designers who respond to your request. One option I don't recommend (though other lawyers disagree) is so-called *crowdsourcing* or contest sites like www.99designs.com or www.crowdspring.com. As with other freelance sites, users post a project description and offer a "prize" for the winning concept. Designers then create logos for your consideration, with the best receiving your prize as compensation. Though many users like contest sites because they generate a range of different concepts for no charge, they're problematic. Because designers aren't paid to submit a proposed logo, you may attract inferior or even plagiarized designs. As a lawyer, you wouldn't want to work on spec, so why should your designer?
- At the **low end**, there are many free or cheap do-your-own logo design options. At www.logoease.com, you can select a few basic designs and create and download a simple logo at no cost. At www.LogoYES.com and www.Vistaprint.com there are similar options with a little more choice. Their logo design services range from free to $99 (business cards included).

Marketing #3: The Elevator Speech

You're at a party with a roomful of strangers, and someone extends a hand and asks, *"So, what you do?"* If you ever struggled to find just the right few words, you understand the concept of "elevator speech"—a description of professional services so succinct it can be delivered riding up to the third floor. Whether or not you actually have an elevator speech, most legal marketing experts are in agreement: you need a brief summary of your practice. Whether it's something snappy or something simple and direct is up to you.

Avoid vague legal terms. Most non-lawyers won't have a clue what sort of work you do if you say you're a trial lawyer or a transactional or regulatory lawyer. But if you say, *I'm a lawyer who helps clients resolve disputes in court*, it's more descriptive than, *I'm a litigator.*

Use plain English. Imagine you've been asked to speak at a sixth grade career day. Now, how would you explain the nature of your work, and—even more challenging—to make them care about it? Use plain English; it has the highest retention value. What follows are a collection of short, descriptive elevator speeches collected by attorney Sarah Holz (www.womenrainmakers.com), and posted at Tom Kane's Legal Marketing Blog, www.legalmarketingblog.com/marketing-tips-what-message-does-your-elevator-speech-convey.html):

- I'm a bond lawyer. I help hospitals and nursing homes raise cheap, long-term money for projects. Over the last 15 years, I have helped hundreds of institutions raise billions of dollars.
- I'm a corporate lawyer. I help companies of all sizes, both public and private, buy and sell businesses, and come out of it still liking each other.
- I'm an employment lawyer. I help employers do what they really want to do, run their businesses, without being side-tracked by discrimination claims, strikes or other employee problems.
- I'm an insurance coverage litigator. When my clients get sued, I make sure that their insurance companies, and not my clients, pay the claims.

If you get stuck creating your own, go to www.15secondpitch.com/new or www.elevatorspeech.com. Above all, create an elevator speech with which you feel comfortable. If it seems appealing but comes across as gimmicky or overly promotional, use something more straightforward instead.

Marketing #4: Yellow Pages Ads

When was the last time you reached for the Yellow Pages? I thought so. But if *you're* not using them, how can you be sure prospective clients are? In fact, it might be helpful to know that a study found that Yellow Pages searches had fallen by at least half… and that was in 2006! Four years later, Verizon sought permission from New York state regulators to end delivery of phone listing books (the White Pages) because only one of every nine households was using them (a statistic similar for Yellow Pages, according to the New York Times). So, at a time when more and more consumers are going on-line to find lawyers and other service providers, the question arises whether new solos should even bother with the Yellow Pages? Probably not. Of course, it's true that some established law firms still generate the bulk of their business this way… but they also spend $1,000/month or more on ads to generate those results. If you have that much cash on hand for marketing (and let's face it, most solos don't), you're better off investing in more forward-looking activities such as enhancing your Web presence, purchasing Google Ads, or paying for a professional video on YouTube. A caveat: residents in some rural or lower-income communities may still rely on the Yellow Pages because they can't afford, or lack, reliable Internet access. If you practice in such a community, it might make sense to explore the Yellow Pages option provided the ads are not too expensive and they target your desired clients. Often, smaller local versions of the Yellow Pages are a more affordable option for those considering this route.

Marketing #5: Lawyer Directories

Martindale-Hubbell (part of LexisNexis, and a division of Reed Elsevier, Inc.) is among the oldest and most familiar lawyer directories in the country. In addition to lawyer profiles, it includes a peer-review rating system by which lawyers are assigned a grade of CV, BV or AV (the highest), based on peer-assessment of one's legal ability and ethics. In addition, you can now pay to display your rating on their Web site (www.mhur.com/home). But like the Yellow Pages, Martindale-Hubbell—first published in 1868—feels less relevant than in the past. In recent years, an entire cottage industry of other lawyer directories and ratings services has developed, including *SuperLawyers* (which ranks consumer and corporate practices), and *Chambers* (which has a rating system for corporate and largely large firm practices). Even US News & World Report has a Best Lawyers list of 9,000 "top" firms nationwide (http://bestlawfirms.usnews.com). These directories purport to be merit-based; that is, they solicit nominations from lawyers and clients, and do not charge for a listing. Still, they are heavily biased in favor of well-connected, established firms. But most general counsel do not use these directories anymore. The Internet, and, more recently, social media, has made lawyers' work product, testimonials, and credentials, freely available and easier to find than a directory. According to Jane Navarre, a law marketing consultant, general counsel attach more interest to your familiarity with their company's business, and how you can save the company money. *See* http://virtualmarketingofficer.com/2010/01/how-general-counsel-evaluates-and-hires-law-firms-marketing-partner-forum-recap/ .

Marketing #6: Outdoor Advertising

In some regions, and for some clientele, consider adding "outdoor"—e.g., billboards—to your marketing mix. One Texas solo used billboards to help promote his new family law practice a few years ago. He says the campaign cost about $1,000/month, and the phone started ringing soon after it began. Of course, $1,000/month is no small expense. In order to defray it, some solos who share practice areas—such as consumer credit or bankruptcy—should consider pooling their resources for a general public service message (e.g., "avoid foreclosure scams"), and add a Web address for each participating firm. Expense aside, though, outdoor lawyer advertising still has an image problem. In a 2009 blog post, solo Ken Shigley, a veteran trial lawyer and president-elect of the Georgia State Bar, vented his feelings about what he called "TV and Billboard Lawyers":

> *"… As a serious personal injury attorney in Atlanta, Georgia, I am frankly embarrassed by the inundation of billboards and TV ads for personal injury lawyers who have little*

respect within the profession and seldom if ever set foot in a courtroom. If you or a loved one has a serious injury or wrongful death case, you would do better throwing a dart at the attorneys section of the phone book than choosing a lawyer on the basis of a billboard or a 30-second TV ad. At least you would have a chance of getting to a decent, honest attorney who would know how to identify a specialist for an appropriate referral, rather than a "mill" that focuses on volume and accepts low offers rather than doing the hard work of litigation. The subtly misleading slogans of the billboard and TV lawyers, e.g., 'one call that's all' and 'all the help the law allows,' and their use of celebrity spokesmen on TV, does a real disservice to members of the public who are drawn into personal injury 'mills' rather than to serious lawyers who would fight for them ..."

So, while billboards might help you attract clients directly, they might also convey a negative impression that would deter referrals.

Marketing #7: Pro Bono Publico

Most lawyers overlook pro bono work as a potential networking technique ... and it's a big mistake. Getting involved in a pro bono program, particularly those sponsored by prominent community organizations (e.g., the ACLU or Washington Lawyers Committee for Civil Rights), gives you a chance to let other attorneys with whom you're working to see first-hand the quality of your work. And it's worth noting that lawyers who are familiar with your work are more likely to refer you cases or to call you for contract work. Moreover, if you do a really good job, your name is likely to come to the attention of other lawyers who sit on the organization's board. Finally, some pro bono participation can lead to paying work by clients who don't meet the organization's qualifications. You may think that marketing through pro bono is crass. But let's face it ... everyone does it. Large law firms use pro bono programs to provide hands-on experience to associates, and to generate positive publicity for the firm. What's important is that you take pro bono work seriously for its own sake, and represent your clients in a professional, high-quality manner. If you do, your motives for getting involved are beside the point. Remember, there is nothing wrong with doing well by doing good.

Marketing #8: The Media

Even though blawg readership is soaring, you need a broad mix of marketing initiatives. Both new media and old (traditional) media offer attractive opportunities.

New media. More than ever, your prospective clients are going online to educate themselves about the legal issues relevant to their case. That's why education-based marketing—e.g., teleseminars, webinars, podcasts, etc.—are so important right now. They cater to the public's need for authoritative information (see Chapter 17). And if you *really* want to take advantage of new media, bring your message to the new generation of e-book readers (e.g., Amazon's Kindle, Apple's iPad, etc.). For now, Kindle's e-book format is the easiest platform on which to get "published". It only requires that you download a PDF file onto its publishing platform (www.KindleDirectPublishing.com).

Old media. Whether a daily newspaper lands on your front door or arrives as an app on your iPad, we are a nation of news and information junkies.

There are two ways to break into the world of traditional media: write an op ed on a contemporary issue related to your practice. Newspapers everywhere—from your local daily and weekly to the Wall Street Journal—welcome authoritative content with a point-of-view. Just e-mail the paper's section editor with your idea. If accepted, your finished piece—from 750 to 1,500 words—can be used later for mailed reprints to your clients, or digitized for your Web site or blog. You can also provide copies to prospective clients who are dealing with similar issues.

The second approach is more strategic. When you seek publicity about a controversy or trial with which your firm is involved, either hire a PR firm or develop a guerilla campaign of your own. One element of a campaign is the PR release. It's a powerful tool; not just for publicity anymore, but for search engine visibility. But use it sparingly; PR releases are for significant accomplishments like a major jury win or appointment to a corporate board, not for trivial events like attracting the 10,000th visitor to your Web site. There are many companies who will distribute your media release, among them *BlackPRWire.com, Businesswire.com, HispanicPRWire.com, Marketwire.com, GlobeNewswire.com, PRNewswire.com, PRWeb.com, USAsianwire.com,* and *Vocus.com.* For a midpriced service, expect to pay$80 to $200 to distribute a release to several markets. Editors at all the biggest media outlets routinely assign stories based on commercially distributed publicity releases, and reporters use them often to identify sources for future stories.

A simpler, cheaper way to get your name in the papers is by positioning yourself as a knowledgeable expert on a given topic. Like everyone else, journalists track blogs and follow Twitter. If you're covering a topic of interest to them, they will reach out to you for comment. Conversely, you can follow many reporters on Twitter. There is also a site called Help A Reporter Out (www.helpareporter.com). At no cost to you, the site makes available a daily list of two dozen or so inquiries from reporters nationwide on a variety of topics. It only takes a few minutes for you or your assistant to scan the list, and respond to inquiries for which you are qualified.

WRITING THE PRESS RELEASE *by Gina Furia Rubel, Esq.*

The press release, otherwise known as a news or media release, remains one of the most commonly used tools to solidify one's message and to get it out there. Many factors go into writing a good press release, and, if done well, will influence the amount and type of coverage your item will receive. Here are some guidelines:

Include the date and time your news is to be released. The terms most often used are, For Immediate Release, For Release Before [date], or For Release After [date]. This should appear at the top of the release and be all caps, underlined or bolded.

Include contact information. If you mail the release, print it on letterhead and include contact information for yourself or your firm's marketing or PR manager. If you e-mail it, place the contact information (including business and cell phone) at the top.

Include a creative headline. News organizations get hundreds of releases every day. Your headline must be catchy in order to entice recipients to read your release. Include a subheadline if it will add value.

Summarize the release in the first paragraph. The first graph, known as the "lead", should help the editor or reporter determine what the release is all about. So get straight to the point. The lead should answer the who, what, when, where, and why of the story.

Keep your release short. Stick to the facts; use only enough words to tell your story. Typically, a press release should be no more than two pages; one is preferable. Make sure you use one or two quotes to give the release greater authenticity and interest.

Include a paragraph of boilerplate. A boilerplate is the standard block of text that is used at the end of every release. Your boilerplate should contain a brief description of your firm.

Gina Furia Rubel, a graduate of Widener University School of Law, is the founder of Furia Rubel Communications, a PR agency with a niche in legal communications, and she is the author of *Everyday Public Relations for Lawyers: A No-Nonsense Strategic PR Guide.*

Marketing #9: Client Communications

When existing or prospective clients have a problem, who do they call? They call the first lawyer who comes to mind. That's why client communications—reminders, alerts, mailings, newsletters—are so important to keep your name on the client's radar. Some suggestions:

Client reminders. If you practice in areas like trusts and estates or corporate law, your clients' circumstances may change following your completion of an initial matter. Example: you prepare an estate plan that names your client's wife as the beneficiary, but the client has since divorced. Or... the corporation you formed three years earlier has disbanded, but the members never formally dissolved it. In practices like this, you might send out annual mailings to clients, asking whether any events require an update of previously prepared documents. In your mailing, invite clients to call you at no cost, or to set up a complimentary appointment to determine whether any updates are required. Or offer a discount for any changes.

Client alerts. In contrast to a client reminder, which is a more individualized communication to specific clients, a client alert informs *all* your clients of recent changes in the law, or a new precedent which might impact their business, or require updates to work that you've prepared. Invite clients to contact you for a brief consultation for additional information on new developments.

Incident-specific mailings. One example is where a lawyer purchases the names of drivers arrested for DUI and sends a letter of introduction. Or, a lawyer might learn from the public record that a federal agency has taken an enforcement action against several companies, and might contact those companies with information about the firm. *Author note*: depending upon the specifics, a lawyer might run afoul of ethics rules prohibiting direct solicitation. Also, prospective clients might take offense that a lawyer could access their names when they've been arrested for DUI, and might not appreciate the mailing. Criminal defense lawyer Mark Bennett says that incident-specific mailings pose an affront to a client's privacy, particularly when the envelope has your law firm's address stamped on it; or worse, you send a postcard that mentions the incident.

Targeted mailings to other attorneys. Most unsolicited mail to other attorneys —whether you're seeking referrals or contract work—usually ends up in the recycling bin. The one possible exception is if your mailing offers some tip or advice valuable enough to pique a busy attorney's interest. For example, a tax attorney seeking to work on personal injury deals with structured settlements might write to PI attorneys, explaining current tax law related to settlements. The tax attorney might even suggest proposed language that PI attorneys might include to minimize their clients' tax liability. This kind of direct mail works because it shows rather than tells what the tax attorney can do to solve problems. In this way, targeted mailings are more likely to generate a response than a generalized letter about a firm's tax expertise.

Newsletters. With today's technologies, it's simple to create and distribute good client newsletters. At www.Mailchimp.com, you can format and send newsletters to a mailing list of up to 500 at no charge. Two other popular services—www.Constant-Contact.com and www.Aweber.com—charge $10 to $50/month, depending upon the level of service. It's a tremendous savings over printed newsletters, and the production efficiencies allow for more up-to-date material. Of course, every newsletter—electronic or printed—competes for attention. Be sure the content is lively, informative, and original, and that it balances news about legal developments with lighter or more personal topics. Example: if you write a newsletter for home-based companies, you might feature an interview with a home-based business owner. Or...include self-help tips from time management or organizational experts. Avoid buying packaged articles from so-called "content farms". Not only might the content be of dubious accuracy, but its use on your site could negatively affect your search ranking and traffic if Google makes a major adjustment to its search algorithm (as it did in February, 2011) to downgrade what it calls "low quality" content. You're better off sending your clients a quarterly newsletter with original content than a monthly with off-the-shelf articles.

Brochures/flyers. When you need inexpensive collateral material for a seminar or conference table—or your marketing packet—look no further than the Internet. Two popular online printing companies that come to mind—www.iprint.com and www. vistaprint.com—produce reasonably priced four-color flyers, brochures, cards, and stickers, in any quantity. Even Costco has jumped into the online printing game, and accepts graphic files online, and keeps your work on file for reprints or changes. If you want professionally looking pamphlets, go to Tips Products International (www. tipsbooklets.com), and at www.Blurb.com you can even convert blog posts into a print format. At my own Web site (www.MyShingle.com), you can also find a free program (www.MyShingle.com/onesheet) that helps you create a single-page document designed to provide a burst of information about your services. The program lets you upload your logo and customize the colors and layout.

Marketing #10: Client Marketing

From bank ATM's to supermarket self-checkout, the do-it-yourself consumer movement is everywhere, and it isn't limited to retail transactions. These days, anyone with a keyboard or smartphone app can find answers on any topic—financial, medical, legal—for which we once turned to professionals. Now and in the future, the self-help trend will be critical to your client-marketing efforts. Consider the following ideas:

Education-based marketing. Educational materials cater to today's information-hungry consumers, and help clients understand the issues related to their case. These days, you need to provide substantive materials rather than making a sales pitch. Blogs, newsletters, and e-books are all excellent platforms. Create materials like Frequently Asked Questions or "The Top 10 Things Everyone Should Know About Foreclosure." Be sure the materials are substantive and not teasers. If prospective clients go to the trouble of downloading an e-book from your Web site, they'll be very upset if it is a sales pitch in disguise.

Make things for clients. Incorporate practice tools that make it easy for your clients to help themselves. Add a client portal so they can log-in and check the status of their case. Client portals save you time (and headaches) by eliminating—or at least reducing—the number of calls from anxious clients.

Offer unbundled services virtually. If you want to capture do-it-yourself clients, offer unbundled services online. Two companies, VLO Tech and Direct Law offer reasonably priced, turn-key systems for serving consumers online. As a virtual lawyer, you provide legal advice, and draft and review documents, but the client does much of the legwork, such as filing their incorporation or executing the will that you drafted.

Change your attitude. Your clients are more informed than ever. Take the time to answer substantive questions, and explain why the blog post by a New York firm about estate planning doesn't apply in Florida. Lawyers who treat informed clients with disdain shouldn't be surprised if they've gone elsewhere.

Freemium. As technology flattens the cost of production, "free" has gone from sales gimmick to new economic model. Of course, with the exception of contingency matters, you can't work for free but you can work *with* free. A few thoughts:

Give more away. By giving away forms for free, you might generate more business. Minnesota consumer lawyer Sam Glover gives away form letters for consumer clients to send to creditors, and a form answer-and-discovery request for consumers if they've been sued by a creditor (http://consumerlawyer.mn/consumer-resources/free-debt-collection-defense-resources/). Once consumers begin to get far along in the case, they realize that they need legal assistance. Naturally, they turn to Glover. And because the consumers used proper legal forms at the outset, they're less likely to botch them or waive defense, which means that the cases are more viable by the time they reach a lawyer.

Use free to create a new market. Use free products as a way to attract clients who might not have hired you otherwise. Example: offer to prepare LLC documents for a certain number of women-owned businesses in your community. If the businesses take off, you could be first in line for the work.

Educate clients about the shortfalls of free. Many consumers don't realize that free—or even low-cost solutions like Legal Zoom—may not be adequate for their case. Organize a free seminar to educate consumers about the dangers of some of these free online services.

Big firm service at small firm rates. Major changes in how corporate clients procure legal services has important implications for solos and small firms that practice in traditionally BigLaw practice areas, according to Jordan Furlong at his blog (www.law21.ca/2011/03/25/the-stratified-legal-market-and-its-implications/). A decade ago, says Furlong, corporate clients used large firms as one-stop shopping for three levels of legal work: mission-critical, ordinary business, and commodity (document review, routine contracts). In today's economy, corporate clients won't tolerate big firm rates for every level of service. They're managing their commodities work with a combination of technology and off-shoring, and are more receptive to solo or small firms comprised of big firm expatriates, who can handle ordinary business matters at reasonable rates. If you hope to pitch corporate clients, there's never been a better time.

WHAT WOULD ARISTOTLE SAY ABOUT CLIENT COMMUNICATIONS?

by Jim Schuster, Esq.

Aristotle would say that a successful marketing communication is a process of persuasion. That it is not enough to merely announce…it is not enough to inform…and it is not enough to persuade prospective clients that they should take action for their own benefit. We must do all of this and motivate the client to hire us. More than 2,000 years ago, Aristotle wrote *the* book on persuasive communication (On Rhetoric). Its three-part structure of persuasion is as valid today as it was in ancient Greece. Here's what Aristotle would say about communicating to your clients:

There are three essential elements of persuasion, and without them communication will not be persuasive. The essential elements are:

Ethos. Your total message must establish your experience, expertise, integrity, and likeability. As communicators, we must persuade the reader that we are worthy of belief and selection.

Logos. The arguments in your marketing communications must convince your audience that they truly need to take action, and that they will benefit from hiring you.

Pathos. Your message must connect with your audience. Your assessment and proposal must align with the audience's values, attitudes, wants, and needs. They must conclude that hiring you is the right thing to do.

—Jim Schuster, past chair of the Michigan Bar's General Practice and Elder Law sections, and author of *The Aristotelian Method: Practice Development and Marketing for Lawyers on a Shoestring Budget.*

Marketing #11: Corporate and Nonprofit Boards

If you're trying to break into a new practice area, or beef up your existing corporate experience…or you're eager to learn new skills…serving on a corporate or nonprofit board of directors may be just the ticket. In this role, you have an opportunity to learn from others with a diverse background, gain an understanding of the responsibilities of corporate governance, and experience the perspective of those who run the corporation…as well as make contacts with those who may hire you or refer you to their colleagues. Plus, your service on corporate and nonprofit boards will look impressive on a resume. If you're trying to increase your stature in the community or build contacts with potential clients, identify the nonprofits that complement your practice area. Example: a lawyer focusing on special needs trusts might want to serve a nonprofit that helps the disabled. A law-related nonprofit, like a legal aid group, will put you in touch with other lawyers. If you have a passion outside of the law—say, cooking or music—you may want to serve on the board of the community orchestra or local soup kitchen. To find a board, check sites like www.BoardNetUSA.org, a site that matches volunteers with nonprofit board positions, or www.Idealist.org, which has a searchable database of volunteer positions.

Marketing #12: Law Review Articles

Law review or scholarly articles require a great investment of time and energy, but they can establish you as an expert in your field and make a solid impression as you market your services. If you want to get published in a legal publication, or use an article to leverage your way into a new practice area, seek out a more experienced attorney as your co-author—an idea suggested by Ari Kaplan (*Summer Associates Can Write Their Way to Success*, National Law Journal, June 19, 2007). Because of the time demands of a scholarly article, I don't suggest attempting it unless you can piggyback the article on research that you've done for other matters. And try to offload additional research and cite-checking to a law student. Once your article appears in print (usually six to eight months after submission), send copies to existing and potential clients, and alert the media and bloggers interested in the topic.

Marketing #13: Conference Speaking Gigs

You have two options for speaking engagements: speak at an event sponsored by another group (e.g., bar association, chamber of commerce, trade group), or market your own seminar. What follows are the pro and con, and some important how-to's:

Pro & Con. Sponsored conferences offer several important advantages. The organizers are staffed to handle all the details, and your presence on the program confers prestige, and brings you into contact with prominent figures in your field. Naturally, the competition for sponsored conference presentations is intense. And, if you practice in a traditionally BigLaw area, you will discover…if you haven't already…that the large firms can skew the selection of presenters in its favor by sponsoring conference events in exchange for speaker slots. In fact, it's not uncommon for conference organizers to pack panels with five or six speakers to attract more sponsorships. So, even if you do get invited, you may have just a few minutes to make your presentation. *A cautionary note*: some conferences are populated by other lawyers who may swipe your information, and use it for their own presentations.

Choosing a conference. Do you want to target clients directly? Then select conferences or trade shows populated with potential clients…not lawyers. Or, do you want an audience of lawyers? A colleague of mine specializing in legal research and writing services for lawyers, speaks a few times a year at bar events and CLE seminars. Other solos find that by speaking at bar events—even on topics that don't relate directly to their practice expertise—can give them exposure and plant the seeds for future referrals. Incidentally, lawyers who practice in consumer-oriented areas (e.g., estate planning, real estate, small business) should think about offering an adult education course sponsored by a local community college or adult/continuing ed provider.

Start small. As a marketing channel, conference presentations rank high among law firms. Competition for speaking gigs is intense. In fact, some of the top conferences in my industry attract hundreds of proposals for just a few dozen speaking slots. If that's also true in your field, don't just limit your efforts to large, prestigious events; focus on the smaller regional events and trade associations overlooked by most large firms. Smaller events, or even adult/continuing ed courses, can be preferable. After all, you're more likely to be a featured speaker than being one of a panel of lawyers who each have just a few minutes to speak. Furthermore, because smaller events are generally more collegial and intimate, you have a greater chance to talk with attendees afterward.

Identifying conferences. You're probably familiar with the handful of conferences where you want to present. If not, go online to find industry newsletters and blogs to identify trade associations where speakers are needed. Some large conferences or adult ed programs have a formal process for submitting a proposal. If they don't, send an e-mail introducing yourself, along with your resume and a list of any previous talks. Another way to find events is to search social networking sites like www.Meetup.com or www.Biznik.com, which many local groups use to create a Web presence and to publicize events. By searching these sites by topic, you're likely to find several that might have an interest in your expertise.

Choosing a topic. Visit a conference group's Web site for clues to prior presentations. This is very helpful, and will let you know what issues the group regards as important, and prevent you from submitting a proposal on a topic covered earlier. Unless the conference is geared towards less sophisticated clients or novices, avoid the basics (e.g., Steps to Getting a Patent). Instead, think of specific problems, such as *Protecting Your Company from Employee Harassment Actions after the Landmark Jones v. Smith Decision*. What's always popular are presentations based on "tips" and lessons-learned. Cross-over talks—applying knowledge from one industry to another—also do well. Example: a presentation on how banks can protect themselves against liability for identity theft could be modified for Internet providers with similar concerns. Note: cross-over talks offer a good introduction into a related industry.

Should I ask for payment? Whether you get paid for your talk depends upon the industry. Keynoters, authors, and subject-matter gurus can demand…and usually get…thousands of dollars for presentations. Lawyers rarely have the same bargaining power. In fact, competition among lawyer/presenters is so intense that if you require compensation the conference may find another speaker. Whether or not you get paid, some groups do pay travel expenses or waive conference fees. And some programs will even share a portion of the proceeds collected with speakers. *Bottom line*: your speaking practice is unlikely to earn much if any revenue...except whatever new business the talk might generate.

Presentation pointers. Most of the larger conferences have strict guidelines about your presentation, and may require you to use PowerPoint or to submit a paper in a specific format. Requirements for small conferences vary; many won't have requirements, giving you discretion over form and content. If you choose to use PowerPoint, be prepared to bring your own projector if the sponsor lacks one. And if you are presenting on a screen, always distribute a handout of your talk, or e-mail it to attendees afterwards. Include a fair amount of real substance in the presentation. You want your talk to have staying power beyond the presentation; to serve as a document that people will keep on hand and reference and call you about in the future. Even if your audience is comprised of novices, they'll be impressed if you provide cites to actual laws or regulations rather then simply paraphrasing them.

Make the most of your presentation. In the weeks before your talk, do a little extra-curricular PR: distribute a short media release as well as sending an e-mail alert to colleagues who might attend; ask permission of the conference organizers to have your presentation recorded or videotaped for posting to your Web site later; and, before your presentation ends, let the audience know you will be available afterward to take questions. Social media can help get the word out as well. You can post about your talk on sites like Facebook, LinkedIn, and Twitter, encouraging participants to "tweet" or blog about your presentation so it will get extra mileage online. If possible, ask a colleague or a law student to tape or record some or all of your talk, and upload it to your Web site.

Laying the foundation for next year. Don't give up if you didn't get a speaking invitation for the conference of your choice. Before the event, contact the conference organizers, and volunteer to live-blog or tweet the proceedings. Your coverage will get added exposure for both you and the conference...and likely ensure an invite for the following year.

Marketing #14: Conducting Your Own Seminar

Sponsoring your own seminar puts you in the driver's seat. You can feature yourself as the sole speaker, and perhaps even charge an entry fee to recover costs. Of course, you're responsible for such mundane (and time-intensive) details as selecting the venue and the promotion. As a general rule, do-it-yourself seminars work best for practices that serve individuals or small businesses. Your audience is less likely to pay attention to your reputation, and more likely to regard you as an expert simply because you're a licensed attorney. And they will appreciate the chance for some free information on issues that affect them, their family, or their business.

The venue. Pick a location convenient for the intended audience. Public libraries work well; they attract retirees and senior citizens interested in estate-planning issues. Libraries are also a convenient location for parents who can drop older children off in the reading room while they attend your seminar. If you're targeting other attorneys, rent a bar association meeting room or office conference room.

Incentives. It doesn't cost much to provide drinks and snacks for 20 or 30 attendees. Also, consider a raffle to maximize attendance. Raffles are an incentive to attend, and provide a means to collect business cards or contact information. The prize might be an iPod, a magazine subscription, or a gift certificate to a local restaurant. And be sure to send participants home with helpful information, branded with your law firm logo or name. Even if attendees don't express immediate interest in your services, a useful handout makes it easy to contact you later.

Advertising. Direct mail is still regarded as one of the best means to drive traffic to a seminar. But graphic production and mailing costs can add up quickly. So, consider some alternative forms of promotion: your daily newspaper probably has an events section that allows you to promote events at no charge. You can post flyers in areas that will attract your target audience. Example: if you plan to talk about legal issues related to remodeling, leave a stack of materials at local hardware and home-improvement stores. Use your blog or Web site to promote your seminar, and ask other bloggers if they would write a post about your seminar. There's always Twitter, Facebook, and LinkedIn's event page. And be sure to e-mail your contacts and clients about your seminar.

No matter what combination of marketing tools you use—direct mail, blogs, articles, speeches, networking—you won't achieve measurable results without taking the following into account:

The 48-hour Rule. After every networking event, gather up the business cards of prospects you collected and send some kind of "enjoyed meeting you" e-mail within 48 hours.

Call every few months. After you've met with a prospect, call every few months to see how they're doing. Sometimes, your call will catch a lawyer in the midst of a busy period and your call reminds him to outsource work to you.

Keep in contact with clients. When you think an issue like a new statute or recent case might impact a client, send a brief e-mail attaching a copy of the statute or case along with a brief description of the implications. If you've helped a client avoid a lawsuit, call a few months later to make sure that the problem hasn't reemerged. You might discover the client has other problems requiring your assistance.

Marketing #15: Trade Groups & Associations

Joining a trade group or bar association is your chance to meet prospective referral sources and clients at sponsored lunches, happy hours, speaking events, and conferences. Opportunities for conversation are limited, though, and often you find yourself competing with others who are also trolling for business. And when it comes to networking events, they can be just as demoralizing as the singles dating scene if you happen to be abandoned mid-conversation for "someone more important". The real value of trade groups or bar associations comes from personal participation. Getting involved lets you work with other lawyers or experts in the industry, and it is these interactions that build long-term relationships with prospective clients and referral sources.

Most trade groups—particularly the smaller local or regional groups—are desperate for help. So even if you're a new law grad, you shouldn't have any trouble finding a role for yourself. From a networking perspective, the best committee job involves arranging a speakers' panel. It allows you to help develop an event agenda and—even better—to contact potential speakers (which gives you a convenient excuse to introduce yourself to some of the prominent names in your industry). Writing the committee newsletter—which involves attending group events and interviewing group speakers—offers additional visibility.

There are dozens of bar associations, trade and local groups (e.g., chambers of commerce, neighborhood advisory committees) you can join. I suggest mixing it up: (a) join a specialty bar association or mentoring group that provides you with substantive information and access to experts in your field; (b) a trade or business group that serves professionals and businesses within one industry rather than just lawyers; and (c) a local bar association or networking group so you can build relationships with lawyers in your immediate community.

If you can't find a trade group or association to suit your interests, form your own. Or, create a subgroup within an existing organization. One attorney I know started a solo and small firm networking group within her local women's bar association. In my own case after years of representing ocean energy developers, I co-founded the Ocean Renewable Energy Coalition (www.oceanrenewable.com) to give ocean energy start-ups access to legal and lobbying resources they otherwise couldn't afford on their own.

Bar associations. I find that in large urban areas, e.g., outside of New York, District of Columbia or Boston, the city and county bar associations offer the best "bang for the buck." Often, they are quite active, and sponsor dozens of events each month. With close proximity to large firms and universities, the city and county bar-sponsored panels and seminars are stocked with leading speakers. Moreover, many of the city bars offer seminars and panels on traditionally BigLaw issues like Sarbanes Oxley, securities, or re-insurance law, at a fraction of the cost of the ABA or professional CLE's. And because city bar events are located so close to many law firms and offer quality panels, they often attract a large turnout so you can meet more people.

Specialty bars. You can find a bar association devoted to virtually every practice area, ranging from the National Association of Elder Care Lawyers to the Defense Research Institute (DRI is a professional group for insurance and civil defense attorneys). Most specialty bars publish have newsletters, journals, blogs, and listservs, and even member-only databases that make available a steady stream of information relevant to your practice. Specialty bars also produce quality forms and practice guides that can help you learn new skills. Whether you already have a specialty, or you're interested in developing expertise in a new practice area, specialty bar membership is vital to keeping abreast of developments and making contacts with experts in the area. Specialty bars will cost more than state or city bars, typically ranging between $150 (for more recent law grads) to $400. They're a good value, and many will grant a no-cost trial membership. Also, if you ask, some groups may be willing to waive or discount fees for new practitioners.

Constituency bars. Just as you'll find a bar association for any practice area, you'll also find a bar association for many different constituencies of lawyers—women, African-, Hispanic-, and Asian-Americans, religious groups, and even lawyers of certain political affiliations, such as the conservative-oriented lawyers division of the Federalist Society. All these special-interest groups sponsor events that address issues of interest to their constituency. For example, a woman's bar association may have events on part-time and contract lawyering or returning to work, while a Muslim Lawyers' association might sponsor events on profiling or immigration issues.

Inns of Court/law school consortiums. Some groups focus on mentoring and skills, creating valuable networking opportunities. If you prefer working closely with others and building relationships rather than meeting large numbers of new people, this type of organization may work best. Law school consortium programs—at www.lawschoolconsortium.net and www.lowbono.org—provide training, mentors, and support to new solos who establish firms to serve low-income communities. Though the programs focus on training through participation, you may meet mentors and other lawyers who have contract work or cases to refer. Inns of Court (www.innsofcourt.org) is another type of training/mentoring group with a goal of "improving the skills, professionalism, and ethics of the legal profession." It specializes in civil and criminal litigation practice, and gives younger attorneys an opportunity for mentoring from more experienced advocates and judges.

Alumni groups and law firms. Your law school and undergraduate university probably sponsor alumni activities. Not only do they provide a way to re-connect with your past, and support your alma mater, but to develop new contacts as well. These days, many large firms are creating alumni networks of their own, attempting to stay in contact with attorneys who departed for in-house positions or other law firms, and who might be in a position to refer business back to their former firm. These alumni programs benefit the departing lawyers as well, providing another way to find potential sources of business. In fact, they may even give you an edge in getting work. For example, suppose you want to take cases too small for large firms to handle. You could call Partner Smith at ABC firm to ask that he send cases your way, but he would probably dismiss your request or, at best, launch into a lengthy check of your references. By contrast, if—like you—Partner Smith once worked at XYZ firm, and you found his name through their alumni network, he might be more receptive to your call. He may not have immediate work, but at least you won't have to overcome the usual credentials hurdle because your previous employment at XYZ would give Smith confidence in your abilities. Granted, this all seems very superficial. But in a credential-obsessed profession, grab the edge where you find it.

Chambers of commerce and advisory groups. If you want to use your law degree to serve your local community, join local business groups. Keep in mind that chambers of commerce often draw very, very small businesses that cannot afford to hire a lawyer. On the other hand, many of these new businesses often don't know other lawyers; if you introduce yourself, or avail yourself of their products, they may call you eventually. Local advisory groups are another way to use your expertise to the community's benefit, and to market your service at the same time. Many communities and local government now have citizen-advisory committees, which advise local government on a wide variety of issues like healthcare, air quality, zoning, and ethics. The committees are typically populated by non-lawyers who specialize in the subject matter within the committee's jurisdiction (for example a healthcare committee might have a scientist from a pharmaceutical company, a nurse and a healthcare policy analyst), thus providing a chance to make contacts with others in your area of expertise. And since advisory groups are often called upon to brief county and local government, you may have a chance to meet government officials who might consider retaining you for other matters. Or you might have a chance to testify at a local hearing, which will earn you some media visibility.

Marketing #16: Business Networking Groups

There are many business networking groups that provide generalized networking opportunities for all types of local businesses. Some provide informal networking opportunities along the lines of a chamber of commerce group. Others, like BNI, a business-referral network, create structured environments that encourage members to actively refer business to each others (e.g., members commit to refer business to a suitable person within their group before sending it to someone outside the network).

Author note: some state bars prohibit lawyers from joining BNI or similar groups, finding that their practice of encouraging cross-referrals violates ethics rules that prohibit lawyers from giving something of value in exchange for receiving a referral. In the bars' view, the "something of value" would be the lawyer's promise to make referrals to other group members in exchange for referrals to the lawyer. The bars also believe that membership in the group compromises a lawyer's independent judgment because lawyers might make referrals based not on the merits of another service provider, but rather, because the group allegedly obligated lawyers to make the referral. For my opinions on the utter irrationality of these rules, read my May/2005 blog post at http://tinyurl.com/3le4mao. Many lawyers who practice in jurisdictions that allow lawyers to participate in referral groups swear by their value. At the same time, even where the bar allows you to join, you may find that the composition of the groups—primarily, small local businesses—aren't a great source of referrals anyway. So whether or not your bar allows you to join a professional networking and referral organization, consider forming your own group.

While you may make some decent contacts at networking events, a group setting doesn't lend itself to closing a deal or delving into specifics about your services. For that, you need a personal meeting with your prospect. Here are some tips to make one-on-one meetings more productive:

Why not breakfast? You'd be surprised how many lawyers and business people welcome a pre-work meeting as early as 7 a.m. It's an excuse to get out of the house early, and doesn't interfere with their day's business. And breakfast is way less expensive.

Don't do lunch. Whatever you do, avoid inviting lawyers or prospective clients to lunch. For one thing, if you work part-time or from home, lunch takes a big chunk out of your work day. Second, the lunch atmosphere is too relaxing, making it awkward to take notes or make an assertive pitch for business. And, let's face it, lunch is costly if you visit a decent restaurant. Of course, where a prospect invites you to lunch, or is visiting from out of town and doesn't have any other openings except lunch, you should accept.

Offer to stop by. Make life convenient for your prospect by offering to come by their office. Even people who are short on time can generally spare a half-hour for a quick meeting.

Come prepared. If you're after contract work, your packet should include a resume, at least two writing samples (an article or two, and some sort of formal legal writing like a brief or memo), contact information, and a few references with current contact information. You might also include a sample contract that the attorney would sign to retain your service, and excerpts from bar opinions on the ethics of marking up rates paid to contract attorneys. If you're meeting with a prospective client, include a resume, a list of similar projects or matters that you've handled for other clients, and copies of relevant articles or speeches that you have given on the client's matter of interest.

Listen, listen, listen. When meeting with a prospective client or referral source, don't brag. Put the focus elsewhere; ask lots of questions. Find out what they do and what challenges they face. Only then should you describe your services in a way that responds to their needs.

Marketing #17: Referrals

As everyone knows, personal referrals are among the most effective and desirable way to find clients. Not only is it flattering to receive a referral from a former client or colleague, but the referral almost always converts into actual business because it comes with a personal endorsement. That's why there are no shortcuts to generating referrals: clients and colleagues most often refer business to lawyers they know, respect, and trust...and such relationships take time to cultivate. Some suggestions:

- *Be generous with advice.* When other lawyers call with basic questions that involve your area of expertise, don't hesitate to help. After discussing the matter, the lawyer might decide it's too complicated to handle, and may either refer the case to you or bring you on as special counsel. If you find yourself repeatedly dispensing advice to the same lawyer without any return, cut the conversation short ...or quote your rates.

- *Be a resource.* Seek out activities in which your initiative and legal skills are more visible. Such activities might include pro bono, bar association, or trade association work.
- *Look for parallels.* Build relationships with lawyers whose practices are complementary to yours. Some practice areas raise the same crossover issues regularly; e.g., a just-divorced family law client who will likely want to change a will, or who may need to file for bankruptcy to escape a spouse's debt.
- *Don't be shy.* Potential referral sources may not know you're actively looking for additional business until you take the time to remind them. And don't be shy; you might have to remind them more than once.
- *Seek out existing relationships.* Look to those with whom you have an existing relationship—friends, family, former law firm colleagues, a judge for whom you clerked. And if you've just completed a matter for a satisfied client, ask them to recommend you to others.
- *Seek out "conflict" clients.* Soliciting referrals from lawyers in the same practice allows you to capture "conflict" clients. Lawyers with a different specialty may send you cases that they don't handle themselves. Suggest you also target referrals within and outside your own practice area.
- *Find the big picture.* Take the time to educate lawyers who may not see the practice area connection. A transaction attorney's business clients may have concerns about the impact of a merger or acquisition on employees. If you're an employment attorney, suggest ways you can assist these types of clients. Or at least assist the attorney who's handling the business transaction.
- *Make it easy for people to pass your name around.* When you close out a client file, include several business cards that the client can distribute to friends.
- *Approach referral arrangements with caution.* Agreeing to refer business to another attorney or business in exchange for their referrals violates ethics rules in many jurisdictions that prohibit lawyers from offering something of value (in this case, a cross-referral) in exchange for referrals. Such arrangements also put pressure on you to refer business to someone who may not be right for the job.
- *Keep the door open.* In some practices, lawyers are plagued by lunch invitations from real estate agents or financial planners eager to discuss cross-referrals. If you're pressed for time, but still want to keep the door open to future referrals, meet for coffee or extend an invitation to drop by your office with materials. Better yet, request information that spells out how a referral arrangement might benefit your practice (for example, a financial planner might explain that she's prepared to refer divorced clients who need to change their wills).
- *Put a limit on "dud" referrals.* Many times, experienced lawyers—perhaps believing they're doing a good deed—will pass off loser cases on a younger attorney. Give the referrer the benefit of the doubt...the first two or three times... with your thanks, of course. If you receive more than three duds, express your gratitude but explain that you aren't interested in handling cases of marginal

merit or representing clients who cannot pay. This puts the referrer on notice to pre-screen cases before passing them on.

- *Don't forget to thank your referral source.* Where a referral converts into a piece of business, send a gracious "thank you". And, if appropriate, a small gift (unnecessary if you pay a referral fee). Even where the referral doesn't become a client, thank the referrer. A simple gesture, but it is the best guarantee of continued referrals.

SHOULD LAWYERS ACCEPT OR PAY REFERRAL FEES?

The pro and con of referral fees are a source of endless debate (though for some lawyers, referral fees are prohibited in their jurisdiction).

Pro: referral fees ensure that cases go to those best equipped to handle them. If a new solo brings in a complex, multi-million dollar medical malpractice case, he or she might be inclined to keep the case…and possibly botch it. A referral fee is an incentive for solos to refer the matter to a lawyer capable of handling it, and collecting from 10 to 30 percent of the amount eventually recovered. Referral fees are also a boon to solos getting their practices off the ground. New solos with rainmaking skills may attract clients for projects beyond their expertise, and a referral fee provides an additional revenue stream for their efforts. In other cases, lawyers who don't like marketing are willing to pay a 20 percent cut of their fees to a referral source instead of spending for advertising.

Con: The referral fee incentive can result in cases being directed to the lawyer who pays the highest referral fee rather than to the one who's best for the job. Another downside: lawyers who rely too heavily on referral fees for business may find that they're generating too little revenue after paying out the 20 percent referral fee share.

Some guidelines if you decide to accept referral fees:

Be sure that referrals comply with bar rules. Those bar associations that permit referrals usually do so where some or all of the following criteria are met: the referral fees are disclosed to clients, the overall fee is reasonable, and/or the fee reflects the portion of work contributed by the referring attorney.

Vet your referrals. If you're going to collect a referral fee, you're likely to be on the hook for negligent referral if they botch the case. Make sure you're familiar with the referral's work, that they've got a clean disciplinary record, and that they carry malpractice insurance. Likewise, don't refer cases to a lawyer simply because he or she is willing to pay the highest referral fee.

Waive a referral fee where a lawyer does a favor. Sometimes you may refer a case to another lawyer because the client can't afford your fees. If you're passing on work that you don't want, but not that you can't handle, a referral fee really isn't justified.

Put it in writing. An agreement to pay a referral fee is an enforceable contract. If you pass on a valuable case to a firm that makes a considerable amount of money from it, you deserve to be paid. At the same time, be reasonable; if the case turns out to have less value than expected (not due to any fault of the referred lawyers), consider waiving or reducing your portion.

DO YOU WANT MORE CLIENTS...OR MORE REFERRALS?

by Brian Tannebaum, Esq.

If you want more clients, here's my suggestion: use direct mail, Google Adwords, billboards. You'll get a ton of calls, and a ton of cases. Most clients will be looking for a low fee, but that's OK. You can do a bunch of cases cheaply, and hopefully you'll have a practice that can handle the volume. But if you want more *referrals*, what you're asking is that another person—lawyer or otherwise—put *their* credibility on the line because they're recommending that you should be hired. Consider:

Be patient. If you just want clients, type away on Google Adwords and start putting stamps on direct mailers. None of your clients will care about anything else except that you charge a "reasonable fee". If you want to have a volume practice of small cases, that's fine; you will get there through advertising. But if you want a smaller practice with better cases and higher fees, you have to stop seeing the computer as the key to your future. Good referrals take time. It requires that you have a reputation; not necessarily as a great lawyer but as a good lawyer. And becoming a good lawyer occurs one client at a time.

Talk to your clients about other things besides the case. If you want referrals, develop a relationship with a client to the point where they feel they can discuss "anything" with you. When that happens, some clients will refer you cases during their representation; others you will need to ask when the case is over (assuming you weren't fired). But if you are not willing to ask a client to refer clients to you, you have a problem.

Meet non-lawyers, go to non-lawyer events, have non-lawyer conversations. If you think you need to sell your practice to get referrals, you'll be the one at the cocktail party standing alone in the corner. Clients aren't hiring your practice, they are hiring you.

Never assume a meeting with someone was a waste of time because you didn't get a referral 10 minutes later. My rule is that within six months of meeting someone who may be in a position to refer me a client, I will get a call. Sometimes it's a year. It just happens that way.

Pay attention to what is going on in the community. Pay attention to people you know, even if you just know them by name or reputation. If someone you know won a case, or received some other type of accolade, congratulate them. No need for a formal letter; e-mail will do. But don't include an invitation to lunch unless you know the person well. There are people who scour media and send letters to lawyers who win awards; most of them are financial advisors looking for clients.

Spend your advertising and marketing money on things that allow you to be in the presence of others. Small ads in the local paper are fine, but your $1,500 is better spent on a foursome at a golf tournament than on a four-color ad in a lawyer's magazine.

Make time to talk to people seeking advice, especially when they're in a position to refer you a client. I take a lot of calls, and receive a lot of e-mails seeking opinions and advice. I return them when I have time, but usually pretty quickly because "thanks for calling me back so quickly," makes you the lawyer who deserves an important client. The best and worst part of having a referral-based practice is that you never know who will refer you a client.

Always, always, always show appreciation (even if it doesn't work out). Yesterday a lawyer e-mailed me that my referral didn't work out, but that he was grateful for the referral. I do this as well. I always let my referral source know if the case doesn't work out. Many lawyers don't like to do this because it appears negative. I think it's essential. If the referral doesn't work out, use it as opportunity to take the referring individual to lunch and talk more about your practice. No one expects anything when a referral doesn't work out, especially a free lunch. This year a few lawyers referred me multiple clients. Even though none hired me, those lawyers all received holiday gifts. The phrase "it's the thought that counts," is actually true.

—Brian Tannebaum (www.MyLawLicense.blogspot.com), a Miami-based criminal defense lawyer. Excerpt used with permission.

Marketing #18: Law Firm Swag

Swag is slang for all those promotional items—pens, calendars, magnets, notepads, tote bags, coffee mugs, etc.—screened with your firm's name/logo and contact information. Effective marketing tools or just more junk? Some lawyers believe swag—especially pens, calendars, and notepads—keep your name in front of clients. It works for Bruce Cameron, a solo in rural Minnesota (www.rurallawyer.com). *"For some reason,"* says Cameron, *"Imprinted pens have been an effective form of marketing for me. I have pens imprinted with the name of my law firm and a contact number, and leave them in check-out lanes, at gas stations, on restaurant tables, and with anyone patting their pockets. Once free from my control, those pens occasionally wind up in the hands of someone who wants a lawyer."* Here's another example: an appellate lawyer I know listed the rules of appellate practice on bookmarks and distributed them to trial attorneys he considered potential referral sources. The bookmarks served as a quick reference for relevant deadlines in appellate cases as well as a reminder of the appellate lawyer's services. My vote for the most useful promotional gadget? Computer flash drives. Not exactly a cheap giveaway at $10 or $15 each. But they do make impressive and useful gifts for all types of clients. Moreover, you can load them with relevant cases or articles that you've authored, or stock them with forms or checklists that your consumer clients may need. And each time you create new content, you can contact your client and remind him to plug in his flash drive and download your new materials.

Marketing #19: Sponsorships

Sponsorships are a time-honored marketing practice in which a law firm goes to the expense of hosting extracurricular bar conference activities—a golf tournament, a lunch, a cocktail hour—in exchange for having the firm's name branded on conference materials. This level of marketing is beyond the budgets of most solos, and besides, few people attending these conferences realize who sponsored the activity, and those who do probably don't care. Instead, sponsor an event to raise money for a good cause or to give back to the community. Many lawyers sponsor kids' sports leagues or local charitable events because they are personally committed to the event. Even if your sponsorship doesn't generate clients, you'll get personal satisfaction from your contribution.

Marketing #20: Contests

Though I'm not sure about their long-term effectiveness for attracting new clients, contests are another way to generate good will and give something back to your community. For example, a law firm might sponsor a competition that invites high school students to produce the best short video on some public service issue like bike safety or the dangers of texting and driving. Or a firm might sponsor a contest in the business community that awards sports tickets or free legal services. Social media (e.g., Facebook, Twitter) is a great tool for announcing contests and building buzz for the firm, but be sure you understand each site's ground-rules. Some sites are more strict than others, and violating them may cost you your account on that site. For details, go to www.legalmarketingblawg.com, and enter "contests" in the search box.

CHAPTER 17

Marketing in an Age of Changing Technology

"Marketing is easier when you reach out to a niche audience instead of to 'everyone' in your general practice area."—David Leffler, author of *Niche Marketing: The Inside Track to Client Development*

New tools for marketing are emerging all the time. The client, too, is changing, so it's important to understand (1) how and where consumers view law firm marketing efforts and (2) what types of services may appeal to them. This section discusses some emerging trends.

Teleseminars & Webinars

Teleseminars and Webinars video aren't just for corporate and business clients. These days, lawyers produce and distribute their own electronic events...often without leaving their office. In a teleseminar, you deliver your material by phone while participants listen in on a conference call; in a webinar, your message—both audio and visual (such as a PowerPoint or shared screen)—is delivered online. In either case, it's a win-win for everyone. For you, teleseminars and webinars are inexpensive to produce, and more convenient than crossing the country to speak on a panel; for the audience, the technology allows for participation from home...even via smartphone in their car! If you have a national practice, teleseminars and webinars are a great way to address "attendees" all over the country simultaneously. And if you practice in an area of interest to corporate clients, you may even be able to turn your teleseminar or webinar into a profit center. With conference and travel fees easily costing several thousand dollars per person, corporations might welcome the opportunity to register one or more staff-members for your "event". Even at $99 each, you still make $2,000 for registering just 20 corporate customers...and you will have made 20 contacts who might become clients.

Basically, teleseminars and webinars let you get paid to market your practice. And they're neither costly nor difficult to set up. If you're holding a free teleseminar or webinar, you can use one of the auto-responder Web sites I described in Chapter 15. For a fee-based program, you simply add a link to Paypal at your Web site, or use a separate registration platform such as those at www.Eventbee.com or www.Eventbrite.com. Both let you create a temporary registration page that users can use to sign up and pay by credit card. Of course, once the registration page is set up, you need a host company. For teleseminars, a service like www.freeconferencecall.com provides a free call-in line for up to 200 people, and you can record the calls in MP3 format. For webinars, one of the free hosting sites is at www.Freebinar.com, which offers free webinar service for up to 100 participants. At www.Glance.net , you get a single pass for up to 100 users for $9.95, or you can purchase a $49.95/month subscription. At www.gotowebinar.com, the fee is $99/month. Most of these services will tape a webinar so you can redistribute it later.

Video

YouTube has an incredibly simple interface for uploading promotional or educational videos, or for posting them onto your Web site and/or blog. And while podcasts still have their place, videos are—in my opinon—more captivating than one-dimensional podcasts, and convey to clients more about you and your effectiveness as an advocate. Lawyers have barely scratched the surface where video marketing is concerned, but a few are headed in the right direction:

- Allison Margolin, a Los Angeles criminal defense lawyer specializing in drug crimes, has an online video commercial. A three-minute clip, it gives prospective clients a chance to see her at the courthouse discussing with her client the motion that she plans to file, and sharing her philosophical objections to criminalizing marijuana. Her video even subtly gets across Ms. Margolin's impressive educational credentials—a BA from Columbia and a Harvard Law degree. The video is interesting, compelling, and it gives clients a glimpse of what Margolin's practice is about even before a client steps into her office.
- Solo Kelly Chang, in Los Angeles, has positioned herself as an expert on family law matters through a series of online videos (available at www.videojug.com/user/USEX0093).
- Medical malpractice attorney Gerry Oginski has created hundreds of two-to-five minute informational videos discussing questions related to medical malpractice or summarizing the results of his cases. Oginski's videos have generated numerous clients for his firm, and serve as a useful educational tool for anyone interested in learning more about medical malpractice (see sidebar).

Until a few years ago, the cost of a 30-second TV spot was well beyond the budgets of most solo and small law firms. Now, thanks to the Internet, even the smallest firm can add TV and video ads to their marketing mix. Google TV Ads, a subset of its popular AdWords program, makes it easy to buy, sell, and measure national cable TV advertising for as little as a few hundred dollars to a few thousand dollars. One Brooklyn bankruptcy lawyer aired a professionally produced, 30-second spot for less than $3,000. Google's TV ad platform is affiliated with the Dish Network's 98 cable channels, and lets you select when, where, and how often your ad will run. For details, go to www.google.com/adwords/tvads. Google is affiliated with dozens of video production companies around the country (see their list of vendors); one that does a lot of TV ads for lawyers is PixelFish (www.PixelFish.com).

How do you get a potential client to sign a retainer agreement during an initial consultation? There are two ways to do it: old school and new school:

Old school: you dazzle them, entertain them, educate them, teach them, and otherwise be brilliant so prospective clients realize you are the best lawyer on the planet, and can solve their every problem. Next new client, same razzle dazzle. This traditional way of closing the deal still works, but you've got to work so darned hard to make it happen… and you must do it every single time a new client walks into your office. It's exhausting and extremely inefficient.

But what if you could demonstrate your legal brilliance, and dazzle them with your courtroom style and sharp tongue, even *before* you meet your clients? You can. Let me introduce you to the future of lawyer marketing:

New School: You create introductory and how-to videos on your Web site so viewers can see you, hear you, and learn from you *before* ever stepping into your office. With video, you've pre-sold yourself.

After being in practice for more than 22 years, and having done Old School for most of my career, I am more than happy to let my videos talk for me. Video works and I'm living proof. My new clients understand I have information they want before I ever meet them… because they've watched my videos. Not just one or two; they watch a lot of them. They trust what I have to say, and when they come into my office I don't have to put on a song and dance.

Years ago, hardly any lawyers had Web sites; now everyone's got one. So, how do you "show" the visitors to your site that you're different? With video. In fact, online consumers expect you to have video. They want to see you. They want to hear you. They want to listen to what you have to say. Are you intelligent? Do you have a deep voice? Are you wearing nice clothes? What does your office look like? Do you have an understanding of their type of legal problem? The most efficient way to answer these questions is with video.

I predict that lawyers who do not adapt to their consumers' wants and desires will not only lose business to their competitors, they will become obsolete. Remember, potential clients searching for an attorney online will compare you to other lawyers online. If you don't have information they want, *in the media they want*, they will go elsewhere.

Gerry Oginski is a New York medical malpractice trial lawyer, and founder of the Lawyers Video Studio (http://lawyersvideostudio.tv).

Video Conferencing

While servicing clients entirely online through a virtual law firm is certainly convenient, it can also be sterile or impersonal. Moreover, sometimes clients are wary of dealing with a lawyer they've never seen. Video conferencing solves this problem. One of the lead video conferencing platforms, Skype, has been around for a while, and the quality has improved to the point where it's ready for prime-time professional use. And you can't beat the cost: Skype-to-Skype calls are free. Law firms are beginning to embrace Skype's potential for serving clients. One California firm, The Trust Store (www.the-trust-store.com/) uses Skype to conduct its online client consultation meetings.

Mobile Marketing

Even if only a small portion of your target clients access the Web through mobile devices (smartphones, tablets), it won't be long before mobile access is commonplace. In fact, a Gartner Research Group study predicts that by 2013, *smartphones will overtake computers as the most common Web access device*. Consider:

The Gartner study speculated that Web sites not optimized for the smaller screen formats will become a "market barrier" for their owners because mobile Web users prefer the speed and convenience of mobile sites over PC's. At some point you will you need to design (or redesign) your site and blog to make it accessible for mobile platforms. Fortunately, several Web and blog applications like WordPress offer a plug-in that let you display your site in a mobile format.

Presumably, users searching for a lawyer via a mobile device will be searching for someone nearby. And they're likely to use the local search function on their smart-phone. The Online Marketing Blog recommends listing your Web site in local search directories to maximize the chances of it being found via a mobile search. Source: http://www.toprankblog.com/2010/01/is-your-website-ready-for-the-mobile-web/.

Of course, as mobile devices gain popularity, advertising will change accordingly. Even now, a Nielsen study shows that 43 percent of users aged 25–44 always or some-times look at ads placed on mobile phone apps, and even adults in the 55-and-over category occasionally look at the ads. You can find a discussion of the Nielsen study at http://bits.blogs.nytimes.com/2010/09/14/report-looks-at-trends-with-mobile-apps/. *Bottom line:* it may be premature to start a mobile ad campaign now... but it is a trend worth watching.

Phone Apps

Behind the Apple and Android phones, there is an army of developers developing new apps every single day. In fact, some law firms are creating apps as well for lawyers on the move. Some of these apps function as vanity pieces, and merely replicate the firm's Web site or blog. But there are also ways to make apps that appeal to potential clients. For example, Florida personal injury attorney Jason Turchin created the My Attorney app (myattorneyapp.com), which includes such features as a checklist of what to do if you've been in a car accident... and a list of verdicts and settlements that his firm has won. In Dallas, Texas, lawyer Michelle May commissioned a divorce app that cal-culates the cost that litigants can expect to pay in a divorce case (itunes.apple.com/us/app/divorce-cost-prep/id369353834?mt=8). And another Texas lawyer, Jimmy Verner, developed a child support calculator app, and has since assisted in the development of apps of various other apps for lawyers (see www.vernerlegal.com/iPhone_Droid_Nex-us_One_apps_law_legal/about.html). The cost of developing apps varies depending upon complexity. You can find app developers at elance.com or odesk.com, but there are also do it yourself programs, such as Build An App (www.buildanapp.com) and EBookapp.com, which converts an e-book into an app.

V. SOLOS IN TRANSITION

CHAPTER 18

Special Situations

From Prosecutor to Solo *by Mark A. Sindler, Esq.*

I was a prosecutor for several years, so it was logical I would choose defense work when I finally started my own firm. What helped smooth the transition was to make sure I could be around people who knew more than me about defense work. So, once I decided to resign—it was several weeks before the actual date—I immediately sent out two dozen letters to some of the best-regarded criminal-defense practitioners in the area where I wanted to open an office. Most of them worked on their own, or in small-firm setups with an empty space here or there. As a result of space-sharing, I was able to count on wiser individuals for tips and experience on topics I never had to confront as a prosecutor. As it turned out, the arrangement worked both ways: my experience was a boon to them because I could provide insights into a segment of the law-enforcement community that isn't usually available.

State and federal prosecutors don't generally affiliate with a city or county bar association. So, I joined the local bar association as well as a sub-committee tailored toward criminal investigation. With meetings every few months, there were opportunities to mingle with judges, get to know others in this segment of the practice, and to obtain updates on the local rules of practice in state and federal trial courts.

So, how does a former prosecutor get clients right from the start?

- Get appointed to the Criminal Justice Act panel for the federal district in which the principal office is located. Every district has a CJA panel, comprised of attorneys who take cases in which the Federal Defender has a conflict of interest. (The Federal Defender can provide details about panel membership. A prerequisite is proof of training or prior experience in applying or using the United States Sentencing Guidelines.) In state trial courts, door-to-door visits may be required with each judge's secretary to hand out cards and let the support staff know that you're available for conflict appointments. The only downside is that payment for services comes only after the case is closed since your invoice for services cannot, with limited exceptions, be submitted sooner. Two other methods of steadying the cash flow include review of court "blotter" sheets, and signing up for mandatory arbitration in certain civil cases:

- Some municipal courts permit attorneys or their paralegals to review recent arrests, which include contact information of the defendant. Some of these defendants have not hired counsel yet. Assuming you are clear on ethical rules regarding soliciting new business, a one- or two-page letter can then be sent to that person that explains your ability to help protect his rights.

- Serving as an arbitrator in certain civil cases not only puts a nominal amount in your pocket, but also exposes you to the basics of personal-injury, landlord-tenant and contract-dispute litigation. It is here, in a non-binding setting, that many courts require cases be heard first when the claimed damages don't exceed a pre-set sum such as $20,000 or $25,000. Three-member panels of lawyers sit as a means of alternative-dispute resolution, hearing and deciding several cases per day. I have found it to be invaluable because if I came across certain pleadings or submissions that were well-researched or well-written, then I eventually got copies to use for later reference.

Note: if you devote your new practice to defending criminal defendants, invest in a membership with the National Association of Criminal Defense Lawyers, and the sister chapter in your state. It is money well spent. Not because it looks good on your resume, but because anyone worth their salt as a defense lawyer associate belongs in these organizations. They devote their careers to this niche, are quick to share their assistance if needed, and can sometimes refer a new matter or two your way. Solidify your status by belonging to NACDL and one of its state affiliates.

Mark A. Sindler (www.marksindlerlaw.com) is a criminal defense lawyer in Pittsburgh.

From BigLaw to Solo *by Carolyn Elefant, Esq.*

Q: My partners say going solo is career suicide. How do I respond?

A: Career-suicide? Just the opposite. In fact, in today's law firm environment starting your own practice is less risky than ever. Clients are tired of associates with little experience handling their cases. As a result, they're leaving large firms in search of more reasonable rates, and better, more personalized service, elsewhere.

Q: I specialize in a BigLaw practice, e.g., corporate securities, antitrust, management side labor and employment, etc. Is that enough to sustain my own firm?

A: Yes, absolutely. As firms continue to grow, they often don't provide the same level of service, and may also be resistant to keeping rates down or to implement flat-fee or alternative-billing arrangements. For these reasons alone, corporate clients are reporting greater dissatisfaction with the service provided by their existing attorneys. My advice is to target disgruntled clients and any who have been priced out of the BigLaw market. To attract clients looking for a high-quality alternative to standard big firm practice, use your Web site and/or blog to let people know you offer flat-fee or value-billing, client newsletters and personal service.

Q: My Ivy League law degree got me my BigLaw job, but do clients really care?

A: Some do, some don't. Some clients don't ask or care where you went to law school as long as you get the job done. Guys like Gerry Spence and the late Johnny Cochran didn't attend top-tier law schools. They built their reputations on fierce trial skills. For some clients, your education and legal credentials may be an added draw, particularly for younger attorneys who don't yet have extensive experience. And if you specialize in an area not typical for a top-tier law grad, your credentials will also help you stand out.

Q: How can I leverage my BigLaw background and judicial clerkship to get more referrals?

A: If you previously had a clerkship, let your former judge know you've gone out on your own. Judges are often asked to recommend attorneys, and if your judge was happy with your work, he or she is sure to pass along your name. Also, consider working with a law school's adjunct faculty. With a top-tier degree and tenure at BigLaw, you would be an attractive hire.

Q: The experts say not to compete on price. So how do I compete with BigLaw?

A: Never pitch a client on price alone. Corporate clients may be cost-conscious, but they're not destitute. And they won't choose a firm just for a bargain price. Does price matter? Of course it does; it's just not primary. Many corporate clients who choose small firms over their large firm counterparts do so both because of quality of service and cost considerations. In many cases, lower rates—in the form of reduced-hour fee or flat-fee and alternative-billing arrangements—can make the difference between a client using your firm or going with a BigLaw competitor. More than anything else, client dissatisfaction with large law firms is associated with poor quality service and lack of personal attention. So, make your pitch based on value. Make clear your rates derive from passing on overhead savings and increased efficiencies. Also make clear that you guarantee personal responsibility for every aspect of a case, from drafting contracts and writing briefs to the accuracy of their invoice, and that you employ the latest technology to resolve your cases and communicate with clients.

From Government to Solo *by Carolyn Elefant, Esq.*

Q: I'm leaving government to start a firm, but I don't have any business and I'm not sure how to build it.

A: As a former government attorney myself, your inside knowledge of how your agency works gives you an edge in several ways:

First, having worked at an agency, you'll be more adept in keeping abreast of newly issued decisions which you can report and analyze on a blog or in an electronic newsletter. Establishing a reputation as the go-to source for the latest information will help attract clients.

Second, most agencies now maintain online dockets with documents filed by companies and trade groups with business before the agency. The documents will generally indicate whether the entities are represented by inside counsel or an outside firm. You can use your familiarity with your former agency's docket system to identify unrepresented entities with business before the agency, after which you can determine through your networking relationships, whether you have a contacts at any of these companies. Moreover, by following the docket, you can anticipate situations where a firm representing two clients in a single proceeding may run into a conflict of interest, either because the clients' interests grow adverse, or the firm merges with another firm that also represents clients. Track these development so that you can position yourself to bid for the client if its law firm is conflicted out of the case.

Third, look for speaking opportunities where you can showcase your expertise. For example, offer to speak to an industry group on topics like, Filing a complaint under Agency X's New Rules, or, Ten Ways to Stay Out of Trouble With Agency Y.

Finally, keep in touch with former colleagues at your agency. When you finally start representing clients before the agency, your contacts can help you set up meetings with staff, provide you with information on your case status, and even move a case more quickly to resolution. Your ability to obtain this special treatment will impress your clients and lead to referrals and repeat business.

Q: I'm concerned I'll be precluded from working on matters my former agency handled, which are exactly the ones where people are most likely to want to hire me. How do I avoid ethics restrictions?

A: You're right to be concerned about ethics, but be sure you're not reading the restrictions too narrowly. As discussed in *Special Consideration for Government Lawyers, and The Revolving Door* (Chapter 5), the ABA Model Rules, and most state ethics codes, prohibit former government attorneys from handling matters where they participated "personally and substantially." So if a group of attorneys in your office were assigned to enforcement matters related to Company A, but handled the Company B file, you would be precluded from representing only Company B. In some cases, a government agency may restrict former employees from making an appearance before the agency on any matters (not just those in which they participated substantially) under their official responsibility. The ban on appearances generally lasts one or two years, and typically affect more senior level employees who are responsible for far more files than junior attorneys. Still, even if you're barred from making appearances, you could advise a client on agency policies behind the scenes without making an appearance, or you could offer your expertise to a firm an of counsel basis where the firm's attorneys could make an appearance. See Giving Notice (Chapter 5). Where you face a ban, regard it as an opportunity to expand your potential practice areas. Most government agencies have state and federal counterparts, and even if you're banned from appearing before one, you can still appear before the other. For example, if you're barred from appearances before your former employer—say, the federal Equal Employment Opportunity Commission—use your knowledge and credentials as a way to attract clients who need employment counsel before state employment or human rights commissions.

Q: I struck out interviewing with private law firms after a decade in government. If law firms don't want me, how can I make my government experience attractive to potential clients?

A: Law firms unfairly assume that former government employees landed there because they couldn't cut it in private practice, or that they are too accustomed to punching a time clock to adapt to a rigors of the law firm lifestyle. Clients look at it differently. Many prospective clients have great respect for attorneys who put time in government service, and they regard the experience as valuable because it gives you an inside track. When it comes to marketing for clients, you needn't be sensitive about your government background.

From Parent to Part-Time Practice *by Nicole Black, Esq.*

Lawyers choosing part-time practice fall into two broad categories: those who wish to accommodate the needs of their family, or who are transitioning back into the profession after having left the workforce to raise young children. The other group includes law students who come to law from a second career, but who have been unable to find a legal job after graduating and are reluctant to forego a paying job in their former field. Both groups look to part-time practice as a way to lay the foundation for a full time practice without giving up a steady stream of revenue.

Q: Many experts say that starting a firm is a full-time job. But can I succeed at it part-time?

A: In order to have a successful and manageable part-time practice, you need to narrow your areas of practice. Litigation is not conducive to part-time practice because of the unpredictable schedule inherent to that area of practice. Areas of practice that are transactional—e.g., real estate, trusts and estates, appeals preparation, and research and writing for other attorneys—are far more manageable as a part-time practitioner. And these areas of practice can often be quite profitable, especially if you minimize your overhead. But whether a part-time practice be successful depends on how you define 'success'. If it isn't tied to a large income not commensurate with a reduced schedule, then, yes, you can be successful as a part-time practitioner.

Q: Some colleagues, even friends, see my home office and part-time schedule, and don't take my success seriously.

A: What's success? Is it about achieving a balance between work and family, or is it about power and prestige? It's both because there is no one definition of success. But the irony is that a lawyer working at a home office part-time can actually earn more... or at least as much as...some law firm associates. So who's the more successful? In my own practice, I perform nearly the same function as I did as an associate in a mid-sized litigation firm...but I practice on my own terms. I choose the quantity of work I accept, I can turn down assignments, my work schedule is under my control, and my hourly rate far exceeds what I earned at any other point in my legal career (assuming you divide my annual salary for my prior jobs by the number of hours that I worked). So, although some lawyers may be disdainful of my practice since it appears to offer no power or prestige, I know better. I'm in charge of my schedule, my workload, and my hourly rate. I've got a busy practice and a fulfilling professional life. I'm successful by my definition, and that's what matters.

Q: How can I network without sacrificing the time needed for billable work?

A: Occasional business lunches are a good way to do some person-to-person marketing. But there many other ways to network that don't involve a meal. If your state requires an accumulation of CLE credits to maintain your license, seminars are a good way to fulfill your education obligations and network with other attorneys who practice in the same area of law. Also, join your local bar association and any practice-area committees relevant to your practice. In this way, you can network while brushing up on important local issues. Other networking options are online message boards, list-servs such as the ABA's solosez.net, and social media. And don't forget blogs: not only does a blog highlight your writing skills and your knowledge of your areas of practice, it also allows you to network with attorneys across the country. You'll be astonished at all the many lawyers you'll meet...virtually and in person...as a result.

Q: I've got young children, and have a part-time practice. But I keep thinking ahead to when my kids are older, and wonder how I should plan for the future?

A: Right now, the smartest thing to do is to keep on networking, and to stay in the loop in your legal community. The more visible you are, the more often people will think of you when you're ready to increase your hours. I can't say it too often: don't isolate yourself. Join your local bar association, get involved in committees, write articles, start a blog. Make your presence known in whatever way that you can. You never know what will come your way if you make an effort to stay involved in your legal community.

Nicole Black (www.nicoleblackesq.com) is of counsel to an upstate New York law firm, a columnist for the New York Daily Record, author of *Sui Generis*, a New York law blog, and co-author with Carolyn Elefant of *Social Media for Lawyers: the Next Frontier* (ABA 2010).

Part-time Practice With a Day Job *by Carolyn Elefant, Esq.*

Just as you need a predictable practice area to make a part-time practice work, you also need a flexible "day job" with limited hours. Some jobs may allow you to work as few as two or three days a week and keep your benefits, leaving other days free for legal work. Or, you might find a day job that allows you to leave early and keep your weekends free. This is especially true for lawyers who teach school. One such lawyer/teacher is Chicago solo Danielle Colyer, a prep school instructor who runs a real estate practice from her home. Though she has an assistant now who shares the workload, Colyer started out reviewing documents in the evenings and dropping them off during her lunch break. These days, she schedules real estate closings after school and on her summer vacation. The subject of an ABA Journal profile in 2007 (www.abanet.org/journal/ereport/jn29solo.html), Colyer says she's content with her arrangement, but that her part-time legal work did not match her teaching salary until her fourth year of practice.

The time you devote to your day job, even one you enjoy, will affect your practice. Working a second job—particularly if it involves similar skills to your practice (e.g., handling contract work for an attorney or a writing job) can interfere with your efficiency. And while putting in 25 hours at your day job may seem like only half a week, it's also time that a solo with a full-time practice would otherwise devote to marketing or building their firm. If you do decide to moonlight, try to limit your day job to 15 hours...or no more than 20 hours if absolutely necessary...to retain your health insurance benefits.

Solos who start out as part-timers—say, handling contract work for another lawyer—often become dependent on their outside income. Example: a solo who agrees to handle 15 hours of contract legal work a week at a rate of $75/hour. Suddenly, the hiring lawyer gets busy and offers the solo another 10 hours of work. The solo, calculating the additional income and goodwill, accepts. Trouble is, the lower-paying contract work prevents the solo from spending time marketing and finding his or her own clients who might pay twice the contract rate...or more. The lesson? If you're handling part time per diem work, you need to set a 15-hour limit and stick to it—and be prepared to lose the work if you're not willing to offer more of your time. And if you are going to start a part-time practice, check your company's policies to find out what kinds of work you can do off-hours. Some companies don't care what employees do so long as they show up for work, but others may have restrictions on outside work.

When you work for law firm and start a part-time practice, there are several additional considerations:

First, you may expose your employer to malpractice liability if you take on your own clients, even on your own time. Consequently, most law firms strictly forbid outside legal work of any kind, even pro bono, without their explicit knowledge and consent. Consider a part-time malpractice policy. Many insurers offer them with plans for less than $600/year.

Second, if you even inadvertently use firm resources like letterhead, phone lines or the law firm LEXIS account, your employer could report you to the bar for misappropriation of resources.

Third, your outside representation could unknowingly create a conflict with existing law firm clients, another potential ethics violation, irrespective of whether the firm where you work has an express prohibition on outside work. In short, don't handle your own clients while still working at a firm unless you disclose the proposed arrangement to your employer and you obtain permission. Of course, don't be surprised if your employer responds by saying that if you want to handle your own clients, you should leave and start your own firm.

Fourth, you can't stay part-time forever. At some point, your practice could reach a point where you're too busy for your day job and you'll have to make the leap. While in transition, your income may take a temporary hit until your practice reaches full capacity.

Except for some rare cases, you can't split your time between a full-time day job and outside law firm forever or your performance at both will suffer. So, have an end game in mind; either a commitment to transition to full-time practice within a certain time frame (e.g., a year, 18 months), or when your practice has reached a certain level of revenues.

Q: Would you still solo given what you've learned?

"I'm glad I decided to solo, and I would do it all over again. My practice and my life are more interesting as a result." —David Abeshouse (class of 1982)

"I wake up loving what I do every day. I look forward to Fridays as much as Mondays." —Gabriel Cheong (class of 2007)

"Given what I've learned, I wish I would have gone solo sooner. I'm enjoying practicing law more than ever, and hope that I am fortunate enough to have my own practice for as long as I practice law." —Kevin Afghani (class of 2004)

"I'm having a great time doing what I'm doing. I look forward to it every day. I can't wait to get to my desk in the morning. I'm not yet on solid ground financially. But I'll always be glad I [solo'd] no matter how it turns out." —Mark Tanney (class of 1998)

"[Solo again]? Yes, in a heartbeat." —Matthew G. Kaiser (class of 2002)

"No regrets at all." —Mitchell J. Matorin (class of 1993)

"Unquestionably and undeniably, without reservation." —Marc W. Matheny (class of 1980)

"Yes. I'm the best boss I've ever had: tough but fair!" —Jan M. Tamanini (class of 1984)

"I absolutely would choose to solo again. For all the financial uncertainty and moments of being over-whelmed by workload and isolation, there are so many more moments of satisfaction and freedom." —D. Jill Pugh (class of 1994)

"I will always have doubts about my decision to go solo, but in the final analysis it has been a fantastic learning experience. Whether or not I succeed as a solo, I am glad to be traveling this path." —Bruce Cameron (class of 2007)

"I love getting up every day to go to the office. I like being able to choose my cases, and how I am going to handle them. It is certainly a sacrifice to go solo, but the sacrifice will pay off in dividends if done right." —Paul Scott (class of 2008)

"Although it was the right decision given my circumstances at the time, I would have preferred to start my career at a multi-lawyer firm and then go solo after becoming more seasoned. But I do not regret the decision." —Adam Neufer (class of 2009)

"I'm still not making the money I want, but my freedom is invaluable. The mere thought of going to work for a firm where my hours are tracked, where my bonuses are poached by senior partners, where I have no say in what clients I have to take, and where I have to beg for days off, makes me queasy. I'm doing the best I can, and the money will come. I just have to be patient." —Gina Bongiovi (class of 2007)

—Excerpt from *Solo by Choice, The Companion Guide: 34 Questions That Could Transform Your Legal Career* (Carolyn Elefant, 2011)

The practice of law is changing in ways unimagined just a few years ago.

Since 2008, law firms have cut more than 15,000 associates, and those positions are never coming back. Law firms are offshoring lower-level work to India, or automating tasks like document review previously performed by new lawyers. As a result, new grads who took on huge debt to attend law school in anticipation of job security are now unable to find employment. Yet with all these changes, law schools are still failing to keep pace:

- Even now, few law schools have classes on how to establish a solo practice.
- Law school placement offices, particularly those at top-tier schools, brim with brochures from the AmLaw Top 100, but rarely provide materials on starting your own firm or even make available contact information for alums who might want to serve as mentors.
- Many law schools are encouraging students to use their law degree outside the law in non-legal positions *instead* of considering the solo practice option.
- Most law professors have never encountered successful solos, since their own experience is often limited to a prestigious federal court clerkship and maybe a short stint at a large law firm.
- The grants or course credits offered to law students who accept summer positions with a public interest group aren't often extended to students who want to intern with a solo, even one representing the same constituency (e.g., clients who qualify for court-appointed counsel fees, or who fall just below the cutoff for legal aid services).
- As for volunteering to work for a solo practitioner, it's even less likely because of the staggering levels of tuition debt with which law students are burdened.

Even though starting a law firm enables unemployed students to use their law degree, and to take advantage of the opportunities available in the profession, most law schools still fail to encourage students in this direction. Though technology may limit traditional employment at large firms, it is—at the same time—creating exciting opportunities for those willing to start a firm. Technologic advancements—from mobile devices and cloud computing to social media and low-cost legal research—have obliterated the financial barriers to starting and operating a law practice. Today, solos can deliver legal services more effectively and affordably than ever before, which means they can compete for business with BigLaw, expand to overseas markets, or earn a profit serving clients in need of affordable counsel.

Fortunately, cultural attitudes toward solo and small firm practice are improving... slowly.

In an entrepreneurial age, starting your own law firm is now appreciated for what it—an act of entrepreneurialism with an enormous potential for success. As I wrote in the Preface, solo and small firm practice makes possible now—as never before—the dream of becoming the lawyer you always wanted to be. And even as you contemplate your decision, remember you are not alone. You're part of a growing trend of lawyers who are either rejecting large firm or government practice outright, or leaving it behind, because they recognize that by harnessing technology they not only can achieve enormous flexibility and provide affordable legal services…but earn a nice living in the process, and take advantage of new opportunities.

Throughout the history of the legal profession, we solos have always lead the way:

Solos developed the concept of the contingency fee…challenged bar advertising rules in *Bates*…and were the first to harness the power of social media to build relationships with colleagues and clients. As the legal profession reinvents itself in the age of fast-changing technology, it is entrepreneurial solos who will lead forward to the future by showing how to enjoy a career in law without sacrificing financial success, work-life balance, or intellectual and personal satisfaction. Which is why your decision to go solo represents more than a personal choice: solo practice serves as an example of, and a catalyst for, change in the legal profession. —CE

APPENDIX SOLOS BY CHOICE

As I mentioned in Chapter 2, the thought of starting your own law firm can seem daunting. You must examine your motivation, analyze your business prospects, engage in exhaustive self-reflection and self-evaluation. In the final analysis, though, your decision may be more art than science, more instinct than reason. And whether your new solo practice succeeds . . . or not . . . may well be determined by your answers to the following four questions:

Are you willing to do what it takes to establish your firm?
Are you confident with your lawyering skills?
Will you regret it?
Do you love the law?

If you love the law and take pride in serving clients or expanding access to justice, and you believe that what you do as a lawyer matters, then don't let obstacles stand in the way. Your passion for what you do will carry you through even the toughest time. This section is an excerpt from *Solo by Choice, The Companion Guide: 34 Questions That Could Transform Your Legal Career.* In the pages that follow, you'll meet five solos who didn't let obstacles stand in the way of their success.

The lawyers profiled are . . .

KEVIN AFGHANI

Education: Tulane School of Law; Class of 2004

Resume: Practicing law 5 years.

Solo practice: Two years

Practice specialty: Patent law

Q: Why did you decide to solo? "Before starting a solo patent practice, I was an IP associate in BigLaw. The money was good, but after about a year I realized it was not a good fit. If I wanted a fulfilling legal practice, I would have to escape. Going solo has exceeded my expectations in every way imaginable. I feel in control of my destiny, and my future no longer depends upon the whims of a partner."

Q: What sacrifices did you make to solo? "I gave up a BigLaw salary and a regular paycheck for no guaranteed income at no guaranteed time. [The sacrifice] was worth every penny."

Q: How did you explain your decision to colleagues? "Some people excel in a BigLaw environment, others in a more structured government or in-house environment. I was cut out for solo practice because I like being my own boss, and because I have a high tolerance for risk."

Q: What did you know about solo'ing before you began? "Everything I knew about solo'ing was based on observing colleagues who had gone on their own. I knew that every aspect of running a business would fall upon me, and I knew about the risks involved."

Q: What about the risks in a solo practice? "One of the most important personality traits of a solo practitioner is a high tolerance for risk. If you are uncomfortable with not getting paid for over a month or two, and not being able to accurately project your income—at least in the starting phase—you should think seriously about your decision to solo. Indeed, the risk factor is *the main force* preventing many of my colleagues from breaking out on their own."

Q: What about job security? "When you work for a law firm, you derive income from a single source, and it can lull you into a false sense of security simply because you're receiving a paycheck at regular intervals. But going solo can actually *increase* your job security by diversifying the sources from which you derive income."

Q: What role does a spouse/partner play in a solo's success? "My fiancé was critical in my decision to go solo. To this day I do not think I would've done it without her support. Since she herself is a patent attorney, she understood very well the stresses that come with being in a law firm. She saw the perfect fit between me and solo practice even before I myself had realized it."

Q: What was your biggest goof, and what did it teach you? "Early on, I failed to identify my ideal type of client or focus my efforts on acquiring this ideal type of client. Instead, my business development efforts tended to follow a scattershot approach."

Q: What are the biggest challenges when you're the boss? "You need to establish a budget for insurance (health, dental, malpractice, disability), and any of the other services normally provided by an employer. Second, set up a time management and appointment system, because you will have to wear many different hats on any given day, including collector, lawyer, accountant, PR expert, or janitor."

Q: How important is a business plan? "To me, a business plan should be a growing organism that takes account of your expanding knowledge and experience base. [In the beginning], I kept my business plan pretty simple, and I continue to develop it to this day. Sometimes, the simple act of committing your plans to writing can help to ensure that you follow through on those plans."

Q: How important are people skills in a solo's success? "People skills are an absolute necessity. When I look at how much my personal interactions have increased since going solo, I don't see how it would be possible without being able to effectively interact with others. For someone trying to build a client base from the ground up, you will be interacting with others extensively. People skills should be developed or practiced."

Q: What business skills are essential? "Unless you're planning on hiring a CPA, you should gain at least some basic knowledge in federal income tax to ensure that you are not over- or under- paying your taxes. I was pretty freaked out to learn that I was required to pay a quarterly estimated tax to the IRS based on my projected income, and that my failure to pay this quarterly estimated tax could result in an underpayment penalty."

Q: Any advice for new solos? "If you are soloing with little or no experience, you might explore project-partnering with an experienced lawyer in your practice area. They will be able to provide you with referrals and the mentoring you need. Of course, they will also probably require you to share fees with them, but this financial sacrifice could yield long-term benefits. I recommend partnering with an attorney who allows you to have direct contact with clients for which you perform work."

Q: Kevin, given what you've learned, would you still solo? "I wish I'd have gone solo sooner. I'm enjoying practicing law more than ever, and hope that I am fortunate enough to have my own practice for as long as I practice law."

GINA BONGIOVI

Education: University of Nevada/Las Vegas, JD/MBA; Class of 2007

Solo practice: Two years

Practice specialty: Part-time general counsel for small businesses

Q: Why did you decide to solo? "In my second year of law school, one of my professors described the typical life of a new attorney: it was the polar *opposite* of what I'd attended law school to become. From then on, I knew I wanted to solo. I couldn't imagine toiling away four years of a part-time law program while working full or part-time, only to lose some of the freedom I'd enjoyed before enrolling in law school."

Q: Is there a solo type? "The successful solo must have self-discipline! You don't have a supervisor breathing down your neck or a time card to punch. No one is taking issue with your billable hour quota, and you don't have a paycheck direct-deposited to your account every two weeks. You have to manage your time, manage your caseload, make your own schedule, and handle all the administrative stuff, too. Some people just don't have the desire to shoulder that much responsibility. And that's okay. Just be honest with yourself about your personality and your motivations, or you'll be a miserable square peg in a round hole."

Q: What are your sharpest memories of starting out? "It was a rough time. For the first eight months, I waited with almost unbearable anticipation for the phone to ring. When it did, I felt like hiding under my desk. I was stuck between the excitement of building my business and terror that I would screw something up. For a few months, the fear was almost paralyzing. I'd find myself in tears some days, wondering what I'd done, whether I'd made the right decision to start my own firm, or to even attend law school."

Q: What sacrifices did you make to solo? "Money is the first and most significant sacrifice. Two years in and I'm still not making the money I want. However, I chose to laser-focus my practice area, and I don't dabble in other areas. This way, I have sacrificed a lot in potential revenue, but I have also become the go-to person for my practice area. And even though clients don't come along as often, the clients I do get now are higher quality."

Q: What role does a spouse/partner play in a solo's success? "If it wasn't for my husband's support, I wouldn't have been able to go on my own. The financial hit we took while I got the firm started wasn't easy, and the emotional turmoil I put myself through wasn't easy either. Watching me vacillate between elation and terror was pretty rough on him because he couldn't really do anything to help."

Q: What frustrations are solos likely to experience? "My biggest frustration was, and still is, the realization that law school did *nothing* to prepare me for actual practice. I thought for sure that toiling those three years under constant stress and anxiety would provide the knowledge I needed to practice law. I am just amazed how precious *little* I learned about real-life litigation in law school, and that feeling has not waned."

Q: What do you like/dislike about the autonomy of solo practice? "I love the autonomy [of being a solo]. It means being able to take care of a friend after surgery, being able to attend my nephew's basketball game, being able to take my dog to the vet."

Q: What role do mentors play in your practice? "Books and CLE's can take you only so far. Mentors and contacts are invaluable. A mentor can help you brainstorm ideas, guide you in making decisions, and keep you from falling on your face. Finding a mentor can be a challenge. But once a potential mentor walks into your life, show your appreciation and ask if you can lean on them for help. Most will find it flattering and a very rewarding way of giving back."

Q: What role do people skills play in your practice? "People skills are crucial. Most solos are the face of their firm in marketing efforts and must be accessible and approachable. No matter your practice area, you will do some amount of counseling and deal with people's emotions. Having the skills to manage your reactions and keep the client calm will serve you well."

Q: What role does risk play in a solo practice? "Risk is the ever-present ghost over your shoulder. From month to month, you can't rely on a steady income. You don't know if your clients will pay; you don't know if the phone will ring; you don't know if any consultation will turn into a client; you don't know if your particular niche will be eliminated due to some new legislation. Risk is probably *the biggest factor* in a solo practice. The trick is to figure out how to manage it, strategically and emotionally, so that dips don't sideline you, and you don't overspend in the good months. Budgeting is a great tool, as is having a solid business plan that you revisit every few months to make sure you're on the right track."

Q: What would you say to new solos about marketing? "Advertising is usually a waste of money unless you have a war chest to throw at a campaign designed to put your name in front of people at least seven times. Instead, I find networking to be the most profitable. Not just any networking, though. *I spun my wheels in networking groups for about six months, signing very few clients because I was marketing to the wrong audience...potential clients.* Now, I network and market to my *referral* sources, and it has made all the difference."

Q: What's your advice to new law grads who want to solo? "Be prepared for the fear... market like crazy when business is slow... stay in contact with everyone you meet... don't be a general practitioner unless you're in a small town... keep your expenses low... and be honest with yourself: not everyone is cut out for having their own practice. You'll be miserable if you try to be a business owner when you might be happiest as an employee."

Q: What about job security? "I see friends who worked as loyal employees for over a decade laid off with an hour's notice. No one these days has any job security. I might go so far as to argue the highest degree of job security is enjoyed by the self-employed."

Q: Gina, would you still solo given what you've learned? "I'm still not making the money I want, but my freedom is invaluable. The mere thought of going to work for a firm where my hours are tracked, where my bonuses are poached by senior partners, where I have no say in what clients I have to take, and where I have to beg for days off, makes me queasy. I'm doing the best I can, and the money will come. I just have to be patient."

BRUCE CAMERON

Education: Hamline University School of Law; Class of 2007

Resume: Practicing law for three years; previously, a research scientist

Solo practice: Three years

Practice specialty: Collaborative family law, probate, and real estate work

Q: What role does a spouse/partner play in a solo's success? "If it weren't for my wife's support, I don't think I would have made it through law school... much less have the courage to go solo."

Q: Why did you decide to solo? "Going solo right out of law school, AND practicing in a small rural town, was the last thing I wanted to do. My plan had always been to find an associate position with a firm doing IP work. After all, what firm *wouldn't* want an experienced software engineer/biomedical researcher-with-multiple-graduate-degrees-turned-lawyer? As it turns out, hiring partners aren't much interested in an over-40, second career, 'night school' lawyer (actually, I took all my classes on the weekends) who graduated from a tier 3 school."

Q: What did you know about solo'ing before you began? "I had no idea how complex a solo practice is, or that you that most of your time is spent on marketing and managing the business and a minority of time actually practicing law. Nor did I know that being a solo would be the scariest, most exhilarating, dullest, stimulating, stressful, challenging, satisfying thing I ever attempted."

Q: What role does risk play in a solo practice? "Going solo means spending large amounts of time and money in a venture with no defined return, and with odds that are undefined, unpredictable, and continuously variable! It's an intricate dance with risk... but *not* a gamble. [To manage risk], you need to think strategically, making decisions based on information and a cost/benefit analysis rather than reacting to immediate events. Risk is what makes my solo practice fun, exhilarating, worrisome... and scary at the same time. It's what keeps me sharp and drives me to do my best work."

Q: What are your sharpest memories of starting out? "There was an intense rawness to those first days and months [of solo practice]. But my sharpest memories are more internal than external: the feeling of dread when I walked into the office each morning; the elation of that first client; the surprise when I got a referral; the exhilaration that came from getting a positive result for a client; and the contentment of earning that first fee."

Q: What sacrifices did you make to solo? "It's not a 'sacrifice' as much as making trade-offs or substitutions. For example, date night for my wife and I changed from restaurants and theater tickets to take-out and a rented DVD. And those leisurely, two week vacations are now a hectic three-day weekend."

Q: Can you solo on a shoestring budget? "You *can* set up a solo office on a shoestring; you just can't *run* a solo practice on one. All those articles on the '$10,000 law practice', the '$5,000 law office', are correct as far as they go. But they don't consider what it costs to live AND maintain your practice. You need to factor in rent or mortgage payments, and those pesky bills for food, utilities, telephone, transportation, health insurance, and taxes. On top of that, costs for marketing, maintaining your license, and advancing court costs or filing fees on your client's behalf. On top of THAT, there are *unexpected* costs like the $500 brake job or the thousand-dollar medical bill."

Q: Any financial advice for new solos? "You'll need an accountant at least three times during your first year: to set up your books and learn how to maintain them, to start planning for the year's taxes, and again at tax time."

Q: How you feel about business plans? "It doesn't have to be fancy or follow any formal outline; nor does it have to be more than a set of bullet points. All it needs to do is outline what you are going to do, with whom you are going to do it, and how you are going to do it. But don't just write it and put it away. Refer to it regularly, and update it when necessary. But stay focused on your original purpose. Without a road map, you won't know how to get there...or know when you've arrived."

Q: What would you tell new lawyers about malpractice insurance? "Check with your local bar; it may be a requirement. If it's not, get it anyway. It helps you sleep at night."

Q: What would you advise new solos about marketing? "The more you know about your ideal client, and the more detailed description you have of that ideal client, the more cost-effective your marketing will be. Three suggestions: a) Tailor your marketing to your ideal client, and don't waste time, effort or money on methods that will not reach that ideal client...b) When preparing materials, you need to get across who you are, what you offer, why you should be hired, where you are located, and how to contact you in an efficient manner...and c) Have a uniform look across all your materials and a consistent presence. If you take an ad out in the local shopper, keep it going for several weeks, even months. Name recognition takes time and patience."

Q: Any other marketing advice? "One big marketing *don't* concerns phone directory advertising. If you can't afford to put a full page ad on the cover, or in the front of the attorney's section, don't bother spending money on anything other than the minimal listing."

Q: What's your advice to new law grads? "Have a mentor or two. Don't try to spread yourself across multiple practice areas. Focus on one and become competent in that field before adding additional practice areas. And attend all the CLE's in your practice area that you can afford.

Q: Bruce, what's the future for solo practices? "The practice of law is swinging towards an era of solo and small firm practices because of their flexibility and ability to innovate. It will be the solo/smalls who evolve their practices to fill niches as they become available, and to respond to the ebb & flow of the practice of law. We are facing a period of time where we have a glut of lawyers. My guess is that most of the attrition will come from those firms would fund their operation by borrowing on their accounts receivable, followed closely by those who maintain rigid adherence to the billable hour fee model. This may not be an extinction event, but you can see it from here."

MITCHELL MATORIN

Education: Duke University School of Law; Class of 1993

Resume: Practicing law for 18 years

Solo practice: Four years

Practice specialties: Business litigation, IP litigation, Appellate practice

Q: Why did you decide to solo? "I practiced for 18 years, three-and-a-half at the Department of Justice, and the remainder at two large law firms. I wasn't happy with my career choice after leaving DOJ. Not because there was anything wrong with my firms; they were both good places with smart, caring people, and interesting work. I just wasn't cut out for the big law firm culture. So, I cast about for years, trying to figure out what else I could do. I had never seriously considered [solo'ing], but after scratching out some calculations on a pad of paper, multiplying hourly rate by billable hours, I realized that even if I didn't have a ton of work at first, the numbers were actually very favorable. So I leaped."

Q: Now, four years later, how do you feel about the decision? "No regrets at all."

Q: What's your plan B if things don't work out? "Plan B? See Plan A."

Q: What about job security? "You don't have much job security in a law firm anyway, as the last few years have demonstrated quite nicely. My job security now lies in my ability to get the job done, and to have clients who think highly of me, and respect what I've done for them."

Q: What are your sharpest memories of starting out? "[When I started my firm], I didn't have much in the way of savings, and I financed my practice by drawing on my home equity line of credit. We lived frugally for a few months; not nearly as frugally as we could have or should have, but frugally enough."

Q: How did you create a revenue stream in the beginning? "My practice was, and still is, heavily dependent on referrals from other solo attorneys, and from my old firm (a word of advice: *never burn bridges*). With a litigation practice, it only takes one or two cases to get a reasonably consistent and lasting revenue stream. If I had a transactional practice or a family-oriented practice where I had to hustle for each client and each client offered only a discrete revenue potential, things would have been far more difficult for me."

Q: What sacrifices did you make to solo? "The biggest 'sacrifice' has been of perceived prestige. Like most law students, I was indoctrinated [to believe] that success is measured by the name of your firm and the size of your paycheck. It took some time to get my mind around the idea that it might not be that way, and the number of big firm attorneys who have told me that they envy me—or who have sought me out to talk about my career path—never ceases to amaze me."

Q: How do you balance parenting with a solo practice? "It's more than a little unnerving not having a guaranteed monthly income when you have kids who insist on eating every day, [and on top of that] a mortgage and living expenses. [As a solo], it's great to be able to control my own schedule—somewhat— and to be able to guarantee that I can attend certain things. On the other hand, I also feel compelled to work late because everything depends on me, with the unfortunate result that I'm usually not home for dinner. Somewhere, there's a happy medium…but I haven't found it yet."

Q: Describe your most difficult client experience, and what you learned? "My worst client was my first. It was a non-litigation matter, and I had offered him a choice of hourly or fixed fee and he chose fixed. The client turned out to be extremely demanding and required constant hand-holding, and did a lot of things on his own that made things unnecessarily complex. I finally lost my patience and told him he should find another attorney. Lesson learned: sometimes you have to fire a client to stay in business…and it's OK to do that."

Q: What was your biggest goof? "Letting a client accrue a huge outstanding balance on a litigation matter that took a tremendous amount of my time (and many all-nighters). I let the empathy I felt for the client, who had to defend against a full-blown lawsuit over a dispute that easily should have settled, get in the way of good business sense. Although empathy is a good thing, when it comes to running a solo practice it has to be backed up with a somewhat cold-hearted view of the bottom line."

Q: How important is it to prepare a business plan? "Whether or not to write a business plan, probably depends on experience level and practice area. For me, it was not important at all. At least, I didn't have one, and I wouldn't know how to write one. It's possible, though, that I might be vastly more wealthy and nearing financial security if I had had a business plan. I guess ignorance is bliss."

Q: Can you solo fresh from law school? "If you have to [solo without previous legal experience], or if you have always felt that this is what you want to do, then go for it. But if you have the option of working in a firm for a few years, do it instead. You'll see how things are really done, and that will translate into self-confidence that you actually can do it."

Q: How would advise new solos about marketing? "Network with other attorneys. Go out of your way to be helpful, and to go beyond the expected when somebody asks for advice. Join the ABA's Solosez listserv and actively participate and show your experience and willingness to help. And always be available for brainstorming with other attorneys. Get a good Web site; it doesn't have to be expensive, but it does have to be professional, informative, and most of all, it has to exist."

Q: Mitchell, where do you see the practice of law, and solo practice, headed? "Big firm layoffs and increasing client cost pressure have opened up new opportunities for solos and small firms to take a piece of the work that always went to the big firms by default. [For this reason], I think the last few years have been transformative for the solo/small firm practice. I'm fairly hopeful about the future of solo/small firm practice generally, and about my own prospects specifically."

KARA O'DONNELL

Education: University of Miami; Class of 1995

Resume: Practicing law for 14 years

Solo practice: One year

Practice specialties: Bankruptcy, family law, civil

Q: Why did you decide to solo? "After buying my first home only three months before, I was suddenly laid off. After a few months of no job prospects, I decided to start my bankruptcy law practice."

Q: What was the reaction among your colleagues? "Many were surprised. Give up a weekly paycheck and health insurance? *How dare I rock the boat*! But the time was right to start my firm, so I chose to take the risk rather than to look for another uninspired job with a paycheck and a few benefits.

Q: What are your sharpest memories of starting out? "[I remember] the ups and downs: having many new prospects call in a single day, and then have no one call for a week or two. I also remember working late nights to file bankruptcy cases, and then realizing happily that I could sleep late the next morning. After all I was a solo! [What I failed to consider] is that bankruptcy court usually calls at 8:30 a.m.! Now, I work into the wee hours only if I can answer calls in a coherent fashion at 8:00 the next morning."

Q: How do you handle the risks associated with solo practice? "I [used to have] high anxiety whenever my firm's bank account was low. It was scary wondering what would happen month-to-month. After only nine months of being a solo, though, that anxiety is rarely an issue. [But] the other risk involves being able to do the legal task in a professional manner *without* the benefit of another attorney "down the hall" to bounce questions off. The only solution? Read...research...read more. Repeat."

Q: What are the biggest challenges when you're The Boss? Making money. Getting clients. Knowing your field of law."

Q: What do you do to make sure your business maintains profitability? Keep all expenditures low, and don't spend your money unless you really need to."

Q: What did you sacrifice to solo? "I can't go to restaurants like I used to, and my hair stylist has forgotten my name. But business is improving...slowly. It takes a while to develop that happy client base that will refer you to new clients. It's been nine months and I just got my first one of those yesterday."

Q: What are some of a solo's frustrations? "I'm constantly rattling my brain, wondering how to get more clients. Where are they...why do they go to Attorney X...how does Attorney X have such a huge caseload? It's sleep-depriving."

Q: Describe your most difficult client experience, and what you learned? I have had clients that lie to you or *conveniently* forget to tell you something. I have since learned to ask anything and everything, and I watch them closely. It's a skill I learned conducting depositions for years in auto injury litigation. A facial expression can tell me there's more to the story, and I have to keep probing. My favorite client has come to my house and helped with drywall. Who wouldn't love that?"

Q: How important are people skills in a solo practice? "An attorney's personality can be the difference between a potential client wanting to come in to sign up, and wanting to call a few other places. In general, clients like that I care about their problem, and take (a lot of) time to talk to them even on the first call."

Q: What role does networking play in a solo's success? "A prospective solo should consider what kind of network they have available, and how they can make use of it. I started soloing in a community where I have lived for many years. I have many contacts through my extended family, my old work, my kids' school and activities, my hobbies, and my husband's work, etc. I use these contacts all the time. I couldn't imagine being successful without having this network. I don't think I would be as successful if I just opened shop in some random area."

Q: What role do mentors or contacts play in your practice? "I wish I had more, but so many other attorneys are too busy to mentor."

Q: What do you like/dislike about the autonomy of solo'ing? "I miss having co-workers. Sometimes I feel like the Tom Hanks character [in *Castaway*], talking to a volleyball when he was marooned on an island in the Pacific."

Q: What's your impression of social media as a marketing tool? "Social media makes practicing more affordable in that you can get your message out faster and cheaper than old fashioned print ads and articles."

Q: What would you tell a roomful of new law grads about solo'ing? "Have a slush fund for the first two to three months. Do doc review if you have nothing in your bank account; intern if you have to. Just get experience, and always be hungry for the next opportunity. You never know where it will lie. Just don't quit even when business gets slow... even if it is slow for two months! And keep reading and educating yourself. There is a wealth of information on the listservs [e.g., Solosez], where much more experienced solos are posting their opinions and helpful hints."

Q: Your advice to new lawyers about malpractice insurance? "Buy it. In large amounts."

Q: Kara, what does the future hold for solo practice? "Like all businesses, the truly hungry [solos] will be in it for the long haul, and the meek will move into paycheck jobs. I have hope for me; if I don't, who will?"

CAREER RESOURCES for a LIFE in the LAW

Made in the USA
Middletown, DE
27 September 2016